On a Grander Scale

On a Grander Scale

THE OUTSTANDING CAREER OF
SIR CHRISTOPHER WREN

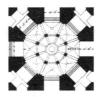

LISA JARDINE

HarperCollins*Publishers*

HarperCollins*Publishers*
77–85 Fulham Palace Road,
Hammersmith, London w6 8jb

www.**fire**and**water**.com

Published by HarperCollins*Publishers* 2002
1 3 5 7 9 8 6 4 2

A catalogue record for this book is
available from the British Library

ISBN 0 00 710775 7

Set in PostScript Linotype Minion with
Janson and Trajan display by
Rowland Phototypesetting Ltd,
Bury St Edmunds, Suffolk

Printed and bound in Great Britain by
Clays Ltd, St Ives plc

for John

CONTENTS

PREFACE

Reader, if you require a monument, look around you.

(inscription on the plaque above Wren's tomb)[1]

London's St Paul's Cathedral is Sir Christopher Wren's lasting memorial, as the plaque on the crypt wall, above his tomb, anticipated with vision-ary eloquence. Since his death in 1723, the Cathedral has come to stand for the man, to such an extent that its bold, imposing beauty tends to blot out the brilliant diversity of the career of the man who designed and built it.

Wren's son, Christopher, proposed an alternative tombstone in-scription, which might have served his father better, by making a clear distinction between the man and his work:

> Visitor, if you require a tomb, look down
> If you require a monument, look around you.[2]

Nor should we forget another phrase which figures in both versions: 'he lived more than ninety years, not for himself, but for the public good'.[3] The much repeated suggestion that his best-known building is a monument to its architect is entirely out of character – at odds with the way Wren saw himself and his role as a prominent public servant. St Paul's was built, he believed, 'for eternity', as a monument to the Angli-can Church (the first new-build cathedral in post-Reformation England). It commemorated both his beloved sovereign, the restored King Charles II in whose reign it was begun, and King Charles 'the martyr' (as Wren referred to the previous monarch) whom Wren's own father had devot-edly served. The least self-regarding of men, Wren dedicated a long life to making his mark on the world on behalf of others.

Writing a book about the career of Sir Christopher Wren has been a remarkable experience. Wren was an outstandingly gifted individual, born at a defining moment in English history, when the intellectual world was changing with astonishing rapidity, providing a fertile

ix

Wren's lasting monument – St Paul's during the Blitz.

environment within which his extraordinary mind burgeoned and blossomed. Politically, his world could hardly have been more unstable (it might be argued that those difficult times contributed to the reshaping of the intellectual agenda). His long life spanned almost a century – a century of revolutions (both bloody and bloodless), restoration (of the monarchy, of the established Church and of a capital city devastated by fire), and expansion (of ideas, aspirations and commercial and imperial power), which permanently reshaped the face and temper of Britain. Against that backdrop, Wren's virtuoso mind produced innovative solutions to an extraordinary range of difficult problems – reaching far beyond architecture and design. His diverse talents were more exceptional by far than a single building, however magnificent, could convey. He was a landmark figure in a landmark age.

Wren has been written about at length and repeatedly since his death, both as an architect and as a significant innovator in science, astronomy, mathematics and medicine. This is, however, the first integrated modern account of his career. It is no accident that I should have felt the need to undertake the daunting task of bringing together the many aspects of Wren's richly active career and the diversely innovative details of his intellectual life. Wren is a type I have always particularly admired – the person of many talents, whose enterprises regularly transgress, fearlessly and with apparent ease, the disciplinary boundaries traditionally policed under the labels 'arts' and 'sciences'.

Wren, then, is my kind of hero. Still, I was unprepared for the extent to which my admiration and respect for him would increase in the course of exploring his life and work.

At a critical moment during my research a single momentous discovery crystallised my ideas, focused my esteem for his intellect and set the course of the book that follows. Invited to contribute to a Channel Four documentary on the Great Fire of London, I spent three early hours of an unseasonably cold April morning at the Monument to the Great Fire, collaboratively designed by Wren and his close friend Robert Hooke, and completed in 1677. While I was waiting forlornly in the entrance-way at the bottom of the 200-foot column for the camera crew to finish setting up for filming at the top, the attendant – to cheer me up, I think – asked me if I had ever seen the basement. Removing the chair from his ticket booth, he rolled back the carpet, lifted a hinged trapdoor in the floor, and there, like something from a Brothers Grimm fairy story, was a flight of stone steps, curving down to a sizeable room beneath. Nothing I had read about the Monument and its construction, and none of the many experts in a whole range of fields relating to my project, had ever mentioned an underground chamber.[4]

There followed one of the happiest half-hours of my life, as I explored what I immediately recognised to be the laboratory Wren and Hooke had designed together, as the purpose-built setting for a whole series of scientific experiments requiring 'heights' – available to be used, most notably, as a zenith telescope, with lenses at ground and upper-platform levels, to attempt to track the minute shift in position of a selected fixed star, and prove the rotation of the earth. Some months later I returned, on a slightly more clement early-November morning, to take detailed measurements of the basement for a drawn cross-section of the building which would include the underground room (no extant drawing, either at the time of construction or thereafter, shows it). This time, while my architect husband was taking the measurements, I climbed the 345 steps of the beautifully crafted cantilevered stone staircase to the observation platform (a favourite tourist attraction, offering a panoramic view of London), unlocked two further heavy doors, and found the iron ship's-ladder which rises vertically inside the drum. I lifted – with difficulty – the heavy iron trapdoor (two semi-circular doors, in fact, like a ship's hatch) at the very top of the flaming urn which crowns the column. To my amazement, I found myself once again in the open air, high above the City, and vertically above the three-foot-diameter circular aperture in the domed roof of the basement laboratory.

Now I knew with absolute certainty that the Monument had indeed (as one or two comments by contemporaries had suggested) been designed by Wren and Hooke as a unique, hugely ambitious, vastly oversized scientific instrument. From the basement laboratory area an absolutely clear view could be had of the sky, via another aperture at platform level, then via a third at the base of the upper drum, and finally via a two-foot aperture at the top of the gilt flames issuing from the ornamental urn, hundreds of feet above. The upper observation platform also provides a suitable place where one could conveniently swing a long pendulum, or lower a barometer or thermometer on a rope (as Hooke records having done from the tower of Old St Paul's in the 1660s). From the strategically located man-sized niches set into the wall alongside the beautiful, regular stone spiral stair, with its black marble treads, one can take measurements using a delicate instrument calculating, say, atmospheric pressure variation with height, carried down, step by step (as Hooke records doing with a barometer, on this very stair, in 1678).

It seems incredible that such an achievement should have been so totally lost from view – hidden in clear sight from successive generations of admirers of both Wren and Hooke. How could we have overlooked the extraordinary precision in construction (every step exactly six inches high, each aperture a perfect multiple of feet), the careful, tailor-made functionality of the building for scientific use (Hooke used it for scientific experiments for many years after its completion)?

But the moment for such grandiose gestures on behalf of what one might call a unified creative agenda was a fleetingly brief one; by 1720 the ambition to advance knowledge on all intellectual fronts simultaneously was over. When Wren's ex-clerk and architectural pupil Nicholas Hawksmoor praised the Monument in 1728, it was as an architectural masterpiece, which vied in its neo-classical beauty and proportion with Trajan's Column in Rome – this in spite of the fact that Wren himself had cautioned that the proportions of the huge doric column were not correctly as specified by classical architectural theory. The underground laboratory was forgotten, as was the hinged lid, and the other features designed to make the building useful for experiments. No one any longer noticed the Monument's many strategically placed

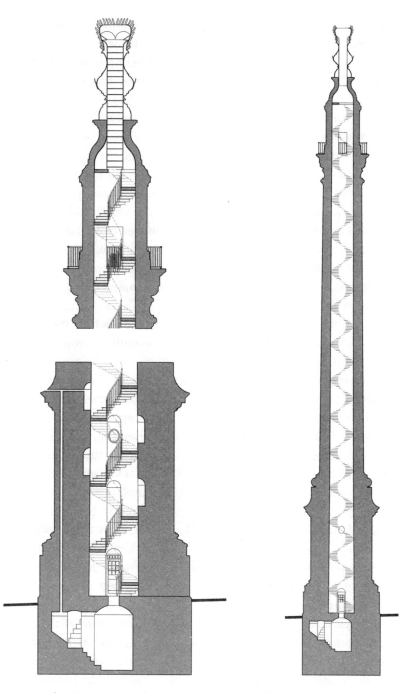

The Monument to the Great Fire which doubles as an oversized
scientific instrument – section showing basement laboratory and
stairway to hinged 'lid' to the flaming urn.

vents and vantage points – a small spyhole close to the top through which bearings could be taken from other buildings; a narrow vertical shaft within one of the stairway alcoves down which a plumbline could be dropped. Wren the versatile genius had become, simply, Wren the greatest architect England has ever had.

I determined that first day when I descended into the forgotten underground room in what Hooke always called 'the pillar at Fish Street' that my book about Wren's multi-faceted career would do justice to the brilliant versatility of the mind which had conceived of it and built it. The more I burrowed in the archives for additional evidence to fill out Wren's life into a rounded whole, the more the Monument became an apt metaphor for the entire enterprise. Alongside the familiar triumphalist tale of the great architect and the building of St Paul's, Wren's real life is a concatenation of now-buried chambers, each a vital part of his remarkable, rounded career, each richly in use during his lifetime, and each rapidly forgotten after his death.

In what follows I have tried to restore to Wren's career the complete shape which allows us to grasp just how extraordinary and innovative it was – the counterpoise at the end of the seventeenth century for the correspondingly astonishing and original career of his colleague Sir Isaac Newton, who has had, in terms of career, a far better press. Newton was an intellectual giant, whose inverse-square law of gravitational attraction we all take for granted, and whose laws of motion continue to be used today to explain mass and momentum. Still, what I aim to uncover here for Wren – like the secret chamber and the oversized telescope – is a career on a yet grander scale.

Having attempted the complex task of weaving together the threads of Wren's varied life convincingly into a coherent whole, there are a few caveats to be made. In the first place, it has inevitably proved impossible completely to do justice to each of the many separate branches of knowledge to which he so vigorously contributed over an active career spanning close to seventy years. The scale of a book-length enterprise dictates that some aspects of each field covered have of necessity had to be left out: full discussions of, say, his innovative work on the trajectories of comets; his work in mathematics on the rectification of the cycloid and impact between solid bodies. Jim Bennett's ground-breaking book is still the place for readers to turn for these.

Neither have I been able to give the treatments they deserve to all of the many surviving buildings designed and built by the Wren office, let alone the many projects either unbuilt or subsequently demolished. In each of these areas, wonderful work by experts exists in the large Wren secondary literature, and I refer the reader to my bibliography for fuller discussion of topics only dealt with here in passing. As I write, new vistas in Wren studies are being opened up by younger scholars like Dr James Campbell, Dr Anthony Geraghty and Dr Gordon Higgott – names, I have no doubt, that will rank with those of John Summerson, Kerry Downes and Margaret Whinney, whose work still sets the gold standard in studies of Wren by architectural historians.

An interesting dilemma arises, too, for the intellectual biographer, as to what to do when Wren's solution to a problem was misguided or simply wrong. A central theme of this book is how remarkable, how ground-breaking, Wren's many intellectual and technical innovations were in fields as diverse as micrometer-screw gauges for telescopes and the construction of stable stone arches in building. But Wren lived on the cusp of the modern era, between a world saturated in received wisdom and one whose fundamental scientific beliefs were grounded in observation and meticulously recorded data. Sometimes he was misinformed; on a number of occasions he clung to an explanation given him by his father, which common sense should have told him had no place in his fundamentally rational explanation of natural phenomena.

A good example of the contradictions between old and new styles of knowledge with which Wren and his contemporaries lived can be found in the diary kept by his devoted friend Hooke – a diary which fortunately gives us many glimpses of Wren out of the public eye. On Thursday, 16 August 1677, Hooke recorded:

> At Sir Chr. Wrens. . . . At the Crown [public house], Sir Christopher told me of killing the worms with burnt oyle . . . and of curing his lady of a thrush by hanging a bag of live boglice about her neck. Discoursed about theory of the Moon which I explain. Sir Christopher told his way of solving Keplers problem by the Cycloeid.[5]

While animatedly discussing such important topics as the lunar orbit (the problem of determining the motion of a body on which gravitational attraction is exercised by both the sun and the earth), and Wren's sophisticated mathematical attempts at solving it, the two men exchanged opinions also on superstitious cures for humdrum diseases. The former remain the object of our interest and attention, the latter have receded into the domain of the superstitious and quaint.

I have not dwelt unduly on Wren's mistaken beliefs (nor, I hasten to add, have my predecessors in the field of Wren biography). Nevertheless, I would contend that some of them are important for our understanding of the way his mind worked. For that reason the reader will find a surprising amount in this book about curious beliefs of Wren's to which we no longer usually consider it appropriate to give attention: his passionate commitment to – amounting to worship of – the memory of the 'martyred' King Charles I; his lasting loyalty to the mystical elite fraternity of the Order of the Garter which had meant so much to his father, and to the fraternity of Speculative Freemasons which meant just as much to the master craftsmen he employed on his construction sites. Wren's contributions to knowledge and to beauty are lasting and timeless. The social and political contexts in which they were made were local and historically specific, and played a vital part in the particular way in which Wren thought and worked.

We are the lasting beneficiaries of Wren's genius. The consequences of his inspired ideas and innovative practices are all around us, as are the great buildings he built so solidly that they have – as he hoped – stood the test of time. Everything Wren undertook, he envisaged on a grander scale – bigger, better, more enduring, than what had come before. The work stands. It is for the reader to decide whether I have done justice to the man behind the work.

LISA JARDINE
December 2001

ACKNOWLEDGEMENTS

The process of writing this book has involved two kinds of exploration: a detective-style investigation of the archives, and a series of dialogues with a wide range of people with abundant funds of information on Wren and his age which they generously shared with me. I am deeply indebted to all who were prepared to give time and enthusiasm to responding to my, I am sure sometimes tiresome, requests for information and enlightenment. These include: Dr Jim Bennett, Professor Jacques Heyman, Sir Alan Cook, Professor Charles Webster, Dr James Campbell, Dr Michael Cooper, Dr Gillian Darley, Dr Douglas Chambers, Dr Alan Stewart, Dr Alison Stoesser-Johnston, Dr Rob Iliffe, Dr Vaughan Hart, Dr Frances Harris, Professor Michael Hunter, Professor Moti Feingold, Dr Charles Saumarez-Smith, Professor Pat Rubin, Professor Andrew Prescott, and Professor John Knott.

The many librarians and archivists who have assisted me along the way include: Jo Wisdom, Librarian St Paul's Cathedral Library; Professor Ian Maclean, Librarian of the Codrington Library, All Souls College, Oxford; the librarians of the Guildhall Library and Guildhall Record Office, the Royal Society Library, Soane Museum Library, Wellcome Library for the History and Understanding of Medicine, Warburg Institute Library, Institute of Historical Research Library, British Library and Cambridge University Library. The librarians at my own university Queen Mary, University of London, deserve special thanks for defending me from persistent recalls at crucial moments of volumes of the Wren Society publications, for which they granted me extended, uninterrupted loan. Jonathan Clark of Sotherans Rare Books in London helped locate vital Wren secondary sources.

Rachel Jardine did some essential research for me on the Isle of Wight and in the PRO and Hampshire Records Office. Jerry Brotton was a tireless and exemplary picture researcher, locating images I never dreamed we would be able to find. John Hare gave freely of his architectural expertise, and measured and drew the Monument.

My HarperCollins editors, Michael Fishwick in the UK, and Terry Karten in the USA, have been wonderfully supportive throughout, as have also Maggie Pearlstine and John Oates of Maggie Pearlstine Associates. The production team at HarperCollins shared my enthusiasm from the beginning, and went to enormous lengths to ensure that the final book came up to all our expectations.

This book could not have been written without access to the important published works of great scholars in the field. These sources include above all the ground-breaking work on Wren's science and mathematics by Jim Bennett. Other scholars have given me access in advance to vital material: Charles Webster generously allowed me to read the new introduction to his *Great Instauration* in typescript, while Michael Hunter gave me early access to his new edition of the complete correspondence of Robert Boyle. Margaret 'Espinasse's book on Robert Hooke first got me intrigued by the relationship between Wren and Hooke, and the articles by Mike Cooper on Hooke's surveying deepened my understanding of Hooke's virtuosity. I have relied heavily on the definitive architectural work of Howard Colvin, Kerry Downes, John Summerson and Margaret Whinney. Recent work by James Campbell, Anthony Geraghty and Gordon Higgott on Wren has proved invaluable.

Finally, my colleagues at Queen Mary, University of London have given me the kind of unstinting intellectual support and encouragement that every scholar hopes for, but few are fortunate enough to find. They are my constant inspiration.

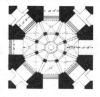

1

Loyal Sons of Delinquent Fathers

On the afternoon of 10 January 1642, King Charles I left his Palace at Whitehall in London without warning, accompanied by his wife, Queen Henrietta Maria, his eldest son, the twelve-year-old heir to the throne, Charles, Prince of Wales, and his daughter Princess Mary (who had been married to William, Prince of Orange the previous year, but who, at barely ten, was too young permanently to join the household of her new Dutch husband).[1] Their departure from the capital was so sudden that the royal servants at the party's first stopping-place, Hampton Court Palace, two hours or so away by barge down the River Thames, had no time to prepare for their arrival – we are told that it was so cold in the closed-up royal apartments that on their first night the King and Queen and their children were obliged to sleep together in one bed for warmth. The Palace at Whitehall, summarily abandoned by its royal owner and left vacant and unsecured, swiftly became a tourist attraction – curious Londoners wandered around its twenty acres of opulent grounds and buildings, staring at the King's picture collection, and even, apparently, trying out the throne for comfort.[2]

Two days later the King and his party moved on further down the Thames to Windsor Castle, where they stayed until 7 February. The King then escorted his wife and daughter to Dover, from where it had been decided that Princess Mary and Queen Henrietta Maria should embark for the safety of the Netherlands, and the protection of the royal couple's new son-in-law William of Orange. Carefully skirting London, the party reached Dover on 16 February, where the royal couple lingered, reluctant to take leave of one another; a week later, after emotional farewells, the Queen and Princess sailed out of Dover on a modest ship, the *Lion*, with a small escorting flotilla. King Charles galloped along the White Cliffs, waving desperately to his wife and daughter until they were long out of sight. The King then rode directly to Canterbury, from where he sent word to his eldest son, still at Windsor, that he should join him at the Royal Palace of Greenwich.

Now, as relations openly deteriorated between the King and the elected representatives of his people, Parliament countermanded the King's instruction to his son, hoping to take the heir to the throne into their custody along with the three of the royal children (James, Elizabeth and Henry) who had remained at St James's Palace in London. The Parliamentary Commission and the King with his entourage arrived at Greenwich together where, just in time, Charles dismissed the Commissioners, and set off again with his son for his favourite palace in Hertfordshire, Theobalds. On 19 March they reached the royalist stronghold of York; in August, at Nottingham, with his son by his side, the King formally declared war on his own people.[3]

For the next four years the two royal Charleses, father and son, lived hand to mouth, itinerant and to all intents and purposes homeless. Sometimes they marched into battle flamboyantly side by side, sometimes they retreated to the shelter of the castles of royalist sympathisers. For a period the King's headquarters was Oxford, his son's Bristol. Theirs was a fundamentally comfortless, soldier's existence, in stark contrast to the pampered, court-based years of the younger Charles's early childhood. From the make-believe world of chivalric pageantry and court ceremonial the Prince and heir to the throne was catapulted into a real-life world of battles, fear and pain – even his father was apparently shattered when he confronted the carnage and loss of life after the first clash between royalists and parliamentarians at the Battle of Edgehill in the autumn of 1642.[4]

In 1646, with things looking increasingly dark for the monarchy, and following several narrow escapes when the young Prince was nearly taken by the parliamentary forces, the King gave in to pressure from the Queen (now at the French court), and ordered a reluctant Prince Charles out of the country for safety – first to the Isles of Scilly, and thence to Paris to join his mother. Three years later, in January 1649, almost exactly seven years after his precipitate departure, the King returned to his Palace at Whitehall, now under close arrest, to spend his last night in the royal bedroom (stripped of its sumptuous furniture and fittings). On 30 January 1649, King Charles I was beheaded on a public scaffold outside the Banqueting House at Whitehall, his last sight as he walked calmly to his 'martyrdom' (as he deemed it to be) the gorgeous ceiling painted for him by Rubens. The ten-year English Commonwealth and Protectorate, under the rule first of Parliament and then of Oliver Cromwell, was about to begin.

The story of Charles I's flight from London and subsequent peripatetic existence during two periods of civil war (1642 to 1646 and 1647 to 1648), leading up to his trial and execution, has been told again and again – sometimes as tragedy, sometimes as farce, depending upon the inclination of the times of writing and the political affiliations of the writer. The Dutch engravings of the King on the scaffold and the English poet Andrew Marvell's lines recalling Charles's dignity and composure at the end ('He nothing common did or mean / Upon that memorable scene') are familiar, lastingly vivid images in English history.

After the death of Charles I, however, attention tends to shift briskly away from the Stuart dynasty to Cromwell, the Commonwealth and the Protectorate. For the purposes of this story, though, it is the sturdy dark-skinned boy who survived his executed royal father that we should watch. His story and, most importantly, his intellectual and cultural development continued in exile, as the tolerated, but not-quite-welcome guest first of the Dutch and then of the French, watching the courts of William of Orange and Louis XIV from the wings. When that boy who had been exiled from family and country at the age of fifteen returned in triumph in 1660 as King Charles II – unexpectedly, at the invitation of the English government – the years in exile left a lasting impression on him. Nevertheless, it was his childhood experiences in his native land which most distinctively shaped and coloured his outlook, from the friendships he made and the favours he bestowed to the domestic details of his everyday life, and the very style in which he chose to reign.

Back at last in the Palace of his happy childhood at Whitehall in 1660, Charles II gathered around himself a band of small boys (now grown men) who had shared his bewilderingly sudden, downward-spiralling fall in fortunes, from charmed, golden childhood to fearful, penurious adolescence, and for whom, too, the King's Restoration marked a glorious return to centre stage.[5] Together they reinvented English 'civility', drawing deep on the ideas and activities that had sustained them through the years of personal and political uncertainty. Many of them, too, had lost their fathers under traumatic circumstances, or had seen them sink from positions of rank and influence to humiliation and hardship. All of them owed their survival to acts of generosity on the part of more fortunate men of their fathers' generation. In the new world of Restoration England these compassionate mentors provided the missing generation of father-figures for a generation of lost boys. It is, as we shall see, this peculiarly post-civil-disorder society which frames and shapes the career of Sir Christopher Wren.

THE BLACK BOY

Unlike his father, who as a child could barely walk for his rickety legs, and who suffered from a lifelong pronounced stutter, the future Charles II was a large, sturdy child.[6] At four months the heir to the thrones of England and Scotland could pass as a one-year-old. He apparently inherited his bulk from his Scandinavian ancestors on his father's side. His swarthy complexion, on the other hand, supposedly came from his Italian, Medici forebears on his mother's: 'He is so dark I am ashamed of him,' the Queen wrote shortly after he was born, and that colouring earned him the nickname 'the black boy'.[7] Still, by the time he was four months old she could write proudly, 'his size and fatness supply the want of beauty. I wish you could see the gentleman, for he has no ordinary mien; he is so serious in all he does, that I cannot help fancying him far wiser than myself.'[8] In an age when a quarter of all children died before the age of ten (and several of Charles's own siblings failed to reach adulthood), the future Charles II reached maturity having suffered nothing more serious than a gastric infection, a fever and a broken arm.[9]

Prince Charles's father, Charles I, James I's second son, had not been born to rule. His early childhood was spent watching from the sidelines as his father's handsome and talented first-born, the heir to the throne Prince Henry, received all the public and private adulation. Not until Henry died, when Charles was twelve, did the spotlight shift

The infant Charles II
in royal splendour,
with his pet spaniel.

to him, and even then Charles was permanently overshadowed by the
memory of his beloved elder brother. The future Charles II, by contrast,
was the centre of everyone's attention from the moment he was born.
His first household at St James's Palace consisted of almost 300 servants,
at an annual cost of £5000.[10] Before his third birthday (when the royal
household had moved to Richmond Palace) the annual wardrobe
expense for his sister Mary and himself totalled £3000. Thus sumptuously attired, he entertained his first distinguished foreign guests at
Whitehall at the age of five, and at six presided over a masque as
Prince Britomart, dressed in blue and crimson taffeta 'after the Roman
fashion'.[11]

As Prince Charles approached the age of eleven, when the political
situation between Charles I and the House of Commons started seriously
to deteriorate, the heir to the throne was a good-natured, lively, utterly
pampered child, an excellent horseman and tolerably well-educated
schoolboy, accustomed to being the focus of any public event in which

The future Charles II and his brother James armed and ready for battle before Edgehill in 1642.

he participated. Even as he and his father rode towards York, after their precipitate exit from London in 1642, it was the Prince of Wales who, riding ahead of his father, received the expression of loyal support on the part of the University of Cambridge, in the shape of an honorary MA, awarded in a lengthy and elaborate ceremony, followed by a three-hour Latin play. At early appearances of the gathering royalist army in the same year, Prince Charles and his younger brother James, Duke of York (the future James II) appeared as gorgeous figureheads, Charles dressed in oyster-coloured silk decorated with gold bands and lace at the cuffs, with a red sash around his waist and a sword at the side of his buff leather jerkin.[12]

Less than four years later, shortly after his sixteenth birthday (which he celebrated to the firing of cannon on the island of Jersey), Charles entered exile in France, landing there so ill-clad that others had to vouch for him before the locals could be persuaded to provide him with food and lodging. In France the heir to the English throne was dependent on the charity of the French court, painfully conscious of the humiliatingly reduced lifestyle of himself and his mother. Without a royal role, no longer the centre of political or domestic attention, dependent for the least thing on other people's good will, it would be fourteen years before he was at last in a position to resume the role for which his childhood had so thoroughly prepared him.

THE DEAN'S SON

The future Sir Christopher Wren was not yet three when his father was appointed Dean of Windsor and Register of the Order of the Garter in 1635, a privileged servant of key significance within the baroque, absolutist court world created by King Charles I. The King was Supreme Head of the Order, which at any time consisted of just twenty-five Knights or Knights Companion, elected for life at a convocation of the other Knight-members held annually on St George's Day (23 April), and bound by an elaborate chivalric code of conduct. Much of this code had been reinvented by Charles I in close collaboration with his then Dean of Windsor, Christopher Wren senior's elder brother Matthew; in particular, the ceremonial procession and dinner at Windsor on the eve of the annual Garter convocation was introduced at Matthew Wren's suggestion in 1629. Herbert, Charles's gentleman of the bedchamber, informs us that the King put on his 'George' (his jewelled insignia of the Order, worn on a ribbon round his neck) first thing in the morning and never failed to wear it.[13]

In addition to English members of the Order, a small number of crowned heads of foreign territories figured among the Garter Knights. The Dean of Windsor and Register of the Order presided over all official functions, kept records of the secret conclaves, and generally orchestrated the ceremonies. Where Garter matters were concerned, he took precedence over all other clerics, and, by virtue of his role, he rubbed shoulders with the highest nobility in the land, and the representatives of crowned heads of allied nations such as (during Charles I's time as Head of the Order) Denmark, Bohemia and Sweden.[14]

A grand house at Windsor came with the job of Dean, and Christopher Wren senior and his family took up residence in 1636. Not that their previous residence, the rectory at Knoyle Magna in Wiltshire – the living Christopher Wren senior had held before being invited to

Ceremonial portrait of Charles I in full regalia of the Order of
the Garter.

replace his brother Matthew as Dean of Windsor – was anything but
comfortable. Like Matthew, Christopher Wren senior had been a protégé
and chaplain to Lancelot Andrewes, Bishop of Winchester and close
personal adviser to Charles I (Bishop Andrewes, a leading prelate of
Elizabeth I's reign, died in 1626). A note among Dean Christopher
Wren's papers tells us that on 6 August 1620 he joined his brother

Matthew as a member of the Bishop of Winchester's household, 'following the special assembly held by him that day in the chapel at Windsor Palace', and that afterwards they both accompanied the Bishop to Farnham Castle 'where the King with his entire royal court was entertained by the bishop over a period of three days, with the most sumptuous pomp, and at a cost of more than 3000 pounds. Bravo!'[15]

It was Bishop Andrewes who subsequently placed Christopher Wren senior in the substantial Knoyle Magna living, which remained Wren's after his promotion to Windsor. Shortly after his appointment as Dean, Christopher Wren petitioned the courts over a dispute with 'one Thornhill' who had, it was claimed, undermined the foundations of the pigeon-house at the rectory of Knoyle Magna 'under pretence of digging for Salt-Petre'.[16] Wren invoked his right of protection and restitution under the ancient privilege of the Order of the Garter, and a ruling was indeed issued on Wren's behalf to that effect. In the end, however, Thornhill was 'indicted for conveying Salt-Petre to Dunkirk [that is, supplying it to the enemy], fled: and so the prosecution of this business fell'.[17]

Dean Christopher Wren's only son, also named Christopher, was born at East Knoyle on 20 October 1632. He was one of ten children (one further boy was still-born), of whom five appear to have survived beyond infancy. Three sisters (Catharine, Anna and Susan) reached adulthood.[18] At the time of the move to Windsor the family consisted of three little girls and the three-year-old Christopher.[19]

In fact, Dean Christopher Wren's family may have had to wait a while before they could occupy the fine domestic apartments in the Dean's House at Windsor. In 1635 Dean Christopher Wren's brother Matthew, who had married just months after his own appointment to the Windsor post in 1628, had eight children, including four-year-old twin boys, and a ninth was on the way.[20] (Matthew's eldest son, born in 1629 and named Matthew like his father, was to become one of Christopher Wren junior's closest friends.) The logistics of transporting so large a family to new homes in London and (then) Ely were considerable, and certainly not to be rushed.

Once installed at Windsor, the boy Christopher Wren found himself effectively part of the royal household, in close proximity to the royal family whenever they were in residence. The Dean's House was located within the perimeter fortified wall of Windsor Castle, on the river side, close to St George's Chapel; it was a substantial detached house with a garden.[21] Some sense of the lavishness of the lifestyle to which the Wrens quickly became accustomed is to be gained from a passing remark made by Elias Ashmole in his 1670 *History of the Order of the Garter* (a book in which both Dean Christopher Wren and his son had a hand, and to which we shall have occasion to return):

> It was the manner heretofore, for the Soveraign's Lieutenant (when the Soveraign thought fit to appoint the Installation at the same time with the Feast of St. George) to ride to Windesor, attended by a gallant Train, and no small number of his own Gentlemen and Yeomen richly habited, and in all things well appointed. . . . The Lieutenant and his Assistants (or otherwise the Knights-Commissioners, if the Feast of St. George be not then held) being arrived in the Castle, forthwith retire to their Lodgings, which most usually have been prepared at the Deans house, the Rooms therein being the fairest, and best fitted for accommodation in the Castle (next those of the Soveraign's in the upper Ward).[22]

It was in the Dean's House that Charles Louis, Elector Palatine, the eldest son of Charles I's sister, Elizabeth of Bohemia, lodged during the summer of either 1640 or 1641 (or possibly both). The King had become unofficial guardian of his sister's family after the death of their father in 1632 (since their expulsion from the throne of Bohemia and their Palatinate territories by the Habsburgs in 1621, Elizabeth and Frederick had lived ignominiously in exile in Holland), intermittently pursuing the 'Protestant cause' of returning the family to their throne. Various of Frederick and Elizabeth's children resided almost permanently in England, from 1635, drawing substantial English pensions. At the Elector Palatine's departure from Windsor on this occasion he presented Dean Christopher Wren with two large silver tankards, 'in Acknowledgement of the many Civilities, and respectful Entertainment, his Royal Highness had occasionally received in the Deanery-house, where he lodged when he was pleased to reside, for a Season, at Windsor'.

> The Elector usually expressed a great Satisfaction with this his commodious Retirement from Whitehall, (where the Parliament had allowed him a Lodging) and the Opportunity of conversing

Detail from an engraved view of Windsor Castle – the Dean's house is inside the castle walls, immediately to the left of the bell tower.

with the Dean, and some other Persons of Learning, his Friends, who used to resort there.

Here the Prince lived in a very private Way, with two Gentlemen only of his Retinue, a Secretary, and one who waited in the Bed-chamber; and a few inferior Servants. He dined at a little Table by himself; the others, with the Dean and his Family.[23]

Christopher Wren junior recalled that stay later, when, around the age of seventeen, at the beginning of his association with Wadham College, Oxford, he was persuaded by the Warden, Dr John Wilkins, to present some of his precocious scientific work to the Elector Palatine (Wilkins had been chaplain to the Elector Charles Louis during his residence in England). These comprised a mechanical device for assisting the planting of corn ('which being drawn by a Horse over a Land ready plow'd and harrow'd, shall plant Corn equally without Want and without Waste'), a device for double-writing, and two drawings of mites viewed under a magnifying lens.[24] In the accompanying letter, in a careful bid for patronage, he wrote:

Now if it is possible for your Highness to force your self to accept such extreme Littlenesses as these [the microscopic drawings], you will therein imitate the Divinity, which shews it self *maxime in minimis*, and preserve that Devotion towards your Highness, which I conceived while yet a Child, when you were pleased to honour my Father's House by your presence, for some Weeks.[25]

Christopher Wren would have been eight or nine during the summer in question – an impressionable age for a child, and the same age at which, in 1638, Prince Charles, the future Charles II, had been installed as a Knight Companion of the Order of the Garter at Windsor Castle, in a particularly elaborate ceremony, under the proud eye of his father the King, with Wren's father Dean Christopher Wren officiating. Since the young Christopher's early education was at home, under a personal tutor, the Reverend William Shepheard (because of his frail health), the boy was probably present at Windsor on this auspicious occasion – one which, throughout his own later life, the future Charles II recalled repeatedly, as a touchstone for the legitimacy and continuity of Stuart rule and a symbolic moment of father-son trust.[26]

Although after the Restoration Sir Christopher Wren chose not to draw attention to the fact, until the age of twelve his was a golden childhood, one of comfort and privilege, close to the innermost circle of the King of England himself. Both his father and his uncle occupied public positions of importance and influence, which brought them into day-to-day contact with the most powerful people in the land. Prior to 1642, Bishop Matthew Wren and Dean Christopher Wren were certainly justified in having the highest expectations of glittering future lives and careers for their first-born sons. In that year, however, the Wren family's fortunes changed dramatically, and for ever.

In August 1642, King Charles planted his royal standard at Nottingham, and, as we have seen, declared war on his disobedient people. From that moment the parliamentary party proceeded swiftly against those of the King's allies and advisers who lived near London, and were hence within easy reach of the parliamentary forces who controlled the capital. On 30 August, Bishop Matthew Wren was violently seized from his home and imprisoned in the Tower of London.[27] One small comfort to him was that that autumn his eldest son Matthew was admitted as an undergraduate to Peterhouse College, Cambridge, where in better times his father had held the Mastership. A few years later, however, when Matthew Wren junior moved to Oxford, his family could no longer afford the residence fees. Bishop Wren was to remain in prison until the Restoration in 1660.[28]

The first battle of the civil war was fought at Edgehill, a few miles north-west of Banbury in Oxfordshire, on 23 October 1642. The forces were supposedly commanded by the King and the twelve-year-old Prince of Wales together. In fact, the Prince of Wales's troops (and effectively the engagement as a whole) were under the tactical command of Prince Rupert of the Rhine, younger brother of Charles Louis, Elector Palatine, and Charles I's favourite nephew (already at twenty-two a seasoned campaigner after years fighting for the Palatinate in Europe in the thirty years war). The battle was bloody and did not deliver outright victory for either side (though both claimed it), but the opening of actual hostilities had immediate political consequences. By the end of the year Parliament had introduced legislation empowering them to confiscate and dispose of all property belonging to known royalist supporters, officially dubbed 'delinquents'.[29]

The King had responded to this legislation by insisting that certain of his key officers (including the Dean of Windsor) should be protected from any such proceedings, and Parliament had apparently conceded that seizure in this case would be inappropriate. On 25 October 1642, however, a troop of soldiers arrived at Windsor Castle (already requisitioned by Parliament as a garrison and prison, and placed under the Governorship of Colonel Venn), and made their way to St George's Chapel, where 'one Captain Fogg pretending a Warrant from the King, demanded the Keys of the Treasury at Windsor, in presence of Colonel Manwaring, with Threats'. None of the three official key-keepers – neither Dean Wren nor his two prebends – was at Windsor, so the soldiers forced their way into the Chapel. There they gathered up the valuable Garter ceremonial trappings (banners and insignia) from the Chapel stalls and tombs, and then, using iron bars, broke down two doors and the stone door-jambs to get into the Treasury in the vaults, where they impounded the fabulous collection of Garter-related gems, plate and armour it housed.[30]

Three days later soldiers returned and broke into the Dean's House, plundering it of all its valuables. The only thing the Dean ever succeeded in retrieving was a harpsichord 'of about ten pounds value' which was returned to him in London six years later.[31] Dean Wren was not there, having accompanied the King on his journey northwards.[32] But his wife was at Windsor at the time of the sacking of the family home, pregnant with their last child, Francesca. The baby was born at Windsor in 1643, and she and her mother and sisters moved back to Knoyle Magna shortly afterwards for safety ('She fled to Knoyle in the loving embrace of her mother and sisters'). Like so many of her siblings she too died in infancy – Dean Wren described her as 'a very sweet baby'.

Christopher Wren senior (officially deprived of his Deanship, and subsequently of the Knoyle Magna living by Parliament) was now itinerant, he and his family dependent upon the hospitality of friends and colleagues. Still Register of the Order of the Garter, he joined the King and his entourage, who at the beginning of 1643 had set up their official headquarters in Oxford, a staunchly royalist town which would be Charles I's main base for the next three and a half years. Then, in April 1646, when the King left Oxford surreptitiously and went on the run again, Dean Wren and his family withdrew to the safety and seclusion of his son-in-law the Reverend William Holder's house at Bletchingdon, a short distance outside Oxford in the direction of Bicester.[33]

There, in rural seclusion, the hitherto prominent and prestigious Wren family to all intents and purposes 'disappeared'.[34] Aside from regular appearances by Christopher Wren senior at court hearings in London to try, unsuccessfully, to retrieve his illegally seized possessions, he was forced to withdraw completely from public life.[35] For the next fourteen years, with no way of earning a living, he and his family, like so many other royalists and minor clergy, identified as delinquents and deprived of all lands, livings and income, had to rely on the goodwill of friends and relatives to save them from utter ruin. From now on all the family's hopes and prospects rested with Dean Wren's able, but barely adolescent, only son, Christopher.

THE BOY FROM THE ISLE OF WIGHT

On 11 November 1647, Charles I slipped out of Hampton Court Palace, where he was a prisoner of the parliamentarian forces on his own premises, down a back staircase, under cover of darkness, crossed the Thames in a rowing boat, mounted a waiting horse and escaped to the Isle of Wight. He arrived there on 13 November, and took up residence in Carisbrooke Castle, a mile south-west of the island's capital, Newport. The twenty-six-year-old Governor of the Castle, Colonel Robert Hammond, was not altogether happy at the sudden arrival of his royal guest, but to begin with at least he was prepared to provide him with a base for what turned out to be a kind of last, lingering Indian summer of Charles I's life and reign.

After lunch on the following day the King received the royalist-sympathising gentry of the island who came to pay their respects. We have an eye-witness account of this arrival from the diary of Sir John Oglander – one of the Isle of Wight's most prominent residents, an ardent royalist, and the only person to have the honour of entertaining the King privately to a formal dinner, at his family home in Nunwell, during his year-long residence on the island:

> Sunday morning at church I heard a rumour that the King was that night, being the 14th November, landed at Cowes. I confess I could not believe it, but at evening prayer the same day Sir Robert Dillington sent his servant to inform me of His Majesty's coming into the Island and that our Governor, Colonel Hammond, commanded me and my son (as he had done to all the gentlemen of the Island) to meet him at Newport the next day, being Monday, by nine in the morning.
>
> Truly this news troubled me very much but on the Monday myself and most of the Island gentlemen went to Carisbrooke Castle to him, where he used us all most graciously and asked the names of those he knew not and, when he asked my eldest son his name, he asked me whether it was my son.
>
> And not long after, Hammond came, when he made a short speech to us, which – as well as my old memory will give me leave – was thus, or to this purpose: 'Gentlemen, I believe it was as strange to you as to me to hear of his Majesty's coming into this Island. He informs me necessity brought him hither and there were a sort of people near Hampton Court, from whence he came, that had voted and were resolved to murder him, or words to that effect, and therefore so privately he was forced to come away and so to thrust himself on this island, hoping to be secure here. And now, gentlemen, seeing he is come amongst us, it is all our duties to preserve his person and

to prevent all comings over into our Island. I have already stopped all passages into our Island except three, Ryde, Cowes and Yarmouth, and at them have appointed guards. Now I must desire you all to preserve peace and unity in this Island as much as you can. I hear there are some such persons as his Majesty feared but I hope better, but to prevent it I would give you these cautions. If you see or hear of any people in any great number gathered together, whatsoever their pretence, I would have you dissipate them, and timely notice given to me of it. Also, if there be any of those formerly spoken of, such as his Majesty fears, that shall offer to come into this Island, you must do your endeavours to suppress them, and all things for the preservation of his Majesty's person. And to this end I shall desire all the captains to come and renew their commissions that they may be the better authorised thereunto. And lastly I must tell you I have sent an express to Parliament to signify his Majesty's being here and, as soon as I receive my answer, I shall acquaint you with it.'

After this speech Sir Robert Dillington moved the Colonel to know whether the gentlemen might not, after dinner, go up to his Majesty to express their duties to him. The Colonel answered, 'Yes, by all means. It would be a fit time when the King had dined. And, truly, I would invite you all to dinner, had I any entertainment, but truly I want, extremely, foul [fowl] for his Majesty.' Intimating thereby that he wanted the gentlemen's assistance. Whereupon I and others promised to send him what we had. So he thanked us and returned to the Castle to his Majesty.

Now, when we had dined, we all went up to Carisbrooke Castle, where we had not stayed half an hour before his Majesty came to us and, after he had given every man his hand to kiss, he made this speech, but not in these words but, as well as my memory will give me leave, to this effect: 'Gentlemen, I must inform you that, for the preservation of my life, I am forced from Hampton Court. For there were a people called Levellers that had both voted and resolved of my death, so that I could not longer dwell there in safety. And, desiring to be somewhat secure till some happy accommodation may be made between me and my Parliament, I have put myself in this place, for I desire not a drop more of Christian blood should be spilt, neither do I desire to be chargeable to any of you. I shall not desire so much as a capon from any of you, my resolution in coming being but to be secured till there may be some happy accommodation made.'

After this he caused Mr William Legge, one of his servants, to read a kind of remonstrance, which it seemeth he left at Hampton Court when he came thence, but I shall forbear writing of that, it being in print. Mr Legge demanded of me, 'What if a greater number of these Levellers should come into our Island than we were able to resist? What course could then be taken for his Majesty's preservation?'

I answered, 'None that I knew, but to have a boat to convey him unto the mainland.'

These were all the passages on that day and, on the Thursday following, he came to Nunwell and gave a gracious visit there, and in the Parlour Chamber I had some speech with him, which I shall forbear to discover. I pray God send him happily hence and to regain his crown as his predecessor King John did here.

While his Majesty was in our Island I went (most commonly) once a week to see him, and seldom went but his Majesty would talk with me, sometimes almost a quarter of an hour together, but all (since his close imprisonment) openly.[36]

Oglander records here the setting up of a modest kind of court in exile, with the minor gentry of the Isle of Wight in the role of courtiers in attendance. As his account makes clear, when the King came to the Isle of Wight, gentlemen of rank on the island treated him as their honoured guest. So, too, apparently, did Governor Hammond (although the following February he would quietly comply with Parliament and change Charles's 'residence' in Carisbrooke Castle to close arrest). In early December 1647 the King's coach was shipped to the island, and Charles proceeded to tour his tiny island kingdom, much to the delight of the inhabitants, who had never before had such glamour in their midst.[37] It is not surprising that the islanders stayed determinedly loyal to the King when his relations with Hammond turned sour – islanders assisted in at least three attempts to rescue Charles and get him away to the continent between January and September 1648. As Sir John Oglander indicates in his memoir, he for one was ready and willing to provide a boat to effect such an escape, should the need ever arise.[38]

One of those loyal islanders who is likely to have attended the November dinner held for the King at Oglander's Nunwell country house near Sandown was the Reverend John Hooke. In the 1620s the young John Hooke had tutored Oglander's eldest son George (he died of smallpox in France in 1632).[39] At that time Hooke was curate of Brading Church near Nunwell; later he became curate of Freshwater Church.[40] John Hooke was a committed royalist and High Anglican, father of four children, three of whom had left home by 1648 – the eldest son John to serve an apprenticeship as a grocer, the two daughters apparently married.[41] Only his frail, clever thirteen-year-old son Robert remained with his parents at the vicarage, where he was first tutored by his father (like the young Christopher Wren, because of his ill health), and then either attended Newport Grammar School or perhaps was taught at home under the guidance of its headmaster, William Hopkins (a close friend of Sir John Oglander). If John Hooke had a brief taste of life in the royal circle because of his close association with Oglander and Hopkins, so too did his intense, intellectual son Robert.

Robert Hooke's teacher Hopkins was also a committed royalist, who played a prominent role in events during the King's stay on the Isle of Wight.[42] Like Matthew Wren, his house had been sacked by a parliamentary mob in August 1642, because of his declared support for the King's cause. It was in Hopkins's household that Charles I lodged for the final negotiations in September which culminated in the Treaty of Newport.

> In agreeing to open talks parliament also let Charles leave Carisbrooke Castle ... for more congenial quarters in Newport. In Newport Charles stayed with his friend, William Hopkins. Once more faithful servants, Will Murray, Ashburnham, Firebrace, Mrs Wheeler, and trusted advisers, Richmond, Hertford, Southampton and Lindsey, and sober chaplains, Sanderson, Sheldon, Hammond, and even his old secretary, Sir Edward Walker, attended the king. Allowed out riding again, he showed his old skills had not gone rusty; when going down the steep hill to Newport the bridle broke, but he was able to stop his horse without reins or breaking his neck. Charles seemed to be acting

as if he were a real king once more. His coachmen were issued with new livery, he encouraged efforts to discover silver in Somerset, requested a favour from the governor of Newfoundland, a pardon from the sheriffs of London, granted safe conducts to John Kerckhoven and Lady Stanhope to return to England, and appointed Sir Simonds D'Ewes, keeper of the royal libraries and medal collection.[43]

Charles I, famous throughout his reign for his lofty detachment from his people, became, in those final months of illusory regal dignity on the Isle of Wight, the people's sovereign, a man of the people. It is easy to see how the island's inhabitants, their heads turned by their King's personal attentiveness, became his most loyal subjects. In the schoolmaster's house the King treated Mrs Hopkins 'with a solicitude he had rarely shown the wives of his great officers of state'. 'As for yourself, be sure,' the King promised them, 'when I keep house again there will be those, who shall think themselves happy & yet sit lower at the table than you.'[44] What delusions of grandeur might ordinary families like the Hopkinses and Hookes have harboured, what dreams of future wealth and prominence, should the King, at this eleventh hour, regain his kingdom?

Yet, even as the King deluded himself that he might still negotiate his way back to power, and reach accommodation with his political opponents in Westminster, there were several good reasons for the residents of the Isle of Wight to feel increasingly depressed about their own futures. In the first place, the weather that year was terrible. As Sir John Oglander wrote in his diary:

This summer of the King's being here was a very strange year in all His Majesty's three kingdoms, if we duly consider the heavens, men and earth. To leave men and their nature to themselves, for it was never more truly verified than now – *homo homini lupus.*

I conceive the heavens were offended with us for our offence committed to one another for, from Mayday till the 15th of September, we had scarce three dry days together. . . . His Majesty asked me whether that weather was usual in our Island. I told him that in this 40 years I never knew the like before. If it doth not please the Almighty to send more seasonable weather, we shall save little pease and barley.

As for the earth, it is turned almost to water. The rivers in the Main have overflown all their neighbouring fields, the rich vales stand knee deep with water and, with the current, much corn is carried away and haycocks swimming up and down. In our Island the earth was drunk, and you might in August have gone with boat from Sandham two miles beyond Heasley. . . . God mend all. First let us repent all our bloody sins, then we shall find His mercy, and the earth will be again propitious unto us – which God grant.

But they tell us the Treaty [of Newport] will begin on Thursday the 14th of September at Newport, and that then we shall have peace and the issue of blood will be stopped, fair weather and all things according to our hearts desires.[45]

The islanders, identified, because of the positive welcome they had afforded the King, as out-and-out royalist supporters, were also assailed by punitive fines and levies exacted from them by the parliamentary administration in London as delinquents.[46] Oglander recorded the heavy impact of fines on the Isle of Wight in his diary, and commented that, because of the level of fines raised, Parliament had more money to play with than the average legitimate prince:

Besides Excise, Customs, Tonnage and Poundage, all the King's lands, delinquents' lands under sequestration, all the King's goods, subjects that have been plundered, the Bishops' lands, the Deans' and Chapters' lands, all the Prince of Wales' estate and the tin and lead mines, the Parliament lays a tax on the Kingdom of £90,000 for the Army. Of which the Isle of Wight pays every month £305, and the parish of Brading pays every month £21/ 10s, and of this Sir John Oglander payeth £3/10s, and every week 18s. I believe few princes in Christendom have such a coming in.[47]

At the Restoration, ordinary men resident on the Isle of Wight in 1648 would recall their involvement with the King's short residence there with pride.[48] Close to the Oglander family (who certainly were thus involved) the Reverend John Hooke was probably part of the island's intimate circle around the King in those last days. There seems, indeed, a *prima facie* case for linking his death in 1648 to the declining fortunes of the King's cause. John Hooke made a will on 23 September, five days after the talks opened in Newport. On 25 September, the Commissioners for Parliament presented their second major set of proposals: the abolition of the prayer book and of bishops, the sale of their lands, and the establishment of Presbyterianism. On 8 October the King accepted all these demands, sticking only at the total abolition of the bishops.[49] That week or the next, John Hooke died. The Freshwater Parish Register records: 17 October 1648 'Buried Mr. John Hooke'.[50] The post-mortem inventory of his goods which accompanied the will when it was proved on 18 December 1648 was taken on 9 November.[51]

Like other islanders John Hooke had been reduced to straitened means by the heavy fines imposed for delinquency. The King's settlement with the Parliamentary Commissioners would have deprived him of his living too. If he was already sick, the strain may have been too much for him. He may even have taken his own life, as his son John, heavily in debt and involved in a difficult lawsuit, did in 1678. Throughout his life, Robert Hooke too suffered from depression.[52]

Whatever the cause of the death of John Hooke, he had already made arrangements for his son Robert to leave the island for London, in the care (and at the expense) of a likeminded friend or colleague. The boy may indeed have already been gone when his father died – safely conveyed away to set his mind at rest. In John Hooke's will he left Robert 'forty pounds of lawful English money, the great and best joined chest, and all my books'.[53] Whereas his other children received large household goods, Robert's bequest was entirely portable – cash, books and a chest to carry them in. One of those who witnessed John Hooke's will was Cardell Goodman, vicar of Freshwater, with property in Freshwater village, a gentleman, who had been a pupil at Westminster School in London, and then at Christ Church, Oxford. By the end of 1648 Robert Hooke too was at Westminster School, making Goodman a good candidate as his royalist sponsor and patron.[54] Like Christopher Wren, Robert Hooke never spoke in later years about this traumatic period which abruptly ended his childhood.

When Robert Hooke rose to prominence after the Restoration, as a key figure in the Royal Society, as the City of London's Surveyor after the Great Fire of London, and above all as Sir Christopher Wren's devoted and lifelong friend and associate, he kept the manner of his arriving in London a mystery. All we know is that someone took him to London (someone who continued to subsidise him financially, since the forty pounds his father left him would not have gone a long way in the circles in which he henceforth moved), and that he was briefly apprenticed to the Dutch émigré painter, much patronised by the King and his circle, Peter (later Sir Peter) Lely.[55] By the end of 1648, however, the young Hooke was in the care of the great royalist educationalist Dr Busby, headmaster of Westminster School in London.

Hooke never married, and for most of his life lived in rooms at Gresham College which came with the job of Curator of Experiments to the Royal Society. Until his death he kept his valuables, and a large sum in cash, in a fine, large chest. One of his 'valuables' not in the chest but on the shelf of his extensive library was a folio Italian Bible, recorded in the inventory of his books taken after his death as: 'The Bible of Giovanni Diodati in folio, gilded, paper, belonging to his Majesty the King and with annotations by the same.' It fetched an exceptionally high sum at the post-mortem auction of Hooke's library. Was this a precious gift received by John Hooke from his sovereign and willed to his son?[56] The mere fact that the fiercely rationalist and pragmatic Robert kept such a book on his shelves alongside the miscellaneous volumes that clearly had come from his father testifies to his commitment to the ideals of 1647–48, and to the emotional legacy of his father's death.

One further clue to the Hookes' involvement with the royalist circle on the Isle of Wight comes in the form of an anecdote told by John Aubrey in his 'Life' of Hooke, written some fifty years after the event. Hooke told Aubrey that the idea of a 'tryall' with the painter Lely came as the result of a visit by the English painter John Hoskins to the Isle of Wight. We are told that he found the young Robert Hooke an able assistant, and recommended that he be apprenticed to a painter.[57] John Hoskins was Charles I's official miniaturist. The most likely reason for his being on the Isle of Wight, executing a commission (in the course of which he was helped by a willing small boy who was unusually deft at small-scale drafting work, and generally good with his hands), is as part of that entourage that assembled round the King at Carisbrooke in 1647–48. Whoever the sitter was for Hoskins on the occasion of his visit the Hookes were on familiar enough terms with that person to come and go in their household.[58]

Here we have a third small boy left fatherless by the fall of King Charles I, who was supported through adolescence during the Commonwealth period by unnamed royalist sympathisers, and who emerged at the Restoration as a figure with the same array of skills and interests the new King himself had gained during his years on the margins of public life. Until his death, Robert Hooke fasted every year on 30 January – the anniversary of the execution on the scaffold in front of Inigo Jones's Banqueting House at the Palace of Whitehall of the 'royal martyr', Charles I.[59]

ORDER OUT OF CHAOS

Before we leave the civil war years, and the personal histories on whose details, come the Restoration, those concerned would choose not to dwell, there is one link, altogether unnoticed today, which deserves our further attention – one which has already cropped up several times in the course of our story. Criss-crossing the lives of our main protagonists is the connecting thread of the Order of the Garter Knights, the secretive chivalric association especially dear to Charles I's heart (and subsequently, in part as a homage to his father's memory, to that of his son, Charles II).

King Charles I's last act, as he stood on the scaffold in Whitehall just minutes before his execution, in full view of his subjects, was to hand the 'Great George' which hung around his neck – the gorgeous, bejewelled emblem of the Order of the Garter – together with his Garter cloak, to Bishop Juxon who stood beside him to provide spiritual comfort at the end:

> *Dr. Juxon:* 'There is but one stage more. This stage is turbulent and troublesome. It is a short one. But you may consider it, it will soon carry you a very great way. It will carry you from earth to heaven, and there you shall find your great joy the prize. You haste to a crown of glory.'
>
> *King:* 'I go from a corruptible to an incorruptible crown, where no disturbance can be.'
>
> *Dr. Juxon:* 'You are exchanged from a temporal to an eternal crown, a good exchange.'

Then the King took off his cloak and his George, giving his George to Dr. Juxon saying, 'Remember!' (it is thought for the Prince), and some other small ceremonies passed. After a while the King, stooping down, laid his neck upon the block; and after a little pause, stretching forth his hands, the executioner at one blow severed his head from his body.[60]

Asked later to explain that 'Remember', the Bishop of London insisted that it was simply a precautionary measure on the doomed man's part: the Bishop was well known for his absent-mindedness, and the King wanted to be sure he did not forget to pass on the precious jewel (Charles's personal Great George was set with priceless diamonds) to his son, the Prince of Wales.[61] The King's last act was, however, more richly symbolic than Juxon, in those politically dangerous times, was prepared publicly to admit. In the course of Charles I's reign, and particularly during the period of turmoil through two civil wars when he lacked a physical centre for the exercise of his authority, Charles had repeatedly made the ceremonial and rituals of the Order of the Garter the focus for reaffirmation of loyalty to himself and the Crown of England on the part of his senior nobles.[62] Returning the George and Garter mantle to the reigning sovereign – Supreme Head of the Order – and to St George's Chapel, Windsor, to the safe-keeping of the Dean, was the final official duty expected of any Knight Companion of the Order. In December 1612, for example, Frederick, Elector Palatine, husband of the future Charles I's sister Elizabeth, at his introduction to the Order, was formally presented by his father-in-law James I with the Garter insignia of James's son, Prince Henry, who had died only a month previously.[63]

If we are to understand the way in which Charles I held on to the conviction that he continued to command the affections of his most important subjects, and, above all, if we are to understand his son Charles II's elaborate strategies for re-establishing the Stuart dynastic order and reaffirming the continuity of English kingship after the Restoration, we need to take a closer look at the fortunes of the Order of the Garter, and the Knights Companion and Officers of that Order, in the period leading up to that ultimately theatrical gesture on the Whitehall scaffold. It is a story in which the young Sir Christopher Wren plays a not insignificant part.

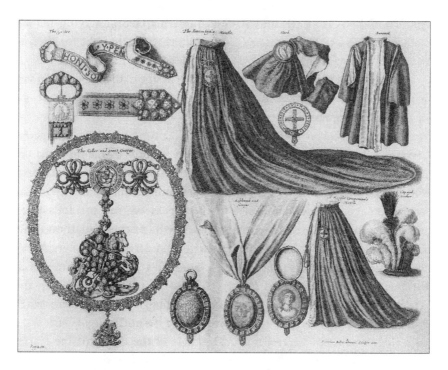

Garter regalia – the George medallion at the bottom centre (seen in three views) is supposed to be the one Charles I wore on the scaffold.

DEANS MATTHEW AND CHRISTOPHER WREN

The two Doctors of Divinity who, one after the other, held the crucial ceremonial title of Dean of Windsor and Register of the Order of the Garter during the reign of Charles I were brothers, Matthew and Christopher Wren. As key functionaries in the monarch's favourite royal institution, their influence during their tenure of the Deanship of Windsor was considerable. According to Dean Christopher Wren's grandson, who assembled the family papers for publication into a folio volume entitled *Parentalia*, and according to Elias Ashmole, who in 1670 published an equally lavishly illustrated volume containing the *History of the Order of the Garter*, it was the two Wren brothers who, during the reign of Charles I, formally established the rituals and records of the Order of the Garter, and codified them in their definitive form. The Statutes of the Order were organised by Matthew Wren in 1631; the Register, or

Black-book, put in order; and a 'short historical Account of the sacred Offerings, and Gifts' provided by his younger brother Christopher in 1637.[64]

Matthew Wren's rapid rise within the Stuart court began in 1621, when he was appointed by James I as personal chaplain in the household of Charles, Prince of Wales (later Charles I), at the direct suggestion of Bishop Lancelot Andrewes, whom he at that time served as secretary. Two years later Matthew Wren accompanied Charles and the Duke of Buckingham to woo the Spanish Infanta as Charles's bride – an incident which ended in humiliation for the Prince, and caused panic across the British Isles as it seemed the heir to the throne might take a Catholic wife. Although his father found it convenient to let it be believed his impetuous son had set out for Spain without his permission, letters sent by James to the two young men clearly sanction the journey, and reveal, furthermore, that in spite of proper hostility to papal authority on the part of all concerned their religious beliefs and observance were effectively Catholic:

> I have sent you, my baby [James I's pet name for Prince Charles], two of your chaplains fittest for this purpose, Mawe and Wren, together with all stuff and ornaments for the service of God. I have fully instructed them so as all their behaviour and service shall, I hope, prove decent and agreeable to the purity of the primitive church and yet as near the Roman [Catholic] form as can lawfully be done, for it hath ever been my way to go with the Church of Rome *usque ad aras* ['even unto the altars' – as far as is allowable].[65]

Wren family documents record clearly and with pride that James himself had instructed Matthew Wren to accompany Charles ('Whom, <by K. James special Directions> in 1623, he attended in His Journy to Spain'). Wren was also entrusted with transporting the two young men's Garter robes and jewels, to be worn by them at the Spanish court on St George's Day, 'for it will be a goodly sight for the Spaniards to see my two boys dine in them'.[66]

On their return, Matthew Wren was closely questioned by the Archbishop of Canterbury and others concerning the Prince's demeanour during the Spanish visit. Wren loyally vouched for the *bona fides* of his young charge, denied that he had seen in his behaviour the slightest sign of Catholic religious sympathy, and thereby won the young Prince's lifelong gratitude.

Matthew Wren gave his own vivid account of this episode as follows:[67]

After our Return from Spain, my Lord of Winchester (among other great Expressions of his Respects to me) made me promise to him, that, upon all Occasions of my coming to London (for I abode still at Cambridge) I would lodge with him; to which End, he caused three Rooms near the garden to be fitted and reserved for me; and twice or thrice I had lodged there.

And in another Time coming suddenly to London and late, I lodged at my Sister's in Friday-street, and the next Day, being Friday, I went to Winchester-house to Dinner, and craved his Lordship's Pardon, that I lodg'd not there; because that my Business was to treat with some Country Gentlemen, who lay in Holbourn, whom I should not meet with, but in the Evening and Morning, when it would not be sage for me to pass the Bridge, or the Thames; and so after Dinner I took my Leave of him, hoping to return to Cambridge on Monday.

But on Saturday, going to do my Duty to my Lords of Durham and St. David's and telling them of my sudden Return, they would needs over-rule me, and made me promise them, though I had taken Leave of my Lord of Winchester, yet, to meet them next Day at Whitehall, at my Lord's Chambers, at Dinner; I did so, and there we sat, at Dinner, above an Hour. And then, I shewing them, that on the Morrow my Business would be dispatched, and I would be gone on Tuesday, I took my Leave again of them all. But, on Monday Morning by Break of Day, (before they used to be stirring in Friday-street) there was a great knocking at the Door where I lay; and at last an Apprentice, who lay in the Shop, came up to my Bed-side, and told me, there was a Messenger from Winchester-house to speak with me; the Business was to let me know, that my Lord, when he came from Court last Night, had given his Steward Charge to order it so, that I might be spoken with, and be required as from him without fail, to dine with him on Monday; but to be at Winchester-house by ten of the Clock, which I wonder'd the more at, his Lordship not using to come from his Study till near twelve. My Business would hardly permit this; yet because of his Lordship's Importunity, I got up presently, and into Holbourn I went, and there made such Dispatch, that soon after ten o'Clock I took a Boat, and went to Winchester-house, where I found the Steward at the Water-gate, waiting to let me in the nearest Way, who telling me, that my Lord had called twice to know if I were come; I asked where his Lordship was? He answered in his great Gallery (a Place where I knew his Lordship scarce came once in a Year) and thither I going, the Door was lock'd; but upon my lifting the Latch, my Lord of St. David's opened the Door, and letting me in, lock'd it again.

There I found none but those three Lords, who causing me to sit down by them, my Lord of Durham began to me, 'Doctor, your Lord here, will have it so, I that am the unfittest Person, must be the Speaker; but thus it is, After you left us Yesterday at Whitehall, we entering into farther Discourse of those Things, which we foresee and conceive will e're long come to pass, resolv'd again, to speak to you before you went hence.

We must know of you, what your Thoughts are concerning your Master the Prince. You have now been his Servant above two Years, and you were with him in Spain; we know he respects you well; and we know you are no Fool, but can observe how Things are like to go. What Things, my Lord? (quoth I.) In brief, said he, how the Prince's Heart stands to the Church of England, that when God brings him to the Crown we may know what to hope for.'

My Reply was to this Effect, that, however, I was the most unfit of any to give my Opinion herein, attending but two Months in the Year, and then at a great Distance, only in the Closet, and at Meals, yet seeing they so pressed me, I would speak my Mind freely; so I said, 'I know my Master's Learning is not equal to his Father's; yet, I know his Judgment to be very right; and as for his Affections in these Particulars, which your Lordships have pointed at, for upholding the Doctrine and Discipline, and the right Estate of the Church, I have more Confidence of him, than of his Father, in whom they say (better than I can) is so much Inconstantcy in some particular Cases.'

Hereupon my Lords of Durham and St. David's began to argue it with me, and requir'd me to let them know, upon what ground I came to think thus of the Prince; I gave them my Reasons at large, and after many Replyings (above an Hour together) then my Lord of Winchester, (who had said nothing all the while) bespake me in these Words; 'Well Doctor, God send you may be a true Prophet concerning your Master's Inclinations in these Particulars, which we are glad to hear from you; I am sure I shall be a true Prophet; I shall be in my Grave, and so shall you, my Lord of Durham, but my Lord of St. David's, and you, Doctor, will live to see that Day that your Master will be put to it, upon his Head and his Crown, without he will forsake the Support of the Church.'

Of this Prediction made by that holy Father, I have now no Witness but mine own Conscience, and the eternal God, who knows I lie not; no Body else being present when this was spoken, but these three Lords.

The future Charles I rewarded his chaplain's loyalty handsomely. When he ascended the throne in 1625, he immediately made Matthew Wren Master of Peterhouse, Cambridge, and shortly thereafter Vice-Chancellor of the University. In 1628 Charles made Matthew Wren Dean of Windsor, and Register of the Order of the Garter (the two jobs went together) – a ceremonial office of real importance, particularly in the eyes of the King. The appointment carried significant status – on occasion the Dean of Windsor might take precedence in officiating over the Archbishop of Canterbury himself – and had considerable financial rewards attached in the form of lands, livings and stipends, and a substantial tied residence in the shape of the magnificent Dean's House at Windsor Castle. So sumptuously appointed was the Dean's House – second only to the royal apartments at Windsor themselves – and so conveniently located, immediately outside the King's Gate to the Castle, that visiting dignitaries were regularly lodged with the Dean (as we saw in the case of the Elector Palatine), and the lavish dinner which preceded the annual St George's Day ceremony for the Knights Companion of the Order was held there (as indeed it still is today).

In 1635 Matthew Wren was once again promoted by the King, succeeding Bishop Juxon as Dean of his Majesty's Chapel, 'one of the highest Dignities of the Court, because nearest the King'.[68] Shortly thereafter, the King made him Bishop of Norwich, and then Bishop of Ely – each time tying his promotion to some supposed act of particularly loyal behaviour. It was a feature of Charles I's 'personal rule' (after he had dismissed his Parliament and rejected its authority) that he rendered personal favour for personal favour – an honour given in exchange for an act of fealty towards the King.[69] Thus in 1641, it was Bishop Matthew Wren who officiated at the quiet wedding ceremony which united the nine-year-old Princess Mary and twelve-year-old William of Orange (an event he later proudly recorded on a blank page of his almanac for the year 1652, from his cell in the Tower of London).[70]

Matthew Wren was by this time one of the three most powerful and influential bishops in the kingdom, alongside William Laud, Archbishop of Canterbury, and William Juxon, Bishop of London. It is only because subsequent events associated these three men all too closely with the final years of Charles I's reign (partisanship in which remained a politically sensitive issue after the Restoration) that the Wren family later chose to make less of Matthew Wren's former elevated status than they might otherwise have done – a question of tact, observed by many such resolutely royalist families.

We should not, however, overlook the fact that it was the direct descendants of those individuals who had stood by and remained true to Charles II's father in his final years (years, we should remember, when as Prince of Wales he had witnessed in person both loyalty and disloyalty to the Crown) whom the returning King discreetly rewarded. In 1660, the elderly Matthew Wren was restored to the bishopric of Ely (to the annoyance of the current incumbent and his parishioners), while his eldest son Matthew was created secretary first to Edward Hyde, Earl of Clarendon, and then to James, Duke of York, Charles II's brother.

When Matthew Wren senior vacated the Deanship of Windsor (and the associated post of Register of the Order of the Garter) to take up the bishopric of Norwich in 1635, he persuaded the King to appoint his younger brother Christopher Wren in his place, 'by his Majesty's special Appointment'.[71] Thus it was Dean Christopher Wren who officiated at St George's Chapel, Windsor Castle, when Charles I's eight-year-old son, Charles, Prince of Wales, was introduced into the Order of the Garter in 1638 (a service for which the Dean was rewarded by being presented with the 'rich Rectory of Hasely in Oxfordshire'). Dean Wren ordered some swift improvements, particularly to the chimney arrangements in the Dean's house, in anticipation of the exceptionally grand dinner which would precede the ceremony on this occasion.[72]

When he took over the office, Dean Christopher Wren (as Ashmole indicates in his *History*) put considerable effort into bringing the Garter records contained in the official record books up to date. This was an undertaking begun by his elder brother in 1631 – a meticulous draft of 'Statutes of the Order called in English "of the Garter", with marginal notes' survives among the Wren family papers.[73] He himself has left us a vivid account of the sumptuous ceremonial of that 19 May 1638 – an occasion the memory of which we may well imagine lastingly remaining in Charles II's memory, since it was the single great symbolic ceremony of sovereignty of his youth, before the collapse of monarchy and the onset of the civil war period. The twenty-five Knights Companion of the Order of the Garter (King Charles among them), summoned as was customary to attend, assembled at Windsor. On this occasion they were welcomed (unusually) by 'family': Queen Henrietta Maria, the baby Duke of York ('parvulus'), with the French Duchess of Chevreuse in attendance.

On 21 May the Knights Companion met *in camera* in a private room to conduct their secret ceremonies, and then, having readmitted the Queen and the Duchess of Chevreuse, announced their intention to elect Prince Charles to their number. First, however, the boy had to be made a Knight Bachelor, since, as Dean Wren explains, no British member could be admitted to this, England's most prestigious military Order, who had not already been knighted. Once this had been done, the solemn invitation was delivered by the Garter King of Arms to the Prince (in English rather than in Latin, out of deference to his age):

Charles R.

Our most dear, and entirely beloved Son, having to our great Comfort seen, and considered the Ripeness of your Youth, and conceiv'd joyful and pregnant Hopes of your manly Virtues, in which we are assured, you will increase to your own Honour, both in Prowess, Wisdom, Justice, and all princely Endowments; and that the Emulation of Chevalry will in your tender Years provoke and encourage you to pursue the Glory of heroick Actions, befitting your royal Birth, and our Care and Education.

We with the Companions of our most noble Order of the Garter, assembled in Chapter, holden this present Day at our Castle of Windsor, have elected and chosen you one of the Companions of our Order. In Signification whereof we have sent to you by our trusty, and well-beloved Servant, Sir John Burroughs, Knight of the Garter, and our principal King of Arms, these our royal Letters, requiring you to make your speedy Repair unto us, to receive the Ensigns of our most honourable Order, and to be ready for your Installation, upon the twenty-second of this present Month.

Given under the Signet of our Order, at our Castle of Windsor, the 21st of May, in the 14th Year of our Reign, 1638.

To our dearly beloved Son, Prince Charles.[74]

There followed an elaborate ceremony, during which the eight-year-old was dressed in the full Garter regalia, and which must have gone on for hours, taxing the patience and stamina of an adult, let alone a child.[75] It is hardly surprising that his father had second thoughts about the original plan that the entire assembly should process from Westminster Abbey to Windsor between a first installation ceremony of the boy Prince as a Knight of the Order of the Bath in the Abbey, and the Garter ceremony in St George's Chapel.[76] A drawing by Van Dyck survives, depicting the proposed event, probably intended as the basis for a series of tapestries to mark the occasion, to be hung in the Banqueting House at Whitehall. When the procession did not take place, the tapestry project was abandoned.[77]

Finally, the three most powerful figures in the Anglican Church officiated in the service of thanksgiving to celebrate Prince Charles's admission – the Archbishop of Canterbury, the Bishop of London (Bishop Juxon) and the Bishop of Ely (Bishop Matthew Wren). Thus both Wren brothers participated in this – as it turned out – historically most significant of Garter installations.[78]

One further ceremony was performed in the Chapel at Windsor on this occasion in the Prince's presence. The Great George and Garter presented to King Gustav Adolph of Sweden at his own installation as Knight Companion in 1627 (and which 'did excel all others, presented by former Sovereigns, for Richness and Glory') was formally returned by an ambassador,[79] following his death in battle, defending the

Protestant cause, as was stipulated under the rules of the Order. These regalia were reconsecrated on the altar of St George's Chapel before being placed in the Treasury for safekeeping.[80] His 'blew Velvet Robe' 'with a Train, and embroidered with a Garter, Pearl and Gold' was hung permanently alongside the altar, above the tomb of Edward IV.[81] King Gustav Adolph had proved himself a Garter Knight in the truest of heroic modes envisaged by Charles I. He had died in battle, fighting to restore the Protestant Elector Palatine to his territories, in the thirty years war (a war in which first James I and then Charles I had studiously avoided taking an active part).[82]

The later loss of King Gustav Adolph's priceless insignia – pillaged along with all the other Garter gems and properties during the civil war – remained a permanent source of remorse for those who had been present in St George's Chapel that day, and who had pledged to keep these treasures safe in the dead King's memory. The items were worth a king's ransom, and if recovered would have solved the financial problems of any of those royalists impoverished by the civil wars.

When the King left Windsor and set off north in February 1642, his devoted Register of the Garter, Christopher Wren senior, secured the records and regalia of the Order before he too left to join the itinerant court. He closed up the Chapel and locked the Garter office in the Dean's House ('the Closet called the Registry of the Order of the Garter'). This office contained a cabinet of eleven drawers, filled with the writings and records of the Order, 'and other Things of Value'; another large iron-bound cabinet, 'with Partitions, and Boxes, gilt, and filleted, with special Records and Papers therein'; a table of all the Knights of the Garter from the origin of the Order, with their coats of arms; and three fine paintings in gold frames.[83] He also, at some personal risk, took the precaution of burying the Great George and Garter of King Gustav Adolph of Sweden under the floor of the Treasury in St George's Chapel, 'and deposited a Note in the Hands of a worthy Person, intimating where they might be found, in case of [his] Death'.[84]

On the first occasion on which St George's Chapel was ransacked in October 1642, King Gustav Adolph's jewels went undiscovered, though his Garter cloak was taken along with the other decorations from the Chapel itself. Three days later the Dean's House was ransacked, and the Garter records and other documents taken from the Closet. But it was not until March 1645 (according to Ashmole) that Cornelius Holland

Bird's-eye engraved view of Windsor Castle – St George's Chapel is on the upper left, the Dean's house is the detached house with garden, inside the walls and immediately behind the Chapel, right of the bell tower.

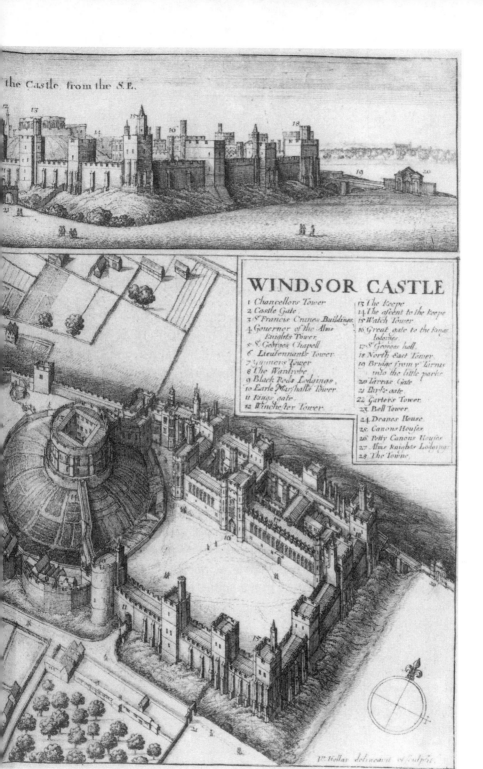

the Castle from the S.E.

WINDSOR CASTLE

1 Chancellors Tower
2 Castle Gate
3 St Frances Crimes Buildings
4 Governor of the Alms
   Knights Tower
5 St Gebrius Chapell
6 Lieutenants Tower
7 Gunners Tower
8 The Wardrobe
9 Black Rods Lodgings
10 Earle Marshalls Tower
11 Kings gate
12 Winchester Tower

13 The Keepe
14 The ascent to the keepe
15 Watch Tower
16 Great gate to the kings
   lodgeing
17 St Georges hall
18 North East Tower
19 Bridge from ye Tarras
   into the little parke
20 Tarras Gate
21 Parke gate
22 Garters Tower
23 Bell Tower
24 Deanes House
25 Canons Houses
26 Petty Canons Houses
27 Alms Knights Lodging
28 The Towne

W. Hollar delineavit et sculpsit.

and one-time Windsor Governor Colonel Venn unearthed the buried items under the floor of the Treasury. They were handed to the current Governor, Colonel Whitchcott (Windsor Castle was used as a parliamentary barracks throughout the civil war period), and subsequently sold to Thomas Beauchamp by the 'Trustees appointed by the long Parliament for the Sale of his Majesty's Goods'.[85]

Right up until his death in 1658, Dean Christopher Wren spent his enforced retirement trying to retrieve the registers, papers and treasure of the Order of the Garter, with which he had been entrusted by virtue of his office as Register, and for which he felt personally responsible. He had, indeed, never been dismissed from his post as Register, and therefore, in his own mind, continued to exercise that office (the Garter King at Arms, another official of the Order, did indeed remain officially in post, since he went into exile and continued to exercise his traditional duties on behalf of the deposed King, Charles II).[86] Those were tough, unsentimental times for a doggedly loyal old royalist retainer: he failed to retrieve a single item from among the Garter jewels, plate and furniture, all of which had presumably been dismantled or melted down for their precious materials.

He was more successful where the records and papers were concerned:

> The Dean by great Application, Expence and long Attendance on the Trustees and their Meetings in Somerset-house, by Favour of their Chairman, Major Wither's, performed, at Length, a memorable Piece of Service to the Order, and recovered out of the Hands, First, the two old Registers, stiled the Black, and the Blue; and some Time after retriev'd the Red also, with other Books and Papers, relating to the Statutes and Annals; all which were carefully concealed and preserved by him to the Time of his Death.[87]

Ashmole records having spent many hours consulting these precious manuscripts with Dean Wren during the dark years (as he saw it) of the Commonwealth, when he too had time on his hands; it was then that he first conceived the idea of writing a full antiquarian history of the Order of the Garter.[88]

True to the martial, chivalric spirit of the Order of the Garter, it was to the Knights Companion that Charles I turned for backing when, having fled London in 1642, he found himself, in March of that year, in York, without a plan. His rallying cry came in the form of a special summons issued on 28 March, and sent by personal courier to every Garter Knight. That year, exceptionally, the Knights, officers and heralds were ordered to attend the annual congregation of the Order at York, rather than at Windsor:

> The King's Majesty, Sovereign of the most noble Order of the Garter, having prorogued the Solemnization of the Feast of St. George, to the 18th, 19th, and 20th Days of April next, at the City of York, these are to certify you, that you may take Notice both of the Time, and Place, and to accompany in that Service the rest of the Officers of the Order; and therefore in Assurance of your Presence accordingly, I rest,
>
> Your very assured Friend,
>
> James Palmer [Chancellor of the Order][89]

Here was a coded message for the King's inner circle of supporters. To fail to respond as a Garter Knight to the summons of the Supreme Head of the Order was an act of unthinkable chivalric disloyalty, an infringement of the most fundamental rules. Recognising the challenge to their authority this summons represented, Parliament countermanded with their own order. Those Knights who were members of the Long Parliament were ordered to be in attendance at the House of Lords on 18, 19 and 20 April, 'that they attend the weighty Affairs of the Kingdom, discussed in Parliament, whereunto they are obliged by his Majesty's Writ, and the Law of the Land'.[90] Although a number of Knights sent urgent letters to the King pleading leave to be absent from York, on grounds of government business, Charles refused to grant the necessary permissions, under the rules of the Order. He had tried his Knights, and learned who were true and who false. Indeed, it is by and large the case that those who went to York remained staunchly royalist throughout the entire ensuing civil war period.

At the secret conclave held in York in April 1642, the Knights present

Prince Rupert, second
son of Charles I's sister,
Elizabeth of Bohemia,
flamboyant military
commander, and
Charles's favourite
nephew.

expressed their intention to bestow the Order of the Garter on nine-year-old Prince James, Duke of York and on the King's favourite nephew, Prince Rupert, younger brother of Charles Louis, Elector Palatine (who had already rushed to his uncle's side to take command of his troops). The two would be installed, it was agreed, as soon as the royal forces regained possession of Windsor Castle.

Two and a half years later it was clear that it would not be possible to conduct Garter ceremonies in St George's Chapel for some time. Prince Rupert was by now Charles's foremost military commander – a royalist hero, who was currently holding the besieged city of Bristol. Accordingly, from his headquarters at Oxford, the King issued a special dispensation, granting James, Duke of York and Prince Rupert the full status of Garter Knight without requiring that they go through the Windsor Chapel initiation ceremony:

Charles R.

Charles by the grace of God King of England, Scotland, France, and Ireland, Defender of the Faith, &c. and Soveraign of the most Noble Ordre of the Garter. To all and singular unto whom these our Letters Patent shall come greeting. Whereas by the Statutes of our said most Noble Order, all Knights elected to be Companions of the same are (according to usual form and Ceremony) to be installed at the Stalls of the Order, in the Chappel of our Royal Castle of Windesor, before they can be admitted to have their Stalls, Places, and Votes amongst the rest of the Companions there. And whereas our dearly beloved Son James Duke of York, and our intirely beloved Nephew, Prince Rupert, Count Palatine of the Rheyne, Duke of Bavaria and Cumberland, and Earl of Holderness, were in a Chapter held at York, the twentieth day of April in the eighteenth year of our Reign, elected and chosen Companions of our said most Noble Order; but, by reason of the succeeding distractions and Rebellions in this our Kingdom, their Installations at our said Castle of Windesor, could not according to the Statutes aforesaid be celebrated and performed, by reason the same hath been ever sithence, and still is in the possession of the Rebels.

Know ye, that we as Soveraign of the said most Noble Order (unto whom the power of dispensing with any of the said Statutes is reserved) have thought fit to dispence (in regard the not performance of the Statutes hath not been by the default of these elected Knights) and by these presents do accordingly dispence with the Installations of our aforesaid Son and Nephew, both for time and place, when and where those Installations are and ought to be made, willing and ordaining that they and either of them, shall by virtue of this our Dispensation, at all times hereafter, be held, reputed, and taken to be Companions of our said most Noble Order; And shall have, possess, and enjoy all manner of Titles, places preheminencies, Votes, Ornaments, and Priviledges of the same, as if they or either of them had been formally and actually installed at our said Castle of Windesor; any Law, Statute, or Ordinance made to the contrary in any wise notwithstanding.

Provided always, and we do hereby declare, that our said most dear Son, and our entirely beloved Nephew, shall (notwithstanding these our Letters of Dispensation) first take the Oath usually taken by the Knights at their Installation, and hereafter act and perform all such Rights and Ceremonies as are accustomed at the Installations of the Companions of our said most Noble Order of the Garter, when it shall be thought fit, and possible for them to perform the same at our Castle of Windesor aforesaid. And that this our Dispensation made upon such most weighty and urgent necessities shall not be drawn into consequence or example in time to come. Given under the Great Seal of our Order, and our hand first superscribed thereunto, at our Palace at Oxford, this seventeenth of January in the twentieth year of our Reign, 1645.[91]

In the midst of the rigours of war in earnest – in which the King's forces were doing increasingly badly – King Charles seems to have regarded the charmed, ceremonial Order of the Garter as his secret military weapon. In early March 1645 he ordered the fourteen-year-old Prince Charles to Bristol, as the newly appointed Commander of the Western Forces, while he and Prince Rupert set off eastwards with the bulk of the royalist forces (11,000 men). By June these forces had been comprehensively beaten at the Battle of Naseby, and Rupert too went west to Bristol, which by August was being besieged by the parliamentary forces under General Fairfax. Rupert told the King by letter that he could hold Bristol for up to four months. On 9 September the King wrote to Rupert assuring him that relief troops under his personal command were on the way.

Then, on 10 September, Rupert surrendered Bristol to Fairfax. The King was devastated.[92] When he received the news on 11 September he told the messenger that the news 'hath given me more grief than any misfortune since this damnable Rebellion'.[93] It did not matter that Rupert's had been a strategic decision to surrender the city. For Charles I the surrender was a matter of honour, a fundamental breach of the chivalric code of conduct of the supreme military order into which Prince Rupert had so recently been admitted. On 14 September, the King wrote to Prince Rupert summarily dismissing him from his command, and banishing him from his kingdom:

Nephew:

though the loss of Bristol be a great blow to me, yet your surrendering it as you did, is of so much affliction to me that it makes me forget not only the consideration of that place, but is likewise the greatest trial of my constancy that has befallen me; for what is to be done after one who is so near me both in blood and friendship submits himself in so mean an action? (I give it the easiest term). Such – I have so much more to say that I will say no more of it: only lest rashness of judgement be laid to my charge. . . . My conclusion is to desire you to seek your subsistence (until it pleases God) to determine my condition, somewhere beyond the seas. . . .

Your loving uncle and most faithful friend

Charles R.[94]

The same day, Charles wrote to Sir Edward Nicholas, who had custody of Prince James. 'Tell my son', he wrote, 'that I should be less grieved to hear that he is knocked on the Head, than that he should do so mean an action.' If either of his own sons, Companion Garter Knights both with Rupert, had behaved with equivalent dishonour, the King insisted, he would have treated them in the same manner.[95] The King never forgave Rupert (and, although Rupert did not obey his orders, he was banished from the country by Parliament after the fall of Oxford). In 1660, however, the three boy-soldiers and Garter Princes – Prince Rupert of the Rhine, James, Duke of York and Charles II – were reunited in London in chivalric brotherhood. Theirs became the key collaboration of the Restoration royal administration.

Dean Christopher Wren was in attendance on the King in Oxford throughout this period. As Register or ceremonial Secretary, his official services were required in all activities involving the Order of the Garter. Thus he needed to be at hand, and duly consulted, when the discussions took place concerning waiving the installation procedure for Rupert and James. The only record we have of him there, however, dates from December 1643, when the King issued his Register of the Garter with a special safe conduct to allow him to leave Oxford:

Charles R.

Whereas by the ancient Constitution and Laws of our most noble Order of the Garter, the Register of our said Order is to have his Person, and Estate secured from Violence and Injury, to the End he or his Ministers may securely live under our perpetual Protection and Safeguard; and as often as he shall be molested for himself, or for any Thing that belongs unto him, he is to receive our Protection, and the Assistance of the Companions of our Order, according to Equity and Right. These are therefore to will, and command all Men of what Condition soever they be, not to trouble or molest Doctor Christopher Wren, Dean of Windsor, and Register of our most noble Order of the Garter, or any of his Ministers whomsoever, or any Thing that belongs to him whatsoever; but to suffer his Person, Servants, and Estate, to be in Quiet, Security, and Peace, without any Injury, or Violence to be offered by any to him, or his, as they, or every of them shall answer to the contrary at their Peril.

Given at our Court, at Oxford, under the signet of our Order, the 12th Day of December, in the 19th Year of our Reign [1643].[96]

This safe-conduct was in all likelihood granted on compassionate grounds – Christopher's brother Matthew, locked up in the Tower of London, had suffered a succession of family tragedies, and Christopher may have been needed to help his family, some of whom were still based in Ely.[97] The document can have been of little practical use as the Dean crossed territory controlled by the parliamentarians. Loyal to the end, however, he kept the precious scrap of paper, treasured among his few remaining family possessions.

The years of exile in France and the Netherlands were, for Charles II, wilderness years of uncertainty and impoverishment, surrounded by sycophants, and offered conflicting advice by largely unsuitable counsellors. Plucked from obscurity and reinstated as King of England in 1660, he drew on the powerful childhood memories of the ceremonies of the Garter, and their chivalric mystique. On 22 March 1660, when Charles II already knew that he would shortly return to his English kingdom, he wrote to his Garter cousin Rupert from Paris, where he was staying with his mother, expressing an almost childish delight at the news that Rupert was proposing to join him in London:

My dearest Cousin

I am so surprised with joy in the assurance of your safe arrival in these parts, that I cannot tell you how treat it is, nor can I consider any misfortunes or accidents which have happened, now I know your person is in safety, if I could receive the like comfort in a reasonable hope of your brother's [Maurice had been lost at sea off the West Indies some years previously, but his family still vainly hoped he might have survived]: I will not tell you how important it would be to my affairs, when my affection makes me impatient to see you, I know the same desire will incline you, after you have done what can be only done by your presence there, to make what haste to me your health can indure, of which I must conjure you to have such a care as it may be in no danger.

I have sent Colonel Owen whom you know to be a very honest man, to do you such service as you shall direct him. Mr. Anthony will write to you more at large of all things, so that I will say no more to you at present, only to assure you I shall be very impatient till I see you, that I may myself tell you how much kindness,

I am, My dearest Cousin
Your most affectionate Cousin

Charles R.[98]

ABSENT FATHERS

On 25 May 1660, King Charles II sailed from the Netherlands to England and, in the company of a large retinue of royalist gentlemen and noblemen who had travelled out to greet him (including Samuel Pepys), re-entered his kingdom. Prince Rupert saw him off from The Hague, with the promise that he would shortly join the King permanently in his newly restored kingdom.[99] Even before the King left The Hague he was re-creating his lost childhood. When representatives of the City of London presented Charles with £10,000 as evidence of their goodwill, he responded with a speech in which he stressed his 'particular affection' for the capital 'the place of my birth', and proceeded to knight the delegates (by contrast, he snubbed the parliamentary delegates).[100] Once back in London he moved into Whitehall Palace and set about restoring it to its previous splendour, including attempting to reassemble his father's magnificent art collection – dispersed by auction shortly after his execution.[101] In this case, too, he self-consciously revived his father's plans – the plans of his childhood. Bit by bit he began painstakingly piecing back together the shattered and dispersed memories of English sovereignty, so much of which, like the Garter regalia, had been dismantled and destroyed during and after the civil war.

Following negotiations conducted between the King and the English Government from The Hague, the elderly Matthew Wren had already been released from the Tower in April, and reinstated as Bishop of Ely. His brother, Dean Christopher Wren, however, had died at Bletchingdon two years previously. The Restoration came too late for him to return the precious Garter records to the new monarch in person. Instead, in August 1660, the twenty-eight-year-old Christopher Wren junior handed the precious books of Garter records, retrieved with so much pain by Dean Wren, to the new King on his father's behalf. Their restoration was a highly symbolic moment in the process of rebuilding the dignity and authority of the Crown. Reconnecting the chain of tradition which ran, according to Dean Christopher Wren's documentation of the Order, unbroken from the reign of Edward III to the present day, was a vital part of Charles II's own personal sense of lineal continuity. That unbroken tradition, which had survived both the civil war and the Commonwealth, symbolically erased the interruption in Stuart dynastic rule (just as Charles I had created Knights of the Order in the period 1642 to 1648, so Charles II had done so in exile, for services loyally rendered to the Crown).

Receipt of the precious records was provided by Bruno Ryves (Reeves), the newly appointed Garter Register:

> I do acknowledge, that I have received of Mr. Christopher Wren, the Son of Mr. Dean Wren, a Box, in which are three Register-Books, and other Note-Books, all relating to the most noble Order of the Garter; in Testimony whereof, I have hereunto set my Hand, this 11th Day of August, in the Year 1660. Bruno Ryves.[102]

At the height of Charles II's triumph, Christopher Wren stepped centre stage and performed one of the key ritual 'restorations' on which the new King's rule was to be founded. Devoted son of a loyal father himself, Christopher Wren here re-established a crucial emotional bond between another devoted son and his royal father's memory. So began Christopher Wren's special relationship with the Crown, which would last for more than sixty years, and through the reigns of six English monarchs.

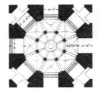

2

Precocious Students at Invisible Colleges

Between the collapse of Charles I's baroque, absolutist court culture and the bright new dawn of the Restoration of Charles II the fortunes of the Wrens went (through circumstances beyond their control) into increasingly rapid decline.

The bright prospects of Dean Christopher Wren and his children evaporated when the King left Oxford by stealth on 27 April 1646, abandoning the remnant of his court and administration there. The King having fled, the besieged City of Oxford surrendered to the parliamentary forces under General Fairfax on 24 July (Midsummer's Day), the remaining members of his court and armed forces dispersing rapidly into the surrounding countryside. The next ten years of Christopher Wren junior's life would be years of struggle and graft. In later life, when he had restored the Wren family fortunes to splendour through his own efforts, he rarely referred to them at all.

For the previous three and a half years Oxford had been a garrison town, during a period of continuous hostilities. Although the colleges of the University continued to operate (and the King made generous use of his powers to grant degrees and academic posts by royal mandate), it is worth remembering that those whose qualifications date from these troubled years conducted their studies surrounded by billeted soldiers, penned livestock, camp followers, disease (overcrowding produced frequent epidemics) and field hospitals.[1] Even some of those with strong royalist sympathies found conditions intolerable, and withdrew from their studies until the end of the civil war. John Aubrey was in his first year at Trinity College when the royalists occupied Oxford. In August 1643 his father called him home for safety, and although Aubrey returned briefly early in 1644, he was home again by June, and did not return to the University to complete his degree until after the King had left, in autumn 1646.[2]

Nevertheless, during the period 1642 to 1646 it had seemed out of the question to those in the sovereign's close entourage that the King's cause might fail. In spite of the makeshift arrangements, court and King's administration continued to operate with much of their usual pomp and circumstance (right up until his arrest on the Isle of Wight in 1648, those serving Charles his meals continued to do so from gilt plates, on bended knee). At the beginning of 1646, though, the atmosphere of impending disaster must have communicated itself to even the most devotedly loyal of royalists. Food was short (the soldiers were eating horsemeat), the conditions in the cramped living accommodation were poor, and Charles had to scrounge £30 a month to pay his household expenses. It was no longer possible to leave the town without being detained.[3]

As spring arrived, and with it the moment to launch the 1646 military campaign, even the King himself finally began to lose his nerve. Never decisive, he now became paralysed with indecision over what to do next. At the beginning of April he dithered: should he march on London for a military showdown with Parliament, should he leave England for temporary safety in France, or should he respond to the overtures of the Scots, and move north to relaunch his campaign with Scottish and French backing?

In the end it was the determined lobbying of the Scots that decided it. The chief negotiator for the Scots was Sir Robert Moray, a staunchly royalist member of the Scottish administration, knighted by Charles in Oxford in 1643, who had been deliberately chosen for his capacity to conciliate.[4] (His skills at placating difficult groups of opinionated individuals would later come in handy, at the Restoration, when he became the first President of the Royal Society.) Moray urged the King to reach a settlement with his Scottish subjects (he was, after all, King of Scotland also), and to move his headquarters to Scotland. Charles was persuaded: 'I am ready to go at an hour's warning,' he wrote on 13 April. That decision implied that the King would yield to the Scottish demand that the institutions of the Church of England be dismantled, and its bishops, deans and chapters replaced by those of the Scottish Presbyterian Church. Yet, still wishing to hedge his bets, on the same day King Charles gave Gilbert Sheldon, Warden of All Souls College, a secret signed vow that if 'God restore me to my just kingly rights', he would return to the Church of England 'all impropriations held by the crown'.[5] Still, to Scotland (or rather, to the Scottish-occupied north of England) Charles eventually went. By May, however, the Scots had rejected Charles's overtures, and placed him under virtual imprisonment at Newcastle (a final attempt to effect an escape, planned by Moray in December 1646, failed).

With the King's flight northwards, Dean Christopher Wren's ten years as a respected figure in the King's immediate entourage abruptly ended. Indeed, without the protection of the Oxford garrison, it was not simply his career, but his life itself that was now at risk. As a member of the much reviled band of 'Bishops and Deans' against whom Parliament regularly vented their anger during the civil war period, his lands and livings had already been proclaimed forfeit. Like the properties of all delinquents, they were let to Parliament-sympathising tenants, a bare fifth of the revenue reverting to Wren and his family for subsistence.[6] He could no longer count on any of the customary perquisites which had come to him by virtue of his tenure of the Deanship of Windsor, and his royal chaplaincy. Now he was fortunate simply to have family near by to shelter him, in the shape of his daughter Susan and her husband William Holder, at Bletchingdon.

He did, however, make one last attempt at exercising the authority of his Register office. As the Parliamentary Commission set off for Scotland with instructions to arrest the King and return him to London for trial, on 23 January 1647, Dean Wren managed to present a petition to Parliament ('before they sat'), summoning a meeting of the members who were Knights Companion, presumably to discuss intervention in the decision-making process on behalf of the King:

To ye right Honorable ye Knights of ye most Noble Ordre of ye Garter

Dr. Christopher Wren, Register & Secretarye of ye said most Noble Ordre

Prayeth

That according to ye Commission directed to all ye Honorable Peeres of ye said moste Noble order, or To any Three of them <To Meete & Consult in ye absence of ye Soueraine vpon all such emergent occasions, as may concerne, ye Advancement or Indemnity of ye said most Noble Order.>

Itt may therefore please your Honors, to giue your consent, for some sett Time & Place of Meetinge, with such convenient speed, as may best stande with your great Affaires. That your humble Servant ye Register, may Represent to your Honors, some four Things, which hee humbly conceaues, may much concerne ye Honor & Interest of your most Honorable Order, to bee prouided for:

I Deliuered this Petition, in ye Parliament House, before they sate [sat].

Jan: 23°: 1647.

A draft of this letter survives among Dean Wren's papers. It is accompanied by a copy of a second letter addressed to 'the Deputee Chancelor' (which Wren has substituted for the original 'Chancelor', the latter presumably being absent at the time), requesting permission to deliver a similar petition to the Privy Council:

Honorable Chancelor,

I haue noe particular aime in this my humble suite to ye Lords of ye Order, To propose any priuate, or Personal Interest, of my owne or of any other Mans; much less to Engage their Honors in anye thing that may seeme to contest with, or Dissent from ye highe Court of Parliament wherein they now sit, & from whence, I am not ignorant, ye most Honorable Society of ye most Noble Order, receaued, as at first Life & Being, soe now holds, its establishment. My humble & earnest desires, are to represent such Things only, as I humbly conceaue may neerly concerne ye Honor & Interest of their most Noble Order. To wich (next as your selfe, Honord Sir) I am by oath obliged; <To preserue ye Honor thereof, & of all in itt, to my utmost Power> In zeale of this duety, wich (vpon your intimation of

what I heere profess) I presume they will not reject, I beseech
you to giue them [ym] this assurance, as yf itt were from ye
tender of my owne Mouthe, who am att this presente, Gods
Prisoner, & vnder him

your servant. CW:[7]

It seems, from the final sentence of this letter, that when Wren had
delivered his petition to Parliament he may have been, for a short time,
placed under arrest. In any case, the two letters poignantly testify to
Dean Wren's sense of obligation, under the terms of his appointment
as Register of the Order of the Garter, to continue to act in accordance
with its oath and rules, even under these extreme circumstances.

For the time being, though, his son Christopher Wren's circumstances partially protected him from the consequences of the collapse
of his father's world. In the autumn of 1641, shortly after Charles, Elector
Palatine had lodged with his family at Windsor, Christopher started at
Westminster School in London, under its distinguished headmaster, Dr
Richard Busby. To the end of his life, Dean Wren kept among his
personal papers a painstakingly composed formal letter in Latin, from
his just-turned nine-year-old son, sent to him as a New Year's gift that
year, which closed with the little jingle:

> To you, Dear Sir, your Son presenteth heere,
> The first fruits of his pains, and of the Yeare:
> Wich may (though small) in time an harvest grow,
> If you to cherish these, your favour show.[8]

During the unstable early 1640s, Christopher Wren was receiving
probably the best education available in England (since it included some
mathematics and science as well as the classics). He was sheltered from
the civil war, even though his school was located in the heart of Parlia-
ment-controlled London, adjacent to the very Hall in which Parliament,
in March 1643, handed down the legislation that stripped his father of
his titles, lands and revenues. Dean Wren's son was thus cushioned
from the kinds of personal adversities that had by this time marked the
experience of Charles, Prince of Wales – a mere two years older than
Christopher Wren, but already having exchanged a charmed childhood
for active military service.

The first alteration in circumstances to affect Christopher Wren

Dr Richard Busby, Headmaster of Westminster School, who continued to admit bright royalist boys throughout the Commonwealth period.

junior's lifestyle directly was the drop in his father's income, and the consequent deterioration in his own standard of living. Although no portrait exists of the young Wren in the condition of affluence which his family enjoyed at Windsor (unlike the many glittering images of the infant Prince Charles), it is not difficult to imagine how directly the alteration in circumstances affected the fourteen-year-old. 'Want' is a spectre that stalks the families of royalists and Anglican clerics through-out the Commonwealth and Protectorate periods; it was not something the boy Christopher – cherished only son of affluent parents – had ever encountered. Now it would become part of his everyday life.[9]

Nor is it hard to detect the deep scars of that experience in Wren's subsequent life. Throughout an unusually long career (he remained in post, in royal service until only a few years before his death in his ninety-first year), Wren was preoccupied with lasting fame and perma-nent memorials, consistently determined to distinguish the enduring from the ephemeral. On a 1665 fact-finding visit to Paris, for example, at the beginning of his architectural career, he expressed distaste for the voguishness of the new buildings at Versailles:

> The Palace, or if you please, the Cabinet of Versailles call'd me twice to view it; the Mixture of Brick, Stone, blue Tile and Gold make it look like a rich Livery: Not an Inch within but is crouded with little Curiosities of Ornaments: the Women, as they make here the Language and Fashions, and meddle with Politicks and Philosophy, so they sway also in Architecture; Works of Filigrand, and little Knacks are in great Vogue; but Building certainly ought to have the Attribute of eternal, and therefore the only thing uncapable of new Fashions.[10]

Not for Wren the brief period of transitory glory his father had experienced – his lifelong ambition was to create monuments without 'Fashions' that would last to all eternity, permanently preserving and memorialising the Wren name. Moreover, if we detect a tinge of disdain or diffidence at the involvement of women in such projects, that too deserves a moment's reflection. Of the eleven children Mary Wren bore Dean Wren between 1631 and 1643, two (both boys) died within an hour of birth, while of the girls, apparently only Catharine, Anna and Susan were still alive in 1665.[11] His uncle Matthew's family had been similarly all but wiped out by childbed misfortune, childhood disease or hardship – of his twelve recorded children, only four appear to have reached adulthood.[12] Christopher Wren was simply a realist in not putting his trust for the enduring fame of families in the poor prospects of life-expectancy the period afforded (at least for those who had fallen on hard times).

The family's plunge from affluence into penury formed young Christopher's intellectual outlook and attitudes. Instead of indulging in esoteric mental gymnastics of the kind his father and his circle of friends had tended to pursue, in comfort and at leisure during long summers at Windsor, Christopher Wren junior, from the beginning of his adult life, was determinedly pragmatic in his goals. His early interests focus squarely on the practical, and, indeed, on the possibility of making money by marketing one of his early inventions. The first invention of his of which we have a detailed record is a device for mechanically assisting the sowing of grain, and in his letter to Charles Louis, Elector Palatine Wren represents this as planting corn 'equally' (drilling and dropping seed at regular intervals), but, most importantly 'without Want and without Waste'.[13] By 1648 Christopher Wren had adapted to a frugal life in the family's country retreat, and had learned about 'want' and the merits of avoiding 'waste'.

Some time in 1646 Dean Wren removed Christopher from Westminster, worried now for his son's safety. Westminster School had been put under the management of a Commonwealth-friendly board of governors in 1645, who none the less retained the royalist-sympathising Busby as headmaster. Throughout the late 1640s and 1650s, Busby contrived to continue to admit to the school a good number of academically gifted sons of royalist sympathisers as scholarship boys, including, in 1648, the fatherless Robert Hooke. Still, a Wren was perhaps too prominent a charge to keep surreptitiously in the school's midst. There were practical difficulties now, too, in Christopher's remaining in London. In April 1646, Parliament passed legislation prohibiting delinquents from coming to London, and confining them to their provincial places of residence, unless a special dispensation had been issued (such a safe-conduct was presumably necessary to allow Dean Wren to present his petition 'at the Parliament House' in 1647). In February 1650 delinquents were further confined to within a five-mile radius of their houses – sentencing Dean Wren to a kind of moderate house arrest, and presumably putting paid to his efforts to retrieve the King's Garter properties via the courts until the restrictions eased.[14] A vulnerable boy could hardly be left beyond the reach of his father or of family friends (most of whom were also delinquent royalists). So Christopher joined his father and mother in Bletchingdon, where, fortunately, his brother-in-law, William Holder, ran the local grammar school. There his schooling continued for a further two years.

So in 1646 it was Christopher Wren junior's sister Susan – five years his senior – who rescued the family and gave them a place of refuge from the political storm raging across the country. In 1642, at the age of fifteen, she had been married to William Holder – a graduate of Pembroke College, Cambridge (Bishop Matthew Wren's old college), and appointed in the same year to the living of Bletchingdon in Oxfordshire. Susan Wren and her husband took in the family permanently when her father was ejected from East Knoyle in 1647 – just as Charles I's daughter Princess Mary and her family by marriage took in the future Charles II (also following the collapse of the siege of Oxford) at the Dutch court in The Hague. The Wren family remained with the Holders at Bletchingdon until Dean Wren's death in 1658.

When the King had abandoned his London home in January 1642, there were other residents of Whitehall Palace besides the royal family who lost everything they owned. The sprawling Palace contained a number of suites of rooms assigned to prominent court officials. One of these was the King's personal physician, Dr William Harvey, already internationally famous for his discovery of the circulation of the blood, which he had published in 1628.[15] Since 1639 Harvey had been the King's principal 'ordinary physician', in charge of those doctors who were permanently in attendance, as opposed to the various extraordinary physicians who attended occasionally. Whereas protection orders were placed on the King's possessions following his flight, reserving them for seizure and subsequent sale by Parliament, William Harvey's rooms were simply ransacked, his papers destroyed, and his personal possessions irretrievably dispersed.[16] Harvey himself, meanwhile, continued to serve the King as his trusted doctor, following him first to York, and then to Oxford. According to Aubrey, it was he who had charge of the royal children, Prince Charles and Prince James, at the Battle of Edgehill.[17]

Nevertheless, of all the professional groups caught up in the civil war, none had more resilience (or greater practical bargaining power) in the face of the ups and downs of factional politics than the physicians. Able practitioners were vitally important to both sides in the conflict, giving royalist physicians much more flexibility than Anglican clergymen or royalist gentlemen to 'compound' (pay a statutory fine to Parliament to buy a full pardon).[18] From 1643 to 1646 the circle of physicians serving the King at Oxford included George Ent, Thomas Willis, Walter Charleton, Nathaniel Highmore, Ralph Bathurst and Charles Scarburgh. All claimed later to have been pupils of Harvey's (a claim for which there is documented evidence in the case of Ent).[19] All continued to practise lucratively during the Commonwealth and Protectorate periods, and those who outlived the Commonwealth rose to further prominence under Charles II at the Restoration.[20]

The career of physician George Ent during this period is a typical one. Born in Kent in 1604, to a Dutch merchant family, he was taught at Cambridge by Samuel Ward and gained his MA at Sidney Sussex College in 1631. He practised medicine in London in the late 1630s, and

William Harvey, eminent medical scientist who discovered the circulation of the blood in 1616, and royal physician to both James I and Charles I, painted at about the time of Charles's execution in 1649.

like William Harvey was a fellow of the Royal College of Physicians. He was in Oxford as one of the King's physicians from 1643 to 1646, closely associated with Harvey, whom he persuaded to publish his *Anatomical Exercitations Concerning the Generation of Animals*, which came out in 1651. He apparently passed seamlessly into Commonwealth London medical life after the execution of the King: in 1650 he was one of three fellows of the College of Physicians (now without the 'Royal') who supervised the revised edition of *The Pharmacopoeia londonensis*. At the Restoration Ent passed equally seamlessly back into royal favour – he was knighted by Charles II in 1665, after an anatomy lecture at the Royal (again) College of Physicians which the King attended. Ent was one of the founding fellows of the Royal Society and was named in the original Council in the royal charter of 1662. He was President of the Royal College of Physicians for seven of the years between 1670 and 1684.[21]

Since Oxford was a garrison town, during a period of active military combat, the circle of royalist-sympathising physicians there was afforded an unparalleled opportunity to conduct experimental research in medicine. In more settled times, very large quantities of large and small animals killed by the King on his hunting trips had provided Harvey with a ready supply of recently slain bodies for dissection, leading ultimately to his discovery of the circulation of the blood (Harvey used to accompany the hunting party, to make sure his carcasses were as freshly slaughtered as possible).[22] Now, force of circumstances meant that human cadavers were available in comparable numbers, and that the physicians, mostly unable to leave Oxford, had the opportunity, alongside their field-hospital duties, to pursue their dissections and other experiments. There is, of course, something rather distasteful about this – medical men exploiting the pain and suffering of casualties of war in the interests of science. Typically, in such circumstances, medical men from Oxford drew a veil over their occupation activities, and fudged the dates of their research materials. This is a feature of these difficult years which we shall see intensifies around the execution of the King (when no one knew what the future held), and which directly affects Christopher Wren's later-life account of his own activities around this time.[23] When we learn that intravenous injection of opium and other painkillers was developed in the Oxford group in the early 1650s, we should remember the prevailing conditions when the physicians concerned began their researches in the 1640s.[24]

Some lasting traces of the dissecting activities of the Oxford physicians can be found in books published shortly after the civil war. Nathaniel Highmore, like Bathurst a fellow of Trinity, like Ent worked closely at Oxford with Harvey. In 1651 Highmore published in London his own *History of Generation* (in the same year in which Harvey published his work of the same name, edited and seen through the press by Ent), presumably drawing on work done in the Oxford circle during the 1640s.[25] In that year, too, he published discreetly in The Hague (the Dutch city which had been the home of the exiled Elizabeth of Bohemia, widow of the Elector Palatine Frederick, and Charles I's sister, since 1621) a book entitled *Anatomical Disquisition on the Human Body*. Safely out of reach of the parliamentarians in power in England, this latter work was dedicated to William Harvey (gratefully acknowledging Harvey's support for his research during 1642–43), and vigorously defended the circulation of the blood. It also contained anatomical materials evidently based on Highmore's access to human bodies during the Oxford occupation – not the sort of thing to draw attention to under an administration which had presumably inadvertently supplied some of the experimental specimens in question.[26]

Christopher Wren junior moved into this circle of medical practitioners when he was withdrawn from Westminster School in London and came to live at Bletchingdon with his family.[27] His father, like the royal physicians, belonged to the intimate inner circle around the King.[28] Annotations from this period in some of Dean Wren's books show that he was aware of, and interested in, the researches the Oxford physicians were conducting. They include notes on the way poisons enter the bloodstream after a snakebite or insect-bite – a topic on which Christopher Wren junior was later to do important work.[29] The projects members of this circle were working on were inevitably those Harvey had mapped out in the wake of his discovery of the circulation of the blood: respiration, the functions of the brain and spleen, animal locomotion, comparative and pathological anatomy. Harvey's preliminary research data on these topics had been lost to looters from his rooms in Whitehall Palace. Now the work was redone with the collaboration of Harvey's students, including Ent, Charleton and Scarburgh. Harvey did his experimental work on the development of the foetus, for example, on eggs from a hen which he kept in the rooms of George Bathurst (Ralph Bathurst's elder brother)[30] at Trinity College: 'which they dayly opened to discerne the progres and way of generation'.[31]

For the rest of his career Christopher Wren retained a strong interest in medical experimentation, particularly in respiration, muscular action, intravenous injection and blood transfusion, all of which were areas of research deriving directly from Harvey's experimental work on the circulation of the blood. Long after he had made his professional name as an architect, he continued to dabble in dissection – sharing this slightly macabre pastime with his surveyor colleague and employee Robert Hooke.[32]

In 1647, after his personal circumstances as a delinquent became increasingly constrained on account of his intervention with Parliament at the beginning of the year, Dean Wren put his son Christopher into the care of the physician Charles Scarburgh. Scarburgh had presumably compounded immediately after the fall of Oxford, since shortly afterwards he returned to residence and medical practice in London, where he lived 'magnificently, his Table being always accessible to all learned Men, but most particularly the distressed Royalists and those ejected from the universities'.[33] There the Royal College of Physicians provided a university-style focus for medical researches which remained continuously active throughout the 1640s and 1650s.[34] After 1646, Scarburgh's home became the regular meeting place for 'virtuosi' or intellectuals of broadly royalist persuasion. This was the group which the fifteen-year-old Christopher Wren now had the good fortune to join.[35]

Wren himself later let it be understood that he had first entered Scarburgh's household as a patient (he was always physically frail), and that he then stayed on as a pupil-amanuensis. There is also a suggestion that it was Susan Holder, active in therapeutic remedy-preparation and tending the sick, who knew Scarburgh. What matters is that within Scarburgh's household, over a period of about two years, Wren was employed as technician-assistant to the physician's scientific and mathematical activities. In Scarburgh's care, and removed from the decisively royalist taint of his father's milieu, the young Wren took his first steps in the two fields in which Scarburgh was competent to act as mentor and patron – medicine and mathematics.

It is at this point that Christopher Wren's giftedness harmonises with the prospects his father could offer him by calling in old favours. It is clear from the fragments which survive among his father's papers that the young Wren had by this time already been recognised as a mathematical prodigy, with an astonishing aptitude in the kind of complex calculations required to produce original work in astronomy. In addition, his drawing and drafting skills were exceptional – Wren's 'hand' is remarked on in every graphic representation he produces, in whatever field, throughout his life. Surviving freehand sketches show he had unusual artistic flair, and he combined this with a fastidious attention to detail in measured drawings. In other words, Dean Wren's son stood out as particularly talented in areas in which potential sponsors or patrons like Scarburgh and Wilkins – now desperately necessary to the suddenly unfortunate Wren family – were especially interested.

No details survive of Wren's life in the Scarburgh household, apart from a single letter home (written in Latin) from Wren to his father. Like other accounts of Wren's adolescent activities, this amounts to a checklist of 'clever things the boy has done', including astronomical instruments (designed and constructed) and mathematics (specifically, spherical trigonometry, needed for astronomical calculations). Somewhat insistently, Wren boasts of his achievements since he arrived at

Scarburgh's, remembering to stress the part that his father has played in preparing him for such successes. The tone of this suggests that Christopher Wren was under some pressure from his father to perform as a prodigy – a familiar kind of strain placed on the offspring of a man whose own ambitions have seen a sudden and permanent downward turn:

Reverend Father,

I am enjoying the companionship of the most distinguished Dr Scarburgh, who is loving beyond measure towards me. Nor does this approachable and most modest man, who has done many things in mathematics which have earned him applause, think it beneath him to pay attention to my – I won't say judgement – to my inept fantasies, and to listen with a most attentive ear to what I think. Often, indeed, he depends upon my inferior argument, then I in turn, to his great delight, offer him something beautiful in the way of abstract or applied thinking which I have discovered, or which I have learned from you.

One such invention of mine I constructed out of bronze/copper, skilfully fashioned for him with extreme care, I put in place yesterday: it is, an *Aetherocriticon* and Memorial Cylinder, for which I wrote the text at night and in darkness.

Recently I wrote a treatise on Trigonometry, in which, using a new method, the whole of spherical trigonometry is concisely comprehended in a small number of rules. Of which I have copied afresh an epitome on to a little bronze/copper wheel, the size of a gold James [coin]. I engraved much of this with my own hand, having mastered the technique for that process as executed by an artist. When the doctor saw the wheel, he would not rest until I had made him a similar one. There is a tract in English by the most celebrated Oughtred, entitled *On Geometrical Time Measurement* which the author (tired out with age) had many times asked Dr Scarburgh to translate into Latin. He, truly overwhelmed with his own work, passed the business over to me. When I had barely finished, he made me add a letter to the author, by means of which (so the doctor promised), most opportunely for me, I might win the approval of the aged author, and at the same time that of the band of distinguished mathematicians, who recognise Oughtred as a kind of father and teacher.[36]

All these activities, we might note, are compatible with Wren's providing the skilled services of an amanuensis (secretary and assistant) in exchange for his board and lodging – not, however, a version of the arrangements which Wren would have emphasised, since it would draw undue attention to the fact that his father could no longer afford to pay for his keep.[37]

As Wren indicates, one of the tasks Scarburgh had encouraged him to undertake was to make a Latin translation of a short treatise on constructing sundials, written by the distinguished English mathematician William Oughtred. Wren's qualifications for executing this task, in spite of his youth, were impeccable. As son of the Dean of Windsor, and an ex-pupil of Westminster School, he was an accomplished Latinist – his surviving letters testify to his Latin eloquence and command of high Latin style. We also have documentary evidence that the young Wren had constructed sundials before at the family home (which was now at Bletchingdon).[38]

When the new Latin edition of Oughtred's *Key to Arithmetic* appeared in 1652 it included both Wren's translation of the treatise on sundials and the elaborately complimentary prefatory letter to Oughtred that Scarburgh had also pressed him into composing 'when the translation was barely completed'. This carefully judged juvenile publication (orchestrated by Scarburgh) had the desired effect of drawing Wren – as a mathematical prodigy rather than as a Commonwealth supporter – favourably to the attention of the Parliamentary Commissioners for the University of Oxford. The new Oughtred *Clavis* Latin edition gained a number of its participants significant preferment from the Commissioners.

The prime movers behind the mathematical 'fashion' for Oughtred, as flagship text for Commonwealth practical studies at the universities, and, specifically, behind the 1652 edition of his key work were Seth Ward and John Wallis. Both were in need of solid credentials for academic preferment under the new government, around 1649–50. Although a talented mathematician, Wallis had not strictly held a mathematical post before he was appointed to the Savilian Professorship of Geometry at Oxford in 1649, but he had served as a cryptographer to the Parliamentarians during the civil war.[39] He also clerked for the Westminster Assembly which sat continuously throughout the civil war period, redrafting the Anglican prayer book and liturgy. His Savilian chair (in which

John Wallis, mathematician and cryptographer whose career survived the Restoration, probably because he had deciphered coded documents for both sides during the civil wars.

he replaced the dismissed royalist Peter Turner) was probably a political reward for these services rendered to the victorious parliamentary party in the civil war. In fact, Wallis's work as a cryptographer, throughout the Commonwealth period and into the Restoration, probably helped keep him in favour in successive regimes. It is perhaps significant that Wallis insisted on inserting a sentence drawing attention to his code-breaking skills into the preface to Oughtred's *Key*, thereby annoying Oughtred.[40] Wallis's *De cycloide* (1659) contains original work on the properties of the cycloid by Wren and William Neile (son of Sir Paul Neile).

Seth Ward's mathematical credentials were in no doubt, in 1649, but his political credentials were. In 1644 he had been ejected as a royalist sympathiser from his fellowship at Sidney Sussex College, Cambridge, where he had already lectured on Oughtred's *Key*. In 1649, however, the Parliamentary Commissioners were prevailed upon to appoint Ward to the Savilian Professorship of Astronomy at Oxford (in this case with the full approval of the ejected Professor, John Greaves, who respected Ward's mathematical competence).[41] A letter from Oughtred to Ward

Seth Ward, mathematician and cleric, who became Bishop of Salisbury and Chancellor of the Order of the Garter after the Restoration.

in April 1651 explains that he has sent the volume to Robert Wood for checking (Wood was the original translator of the main text from English into Latin), and that to Wood, Wallis and Ward 'I commit all my right and interest for the printing thereof at Oxford'.[42] This, then, was very much an Oxford volume, with the preferment of Oxford individuals to appointments vacated by delinquent royalists the main issue.

In his prefatory letter to the text published in 1652, Oughtred made a special point of singling out the adolescent Christopher Wren's remarkable talents:

> a youth generally admired for his talents, who, when not yet sixteen years old, enriched astronomy, gnomics, statics and mechanics, with brilliant inventions, and from that time has continued to enrich them, and in truth is one from whom I can, not vainly, look for great things.[43]

The 1652 Oughtred edition was the high-point of the author's celebrity on the mathematical scene in England. The volume earned all its participants – translators, editors, proof-correctors, encouragers of the author – parliamentary recognition. It should come as little surprise, then, that in 1653 Wren, in spite of his strong royalist connections, was appointed by the Parliamentary Commissioners, unusually young, to a fellowship at All Souls College.

It was as a result of Scarburgh's political astuteness that Wren's career took this first upward turn. Scarburgh had evidently begun to work with Wren on a topic in experimental medicine of his own – how the muscles of the arm function. This was a subject on which Scarburgh later published, and to which Wren repeatedly indicated in later life he had contributed, by assisting in making pasteboard models of the working muscular systems. Had he continued in Scarburgh's household his career might, like those of other talented scientists among the royalist 'orphans' – like Robert Hooke – have consisted of sequential employments by patrons prepared to hire him for his technical skills.[44]

The proposal to produce a new Latin text of Oughtred's *Key to Arithmetic* was from the outset intended to promote talented mathematicians looking for backing from the new Commonwealth administration, which itself was anxious to promote 'useful knowledge' of the kind Oughtred-trained mathematicians practised.[45] The slight tract on sundials which Wren translated was of little intrinsic importance (Hooke, who owned a copy of the edition, apparently never bothered to read it).[46] The elaborately complimentary prefatory letter by Wren stood out, however, as did Oughtred's own flattering remarks on both Wren and Scarburgh. With the translation and letter in press, Wren moved into the academic community at Oxford. Thanks to Scarburgh, his reputation as a mathematical prodigy went ahead of him.

FRIENDS IN HIGH PLACES

As Oxford gradually returned to normal after its more than three years as a royalist garrison town, Parliament took action against those prominent academics who had supported the King. In 1648, even before the King's trial and subsequent execution, a Commission of Parliamentary Visitors assessed the political loyalties of the fellows of all the Oxford colleges, removing the heads of houses and fellows who had actively supported the royalist cause.[47] These included Gilbert Sheldon at All Souls, and

William Harvey, who had briefly been made Warden of Merton College by the King himself. Their coveted places – since the post of head of a college was a recognised step along the direct route to high public preferment – were taken by loyal servants of the parliamentary cause, or at least those who were considered to be useful allies.

Dr John Wilkins, who in April 1648 became Warden of Wadham College, fell into this latter category. Wilkins had served as chaplain to Charles Louis, Elector Palatine in exile since the early 1640s. His background, therefore, was as royalist as Wren's (they moved, indeed, in the same circles). But in summer 1642, shortly after the beginning of the English civil war, the exiled Elector changed sides – from King to Parliament – judging that any chance there might be of retrieving his territories depended on continuing financial support from the English Government. Charles Louis (and his mother, Charles I's sister Elizabeth) received that commitment from Parliament (prayers said before sessions in the 1640s included a sentence praying that the Elector Palatine be returned to his rightful kingdom).

So while his younger brothers Rupert and Maurice continued to fight on the side of the King, the Elector and his mother came out publicly in support of the Commonwealth, a position they sustained right up to the end of the civil war. When the King had been detained and was on his way back to Hampton Court in early July 1647, it was the Elector Palatine and Generals Cromwell and Fairfax who met him at Windsor to discuss peace terms. After Charles had been condemned to death in January 1649, the Elector Palatine was one of those who sought – and was refused – a last audience with the King ('the Bishop of London made his excuses on account of the distress [the King] was in from the sight of his children').[48]

In spring 1648, when Wilkins was appointed Warden of Wadham, Charles Louis was in London, his presence an endorsement, giving a measure of respectability to the revolutionary Government. Appointing his personal intellectual and spiritual adviser to a prestigious academic position in the University of Oxford was a prudent move on the University Visitors' part. When, under the Treaty of Westphalia which ended the thirty years war in autumn 1648, a portion of the Upper Palatine, together with the royal palace in the old university town of Heidelberg, were restored to Charles Louis, Wilkins became an important figure in efforts to retain the Elector Palatine's support for the parliamentary cause.[49]

John Wilkins, Chaplain to Charles Louis, Elector Palatine, Warden of Wadham College, Oxford, and, after the Restoration, founder of the Royal Society and Bishop of Chester.

After the execution of the King, Wilkins was virtually uniquely placed in terms of political influence (and access to patronage). He had been a committed royalist (albeit a middle-of-the-road Anglican churchman), an aspirant to high public office with a fellowship at Magdalen Hall, Oxford, whose intellectual services had, until summer 1642, been assiduously placed at the disposal of members of the court circle (albeit those critical of Charles I's more extreme policies, particularly in taxation).[50] He had published a work on cryptography in 1641, which suggests that he may already have been used in a sensitive position of cypherer, possibly by the Palatine circle. As chaplain to Charles Louis from 1644, he had joined an intellectual coterie around the Elector in exile, which took a particular interest in science. Wilkins's early published works fit precisely the profile of speculative, slightly whimsical, well-informed discussion centred on mathematics and astronomy which had characterised the Palatinate circle since the halcyon days when Frederick and Elizabeth were briefly King and Queen of Bohemia, and which may have helped him to his chaplaincy appointment.[51]

At this delicate political moment, Wilkins's previous position as trusted personal spiritual adviser to the newly restored Elector Palatine meant that he also enjoyed the goodwill of the new parliamentarian government in London.

Although Prince Charles Louis technically regained his Palatinate territories in 1648, he did not leave London to reclaim them until March 1649. In the meantime he continued to receive his parliamentary pension, and to be highly regarded by the parliamentary authorities (it was widely rumoured that he might be invited to replace Charles I as an appropriately Protestant Stuart king of England). When he did finally return home, he left in England two close personal contacts, both of whom became long-standing members of the English scientific community (first as part of the so-called 'invisible college' at Oxford, and subsequently as members of the Royal Society). They were his personal chaplain, Wilkins, and his secretary (a native of Heidelberg), Theodore Haak.[52] In 1648 Haak had refused the offer of a post as secretary to the Elector back in Germany, but had agreed to remain as trusted contact and intelligencer for him in England (a role he fulfilled with his prolific correspondence over the following years).[53] It was as a vital go-between with one of the only foreign powers ostensibly sympathetic to the parliamentary regime that John Wilkins was given the prestigious post of Warden of Wadham College, Oxford.[54]

Wilkins's appointment at Wadham was of critical importance for a number of scholars and intellectuals from known royalist-sympathising families, who found in him a supportive academic patron for their activities in this period of their own enforced retirement from public life. Among them was Dean Wren, who rapidly recognised that Wilkins offered a lifeline for his gifted son, otherwise likely to be consigned to obscurity by the vagaries of fortune, because of his father's previous position. The official line, as in the case of the royalist Busby's continuing headship of Westminster School, was slightly different: Wilkins's utter commitment to intellectual excellence and above all the advancement of the new scientific and technical research on which the future prosperity of England depended overrode all party and faction. He recruited, and appointed at Oxford, anyone of tested and tried intellectual calibre, regardless of their origins or past allegiances.[55]

Wilkins and Dean Wren already knew one another. Wilkins may even have been one of those 'Persons of Learning, [the Dean's] Friends', who entertained the Elector Palatine with intellectual conversation when he stayed at Windsor in 1640–41. On that occasion, we are told (as we saw in the last chapter):

The Elector usually expressed a great Satisfaction with ... the Opportunity of conversing with the Dean, and some other Persons of Learning, his Friends, who used to resort there.

Here the Prince lived in a very private Way, with two Gentlemen only of his Retinue, a Secretary, and one who waited in the Bed-chamber; and a few inferior Servants. He dined at a little Table by himself; the others, with the Dean and his Family.[56]

In 1640–41 John Wilkins was officially chaplain to George, Lord Berkeley, having recently left university life in search of swifter preferment in private service; from there he moved to become chaplain to Charles Louis around 1644.[57] It is tempting to trace back to those summer discussions at Windsor, in the circle of Charles Louis, Elector Palatine, at Dean Christopher Wren's table, the beginnings of those entertaining intellectual conversations concerning 'useful knowledge', hosted by Wilkins, which, as the 'invisible college', the Royal Society claimed as the origin for its own scientific activities.[58] At any rate, Christopher Wren, the Dean's son, emerges as a young protégé of Dr John Wilkins at Wadham College from shortly after Wilkins's arrival there. Wilkins had lost his own father at the age of eleven – perhaps that accentuated his sense of the neediness of young Wren, left effectively fatherless by Dean Wren's fall from political favour.

Wilkins had a dream of a scientific institute which would produce a new kind of active scientific practitioner. One could hardly imagine a more suitable training ground for a bright, imaginative young man of a practical bent, already interested in instrumentation and astronomy, and able to turn his hand to any laboratory task, from drafting to experimentation.

At the beginning of young Wren's career in Oxford, there was a further individual fortunately placed with the new government, who took a significant paternal interest in him. In terms of formative influence on Wren's subsequent outlook and career, William Petty should probably be counted as second only to Wilkins among his early backers and mentors (although after the Restoration Petty's fortunes never rose as high as those of Scarburgh, Moray and Neile, whose impeccable royalist credentials guaranteed them real riches and power).

The same Parliamentary Commissioners who gave Wilkins his

The young William Petty, physician and anatomist, who became a celebrity when he revived a hanged woman on the dissecting table.

Wardenship at Wadham also installed William Petty in a fellowship at Brasenose College. In Petty's case, his acceptability to the parliamentary regime was based on his wholehearted commitment to the Common-wealth cause, and his being a 'Commonwealth man' in the pragmatic sense of being both a respected physician and an applied mathematician and economist, with particular expertise in economic theory and tax-ation distribution. He had spent the period of the civil war in mainland Europe, in Utrecht, Leyden, Amsterdam and Paris, where he had studied languages, chemistry and medicine (in Paris he became a friend of another civil war émigré with mathematical ability, Thomas Hobbes).[59]

William Petty came back to England somewhere around 1647 (like so many others he was later a little vague about precisely when) and was one of those physicians whose rise in fortunes resulted from their practical medical services to a powerful patron. From 1651 to 1652 Petty was on official leave from Brasenose College, serving as Cromwell's surgeon-general in Ireland. He probably became Clerk to the Council there in 1652, a post which he held until shortly before the Restoration. In addition to his flair for medical diagnosis and treatment, Petty turned out to be a consummate organiser – a skill much in demand in the early, administratively disorganised years of the Commonwealth. In 1652 he won the patent to execute the so-called Down survey of the forfeited lands of the rebellious Irish, for the redistribution of lands implemented and administered under Cromwell's son Henry.[60] The Irish survey was a model of large-scale organisation of manpower and technical resources:

> He engaged about 1,000 persons, including 40 clerks at his Dublin headquarters. To prepare for the fieldwork he had one wiremaker to make nothing but the measuring-chains, one watchmaker solely for the compass-needles and their pivots, a turner for the boxes and the wooden tops of the tripods, of which a pipe-maker made the legs, a founder for all the brass-work, and another craftsman 'of a more versatile head and hand' magnetized the needles, adjusted the sights and cards, and assembled the instruments. The scales, protractors and compass-cards were ordered from the ablest artists of London, as were the writing materials, ruled field-notebooks specially made to a uniform size, and squared and scaled paper, besides a whole range of articles, from tents to rulers, for the field-workers. . . . Most of [the surveyors] were soldiers who had been bred to trades and could write and read enough for the purpose, and were judged 'headfull and steddy minded though not of the nimblest witts'; they had to learn not only the technique of their measurements but also to distinguish profitable land from unprofitable. Others, drafted from suitable occupations, translated the measurements into maps and brought these to prescribed scales; and some did the colouring. Over and above all these diverse people were put 'a few of the most astute and sagacious persons' to inspect the field-records and calculations, to guard against inaccuracy, slackness and fraud, and to reckon the individual men's work in terms of 'linary content', according to which Petty paid them. He himself was paid at £7 3s 4d per 1000 Irish acres (equal to 1600 English [ones]) of forfeited profitable land, and for Crown and Church land at £3 an acre; and out of these receipts he paid the whole expenses of the work, and cleared £9600 for himself. The total quantities measured, expressed linearly, equalled about five circuits of the world.[61]

In the process of completing the Down survey successfully, on schedule, Petty built up a sizeable Irish landholding of his own; he also speculated in land debentures, and laid the foundations of a large personal fortune. In 1661 he was knighted by Charles II (fortunately for Petty, his financial skills were as necessary to the returning monarch as they had been to Cromwell); and, for the first time in a decade, turned his attention once more to science, helping to set up and organise the Royal Society.[62]

Petty was a man who understood the need for technical and development skills in the field of the 'new philosophy' and the development of 'useful knowledge', and he was himself trying to make a living from his inventions. In spite of (or rather, because of) his family pedigree, Wren was a young man looking for a way to earn his way through college. Several years before he became an undergraduate, William Petty took Christopher Wren on as a junior research assistant and amanuensis for the group, his mathematical, drafting and experimental skills earning him lavish praise from all members.

For a man who in later life would be required to run three separate architectural offices, employing large numbers of skilled and unskilled workmen, and (after the Great Fire in 1666) administering a number of complex building projects simultaneously, Petty's could hardly have been a more useful influence. Petty knew how to organise projects, how to direct semi-skilled, intelligent workers to execute complex schemes through astute instruction and structured teamwork. He also apparently recognised in Wren a talented individual, with an aptitude for responding well to his kind of direction.

Wren may have continued living at Bletchingdon when he began his undergraduate studies early in 1650, since by then his father certainly could not have afforded to pay the full expense of a gentleman commoner's board. His circumstances only improved in 1653, when, shortly after he had gained his MA, and as a result of his various precocious mathematical publications, he was awarded a fellowship at All Souls, an appointment which carried with it the right to a set of rooms within the college.

As we might expect, the young Wren settled with enthusiasm into the life of college fellow, with its reassuringly regulated, bachelor way of life. He is credited with contributing to the design of a sundial erected in the year of his arrival at a cost of £32 11s 6d on the southward-facing side of the chapel.[63] Beginning a lifetime as an efficient administrator, he became the college's Bursar (its financial manager).[64] So it is curious to find a letter from Wren to Petty (who had left Oxford for Ireland in 1651), taking advantage of the fact that Robert Wood (the translator of the Oughtred *Clavis* volume) was travelling to Ireland to take up a government position there himself, to thank his old mentor for allowing him the continued use of his rooms at Buckley Hall in the High Street:

> It's much above my desert that you have been pleas'd to let me be frequently sensible, as you have had occasion to write to Whadham College, that you allow me a room in yr. memory: you doe me too much honour to let me croud in there amongst so much select and improv'd literature, by w[ch] you have often challeng'd the Divine Title, Inventor: and now especially you extreemly highten the obligation, if you suffer me to have any lodgement in yr. thoughts, when Sacred Business fills you, when you sit at the Helme and Steer a Kingdom. From these encouragements, I take this opportunity of my Worthy friend Mr. Wood's Voyage to Ireland, to present you my humble service, and sue for the continuance of yr. affection.[65]

The rooms, however, were not for the use of Wren himself at all, but for his yet more unfortunate and impoverished cousin Matthew Wren (and later Matthew's brother Thomas too). *Parentalia* notes that between 1651 and 1657, after Matthew Wren moved to Oxford from Peterhouse, Cambridge after completion of his undergraduate degree, he lodged outside the University: 'Matthew Wren, the eldest Son of Dr. Matthew Wren, Lord Bishop of Ely, was originally a Student in Cambridge, and afterwards for several years (in the Time of the Usurpation) in the University of Oxford, not in a College or Hall, but a private House.'[66]

When Thomas Wren was awarded the degree of 'Doctor of Physick' at Cambridge in 1660, without having to perform the usual exercises, the Chancellor's letter granting him this special dispensation specified:

> That by Force of the late unhappy Times, he was constrained to leave the University of *Cambridge*, (in divers Colleges whereof his *Father* was *Visitor*) and for his Proficiency of Studies, was fain to settle himself in the Verge of the University of *Oxford*: That the Pressures under which his Father lay, for seventeen Years together, were such, that he could not (his Estate being

taken away) allow his Children Bread, much less supply their Expences for living in Colleges, and the taking of their Degrees, only to have the Benefit of the publick Library, &c.[67]

Matthew Wren remained grateful for the rest of his life to his younger cousin Christopher for his support during this most difficult period. After the Restoration, when, as part of the recognition of his father Dean Matthew Wren's exceptional loyalty and suffering during the Commonwealth and Protectorate periods by Charles II's new administration, Matthew Wren was appointed secretary to Edward Hyde, Lord Clarendon, and later to James, Duke of York, he took every opportunity to show his gratitude by recommending his cousin for preferment and proposing his name for a series of lucrative commissions and employments.[68]

Petty was a down-to-earth, practical man of humble origins, who had worked his way up from the bottom, and who understood the concept of hardship and want. He had identified Christopher Wren as having potential as a skilled scientific technician, and had benefited himself from Wren's ability to turn ideas into machines that worked. When he left Oxford to serve Cromwell in Ireland, Petty acknowledged Wren's potential by contributing to his able young amanuensis's running costs at Oxford (and, incidentally, to those of his protégé's relations as well).

The Wilkins connection and Petty's attention assisted Wren in getting his foot on the first rung of the ladder of academic preferment. Nevertheless, it was Wren's precocious brilliance and genuine talents which, even in the short run, and certainly in the long, ensured that both men's patronage was effective.

DOCTORING THE RECORD

But before Wren joined the group of scholar- and gentleman-scientists who gathered in Oxford at the beginning of the Commonwealth period, there was an interruption. Shortly after the execution of the King on 30 January 1649, it appears that Dean Wren sent Christopher abroad as a precautionary measure. The prospects for a family like the Wrens must at that moment have seemed extremely bleak – Bishop Matthew

Wren, Christopher junior's uncle, was in the Tower of London,[69] and leading royalists were being arrested with the threat of imminent execution (three royalist peers were indeed beheaded in the following months).[70] The evidence for Christopher Wren's quietly being shipped off to safer territory comes in two surviving Latin letters reproduced in the *Parentalia* volume: one from Wren to his father, dated 6 April 1649, the other from the Reverend Thomas Aylesbury to Wren, dated 10 April. Two months after the death of the King, Wren is away from home, in a safe location of considerable splendour, away from 'lands full of wickedness'. This trip overseas is never mentioned in any 'life' of Wren, nor in his own recollections. The first of the two letters (of which we have only a part) describes the refuge in which Wren finds himself. If we take its details seriously, it clearly lies outside the British Isles:

Reverend Father,

I have spent these Easter holidays enjoyably, thanks to the hospitality of the best of friends. With how much happiness am I permitted to send you this very brief letter of praise for the place where I am. This remarkable house (or rather this palace, not unworthy of a prince, either in size, or in the beauty of its architecture, or in the splendour of its furnishings) sits on a rising slope from which you may look back at almost the summit of the highest of mountains. The most delightful gardens surround it, filled with innumerable tree-shaded walks, strewn either with gravel or with mountain turf. Nor are huge man-made pools lacking, nor most noble groves of trees on the mountainside, on whose summits live a large, noisy republic of goats, organised into herds or 'cantons', or should I say, rather, into blameless states [*civitatibus integris*]. Beside the house is an attractive and ample park.

You would say that this was truly paradise on earth, nay, part of heaven itself (and indeed, it can be said of this palace more truly than of Caesar's, 'it is a house equal to heaven, but the owner is better still'). Why, indeed, should I not call this most beautiful place, heaven? A place where original piety and religion, fleeing lands full of wickedness, might be said to have discovered a refuge at last, where all virtues do not simply like to spend a little time, as they do elsewhere, but rather here love to dwell continuously. All the three graces (manifestly divine) would nominate this as their Parnassus or their evangelical Pindus – the seat of the evangelical muses. Here, finally, holy mothers, and virgins, continuously singing divine songs, or offering the most chaste incense of sermons, or reading, meditating upon, or composing sacred texts, are assumed into the fellowship of the most blessed god and his angels.

Among such delights, what more shall it avail me to write however eloquently which will not be tautologous? With so many happinesses, I could scarcely desire anything further, unless it was that you might be in good health, and might give your blessing to your most obedient son.[71]

Although, in the version of this letter which survives, all specific clues to location have been omitted, the description of the villa or country house, with its walks and ornamental baths, situated in a hilly region, in which graze herds of goats, and with an adjacent convent (which might be either Protestant or Catholic on mainland Europe), narrows the possibilities, and at the very least makes it clear that, less than three months after the King's execution, Wren is outside England.[72]

The second letter, from a royalist clergyman friend of Dean Wren's, and, like him, an amateur mathematician and astronomer, was written four days later ('Die salutiferae passionis, 10 April. 1649'), and shows all the signs of being a kind of testimonial or reference. It thanks Wren junior for the gift of his illustrated treatise 'Sciotericon' (presumably as a manuscript copy in his father's possession) in the most fulsome tones, and remarks with admiration on astronomical instruments built by Wren junior, which Aylesbury has seen at Dean Wren's house:[73]

Most observant young man,

I have indeed received your precisely constructed Sciotericon, and your faithful interpretation of helical motion, and I have examined them with the greatest pleasure. For the rest, I am perplexed as to whether I should congratulate more the ingenuity of the work or the generosity of the author. Astounded, I wonder at and praise both to the skies. Where the daily revolving of the sun is measured out, and the limits are fixed between solstitial end-points by the advance and retreat of the sun. Nay even the very appearance of the heavens and the variegated regions to be surveyed are explained within a single framework.

This piece of work deserves to be praised by no other title than the exclusive one: Organon of Organons. And if the magnetic needle you have invented is less remarkable, it is certainly more [practically] reliable, in that what was started excellently by another you reduce to precepts, and without any assistance from him you bring together in harmony the true precepts, and you confirm those (separated by your own calculations) which make up your system. Of those devices you have constructed, your solar circle ranks no lower than those already mentioned.

In your father's house, examples of your ingenuity and of your having transcended the existing limits of philosophy are suspended from every curtain, to be reflected upon. And as things are now, in chambers, dining rooms and wherever windows let in the sun's rays, these are subjected to the rules of your gnomicon [sundial treatise]. Nor by arranging the contrary motion of the heavens (which were customarily organised somewhere between a sundial which shows latitude and meridian, and a clock), but rather (by means of reflected light) it emulates the circuit of the sun itself by projection. As the sun is escorted from its Sphere like 'a bridegroom emerging from the marriage bed, who springs vigorously with giant strides as he leaves at a run'.

O happy you! Who advances Phoebus himself before our eyes. What scale of harvest is promised by seeds sown at such a tender age? Nor does that genus of studies which concerns ploughing and your first entry into agricultural invention auger any less favourably for you (designed to advance those delights), and those also which open fully by the key of your disquisition lands hitherto unknown on this globe. So far in this do you stretch your sinews.

I pray that it will all turn out exceedingly happily for you. Farewell little eye of mathematics, and love your most respectful, Thomas Aylesbury.[74]

This eulogy is obviously written in the absence of Wren's son. Presumably Dean Wren is to forward it to its addressee. The fact that Aylesbury has admired Wren's astronomical instruments at his father's house, while the gifted maker is away, is also suggestive (according to the standard accounts, Wren was supposed to be living at home throughout this period).[75]

We should not be surprised that Wren suppressed all mention of this trip after the Restoration (nor that his grandson, in the *Parentalia* volume, omitted to reproduce the portion of the letter which referred explicitly to Wren's location, and the purpose of his visit). It is entirely typical of the select band of those broadly royalist individuals who eventually flourished under the Protectorate, and whose fortunes revived still further at the Restoration, to draw a veil over their movements in the 'dark days' immediately following the King's execution.[76]

After the Restoration, the diarist and gentleman gardener John Evelyn, for example, tended to represent himself as having resided safely abroad during the 'troublesome times' of 1647 to 1652. In fact, he was in England at the time of the King's execution, securing the property of his father-in-law Sir Richard Browne, who was Charles I's resident ambassador in Paris.[77] The entries in his diary for late January and early February 1649 clearly demonstrate the problem of admitting openly to having 'been there'. Although privately devastated by 'that execrable wickedness', he is obliged to keep up appearances of normality or risk arrest himself:

> 22nd [January 1649]. I went through a course of chymistry, at Sayes Court. Now was the Thames frozen over, and horrid tempests of wind.
>
> The villany of the rebels proceeding now so far as to try, condemn and murder our excellent King on the 30th of this month, struck me with such horror, that I kept the day of his martyrdom a fast, and would not be present at that execrable wickedness; received the sad account of it from my brother George, and Mr. Owen, who came to visit me this afternoon, and recounted all the circumstances.
>
> 1st February. Now were Duke Hamilton, the Earl of Norwich, Lord Capell, &c. at their trial before the rebels' *New Court of Injustice*.
>
> 15th. I went to see the collection of one Trean, a rich merchant, who had some good pictures, especially a rare perspective of

Stenwyck; from thence to other virtuosos. The painter, La Neve, has an Andromeda, but I think it a copy after Vandyke from Titian, for the original is in France. . . . Bellcar showed us an excellent copy of his Majesty's sleeping Venus and the Satyr, with other figures; for now they have plundered, sold, and dispersed a world of rare paintings of the King's and his loyal subjects.[78]

At the time Evelyn took considerable risks by sending regular intelligence to his father-in-law in Paris detailing unfolding events – sometimes in cypher, and both sender and recipient using pseudonyms. He records in his diary that on 21 March, 'I received letters from Paris from my Wife, and from Sir Richard [Browne], with whom I kept up a political correspondence, with no small danger of being discovered.'[79] Later on, the most prudent course of action was simply to draw a veil over precisely where one had been and what one had been doing in the early months of 1649.

Travel abroad was severely restricted in the tense, unstable early months of Commonwealth government. There was, however, one obvious occasion on which Christopher Wren might have travelled overseas without attracting adverse attention. In March 1649, Charles Louis (soon to revert to the Germanic form of his name: Karl Ludwig), Elector Palatine, left England to return to his restored territories along the Rhine.

Since January of that year the Elector Palatine had found himself in an extremely awkward position politically. At the time of the trial and execution of Charles I Charles Louis was the guest of (and financially supported by) the parliamentary party. He was, therefore, in the eyes of the rest of the crowned heads of Europe, deeply implicated in these events. His rapid departure (by the standards of the period) shortly after the execution was kept as low profile as possible. On 13 March, Sir Henry Mildmay notified the House of Commons that 'the prince Elector intends travelling to his own country on Thursday', and inquired 'whether persons should not be sent to offer the civilities usual on the departure of princes and their ambassadors'.[80] In a letter dated 22 March, John Evelyn informed a correspondent in Paris that 'The Prince Elector (with some ceremony) is gone for Holland.'[81]

The Palatinate party was in The Hague in early April (on mainland

Charles Louis, Elector Palatine, eldest son of Elizabeth of Bohemia, who spent most of the 1640s in England, and was Wren's most prominent early patron.

Europe, in the seventeenth century, the calendar ran ten days ahead of that in England). Charles Louis paid formal visits there both to his mother, Elizabeth of Bohemia (Charles I's sister), and to the new King-in-exile, Charles II, at Elizabeth's summer palace at Rhenen.[82] He had an intense and angry audience with his mother, who was devastated at his involvement in her brother Charles I's death (their relationship never really recovered). By contrast, at an occasion contrived by his mother for him to pay court to his cousin Charles II, Charles received him amiably.[83] Matters may have been helped by the fact that Charles Louis had been entrusted with carrying to Charles II the Great George which his father had ceremoniously divested himself of on the scaffold, and instructed to be handed on to his son.[84]

Between Rhenen and Kleve the party passed through one of the few 'mountainous' areas in the Netherlands – the Veluwe hills. Christopher Wren's description of the location where he found himself on 6 April 1649 (16 April, European style) is consistent with a large country house in this area. The match between the date of this letter and the dates we have for Charles Louis's progress from The Hague to Heidelberg in April allows the possibility that Wren may have left England in the train of the newly restored Elector Palatine Karl Ludwig (as Charles Louis would become when he reached his German territories).[85]

Better-documented experiences of other, similarly placed gentlemen make suggestive comparison with our fragments from this vanished episode in Wren's life. From late March 1649, the distinguished Dutch diplomat Constantijn Huygens, a cultivated anglophile who had served as Dutch ambassador to London during the reigns of both James I and Charles I, spent about a week at the Villa Klarenbeeck near Apeldoorn – an elegant country house a short journey from Rhenen. This was House of Orange territory, a country retreat where William III would build the magnificent Het Loo palace, with its formal gardens and spectacular fountains in 1685.

Among Huygens's many talents (he was a fine painter, and a connoisseur and patron of art), he numbered that of being a poet of some stature. Our evidence for his stay at Klarenbeeck – or 'Clarivium' as he Latinises it – is a sequence of poems he wrote for his host during his stay. In his finely honed Latin verses Huygens elaborately compliments his host, 'District Governor Rutger', on his hospitality, his house and, above all, the bucolic beauty of the Villa and its surroundings.[86] The poems play on 'Clarivium'/Klarenbeeck – a clear ('clarus'/'claren') stream ('rivus'/'beeck'):

Inscriptions at the Villa Clarivium, Klarenbeeck,
Huygens in gratitude to District Governor Rutger

Do you see the splendid springs, silvery, murmuring?
Do you see the hero brothers who preside over them?
Either I am mistaken, unless you are in doubt, yet more pellucid,
    clear,
And spotless are the hearts of these [brothers], than the waters.[87]

Clarivium Klarenbeeck II

If anyone, as an overly ardent explorer of these precious waters
Shall be wanderer in the mountains;
If, dripping with sweat and panting in the summer heat
He has hurried to this spring to quench his thirst,
With whatever languishing fever, or multiplying misfortunes,
He will proceed more happily, his thirst more sated,
Because medicinal cure lies close by the villa; that Clarivium
Whose master instantly insists that he enter:
Here a liquor will cleanse him of blemishes, which comes not from
    those mountains,
But which is said to come from the sources of the Rhine itself.
30. March. [1649][88]

Huygens wrote these celebratory poems as he waited (within easy reach of Elizabeth of Bohemia's Summer Palace at Rhenen) for the Elector Palatine's party to arrive from England, en route to Heidelberg (the group may have included Huygens's son Constantijn, who had been on an embassy from William of Orange in London, and had also witnessed the execution of Charles I).[89] He was certainly thinking of his boys – Christiaan and Lodewijck, who had been studying for four years at Breda, were about to come home in August, and one of his short poems refers to their imminent return.

The next three poems he wrote, however, took a very different tone. They were sharp, anguished verses about the 'English Parricide' – the execution of Charles I. Had Constantijn brought his father his horrifying eye-witness account of the execution?[90]

Sir Constantijn Huygens, Secretary to both William II of Orange and his
father, poet, and connoisseur of art and literature – he was responsible
for the education of William's son (later William III of England), born a
fortnight after his father's death in 1650.

If the seventeen-year-old Wren was with the Elector Palatine's party
at Klarenbeeck, he was not travelling without a mature companion. We
have contemporary testimony to the fact that Wren's mentor John

Wilkins left England with his old employer the Elector Palatine in March 1649. In his 'Life' of Wilkins, John Aubrey includes some telling remarks about Wilkins's swift rise in the 1640s, concluding with a firm statement that he chose to remain in the service of the Elector Palatine for a period after he returned to Germany:

> He sayd oftentimes, that the first rise, or hint of his Rising, was from accidentally a courseing of a Hare: where an ingeniose Gentleman of good quality falling into discourse with him, and finding him to have very good partes, told him, that he would never gett any considerable preferment by continuing in the University: and that his best way to betake him selfe to some Lord's, or great person's House, that had good Benefices to conferre. Sàyd Mr John Wilkins, 'I am not knowne in the world; I know not to whom to addresse myselfe upon such a designe.'
>
> The Gentleman replied, 'I will recommend you myselfe', and did so, to (as I thinke) the Lord Viscount Say and Seale,[91] where he stayed with very good likeing till the late Civill warres, and then he was chaplain to his Highnesse [Charles Louis] Prince Elector Palatinate of the Rhine, with whom he went (after the peace concluded in Germany was made) and was well preferred there by his Highnesse. He stayed there not above a yeare.[92]

Corroborating evidence for Aubrey's assertion that Wilkins left for Heidelberg with Charles Louis is to be found in the records of the University of Oxford. On 13 April 1648, the Parliamentary Visitors appointed Wilkins Warden of Wadham College. The holder of this office was required to take the degree of Doctor of Divinity, but on 5 March 1649 the Visitors gave Wilkins a year's dispensation since he was 'at this time in attendance on the prince elector and cannot in regard of that service have time to do his exercise, and all other things necessary unto that degree'.[93] Wilkins eventually took the degree on 19 December 1649. We may conclude that Wilkins was abroad with the Elector Palatine from March until early December. It appears that Christopher Wren travelled with him.

To an ambitious man like Wilkins, the prospects in the newly restored Palatinate must have looked more promising in early 1649 than those at home in England. He may even have believed (as many did) that the victorious parliamentarians, having legislated to remove Charles I's sons from the succession, might invite Karl Ludwig back, as a suitably committed Protestant Stuart claimant to the English throne.[94] In the interests of continued close communication between Parliament and himself, the Elector Palatine's second trusted personal servant in England, his private secretary Theodore Haak, remained in London to oversee correspondence and intelligence.

Christopher Wren's trip was directly sponsored by Wilkins, acting as trusted family friend and protector. 'By means of Dr. Wilkins, who was Chaplain to his Royal Highness Charles Elector Palatine, while resident in England, he had the Honour to be introduced to the Acquaintance and Favour of that Prince, a great Lover and Encourager of Mathematics, and useful Experiments,' writes Wren's son Christopher in *Parentalia*.[95] The possibility that Wren embarked for mainland Europe in the train of the Elector Palatine, accompanying the Elector's chaplain and close adviser John Wilkins, casts the patronage-soliciting letter which Wren wrote to the Elector Palatine in a somewhat different light. We have already quoted selectively from that letter; now it deserves closer inspection:

> To his Most Illustrious Highness Charles, Prince Elector Palatine of the Rhine, &c.
>
> Most Illustrious Prince,
>
> When of old a Votive-Table was hung up to some Deity or Hero, a few small Characters, modestly obscuring themselves in some shady Corner of the Piece (as yet the modern Custom is) were never prohibited from revealing the poor Artist, and rendering him somewhat a Sharer in the Devotion: Indeed I was almost prompted to such a Presumption out of my own Zeal to a Prince, so much *mercurialium custos virorum* [protector of men of intellect], but the learned Votary who consecrates these Tables to your Highness (being one who suffers me to be a most addicted Client of his)[96] civilly obstetricated my Affection to your Highness, by adding his Commands to me to tender this Oblation: And had not my too indulgent Patron by undeservedly thinking them not unfit for his own presenting, (tho' exceedingly beneath your Highness's Acceptance) robb'd me of my Humility, and taken away the extreme low Thoughts I should

otherwise have had of them, I must needs have called the first Device, but a rustick Thing concerning Agriculture only, and therefore an illiberal Art, tending only to the saving of Corn, improper in that glorious prodigal Soil of your's. where every Shower of Hail must necessarily press from the Hills even Torrents of Wine. The other Conceipt I must have deplor'd as a tardy Invention, impertinently now coming into the World, after the Divine *German* Art of Printing. Of the third Paper I cannot say any Thing too little, 'tis Extenuation enough to say that they are two Mites, two living Nothings, nay, but painted Nothings, the Shadow of Nothing; and this Shadow rarified too, even to forty thousand Times its former Extension; if it presents you with any Thing in Nature, 'tis but with a Pair of Atoms. Now if it be possible for your Highness to force your self to accept such extreme Littlenesses as these, you will therein imitate the Divinity, which shews it self *maxime in minimis*, and preserve that Devotion towards your Highness, which I conceived while yet a Child, when you were pleased to honour my Father's House by your Presence, for some Weeks, who therefore must eternally retain a Sense of being

Your Highness's most humble and most devoted Servant,

Christopher Wren.[97]

In this letter Wren represents himself as an amanuensis and draughtsman/technician, skilfully executing works on behalf of his well-connected patron (Wilkins), who urges him to present these to a yet greater Maecenas, in the hope of gaining his support. The most plausible practical purpose such a letter could have served was to have earned Wren a position either in the Elector Palatine's departing household as a secretary (the job Haak had turned down), or at the University of Heidelberg – the Palatinate was notoriously short of money, and not likely to support a young scholar back in England. Wilkins chose the moment at which his employer, restored by the Treaty of Westphalia to something of his former princely glory, returned to his much reduced and war-damaged kingdom, to recommend his young amanuensis to him for a fresh start abroad.[98]

Whatever their original plans, neither Wren nor Wilkins remained in the Elector Palatine's service. Karl Ludwig's Palatine kingdom, and

Heidelberg in particular, had been devastated by the thirty years war, the population reduced to a tenth of that in 1620, industry and commerce at a standstill, and the University closed (it reopened in 1652). Intriguingly, a manuscript note by Dean Wren on the state of the great library at Heidelberg following the thirty years war, written in 1651, is to be found in the margin of an Oxford-published book which contains an early (anonymous) tract by Christopher Wren junior on the Julian calendar. It reads:

> 1622: The Library at Heidelberg, the most celebrated in all Europe, boasted a letter written in the hand of Saint Paul, of which one part was carried away to Rome, the other part elsewhere. And as well as this Saint Paul letter, they say that a manuscript of the Pentateuch – of such antiquity that the Jews used to kiss it while genuflecting before it – was also taken from thence to Rome, along with other famous documents.[99]

Perhaps it was specifically the state of the ransacked University and its library which led to plans drawn up by Wilkins and Dean Wren for Christopher Wren's future at Heidelberg being revised. The publishing of a small work by Wren at Oxford the following year was certainly part of a campaign on the part of Wilkins, Scarburgh, Petty and others to bring Wren to the attention of the University authorities as a mathematical prodigy.

One can only speculate on the route of Wren and Wilkins's return journey to England. Nevertheless, it can be plausibly proposed that the route they took home was the other established one between the Palatinate and England – one along which both Karl Ludwig and his father and brothers had travelled on many well-documented occasions. This involved crossing into Switzerland, and thence into France, a route which inevitably took the traveller through Paris. By June 1649 Charles II had joined his brother James in residence there, close to the court of his own mother. If Wilkins had decided (and had decided for his young protégé Wren) that a more promising future now lay with English rather than with Palatine patrons, it is highly likely that they returned via the English court in exile. On 18 September 1649, a warrant was issued by the parliamentary authorities in London 'for the apprehension of —— Wren on business of consequence' – was Dean Wren summoned to account for his son's movements?

In terms of Wren's subsequent career, the suggestion that he had travelled from London to the Palatinate in his late teens, and spent nine months travelling on the continent of Europe, solves one of the long-standing mysteries about his later career – how a man who had never seen the great new buildings of Europe could have embarked so confidently on an architectural career shortly after the Restoration. If Wren's return journey took him through Paris, then the visit of 1665, whose purpose was to allow him to inspect Louis XIV's great new building projects there, and to meet the great Italian architect Bernini, would have been his second visit. It is surely more likely that the man selected by Charles II to rebuild London in the grand style of Louis XIV's Paris, after 1660, would have been someone who had already experienced the dazzling splendour of that renewed city – someone indeed who had experienced that great city at a similar age, and under similar circumstances, to himself.[100]

On the other hand, in his recollections of Wilkins, Anthony à Wood writes that he was 'bred in the court, and was a piece of a traveller, having twice seen the prince of Orange's court at The Hague, in his journey to, and return from, Heydelburg, whither he went to wait upon the prince elector palatine, whose chaplain he was in England'. This would suggest that if Wilkins and Wren did take in Paris on their return journey, they also revisited The Hague.[101]

The Hague, too, was one of the great courtly cities of Europe in the late 1640s, housing no fewer than three royal courts, two of which were reassuringly English in culture and ambience – that of William of Orange and his English wife Mary Stuart; that of her aunt (and Charles I's sister) Elizabeth of Bohemia, widowed Queen of the Winter King Frederick; and that of the widow of Frederick of Orange, William's father and the previous Stadholder (the elected ruler of Holland and adjacent provinces).[102] The teenaged couple William of Orange and Mary Stuart, in particular, were renowned for their love of luxury and ostentatious courtly display. Mary – surrounded by her émigré English court, and dressed and bejewelled with all the splendour of the old days at Windsor Castle – was the same age as Wren. As for the city as a whole: Dutch Republic architecture was in the vanguard of the classical revival – more minimalist and less cluttered with 'fashionable' detail than the French. Views of the period show a skyline of landmark buildings and churches very like that which Wren would eventually create for London.[103]

By the end of 1649 the situation had stabilised somewhat in England, and Dean Wren might reasonably have judged that it was safe for his son to come home. Christopher was back in England by early in 1650, when he entered Wadham College as a gentleman commoner, and Wilkins's personal protégé ('a most addicted client of his', as he had described himself to the Elector Palatine).[104] He joined a growing group of talented physicians and mathematicians, assembled by the Warden (a substitute, perhaps, for the sophisticated intellectual circle with whom he might have thrown in his lot in Heidelberg). And Wilkins continued to promote the young Wren assiduously at every possible opportunity. Already in 1650 the Savilian Professor of Geometry, John Wallis, told the prolific letter-writer and co-ordinator of amateur intellectual activities Samuel Hartlib[105] that Wren was highly commended by Wilkins.[106] When John Evelyn visited 'that most obliging & universally Curious Dr. Wilkins's at Waddum', Wilkins proudly showed him a large number of 'artificial, mathematical, Magical curiosities', including 'Shadows, Dyals, Perspectives ... A Way-Wiser, a Thermometer, a monstrous Magnes [sic], Conic & other Sections, a Balance on a demie Circle, most of them his owne & that prodigious young Scholar, Mr. Chr: Wren'.[107]

Wren and Wilkins were not the only ones to draw a discreet veil over their movements around the time of the execution of Charles I and during the early years of Charles II's exile. Evasions, convenient fictions and downright lies characterise the surviving accounts given by individuals of their behaviour from the early months of 1649 to the mid-1650s. Being economical with the truth started during the Commonwealth period; the stories told were revisited and revised to suit the altered times after the Restoration.

Katherine Jones, Lady Ranelagh, sister of Irish gentleman scientist Robert Boyle, whose salon and dinner table in London both Wren and Hooke later regularly attended, is a striking case in point. After the Restoration, some of the most important contacts between men of science and cultivation were formed at Lady Ranelagh's table. During the Commonwealth and Protectorate period, however, Lady Ranelagh was equally prominent as a notable Anglo-Irish supporter of the parliamentarians, whose house was frequented by gentlemen hoping to bring themselves to the attention of influential figures in the Cromwellian administration by their money-making schemes and inventions. This circle overlapped significantly with Wilkins's circle in Oxford, and, indeed, in the mid-1650s, Lady Ranelagh's brother Robert Boyle moved regularly between his home in Oxford and Lady Ranelagh's in London. He equipped and ran laboratories in both places. In Oxford he was assisted by Robert Hooke as hired assistant; in London Lady Ranelagh and he carried out experiments together (chemical and medical), presumably with London-based assistants.

Throughout the 1650s Lady Ranelagh was in continual contact with the circle of 'virtuosi' who corresponded with Samuel Hartlib, as with Hartlib himself. The authors of many letters addressed to him ask to be reminded to her, and there is a constant flow of letters to her. Hardly any of her own letters, however, survive in the Hartlib archive, and there is good reason for this. At the Restoration, Hartlib allowed any of his correspondents who believed that the contents of letters he held might prove awkward, given the change of regime, to remove them and destroy them.[108] Lady Ranelagh (and thus her brother Robert Boyle) successfully straddled Commonwealth and Restoration periods. The absence of her letters from the Hartlib archive is confirmation that, following the announcement of the King's imminent return, prominent individuals were invited by Hartlib to 'purge' sensitive material from his letter archive.[109]

Indeed, one cannot help feeling that the list of important inventions, mathematical discoveries and astronomical observations which keeps getting repeated after the Restoration by those deprived of more useful occupation during the Commonwealth period conveniently covers for long periods of unaccounted-for time which the author of the reminiscence would rather not recall. Thus John Aubrey writes in his *Brief Lives* as follows:

> Memorandum: that at the Epiphanie 1649 when I was at [Mr Francis Potter MD's] house, he then told me of his notion of curing diseases etc by Transfusion of Bloud out of one man into another: and that the hint came into his head reflecting on Ovid's story of Medea and Jason: and that this was a matter of ten yeares before that time.
>
> About a yeare after, he and I went to trye the experiment, but 'twas on a Hen, and the creature too little and our tooles not good: I then sent him a Surgeon's Lancet.
>
> Anno [1652] I recieved a letter from him concerning the

Subject, which many yeares since I shewed and was read and entred in the bookes of the Royall Societie, for Dr Lower would have arrogated the Invention to himselfe, and now one [R Griffith] Doctor of Physique of Richmond is publishing a booke of the Transfusion of Bloud, and desires to insert Mr Potter's letter.[110]

TEAM VENTURES

In whatever field Wren's mentors encouraged him to develop a career, in those early days he was always thought of as a talented member of a team – part of a collaborative enterprise – not as an isolated genius. In the patronage letter to the Elector Palatine, none of the three 'inventions' whose detailed description presumably accompanied it was actually entirely his. Rather, the young technician is allowed by Wilkins to lay claim to devices which were actually being developed as group ('club') projects, in which Wren had assisted. They were in fact three key projects which the Wilkins–Petty circle had been working on, first in London and then in Oxford, since early 1648 – before Wren could possibly have taken an active part of their discussions. All three 'inventions', indeed, are itemised repeatedly in 'histories' of the group as 'useful knowledge' discovered by the pre-Royal Society scientists. They are attributed to different members of the group on different occasions, and purport to be 'newly' discovered at any time between 1648 and the mid-1660s.

The chief instigator of projects aimed at making serious money for the members of the Oxford group out of their activities was that galvaniser and organiser of the group's activities, William Petty. Among those associated with such 'useful' knowledge, Petty seems to have been the most decisive in pursuing them beyond the speculative preliminaries, and he was the only one who speculated financially on them. The first two of the 'Devices' the young Wren represents as his own to the Elector Palatine were both pet projects of Petty's: an agricultural machine for sowing seed efficiently, and a machine for producing a second, near-identical copy of a piece of writing. Both were practical proposals Petty tried hard to exploit commercially shortly after his return to England in 1647.

In 1648 Petty took out patents on both a mechanical sowing machine and a double-writing machine. In 1648 Hartlib noted in his journal:

The 4 of Juli he [Petty] told mee also of a new invention of his for setting of corne not according to Sir Cheney's contrivances (for these would not doe) but of his owne whereby hee is able to doe all that either Plats or Denmock undertake by way of Instrument.

He hath also scanned and corrected Plats his calculations about the encrease in corne.

The benefit of this new kind of agriculture will be bee [sic] 1. for saving so much in that which is otherwise sowen. 2. in getting of that lesser quantity so much more of encrease. Petty.[111]

In late February 1649 Hartlib reported that 'Petty's agriculture instrument hath beene really and sufficiently tried'. By the middle of that year Hartlib had further news about the trials of the prototype, the fact that it could be marketed in such a way that its machinery could not be copied:

The 6 of July Petty came to mee acquainting mee with the success of his instrument for setting of corne which he hath sent formerly to his friend Dency in the country, that it hath fully succeeded and answered expectation so that the husband-men there judged it the best corne.

The setting of 2 at once doth better then one alone.

The instrument can bee kept secret that none can find out the mysterie.

The whole instrument costs no more than 50 shillings and his joyner or carpenter, who is bound to secrecy, is very greedy of making it. Hee is now making another, friends affording him the lands to make more of his experiments. Petty.[112]

Plainly Petty had plans for marketing his corn-planting apparatus. On September in the same year Hartlib noted that Petty was once again going down to the country to 'trie his engine for corne-businesse'. The tests, however, evidently ran into difficulties, because in the spring of 1651 his agricultural engine was 'not yet altogether compleated'.

It appears that Petty lodged the patent for his sowing engine, then took the problem to the Oxford group for elaboration. Specifically, he (newly arrived in Oxford himself) took on the manually dextrous and mechanically able Christopher Wren for research and development work

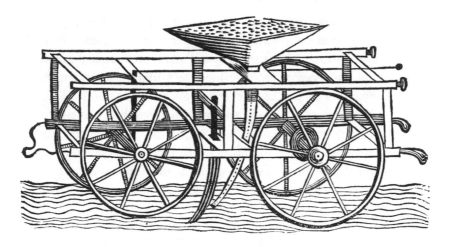

Experimental seed-drill for sowing corn evenly and without waste,
contemporary with the one whose patent was disputed between
Wren and Petty.

– hence Wren's appearance working on precisely the ventures which
interested Petty. The 1651 report on the sowing engine's progress comes
in a letter from John Lydall, fellow of Trinity College, to his ex-pupil
John Aubrey in London:

> Here have been some late inventions with us of some new
> engines, one is how to set a field of corne as soone as otherwaies
> it can be sowne & [harrow] invented by Dr Petty but not yet
> altogether compleated. Another is how with ye same weights to
> weigh graines & scruples, & dramms & ounces, both the scale
> & weights hanging slid at an aequall distance from the centre
> of the ballance, invented by Mr Wren a Bac[helor] of arts of
> Waddham, who likewise invented another engine for double
> writing.[113]

Wren lists the 'balance without weights' elsewhere as one of his inventions. In the case of the double-writing machine, this too had been
patented by Petty in 1648, when he published *A Declaration concerning
the Newly Invented Art of Double Writing* (London, 1648).[114] This carried
a dedicatory letter to Robert Boyle, the Irish virtuoso and younger
brother of Lord Broghill (a leading figure in the Anglo-Irish community).[115] In a letter dated 21 June 1648, Petty indicated that he was
not himself adept at the technical side of inventions: 'my study and

ends being enquiries into nature, and useful arts, and finding how ill my abilities to make experiments answer my inclinations thereto'.[116] Once again, therefore, Petty turned to his adolescent research assistant, and it was Wren who did the subsequent technical development of this piece of apparatus, which allowed an identical copy to be prepared of any formal document, as it was written. The movement of two pens, attached to a wooden frame, and each with a sheet of paper beneath it, was smoothly co-ordinated using hinges and sliding parts. Long before xeroxing, the device allowed authenticated, identical copies of binding contracts to be produced, for signing if necessary at separate locations.

In 1651 Wren wrote to Petty with an advanced prototype of the instrument, following the encouraging reception of an earlier design by his patron and backer:

Sr.

I should be ungratfull not to satisfie yr. affectionate desire of a copy of my Double-Writing, after a larger form; since you was pleas'd to make so much of a little script of It. I now send you a Twin of the Like Production to officiate in its place; and something it would say to you too, concerning its Parent, its Birth & Original; for It fears when the meaness of its Birth is discover'd, it may be slighted: the misapprehending World measures the Excellence of things by their Rarity, or Difficulty of Framing, not by the Concinnity and apt Disposal of Parts to attain their End by a right Line as it were & Simplest way. Any New Invention in Mechanicks perform'd by an Operose way of divers unessential though well compacted Parts, shall be admired together with the Artist, meerly for the Variety of the Motions and the Difficulty of Performance; comes a more judicious Hand and with a far smaller number of Peeces, & those perhaps of more trivial Materials, but compos'd with more Brain and less ostentation, frames the same thing in a little Volume, & such a one I shall call a Master, the other but an Experimenter that hath beat out a thing by chance or unguided Pains. Indeed all Kind of Inventions are much like Fractions in Arithmetic, where I count him no good Proficient, that is satisfied with the first Emergent Fraction, unintelligible by reason of its number of Places, but him that reduces it to the lowest

Denomination, that instead of $\frac{48}{144}$ says $\frac{2}{6}$ or $\frac{1}{3}$, which is the same. And He that aimes not to bring his Invention *Caeteris paribus* to the lowest and directest method and the most parable ways & materials that it is capable of and so that it may deviate not the least from any Particle of that essential Perfection, wch may be justly requir'd for the convenient performance of that end 'twas made for, makes not a thing for Publick use but Ostentation.

Thus would I prepare those that desire the Instrument, and would tell them what they shall find it; an Easy, Parable, Cheap thing; such as every one when he sees it, will be ready to say, I could have thought of this myself, and think it Kin to the Mountain in travail; as indeed he may; for to Produce this slender thing, *Tantae Molis erat* – that I have thrown aside vast heaps of Fancies, every one successivly mending the next preceeding Thoughts, that it might be more Convenient in Handling & of a more single Composure; thus through many several Types of it, and not a few Actual possible, I conceive I have rais'd it to the best perfection in its own kind: Yet am I not ignorant it may be Varied divers ways, that will every one perform the business; however I dare be confident, that such shall be more Complicated, & Costly, or else more Unhandy and Defective then this: nor is this Presumption or guess, for I could tell any man before hand, who thinks he can varie it in any essential part to a better Performance, not only this or that, but a 1000 Variations by an easy Manuduction and Method to the discovery of all possible usefull ways, not only in this but any other Mechanical Invention; and that (granting Experimental Principles) with Mathematical Certainty. And surely otherwise our Inventors (unless it be in such things as depend only upon yet Unexperimented Parts of Natural Philosophy) if they cannot drive up their own Inventions, beyond the Amendment of their Successors, are but *Servum Pecus*, or Low Crab-Stocks for Posterity to graft on. But this method may not possibly be much longer a stranger to the World. And for this particular I shall when I Publish it, satisfie every one in a sheet, concerning those ways that I shall Contend to them; & I wish to find such Candours from them, as I found in you upon the first sight of an imperfect thing, and I shall reckon myself as happy as those firn [? sic] Deified Inventors of rude Antiquity for being General Benefactors to Mankind; and next, Dear Sr, not less happy for being

Yrs – Chr: Wren[117]

A description of the key selling points of the 'diplographical instrument' by Wren survives – presumably part of the marketing plan which Petty and Wren proposed for their invention:

First, That by the Help of this Instrument only, every ordinary Penman may at all Times be suddenly fitted to write two several Copies of any Deeds and Evidences, from the shortest to the largest Length of Lines, in the very same Compass of Time, and with as much Ease and Beauty, without any dividing or ruling, as without the Help of the Instrument, he could have dispatch'd but one.

Secondly, That by this diminishing the tedious Labour of Transcriptions of the greater Sorts of Deeds, Indentures, Conveyances, Charters, and all other Duplicates, the Works of the Pen, (which in so many several Kinds, and several Offices are yearly numberless) are not only shorten'd, but the Penmen themselves both reliev'd, and recompensed by an honest Gain, with half the wonted Toil.

Thirdly, There will be in both Copies thus drawn, such an exact Likeness in the same Number, and Order of Lines, and even of Words, Letters and Stops, in all Places of both Copies; that being once sever'd, there shall hardly be discern'd any Difference between them, except such as is meerly casual, as Spots or Marks in the Parchment.

Fourthly, This Instrument will undoubtedly prevent the mischievous Craft of Corruption, Forgery and Counterfeiting of Hands and Seals, or if any such foul Practice be attempted, will effectually and manifestly discover it; for what will it avail to counterfeit a Seal, or the Hand that signs, unless a Duplicate could be made in every Line, Letter and Dot, like the twin Copy? Which without the Help of the same Instrument is impossible: so expedient might it be to all Intents and Uses of the State, in Matters of the greatest Consequence, that publick Acts be written by this Instrument, for Testimony and Assurance to all Times.[118]

In this case the proposed invention had a valuable and clear purpose. A working prototype designed by Wren was shown to Oliver Cromwell some time around 1650–51.[119] When it came to the final commercial benefit, however, it looks as if Petty found it irresistible to claim the invention for himself, under his original patent. It might be argued that with Wren acting as his technician this was the appropriate outcome (but Wren's position in the Oxford club remained ambiguous, because of his social status). Wren wrote an unusually agitated letter to a friend in London, reaffirming his claim on the machine and, more importantly, on its commercial exploitation:

I am apt to believe from good Information, that those who now boast of it, had it from one, who having fully seen the Author's [that is, Wren's], and examin'd it carefully (as it is easy to carry away, being of no complicate Composure) describ'd it justly to his Friend, and assisted him in making of it; and the very glorying in a Thing of so facile Composure sufficiently discovers a Narrowness of Spirit in Things of Invention, and is therefore almost Argument enough, that he was not justly so much as a second Inventor; nor hath the Author reason to take it for an Injury, that one reported a deserving Person in other Abilities, would please to own a cast-off Toy of his, but rather owes him a Civility out of Gratitude for fathering it, and saving him that Labour of Education he intended, which will now be needless, the dispersing of divers Instruments among the Merchants, with Directions for the Use.[120]

Apparently Wren was successful in his claim that he was the person who ought to benefit financially from the working double-writing engine. Hartlib recorded in early March 1653 that 'Wren is to receive this week the sume of 80 lib. for his invention of double-writing.' As far as we know, this is the first financial benefit gained by the young Wren for his scientific activities. Wren did not come from a background accustomed to selling services for cash, but Petty did. We might argue that once again it was Petty (rather than Wilkins) who set Wren squarely on course for the kind of high-earning employment based on technical skills that was to raise him to greater heights in the public sphere and the memory of posterity than his father or uncle could ever have dreamed of.

The Petty–Wren double-writing machine was envisaged as a tool in diplomacy and commerce, allowing two parties to sign and retain indistinguishable copies of the same document, thereby avoiding the risk of scribal errors, omissions or interpolations. When Wren ran a large architectural practice, however, he found that two indistinguishable copies of blueprints played a vital part in a well-run projects office – one to be signed by architect and client as the agreed plan, the other for the contractor to work from.[121] Among early ideas for labour-saving 'machines' in Wren's papers are a number which either help with production of multiple copies of drawings, or (like his mechanical perspective machine) allow less skilled draughtsmen to produce competent versions of a view or an image.[122] All these devices show Wren sharing that habit of mind of his mentor Petty, whereby best use can be made of willing workers, to produce high-quality documentary material efficiently and economically.

Come the Restoration such mechanical 'toys' proved useful for another purpose – gaining the attention and securing the patronage of the technically minded King. A note in one of the manuscript copies of *Parentalia* records Latin verses composed by Wren to accompany a specially made double-writing machine, perhaps presented to Charles in 1660. The arch little poem assures the King, 'happily restored', that with the help of Wren's double-writing instrument every military treaty to which he puts his signature will be worth double.[123]

'DIMINISHING A COMMONWEALTH AND MULTIPLYING A LOUSE'

The third 'paper' which Wren presented in his patronage bid to the Elector Palatine was the most straightforwardly entertaining, and in drafting terms the most skilled:

> Of the third Paper I cannot say any Thing too little, 'tis Extenuation enough to say that they are two Mites, two living Nothings,

nay, but painted Nothings, the Shadow of Nothing; and this Shadow rarified too, even to forty thousand Times its former Extension.

Wren's line drawings of a louse and a flea (and the wing of a fly) highly magnified charmed everyone who saw them, and have become permanently associated with his reputation as exceptionally able in both science and art – the one to develop the microscope techniques which allowed him to observe and measure accurately, the other to enable him to represent the results as things of beauty. When, after the Restoration, Robert Hooke published his best-selling illustrated book of microscopically enlarged scientific curiosities, *Micrographia* (the book that made Hooke's own name professionally) – which included the flea, the louse and the fly's wing – he made a point in his introduction of crediting Christopher Wren with the original work behind the enterprise:

> By the Advice of that excellent Man Dr. Wilkins, I first set upon this Enterprize, yet still came to it with much Reluctancy, because I was to follow the Footsteps of so eminent a Person as Dr. Wren, who was the first that attempted any Thing of this Nature; whose original Draughts do now make one of the Ornaments of that great Collection of Rarities in the King's Closet. This Honour which his first Beginnings of this King have received, to be admitted into the most famous Place of the World, did not so much incourage, as the Hazard of coming after Dr. Wren did afright me; for of him I must affirm, that since the Time of Archimedes, there scarce ever met in one Man, in so great a Perfection, such a mechanical Hand, and so philosophical a Mind.[124]

It is true that around 1661 Wren presented his party-piece drawings of the flea and the louse to Charles II for his diversion. The King showed them off to distinguished visiting overseas diplomat-scientists: Christiaan Huygens from the Netherlands and the Frenchman Balthasar de Monconys record seeing them (Monconys also mentions the magnified fly's wing).[125] By 1665, so the story went, Wren was too busy to make more microscopical drawings, and the project was passed to Hooke.

Here too, however, it seems that the project had started far earlier, and that originally Wren was simply the talented apprentice who

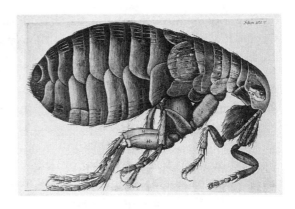

Minutely detailed engraving of a flea observed under the new two-lens microscope, possibly based on a drawing by Wren, from Hooke's *Micrographia* (1665).

executed ideas devised by others. The Wadham group were already using microscopes to examine the detail of living things in the late 1640s. Once again we might point to the circle of physicians around William Harvey as responsible for this particular piece of research interest in the club – in his treatise on the circulation of the blood Harvey indicates that in the 1620s (or earlier) the idea that the blood might circulate had come to him when he examined a transparent water shrimp under a lens and saw the circulation of matter in its digestive tract.[126] And already in his published work on science for entertainment *Mathematical Magick* (1648) John Wilkins had noted: 'We see what strange discoveries of extreme minute bodies (as lice, wheal-worms, mites, and the like) are made by the microscope.'[127] While in 1649 he wrote:

> there are many common things of excellent beauty, which for their littleness do not fall under our sence; they that have experimented the use of Microscopes, can tell, how in the parts of the most minute creatures, there may be discerned such gildings and embroideries, and such curious varietie as another would scarce believe.[128]

The fullest account from these early years of the way Wren fitted into the group's investigations using microscopes at their weekly meetings, and the circumstances under which he produced his captivating images showing the beauty in detail of the minute parasites which plagued seventeenth-century bodies, is to be found in a volume on quite another subject, written by Christopher Wren's cousin Matthew. Matthew, too, had joined the Wadham circle – another highly educated and well-bred young royalist with no clear role (and no clear means of earning a living) under the Commonwealth. Matthew Wren does not seem to have had any particular mathematical or scientific skills, beyond those appropriate to a general secretary or amanuensis (at the Restoration he became personal secretary to James, Duke of York). But in 1659, Matthew Wren did his own bit for the Oxford philosophical club. With Wilkins's encouragement, he wrote an erudite response to an anti-royalist pamphlet which had incidentally implied (in its preface) that Wilkins's Wadham circle of 'new philosophers' might be dangerously royalist in their politics. Matthew's response to this damaging slur nicely captures the club in action:

> [The author] has said in his Epistle Dedicatory, *That the University Wits or good Companies, are good at two things, at diminishing a Commonwealth and at Multiplying a Louse.* In the first place it must be known that the thing he alludes to is a limbe of Mathematiques, and therefore it is not to be expected that *Mr Harrington*, who holds no understanding either with Mathematiques or Mathematicians, should take care for expressing himself properly about it; What he calls Multiplying a Louse ought to have been Magnifying, for the thing is done by a Microscope or Magnifying Glass; But about this no man need be troubled. We are then to vnderstand That a Gentleman in the *University* who is both a Divine, a Doctor, an head of a College, and a Mathematician, has the Satisfaction to see frequently at his Lodging an assembly of Men who are known both at home and abroad to be the most learned persons of this Age; The imployment of this Company is by making Experiments and by communicating their Observations to carry on a discovery of Nature, in order to which They have sometimes had occasion to inquire by the help of a Microscope, into the Figure and position of those smaller parts of which all Bodies are composed; At other times applying the Microscope to some little Animals, as a Flea, a Louse, or a Mite, They have been convinced that the Fabrik of them is Artificiall to wonder, and that the Wisedome of the great Architect of Nature is not more conspicuous in the larger Bulks of an Elephant or Camel, then in these little Creatures.
>
> The pictures of these Animals in that enlarged proportion

which the Glass represents them in are drawn by a Mathematician a member of this Assembly, who has invented a way to measure the apparent magnitude of them, and are seen with Delight and Instruction by all Strangers; And not only so, but have been received with applause by Foreign Princes.[129]

Here Matthew Wren portrays Wilkins as the originator of the microscopical investigations, sharing them with the club at Wadham, and Christopher Wren as the technician who has devised a way of calibrating the observed images, and recording them on paper (the Animals 'are drawn by a Mathematician a member of this Assembly, who has invented a way to measure the apparent magnitude of them'). Such an account is consistent with what we have seen of Wren's other activities in the group. It also suggests that Wren was using the micrometer gauge which he was developing for measuring observed telescopic distances on his microscopes too.[130]

Having diverted his readers with his explanation of the respectable scientific purpose in that 'multiplying a Louse' on which the pamphlet-writer has chosen to pour such scorn, Matthew Wren dodges the issue of the Wilkins circle's political leanings. Under the rules of the Oxford Philosophical Society, drawn up in the mid-1650s, political discussion was not allowed at the weekly Wadham meetings in any case.

Matthew Wren's eloquent published defence of the Wadham club under Wilkins's leadership may be regarded as a kind of thank-you to Wilkins, for having taken him in – as he had so many other bright boys whose fortunes had been shipwrecked by the civil war. Matthew says as much in his dedication to Wilkins:

> To the Reverend Dr Wilkins Warden of Wadham College in Oxford.
>
> The Present I am about to make You is like the Legacy, of that old Graecian, who bequeath'd his Friend, a Widow without a Joynture, and a Daughter without a Portion: These Papers come to live upon You, and to put You to charges to maintain them.[131]

Like his cousin Christopher, Matthew at this point in his life had no family financial prospects whatsoever (there were no legacies, not even in the form of jointures or dowry portions, left after sequestration and fines, for any surviving Wren family members). He owed his very presence in Oxford, and his participation in the Wilkins circle scientific activities, to the charity (albeit indirect) of William Petty, and to his cousin's compassion and goodwill. It looked as if providing services for others – secretarial work, treatises written to order, or laboratory assistance to gentlemen virtuosi – was all the career that would ever be available to either of the younger Wrens.

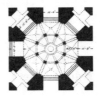

3

Making the Most of One's Talents

COOKERY AND KITCHEN-PHYSIC

'It breaks my heart to be out of action,' an English royalist wrote to a friend in mainland Europe, soon after Charles I's execution.[1] The ingenious, practical activities, described by Wren in his letters sent to his father, William Petty and the Elector Palatine, with their slightly arch tone suggesting that these pastimes are somehow not quite to be taken seriously, is typical of the times. Deprived of occupation, disgraced royalists shifted their intellectual emphasis to match their fallen fortunes.

In the early years after the death of the King, men who were accustomed to busy public lives and a constant whirl of activity at court and in the city found themselves, willy-nilly, with time on their hands. Prominent royalists withdrew to their country estates, where (once they had 'compounded') they lived as unobtrusively as possible, on drastically reduced incomes, prevented from holding even minor regional office. It was out of the question for them to risk a journey to London. A pall of gloom settled over the circles in which Christopher Wren had moved as an adolescent. Their circumstances were such as to tempt some into subversive activity in support of the exiled King Charles II. As one major participant in the affairs of the time, Sir Edward Hyde, Earl of Clarendon, later wrote in his *History* of the period: 'It is a very hard thing for people who have nothing to do to forbear doing somewhat which they ought not to do.'[2]

This inaction, of course, related exclusively to the public sphere. Those deprived of occupation of the customary kind, like the Wrens, turned to other sorts of pursuit, which were characteristically provincial, within the domestic household, and hitherto the domain of women and artisans. Such activities were no longer merely recreational – the hardship endured by disgraced royalists and their families was real, their need to find ways to replace their lost revenues urgent and pressing.

The change of circumstances, from pampered affluence to great want, was often dramatic. In February 1650, Sir Edward Hyde, exiled in France, wrote to console his wife and children, left at home: 'Keep up the spirits of thy company . . . and be as merry as poor, honest, undone people can be.'[3] One of those children was twelve-year-old Anne Hyde. Ten years later Anne, now one of Mary Stuart's ladies in waiting at The Hague (Mary made a habit of taking the children of exiled royalists into her service as part of her support for her deposed brother), fell pregnant after an affair with the King's brother, James, Duke of York (later briefly James II), who duly married her. Two of Anne Hyde's daughters, Mary and Anne, subsequently became queens of England. Such were the dramatically extreme fortunes of the times.

Maintaining one's dignity under these circumstances was, for distressed royalists, part of a strategy for survival. In 1650, those loyal to the Stuarts had only a long future of exclusion from fame and good fortune to look forward to. Lacking the wherewithal for lavish hospitality, previously wealthy individuals reinvented the old courtesies. They redesigned the tokens of status – things to be treated as valued items and treasured possessions – to suit their depleted assets. Now a gift to a friend might be a natural 'rarity' like a fossil or a salvaged archaeological object, a particularly interesting book or an 'ingeniously' designed piece of equipment (a piece of machinery, or an item of new technology like a telescope). Collections of rarities, which had been curiosities to entertain a gentleman and his friends, became the centre of enthusiasm for those no longer able to buy and sell more self-evidently costly items (like paintings and sculpture).[4]

It is this world of straitened circumstances, in retirement after defeat, which provides the context for the key period in the young Christopher Wren's intellectual development. In the domestic setting of the Holder household, Wren – removed from the bookish ambience of Westminster School and no longer being groomed for professional life – began to

A youthful, impoverished and soberly dressed Edward Hyde. Destitute during the Commonwealth period, after the Restoration he became Earl of Clarendon, and his daughter Anne married James, Duke of York, later James II.

direct his technical, drafting and mathematical skills towards more immediately practical, labour-saving inventions. These were the kind of intellectual pursuits which counted in his sister's kitchen-garden, and the agricultural fields around the vicarage.[5] For a period of more than five years the Holder house at Bletchingdon was Wren's world, and his beloved elder sister Susan was at the centre of it.

Susan Holder was clearly intelligent and able, with remarkable skills in the area of domestically manufactured medical remedies and nursing. There is an account of her talents among the surviving Wren family documents which went to make up the published *Parentalia* volume of 1750, though tellingly this passage is already bracketed in the manuscript, as presumably not important enough for inclusion in the final text (it does not figure there):

> Susan [Holder was] a Woman of great Ingenuity, and many rare Endowments, who from a Natural propension to the <study &> Practice of Physick and Chirurgery <and by an intimate acquaintance, and conversation with Dr. Willis, Dr. Scarborough & other eminent Physicians of that Time, who had

a great Esteem for her>; arriv'd to such skill and success, more especially in the latter, as to be the Wonder and Envy of the most Celebrated in that Profession; of which <her chirurgical skill,> among numerous Examples, His Majesty King Charles the Second was a most happy Instance, by the expeditious and perfect cure of a sore <on his Finger,> after He had been long tortur'd, and His health impair'd, by his own Surgeons; for this Service his Majesty, in his Princely Munificence, was Pleas'd to Honour Her with a rich Present of Plate ingrav'd with ye. Royal Ensigns Armorial, and to Continue his Gracious Favours to her Husband Dr. Holder, who in his own Merit highly deserv'd the Esteem of his Prince, and the Dignity He injoy'd in the Church.[6]

John Aubrey also gives us a glimpse of her presence in his 'Life' of Susan Wren's husband, William Holder:

It ought not to be forgott the great and exemplary love between the Doctor and his vertuose wife, who is not lesse to be admired, in her sex and station, then her brother Sir Christopher; and (which is rare to be found in a woman) her excellences doe not inflate her. Amongst many other gifts she haz a strange sagacity as to curing of wounds, which she does not doe so much by presedents and reciept bookes, as by her owne excogitancy, considering the causes, effects, and circumstances.[7]

According to the inscription on her monument in St Paul's (where Holder was a prebend from the 1670s) Wren's sister, Susan Holder, had skills in 'medicinal remedies' and cultivated her gift 'in compassion to the poor'. 'Thousands were happily healed by her, no one ever miscarried.' A tribute written some time after her death adds that 'King Charles the second, queen Catharine, and very many of the court, had also experience of her successful hand.'[8] Although all these eulogies refer to the post-Restoration period, we may take it that she was a formidable presence in the Bletchingdon household, and that it may have been she who first aroused her younger brother Christopher's interest in medicine.

After the Restoration, those who had frequented the Oxford University Wadham circle liked to give the impression that their activities there had been fundamentally serious, scientifically focused and professionally executed. At the time, however, its influential organiser, Dr John Wilkins, was most interested in the kind of diverting mechanical 'toys' he discussed in his popular published book, *Mathematical Magick, or the wonders that may be performed by mechanical geometry* (1648). The project he began when he assembled his group of virtuosi – men of talent from all kinds of background – was an extension of those leisurely afternoons spent at Windsor with the Palatinate court in exile. Wilkins explains in his preface to *Mathematical Magick* that the book was written for his own 'delight and pleasure'. Increasingly, however, the entertaining devices it contained were developed to more serious ends: 'for real benefit [as his preface continues] for such gentlemen as employ their Estate in those chargeable adventures of draining mines, coalpits, etc.... and also for such common artificers who are well skilled in the practice of their arts, who may be much advantaged by the right understanding of their grounds and theory'.[9]

When John Evelyn visited Wilkins at Wadham College in 1654, he was shown the Warden's garden (Evelyn had become, in enforced retirement, a Europe-wide traveller who was something of an expert on gentlemen's gardens). Wilkins's garden reminded him of the kind of fashionable private pleasure-park he had seen in the grounds of castles and palaces of mainland Europe:

> We all din'd at that most obliging and universally Curious Dr Wilkins's at Waddum, who was the first who shewed me the Transparent Apiaries, which he had built like Castles and Palaces and so ordered them upon another, as to take Hony without destroying the Bees; These were adorn'd with a variety of Dials, little Statues, Vanes, etc: and he was so aboundantly civill, as finding me pleased with them, to present me with one of these Hives, which he had empty, and which I afterwards had in my Garden at Says-Court, many Yeares after; and which his Majestie came on purpose to see and contemplate with much satisfaction.

He had also contrived a hollow Statue, which gave a Voice, and uttered words, by a long and concealed pipe that went to its mouth, whilst one spake thro it, at a good distance, and which at first was very Surprizing.[10]

He had above in his Gallery and Lodgings variety of Shadows, Dyals, Perspectives, places to introduce the species, and many other artificial, mathematical, Magical curiosities; A Way-Wiser, a Thermometer, a monstrous Magnes, Conic and other Sections, a Balance on a demie Circle, most of his owne and that prodigious young Scholar, Mr. Chr.: Wren; who presented me with a piece of white marble, which had been stained with a lively red, very deep, as beautiful as if it had been natural.[11]

The precocious twenty-two-year-old Christopher Wren was given sole credit by Wilkins for designing and building the transparent beehives, complete with their architectural features, miniature sundials and statues. One might argue that this was in fact the first of many much admired buildings whose design would be attributed to Wren. As an elegant jeu d'esprit, the beehive, more than any of the other 'instruments' Evelyn lists, is the kind of project a gentleman might contrive for the entertainment of his friends. Indeed, Wilkins and Evelyn were still corresponding about their apiaries two years later. Wilkins wrote to Evelyn from Wadham on 16 August 1656:

For that unusual way of the combs in the hive, it may sometimes so happen, and hath done so with me, though according to the usual course they are built edgewise from the place of their entrance. A window in the side hath this inconvenience in it, that in hot weather when the bees are apt to be busy and angry, a man cannot so safely make use of it. There are several means prescribed by Mr. Rutler in his book of Bees to force such as lay out to rise or keep within, to which I shall refer you.[12]

By the mid-1650s such exchanges of opinions among keen gentlemen horticulturalists were being collected together for publication by facilitators like Samuel Hartlib – co-ordinator *extraordinaire* of letters exchanged between intellectuals and amateur enthusiasts. The flood of practical books on husbandry and housekeeping published in England

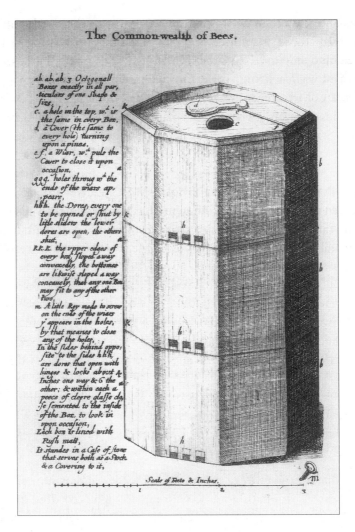

Wren's first architectural project – a transparent beehive constructed for John Wilkins's garden at Wadham College. John Evelyn later had a copy of this hive made for his garden at Sayes Court.

in the mid-1650s also helped distressed gentlemen to modest financial gain. Hartlib's volume on beekeeping, entitled *The Reformed Common-Wealth of Bees* (1655), contains a fine illustration of Wren's design for a three-storey transparent hive, as executed in 1654 for Wilkins.[13]

Wren was comfortable, in later life, to own up to having designed the transparent hive, in a way he was not interested any longer in claiming credit for having worked on the prototypes of thermometers and balances. By then he was a man of means, a celebrated name who could bury those memories of early, anxious efforts to get himself noticed (and employed) by other gentlemen, fallen on hard times, simply to earn himself a living, preferring to remember himself as a young gentleman of leisure, messing about in the garden.[14]

PHILOSOPHICAL CLUB-MEN

In fact what Wren joined when he arrived at Wadham College, Oxford was not so much a 'philosophical society' as an assorted crew of similarly placed, more or less academically able, politically disorientated individuals with a shared set of practical interests. For many years now, historians of science have argued over whether or not what was going on in the circle around Wilkins, Willis and Petty, first in London and then in Oxford, constitutes evidence for an embryonic Royal Society. Because we have followed the youthful Christopher Wren from his father's failed career in the train of Charles I to burgeoning recognition in the Oxford circle, we are in a good position here to assess this claim afresh.

Modern accounts of the activities of the Oxford philosophical club rely heavily on John Wallis's 1700 memoir (supplemented by a second version which he included in his *Defence of the Royal Society* [1678]):

About the year 1645, while I lived in London (at a time when, by our civil wars, academical studies were much interrupted in both our Universities), beside the conversation of divers eminent divines, as to matters theological, I had the opportunity of being acquainted with divers worthy persons, inquisitive into natural philosophy, and other parts of human learning; and particularly of what has been called the *New Philosophy*, or *Experimental Philosophy*. We did by agreements, divers of us, meet weekly in London on a certain day, to treat and discourse of such affairs; of which number were *Dr. John Wilkins* (afterward *Bishop of Chester*), *Dr. Jonathan Goddard*, *Dr. George Ent*, *Dr. Glisson*, *Dr. Merret* (Drs. in Physic), *Mr. Samuel Foster*, then Professor of Astronomy at Gresham College, *Mr. Theodore Haak* (a German of the Palatinate, and then resident in London, who, I think, gave the first occasion, and first suggested those meetings), and many others. These meetings we held sometimes at *Dr. Goddard's* lodgings in *Wood Street* (or some convenient place near), on occasion of his keeping an operator in his house for grinding glasses for telescopes and microscopes; sometimes at a convenient place in *Cheapside*, and sometimes at *Gresham College*, or some place near adjoining.

Our business was (precluding matters of theology and state affairs), to discourse and consider of *Philosophical Enquiries*, and such as related thereunto: as *physic, anatomy, geometry, astronomy, navigation, statics, magnetics, chemics, mechanics*, and natural *experiments*; with the state of these studies, as then cultivated at home and abroad. We then discoursed of the *circulation of the blood, the valves in the veins, the venae lactae, the lymphatic vessels, the Copernican hypothesis, the nature of comets and new stars, the satellites of Jupiter, the oval shape* (as it then appeared) *of Saturn, the spots in the sun, and its turning on its own axis, the inequalities and selenography of the moon, the several phases of Venus and Mercury, the improvement of telescopes, and grinding of glasses for that purpose, the weight of air, the possibility, or impossibility of vacuities, and nature's abhorrence thereof, the Torricellian experiment in quicksilver, the descent of heavy bodies, and the degrees of acceleration therein*; and divers other things of like nature. Some of which were then but new discoveries, and others not so generally known and embraced, as now they are, with other things appertaining to what has been called *The New Philosophy*, which from the times of *Galileo* at *Florence*, and *Sir Francis Bacon (Lord Verulam)* in England, has been much cultivated in *Italy, France, Germany*, and other parts abroad, as well as with us in England.

About the year 1648, 1649, some of our company being removed to Oxford (first *Dr. Wilkins*, then I, and soon after *Dr. Goddard*), our company divided. Those in London continued to meet there as before (and we with them when we had occasion to be there), and those of us at Oxford; with *Dr. Ward* (since *Bishop of Salisbury*), *Dr. Ralph Bathurst* (now *President of Trinity College in Oxford*), *Dr. Petty* (since *Sir William Petty*), *Dr. Willis* (then an eminent physician in *Oxford*), and divers others, continued such meetings in Oxford, and brought those studies into fashion there; meeting first at *Dr. Petty*'s lodgings (in an apothecary's house), because of the convenience of inspecting drugs, and the like, as there was occasion; and after his remove to Ireland (though not so constantly), at the lodgings of the *Honorable Mr. Robert Boyle*, then resident for divers years in Oxford.[15]

The London group appears to have developed directly out of the Palatinate 'court-in-waiting': '*Mr. Theodore Haak* (a German of the Palatinate, and then resident in London, who, I think, gave the first occasion, and first suggested those meetings)'. In a letter to Mersenne, written in the spring of 1648, Haak reports that at several meetings during this winter of 1647–48 the group had tried the Torricelli experiment with mercury, testing barometric pressure at different heights above ground – the protocols for which experiments had been communicated to Haak by Mersenne some months earlier. In the middle of the summer of 1648 the experiment was repeated, this time in the presence of Lord Herbert of Cherbury and the Elector Palatine, Charles Louis – a fact to which Haak alludes coyly in his closing lines to Mersenne:

> We remain, Sir, deeply indebted to you as ever for the communication of your experiment with the tubes and mercury [barometers], for we ourselves have conducted two or three experiments with these, in the company of men of letters and of quality, with much pleasure and astonishment.[16]

Wallis's memoir makes smooth reading. Here is that 'invisible college' in the making, whose offspring, ultimately, was the great Royal Society (originally called the 'Royal Society of London, for Improving of Natural Knowledge').[17] Like so many contemporary accounts of the same period, however, it neatly obscures the diffences between parliamentary and royalist affiliations at the height of the civil war. To the adolescent Christopher Wren, however, the distinctions would have been clear-cut between the London group (broadly parliamentarian, or, in the case of Wilkins and Haak, part of the Elector Palatine's entourage, who had conveniently declared for Parliament) and the Oxford one (staunchly royalist to 1646, but, after 1648–49 and the defeat and execution of the King, leavened with members of the London group who had replaced heads of houses, professors and fellows of colleges ejected under the Commonwealth).

Christopher Wren's peculiar piece of good fortune as the son of the most ardent of royalists was that he could combine a family connection with John Wilkins and the Palatinate circle and a set of skills which gave him access to the Oxford group. His exceptional mathematical ability, manual dexterity and drafting skill all made him a perfect young amanuensis for the Oxford circle in the years after 1650.

We need to pause for a moment here to consider that repeated choice of the word 'club' in connection with the embryonic Royal Society. Used in the sense here of a 'clique' or 'secret society', it is a civil war neologism.[18] It was a term with strong overtones for someone of Wren's background and generation, overtones which are entirely lost today, since we use the term casually for all kinds of societies or associations of like-minded individuals for a purpose. As coined in a popular pamphlet, issued in the first year of the civil war, 'club-men' were those who deliberately suppressed political difference, in order to combine and protect their interests against all comers. The original pamphlet was entitled:

> The Bloody Game at Cards, as it was played betwixt the King of Hearts. And the rest of his Suite, against the residue of the Packe of Cards. Wherein is discovered where faire play; was plaid and where was fowle. Shuffled at London, Cut at Westminster, Dealt at Yorke, and Plaid in the open field. by the Citty-Clubs, the Country Spade-men, Rich-Diamond men, and Loyall-Hearted men. (Woodcut of King of Hearts.) Summer 1643.[19]

This satirical publication represented the continuing civil disturbances luridly – just after the Battle of Edgehill – as conflicts between the suits in a pack of cards. The Citty-Clubs, and hence the club-men who belonged to them, were anxious trimmers, many of them clerics and intellectuals, 'clubbing together' in self-defence. The term caught on. Associations of 'club-men' were founded in the southern and western counties of England, to restrain the excesses of both royalist and parliamentarian armies. They professed neutrality, but inclined towards the King, and were considered enemies by his opponents.[20] In 1645 the Reverend Thomas Aylesbury, friend of Dean Wren (the clergyman who penned the 'testimonial' Christopher Wren carried with him to Heidelberg in 1649), called himself a 'club-man'.[21] Captured by the parliamentarians after a 'club-men' rearguard action against their forces (which were plundering the neighbourhood), he was imprisoned for a year for his activities. When in July 1646 the Committee for Plundered Ministers took evidence regarding delinquent ministers one witness said that 'the said Mr Aylesbury was very forward in the Club business'.

It looks as if the term 'club' was adopted, by analogy, around 1650, for groups of individuals with shared intellectual interests (and whose career prospects had stalled following the King's execution) deliberately trying for middle ground between royalists and parliamentarians. Clubmen also always seem to have pooled their financial resources, contributing to a 'kitty' for equipment and any meal they shared – a necessary and new convention for those not able to distribute gentlemanly largesse. Thus Samuel Hartlib records William Petty writing to him on 12 February 1652 about activities in the circle of physicians and mathematicians still at Oxford as follows:

> The Club-men have cantonized or are cantonizing their whole Academia to taske men to several imploiments and amongst others to make medullas of all authors in reference to experimental learning.
>
> Thus they intend to doe with Kircherus Workes and others whatsoever. Petty.
>
> Dr. Petty is to write the History of Concoctions, with some other pensa.[22]

Shortly afterwards Hartlib records more specifically in his diary: 'They are making an accurate catalogue upon Oxford Library. Id. [Petty]'. Gerard Langbaine, Provost of Queen's College, Keeper of the University Archives and amateur mathematician, was in charge of the project. The assignments of the members of the group, written up by Langbaine in the spring of 1652, survive, and include the names of Wilkins, John Wallis, Seth Ward, Thomas Willis and Ralph Bathurst. It was to this group of men that Seth Ward was referring when he wrote to Sir Justinian Isham on 27 February 1652 that the current work of the 'Clubb' was as follows:

> We have (every one takeing their portion) gone over all or

most of the heads of natural philosophy & mixt mathematics collecting onely an history of the phenomena out of such authors as we had occasion and opportunity, our first business is to gather together such things as are already discovered and to make a booke with a generall index of them, then to have a collection of those which are still *inquirenda* and according to our opportunityes to make inquisitive experiments, the end is that out of a sufficient number of such experiments, the way of nature workeing may be discovered, but because (not knoweing what others have done before us) we may probably spend our labour upon that which is already done, we have conceived it requisite to examine all the bookes of our public library (everyone takeing his part) and to make a catalogue or index of the matters and that very particularly in philosophy physic mathematics & indeed in all other facultyes, that so that greate number of books may be serviceable and a man may at once see where he may find whatever is there concerning the argument he is upon, and this is our present business which we hope to dispatch this Lent.[23]

This group (if such it can be called) seems to have consisted of a diversely qualified band of under-employed data-collectors, rather than a specially formed community of research scientists. What all its members had in common was a good education, depleted means, slim professional employment prospects, precarious futures under the Commonwealth and a range of intellectual interests, from theology and antiquarianism to mathematics and medicine. Here we have a collection of washed-up gentry, clerics and academics, anxiously waiting to see what will happen next politically, and carrying on with intellectual activities which are as little faction-based as possible (compiling histories and archives is exactly what others waiting in the wings were doing elsewhere at this time). This might indeed mean that Dean Wren's scientific marginalia from this period, which range over medicine, astronomy and theology, belong to his assignment as part of this club project.[24]

On mainland Europe, meanwhile, other men of substance with royalist connections – including the royal princes Charles, James and Rupert Palatine themselves – turned their attention to the fashionable new sciences, for want of anything better to do. After his unsuccessful attempt to rescue Charles I and frame an acceptable Scottish settlement for Charles II, the powerful Scottish courtier-administrator Sir Robert Moray withdrew to Maastricht in the Netherlands, where he built and equipped a considerable chemical laboratory, and engaged in vigorous correspondence concerning his scientific findings with other men of the royalist diaspora. Notable among these was Alexander Bruce, second Earl of Kincardine, who was in Germany and the Netherlands from 1657, and who in 1659 married a Dutch wife from a prominent Orangist family, Veronica van Aerssen van Sommelsdyck.[25] The Elector Palatine's brother, Prince Rupert, meanwhile, was also dabbling in experimental science, particularly in chemistry, in Frankfurt in 1657.[26]

Within such circles of intellectual club-men, the seventeen-year-old Christopher Wren – charming, gracious, biddable – perfectly exemplified those club qualities of skilled, non-partisan inquiry. His background and circumstances made him politically careful; his fine, gentrified education, and early intellectual grooming under Scarburgh and Holder, had furnished him with a whole range of technical skills which, put to practical, research and development use, would give credibility to the group's activities. For the members of the Oxford philosophical club – those for whom 'societies' free from political bigotry seemed to be the only way forward – the adolescent Wren symbolised the youth, talent and hope denied them by the accidents of political fortune. They adopted him as their mascot, as their investment for the future and as possible mender of dashed hopes for an entire generation.

THE BOY FROM THE ISLE OF WIGHT JOINS THE CLUB

While the exiled Charles II lived in impecunious retreat, first in The Hague and then in Paris and Germany (where he too dabbled in science), and while young Christopher Wren worked his way through college, assisting Wilkins, Neile and Petty, that other lost royalist boy Robert Hooke arrived in Oxford in 1653, having been awarded a Westminster School place at Christ Church (which admitted poor scholars from Dr Busby's school under special arrangements).[27]

Robert Hooke's world, too, had been turned upside down with the execution of Charles I. Thirteen years old, fatherless, in January 1649 he had been in London only a matter of months, and had just entered Westminster School. Busby held whole-school prayers on 30 January, the day of the King's execution. For the rest of his life Robert Hooke would keep that anniversary, privately, as a fast day.[28] For the remainder of both their lives, Hooke and Busby stayed remarkably close (Hooke was still dining with Busby regularly in the late 1680s, when his old headmaster was in his eighties).[29]

Hooke may have been selected by Busby (in whose house he lodged during his time as a Westminster schoolboy)[30] because he fitted Wilkins's job-specification for a laboratory technician to the Oxford Experimental Club. Even before Hooke set out from London, he had received from Dr Wilkins an inscribed copy of his popular book on practical science, *Mathematical Magick*.[31] Once at Christ Church, Hooke was given paid employment by the anatomist Dr Thomas Willis as a chemical assistant, to help him earn his keep. The Christ Church records list Hooke as 'servant to Mr Goodman', which may have meant that his father's old friend Cardell Goodman, rector of Freshwater, was responsible for some of his basic living expenses. It was through the same kind Isle of Wight family connections that Hooke was recommended as laboratory assistant to Willis: Willis's father-in-law Dr Samuel Fell had been rector of Freshwater Church at the time Hooke's father became curate there in the 1620s.[32]

From Willis, the gifted experimenter Hooke rapidly moved to become laboratory assistant to the Irish nobleman Robert Boyle, recently arrived in Oxford (at Wilkins's personal invitation) from Ireland, though he appears to have remained an assistant to Willis also. In November 1654 Hartlib noted: 'Dr Wellis [Willis] of Dr. Wilkins acquaintance a very experimenting ingenious gentleman communicating every weeke some experiment or other to Mr. Boyles chymical servant, who is a kind of cozen to him.'[33] The family connection claimed here between Willis and Hooke refers to the Isle of Wight, Freshwater Church connection. Samuel Fell was kin to Willis, and as rector to the church where John Hooke served as curate was 'father' to Robert Hooke's own father. So Thomas Willis was 'a kind of cozen' of Robert Hooke, helping him to get his foot on the bottom rungs of the ladder of preferment within the emerging scientific community.

The Boyle–Hooke technical scientific partnership (with Hooke as the paid experimentalist to the scientific enthusiast Boyle) proved extremely productive and successful. Hooke built and operated the air-pump Boyle needed to pursue a vigorous research programme on respiration, which made Boyle the centre for respiration-related theories and experimental investigations throughout the later 1650s (before that Boyle's other interests in chemistry and alchemy had tended to keep him slightly outside the programme). Hooke eventually moved on (with Boyle's encouragement) to become the first Curator of Experiments to the Royal Society.[34]

During the early days of Hooke's studies in Oxford, he and Wren became close friends, their shared intellectual interests reinforced by their closely similar family circumstances (despite their difference in social status). Both Wren and Hooke belonged to Thomas Willis's circle of 'chemists' (medical and pharmaceutical experimenters). In December 1650, Willis and Petty achieved instant notoriety when they discovered that the felon's cadaver they had gathered to dissect at Petty's Buckley Hall Lodgings in the High Street was not in fact dead. Nan Greene – a hapless young woman who had been hanged for infanticide – was duly resuscitated and nursed back to health. Her revivers then petitioned the authorities successfully for a pardon, in the light of the extraordinary nature of her survival.[35] Numerous broadsheets and poems were published, including witty verses by Walter Pope (Wilkins's half-brother) and Wren, indicating that Wren was already part of the Petty–Willis circle by this date, three years before Hooke's arrival and employment as Willis's laboratory 'servant'.[36] On the strength of the publicity surrounding the Nan Greene 'miracle' revival, Petty (hitherto a kind of freelance anatomy tutor, based at Brasenose College) was appointed Tomlins Reader in anatomy by the University.[37]

Both Wren and Hooke were the frail, adored, mathematically brilliant sons of fiercely royalist, Laudian clergymen fathers; both boys had moved, for a short time during their formative years, within the court circle of Charles I. Both had seen their fathers personally devastated, and their family fortunes wrecked, by the King's fall. Both had gone from being cosseted, tutored and encouraged academically by their families to serving as live-in help, dependent on the uncertain attentions of mentors and patrons. Both remained devout High Anglicans, like their fathers, throughout their lives, with a lasting fondness for ceremonial pomp and grand designs – the trappings of 'papistry'.

They worshipped in the same discreet Laudian congregation. In the early 1650s, Dr John Fell (ordained 1647) – Samuel Fell's son and Thomas Willis's brother-in-law – conducted clandestine High Anglican services in Willis's lodgings at Beam Hall, opposite Merton College.[38] Given the connection between Fell, Willis and Hooke (and their shared High Church leanings) this is likely to be the milieu in which they first got to know one another outside the laboratory and classroom.

Hooke's career, in the perpetual service of others, was the life Christopher Wren might have lived had things not turned out differently (and those differences, with hindsight, may have looked like divine providence – not any difference in entitlement, nor any fundamental difference in intelligence or skills).[39] Wren recognised this, and supported Hooke, accordingly, with passionate dedication and determination. In return Hooke loved Wren unwaveringly (though in general he was notorious for his tendency to fall out with colleagues), and defended Wren with absolute, loyal intensity. It was Hooke who regularly insisted, when some claim to priority on the part of an English or continental scientist was made, that Christopher Wren had in fact invented the device many years earlier, but had disdained to write up his discovery. Neither Hooke nor Wren ever formed as lasting a relationship with any other person. It might, indeed, be argued that the glaring absence of a sustained, passionate relationship with a woman on either man's part derived in some way from their shared traumatic childhood experiences, which permanently eclipsed and overshadowed all other kinds of feeling.

As the Commonwealth and Protectorate wore on, royalist intellectuals (denied posts or preferment) began openly to plan for a monastic institution to which they would retire, having pooled their dwindling funds, to pursue celibate academic lives. Among the jottings towards his own 'Life' noted down by John Aubrey is the following:

> *Monastery*: I wished Monastrys had not been putt downe; that the reformers would have been more moderate as to that point. Nay, the Turkes have Monasteries: why should our Reformers be so severe? Convenience of Religious houses. Sir Christopher Wren: fitt there should be receptacles and conveniences for Contemplative men.[40]

In 1659, Evelyn seriously proposed such a college to Robert Boyle (one of the few members of the Oxford circle without dependent family, and with sufficient funds to finance anything on such a scale):

Might not some gentlemen, whose geniuses are greatly suitable, and who desire nothing more than to give a good example, preserve science, and cultivate themselves, join together in society, and resolve upon some orders and economy, to be mutually observed, such as shall best become the end of their union, if, I cannot say, without a kind of singularity, because the thing is new: yet such, at least, as shall be free from pedantry, and all affectation? . . . Were I not . . . obliged, as well by my own nature as the laws of decency, and their merits, to provide for my dependents, I would cheerfully devote my small fortune towards a design, by which I might hope to assemble some small number together who would resign themselves to live profitably and sweetly together. . . .

I propose the purchasing of thirty or forty acres of land, in some healthy place, not above twenty-five miles from London. . . . If there were not already an house which might be converted, &c., we would erect upon the most convenient site of this . . . our building.[41]

Six months after Boyle and Evelyn began discussing these plans, Parliament had invited Charles II back on to the throne of England, the prospects of men like Wren, Evelyn and Boyle looked up markedly, and talk of monastic, residential colleges ceased.[42]

The project of a scientific society, however, remained very much in play. As a viable project – a symbol of restored national pride, with hoped-for economic prospects to match – it became crucially bound up with the chronology of the King's Restoration itself. Evidently by the 1590s a kind of embryonic Royal Society was meeting regularly at Gresham College, under the auspices of John Wilkins (now decamped from Oxford to the Mastership of Trinity College, Cambridge). On 17 February 1660, Evelyn wrote to Wilkins 'President of our Society at Gresham College':

Sir – Though I suppose it might be a mistake that there was a meeting appointed to-morrow (being a day of public solemnity and devotion), yet because I am uncertain, and would not disobey your commands, I here send you my trifling observations concerning the anatomy of trees, and their vegetative motion.[43]

In early February 1660 General George Monck, commander of the parliamentary army of occupation in Scotland, had entered London with two regiments of horse and three of foot, having lost patience with the indecisive Rump Parliament, which was sitting at Westminster. On 21 February Pepys watched as, in response to Monck's demands, the first batch of about twenty MPs of those who had been 'secluded' (expelled) in Pride's Purge at the beginning of the Commonwealth was reinstated. That night Pepys wrote: 'It was a most pleasant sight to see the City from one end to the other with a glory about it, so high was the light of the bonfires.' Church bells were rung, and for the first time in ten years men could be seen drinking the King's health in public 'without any fear'.[44] The 'day of public solemnity and devotion', then, which took precedence over the regular meeting of 'our Society at Gresham College' was undoubtedly one to give thanks for the imminent reinstatement (by now a *fait accompli*) of Charles II.

THE ENTERPRISE OF SCIENCE

For the royalist survivors with scientific interests collaborating in Oxford in the 1650s, the great physician William Harvey was a symbol of hope for an explicitly monarchist intellectual tradition – a scientist with an international reputation, who combined extraordinary acumen as an anatomist with celebrated skill as a royal doctor. He had, after all, personally protected the royal princes at the Battle of Edgehill. During the 1650s the Oxford physicians participated together in an energetic programme of advanced research, developing the physiological consequences of Harvey's discovery of the circulation of the blood, a programme which (like the High Anglican celebration of daily worship) centred around Dr Thomas Willis at his lodgings in St John Street.

Thomas Willis's interest in chemistry went back to the years of the Oxford siege. Before being ejected from Christ Church in 1648, he 'studied chymistry in Peckewater Inne chamber', according to Aubrey. In 1649 he was making 'aurum fulminans' – an unstable, gold-based compound, experimentation with which formed part of the research aimed at supplementing the short supply of saltpetre for essential civil war explosives. By 1652 Willis was one of those who, at Wilkins's urging (according to Seth Ward), 'have joyned together for the furnishing an

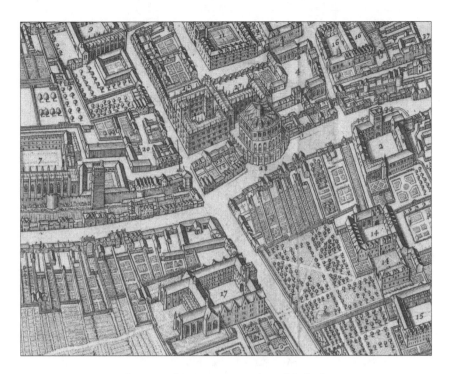

Seventeenth-century engraving of Oxford.

elaboratory' at Wadham; Willis neatly recorded the expenditure on the laboratory equipment in his notebook. By 1654, Hartlib was reporting that Willis, Wilkins and Boyle were exchanging data and experimental protocols, for research in 'chymistry'. These researches culminated in Willis's treatise *De fermentatione* ('On fermentation' – of which Robert Wood later recalled 'having formerly seen some sheets . . . when we met at a Club, at Oxford'). This was published, together with his *De febribus* ('On fevers') as his *Diatribae duae medico-philosophicae* ('Two medico-philosophical arguments') in 1659.[45]

In spite of a later tendency on the part of individual Oxford scientists to discuss work carried out during the Commonwealth years as if it had been solitary, and attributable to a single practitioner, it is clear from the surviving materials that these were resolutely communal, group activities. Important advances of a general, theoretical kind were made as a result of vigorous exchanges of ideas and practices among the members. The shared 'club' research which lay behind Willis's influential published work on chemical compounds, for example, involved an identifiable team of members skilled in chemical analysis and anatomical dissection, and meant that aspects of Willis's theory of chemical composition informed the opinions of others in the group. Wren's conviction in later life that muscle movement is triggered by chemical explosion, for example, combines arguments concerning mechanical movement, developed when he worked with Scarburgh, with arguments about chemical reaction from Willis's chemical anatomy.[46]

Willis's theory of chemical compounds led directly to his theory of fermentation in the blood, and a chemically based explanation for the way heat is generated in the body as blood passes around it. As a skilled chemist, he based this upon chemical analysis of samples outside the body. But his results encouraged a younger group of Oxford scientists with highly developed anatomical skills – a group which included Boyle, Richard Lower, Walter Needham, Thomas Millington and Wren – to undertake further research based on vivisection (or at least interventive experiments using living animals).

The idea was to investigate the effect of intermingling of substances with the blood, as these circulated round the living body. In the *De motu cordis* ('On the Motion of the Heart and Blood in Animals') Harvey had noted, among the significant facts which supported his experimentally established theory that blood circulated constantly in the body, the swift action of poisons and medicines: how else but by circulation could the effects of a septic wound or the bite of a mad dog or of a venomous serpent so swiftly incapacitate an entire organism? Boyle was especially fascinated by these ideas about poisons; so also was Dean Wren, as evidenced by marginal notes he made in the course of his reading in the 1650s.[47] Boyle proposed pricking a dog's veins with needles dipped in poison to see whether poisons 'carried by the circulated Blood to the Heart and the Head' acted faster than those taken by mouth.[48] John Wallis later recalled that the idea of transfusing blood 'from one live animal to another' was discussed in Oxford 'as far back as the year 1651 or 1652', or at least to the time when he, Wilkins, Ward, Wren and others 'were in the habit of exchanging talk on philosophical matters'.[49]

In early 1656, Boyle, Wilkins and Christopher Wren were discussing the action of poisons in Boyle's Oxford lodgings, when Wren made the claim that he could 'easily contrive a way to convey any liquid Poison into the Mass of Blood'. Boyle provided a large dog, and summoned Willis and Bathurst to assist in the experiment. Wren and his helpers freed a large vessel in the hind leg of the dog (probably the crural vein) and ligatured it. They slit open the vein nearest to the ligature, and the 'dextrous' Wren, having 'surmounted the difficulties which the tortur'd Dogs violent struglings interpos'd', inserted the slender pipe of a syringe into the vein and infused 'a warm solution of Opium in Sack'.

Once in the bloodstream, the injected drug 'was quickly, by the circular motion of That [the blood], carry'd to the Brain, and other parts of the Body'. The dog was quite stupefied for a time, but recovered completely from the experience, and even grew fat afterwards (presumably from the petting and attention of the delighted Boyle). Having become famous as a result of the experiment, Boyle reports laconically that 'he was soon after stoln away from me'. The technique was improved in subsequent experiments on other dogs. The group soon found that a bladder attached to a slender quill was a better tool than a syringe, and that 'unless the Dog were pretty big, and lean, that the Vessels might be large enough and easily accessible, the Experiment would not well succeed'.[50]

When Wren wrote to Petty in Ireland in June 1656 with a full report of the experimental work he and other members of the Oxford club had been conducting since his departure in 1651, dissection, microscopic observation of kidneys, brains and nerves, and the dog-injection experiments figured prominently:

Shall I trouble you with what we doe in Anatomy? We have schemes of several Fishes dissected, in which the Fabrick of of [sic] the Parts is often very irregular, and differring much from Brutes & one another. Several things we have observ'd very considerable in Fowls. Some Parts of Animals we have more exactly trac'd by the help of Glasses, as the Kidnies; the Plexus in the Brain. The Nerves we have found to have little Veines & Arteries in them. We find the Lymphae-ducts to empty themselves into the Receptacle of Chyle from all Parts both of ye Bowels and Limbs. – But the most considerable [Experiment] I have made of late is this. I Have Injected Wine and Ale in a living Dog into the Mass of Blood by a Veine, in good Quantities, till I have made him extremely drunk, but soon after he Pisseth it out: with 2 ounces of Infusion of Crocus Metall: thus injected, the Dog immediately fell a Vomitting, & so vomited till he died. It will be too long to tell you the Effects of Opium, Scammony & other things that I have tried this way: I am now in further pursuit of the Experiment, which I take to be of great concernment, and what will give great light both to the Theory and Practice of Physick.[51]

By 1656, then, Wren and his associates had taken the opium-injecting experiment further, conducting trials with toxic rather than intoxicating substances. They had injected a toxic emetic (*crocus metallorum* [antimony sulphate]) which had the predicted effect: the dog 'immediately fell a Vomitting, & so vomited till he died'. As for Wren's final promise to Petty that he had already injected 'Opium, Scammony & other things' and that he was 'now in further pursuit of the Experiment, which I take to be of great concernment, and what will give great light both to the Theory and Practice of Physick': he seems to have done exactly that. He related some of the results to his Wadham contemporary William Neile (Sir Paul Neile's son), who later recalled that Wren 'did propose the giving a man nourishment in a kind of Tappe into the guts', and that he had even attempted transfusing blood, though 'without much successe'. Neile also recalled that Wilkins was involved with these trials.[52]

In 1657, when Wren moved to London, the collaborative research by members of the old Oxford club on injection and transfusion split into two centres, one in London and one in Oxford. In London, Wren re-established contact with another ex-Oxford physician who had a long-standing interest in 'the nature of blood', Dr Timothy Clarke. Like Willis, Clarke believed that 'one of the best keys to the secret recesses of nature' – in particular, identifying the nature of the blood, and the processes by which nutrition and heat took place – was 'chymistry'. Together, he and Wren undertook an enthusiastic programme of associated anatomical experiments, injecting 'many different kinds of waters, beers, milk, whey, broths, wines, alcohol, and even blood itself'.[53] In the autumn of 1657, at the home of the French Ambassador to the Commonwealth, Clarke and Wren attempted to inject an infusion of *crocus metallorum* into 'an inferior Domestick of his that deserv'd to have been hang'd', to see how quickly the poison took effect. The victim, however, fainted as soon as the experiment began, putting to an end 'so hazardous an Experiment'.

At the end of the same year, Wren, Clarke and others injected a moderate dose of emetic into the vein of a large dog at the house of one of Harvey's old patients, his close friend the Marquis of Dorchester. Wren passed on to Petty in Ireland the news that the emetic had little effect, and Petty in his turn suggested to Boyle in Oxford that the club, now meeting at Boyle's lodgings, might do well to pursue a similar series of injection trials. Hartlib duly noted in March 1658 that 'A new anatomy experimented at Oxford to open veines and spout medicins into it.'

Wren returned to Oxford in late 1658 or early 1659, leaving Clarke to continue the programme of experimental injections in London. These continued uninterrupted into the Restoration period. On two occasions in 1661 Clarke was requested to supply Gresham College with a written account of 'his injection of liquors into the veins'; he did so, briefly, in 1662. In 1664 Pepys recorded going to the Royal Society with the Duke of York to see an experiment 'of killing a dog by letting opium into his hind leg': 'Mr Pierce the surgeon and Dr. Clerke [Clarke] did fail might-ily in hitting the vein, and in effect did not do the business after many trials; but with the little they got in, the dog did presently fall asleep and so lay till we cut him up.'[54]

In 1665, the Royal Society's secretary, Henry Oldenburg, reported that a German physician had published a book advocating injection for therapeutic purposes. In the ensuing, renewed flurry of excitement over injection, Wilkins (now permanently in London) suggested 'that the experiment of injecting the blood of one dog into the vein of another might be made'. On 7 June 1665 Wilkins announced that he, Hooke, Petty, Daniel Cox and Francis Willoughby (all ex-Oxford club) had succeeded in open-ing a dog, letting five or six ounces of blood from the *vena cava* into a bladder, and then, using a brass nozzle, injecting about two ounces of this blood into the crural vein of another dog. This was achieved, they reported, without 'any sensible alteration in the bitch'.[55]

In 1666, John Ward, visiting Oxford, reported that:

Dr Lower let one doggs blood into ye bodie of another by opening ye veins of one and ye arteries of another and putting a quill into each and so letting one blood on ye other side: ye one died, ye other lived: another dog yt had 2 Vena Cavas as they say: – Dr. Lower. They had siringed in beer into ye Crurall areries and likewise infus. Cros. metallorum.[56]

Experiments such as these were to lead, eventually, to the much reported attempts at transfusing animal blood into the bloodstream of an unfortunate human volunteer, carried out by Richard Lower (in front of sizeable audiences) in London in 1667.[57]

Meanwhile in Oxford, largely under the direction of Wren, who had become an enthusiast, injection was developed into a standard anatomical and physiological tool. Wren carried on with injections of medicaments, as John Ward noted in his diary in April 1659. When Boyle was in Oxford he did the same. Ward noted in February 1661 that Boyle had killed a dog with opium, 'as I heard Mr Wren did with *Infus. Croci*'.

The most scientifically successful application of the injection techniques developed by Wren and others, however, turned out to be in Willis's researches into the functioning of the brain, published in 1664 in his anatomical masterpiece *Cerebri anatome* ('The anatomy of the brain'). Injections of ink and other coloured fluids into the bloodstream proved highly effective as a way of showing unambiguously the course and speed of bloodflow. Willis and his associates injected ink into the vessels of the *dura* and *pia mater*. They did the same to trace the intricate patterns of veins in the *rete mirabile*, and to show the passage of the blood from the carotid artery to the interior of the pituitary. Their most important use of injection, however, was to confirm the function of what is still known today as 'Willis's circle' – the 'circle' of anastomosed arteries at the base of the brain by which, if any carotid or vertebral artery is blocked, the remaining ones continue to maintain full bloodflow to all parts of the brain.[58] Lower wrote to Boyle in June 1663 that he had tied both carotid arteries of a dog very tightly and observed that circulation to the brain was unimpaired: 'But this I might have told you in a shorter time; for if one artery be syringed with any tincted liquor, all the parts of the brain will equally be filled with it at the same time, as several times we have tried.'[59] Without syringes, Lower noted a fortnight later, in another letter to Boyle, 'anatomy is as much deficient, as physic would be without laudanum'.[60]

In his published text, Willis paid tribute to Wren's participation, with medical doctors Lower and Millington, in the dissections which formed the basis for his research on the brain. They 'were wont frequently to be present at our Dissections, and to confer and reason about the uses of the Parts'. He went on to single out for thanks Wren's help in making the drawings on which the compelling engravings used to illustrate his book were based:

> Dr Millington, to whom I from day to day proposed privately my Conjectures and Observations, often confirmed me by his Suffrage, being uncertain in my mind, and not trusting my own opinion. But the other most renowned Man, Dr. Wren, was pleased out of his singular humanity, wherewith he abounds, to delineate with his own most skilful hands many Figures of the Brain and Skull, whereby the work might be more exact.[61]

However, Wren certainly also participated fully in the preliminary procedures for injecting tracer inks – a procedure in which he and Lower had become particularly skilled. Wren's unusual manual dexterity (on which Willis commented) made him an invaluable participant in medical experiments in Oxford in the early 1660s. During the same period he was building pasteboard models to illustrate the statics of muscular motion, along the lines developed by Sir Charles Scarburgh.[62]

In spite of its sensationalist value as 'news' and gossip, the injection experiments conducted by Boyle, Wren, Willis and Lower and the transfusion attempts of Boyle and Lower constituted serious scientific work, conducted by groups of virtuosi as part of a programme of research investigations in anatomy and physiology. Its senior practitioners made their reputations conducting carefully designed sequences of related experiments, and recording, exchanging and publishing their results. Willis's fame as a physician, combined with his staunch Anglicanism, and the fact that his equally royalist and Anglican brother-in-law John Fell had recently been appointed Dean of Christ Church, made him the obvious choice as Professor of Natural Philosophy, to replace the Commonwealth incumbent forced out by the Restoration Visitors in August 1660 (his most prominent backer for this appointment was Archbishop Gilbert Sheldon, to whom he dedicated Cerebri anatome). Willis rose rapidly to become one of the richest and most respected medical men in Oxford, sharing his practice with his younger collaborator Richard Lower, who became almost equally wealthy and successful as a result. Patients visited them from all over the country, particularly on their way to take the medicinal waters at Bath. In 1666 Sheldon had a stroke in Oxford, and Willis successfully treated him. Sheldon persuaded him to move his practice to London, where he continued his success from 1667 to 1675.[63] The careers of other medical experimentalists from the Commonwealth years in and around Oxford also became once again successful and lucrative with the Restoration. Sir Charles Scarburgh's London practice boomed, and he regained his employment as the returning King's most senior personal physician.

Reflecting on his career at the end of his life, Wren suggested to his son that it would have been more distinguished, and certainly more lucrative, had he not been diverted by Charles II 'to spend all his time in Rubbish' (that is, in building and architecture), and had instead joined the ranks of leading London physicians:

> In the latter part of his life, he has been often heard to complain;
> That King Charles the 2d. had done him a disservice in takeing
> him from the pursuit of Those Studies [medicine], and obliging
> him to spend all his time in Rubbish; (the expression he had
> for Building:) for, had he been permitted to have follow'd the
> Profession of Physick, in all probability he might have Provided
> much better for his Family.[64]

THE BUMPY ROAD TO COMMONWEALTH PREFERMENT

In the spring of 1656 the Professor of Geometry at Gresham College in London, Daniel Whistler, let it be known that he intended to marry, and would therefore be resigning his position the following year (celibacy was a condition of tenure of the Gresham Professorships).[65] Among observers with power and influence in London, Christopher Wren's name quickly emerged as the front-runner to replace him. Wren's mentor, John Wilkins, was particularly in evidence in London intellectual circles that year. He had recently married Cromwell's sister, Robina French, and was therefore in a strong position to lobby the Protector directly.[66] Gresham College was an independent, technology-orientated academic institution in the heart of London, which offered free public lectures on cutting-edge developments in art and science.[67] The Protector was known to take a particular interest in its appointments – in 1655 Jonathan Goddard, who had acted as physician-in-chief to the parliamentary army in Ireland, was appointed to the Gresham chair of Physic 'through the favour and power of Cromwell'.[68] Wilkins was now alternating his time between his Wadham lodgings and his household in London; his special protégé might have been expected to do likewise. Once Wren's name was raised, then, his election seemed almost a foregone conclusion.

On 12 April, John Evelyn recorded in his diary: 'Mr. Berkeley and Mr. Robert Boyle (that excellent person and great virtuoso), Dr. Taylor, and Dr. Wilkins, dined with me at Sayes Court [in Deptford], when I presented Dr. Wilkins with my rare burning-glass. In the afternoon, we all went to Colonel Blount's to see his new-invented ploughs.'[69] Evidently the subject of the Geometry Professorship came up in the course of the day's conversations; at any rate, it was soon known throughout the extended circle of virtuosi that Wren was tipped for the Gresham position. By 20 May Boyle was confidently reporting in a letter to Samuel Hartlib the fact that Wren was likely to succeed Whistler.[70]

In early 1656 Evelyn was spending a lot of time with Wilkins and his circle of gentleman scientists in London, now that that circle had gained markedly in its political influence. When the arch-royalist Evelyn, who had kept his distance from the Commonwealth administration, recorded in his diary, on 11 January, that he had 'ventured to go to Whitehall, where of many years I had not been', it was probably in order to visit his friend Wilkins, newly installed in marital accommodation there as the Protector's brother-in-law.[71] Since 1654 Whitehall Palace had been the official residence of the Lord Protector and his family (including, presumably, his sister), as well as the location for the Protectorate's government departments and offices (a function it had fulfilled since the execution there of Charles I in 1649).[72]

On 8 May 1656, John Evelyn again visited Wilkins at Whitehall Palace. On this occasion he was introduced to Sir Paul Neile, 'famous for his optic-glasses'.[73] A day later the Lord Protector himself intervened in the matter of the successor to Whistler for the Gresham College Geometry Professorship. On 9 May Cromwell sent a letter to the electors responsible for making the Gresham appointment, addressed 'For Our worthy Friends the Committee of the City of London for Gresham College': 'We understand that you have appointed an election this afternoon of a Geometry Professor in Gresham College, We desire you to suspend the same for some time, till We shall have an opportunity to speak with some of you in order to that business.'[74] It looks as if Wilkins had drawn Cromwell's attention to the Gresham electors' intention to appoint Wren to the vacant chair. Wilkins may, indeed, have been looking to the Protector to give Wren's appointment his stamp of approval, to secure the election.

But Wren was not, after all, appointed to the Geometry Professorship. Instead, Lawrence Rooke, already Gresham Professor of Astronomy, got the job. Something apparently happened in the aftermath of the Lord Protector's issuing the order to the Gresham electors to await further instructions from him. The most plausible explanation for Rooke's appointment is that, far from endorsing Wren's appointment, Cromwell actively sought to block it.

It does indeed look as if the Warden of Wadham's and Sir Paul Neile's purpose on 8 May was to lobby Oliver Cromwell on Wren's behalf. But in spite of Wilkins's strong backing, Wren's personal credentials were still strongly royalist, as indeed were Neile's. It seems the two senior men were unable to persuade Cromwell to support their nomination of Wren. In the matter of academic appointments, Cromwell had regularly shown himself just as capable of opposing a candidate for preferment whose politics he did not like as of promoting one who had served him well. A year later, in 1657, for example, when Seth Ward (a talented mathematician from the Wilkins circle, but similarly royalist-tinged in his sympathies) was elected Principal of Jesus College, Oxford, by the fellows, Cromwell failed to endorse Ward's election, and installed another man in his place.[75]

By the time Wilkins and Neile left Whitehall they probably knew that it would be pointless to go ahead with pressing the committee for Wren's election, since the Protector would simply overrule it. So they returned to the Gresham electors with an alternative proposal. They persuaded the politically acceptable Lawrence Rooke, who had held the Gresham Professorship of Astronomy since 1652, to move to the soon-to-be-vacated Geometry chair (in which the Protector was not taking such an active interest), thereby freeing the Astronomy chair for Wren. Rooke was duly appointed to the Gresham Geometry chair. Meanwhile, Christopher Wren was appointed to the chair of Astronomy vacated by Rooke instead.[76]

Wren delivered his inaugural address as Professor of Astronomy at Gresham College on 7 August 1657.[77] In it he indicated gracefully his reluctance to emerge from the protected privacy of the Oxford circle. He would have preferred to 'exercise [his] radius in private dust' – that is, to have remained a mere private scholar, instead of entering the world of public service.[78] This is a phrase more characteristic of his father's lost world than of his Commonwealth backers (Wilkins and Petty). In Dean Wren's old-style scheme of things, families of the standing of the Wrens served in 'privy' places, not salaried posts. But the charmed world of the old nobility was gone for ever. In fact, from this point forward, for the rest of his life, public place was where Christopher Wren would belong, and his salaried remuneration would make him a comfortable living compensating for that affluence and status lost traumatically by his father, the Dean of Windsor, and uncle, the Bishop of Ely, before the civil wars.

In May 1658, Wren's benefactor Neile presented a thirty-five-foot telescope to Gresham College, for the use of the fellows.[79] By October, however, Gresham College had been occupied by soldiers, in the disturbances following the death of Cromwell. Wren's friend Thomas Sprat wrote to him in Oxford that Gresham was 'in such a nasty Condition, so defil'd, and the Smells so infernal, that if you should now come to make Use of your Tube [telescope], it would be like Dives looking out of Hell into Heaven'.[80] Wren's cousin Matthew, too, wrote to tell him there was no point in attempting to deliver his first Gresham lecture of the academic year, 'the College being reform'd into a Garrison'. Characteristically concerned for his cousin's reputation, he suggested that Wren should write 'a short and civil Letter to the Committee, signifying, that you hope you have not deceiv'd their Expectation, in choosing you, and that you are ready to attend your Duty, but for this publick Interruption and Exclusion from your Chamber'.[81]

HEAVENLY DISTRACTIONS

Evelyn recorded in his diary for 8 May 1656 that the meeting that day at Whitehall Palace was the first time he had met Sir Paul Neile. Like other prominent royalists Neile had only recently emerged from the safety of semi-retreat in the provinces. He had spent the early years of the Commonwealth confined to his country properties near Windsor, as a notable delinquent. Now, in steadier times, and with his friend and colleague Wilkins installed with his household at Whitehall Palace, he could once more afford to venture into public life in the City. Neile remained, nevertheless, an unreconstructed royalist – as is confirmed by the fact that at the Restoration he became an influential courtier in the King's innermost circle (residing at Whitehall Palace, along with Sir Robert Moray, another enthusiastic early backer of the Royal Society).[82]

Neile had not, however, been idle during his period of political inactivity in the country. In the early 1650s he had become involved with the Wilkins circle of amateur astronomers at Wadham, observing the fixed stars and the movements of the planets using the latest in long telescopes.[83] Soon after his arrival at Wadham Wilkins had persuaded the University to sanction expenditure on instruments, books and an observatory. The sum of £25 was approved by a committee, which included Wilkins and Wallis, to build an observatory in the tower of Wadham College, and procure telescopes and other instruments for it.[84] In 1655 one of Hartlib's correspondents claimed that Wilkins and Wren were attempting to construct an eighty-foot telescope, 'to see at once the whole moon'.[85] Although this report was far-fetched, they did apparently succeed in making a twenty-four-foot telescope, with the aid of which Wren proposed to prepare a 'Selenographia [moon map] which will be far more accurate than that of Hevelius, doing all by rule & demonstration which hath been hitherto done by guesses'.[86]

Sir Paul Neile became a major contributor, in terms of both money and resources, to the astronomical activities of the Wadham club. Deprived of a role in public life, he threw himself with gusto into the surrogate activity of overseeing the production of custom-made technical equipment, wrestling with lenses and tubes, and participating in vigorous exchanges with others similarly infatuated with the new telescopes in exploring the secrets of the heavens. He introduced his son William – also now without an obvious career-path, through the accidents of English politics – to the Wilkins circle (as an undergraduate at Wadham), where he developed into a considerable mathematician. He established his own well-equipped astronomical observatory at his house at White Waltham, near Windsor ('Hill House', thus conveniently located for observing the heavens).[87] He invested heavily in the latest and longest telescopes, and employed his own skilled instrument-makers to grind state-of-the-art lenses, of exceptional accuracy. And he collected around him a group of astronomical enthusiasts among other unemployed royalist gentlemen – William Ball, later a keen member of the Royal Society, was also observing Saturn with Wren and Neile.[88]

Although ostensibly the 'gentlemanly pursuit' of a man with time on his hands, Neile's engagement with other lens-grinders and telescope-builders was expert and highly competitive – particularly, as we shall see, when it came to achieving results comparable with those of well-funded foreign practitioners like the young Dutch aristocrat Christiaan Huygens.[89]

In Sir Paul Neile, Christopher Wren once more found a generous and supportive patron, with a particular enthusiasm for the fields of geometry and astronomy, in which his special talents lay. Like his previous protector, Charles Scarburgh, here was a man who had managed to hold on to some of the status and influence which his own father had so irrevocably lost with the fall of the King. Here, too, was another benefactor with the resources to provide the precision technical equipment which would enable Wren to achieve an exceptional level of accuracy in his measurements and calculations during their shared astronomical observations. When Wren came reluctantly to write up his ground-breaking work on the strange appearance of Saturn, under the title *De corpore Saturni*, he gave fulsome acknowledgement of the important part Neile's patronage (and equipment) played in his discoveries:

> [My explanation of the changing shape] of Saturn was long before hatched by your influence at White Waltham, upon the Observation of Decemb. 3 1657, when first we had an apprehension, that the Armes of [Saturn] kept their length, w.[ch] produced this Hypothesis, made first in two pastboards, not to say any thing of our attempts in Wax, in Jan 1655. The Hypothesis made more durable in metall was exposed on the top of that Obeliske, w.[ch] was erected at Gresham College, in May 1658 (if I mistake be please to rectifie me), to rayse the 35 foot Telescope of your donation.[90]

In the published *De corpore Saturni* text itself Wren again gave pride of place to an account of the importance to his enterprise of the observatory and scientific instruments made available to him by Neile:

> Because observers did not often use very long tubes and absolutely perfect lenses (of which there is need) and did not take good enough care to remove all superfluous light fringes from

the aperture in the customary manner, or because they were unaccustomed to depict graphically on the spot just what they saw distinctly . . . it came about that they left us very disparate figures, so that . . . nothing agreeable to the uniform and beautiful harmony of natural motions is portrayed. . . .

But these are . . . things that cannot be concealed from the experienced observer and practised optician, so that he readily takes notice of them and substitutes genuine phenomena for erroneous ones, especially if he makes use of not one, but several telescopes at the same time.

And therefore, since it was granted to us to have the use of very well worked telescopes of 6, 12, 22 and even 35 feet long, together with a supply of all sorts of lenses of English manufacture, and to have at hand many observed appearances of Saturn in a continuous series from 1649 onward (some of which, from the last four years, we have depicted with the greatest care) we have not hesitated to unveil at last the hypothesis of Saturn which for a long time has been kept secret from very learned men; especially lest the stars would seem to have granted us the friendship of that very distinguished man, Sir Paul Neile, in vain.

This is the man who, having hired the best workmen, ordered the making of these above mentioned celestial devices, and even greater ones, of 50 feet, in his own house, he himself supervising the work (by virtue of the remarkable strength of his judgment in mathematics). And not less sincerely does he rejoice to share his hospitality at the same place with his chosen astronomical friends; and I am also grateful for the gift of certain remarkable lenses and very many observations of Saturn.[91]

The fruit of these group observations, using the newest long telescopes and the best lenses, was a sequence of meticulously represented images, depicting Saturn and its curious surrounding 'rings' at various phases in its cycle (in the course of these investigations Wren and others arrived correctly at the view that these occur over a thirty-year cycle). In its final form, this fundamental piece of observational astronomy by Wren depends upon data collected collaboratively, beginning around 1649 (before he joined the Oxford circle). Already, then, in this early work, Wren has acquired the habit of combining data meticulously collected by 'trusted informants' (later it would be 'trusted skilled crafts-men') into a whole whose weight and importance significantly exceeded anything he might have arrived at on his own. Wren's own observations began in about 1654 and continued until at least 1659, and were resumed thereafter at Whitehall, in the company of Christiaan Huygens, in spring 1661. Thanks to Neile, Wren had access to a series of first-hand observations going back to 1649. Thus the hypothesis he arrived at, as to the form and material of Saturn's 'ring', was made on the basis of more than ten years' continuous observation of its appearance at different points in its cycle. That hypothesis in its turn was put to Wren's senior astronomical experts – Neile and Rooke – to be assessed for its plausi-bility.[92]

As early as 1654 Wren was making wax models of Saturn for Neile. In 1655 he and Neile observed one of Saturn's satellites, but apparently did not recognise it as such until a year later they read Christiaan Huygens's published paper *De Saturni luna* ('On a moon of Saturn' [1656]). Also in 1655, one of their fellow astronomers, Ball, first saw the shadow of the ring on the body of Saturn, and, as Wren later recalled, 'showed it to us at once'. Wren saw 'a certain zone, darker than the rest of the area of the disc and slightly narrower than Jupiter's belts'. He also thought he could make out a series of spots on the planet's surface. All these observations, it should be understood, were being made with lenses containing flaws and imperfections, and telescopes which did not yet compensate for distortions and light fringes which interfered with clear sight. A claim to have seen something new required the confidence of an experienced observer, and repeated observations to check that the phenomenon observed was not in fact being produced by the viewing equipment.

Once again, the group of instrument-makers and observational astronomers working at White Waltham thought of themselves as a team, much like any modern scientific laboratory, operating under the auspices of the Wadham club. In his 1656 letter to Petty, Wren reported:

> It is not I suppose new to you what we have been doeing in Dioptricks, which we have improv'd both as to the Theory in giving a true account of Refraction and of Vision (as that the Crystalline Humor is not the Principal Instrument of Refraction

in the Eye, nor essential to vision but meerly to Convenient Vision.) [sic] Perspectives & Microscopes, in which we give the Reasons & Rules for charging them, or suiting the Eye Glasses, and giving them their due appertures, things formerly done by Experiment only; and as to the Practick, thô we have no[t] yet arriv'd to a good 50 fᵗ Glass, yet we have very long ones from 12 to 36 fᵗ by which we have drawn many exact Pictures of [Saturn] not only of his Ansulae but his Spots, and attain'd to a Theory of his Rotation & various inclinations of his Body; and have drawn the spots [of Mars]. We make the Tube and Astronomical Instrument, observe to Seconds, by which we take the Motions [of Jupiter's] Satellites, and [Saturn's] moon; and not only draw Pictures of the Moon, as Hevelius has done, but Survey her & give exact maps of her, & discover exactly her various Inclinations, and herein Hevelius's Errors. I have lately caused a Needle to be made of 40 Inches, by which I hope to discover the Annual Motion of Variation & Anomalies in it.[93]

In the same period, the White Waltham observers and Christiaan Huygens became aware of each other's work and began to correspond, facilitated by John Wallis. Wallis had been in correspondence with Christiaan Huygens on various mathematical problems since 1652. In March 1656 Huygens responded to a request from Wallis for his own views on the orbit of Saturn, committing them to anagram form (as was customary), but providing Wallis with the translation; a week later Wallis replied with a much longer anagram, supposedly encrypting the Neile circle's own observations.[94] In early April 1656, Wallis wrote to Huygens, on behalf of Neile and Wren, acknowledging receipt both of letters concerning the phases of Saturn, its period and moons (with salient details of Huygens's discoveries encrypted as anagrams within them), and of a copy of his published *On a moon of Saturn.*[95] In later annotations in his letter collection, Huygens indicated that he thought Wallis had double-crossed him, and communicated his original observations uncoded to the White Waltham astronomers. He also suspected that Wallis's long anagram did not in fact encrypt the solution finally revealed to him in April 1656 (and felt that the Oxford astronomers' solutions were far too close to his own original formulations to be credible).[96] Wallis (cryptographer to Cromwell's Parliament, and therefore in a position to correspond with whom he wished) acted as intermediary throughout the increasingly technical correspondence between Wren–Neile and Huygens.

In 1659 Huygens indicated in a letter to Wallis that he was annoyed that Wren, in spite of several public expressions of admiration by Huygens of Wren's calculation of the length of arc of the cycloid, had not seen fit to write to him himself.[97] It is clear that Huygens was already irritated with the English astronomers, whom he believed to be taking advantage of his own observations in framing their own theories concerning Saturn. But equally, it looks as if Wren had no time for the spoilt, over-privileged son of a senior Dutch diplomat, who thought far too much of his own individual talents and expected others to treat him with an unreasonable amount of respect.[98]

By 1658, Wren himself felt confident enough to write a paper describing an elliptical shape (as he believed) for Saturn's 'corona', of varying thickness, and touching the planet at two opposed points.[99] He presented this, appropriately, at Gresham College in his capacity as Astronomy Professor (the former Astronomy Professor, now Geometry Professor, Lawrence Rooke, looked it over for accuracy beforehand).

Wren was eventually persuaded by Neile to print and publish his theory of Saturn's rings after the King's return, and the associated dramatic improvement in his own career prospects, in autumn 1661. He did so extremely reluctantly and, in effect, only because he owed it to a prestigious patron, who had funded his research (and to the newly founded Royal Society with which both he and that patron were by now associated), to do so. 'You know of what prevalency your commands alone are with me,' he assured Neile; nevertheless, '*Hugenius* hath outrid me.' By now he was actually convinced that Christiaan Huygens's theory that Saturn's corona was a flat, circular disc, symmetrically surrounding a spherical central planet, was the correct one – more plausible because simpler and more beautiful, criteria of excellence Wren would invoke again and again in a wide range of areas of inquiry:

> When . . . the Hypothesis of Hugenius [Huygens] was sent over in writing, I confesse I was so fond of the neatnesse of it, & the Naturall Simplicity of the contrivance agreeing soe well with the physicall causes of the heavenly bodies, that I loved the Invention beyond my owne.[100]

The Dutch virtuoso mathematician and astronomer, Christiaan Huygens, favourite son of Sir Constantijn Huygens, and inventor of the precision pendulum clock.

There was a good reason for Wren's diffidence about publishing his *De corpore Saturni* in 1661. More than mere modesty can be detected in the self-deprecating tone of his letter to Neile. At the end of March that year, Wren had finally met in person the brilliant Dutch mathematician and experimentalist, Christiaan Huygens.

MORE BRIGHT BOYS, WITH BRIGHTER FORTUNES

Wren's father would certainly have known of Christiaan Huygens's father, even if he did not know him personally – a colourful, cultivated, versatile, artistically gifted intellectual, and go-between between the Stuart and Orange courts, whose long life covered almost the entire seventeenth century (as would Wren's). Sir Constantijn Huygens senior, secretary and close adviser (on everything from politics to architecture) to the Dutch Stadholder, which meant, in practice, to successive Princes of Orange, was ambassador extraordinary from the Dutch Republic to London, serving on a number of occasions, under both James I and

Charles I. James I knighted him in the 1620s – perhaps for his skill as a lutenist. He was also a poet of distinction in Latin, Dutch, French and occasionally English (he spoke all these languages fluently).[101]

Huygens senior acted as acquisitions adviser for the purchase of artworks to Frederick Henry of Orange and his wife, and architectural adviser to a sequence of great houses (he also designed and built several impressive Dutch neo-classical buildings for himself). When the States-General suspended the role of Stadholder in 1650, thereby depriving Huygens of his job, he became adviser to William II's widow, Mary Stuart (Charles II's sister), designing a full programme of education for her son, the future William III of England. After Mary's death, he assumed an even more important role as William's guide and mentor, and lobbied consistently for his reinstatement as Stadholder, and for his recognition by the French and English administrations.[102]

Christiaan Huygens was the second of Sir Constantijn Huygens's four talented sons. Christiaan's elder brother Constantijn became, in his turn, secretary to William III, and accompanied him in London, when William and his wife Mary were invited to reign as joint monarchs in the place of her father, the disgraced Catholic King James II, in 1688. Constantijn Huygens junior was in London at the time of the execution of Charles I (to his father's dismay and embarrassment), which he witnessed, along with the Elector Palatine, Charles Louis.

There are at once striking similarities between the upbringings and careers of Christiaan Huygens and Wren, and yet equally telling differences, of which Wren was clearly acutely aware. Three years older than Wren, Huygens too had lost his mother when young and been brought up by his father to expect employment worthy of his high level of education.[103] But in 1661, when they met, Wren was fatherless, and struggling to make his way following the successive upheavals of the English Revolution and the Restoration of Charles II. His future career remained precarious, largely dependent on the whims of others, as claimants for their loyal service to the King in exile jostled with one another for preferment. The only family member surviving, to exert the kind of personal lobbying pressure at court which Wren recognised as invaluable for a man to rise in the new regime, was his aged uncle, Bishop Matthew Wren, recently released from the Tower.[104] The Huygenses, by contrast, were a celebrity family of cultivated gentlemen of substance, moving freely around Europe, in lavish style, effortlessly exchanging high-level artistic and intellectual opinions and information with the great and the good. Christiaan arrived in London from Paris (where he had spent the previous months) in spring 1661 to join the personal train of the renowned Dutch general and administrator John Maurice of Nassau, in London on a prestigious extraordinary diplomatic mission from the Low Countries.[105]

John Maurice was in London to assist at the installing of Frederick William, Elector of Brandenburg, and his nephew William III of Orange, as Knights Companion of the Order of the Garter.[106] Both were 'family' of Charles II (brother-in-law and nephew respectively). Both had been awarded the Garter by the English King during his exile, in 1652 (when William was two-and-a-half – the youngest-ever recipient).[107] Huygens's place on the visit had been gained by assiduous lobbying on his father's part. If we were in any doubt as to the advantage Christiaan Huygens enjoyed as compared with the young Wren it is transparent in a letter written by Huygens's father to V. Conrart, in whose train Christiaan was travelling in France in 1661, dated 3 March:

> At last I am able to settle my debts with you, concerning so much favour and civility which it has pleased you to demonstrate to my Archimedes [Christiaan] during the time you have instructed me to leave him in Paris. However, I must warn you that it will be without my making payment, and that it will be necessary for you to add further to that patience you have already stored up in the company of this young man, to wait until either he or I are in a position to discharge so much obligation. . . . Leaving aside such unpleasant conversation, with as much distaste as debtors have for their credit notes, I turn instead to telling you, Sir, that follow- ing the notification that you gave me, I advised my pilgrim that where he is is no permanent City for him, and drag him away from the throng of so much friendship, which he has had the honour of acquiring in your World. And this in order in part to please our excellent Monsieur the Prince Maurice of Nassau, my most worthy and most illustrious Friend, who being on the point of discharging an Extraordinary Embassy in England, on behalf of his Highness the Elector of Brandenburg, has asked me on bended knee, that when my son returns from France I will oblige him to cross the water to join him in London, where

(leaving aside the King, who honours him with a particular esteem) he has the good will of a considerable number of virtuosi and like him mathematicians, who converse with him regularly by letter, and who will welcome his presence. Besides, they are about to have the Coronation of his Majesty, which is one of those spectacles which does not take place very often in any age, and is well worth the trouble of two sea-voyages for someone of his age, capable henceforth of distinguishing the vain from the substantial with some maturity.[108]

So Huygens, having arrived in London, was swept off to lodge with John Maurice's party, and thence on a whirlwind succession of lavish celebrations, culminating in the solemn Garter ceremonies at Windsor, at which Huygens assisted. He records the ceremonies in the diary he kept dutifully to show his father on his return:

20 [April]. Visited by Mr. Wallis and Mr. Rook. Afterwards by Mr. Boyle after dinner. Mr. Moray and Mr. Brouncker came to fetch me and we went to the assembly where I found Mr. Wren. There was discussion of water rising in narrow glass pipes, and a committee was ordered for Saturday at my lodgings, for improvements in telescopes. With Mr. Moray said goodbye to Mr. Bruce and stayed until 10 pm.

23. Dined in my room. After dinner Mr. Moray, My Lord Brouncker, Sir Paul Neile, Dr. Wallis, Mr. Rook, Mr. Wren, Dr. Goddard, met at my lodgings. We spoke of the method for grinding lenses, and I told them my method.[109] I resolved the case they proposed concerning the collision of two spheres.

24. Dined with the Dutch Ambassador.

25. Left with Mr. Moray, Neile, Vermuijden, Wallis for Windsor, where after dinner I saw the ceremony of the reception of the Knights of the Garter, which took place in the Chapel.

Two days later came the Coronation of Charles II, which Huygens did not bother to attend. Instead, he joined members of the Royal Society to observe a transit of Mercury using the best telescopes available:

3 [May]. Was the Coronation of the King, in the Choir of the Cathedral of Westminster. The Bishop of . . . first gave a long

sermon, while the King was seated before the altar. After that the Archbishop of Canterbury anointed his Majesty, who had undressed down to his camisole of red satin, which was open and folded back over his shoulders, which the Archbishop greased with oil, as also his chest, his temples, the top of his head. Then he was dressed again, and put on the coat of royal red crimson lined with ermine, and finally the crown, which was studded with diamonds, a velvet bonnet underneath, and a circlet of ermine at the bottom. The people inside and outside the church shouted loudly, to whom silver medals worth about 15 sous were tossed. The King went and sat on the throne which was beside the altar, where all the Lords came and kissed his hand. There was music of voices and instruments throughout.

All this I have by report, for I was all this time at Reeves's to see the transit of Mercury, which I did. It being 30 years since Mr. Gassendi saw the same thing. . . .

13 May [1661]. Observed the conjunction of Saturn with the moon, in the garden at Whitehall, with Mr. Neile's long telescopes. Saturn passed above very close. The Duke of York was also there.

The next day he returned and with him the Duchess of York, formerly Mrs. Hyde. This time we used my lenses. I bowed deeply to the Duchess, and Mr. Neile praised me highly.

Mr. Moray entertained us often in his room at Whitehall with cakes, bottled ale and wine. I made the acquaintance of Dr. Wilkins, author of a book [claiming] that the moon could be a world, and the earth a planet. He is working on a universal language. I also saw Mr. Evelyn, who is writing a big book on gardening. Mr. Tuke has returned from Paris where he was with M. de Montmor, and said that M. van Beuningen came there often and was much admired. At Milord Brouncker's I saw Sir Kenelm Digby, a large, fat man, who complimented me highly.[110]

Huygens senior proudly reported to his friends that his young 'Archimedes' had preferred astronomy to the spectacle of a Coronation, thereby proving his serious scientific interests. But he knew that Christiaan had in fact dispatched the duties for which he had been sent, at Windsor (Samuel Pepys, who did attend the Coronation, does not

Happy families: (*top*) the five eldest children of Charles I, in pampered finery, in 1637; Charles I in full regalia, with crown and orb, in 1636; the official portrait for the wedding of nine-year-old Princess Mary to twelve-year-old William of Orange in 1641 – William's suit was made for him in London, because his own was not considered lavish enough

Growing up disappointed:
(*top*) Charles I shortly before his
execution, with his second son,
James, Duke of York, who visited
him regularly during his last
imprisonment; James as Lord High
Admiral, in Roman dress in the
1660s – a prince without a proper
role; William III as a boy – orphaned
by the age of ten

Uncertain succession: (*top*) James, Duke of York with his first wife, Anne Hyde, mother of Queen Mary and Queen Anne; Charles II at the end of his life – from modern monarch to Stuart autocrat; Charles Louis, Elector Palatine, and his brother Prince Rupert – a glamorous, Protestant alternative to the main Stuart line; Princess Mary in fancy dress – in the 1640s she and her young husband William lived in opulent splendour at The Hague

New men in Restoration London: (*top left*) Wren in maturity, at the peak of his public career; (*top right*) Irish nobleman Robert Boyle, youngest son of the second Earl of Cork, who settled in England in the 1650s and became one of London's most prominent virtuosi; Sir John Chardin, French traveller and architectural amateur, who settled in London in the 1680s and made his drawings of oriental buildings available to Wren and the Royal Society; Sir Robert Viner and his family, in dynastic splendour in 1673 – Viner presented Charles II with his coronation regalia, and became one of the richest men in London

mention the Garter ceremonies, since he was not of sufficiently elevated rank to attend them).

Wren too, who understood as much about the Order of the Garter as anyone in London, knew what it meant for Christiaan to have had the honour of witnessing their Windsor Chapel initiation ceremonies. Huygens will have explained publicly to his fellow observers of the transit of Mercury (among them Wren), as he had to his father, his nonchalance about the King's Coronation ceremony, in view of his privileged participation at Windsor. It confirmed the fact, if confirmation were needed, that the young Huygens moved easily among the senior courtiers whose favours Wren was obliged so assiduously to pursue. Even if it was not generally in Wren's nature to envy others their advantages, it cannot have endeared Christiaan Huygens to him. If he was diffident about corresponding with the young Dutchman about his rectification of the cycloid, he felt even less inclined to build a relationship with him now. When, later on, Huygens and Hooke became embroiled in controversy over priority for the spring mechanism of the balance-spring watch, the peculiar venom Hooke reserved for his dealings with Huygens may well have derived from his lifelong tendency to mirror and amplify the opinions and attitudes of his beloved friend Wren.

Fortunately for Wren, Huygens, who, during his continental tour, was in the process of weighing up the prospects of a career as a research scientist in Paris or London, decided conclusively in favour of Paris. On his return from his Coronation trip to London he wrote to his younger brother Lodewijk:

> I did not find my stay in London as charming as apparently you did yours. . . . the stink and the smog are intolerable, and very unhealthy, the city is badly built, the roads are narrow and poorly surfaced, nothing but ugly buildings. . . . not much to see, and nothing by comparison with Paris. The people are melancholy, the well-born polite enough but not very friendly, the women are poorly turned out and by no means as spiritual and animated as in Paris.[111]

By the 1670s Wren and Huygens were on better terms, perhaps because Wren had himself become, in the meantime, better established in Restoration London society and more successful. A contributing

Grinling Gibbons, the brilliant sculptor and carver in wood, discovered by Evelyn, and introduced by him to Wren and the court circle.

factor may also have been the fact that Constantijn Huygens senior accompanied William of Orange (whose education he had supervised since his mother's death, and whose personal secretary he had become) to London in early November 1670, when the Prince formally visited his uncle, Charles II. Evelyn dined with the senior members of the party on 15 December, having pronounced the Prince to possess 'a manly couragious wise Countenance, resembling . . . his Mother'. Following the dinner, Evelyn repaired to the Royal Society, ensuring that the contact between Christiaan Huygens's father and those who so admired the virtuosity of his son was established.[112] Evelyn described Huygens as 'that excellent learned man, Poet & Musitian, & now neere 80 yeares of age a vigorous brisk-man'.

This was also the month in which Evelyn introduced the wood-carver Grinling Gibbons to the King; with his interest in art and architecture, Huygens senior is likely to have participated in the court's admiration for and excitement at the virtuosity of Gibbons's work. On

19 February 1671, Evelyn had dinner with Wren and Pepys and 'carried them to see the piece of carving [by Gibbons] which I had recommended to the King'; on 1 March Wren 'promised [Evelyn] faithfully to employ him'. We know that Huygens senior visited Oxford, and that he spent time with the Archbishop of Canterbury, Wren's friend and patron Gilbert Sheldon, because he wrote poems in Dutch about his visits.[113] Although William returned to Holland in February, Huygens senior remained based in England (somewhat against his inclination, to judge from a number of the poems he wrote) until the autumn, attempting to broker continuing peace between England and Holland in the face of threatened French hostilities.

When Christiaan Huygens published his important book on pendulum clocks, the *Horologium oscillatorium*, in 1673, he included a generous passage crediting Wren with 'rectifying the cycloid' – producing the mathematical proof of the length of a straight line equivalent to the cycloid-shaped cheeks which guaranteed the precision of his pendulum clock.[114] A presentation copy of the *Horologium*, inscribed by Huygens 'pour Monsieur Wren', survives.[115]

A ROYALIST WREN, STILL, AT HEART

It is easy, with hindsight, to see the young Christopher Wren's career taking shape around the tinkerings with technology in the garden of the Warden of Wadham in the early 1650s. At the time, though, it was by no means clear what direction Wren's life would or ought profitably to take. Just as we know nothing about his nine months on the continent of Europe in 1649, so we know little, in the early 1650s, about the time he spent outside Oxford, sometimes close to Windsor (at Sir Paul Neile's house in White Waltham), sometimes in London. We do know that he was in the capital on a regular basis. In a letter of 1653, talking about the previous few years, he wrote, 'But Business drew me suddenly from London. . . .'[116]

Similarly, we know nothing about the efforts he made, on his father's behalf, to re-establish the links between loyal royalists, who still entertained real hopes for the return of a Stuart king. In 1652 Wren accompanied Wilkins on a visit to Elias Ashmole, when he perhaps spoke to Ashmole about his father's Order of the Garter records (tellingly,

Ashmole already knew Wren, but met Wilkins for the first time on this occasion).[117] Ashmole later recalled that when in the mid-1650s he began working on his book on the *History of the Institutions of the Order* (which, we should remember, might have remained the nostalgic jottings of an underemployed old royalist had the monarchy not been restored in 1660) Dean Wren had enthusiastically furnished him with access to all the records still in his possession:

> Upon the first communication of my design, to the late Reverend Doctor Christopher Wren, Register of the said Order, it received not only his full approbation, but also his ready assistance in the use of the Annals thereof, then in his custody: From those, and other authentick Manuscripts and Autographs, particularly relating to the Order, and a painful and chargeable search of our publick Records, I had collected the greater part of my Materials, before the happy Restauration of his new Majesty the present Soveraign of this most noble Order; who, being afterwards acquainted with what I had done, was most graciously pleased to countenance it, and encourage me in the prosecution thereof.[118]

After Dean Wren's death in 1658, his son continued the relationship with Ashmole and the Garter project. In May 1659, Ashmole went to Windsor with the Dutch engraver Wenceslaus Hollar, to 'take views of the Castle' for his *History of the Order of the Garter*.[119] Tucked in among Hollar's handsome prints in the volume as it eventually appeared in 1672 is a *Prospect of Windsor Castle from the North*, which is inscribed: 'Christopher Wren delineavit, W. Hollar fecit 1667' ('Christopher Wren drew this, Wenceslaus Hollar engraved it 1667'). Apparently Christopher Wren accompanied Ashmole and Hollar on their pilgrimage to Charles I's favourite palace – home of the ceremonial of the Order of the Garter. Aside from the plates for Willis's *Anatomy of the Brain*, this is the first surviving, published example we have of Wren's exceptional skills as a draughtsman.[120]

The engraving is also a poignant record of Wren's post-Restoration relationship with his old, royal-centred life before the execution of Charles I. Wren's *Prospect* shows his old home – the Dean's House – as seen by an outsider, excluded from the royal household, beyond the

Castle walls. Unlike Huygens, he could no longer wander the Castle grounds at will.[121]

At the same time that Wren the talented young technician was making strenuous efforts to establish himself as an intellectual in his own right, in other words, Wren the son of the former Dean of Windsor and Register of the Order of the Garter was dutifully fulfilling his father's far more conventional expectations.

Lurking in the background in young Christopher Wren's dealings with the Oxford philosophical club, too, is still the Wren family connection, continuing to operate behind the scenes, even in its period of public disgrace and eclipse. William Holder, Dean Wren's son-in-law, was a scientific amateur himself, and provided the Wrens' introduction to the Oxford club (Holder remained closely involved in the activities of the Royal Society scientists for the whole of his life, alongside his celebrity brother-in-law). Dean Wren's marginal annotations from this period reveal that he too was present when the Oxford group observed the 1654 eclipse of the sun (on which Wallis published a treatise). His nephew Matthew Wren junior was by this time also a participant in these scientific amateurs' activities. These were all men at something of a loose end, devising ways of keeping themselves busy in unpropitious political times.

Deprived of real power or influence, the remnants of the royalist circle in Oxford pinned their hopes on a new intellectual world, in which new philosophy and natural science would open new horizons of opportunity. On the shoulders of Christopher Wren junior in the early 1650s are carried a whole generation of uncertain hopes of those whose own expectations have been disappointed. Like the young King-in-waiting, Charles II in exile, the adolescent Christopher Wren must have experienced these passionate expectations as a heavy burden of responsibility.

IMPROVED PROSPECTS AND ENDURING MONUMENTS

Oliver Cromwell died in September 1658 and, amid uncertainty about his successor, the see-saw of preferment and promotions was set violently oscillating once more. It looked briefly as if Dr Wilkins was again going to be one of the main beneficiaries, when in summer 1659 he moved

View of Windsor from the north, from Elias Ashmole's history of the Order of the Garter, drawn by Wren and engraved by Wenceslaus Hollar – the Dean's house, Wren's childhood home, is clearly visible.

unexpectedly to the lucrative and prestigious post of Master of Trinity College, Cambridge.[122] He went with what some saw as unseemly haste: 'Dr. Wilkins gone (*cum pannie*)[123] to Cambridge, and left his great telescope to the library,' one of Boyle's correspondents reported.[124]

In fact Wilkins's departure from Oxford may have been a matter of domestic exigency. Since his marriage to Cromwell's sister, his main

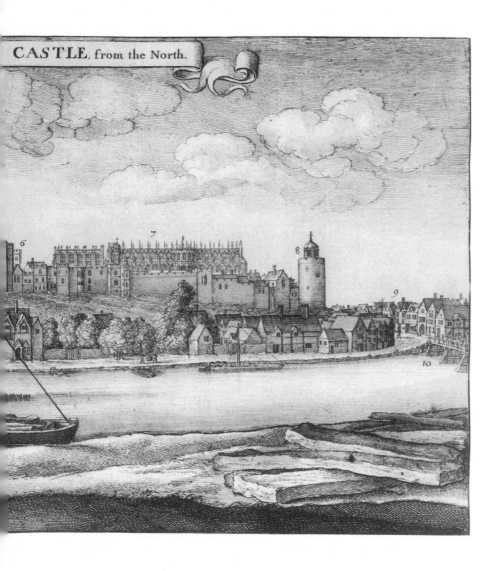

CASTLE, from the North.

residence had been the couple's London apartments at Whitehall Palace. After the Protector's death, Cromwell's immediate family moved out of the royal apartments into more modest accommodation within the Palace precincts. Finally, though, in May 1659 Whitehall was put up for sale (only, of course, to be taken off the market again when the King was recalled to his kingdom the following April). Wadham College had only bachelor apartments for the Warden. Trinity College, Cambridge, by contrast, boasted a magnificent Master's Lodge – more than adequate as the residence for a couple and their household.[125] Such splendour was not to last long. Although Wilkins's appointment had been supported by the fellows of Trinity – in other words, his appointment was based on merit, not mere politics – he was ejected at the Restoration (as a matter of principle). Nevertheless, his service to the Elector Palatine under Charles II's father ensured that he was discreetly preferred to a lucrative, if less prominent post elsewhere.[126]

Protector Cromwell had been quirky and erratic towards the end of his life in his choices of candidates for key posts; the returning King proved far more reliable. Regardless of existing incumbents, or candidates with strong claims, he unhesitatingly appointed those who had personally stood by first his father and then himself during the civil wars, and the continental exile which followed. The closer the association, and the more personal the service rendered, the more elevated the position. If (as in the case of the Wrens) the father was dead (or, in Matthew Wren's case, at the end of his active career), then their son received the honour instead.

The Privy Council appointed by Charles consisted of his brothers and his seven Counsellors from the period of exile. The Earl of Southampton, one of Charles I's wartime Counsellors, became Lord Treasurer; his son-in-law occupied the subsidiary Treasury role of Chancellor of the Exchequer:

> The lesser posts of central government were less completely in the King's gift. In deference to the principle of legitimacy upon which he based his monarchy, he had to recognize the claims of those who had obtained these offices, or the reversion of them, under his father. To displace them was a cumbersome and provocative business. Thus, when Charles wanted to make Sir William Compton [who had participated in an unsuccessful royalist bid to reinstate him in 1651], Master of the Ordnance, he had first to suspend the existing Master and then grant Compton the rights to administer the post and to inherit it. The same procedure was employed to free at least five other important positions for Charles's nominees. . . . The administration that actually emerged resulted from a network of private deals.[127]

The new King seems to have engaged Christopher Wren on royal building projects from shortly after his return, suggesting that Wren's known talents, as developed within the Oxford club, already included building design and the drawing up of architectural plans.[128] It is interesting to reflect on whether Wren's mentor, Dr John Wilkins, had in fact already involved his protégé in building (or at least remodelling) work before the Restoration, in the 1650s, during the most formative (but least well-documented) period in Wren's burgeoning scientific career. This is a compelling idea, because it brings Wren's architectural career in parallel with his scientific one, and, moreover, tethers his ground-breaking work in mathematics and medicine and his innovative structural building work together as related enterprises.

In 1653, Samuel Hartlib reported that the Warden of Wadham was in the process of making building provision for the scientific 'College' it had been his ambition since the late 1640s to set up at Oxford:

> They are now erecting a College for experiments et mechanicks at Oxford, toward which Dr. Wilkins hath given 200 lib [pounds]. It is over the Schooles or in the long gallery, where all the models of inventions, arts etc, are to bee reserved with a treatise added to each of them shewing the structure and use of it.[129]

According to this account, Wilkins was in the process of establishing a repository for the scientific instruments and inventions of the Oxford circle, placed under the supervision of Ralph Greatorex, the London instrument-maker.[130] The Schools quadrangle, where the University disputations required of students before graduation were conducted, is adjacent to the Bodleian Library (of which today its buildings form a part), conveniently close to Wilkins's own Wadham. The Schools buildings themselves dated from 1611 – contemporary with the Wadham buildings (1610).[131]

A year later in 1654, Seth Ward wrote of a 'reall designe' to erect a 'Magneticall, Mechanicall and Opticke Schoole, furnished with the best instruments, and Adapted for the most usefull experiments in all those faculties'.[132] In 1657, Evelyn, in the course of sending Boyle a collection of preliminary materials he had compiled for a history of artistic techniques, referred again to Wilkins's 'College' as if it were a physical reality, suggesting that:

> a true and ingenious discovery of these and like arts, would, to better purpose, be compiled for the use of that Mathematico-Chymico-Mechanical School designed by our noble friend Dr.

Wilkinson [sic – that is, Wilkins] where they might (not without an oath of secrecy) be taught to those that either affected or desired any of them: and from thence, as from another Solomon's house, so much of them only made public, as should from time to time be judged convenient by the superintendent of that School, for the reputation of learning and benefit of the nation.[133]

In a further, post-Restoration reminiscence, Evelyn talked about this 'College' as if it had actually materialised, with an 'elaboratory, and other instruments', but had been dispersed at the Restoration.[134]

A functional conversion project for parts of the building was entirely in keeping with the recent history of the Schools quadrangle:

Rooms in the Schools Quadrangle had been refurbished as the Anatomy School, and the endowment of the [Tomlins] Readership [in Anatomy] invested to produce a regular income [before the civil war]. . . . By 1620 [Sir Thomas Bodley] had rebuilt the fifteenth-century library of Duke Humfrey, added the Arts End, and persuaded the university to consolidate their scattered lecture rooms into a new two-storied Schools Quadrangle, which he crowned with a third story to house the more than 16,000 books donated by him and his friends.[135]

Converting a series of rooms, including the tower of the Schools, into spaces suitable for scientific investigations, together with repository and meeting space would have involved Wren and Wilkins in feasibility studies, plans and drawings of an exploratory kind, comparable with their early experimental work for the Oxford club. This suggestion is also compatible with Wallis's claim that a structurally original roof was built for the tower of the Old Schools in the 1650s, a project on which he gave advice, and whose solution Wilkins found sufficiently intriguing to show a model of it later to the Royal Society.[136]

No free-standing new building, of course, was constructed. However, according to Boyle's notebooks or 'work-diaries' in 1662, the Schools quadrangle was the customary place in Oxford to conduct experiments requiring a long drop:

We went to the Schooles <at Oxford> & with an exact Instrument where single vibrations, were half seconds, we measur'd the encrease of velocity of a descending Ball of Iron fastened by a string to the Instrument, & for the most part our Observations agreed in this That in 4 single vibrations & very little more, the Iron fell the height between the Battlements of the Schoole & the Pavement amounting to 56 [feet]. . . . The same Ball let fall from the Tower [of] the Schooles where it is 80 foot high appeard to fal somewhat less then 5 semiseconds <or perhaps in 4> & a half.[137]

An entry in Evelyn's post-Restoration diary adds further weight to the idea that the 'erecting of a College' 'over the Schooles or in the long gallery' did in fact happen, and that the spaces in question were still in use in the 1660s. In October 1664 he once again visited Oxford:

25 [October 1664] . . . I went to visite Mr. Boyle now here, whom I found with Dr. Wallis & Dr. Chr: Wren in the Tower at the Scholes, with an inverted Tube or Telescope observing the Discus of the Sunn for the passing of Mercury that day before the Sunn; but the Latitude was so greate, that nothing appeared: So we went to see the rarities in the Library, where the Library keepers, shewed me my name, among the Bene-factors: They have a Cabinet of some Medails, & Pictures of the Muscular parts of Mans body: Thence to the new Theater, building now at an exceeding & royal Expense by the L:A:B: of Canterbury, to keepe the Acts in for the future, 'til now being in St. Maries church: The foundation being but newly laied & the whole, Design'd, by that incomparable genius, & my worthy friend Dr. Chr: Wren, who shewed me the Model, not disdaining my advise in some particulars: Thence to see the Picture on the Wall over the Altar at All-Soules, being the largest piece of Fresco painting (or rather in Imitation of it, for tis in oyle <of Terpentine>) in England, & not ill design'd, by the hand of one Fuller: yet I feare it will not hold long, & seemes too full of nakeds for a Chapell: Thence to New-Coll: & the Painting of Magdalens Chapell, which is on blue cloth in *Chiaro Oscuro* by one Greeneborow, being a *Coena Domini* & Judgement <on> the Wall by Fuller, as is the other, somewhat varied: Next to Waddam, & the Physik Garden where were two large Locust

Trees, & as many *Platana*, & some rare Plants under the Culture of old Bobart.[138]

If Wilkins's 'College' was a reorganisation of spaces inside the Schools, then Wren, his 'most addicted Client', is likely to have assisted in the conversion. Wren would therefore have been involved in close structural scrutiny of comparatively recent institutional buildings, in the company of a mentor who, like him, had seen fine neo-classical continental buildings (particularly in The Hague) a few years earlier. In which case, Wren had already been involved in building design some years before first his uncle, Matthew Wren, and then his old Oxford fellow worshippers Dr John Fell and Archbishop Gilbert Sheldon asked him to design their thanks-offering buildings for Oxford in the early 1660s.

In terms of available models which Wren and Wilkins might have consulted for their project, large-scale building work had finally begun again in Oxford in the 1650s, after the disastrously destructive years of the Oxford siege, followed by the early Commonwealth years of punitive treatment of Oxford for its unwavering support for the royalist cause. John Jackson's project for a new library, chapel and cloister at Brasenose College was begun in 1656 – a gloriously showy, somewhat pompous run of buildings, to which Wren's Sheldonian clearly owes some of its ostentation (Jackson had been the master mason on the last great building project of Charles I's reign in Oxford, Arhbishop Laud's Canterbury Quad at St John's).[139]

Wilkins certainly never gave up on the idea of a building to house his scientific College. It was he who proposed a purpose-built college for the Royal Society at a meeting on 30 September 1667.[140] By May 1668 over £1000 towards the building had been promised by members (including Boyle, Moray, Wilkins, Matthew Wren, Evelyn, Haak and Pepys).[141] Plans were requested from Wren and Hooke, and on 11 May Wilkins and Neile were deputed to approach Wren for his design; in June Wren sent a drawing and a full description.[142] The requisite funds were not, however, raised, the moment passed, the site earmarked ceased to be available, and – like so many ideas passionately framed by royalists during the 'dark days' of the English Commonwealth – Wilkins's dream College was never actually built.

The saga of possible purpose-built accommodation for the Royal Society pales into insignificance alongside that of suitable royal accommodation for the restored King himself.

In 1660 Charles II returned from exile to Whitehall Palace in triumph, where he remained without interruption for two years, spending every winter thereafter in residence there for the twenty-five years of his reign.[143] Since opinion had it that fleeing London had been his father's downfall, he was determined to assert a real presence in the capital city – he dined daily in public, and made a habit of walking in St James's Park so that his subjects could catch a glimpse of him. Even after the discomfort of some of his own lodgings while in exile, it must, however, have been a shock taking up residence as sovereign at Whitehall. The sprawling buildings were badly in need of repair, having stood neglected (with the exception of the apartments used by Cromwell and his family) for a decade. During his enforced peripatetic existence in mainland Europe, Charles had spent time in a succession of royal palaces, in the Dutch Republic, France, Germany and the Spanish Netherlands. Louis XIV's new Louvre Palace, in particular, set a standard of grand yet functional royal provision which Charles was keen to follow.

Since continuity with his father's reign was much on Charles II's mind, it was natural for him to turn to his father's builder-architects (Inigo Jones, however, had died in 1652). During the final months of the reign of Charles I, in 1647–48, one of those who had visited the Isle of Wight was John Webb, *de facto* Surveyor-General of the Royal Works (that is, royal architect).[144] He had carried with him a set of architectural plans for the complete rebuilding of Whitehall Palace on an elaborate scale – a project which formed part of Charles I's grand ambition to make London the cultural capital of Europe.[145] Like the arrival of the King's state coach and of the royal miniaturist, Webb's visit formed part of a denial on Charles's part that his reign was almost at an end.

At the precise moment when Charles II needed to signal equally grandiose ambitions for the restored monarchy, it was Webb who emerged to reassert his claim to rebuild Whitehall. On 2 May 1660, just one week after the new Parliament had voted to restore the monarchy and invite Charles II to return, Webb petitioned Parliament to be restored to the post of Surveyor of the Works (the Cromwellian appointment already having been suspended).[146] Given the pressing need for renovations to make Whitehall habitable by the royal party, Parliament swiftly complied. Immediately the King arrived in London at the end of May, Webb presented a yet more elaborate petition to Charles:

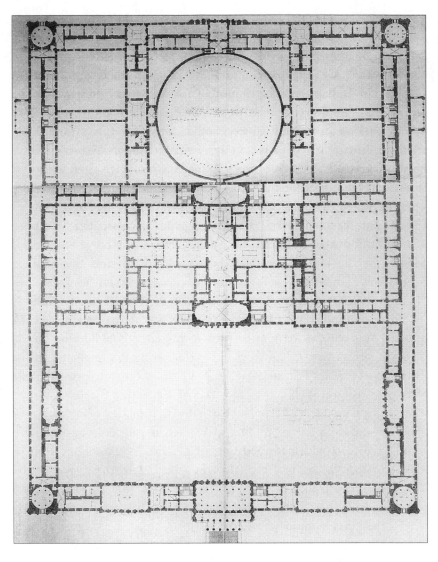

The plan for rebuilding Whitehall Palace on a grand scale, around Inigo
Jones's Banqueting House, prepared by John Webb, and presented to
Charles I for approval on the Isle of Wight in 1648.

To the Kings most excellent Majesty
The humble petition of John Webb Architect
Humbly Sheweth

That your petition was by the especiall comand of yor Ma[jes]-
ties Royall father of ever blessed memory, brought up by Inigo

Jones esq. yor Ma[jes]ties late Surveyor of the Works in ye study of Architecture for enabling him to do yor Royall father and yor Ma[jes]ties service in ye said Office. In order whereunto he was by Mr Jones upon leaving his house at the beginning of the late unhappy warre appointed his deputy to overrule the said place in his absence wch yor petitioner did, until by a Comtee of parliament in ye yeare 1643 he was thrust out, as being entrusted for his Ma[jes]ty since wch time yor pet[itione]r hath patiently acquiesced in confidence of yor Ma[jes]ties glorious returne wch now after so many calamitous years happily succeeding the Lords & Comons in parliam[en]t & Cou[n]cell of State have confess'd none more able than yor pet[itione]r (as he hopes yor Royall Ma[jes]ty shall find) to discharge ye trust of being Surveyor of Yor Ma[jes]ties works, and accordingly he hath & is preparing ye Royall houses for yor Ma[jes]ties reception the charge whereof upon their severall Surveys amounting to 8140 li 5s 2d yor pet[itione]rs credit stands solely engaged for, he having as yet received 500 li only of ye said summe.

Yor pet[itione]rs humble preayer therefore is that yor Ma[jes]ty would be pleased gratiously to cast yor eye upon yor pet[itione]r as yor loyall subject and by yor Ma[jes]ties gratious grant settle upon him the Surveyors office of yor Majesties works whereunto yor Royall father designed him & to that end only ordered his education. Otherwise after his many sufferings and imprisonments during the late warrs for his loyalty to the Crowne yor pet[itione]r standing engaged as above said instead of reaping the fruits of his fidelity and long studyes may together with his whole family be ruined at last for ever without your Ma[jes]ties Royall favour.

And yor pet[itione]r as in duty bound shall continually pray for yor Ma[jes]ties prosperous & happy raigne.[147]

To this petition Webb attached a helpful supporting 'Briefe of Mr Webbs case' as follows:

That hee was brought up by his unckle Mr Inigo Jones upon his late Ma[jes]ties comand in the study of Architecture, as well that wch relates to buildings as for Masques, Tryumphs and the like. That he was Mr. Jones Deputy and in actual possession of the Office upon his leaving London and attended his Ma[jes]ty in that capacity at Hampton Courte and at ye Isle of Wight where he received his Ma[jes]ties comand to designe a Pallace for Whitehall which he did untill his Ma[jes]ties unfortunate calamity caus'd him to desist.

That he was Mr Jones Executor & there is 1500 li due to him in that regard upon Arrears of Mr Jones's wages. Besides 500 li Mr Webb carryed his Ma[jes]ty sewed up in his waistcoate through all ye enemys quarters unto Beverley in Yorkshire wch being afterwards discovered Mr Webb was plundered to the purpose and a long time kept in prison being close prisoner for a month.

That Mr Webb sent to the King at Oxford the designes of all the fortifications about London, their proportions, the number of Gunns mounted on them, how many Souldyers would man them, how they might bee attempted & carried and all particulars relating thereto in writing. That Mr Webb hath made ready Whitehall as his Ma[jes]ty sees in ye space of a fortnight upon his own credit having yet received 500 li only of 8000 and odd pounds.

That Mr Denham may possibly as most gentry in England at this day have some knowledge in the Theory of Architecture but nothing of ye practique soe that he must of necessity have another of his Ma[jes]ties charge to doe his businesse whereas Mr Webb himselfe designes, orders and directs, whatever given in comand without any other mans assistance. His Ma[jes]tie may please to grant some other place more proper for Mr Denhams abilitye and confirme unto Mr Webb the Surveyors place wherein he hath consumed 30 yeares study there being scarce any of the great Nobility or eminent gentry of England but he hath done service for in matter of building, ordering of meddalls, statues and the like.[148]

The procedure by which the returning King made his appointments was a cumbersome one. Out of deference, and to underline the continuity and legitimacy of his reign, Charles had to acknowledge the claims of those who (like Webb) had obtained these offices, or the reversion of them, under his father, before proceeding to use those same posts as rewards for personal loyalties to himself during his exile. Thus (for example) Edward Montagu obtained the important naval office of Clerk of the Acts for his young relative and client Samuel Pepys. First, however, Pepys had to satisfy the previous incumbent, by arranging to pay him a percentage of the salary. Pepys then lobbied vigorously to get his appointment ratified, in case Montagu lost royal favour.

In the case of the post of Surveyor of the Royal Works, Webb's was not the only, nor the strongest, claim.[149] The King agreed to Webb's acting as his architect (since he had begun work on refurbishing the royal apartments), but he conferred upon Sir John Denham the official title of Surveyor of the Royal Works (making him a Knight of the Order of the Bath at the same time). Denham, who had held Farnham Castle briefly for Charles I in the early stages of the civil war, and thereafter had acted as a trusted emissary, at considerable personal risk, was considered more deserving.

Although history has seen fit to pillory Denham as a second-rate poet – author of the long couplet poem *Cooper's Hill* (1642) – who went mad when the beautiful young wife he married in his sixties had a public affair with James, Duke of York, his appointment as Surveyor of the Royal Works was a sensible move on Charles II's part. Denham was no expert in innovative design, but he was a shrewd, competent administrator and an able facilitator of other people's projects. He presided over London's buildings during a decade in which first the Restoration and then the Great Fire created an unprecedented need for fast rebuilding on a limited budget. He left no cathedrals or palaces, but he fixed the tidy, regular pattern of London's residential squares for a century and a half – starting with Bloomsbury Square (for which he gave 'planning permission' to the Earl of Southampton in 1661), and proceeding to St James Square, where, petitioning the Crown (that is, Denham) for permission to build in 1663, the Earl of St Albans wrote that:

> Ye beauty of this great Towne and ye convenience of your Court are defective in point of houses fitt for ye dwellings of Noble men and other Persons of quality, and that your Majesty hath thought fitt for some Remedy hereof to appoint yt ye Place in St James Field should be built in great and good houses.[150]

Sir John Denham, author of the admired poem *Cooper's Hill*, and loyal supporter of Charles I throughout the civil wars – he was appointed Surveyor of the Royal Works at the Restoration.

Lady Denham, whose public affair with James, Duke of York, reputedly drove her husband out of his wits.

Denham duly authorised St James's, as he did numerous other more or less speculative central-London developments. Pepys noted that by no means everybody was happy with the reckless speed with which noble landowners were developing their London lands: 'The building of St. James's by my Lord St Albans, which is now about, and which the city Stomach, I perceive highly, but dare not oppose it.'[151] One might well argue that Denham prepared the ground – softened London up, even – for the dramatic reshaping of London's skyline by his successor, Christopher Wren.

At the outset of his reign, the King – an enthusiast for modern, European-style buildings on the strength of his continental exile – turned to royal servants of his own choice (including Webb), for his major rebuilding projects. In August 1661 the works accounts record a payment for the 'makeing of certayne modells of whitehall by the surveyor of the workes appoyntment'. Whether these were plans for a new palace, or a three-dimensional model, it appears that the King was anxious to proceed immediately with Webb's suggestions, and that Webb continued to work on the project for a time at least – one of the twelve surviving

Webb drawings is dated 9 October 1661. For a number of years the King continued to entertain grand hopes for Whitehall. On 28 October 1664 John Evelyn (himself something of an architectural amateur), 'being in the Privy Gallery at Whitehall', spoke to the King who asked whether he had a crayon and paper. Evelyn 'presented him with both and then laying it on the window stoole, he with his owne hands, designed to me the plot for the future building of Whitehall, together with the Roomes of state & other particulars'. As Webb said in his petition, apparently 'most gentry in England at this day' considered themselves to have 'some knowledge in the Theory of Architecture'.[152]

When Charles came to the rebuilding of his palace at Greenwich in 1661, he appealed directly to the Dutch architects whose work he had seen during his continental exile. In May 1661 Willem de Keyser, son of the great Amsterdam architect Hendrick de Keyser, and himself the architect of several recent classical buildings in the Dutch Republic, drew elevations for the King of proposed new buildings.[153] By December a wooden model of this design had been made, and late in January 1661 the King discussed his ideas on this new building with Evelyn. In 1662, the King took Webb off the Whitehall project so that he could begin work on rebuilding plans for Greenwich, presumably with instructions to modify his own designs to accommodate the Dutch proposals.[154]

In 1660, however, the most immediate need for 'building works' at Whitehall remained the *ad hoc* reorganisation and refurbishment of the existing royal apartments to suit the needs of the new residents. Webb's petition, and accompanying testimonial, specified that he 'hath made ready Whitehall as his Ma[jes]tie sees in ye space of a fortnight upon his own credit having yet received 500 li only of 8000 and odd pounds'. By December 1660 the works accounts record that Richard Daynes had been commissioned to draw 'three drafts and scales of the ground plott of whitehall', presumably to serve as the basis for the drawings and designs to which Charles would give his approval.

Once in residence, the King issued his own instructions. His immediate concerns were for his own comfort, particularly in his bed-chamber, the rooms immediately adjacent to it and his bathing room. A new ceremonial bedroom was created in the French manner, with a railed-off alcove in which a great ceremonial crimson bed was installed, surrounded by carved work, panelling, pilasters and draperies. The cre-ation of this magnificent state bedchamber necessitated the construction of a private bedchamber (where the King actually slept) elsewhere. The King's privy bedchamber was a new room overlooking the Thames, and a new passage was built to link the new room with the existing privy gallery.[155] Accommodation for the Lord Chamberlain and other senior officials was also created by major refurbishment and remodelling in 1660. The King's ground-floor bathroom under the privy gallery was extensively altered and lavishly refitted in 1663; a laboratory was constructed next to the bathroom around the same time, directly beneath the King's closet (or study). In April 1662, only weeks before the arrival of the new Queen, Catherine of Braganza, her bedchamber and privy chamber were completely refurbished:

> The privy chamber was given a new roof 36 feet long and 25 feet wide. This roof was higher than its predecessor, presumably to make way for rooms above it. The 'front' of the room was also built up. At the same time a gutter 43 feet long was inserted 'betweene the roofe of the queenes privie chamber & the roofe of the withdrawing roome' and another gutter was erected at the end of the queen's presence chamber next to the privy chamber. Two small rooms were created north and south of the new privy chamber leading into the presence chamber and withdrawing room. We also learn that the privy chamber had two windows and a balcony facing the Thames. . . . In addition to her lodgings, Catherine, a Roman Catholic, was also provided with a private chapel. This was linked to her bedroom by a short passage and had a small vestry and 'music room' attached. . . . The whole campaign was carried out at great speed, and overtime payments were made to complete the rooms in time for her arrival.[156]

It seems likely that both Webb and Wren worked on these new spaces within the existing Whitehall buildings – their mettle tested by the difficult conditions under which all these works had to be carried out, the speed of execution demanded, and the sluggish timescale for royal payments (the finances of the new regime were far from organised at this point). Both Wren and Webb appear to have been promised the reversion of the title of Surveyor of the King's Works in 1661. Webb was moved to work on Greenwich by 1662; Hugh May was brought in to work on the Duke of York's apartments at Whitehall by 1664. By

1664 Wren too was working on more elaborate plans for rebuilding. A drawing for a Whitehall rebuilding scheme from this period survives which is certainly in Wren's hand.[157] The Venetian ambassador reported in November 1664 that 'The King has decided to have Whitehall rebuilt in the style of the Banqueting hall,' a remark consistent with the Wren drawing.[158]

Denham died in 1669. Webb immediately petitioned once again for the post of Surveyor-General of the King's Works. By now he knew that Wren was the competition:

> The humble desire of yor Petitioner is, to know yor Royall pleasure, how in this conjuncture hee shall dispose of himselfe, for although hee acted under Sr. John Denham, a person of honour, hee conceives it much beneath him, to doe ye like under one, who in whatever respects is his inferiour by farr. May yor Majestie please if not to confirm yor Petitioner's Grant as in the honor of a King you appear to bee obliged, then to Joyne him in Patent with Mr. Wren and hee shalbee ready to instruct him in the course of the office of yor works, whereof he professeth to bee wholy ignorant.[159]

By 1669, however, Wren had fully established his reputation as a practising architect, with a flair for the structural and engineering aspects of the profession, the ability to organise major public works, and a no-nonsense attitude to execution and completion of any project he undertook. Charles II appointed Christopher Wren to be his Royal Surveyor, a post he held, under five successive monarchs, over a period of more than forty-five years.

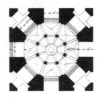

4

Preferred Routes to Success

With extraordinary rapidity, the senior figures in the circle to which Wren had belonged during the years of Charles II's exile established themselves as leading patrons of the newly restored monarchy in spring 1660.[1] Men like Sir Paul Neile and Sir Robert Moray, driven into retreat and continental exile respectively because of their faithful service to Charles I, slipped discreetly back into lodgings as royal intimates at Whitehall Palace.[2] The consequent alteration to Wren's own life was swift and lasting.

He moved back into the familiar relationship with men at the centre of royal power, as if his father were still Register of the Garter, living with his family in the Dean's House at Windsor. Some sense of the completeness of the recuperation of a past life can be gathered from a handwritten account by Sir Robert Moray of a relaxed outing he took with Sir Paul Neile and Wren 'from Faringdon in to Abingdon' (in Oxfordshire), on the journey back from observing tidal movement in the English Channel. Both older men were Wren's patrons. The account – a fleeting glimpse into the largely lost world of Wren's private life – is headed, 'Observations of Sr. Robert Moray, Sr. P Neil and Dr Wren, made by them in their late excursion in to the contry':

On Thursday the 14. of Octob[er] coming from Faringdon towards Abbington, before the sun was up, (there having been all night a great mist and Faringdon standing upon a high ground,) wee saw in the large valleys on both handes lying southwards and northwards the mist lying so thick, low & levell, that it looke lyke a sea, and afforded a very pleasant prospect, the tops of some steeples & trees looking as if they had stood out of the sea, & some rysing grounds looke presently lyke Ilandes. This continued till after the sun was up, & then the mist began to rise as the sun, which shone bright, got up higher. when the mist was risen so high as to make a Circle above the Horizon which was about some 5. or 6. degrees − one might see two places in it distant from one another so farr and in such manner opposite to the sun that they gave us cause to look for some kinde of Rainbow when the mist should bee yet high enough, which accordingly fell out, for by the time the sun had been up about 3. Quartre of an houre, wee saw a Compleat semicircle of the same size & the endes of it distant from one another as rainbowes in such cases use to be, as upon consideration it appeared to them. But there appeared none of the colure usuall in rainbowes. onely the whole bow being of a lighter colour than the rest of the Mist, the insides of it were more darkish. and still as the sun grew hotter the bow grew more perfect & distinct, till it [sic] about 9. a clock. & then by little and little it vanished.[3]

We picture the three men, on horseback, marvelling at a strange phenomenon of deflected sunlight, and the younger man, Wren, ably offering technical comment for the benefit of his two older companions.

Wren's personal rehabilitation began within months of the King's return. Along with many other survivors from the circle of Charles I, he took the first available opportunity to make direct contact with the court at Whitehall Palace. In August 1660, within days of Charles II's appointing Bruno Ryves as his new Register of the Garter, Wren restored the precious books of Garter records to the King on behalf of his father, thereby effecting an early personal appearance. Less than two months later, he was one of a group of court circle figures with scientific interests entertaining Charles with demonstrations of the heavenly wonders to be viewed with a high-magnification telescope. In October 1660 Hartlib wrote to John Worthington:

> His Majesty was lately, in an evening, at Gresham Coll[ege], where he was entertained with the admirable long Tube, w[i]th which he viewed the heavens, to his very great satisfaction, insomuch that he commanded S[i]r P[aul] Neile to cause the like to be made . . . for the use of Whitehall. Sir Paul hath very highly commended Mr. Wren to greater preferment, and there is no question but he will find the real effects of it.[4]

By April 1661 Hartlib reported that he had 'heard great talk of Mr. Wren, and we see frequent changes of preferment'. His sources were accurate. Wren had already been chosen to succeed Seth Ward as Savilian Professor of Astronomy at Oxford in February (like Wren's old friend Wilkins, Ward was found a suitable clerical post elsewhere, and eventually rose to become Bishop of Salisbury). In March, Wren resigned as Gresham Professor, and on 15 May he was installed at Oxford.[5]

In April 1661, too, Christiaan Huygens, visiting from the Dutch Republic, found Wren in the constant company of a clique of elite courtiers, together with various virtuosi:

> 20 April. Visited by Mr. Wallis and Mr. Rook, afterwards by Mr. Boyle. After dinner Mr. Moray and Mr. Brouncker came to collect me and we went to the Assembly, where I found Mr. Wren. They talked about the capillary action of water in little tubes, and arranged a meeting for Saturday at my house, for the advancement of telescopes. With Mr. Moray said goodbye to Mr. Bruce and stayed until 10 pm.

> 23 April. Dined in my chamber. After dinner Mr. Moray, My Lord Brouncker, Sir Paul Neile, Dr. Wallis, Mr. Rooke, Mr. Wren, and Dr. Goddard arrived. We discussed methods for manufacturing lenses, and I told them of my method.[6]

In fact, Wren's problem during the years 1661 and 1662 in settling on a career seemed to be that he had too many, rather than too few, possibilities open to him. The diversity of interests among his various backers made it unclear which career direction he ought now to follow. Sir Charles Scarburgh had been appointed as royal physician ordinary (the head of the King's personal medical team) – we know from Pepys's diary that Scarburgh was one of those who had rushed to Scheveling to pay their respects to Charles II immediately the decision was formalised, inviting the King back to England.[7] He was now in a position to offer Wren a profitable future in the Royal College of Physicians. Sir Paul Neile's encouragement of his astronomical interests had already gained him the Oxford chair of Astronomy by spring 1661. Dr John Wilkins's comprehensive backing for his technical, inventive skills suggested he might make a career in the new entrepreneurial circles in and around the Royal Society for the Improvement of Natural Knowledge (Wilkins's cherished dream of a club, finally realised in early 1661).[8] As the King's most senior courtier, Sir Robert Moray had enormous influence, a finger in most pies, and a strong commitment to furthering commercially orientated projects to improve the new regime's tottering finances. It is something of an irony that the strong steer which directed Wren towards an architectural career seems ultimately to have come from the King himself.

Coming as we do, historically, after the established fact of the Restoration of the English monarchy, it is hard for us to appreciate how dramatically unexpected a revival in personal career prospects it was for Wren, bringing to an end, as it did, the long string of deprivations, setbacks and disappointments of the preceding decade. The later 1650s had seen an easing of the restrictions on known royalist sympathisers, and their gradual access (as in Wren's own case) to modest opportunities in pursuing their careers. But, in a state where real promotion still depended on powerful patronage by those close to the centres of government, prospects for men like Wren were limited. And even after the death of Cromwell at the end of 1658, few imagined the Stuarts would ever return as dynastic rulers in England.[9]

If Wren's return to favour was swift, his cousin Matthew Wren's was even swifter. Even before Christopher's appointment at Oxford, Matthew, eldest son of Bishop Matthew Wren (now, in old age, restored to his bishopric at Ely), was appointed personal secretary to Sir Edward Hyde – Lord Chancellor, and recently elevated to the rank of Earl of Clarendon, as the father of the Duke of York's new wife Anne.[10] A thoroughly political animal (we recall the skill with which he had penned a public defence of the Wilkins circle against Harrington in the 1650s), Matthew Wren discreetly shifted his loyalties during the 1660s from Clarendon to the Duke of York, as the latter's fortunes improved and the former's declined. At the disgrace of Clarendon in 1667 Matthew Wren immediately became personal secretary to the Duke of York. Adding to the complexity of the choices Christopher had to make about a career, the first use Matthew made of his new influence was to propose the advancement of his cousin – recompense for his practical support of himself and his brother Thomas during the 'dark days' in Oxford.

THE NEW QUEEN'S DOWRY

In 1650, Princess Sophie, daughter of the widowed Elizabeth of Bohemia and niece of Charles I, had refused so much as to entertain the idea of marriage to her cousin, the exiled Charles II, in spite of a brief flirtation, on the ground that he was a penniless prince with no prospects. 'He had shown a liking for me with which I was most gratified,' she wrote in her memoirs, but she had had 'sense enough to know that marriages of great kings are not made up by such means'.[11] (She went on to make an unhappy marriage to a minor German prince – their son George, however, became, by a dynastic accident, George I of England.)

By 1661, Charles II (still officially a bachelor) looked distinctly more eligible.[12] Within months of his Restoration, negotiations were under way between England and Portugal to arrange the marriage of the new King to the Portuguese Princess Catherine of Braganza – a deal which included 'the richest dowry brought by any Queen of England'. In addition to a handsome and much needed injection of cash into the English Exchequer, the dowry included Tangier, on the southern side of the Straits of Gibraltar, and Bombay on the west coast of India. Both towns were strategically crucial for strengthening England's trade prospects, via the East India Company, and the English Crown immediately set about securing them from competing claims (whether from the local population or from the competing Dutch and Spanish trading powers in the region).[13]

Henry Hyde, first Earl of Clarendon, was the prime mover in the marriage negotiations with Portugal (manoeuvring adroitly to exclude competing Spanish negotiators from the picture), and one of the chief advocates for the vital importance of a properly defended Tangier to further English trading interests eastwards.[14] Following the successful completion of the contract arrangements, he acted quickly to secure the

Edward Montagu, first Earl of Sandwich, Samuel Pepys's patron and employer, whose enthusiasm for the fortification of the strategically important port of Tangier resulted in the long-running construction project known as the 'Tangier mole'.

new territorial acquisitions, and to make arrangements for surveying and assessing their defence needs, starting with Tangier.

Shortly after ratification of the marriage contract, and before Charles and Catherine's actual wedding (which took place in May 1662), preparations had begun to garrison Tangier and improve its inadequate fortifications (arrangements for Bombay came somewhat later). In January 1662, Edward Montagu, first Earl of Sandwich was sent to take control of England's newest possession, installing a garrison and the first English governor. Sandwich subsequently invested substantial sums of his own money in property there, and over the next decade remained one of the staunchest supporters of Tangier's strategic, commercial and political importance, and the desirability of England's retaining a presence there.[15]

The immediate problem was the port's vulnerability. Shortly after its acquisition, Sir John Lawson told the King that 'if it were in the hands of the Hollanders, they would quickly make a Mole, which they might easily do; and they would keep the place against all the World, and give the law to all the trade of the Mediterranean'. It was agreed that what the port needed was indeed a Mole – an enclosed, fortified harbour on the Dutch model. Matthew Wren proposed his cousin Christopher's name to Clarendon as a suitably qualified mathematician to head the team to carry out a measured survey and mapping of Tangier and its harbour, prior to the design and drawing up of plans for the Mole.

In an explanatory note to a letter from Thomas Sprat to Wren, written in late 1661, which touched on the Tangier appointment, Wren's son later wrote:

> A Commission to survey and direct the Works of the Mole, Harbour and Fortifications of the Citadel and Town of *Tangier* in *Africa*, was at this Time proposed for him, (being then esteemed one of the best Geometricians in *Europe*) with an ample Salary, and Promise of other royal Favours, particularly a Dispensation for not attending the Business of his Professorship, during his Continuance in his Majesty's Service abroad; and a revisionary Grant of the Office of Surveyor-General of the royal Works, on the Decease of Sir *John Denham*: all which was signified to him by Letter from Mr. *Matthew Wren*, Secretary to the Lord Chancellor *Hyde*.[16]

The Earl of Sandwich (Samuel Pepys's patron, who acquired his title and became a senior figure in command of the English Navy at the Restoration) may also have backed Wren. An undated fragment of a piece of astronomical observing for navigational purposes, commissioned by Sandwich, survives in the earliest manuscript copy of *Parentalia*.[17] Wren's son tells us that his father felt obliged to turn the appointment down: 'This Employment he had no Inclination to accept, (being not then consistent with his Health,) but humbly prayed his Majesty to allow of his Excuse, and to command his Duty in *England*.'[18]

Wren's lasting regret at having had to refuse 'an ample Salary, and Promise of other royal Favours' at this crossroads in his career sounds authentic enough. Nevertheless, his practical good sense (and the advice of friends like William Petty) must have told him that the Tangier survey was not an offer it would be wise to accept, in spite of the material benefits it promised. Whatever his experience of surveying buildings and drawing up plans, he had no experience at all of the kind of large-scale land survey required, in difficult terrain, using local personnel as labour, in a foreign country. This was the kind of venture Petty had undertaken with his Down survey of Ireland, where his previous experience in management and the rigours of overseas work under difficult conditions stood him in particularly good stead. Such enterprises were not to be undertaken lightly.[19]

The person eventually sent to survey Tangier town and harbour in 1663 was Sir Jonas Moore – a much more suitable and qualified man for the job. Moore had been chief surveyor to the Dutch dredging expert Cornelius Vermeyden, for the fifth Earl of Bedford's Fen Drainage Company for a period of seven years in the 1650s. The fen-drainage scheme had involved large-scale surveying operations, and had at one point involved a workforce of around 10,000 men.[20] Moore himself had been required to survey the terrain accurately before and after drainage, to calculate the optimum positions for ditches and sluices, and to draw up the boundaries of the packages of land made available for cultivation by the drainage.

Although Moore's highly successful fen-drainage project had been completed under Oliver Cromwell, his kind of expertise was sufficiently in demand to ensure that he – like William Petty – made a relatively smooth transition into the service of the new regime. By early 1661 Moore was hard at work surveying in London for Matthew Nicholas, son of Charles II's chief secretary in exile Edward Nicholas, and the first post-Restoration Dean of St Paul's. This time the lucrative project was the reclaiming of ecclesiastical lands confiscated by Parliament in the 1640s, and particularly the Nicholas family's own seized properties. In September 1661, shortly after Matthew Nicholas's death, Moore wrote to John Barwick, who had been proposed as the next Dean of St Paul's, with some encouraging prospects:

> I was imployed by Dr Nicholas in much of his own affayres. . . .
> I had proceeded in one parcell of his houses in Shadwell, as to make a survey of all the Tenements there, 16 weeks paynes of 4 men; the Fyne wilbe 3000 li [pounds] & above if not 4000 li which is clerely yours if you accept of the Deanery.[21]

In early 1662, at just about the time when Matthew Wren was proposing his cousin's name to lead the Tangier survey expedition, Jonas Moore gained his first government commission of the new regime in the form of a complete survey of the River Thames for navigational purposes, under the patronage of the Earl of Sandwich. The project resulted in a fine map on vellum, entitled:

> A Mapp Or Description of the River of Thames from Westminster to the Sea with the falls of all the Rivers into it the severall Creekes Soundings & Depths thereof and Docks made for the use of his Ma[jes]ties Navy, made by Jonas Moore Gent: by Warrent from Sir Charles Harbord Knt his said Ma[jes]ties Surveyor Generall. In Pursuance of his Ma[jes]ties Warrant and Command under the Royal Signature Anno Domini 1662.[22]

Either Sandwich or the Duke of York (who seems to have become Moore's patron from early 1663) proposed Jonas Moore for the Tangier survey, an appointment he duly accepted. Between June and September 1663, Moore led the expedition to carry out the survey of Tangier and a feasibility study for the proposed fortifications. Each member of this survey group was paid a hundred pounds on their return, for their 'paynes in setting out the Bounds of the Mole &c'. They presented the Committee with 'a brave draught of the Molle to be built', adding that when completed it was 'likely to be the most considerable place the King of England hath in the world'. The 'draught' or preliminary drawing of the proposed Mole, drawn by Moore himself, was subsequently engraved by Wenceslaus Hollar, and published in 1664 for promotional purposes, as a kind of early investment brochure. In its printed form the map is more than four feet by two, made up of three sheets, and bears the title 'A Mapp of the Citty of Tanger; with the Straits of Gibraltar. Described by Jonas Moore Surveyor to his Royall Highnes the Duke of York'. It also carries the royal arms and a dedication to the King and Queen by 'their obedient servant J. Moore by the Commaund & appointment of the Lords Commissioners for the affaires for Tanger'. Pepys liked it enough to frame it: his diary entry pronounced it 'very pleasant and I purpose to have it finely set out and hung up'.[23]

Despite having declined the office of Royal Surveyor at Tangier itself, Wren continued to be involved in subsequent stages in the design and execution of the project. When he was eventually appointed Surveyor of the King's Works in 1669, the Tangier Mole – much of it now constructed – fell within his remit. From Tangier, Sir Hugh Cholmeley (who had been appointed 'Surveyor General of the Mole') sent a 'Modell

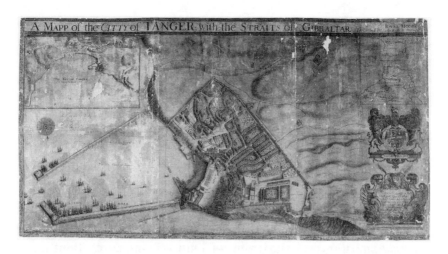

Sir Jonas Moore's map of Tangier, dedicated to James, Duke of York –
Pepys owned a copy, which he framed and hung on his office wall.

[scheme] . . . for the future Governing of the Worke' – 400 of the 600
yards intended for the Mole had by this time been built. Wren, with
the assistance of Jonas Moore, 'perused this modell' and reported the
latest scheme to be 'exact and Sufficient', 'fit & agreeable for the Worke
of the Mole'.[24] In 1676, Hooke recorded several discussions in his diary
in which Moore and members of Wren's office took part, concerning
innovative Italian methods for building harbour defences in deep water,
by sinking wooden chests packed with rubble; William Holder and Wren
were among those who also discussed these ideas at the Royal Society.[25]

Lucrative possibilities opened up for those closely involved with the
Tangier fortifications. Moore became an extremely wealthy man in later
life. No doubt this, too, contributed to the tone of regret with which
Wren told his son of his not accepting the Tangier appointment himself.
Even when his name was on everyone's lips as the 'genius' who was
restoring London to its former glory, Wren never managed to exploit
his position sufficiently to acquire the kind of wealth others of his
generation accumulated. In 1675, Moore was the generous backer of the
Greenwich Observatory, designed and built by Wren, and the flagship
of English navigational science at the end of the eighteenth century.[26]

In the end, the attempt to sustain an English garrison at Tangier
failed.[27] In 1683, with 450 yards of the Mole completed, running east-
north-east (but not the 200 yards return, east-south-east), at a total cost

of some £340,000, the project was abandoned, on the ground that the outpost was simply impossible to defend. Rather than leave the fortifications to be used by Moroccan imperial forces, an expedition led by George Legge, Master-General of the Ordnance (and including Pepys), was dispatched to destroy the Mole and its fortifications. It is some sort of tribute to the skill with which the Mole had been constructed that it took until February 1684, and quantities of explosives, to complete the task of demolishing it.[28]

It is hard to see how Wren could have combined the Surveyorship of the Tangier Mole with his mounting commitments at home. By late 1660, the personal interest shown by the King, the Duke of York and Prince Rupert in the activities at Gresham College had encouraged Wren's original mentor and protector John Wilkins to set about establishing an official royal institution for science and technology on the model of that for physicians and surgeons, the Royal College of Physicians. Wren had been closely involved with the Oxford club from the outset, and his considerable skills as a dissectionist, observational astronomer, instrument designer (and maker) and draughtsman were all actively in demand to support the teams of scientists less talented in practical matters. Where once he had been a mere 'operator' alongside Hooke and others, assisting the gentleman experimentalists, Wren soon became a leading figure in efforts to put the new scientific activities in London on an official footing.

THE ELECTOR PALATINE'S CHAPLAIN
MAKES HIS WAY BACK

Dr John Wilkins may have been deprived of the Mastership of Trinity College, Cambridge at the Restoration, but, back in London, he continued to occupy his central place in the circle of ex-Oxford scientists jostling for position around the new administration. Helped both by his historic links with the court circle through the Elector Palatine and by his personal charm (on which contemporaries of all political persuasions commented), his academic appointments were gradually replaced by ecclesiastical benefices.[29] On 28 January 1661 he was elected preacher at Gray's Inn; at the end of the year George, Lord Berkeley – whom he had served as chaplain before his appointment as Charles

Louis's, and before the civil war – presented him with the living of Cranford, Middlesex. On 11 April 1662 Wilkins became vicar of St Lawrence Jewry in London (the church of the Corporation of London, whose living was in the King's gift).[30] Thus, although no longer the holder of prestigious public appointments, the former chaplain to the Elector Palatine was, from the very beginning of Charles II's reign, in a position of relative influence, and thereby able to promote his two favourite projects: a permanent club for scientists, and the career of Christopher Wren.[31]

In spite of the civil disturbances in London following the death of Cromwell, there was apparently a scientific 'Society' associated with Gresham College, meeting regularly from the end of 1658, with Wilkins as its President. In November 1658, Haak's mathematician friend John Pell, recently returned from a period as Commonwealth ambassador in Switzerland, received an invitation to a meeting:

> There is this day a meeting in the moorefields [presumably because of the troops garrisoned since October in Gresham College itself] of some Mathematicall freinds (as you know the costam hath beene) there will be Mr. Rook and Mr. Wrenn my Lord Brunkerd [Brouncker] Sir Pauel Neile Dr. Goddard Dr. Scarburow etc. I had notice the last night of your being in town from some of the gentellmen now named and of there desire to injoy your company, there will bee no such number as you usually have seen at such meetings 12 is the number invited.[32]

After the King's return, Wilkins moved to have such meetings put on an official footing, and to set about securing the patronage of Charles himself. On 28 November 1660, he used the occasion of Wren's weekly Gresham astronomy lecture to organise a meeting at which it was proposed to found 'a college for the promoting of physico-mathematical experimental learning'.[33] Wilkins took the chair, and was duly voted chairman pro tem, while negotiations continued formally to establish the Royal Society of London for the Improvement of Natural Knowledge (though at this early stage it was simply referred to as the 'Royal Society'). Within two weeks, an ex-Oxford club member, Henry Oldenburg, wrote to a fellow scientist on the continent that Wilkins had been elected 'president of the new English Academy here under the patronage of the king for the advancement of the sciences'.[34] Robert Moray was given the task of informing the King, and soliciting his interest and support.

The minutes of the meeting held on 5 December 1660 record that Moray:

> brought in word from ye Court that The King had been acquainted with the designe of this Meeting. And he did well approve of it, & would be ready to give encouragement to it. It was ordered that Mr Wren be desired to prepare against the next meeting for the pendulum experiment. . . .[35]

Wilkins was still styled President in the first months of 1661. On 6 March 1661, however, Sir Robert Moray was elected official President – the Society was eager to exploit the fact that Moray had the ear of the King.[36]

It was Moray who from the outset encouraged the group to use Wren as bait to arouse Charles's interest in the venture. Knowing the new King as intimately as he did he could be confident of two things: that Charles had already established a sympathetic bond with this son of one of his father's close and faithful servants, with whom he shared troubling memories of a lost golden childhood; and that, by happy chance, the elegantly crafted scientific 'curiosities' which Wren had proved so adept at designing and manufacturing since boyhood were exactly the kinds of thing guaranteed to attract the King's attention and interest.

On 7 May 1661 Moray and Neile, who had evidently succeeded in raising Charles's curiosity with their accounts of the new Society's activities, wrote formally to Wren with the King's personal command for a diverting piece of science created expressly for him:

> The King hath commanded us to lay a double Charge upon you, in his Name, to a perfect Design, wherein he is told, you have already made some Progress, to make a Globe representing accurately the Figure of the Moon, as the best Tubes represent it: and to delineate by the Help of the Microscope the Figures of all the Insects, and small living Creatures you can light upon, as you have done those you presented to his Majesty. If it were needful to add any further Excitement to your Industry, we should tell you how much our whole Society is rejoiced, that his Majesty has a just Esteem of your Parts, and honours you

with his Commands, which we are confident will prevail with you, and therefore we reserve all other Motives for other Things, only we expect you will signify to us your Readiness to comply with his Majesty's Pleasure; and you may be sure we will improve it as much to your Honour and Advantage. as is possible for [a] much honoured Friend.[37]

Wren's globe and microscopical drawings were needed with some haste, because it was hoped that the King might be persuaded shortly to visit the Society, thereby bestowing on it his royal imprimatur. Tellingly, both proposed royal 'diversions' take advantage of a scientific instrument whose significant refinement is credited to Wren – the micrometer eyepiece. For an accurate lunar survey Wren would have needed a method of measuring very small angular distances, both for plotting the moon's features in plan, and for calculating the heights of lunar mountains.[38] Precision drawings of objects and animals viewed under the microscopes also necessitate the taking of minute angular measurements by means of a micrometer eyepiece mounted in the focal plane of the objective lens. Although moving-wire micrometers were in use in France and England in the 1660s, both Hooke and Thomas Sprat attribute the perfection of their use for fine measurement in telescopes and microscopes to Wren.[39] Moray, however, does not suggest that the King's interest could be excited by the precision instrument – it is the 'curiosities' artfully created by means of the micrometer gauge that can be counted on to arouse Charles's interest.

In July Wren responded. The scientific toys requested could not be completed in the time, because he did not have suitable technical assistance in Oxford. Instead Wren proposed some alternatives he could offer – a compilation which gives us a sense of the range and diversity of his personal talents:

The Act and Noise of Oxford being over,[40] I retir'd to myself as speedily as I could, to obey your Lordship and contribute something to the Collection of Experiments design'd by the Society, for his Majesty's Reception. I concluded on something I thought most suitable for such an Occasion; but the Stupidity of our Artists [technicians] here, makes the Apparatus so tedious, that I foresee I shall not be able to bring it to any Thing within the Time propos'd: What in the mean while to suggest to your Lordship I cannot guess; the Solemnity of the Occasion, and my Solicitude for the Honour of the *Society*, makes me think nothing proper, nothing remarkable enough.

For myself, I must profess freely, I have not any Thing by me suitable to the Idea I have of what ought to be perform'd before such an Assembly. Geometrical Problems, and new Lines, new Bodies, new Methods, how useful soever, will be but tastless in a transient Show. New Theories, or Observations, or astronomical Instruments, either for Observation or Facilitation of the Calculus [micrometer gauges], are valuable to such Artists only who have particularly experimented the Defects that these Things pretend to supply. Sciographical Knacks [perspective drawing devices], of which yet a hundred Varieties may be given, are so easy in the Invention, that now they are cheap. Scenographical, Catoptical, and Dioptical Tricks [examples of *trompe l'oeil*], require excellent Painting, as well as Geometrical Truth in the Profile, or else they deceive not. Designs of Engines for Ease of Labour, or promoting any Thing in Agriculture, or Trades, I have occasionally thought about divers, but they are not intelligible without Letters and References, and often, not without something of Demonstration. Designs in Architecture, &c. the few chymical Experiments I have been acquainted with, will, I fear, be too tedious for an Entertainment. Experiments in Anatomy, tho' of the most Value for their Use, are sordid and noisom to any but those whose Desire of Knowledge, makes them digest it.[41]

Wren's proposed solution is to 'retire back to something I have formerly produc'd', and he suggests the construction for the King's amusement of a compass, ingeniously constructed to remain stable in a coach travelling at speed, to be combined with a 'way-wiser' or odometer:

A Needle that would play in a Coach, will be as well useful to know the Coast and Way join'd with the Way-wiser [surveying device for measuring distance], as a pleasant Diversion to the Traveller; and would be an acceptable Present to his Majesty, who might thus as it were sail by Land. The Fabrick may be thus: In a Sphere of Glass of two Inches Diameter, half full of Water, cause a short heavy broad Needle fixed to a Chart [piece of card] to swim, being buoy'd up by the Chart, and both varnish'd; instead of a Cap and Pin, let the perforated Needle play upon a small Wire, or Horse-Hair, extended like a perpendicular Axis in the Glass-Sphere, whose Nadir being made weighty with Lead, and an Horizon as it were cemented to it, let it play in Circles like the Compass: Then let a hemispherical Concave containing the Sphere in its Circles, be hung upon Springs after this manner.

Suppose a Basis upon which are erected perpendicularly three stiff Brass-Springs, from the Ends of which Springs, are String strain'd, forming an equilateral Triangle, the Middle of whose Sides pass through three small Loops on the Brim of the concave, which therefore having on the Strings represents a Circle incrib'd in a Triangle. From the middle of the Basis arises a Worm-Spring fasten'd by a String to the Nadir of the Concave, drawing it down a little, and acting against the other three Springs. These Springs, I suppose, will take off at once much of both the downright and collateral Concussions, the Circles will take off Oscillations, the Agitations remaining will be spent in the Water, and still'd by the Chart; for thus we see a Trencher swimming in a Bucket keeps the Water from spilling in the Carriage: and the *Chinese* have their Compass swimming in water instead of Circles.

Lastly I would have all the Bottom of the Basis bristled round like a Brush, somewhat inclin'd, which is a cheap Addition and will ease it like a hundred Springs: It should be placed on the Middle of the Floor of the Coach, where by opening a Window you might see likewise the Way-wiser on the Pearch.

My Lord, if my first Designs had been perfect, I had not troubled Yr. Ld.ship with so much tattle, but with something perform'd and done: but I am fain, in this Letter, to doe like some Chymist, who when Projection (his fugitive darling) hath left him threadbare, is forced to fall to vulgar Preparations to pay his debts. I must needs acknowledge I am only indebted to the Society, but most particularly to Yr. Ld.ship, to whom I ow a double duty both as our President & as my very good Ld. & Patron.

The royal visit apparently never took place, nor do we know if a compass-cum-odometer was ever built from these clear instructions, for the King's personal use. Wren eventually did agree to complete the lunar globe, though he declined to undertake any more microscopic drawings. On 13 August, Moray wrote with a formal summons into the King's presence:

> Since my last I told the King you had Finished your Lunar Globe, and desired to know what are His further Commands; and he commanded me to let you know, He would have you bring It Hither to Him. I have also to tell you, that in complyance with your desire to be eased of the further Task of Drawing the Figures of Small Insects by the help of the Microscope, we have moved His Majesty to lay His Commands on another, one *Vander Diver*; and we have also perswaded Mr. *Hook*, to undertake the same Thing. This is all the trouble you shall now have from – my worthy friend, – yr. humble Serv[an]t R. Moray.[42]

Wren attended the King as instructed, and presented the globe, which was made of pasteboard, moulded in relief and painted, with a scale in miles, and which bore the courtly, contrived inscription: 'To Charles the Second, King of Britain, France and Scotland, for whom Dr. Christopher Wren has created the new world of this Selenosphere, because, for one of His magnitude, "one [world] is not enough".'[43]

The lunar globe succeeded in drawing a satisfactory amount of attention to the activities of England's virtuosi. Christiaan Huygens, recently returned to The Hague from his first visit to London, was given a graphic account of the globe by Oldenburg (who, to his chagrin, had not yet seen it himself):

> As for Mr Wren's moon, he gave it to the King without showing it to the company, which, however, ordered him to make another, a little larger, to be kept in our college for the Society. I have not yet been so fortunate as to see it, but I shall do so in a few days and then shall answer your questions about its details. I have heard that is is a globe which so accurately represents the Moon that on it are visible all the Moon's inequalities, heights, depths, seas, river, islands, continents, etc., exactly as Mr. Wren saw all

Portrait of Wren, surrounded by his scientific instruments and
holding the ground plan of St Paul's.

these things with the telescope during one whole lunation; thus
this artificial globe presents, according to its various positions
with respect to the Sun, all the different parts of the Moon,
exactly as they appear in the heavens.[44]

Huygens made sure to see it on his next visit, and described it as 'very
pleasant to look at, with all its marks and little round valleys'.[45] So did
visiting noblemen Balthasar de Monconys and Samuel Sorbière. Sorbière
reported that 'His Majesty put me upon admiring it.' The lunar globe
is represented in the foreground of a portrait of Wren which now hangs
in the Sheldonian Theatre in Oxford.[46]

Although credited to the individual 'genius' of that royalist prodigy,
Wren, the three-dimensional lunar globe was, nevertheless, derived from
Wilkins, and produced by Wren under his direction. In his 1657 inaugural
lecture at Gresham College Wren had already remarked that it was possible
to 'depict the moon with more Accurateness, than we can our own Globe'.
The idea of 'mapping' the moon just like the earth, to show 'that on it are
visible all the Moon's inequalities, heights, depths, seas, rivers, islands,
continents, etc.',[47] comes straight from Wilkins's early work:

The central argument [of Wilkins's *A Discourse Concerning a New World and Another Planet in Two Books* (1640)] was borrowed from Galileo: the moon is not a shining disk or whatever else men might have imagined, but a world with natural features much like the earth.[48]

The microscopic pictures, minutely representing a flea and a louse, as we already know from Matthew Wren's reply to Harrington's *Oceana*, had been prepared by Wren for meetings of Wilkins's Wadham club at Oxford in the 1650s. Robert Hooke, who did indeed take over the project from Wren, wrote in the preface to his best-selling *Micrographia, or Physiological Descriptions of minute Bodies made by the Help of magnifying Glasses* (1665):

> By the Advice of that excellent Man Dr *Wilkins*, I first set upon this Enterprize, yet still came to it with much Reluctancy, because I was to follow the Footsteps of so eminent a Person as Dr. *Wren*, who was the first that attempted any Thing of this Nature; whose original Draughts do now make one of the Ornaments of that great Collection of Rarities in the King's Closet. This Honour which his first Beginnings of this Kind have received, to be admitted into the most famous Place of the World, did not so much incourage, as the Hazard of coming after Dr. *Wren* did affright me; for of him I must affirm, that since the Time of *Archimedes*, there scarce ever met in one Man, in so great a Perfection, such a mechanical Hand, and so philosophical a Mind.[49]

All the same, the parties directly involved in the royal transaction to acquire the globe and technical drawings were Wren and the King (with Moray as royal intermediary), rather than Wilkins, or the newly established Royal Society. Responding to the King's personal summons, Wren took the lunar globe to him without pausing to exhibit it as his 'experiment' at one of the weekly meeting of the Royal Society (to whose foundation Council he had been nominated) at Gresham. Henry Oldenburg (already acting as self-appointed Secretary to the new Society) complained in a letter to Huygens of 7 September that Wren had gone directly to the King 'without showing it to the company'. A second,

William Brouncker, 2nd Viscount Brouncker, prominent courtier and President of the Royal Society from the issuing of its royal charter in 1662.

larger lunar globe requested from Wren by the Royal Society for its own Repository was never executed.

The group vigorously, and successfully, promoting the new Royal Society with the King consisted of elite 'returners', already well installed at Whitehall: these included Viscount Brouncker, Sir Robert Moray, Sir Paul Neile and the cousins Matthew and Christopher Wren. Wilkins, his reputation compromised by his highly visible collaboration under the Protectorate, stood back somewhat from this leading group of promoters during the early stages. Nevertheless he was, and remained, the single most significant figure in the setting up of the Royal Society, and its activities during the early years of the Restoration.

The records of these years show that Wilkins was busier than any other member in the Society's affairs. From the beginning until his death, he was re-elected to the Council each year; he also served continuously as one of the two Secretaries, another elective office (alongside Oldenburg), until he became Bishop of Chester in November 1668. He was occasionally referred to as Vice-President, although the statutes made no provision for such an office. As Secretary, he attended practically every meeting, and at most of them he was busy doing something: providing recent information, proposing experiments, chairing special committees, appealed to for advice, and engaged in the Society's endless fund-raising. He proposed a very large number of candidates for membership, and it was he who suggested that Robert Hooke be made curator, and proposed Nehemiah Grew as curator for the anatomy of plants. It was Wilkins who supervised the writing of Thomas Sprat's official *History of the Royal Society* in 1667.[50]

MAKING THE SOCIETY 'ROYAL'

The first letters patent and royal charter were granted to the Royal Society in 1662. These gave the Society legal standing, entitling it to organise its own internal affairs through its President, Council and fellows, by means of appropriate laws, statutes and orders (as long as these were not contrary to the laws of the land). It was granted permission to meet in London, the right to appoint printers and engravers, and the power to authorise them to print matters relating to the Society (in other words, gave it its own 'imprimatur'). It was authorised to correspond with foreigners on scientific subjects (an entitlement which would prove vital during the various Dutch and French wars), and to build a college in London or within ten miles of London. It was also given the same rights as the Royal College of Physicians to carry out dissections of the bodies of executed criminals.[51] In a period of high political sensitivity, these were significant rights, amounting to an endorsement of the collaborative, non-partisan basis on which the Royal Society was established. A roll-call of the first hundred members (roughly down to the time of issue of the royal charter), bears this out. It consists of most of the members of the Oxford and London pre-Restoration scientific circles, with the addition of senior courtiers and returning aristocrats prominent in the circle around Charles II, many of whom had dabbled in scientific activities abroad during the 1650s.[52]

Wren himself wrote a draft for the Society's charter. Although its wording was not that favoured for the final document – something rather more florid was agreed in the end – it perfectly captures his aspirations for a 'company' of scientists.[53] Reflecting his own adolescent experience in Oxford, when the team activities of the Oxford club had rescued Dean Wren's son, he described with characteristic clarity the benefits of collaboration for the community as a whole:

> The Way to so happy a Government, we are sensible is in no Manner more facilitated than by the promoting of useful Arts and Sciences, which, upon mature Inspection, are found to be the Basis of civil Communities, and free Governments, and which gather Multitudes, by an *Orphean* Charm, into Cities, and connect them in *Companies*; that so, by laying in a Stock, as it were, of several Arts, and Methods of Industry, the whole Body may be supplied by a mutual Commerce of each others peculiar Faculties; and consequently that the various Miseries and Toils of this frail Life, may, by the Wealth and Plenty diffused in just Proportion to every one's Industry, that is, to every one's Deserts.[54]

Such were the Royal Society's aspirations. But much as in the case of the clubs which preceded it in Oxford and London, those aspirations greatly exceeded any real scientific successes in its early years. To that extent the Royal College of Physicians had been wise to distance itself from the Society at its formation, and Charles II's reported amusement was typical of a general feeling that the Society's activities amounted to 'much ado about nothing'. As Pepys reported the latter, in 1664: 'The King came and stayed [at the Duke of York's] an hour or two, laughing at Sir W[illiam] Petty, who was there about his [double-bottomed] boat, and at Gresham College in general ... for spending time only in weighing of ayre, and doing nothing else since they sat.'[55] To the extent that 'weighing of ayre' was precisely what Boyle and Hooke were doing with the air-pump, the Society's publicity was clearly getting through. To the extent that it was regarded as a bunch of amateurs – a mere diversion for the King – the assiduous courting of royal favour from the outset had undermined its claim to scientific seriousness. By the mid-1660s, attendance at Royal Society meetings had fallen off badly, and its income (consisting in any case only of its members' dues) had all but dried up.[56]

Behind the din of the promotional literature – of diverting lunar landscapes and hugely magnified fleas – we need to listen for the record of serious, collective scientific activities on the part of the ex-Oxford club in London. Both of Wren's much vaunted curiosities depended for their construction on high-resolution lenses, in whose development and manufacture Wren himself played a significant part. The process of transforming marvellous sights seen through telescope and microscope into attractive graphic representations required accurate devices for measuring minute distances across the field of vision of the apparatus's eyepiece. The graphic records themselves called for exceptional draughting skills.

The telescope-based activities of what became the Royal Society centred on Neile's long telescopes at Gresham College, and were structured around a rigorous programme of astronomical observation which, over the period in question, mapped and measured the surface of the moon through at least one complete cycle (for the globe). It was the same team which had carried out the systematic observations of Saturn in its various phases (including the collection and processing of data provided by other teams of astronomers, at other locations in Europe), as part of the continuing debate with Christiaan Huygens and others over the form of Saturn's ring.

Since Wren (like Moray and Neile) moved between the court circle and the Royal Society in the early 1660s, it was in part his fault that the Society gained a reputation as a mere diversion for his Majesty. He knew at first hand how to cope with the King's notoriously short attention-span, and was passionate enough about pleasing him to give serious effort to coping with his intellectual shortcomings.

Wren's lunar globe and his line-drawings of louse and flea have long since met the inevitable fate of royal playthings and disappeared. Other artefacts which formed part of the royalist propaganda of 1660 have been more lasting. On 29 May 1660, the night of Charles II's return to London in triumph, Sir Charles Scarburgh was, as usual, observing with his long telescope. The star alpha in the constellation Canes Venatici (the Hunting Dogs) seemed to shine more brilliantly than he had ever seen it before, and he immediately renamed it Cor Caroli – the Heart of Charles I. Cor Caroli continues to shines brightly, to the left of the Big Dipper's handle, at the centre of a flat triangle of stars, and continues to bear its celebratory Restoration name.[57]

Royal Society members themselves agreed that one of the problems for the Society's recognition as a serious institution was its lack of a permanent home. In 1668 Henry Oldenburg, the Society's Secretary, confided to Robert Boyle that the lack of proper accommodation was one of the reasons why the Royal Society was not taken seriously: 'who are now looked upon but as wanderers, and using precariously the lodgings of other men'. What was needed was 'a certain place, where we may meet, prepare and make our experiments and observations, lodge our curators and operators, have our laboratory and operatory all together'.[58]

There were difficulties in finding the Society accommodation from the very outset – and some irony in the fact that this was a matter which had bedevilled all of Wilkins's attempts at a properly established scientific club since the 1650s. On 5 December 1660 it was suggested that the Royal College of Physicians would 'afford convenient Accommodation for the meeting of this Society'. On 12 December this proposal was passed to a small committee for further investigation: 'It was then referred to My Lord Brouncker, Sir Robert Moray, Sir Paul Neile, Mr. Matth: Wren, Dr. Goddard, and Mr. Ch: Wren, to consult about a convenient place for the weekely meeting of the Society.'[59] They confirmed the idea, suggesting that members of the Royal College should be admitted free of dues to the Royal Society. The proposal did not, however, find favour with the physicians and was abandoned.[60]

Behind their refusal to share their accommodation with the newer scientific foundation lay a deeper fracture, which impacted directly on Wren's activities. The Royal College of Physicians had continued to operate throughout the Interregnum (merely dropping the 'Royal' from its title), in spite of the arch-royalist William Harvey's continued association with them. The College had continued to promote organised research in clinical subjects – the Gulstonian lectures on pathology, for example, were given with great regularity throughout the 1650s. Regular dissections were carried out, and organised groups of researchers investigated 'arguments to confirm and advance that incomparable invention of Doctor *Harvey*, the Circulation of the Blood'.[61] Between 1651 and 1654 Harvey paid for a building for the College, a magnificent 'Museum', consisting of a library above and meeting room below, which he furnished sumptuously, and to which he donated many of his own books and dissecting instruments (these were the premises the Royal Society hoped to share).[62] Having weathered the previous political upheavals as a non-partisan organisation, the Royal College of Physicians was evidently reluctant to risk compromising itself with the new regime. Since Sir Charles Scarburgh was the most senior figure at the Royal College, however, Wren's leading role in the Royal Society effectively cut him off from one of his available routes to preferment.[63]

At the Royal Society meeting on 19 December 1660 it was resolved 'that the next meeting should be at Gresham Colledge, & so from weeke to weeke till further order'.[64] On 17 December, Hartlib wrote to John Worthington: 'Thus much is certain, that there is a meeting every week of the prime virtuosi, not only at Gresham College in term time, but also out of it, at Mr. Ball's chambers in the Temple.'[65] However, sending Worthington the latest news about the new Royal Society on 1 January 1661, Hartlib told him that the Society had moved back to Gresham, even though it was the vacation, and was meeting in Goddard's rooms there: 'Mr. Boyle, one of [the virtuosi] told me that for the present they are removed to Gresham Coll[ege], to Dr. Goddard's lodgings.'[66]

In September 1667, Wilkins made another attempt to realise his long-standing personal dream of a home for the Royal Society. He moved that a committee be appointed 'for raising contributions among the members of the society, in order to build a college'. Once again the proposal was mooted that the Royal Society and the Royal College of Physicians should pursue such a project jointly. This time it was the Royal Society who rejected the joint project, on the grounds that 'both the name of the place and the honour would be wholly the Physitians'. This was presumably because as direct Fire victims (the College building had been destroyed by the Fire) the physicians were entitled to public monies for rebuilding, and the completed building would therefore be a new 'College of Physicians' building.[67] Instead, first Hooke and then Wren was asked to produce plans for a Royal Society building, to be erected on ground adjacent to Arundel House on the Strand. In spite of considerable enthusiasm for the project, and a substantial sum raised, including £50 contributed by Willkins to start the subscription ball rolling, this attempt too came to nothing.[68]

This new attempt is documented in a series of exchanges between Wren and the Secretary of the Royal Society, Oldenburg in 1668. One half of these exchanges concerns yet another failed attempt to erect such a purpose-built home; the other concerns the Society's emphatic commitment to leaving a lasting legacy in the form of properly recorded breakthroughs in fundamental topics in science and mathematics. In Oldenburg's mind, as in Wren's, legacies of both kinds were vital as fitting memorials to representative individuals and institutions.

The Society had moved temporarily to Arundel House, a property which belonged to Henry Howard, grandson of the great collector (and Evelyn's patron), Thomas Howard, Earl of Arundel, following the requisitioning of Gresham after the Fire. In May 1668 Howard agreed to convey to the Society a piece of land alongside the main house, on which to build its own meeting rooms, library and museum or repository.[69] At the beginning of June 1668, Wren was asked by the Royal Society to 'attend Mr. Henry Howard at Oxford about the draught of the society's buildings'.[70] On 7 June Wren replied to Oldenburg:

His honour Henry [Howard] of Norfolk was extreamely obliging to us in his returne this way. . . . When I waited upon him, he tooke delight to shew me some Designes he had thought of himselfe for your buildings, & commanded me to trace out to him what I had considered, the same in effect I shewed you in London. . . .

The Designe is indeed somwhat greater then was proposed, as being 100 foot long & 30 foot broad, wch. length Mr. Howard doth not scruple to allow you.

It containes in the foundations first a Cellar, & a fair Elaboratory, then a little shop or 2 for forges & hammer workes with a Kitchin & litle larder. In the first story it containes a Vestibule or passage-Hall leading through from both streetes, a fair Roome for a Library & Repository wch. may well be one roome placing the bookes after the moderne way in glasse presses, or if you will divide the roome with pillars it will the better support the floor of the great roome above it, & soe place the presses for bookes in one part & the presses for rarities in the other: upon the same floor is a parlor for the house keeper: & from the Vestibule the great Staire leades you up to the antichamber of the great roome & noe higher: the great Roome for the meeting is 40 foot long & 2 stories high, divided from the Antichamber by a Skreen between columnes, soe that the whole length in case of an entertainment may be 55 foot: upon the same floor is the Councell roome & a litle closet for the Secretary.

[I]n the 3rd story is 2 chambers with Closets for the Curators & backstaires by them wch. lead from the bottom to the top, one of the chambers being over the great staires, upon the same floor is a Closet or Gallery over the antiroome looking down into the great roome very usefull in case of Solemnities. the 4th story is the Timbers of the roofe wch. being 30 foot wide & to be leaded cannot be firme without bracing it by partitions to the floor below. these partitions are soe ordered as to leave you a little passage gallery the whole length of the building for tryal of glasses and other experiments that require length, on one side of the Gallery are litle shops all along for operators, on the other side are litle chambers for operators & servants. the platforme of Lead is for traversing of Tubes & instruments & many experiments, in the middle rises a Cupolo for observations, & may be fitted likewise for an anatomy Theatre, & the floores may be soe ordered that from the top into the Cellar may be made all experiments for hight.[71]

The person brokering the land deal between Henry Howard and the Royal Society was Evelyn. He had served Howard's grandfather, Thomas Howard (as had Inigo Jones), and accompanied him on his European travels in the 1640s, prior to the Earl's death in 1646. The civil wars and sequestrations of the Commonwealth period meant that at the Restoration the Howard family were almost £200,000 in debt – their wealth in assets and artworks largely dispersed and lost.[72] On an occasion when Evelyn visited Henry Howard to inquire whether he was prepared to part with any of the Raphael cartoons 'and other Drawings of Raphael & the great masters', Howard's answer was that 'he would part with & sell any thing for mony', 'but that the late Sir Peter Lely (our famous painter) had gotten some of his best'.[73] The Howards were, in addition, a prominent Catholic family, whose activities after the Restoration were closely watched (Henry's uncle, Stafford, was executed as part of the Popish Plot of 1678). Howard, therefore, had as strong a vested interest as the Royal Society in a building associated with Arundel House which would be a memorial to

Diarist John Evelyn, who had travelled widely on the continent of Europe in the service of Thomas, Earl of Arundel, before the Commonwealth period, and who after the Restoration became a minor official in the court of Charles II.

a great family (now apparently in decline), just as other learning-related buildings, like the Sheldonian Theatre and the Ashmolean Museum in Oxford, immortalised the names of their chief benefactors.

Wren's plan was pronounced over-ambitious and too costly. In June 1668 the Royal Society looked at more modest plans from the Wren office, which Hooke presented on 29 June. Preliminary contracts were even drawn up for the supply of timber. Nevertheless, insufficient funds were raised for the project, and by spring 1669 plans for the building of a permanent home for the Royal Society had once again been shelved.

At exactly the same time that Oldenburg, on behalf of the Royal Society, was negotiating with Wren over designs for a Society building, he was also proposing that Wren make an equivalent contribution to the enduring intellectual reputation of the Society. On 29 October 1668, Oldenburg asked Wren to make a formal presentation of his mathematical laws of motion:

On Thursday last at ye publick meeting of the R. Society it was proposed by some, yt there might be made experiments to discover ye nature & laws of motion, as ye foundation of Philosophie and all Philosophical discourse, to wch proposall wn it was mentioned by others, yt both you and Monsr Hugens had considered that subject more yn many others, & probably found out a Theorie to explicate all sorts of experiments to be made of that nature, I was commanded to desire you, as well as Monsr Hugens, in the name of ye Society, yt you would pleas to impart unto them wt you had meditated & tryed on ye sd argument, assuring yourself, yt these communications of yours shall be registerd by the Society as your productions, and stand in their booke as one of the best monuments of your Philosophicall Genius.[74]

Five days later Wren replied:

I received yours of the 29th. & presently looked out those papers of the Experiments that concerned the Lawes of Motion arising from collision of hard bodies. I found them somewhat indigested as I left them at first. & I could be glad if you would give me a little time to examine them, & in the middle of terme & some businesse at this time, I have but litle leasure. Yet I have noe doubt of the truth of the Hypothesis, but of some of the Experiments wch. I would trie over again. I suppose you may know whither Mr Hugens hath don any thing of this nature or not. if you know it, be pleased to tell me, for I would not *actum agere* [work needlessly].[75]

There followed a series of exchanges between Wren and Oldenburg, and between Huygens and Oldenburg, in which each tried to hedge his bets, and to see the other's work in writing before committing himself finally to paper.[76]

Like the attempt at providing a monumental building for the Royal Society, this attempt at a lasting legacy in the form of the generalised laws of motion also lapsed, left inconclusive and unresolved, without adequate record. It was left to Sir Isaac Newton eventually to produce those laws – the Newtonian laws of motion indeed serving as an enduring legacy to the work of the early Royal Society. It was also, ironically, under Newton that the Royal Society finally secured its physical premises.[77]

The Royal Society did not acquire a permanent home during

Wilkins's lifetime, nor, indeed, during the lifetime of Hooke, remaining at Gresham College (with a brief move to Arundel House on the Strand after the Fire of London, when the buildings were requisitioned under emergency measures as the meeting place for the Corporation of London). While Wren followed two career paths simultaneously for most of the second half of the seventeenth century, the most striking difference between the two domains lay in their relationship with masonry. His career as architect and Surveyor of the King's Works involved creating permanent, monumental buildings; that as a scientist was handicapped by the fact that the Royal Society was unable to provide itself with any accommodation of its own.[78]

ROBERT BOYLE, ROBERT HOOKE AND ANGLO-IRISH AFFAIRS

In the first year following the Restoration, Wren moved from part of a supporting cast for the main scientific characters to the position of lead player (and official star) in the Royal Society. Robert Hooke did not. It is at this point that Hooke's career path diverges dramatically from that of his lifelong friend Christopher Wren. Hooke must have been as delighted as any other diehard royalist at the return of Charles II. But for him there was no question of the sudden catapulting into high places, or tempting career offers, of the kind that showered upon Wren. During the crucial period 1659 to 1661, Hooke continued to work as Robert Boyle's paid scientific assistant or operator, while Boyle moved between his home in Dorset, his Oxford lodgings and his sister Lady Ranelagh's house in London, at all of which locations he had fully equipped and staffed scientific laboratories.

This is the period during which Boyle's famous air-pump was developed – a piece of equipment designed largely by Hooke (based on a much less satisfactory continental prototype), and which only he could ever operate successfully. Thus when Evelyn says that he saw the air-pump in operation at Mr Boyle's London home in 1660 we have to assume that Hooke was there too.[79] Equally, when Wren wrote to Moray in 1661 that he could complete neither his lunar globe nor his collection of microscopical drawings for the King's proposed visit to the Society, because 'the Stupidity of our Artists [technicians] here [in Oxford], makes the Apparatus so tedious, that I foresee I shall not be able to bring it to any Thing within the Time propos'd', Hooke may already have been one of those he had consulted.

Still, in terms of his prospects after 1660, Hooke did turn out in the end to have been fortunate in the employer John Wilkins and Thomas Willis had found for him in 1654. For Robert Boyle, too, had a boyhood history which linked him directly to the intimate court circle of Charles I and his son, and which ensured that his position would be secure and comfortable, following the King's return. He, like Wren, had had his taste of Stuart court life at its most charmed moment, 1638 – the year in which the eight-year-old Prince Charles was made a companion of the Order of the Garter.[80] As a result, through the combined good offices of Wren and Boyle, Hooke, too, eventually found his way to a career and a public prominence he could never have expected under the Protectorate.

Boyle was the fourteenth of fifteen children of Richard Boyle, first Earl of Cork, and the seventh son.[81] His father was an English 'adventurer' who had made his fortune in Ireland and who rose to become one of the richest and most influential men in Britain and Charles I's Lord High Treasurer in Ireland.[82] As his youngest son, Robert had both substantial wealth and complete career flexibility (his elder brothers had taken care of the family titles and responsibilities).

Robert Boyle's personal fortunes were closely tied to those of his slightly older brother Francis, with whom he spent four years being educated at Eton. In 1638, when Francis was fifteen, and Robert going on ten, an advantageous marriage was arranged for Francis, to one of Queen Henrietta Maria's ladies in waiting, Elizabeth Killigrew. Robert and Francis went together to the Palace at Whitehall, to pay court to the bride, ahead of the main Boyle family party. The lavish wedding took place at the Palace shortly thereafter, in the presence of the King and Queen. Four days later, to the young bridegroom's disappointment, the Earl of Cork prudently arranged for his two sons to leave for France, on a Grand Tour which ended only in 1642.[83] Francis's new wife remained at court with the Queen.[84]

Where Elizabeth Boyle was during the Queen's shuttlings to and fro in the early years of the civil war we do not know, but in August 1646, when the situation for royalists had worsened dramatically with the fall of Oxford, Francis and Elizabeth were granted a passport to leave England for The Hague with their entire household, presumably to join the court of Mary of Orange.[85] We know they were there for almost two years. In late February 1648, Robert Boyle went to The Hague, at relatively short notice, 'to accompany his brother *Francis* in conducting his wife from the *Hague*'.[86] Robert – the inveterate intellectual tourist – took the opportunity of visiting Amsterdam and Leiden, inspecting a number of places of scientific interest, including the famous anatomy school on which he reported back to Hartlib.[87] He was back in England by Easter.[88]

The real reason Robert Boyle made the trip to Holland in 1648, however, was to help his brother Francis, and to hush up, as far as possible, a Boyle family scandal. In spring 1648 Francis Boyle's wife, Elizabeth Killigrew, was pregnant by the future Charles II – possibly the first of his many flings during his European exile.[89] Her daughter, Charlotte Jemima Henrietta Fitzcharles – one of a number of illegitimate children Charles later acknowledged – was brought up as a Boyle.[90] Since there was a court wedding at The Hague that autumn, which Francis and his wife might have been expected to attend, we can pinpoint the birth to late summer 1648. In October 1648, Frederik van Nassau-Zuijlenstein, the illegitimate son of the recently deceased Stadholder, Frederik Hendrik, married Elizabeth Killigrew's cousin, Mary Killigrew. The union was to prove particularly important politically for England and for the Dutch Republic, since it was to this couple (conveniently Anglo-Dutch, and Stuart sympathisers) that Mary of Orange entrusted the raising and education of her nine-year-old son William (later William III) in 1659.[91] Elizabeth Boyle went home before the wedding guests assembled, to avoid awkward questions being asked.

Pepys, who was very close to the negotiations just prior to the King's return, records in his diary for 20 March 1660 that he provided 'Mr Boyle' with 'an order for a ship to transport him to Flushing', evidently to meet the King. This can only have been Robert or Francis, since all the other Boyles already held titles.[92] Shortly after his Restoration, Charles II elevated Francis Boyle to the Irish title of first Viscount of Shannon. By contrast with his anglophile brother Robert, Francis took up virtually permanent residence in Ireland with his family thereafter.[93]

In the summer of 1648, Robert Boyle sat down to write *Seraphic Love* – a work referred to in the literature as marking a 'deep spiritual crisis at age 21'. In this semi-fictional series of letters to a jilted male lover and personal friend, Boyle meditates on women's wiles, and contrasts the woes of earthly love of woman to the sublimity of angelic love of God.[94] He also takes a personal vow of celibacy. Ten years later he was still adamant, in response to the uxorious Evelyn's extolling of the bliss of matrimony, and the advantages of the company of a good, educated woman, that celibacy was the only option for a person of intellectual seriousness.[95] Boyle published an expanded printed version of *Seraphic Love* in 1659, which proved extremely popular, and went through several editions.[96]

After the death of his father in 1643, Robert Boyle took up permanent residence at Stalbridge Manor in Dorsetshire, which he had inherited. Towards the end of 1654 his sister, Lady Ranelagh, found him suitable additional accommodation at Deep Hall in Oxford, so that he could participate fully in the work of the virtuosi in the Wilkins club there (when Wilkins left for Cambridge in 1659 the activities at Wadham transferred to Boyle's lodgings). By 1668 most of the key members of the Oxford group were in London, and Boyle moved in permanently with Lady Ranelagh, on Pall Mall. With her brother's arrival Lady Ranelagh's home – already a notable salon – became a haven for scientists and intellectuals. Throughout the 1670s and 1680s Wren visited the Boyles regularly, as did other prominent members of the Royal Society and court circle.[97]

Robert Boyle's first contact with the Oxford scientists came via Wren's protector, William Petty, whom he met shortly after the rescue mission to The Hague, in summer 1648. In June of that year Petty dedicated his double-writing instrument (over which he was involved in a patenting dispute with Wren) to Boyle:

> For my study and ends being enquiries into nature, and useful arts, and finding how ill my abilities to make experiments answer my inclinations thereto, I knew no readier way to become fat from your kind of knowledge, than by being fed with the crumbs that fall from your table.[98]

By 1651 Petty himself was in Ireland, first as Cromwell's physician, and subsequently as the leader of the Down survey. Unlike Boyle, Petty considered Ireland to be a suitable location for intensive scientific activities.[99]

Petty apparently cared for Boyle during one of his many recurring illnesses, and continued to take an interest in his health. On 15 April 1653 his correspondence reveals him taking Boyle to task for reading excessively – something his brothers and friends believe is damaging his health. Boyle is also reproved for hypochondria: Petty comments on 'your apprehension of many diseases, and continual fear, that you are always inclining or falling into one or the other', 'this fear being in itself a disease incident to all, that begin the study of diseases'. Tellingly, given Boyle's preoccupation with chemistry and therapeutics, Petty warns him against 'practising upon yourself with medicaments (though specificks) not sufficiently tried by those, that administer or advise them'.[100]

It was through Petty that Boyle was introduced to the Oxford club, and specifically to its organiser, the Warden of Wadham. Yet again, it was Wilkins's personality and demeanour which secured Boyle's commitment to the club (as against Petty's less genteel encouragement). After an early meeting with Wilkins Boyle remarked that Wilkins's 'entertainment did as well speak him a courtier as his discourse'.[101] It was Wilkins who attracted him to its milieu as one worthy of an Irish nobleman of his standing. On 6 September 1653, Wilkins wrote to Boyle (in a rare surviving letter): 'I should exceedingly rejoice in your being stayed in England this winter, and the advantage of your conversation at Oxford, where you will be a means to quicken and direct our inquiries.'[102]

Boyle established a long-term base in Oxford in 1655, responding to this direct invitation from Wilkins to add his experimental efforts to the Wadham group (Lady Ranelagh secured him appropriately grand and well-appointed lodgings near by).[103] He transferred a large amount of alchemical equipment from Stalbridge, some of which, to his disappointment, got broken in transit. With Boyle's arrival to join the Wadham circle, the aristocratic interest in chemistry and alchemy (at the same time being pursued by princes in the courts of Europe) joined the other types of scientific inquiry already being carried out there.[104] From then on he and Wren shared a scientific milieu, and many of the same scientific interests. And even before he settled in permanent accommodation in Oxford, John Wilkins had found him a laboratory assistant in the shape of Robert Hooke.

BUILDING ON A SMALLER SCALE –
HOOKE, BOYLE AND THE AIR-PUMP

Over the same period during which Willis, Wren and their colleagues, by means of anatomy and vivisection, were conducting medical research in questions deriving from Harvey's theory of the circulation of the blood, and associated anatomical questions concerning respiration, Boyle (with Hooke assisting) began mechanical experiments on the physical properties of respiration.[105] Boyle came to respiration as an experimental chemist, via his long-standing interest in the properties of nitre, and its function as a vital ingredient in air.[106] He had, furthermore, been interested in pneumatics since the 1640s – in early 1647 he wrote to Hartlib from Stalbridge that he had been reading Mersenne's account of a 'pneumatical engine', which would use compressed air to shoot a bullet. It might be possible, Boyle thought, 'by the help of this instrument to discover the weight of the air, which for all the prattling of our book-philosophers, we must believe to be both heavy and ponderable, if we will not refuse belief to our senses'.[107] By 1658, Boyle had heard of the German Otto Guericke's air-suction pump, which used a cylinder and piston with two flap valves to create a vacuum in an enclosure. He set Ralph Greatorex, a London instrument-maker and mathematician, and his own assistant Hooke to work on building a similar machine, with the added feature of a chamber with external access, so that experimental materials could be introduced into the evacuated space.

The impatient Hooke soon dropped his co-designer, pronouncing the device Greatorex produced for testing 'too gross to perform any great matter'. By early 1659 Hooke had built an air-pump to his own specifications, devising customised components as he needed them, and supervising their manufacture by another London instrument-maker. The completed pump consisted of a large glass receiver (about thirty quarts in volume) with a four-inch opening at the top through which experimental apparatus could be inserted. A brass cylinder with milled valves, in which a sucker could be made to rise and fall by turning a handle attached to a geared ratchet, was mounted on a wooden frame below the receiver. A stop-cock was inserted at the bottom of the receiver and a valve at the top of the cylinder.[108]

Boyle moved the air-pump to London in December 1659, and began public demonstrations there in 1660. Thus Boyle effectively used the air-pump to validate his public presence in London at the time of the Restoration. This in turn dovetailed nicely with the emerging Royal Society, which badly needed some impressive experimental evidence to show non-specialists that their activities could achieve striking practical results. Boyle's air-pump became the means of telling the story of the seamless transition from somewhat beleaguered private research in Commonwealth Oxford to full public recognition in the post-Restoration Royal Society. As Hooke recalled, towards the end of his life:

> At these [philosophical meetings in Oxford] which were about the Year 1655 (before which time I knew little of them) divers Experiments were suggested, discours'd and try'd with various successes, tho' no other account was taken of them but what particular Persons perhaps did for the help of their own Memories; so that many excellent things have been lost, some few only by the kindness of the Authors have been since made publick; among these may be reckon'd the Honourable Mr. *Boyle's Pneumatick Engine* Experiments, first printed in the Year 1660.[109]

In terms of research focus, Boyle's experiments conducted with the help of the air-pump belong side-by-side with those being carried out over the same period by Willis and Petty's group of anatomists. In the early 1660s Wren was an active participant in both teams, as was Hooke in the more modest role as 'operator':

> Boyle acceded to the growing volume of requests for information about [the air-pump] by dictating out, in the form of a letter to [his nephew] Dungarvan,[110] his *New experiments physico-mechanicall, touching the spring of the air, and its effects (made for the most part in a new pneumatical engine)*. He composed the book at Oxford in the late autumn, and finished it at an inn in Beconsfield, 20 December 1659, on his way from Oxford to visit his brother (and Dungarvan's father) the Earl of Cork. [Boyle's Oxford publisher, Robert] Sharrock saw the work through the press at Oxford during the winter and spring of 1660, while simultaneously supervising its translation into Latin.

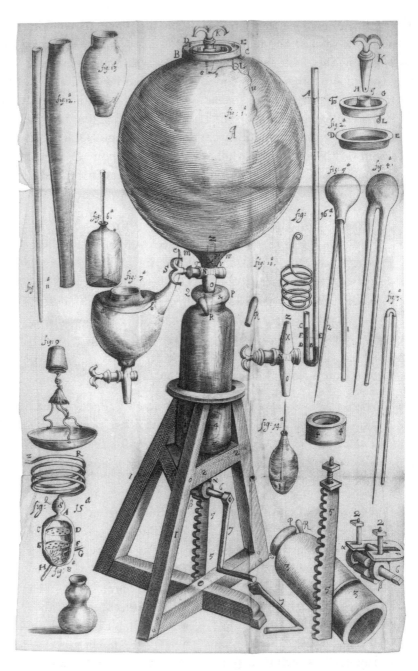

Boyle's air-pump for conducting experiments on the properties of air, and the nature of respiration, designed and built for him by Hooke, who was the only operator who could consistently make the apparatus work.

Boyle, in the meantime had taken his pump to London. There he worked on the *Sceptical chymist*, prepared the *Certain physiological essays* for publication, and showed pneumatic experiments to his friends. Robert Wood had the 'satisfaction' to see some of the experiments there in early 1660, and later, upon reading *New experiments*, noted approvingly that Boyle did not 'affirme all the truth he might have done'. Oldenburg wrote from Paris in March that the virtuosi 'long much' to see Boyle's book of experiments made with his 'pneumatic Engine'. Evelyn too visited Boyle in Chelsea, where he saw Boyle's '*pneumatic* Engine perform divers Experiments'. The printing of the book was completed by June, and the work was available in the booksellers by August.

Although a few of the preliminary experiments in this, Boyle's greatest single work, were done in London, most were performed at his lodgings in Oxford, where he had the benefit not only of Hooke's technical assistance, but of the 'presence of Persons, diverse of them eminent for their Writings, and all for their Learning'. For one crucial experiment Boyle specifically named Wallis, Wren, and Seth Ward as his 'judicious and illustrious Witnesses'. When his receiver once showed a luminous cloud-chamber effect upon sudden evacuation, Boyle immediately sent for Wallis, who was 'not then above a Bow shoot off', and who 'made haste to satisfy his Curiosity'. Repetition of the experiment at first failed to give the effect, and then unexpectedly the engine gave a flash and then subsequent ones, thereby convincing Wallis. Although some of the experiments might seem superfluous, they were not, Boyle assured his readers. They were done to answer objections brought up in the course of research by ingenious men whom, out of modesty, Boyle would leave unnamed. In all, it seems clear that Boyle's research agenda was carried out with the collaboration and conceptual guidance of those gathered at Deep Hall.[111]

The air-pump which Hooke built and repeatedly modified for Boyle became a celebrated feature of Royal Society meetings, since it perfectly fulfilled the royal requirements that science be entertaining – rather than a tedious succession of technical discussions and experiments. Just two days after Evelyn (an early Royal Society member) had attended Charles II's Coronation at Westminster Abbey on 23 April 1661, he went with equal ceremony 'to the Society where were divers experiments in Mr. Boyle's Pneumatic Engine'.[112] Perhaps because of its association with the King's triumphant return, the air-pump was much in demand on occasions when Charles II himself or foreign dignitaries like the Danish and Genoese ambassadors visited the Royal Society. It was produced on the unique occasion known to us on which a woman was permitted to participate in the Society's investigations – when Margaret Cavendish, Duchess of Newcastle visited in 1667 (according to Pepys she was 'full of admiration, all admiration').[113]

Pepys's own first taste of the Royal Society's activities, at the meeting he attended on the day he was proposed as a member by his Admiralty colleague Thomas Povey (Treasurer to the Lord High Admiral, the Duke of York) in February 1665, was a sequence of entertaining experiments on combustion making use of the famous air-pump. Hooke and Boyle were together in attendance to operate the pump and give their explanation of events. 'It is a most acceptable thing,' wrote Pepys in his diary, 'to hear their discourses and see their experiments, which was this day upon the nature of fire and how it goes out in a place where the ayre is not free, and sooner out where the ayre is exhausted; which they show by an engine on purpose'.[114]

The air-pump was extremely temperamental and difficult to operate. Hooke was the only person who could reliably get it to work. The opening to the glass cylinder had to be cemented shut each time it was used (various cements were tried); air entered through the imperfect seal between the plunger and its leather surround; the glass cylinder imploded or cracked. In extended correspondence between Hooke and Christiaan Huygens – the only other consistently successful operator of an air-pump – both men were forced to admit that on numerous occasions they had been unable to replicate a single successful experiment because of some failure in the equipment, a leaky valve, a collapsing receptacle, an imperfect seal.[115]

In November 1662, after a series of damaging fiascos when air-pump demonstrations had to be abandoned as a result of faulty components and incompetent demonstrators, the exasperated Oldenburg persuaded the members to appoint Hooke (on Wilkins's recommendation) as the first incumbent in the permanent paid post of Curator of Experiments

– a job tailored expressly to his talents. They first respectfully asked Boyle to release Hooke from his duties in his laboratory to allow him to accept the offer. Hooke nevertheless continued to carry out a wide range of services for Boyle, including seeing his London publications through the press and overseeing the engravings for them; Boyle apparently continued to pay him until 1664.[116]

Hooke's bravura as an experimentalist – his showmanship and sheer panache – stood the Royal Society in excellent stead in its early years, fulfilling as it did the need to keep the Society's activities before a court circle easily bored with learned treatises and speculative philosophy. On 7 May 1662, for example, Evelyn recorded in his diary that he attended Prince Rupert to a Royal Society meeting:

> I waited on Prince Rupert to our Assembly, where were tried several experiments of Mr. Boyle's *vacuum*. A man thrusting in his arm, upon exhaustion of the air, had his flesh immediately swelled so as the blood was near bursting the veins: he drawing it out, we found it all speckled.[117]

If occasion demanded, Hooke was quite prepared to carry out such experiments on himself. On one occasion in 1671 he devised a man-sized chamber for the air-pump, and volunteered to occupy it while it was evacuated. Fortunately for Hooke, the pump, as usual, under-performed, emptying only about a quarter of air from the container. The sensations he reported when he came out of his airless container were giddiness, deafness and pains in the ears.[118]

Hooke had a reputation throughout his life as a difficult, quarrelsome man, easy to offend, and a long-term bearer of grudges. He remained, throughout his life, devotedly loyal to both Boyle and Wren, even though his relationship with both men was complicated by the fact that he was their paid employee as well as friend. Long after the golden promises of Charles II's Restoration had evaporated, the intensity of their shared memories of the upheavals of the 1640s outweighed any possible differences between them.

The princes of Stuart blood who had left England as adolescents – Charles, James, Duke of York and Rupert Palatine – behaved assiduously, on their return, as if they were simply picking up the threads of their charmed boyhood lives, and as if none of the events of their exile had ever happened. They shared the suddenness and unexpectedness of their restored fortunes with their subjects. Boys who had spent their youth adjusting to disadvantage, revelled together in their new-found access to comfort and opportunity. The result was a culture in which the personalities of successful figures (whether restored nobility or self-made men) loomed unreasonably large – a life, after all, could readily be represented as a continuum in a way that the interruption to Stuart dynastic rule could not.

We have already noted how many of those 'returning' to power discreetly altered the record concerning their activities during the years since 1648. Now court artists like Sir Peter Lely, who had himself continued uninterruptedly painting portraits of prominent Commonwealth figures during the Interregnum, did a roaring trade in studied family portraits, splendidly representing the recently reinstated, or newly ennobled as if behind their wealth and comfort lay a long untroubled past, while in front lay an equally seamless future.

Meanwhile, the fortunes of another young Stuart across the English Channel closely followed the trajectory of that of his English uncles. William III of Orange, son of Charles II's sister Mary Stuart, was born in November 1650, ten days after the sudden death of his father. In spite of vigorous lobbying by Mary and the House of Orange, the baby was not appointed by the Dutch States-General as successor to his father, and in 1654, at the end of the first Anglo-Dutch war, Cromwell exacted from the States-General a pledge that the House of Orange would be permanently excluded from office. Thus William too found himself exiled from power during the Commonwealth and Protectorate periods. One of the first ventures into foreign policy by Charles II's Restoration regime in 1660 was to persuade the States-General to repeal the Act of Seclusion, allowing William of Orange to become Stadholder of the Dutch Republic.[119]

In 1660 William of Orange, too, picked up a lifestyle broken off summarily in the 1650s. For a matter of months he and his mother were able to enjoy the return to royal prominence she had experienced as a young bride; then she too died prematurely, succumbing to smallpox on her first visit to her newly reinstated brother Charles II in England. No one at this point imagined that the distraught, orphaned boy now head of the Dutch Republic would one day also become King of England.

In case we should be inclined to sentimentalise the regrouping of the survivors among Charles I's loyal servants and their families around the King, come the Restoration, we should take note of how strictly success in the public sphere after 1660 was tied to court patronage. Samuel Pepys found his way swiftly to significant preferment by a stroke of personal good fortune: his employer, Edward Montagu, Commander of the Fleet under Cromwell, was one of those strategically placed individuals whose support directly secured the King's return. Accordingly, within weeks of the King's landing in England, Montagu was made a Knight of the Order of the Garter, Privy Counsellor and Earl of Sandwich, and (as we have seen) given the post of Clerk of the Acts in the Navy Office for Pepys.[120]

Royalist gentlemen without Pepys's good fortune had to engineer their own way into favour. Among those who successfully did so were Elias Ashmole and John Aubrey – men whose diaries and memoirs, kept assiduously from the beginning of the Restoration period, have made sure that we are thoroughly familiar with them as, apparently, deservedly successful members of the new post-Restoration English Establishment. Neither had much in the way of marketable skills to offer the new regime, particularly if we compare them with the many talented individuals among the Cromwellians who failed ever to gain significant preferment after the Restoration – notably Wren's former mentor, William Petty.[121]

Ashmole's case is of particular interest here, because his initial introduction to the royal circle relied, as did Christopher Wren's, on his association with the preservation and continuity of the Order of the Garter.[122] Ashmole's own record of his actions during the early days of the restored monarchy gives a vivid sense of the combination of assets an individual needed to produce to find his way into favour: valuable pieces of information or documents allowing the new Stuart regime to piece together its continuity with the last one; some administrative experience and a willingness to take on tedious minor office; and something he could produce which had court entertainment value (in Ashmole's case his embalmed foetuses and other 'curiosities' masquerading as science). On the backs of these Ashmole cautiously chiselled himself out a future in the anterooms – if not the main corridors – of power:

April 11 [1660]. I returned to London.

June 6. 4.15 p.m. I first became acquainted with Sir Edward Walker Garter.[123]

16. 4 p.m. I first kissed the King's hand, being introduced by Mr. Thomas Chiffinch [Keeper of the King's Jewels, 1660].

18. 10 a.m. Was the second time I had the honour to discourse with the King, and then he gave me the place of Windsor Herald [the warrant is dated 22 June].

About this time the King appointed me to make a description of his medals, and I had them delivered into my hands, and Henry the VIIIth's closet assigned for my use.

July 19. This morning Mr Secretary Moris told me that the King had a great kindness for me.

Aug. 6. Mr Ayton, the King's chief gentleman-usher, came to me in the closet, and told me, the King had commanded that I should have my diet at the waiters' table, which I accordingly had.

10. 6.30 p.m. The Officers of Arms took their oaths, and my self among them, as Windsor Herald.[124]

14. This afternoon was the first public meeting of the Officers of Arms in the Herald's Office.

21. I presented the King with the three books I had printed, viz. *Fasciculus Chemicus*, *Theatrum Chemicum Britannicum*, and *The Way to Bliss*.

*

Sept. 3. About 11 o'clock my warrant signed for the Comptroller's Office in the Excise.

4. This morning his Majesty signed another warrant for me, for the Auditors place in the Excise.

*

29. This evening I had my warrant signed by the King for the precedency in the Herald's Office, as also a warrant to the Lord Treasurer to admit me into the Comptroller's place of Excise. Prince Rupert also arrived at London.

Oct. 9. This evening about 7 o'clock Sir Alan Broderick made me acquainted with the Lord Chancellor [Clarendon].

12. This morning I showed the King the young children which Dr. Warner had preserved. The one was a male infant about 4 months, who was cut out of a woman's belly in Covent Garden (she dying of a consumption) and had been (now four years past) luted up in a glass, and preserved by a liquor of his preparation from putrefaccon, the flesh not so much as rumpled, but plump as it was when taken out of ye womb. The other was two girls joyned together by the breast and belly (which monster was borne about the king's coming in), they were dryed, and preserved with spices.

Prince Rupert brought some ladies into my closet at Whitehall that morning after, to see them.

I carried them also to the Princes Royall [Mary Stuart, Princess of Orange, visiting from The Hague – she died of smallpox in December].

*

13. This day about 11 o'clock I brought Dr. Warner to the King, who kist his Majesty's hand, and presented him with an antique gold ring, wherein was a sapphire, and in it a head cut of one of the younger Constantines. His Majesty gave him thanks for this piece of antiquity, and commended very much his invencon of the liquor that had preserved the above monstrous child.[125]

Elias Ashmole is a particularly striking case of someone who did well out of the Restoration through his flair at 'remembering' a largely apocryphal golden Stuart past before the civil war. His lasting fame and 'name' rest (in the title of the Ashmolean Museum) upon his dubious acquisition of another man's lifetime collection of rarities, and his subsequent gifting of them to the University of Oxford.[126] Otherwise, he made a career out of ordering and cataloguing the King's possessions, recording the embellished history of the Garter regalia and ceremonies,

Elias Ashmole, antiquarian and archivist, author of a major, document-based history of the Order of the Garter, published in 1672, for which Wren's father and uncle both provided manuscript material.

and inventing elaborate rituals and ceremonies for royal occasions, from the installations of Knights of various revived Orders, to formal occasions at the universities, all of which would henceforth be regarded as 'authentic', ancient forms.[127] Even so, the officials within the Order of the Garter itself saw through Ashmole. Responding to one of many unsuccessful attempts Ashmole made to be appointed the official historiographer of the Order (eventually he published privately, at his own expense), the Chancellor of the Order Sir Henry de Vic expressed the view that:

> Nothing will Content Mr Ashmole unlesse hee may have all the partes of thee play hee must act Pyramus and thisbee, the beare and the Lyon, Moonshine, and the rest; he must putt out all the officers of the order out of their places, assume to himselfe the honor that is due to all the noble Companions nay indeed play the soveraigne and bee made dictator of this noble Order.[128]

It was because he failed utterly to get himself appointed to any official post associated with the Order of the Garter that Elias Ashmole eventually digested the remarkable body of Garter-related manuscripts he had collected during the Interregnum into his monumental printed Garter history, *The Institution, Laws & Ceremonies of the most Noble Order of the Garter. Collected and digested into one Body by Elias Ashmole of the Middle-Temple Esquire Windesor Herald at Arms. A Work furnished with variety of matter, relating to honor and noblesse,* a work which has, ironically, assured Ashmole some of the enduring reputation denied him by Charles II's entourage.[129]

Ashmole's exploitation of the Garter connection was only a qualified success. Still, Ashmole and Wren had enough in common to remind us how much Wren's career and enduring reputation depended on opportunities offered by his father's close association with the Order of the Garter – an association on which Wren himself was more than happy to capitalise.

Lastingly loyal to the memory of his deceased father, Wren, too, played his personal part in the elaborate fiction of a divinely ordered Stuart dynastic succession which straddled the Interregnum. The relevant incident concerns his old friend Seth Ward – the person Wren replaced as Savilian Professor of Astronomy at Oxford in 1661. Although, like Wilkins, decorum dictated that Ward should be deprived of his academic positions at the Restoration, he too had made his way through ecclesiastical preferment, starting with vicar of St Lawrence Jewry (1660–61 – subsequently held by Wilkins), and rising to Bishop at Salisbury in 1667 (a position he held until his death in 1689).

In summer 1668, shortly before he became Surveyor of the King's Works, Wren responded to a request from Ward, asking him if he would inspect the fabric of the Cathedral at Salisbury, with a view to renovations. Wren produced a report, which drew attention to various urgently needed repairs, particularly to the spire:[130]

Besides the declining of ye Spire from ye foundation it is also bended a little toward ye Top from its right line whether this proceeds from ye sinking below (the point of ye Spire being once carried off from its perpendicular) or whether it hath been since bowed by some tempest, or whither some violent tempest might not at once bend the top, and with ye same Concussion force downe the Pillars and foundation on that side (which is reasonable enough to believe because the Steeple being in heighth 9 times the breadth of its Basis at ye Foundation, any force above would be multiplied as in a Leaver and be 9 times as much upon ye Pillars) I say whichsoever of these were the cause twill be hard to determine; it will be enough to advise the speedy cure, and because the Artist at first hath much trusted to Iron I should advise that this be likewise secured by Iron.

The place of bending is about ye upper Circle <or below it>, there let a curbe of Iron made of 8 peeces be fixed cleane round on ye outside and Joynted at ye corners after this manner and in ye middle of every side let there be an hole, then let 8 upright barres of 12 or 15 foot long with 3 holes in each barre (viz. at ye ends and in ye middle) be fixed to ye middle of each inside wall soe that ye middle hole of ye barrs may be keyed to ye middle hole of ye barres without, and likewise let both ye upper and nether ends of ye inward barres be anchored through the walls. The inward barres may be about 3 inches [broad] and $\frac{3}{4}$ thick. The outward barres $1\frac{3}{4}$ square, the pinne at ye corners made wedgewise to draw ye barres together better than 2 inches broad, at ye top and $\frac{1}{2}$ thick. *Note*, these Irons will be best wrought at some Port Towne where they worke Anchors and other large worke for Shipps for I have found by experience that large worke cannot be wrought sound with little fires and small bellowes.[131]

Wren's letter was carefully illustrated with beautifully executed drawings of the pieces of ironmongery, and technical devices for splicing beams and clamping masonry, which he was recommending. Armed with Wren's pictures an ironworker from 'some Port Towne' could indeed have manufactured the required ties and clamps.[132]

Here, confidently in dialogue with a fellow mathematician and ex-Oxford club member, Wren demonstrates his practical expertise in structural engineering – the kind of informed understanding (at least in seventeenth-century terms) of masonry loading, and how to compensate for non-alignment. The received wisdom is that Bishop Ward failed to raise the necessary funds for the iron brace for his steeple, and that we therefore have no way of knowing whether Wren's proposed correction for its slant would actually have worked. However, in a letter to David Gregory, advising on how to brace the fabric of the Bodleian Library against the massive load of the books, Wren wrote, in July 1700:

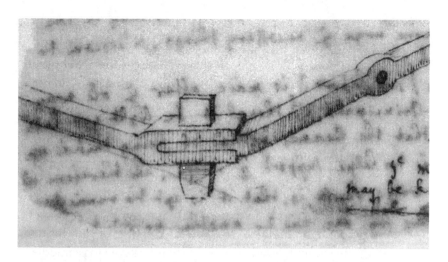

Sketch in Wren's hand of a purpose-made piece of ironwork for use in the repairs undertaken at Salisbury Cathedral for Bishop Seth Ward.

The substantiall way will be to brace each opposite buttresse to one another by two Rods of Iron keyed together upon the outsides or Backs of the Buttresses, these must be good Swedish Iron inch & halfe square, three lengthes will reach over: The skill of the Smith will be to make the Joyntes as trew as a Joyner would make them in wood, leaving a litle liberty for the keys made wedgewise to draw a litle, and bind all to the Crosse barres upon the Backs of the Buttresses. . . .

[B]y such methods I braced the lofty Spire of Salisbury, after the Lightning had rent it with Cracks of 200 foot long; patternes were first made exactly in wood of the full bignesse, which were wrought at Porchmouth by Anchorsmithes, who have the best skill to make great Iron worke sound.[133]

It appears from this that Wren's remedial work on the Salisbury spire was indeed carried out as advised.

Ward benefited from another area of Wren's expertise also. In the course of his visit, Wren seems also to have discussed with Ward the fact that, according to the Garter records, the Bishop of Salisbury had been, *ex officio*, Chancellor of the Order of the Garter – a title which, in addition to the royal honour it carried, entitled the incumbent to pecuniary benefits. Somewhere along the line, the entitlement had been allowed to lapse. Although some efforts had been made to reinstate the connection between Garter Chancellor and bishopric, 'the Scotch War shortly after breaking forth, and troubles growing high at home' meant that nothing was subsequently done about the matter.[134]

Shortly after Wren's visit, Bishop Ward petitioned Charles II. As Ashmole recounts in his *History of the Order of the Garter* of 1672, the office was duly restored to him:

> After which we find not, that the Knights-Commissioners met, either upon this or any other Affair relating to the Order, before the Feast of St. George, begun to be held at Windsor the 20. of May, an. 14. Car. I. and to that, being added the Ceremonies of the present Soveraign's Installation, the Bishop of Salisbury thought it not convenient to interrupt any part of the great Solemnity, with the consideration of this Affair; and the Scotch War shortly after breaking forth, and troubles growing high at home, the further prosecution was laid aside, and not revived until the 19. of November, an. 21. Car. 2. [1669] when Seth Ward now Lord Bishop of Salisbury took encouragement upon the former grounds and the Soveraign's favour, to set on foot this Claim by a petition in Chapter then held at Whitehall, where after a full debate and consideration had of the justness of his Claim, he obtained the following Decree for re-establishment of this Office on the Bishop of that See upon the first vacancy.[135]

When the post next fell vacant, Seth Ward was allowed officially to put his case for *ex officio* tenure of the position, and was duly appointed. He was inordinately proud of his newly regained Garter title (not to mention its perquisites). He included it in the inscription he had carved prominently on the lintel of the Almshouses at Buntingford, Hertfordshire which Hooke later designed and built for him.[136]

SPENDING TIME ON RUBBISH

The first executed building which can be confidently attributed to Wren is the chapel he undertook to design and build for his uncle Matthew Wren in 1663, at Pembroke College, Cambridge – Bishop

Wren's undergraduate *alma mater* (completed 1665). Once again, we may surmise that Matthew Wren junior had a hand in this piece of patronage, which made a relative unknown in architecture his father's preferred choice.

This first solo commission of Wren's is indicative of trends to come in his mature architectural work in a number of ways. In the first place, his appointment underlines the extent to which, for everyone, the early years of Charles II's reign were self-consciously years of repaying personal debts. Wren had rescued his cousin, Matthew; Matthew's father repaid the debt as soon as he was able (the story has it that he allocated the first monies he received as restored Bishop of Ely to the building of his thanks-offering chapel at Cambridge). Secondly, Pembroke Chapel already displays Wren's career-long commitment to the technical, structural side of building. A beautifully constructed wooden model survives, designed to show the precise form of the roof trusses spanning the simple rectangular space. In the Chapel as built, the roof trusses precisely match those specified in the model – here as ever afterwards Wren knew what he was doing, and knew how to pick carpenters and builders who would take him at his word where structure was concerned.[137] Finally, Pembroke Chapel, particularly the façade presented to the world at large (beyond the college) on to Trumpington Street pays deliberate homage to Dutch Republic building of the 1640s and 1650s – a feature of Wren's mature designs to which we will have occasion to return. English building of this period, like English culture in general, tacitly fused and absorbed the influences of the two territories in which royalist exiles had spent their time abroad – the restrained classicism of the Dutch Republic and the more flamboyant classical revival buildings of Louis XIV's France. Designed before Wren's trip to Paris, Pembroke College Chapel is particularly indebted to the former.[138]

Although Pembroke Chapel was Christopher Wren's first building, it was Matthew Wren senior's second. In the 1630s – at the height of Archbishop Laud's power – Bishop Wren had personally overseen the design and construction of a flamboyantly baroque chapel at Peterhouse, Cambridge, across the road from Pembroke (completed and dedicated in 1633).[139] His choice of his nephew as his architect may have had a certain pragmatism about it. In 1663 Matthew Wren was seventy-eight – already a remarkable age considering his eighteen years of imprisonment, and the successive deaths of almost his entire family during that

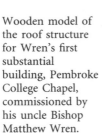

Wooden model of the roof structure for Wren's first substantial building, Pembroke College Chapel, commissioned by his uncle Bishop Matthew Wren.

period. If, as suggested in the last chapter, Christopher Wren had already helped expedite essential building alterations at Whitehall for Charles II, and had demonstrated there his skill at anticipating technical construction problems, as well as directing and organising the work of teams of labourers, that may have decided Bishop Wren in his choice. In the event his confidence was not misplaced. The Chapel took a mere two years from conception to completion, and was dedicated during Wren's absence in France. Bishop Wren died two years later, in 1667, and was buried, with all ceremony, beneath his new Chapel; five years later, in 1672, his son Matthew was interred beside him.[140]

Fortunately, with typical foresight, Wren had made sure that the laying to rest of Bishop Wren would not disturb the fabric of the new Chapel. A pavement flag immediately outside gives access to a purpose built vault beneath the altar.[141]

In 1711, a few years before his retirement, Wren reflected on his long experience of sacred buildings, in a letter to a fellow member of the Commission for Building Fifty New City Churches:

> I could wish that all Burials in Churches might be disallowed, which is not only unwholesom, but the Pavements can never be kept even, nor Pews upright. And if the Church-yard be close about the Church, this also is inconvenient, because the Ground being continually raised by the Graves, occasions, in Time, a Descent by Steps into the Church, which renders it damp, and the Walls green, as appears evidently in all old Churches. It will be enquired, where then shall be the Burials? I answer, in Cemeteries seated in the Out-skirts of the Town.[142]

By 1711 separate mausolea for the wealthy, in designated burial sites, were the vogue.[143]

SECULAR PROJECTS FOR CLERICAL PATRONS —
THE SHELDONIAN

Wren's second major commission, the Sheldonian Theatre at Oxford, although a secular building, was also closely linked with Restoration High Anglican aspirations, and what, at the time, must have seemed like a return to the Laudian tenor of university organisation swept aside during the Commonwealth and Protectorate periods. Proposed by senior Oxford clerics, its chief benefactor was Gilbert Sheldon, who had become Master of Wren's Oxford college, All Souls, shortly before the Restoration, then Dean of the Chapel Royal, Bishop of London, Master of the Savoy and a member of the Privy Council immediately thereafter. Staunchly conservative in Church matters, he had been catapulted from retirement and marginality to become the most powerful cleric in England, with the ear of the King himself, in a matter of months. When he was further promoted to Archbishop of Canterbury on the death of Juxon, the thanks-offering he chose for his old University was suitably magnificent.[144]

It may originally have been Wren's old Oxford friend John Fell (now Dean of Christ Church), who revived Archbishop Laud's proposal that the ceremonies conducted at Graduation in the University of Oxford ought to be clearly separated from Anglican liturgical rituals. Sheldon, indeed, showed relatively little interest in the building he had paid for (and never visited the completed theatre). Fell oversaw the project from conception to completion, and meticulously audited the accounts as it went along.[145]

On 16 April 1663, Oldenburg wrote to Evelyn:

Dr Wren hath brought to town ye modell of a Theater, to be built for ye Oxonian Acts, and for Playes also: wch ye King seeing this very morning, commended highly, and so did all others, yt are severe Judges of such matters. He is desired to shew it on Wednesday next to ye [Royal] Society, to have their approbation likewise.

A fortnight later Wren did indeed make a verbal presentation of his model of the Sheldonian at a meeting of the Royal Society. He was asked to provide in writing 'a scheme and description of the whole frame of it, to remain as a memorial among the archives of the society' (he didn't do so). In May the talk in London (suitably garbled by repetition, one gathers) was that 'Dr Wren has lately brought up to town with him the model of a theatre to be built at Oxford, and used for conferring degrees, dissection of bodies, and acting of plays.'[146]

Separating the Acts of Graduation from the church service celebrating their completion required that Graduation be held somewhere other than its customary location of St Mary's Church. Wren's brief was to design and build a purpose-built space of suitable grandeur and spaciousness. The building had a second and no less important function: its basement was to house the University printer and his presses.[147]

Procession, public performance, overblown oratory and colourful spectacle were the defining characteristics of the graduation ceremonies – the interior of Wren's Sheldonian Theatre fully met the specifications for these, creating an unusually large uninterrupted stage, gloriously roofed in the antique manner. The Sheldonian, like Pembroke Chapel, was rapidly under construction, thanks to the £1000 Sheldon put up to launch the project. Evelyn reported in his diary of 24 October 1664:

> to the New Theater, now building at an exceeding and royal expence by the Ld. Abp. of Canterbury to keepe the Acts in for the future, till now being in St. Mary's Church. The foundations had been newly laide and the whole designed by that incomparable genius my worthy friend Dr. Christopher Wren, who showed me the model, not disdaining my advice in some particulars.[148]

The site acquired for the Sheldonian Theatre was immediately adjacent to the Old Schools quadrangle and the Bodleian Library. Its most significant feature – and the one for which the building was renowned in Wren's day (hence the request for a permanent record of the 'model' from the Royal Society) – is its spanning ceiling. The received opinion (developed by contemporary writers) is that Wren based this structurally innovative form on a piece of applied mathematics carried out by John Wallis. It is therefore interesting to read Wallis's own account, included in *Parentalia*:

I did first contrive and delineate it, in the Year 1644, at *Queen's-college* in *Cambridge*. When afterwards I was made Professor of *Geometry* at *Oxford*, about 1650, I caused it to be framed of small Pieces of *Timber*, prepared by a *Joiner*, and put together by myself.

This I shewed soon after to divers in *Oxford*, and particularly to Dr. *Wilkins*, then *Warden* of *Wadham* College. After the King's *Restauration*, I caused another to be made; and in the Year 1660, presented it to his Majesty, who was well pleased with it, and caused it to be reposited in his Closet.

On the Model first-mentioned, I read two publick *Lectures* at *Oxford*; the one, in the Year 1652, as to the Construction of it; the other, in the Year 1653, as to the Computation of what Weight every Joint of it sustains; whereby it might be the better judged how far it may be safely practised. The greatest Weight charged on any one Joint, doth not amount to ten times the Weight of one Beam; and the greatest Weight borne by one Beam, not to seventeen times its own Weight: And even this, not laid all on the same Part, but distributed to several Parts of it. . . .

I do not know, that yet it hath been reduced to Practice, in more than four Pieces in this Form. Such is one of the Floors in the *Tower* of the public Schools at *Oxford*: The Breadth whereof, to the Length of the Beams, is as three to two. But may doubtless be continued much further; especially in such a Roof, as is not to bear much more than its own Weight.[149]

The Schools quadrangle was the location on which Wren may have cut his architectural teeth, around 1654, refurbishing the Tower as an Observatory and the adjoining rooms as meeting rooms and a repository, for Wilkins's 'College for experiments et mechanicks', at a cost of £200 to the Warden of Wadham.[150] The roof of the Old Schools, however, was structurally completely different from the one devised by Wren for the Sheldonian. As described by Wallis, and clarified by an accompanying diagram taken from Serlio, a copy of which survives in one of the manuscript versions of *Parentalia* compiled shortly after Wren's death and now in the Royal Society Library in London, Wallis's was a lattice of short wooden beams, joined by tongue-and-groove joints at right angles to one another.[151]

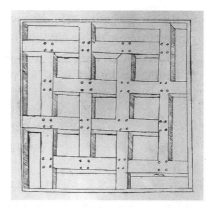

Drawing from the Royal Society manuscript copy of *Parentalia* of Wallis's diagram for a structurally innovative spanning roof or floor, borrowed from Serlio's treatise on architecture.

Nevertheless, it appears from Wallis's account that, before the Sheldonian Theatre, Wren and Wallis had already experimented with a modest version of an unsupported, spanning floor whose breadth considerably exceeded the length of the beams from which it was built, to provide an open space, while capable of supporting Wilkins's telescopes and other astronomical apparatus.[152]

A Pindaric Ode *In Theatrum Sheldonianum, et eius Architectum*, written for the elaborate performances which marked the opening of the Sheldonian in July 1669, celebrates a second extraordinary feature of the space Wren created – its supposedly perfect acoustics. The poem suggests that the open space produces no unwanted echoes, and returns voice and music with pleasing purity.[153] From his work with lenses, Wren may well have imagined that the half-cylinder form of the stage end of the Sheldonian would achieve perfect clarity at its focus (in fact, reflected sound and light behave in different ways).

Wren and his contemporaries were fascinated with the possibility of designing ideal performance spaces for voice and music. In June 1645 on their first afternoon together in Italy (the two had actually met once before in Holland), John Evelyn and Lord Arundel visited the garden of Alvise Cornaro in Padua, where, Evelyn records, they saw the casino, 'a room covered with a noble Cupola built purposely for Musique'. Evelyn also notes the use of earthenware jars in the walls as an acoustical device.[154] In his pre-Fire design for renovating St Paul's, Wren proposed a 'spacious dome' with a cupola, making the middle of the cathedral 'a very proper place for a Vast Auditory' (he held that one of the essential qualities of an Anglican church was an 'auditory' in which every member of the congregation could hear the preacher). In the light of Evelyn's remarks that a 'noble Cupola' produces a desirable space for music, we might ask ourselves whether Wren's commitment to a cupola for St Paul's was linked, in his own mind, not only to the visual aesthetic, but also to an idea of a perfect acoustic space for worship.

RESTORING ST PAUL'S

Matthew Wren's and Gilbert Sheldon's material contributions to their old academic institutions were more than mere architectural gestures. Both men meant to leave marks on the urban landscape – enduring physical traces of the glorious reign of Charles II – which, like the monuments of Rome to which they loved to refer, would stand for posterity as evidence of the lasting importance of the restored Stuart dynasty. They also, it has to be said, saw to it that their own names would remain lastingly on the record. Once again the Roman example is a telling one. Roman emperors rose and fell, but the names of individuals remained lastingly linked to the monuments built under their auspices. When we talk about the Restoration revival of mature Roman classicism, this is an aspect of that revival to bear in mind.

Within a decade such ambitions looked like wishful thinking, but in the early 1660s they were very much of the moment. Christopher Wren was the man of that moment to carry such plans through to completion.

Among the public buildings whose survival seemed symbolic of a divinely willed continuity between the reigns of Charles I and his eldest son, St Paul's Cathedral – battered, but unbowed, still dominating London's skyline – occupied a special place. Even before the civil wars, the Cathedral was already a ruin, its record-height spire having been struck by lightning in the 1560s. The last commission for a large-scale public building carried out by Charles I's Surveyor of the Works, Inigo Jones, had been a refurbishment of the façade and nave.[155] During the Commonwealth and Protectorate periods there had been various proposals to put the redundant place of worship to new, secular use – precisely because its high italianate pillared portico and cavernous interior smacked of Papistry.[156]

The letter of 1661 from Sprat to Wren, warning him that he is in

Engraving of Old St Paul's from William Dugdale's post-Restoration
history of the Cathedral – the spire was destroyed by lightning in the
1560s, leaving a truncated tower, the portico was added for Charles I
by Inigo Jones.

trouble for neglecting his official duties as Savilian Professor in Cambridge, because of the time he is spending on the King's works in London, also already mentions work on St Paul's:

> The Vice-chancellor did yesterday send for me, to inquire where the *Astronomy Professor* was, and the Reason for his Absence, so long after the Beginning of the Term – I used all the Arguments I could for your Defence. I told him, that *Charles the Second* was King of *England, Scotland, France,* and *Ireland,* that he was by the late *Act* of *Parliament* declar'd absolute Monarch in these his Dominions; and that it was this mighty Prince who had confin'd you to *London.* I endeavour'd to perswade him that the drawing of Lines in Sir Harry *Savill's* School was not altogether of so great a Concernment for the Benefit of *Christendom,* as the rebuilding of St. *Paul's,* or the fortifying of *Tangier:* (for I understood those were the great Works, in which that

extraordinary Genius of yours was judg'd necessary to be employ'd).[157]

If, as Sprat's letter maintains, Wren was already involved with the structural surveying of St Paul's by the end of 1661, it was in response to lobbying of the King for the restoration of the Cathedral by Gilbert Sheldon. Sheldon, who had ridden out to meet Charles II at Canterbury on his triumphant return route from the coast in May 1660, was immediately made Bishop of London (Juxon, the aged pre-Restoration incumbent, was elevated to Archbishop of Canterbury, although because of his infirmity Sheldon officiated on his behalf at the Coronation of Charles II).[158] Sheldon had already been reinstated as Warden of All Souls College, Oxford (Wren's college since his appointment to a fellowship there in 1653) in March 1659, following the death of the previous Warden. If an intermediary figure was needed to bring Wren as practising geometrician with experience surveying buildings and drawing up plans to the attention of the King it was Sheldon.[159]

Sheldon's royalist, High Anglican credentials were impeccable, and largely responsible for his meteoric clerical rise after 1660. The aged Brian Duppa, the loyalist Bishop of Winchester, wrote to him on 11 August 1660: 'You are the only person about his Majesty that I have confidence in, and I persuade myself that as none hath his ear more, so none is likely to prevail on his heart more, and there was never more need of it.' A much told anecdote linking Sheldon's fortunes to those of Charles I in his last days captures the flavour of his own symbolic position in the restored Stuart regime. On 13 April 1646, Charles I wrote on a piece of paper for Sheldon (who was in attendance on the King during the siege of Oxford) a vow, to restore all Church lands and lay impropriations held by the Crown to their rightful owners, should he ever be restored to his 'just kingly rights'. Sheldon preserved the piece of paper 'thirteen years underground'. The story once again crucially emphasises continuity over the period of the Interregnum (the making of a promise by Charles I, later fulfilled by his son Charles II). Sheldon was with Charles I during the Indian-summer reign on the Isle of Wight in 1647–48, returning to Oxford in March 1648 to resist ejection from his post at All Souls by the Parliamentary Visitors.[160] He refused to leave the Warden's lodgings, and was finally removed by force and imprisoned (he was released at the end of 1648). Just as Dean Wren rescued and

Archbishop Gilbert Sheldon, staunchly royalist cleric, who became Archbishop of London, at the Restoration, and then Archbishop of Canterbury – he was chief bene-factor of the Sheldonian Theatre at Oxford.

preserved the precious Garter records throughout the Commonwealth and Protectorate periods, so Sheldon did the same for the Laudian statutes of the University of Oxford.[161]

In other words Sheldon was firmly on the conservative wing of the Church, and as such a leading light among the reinstated clergy. The ejecting and reinstating of key clerics took place at the very top of the hierarchy. Below figures like Sheldon, Juxon and Matthew Wren, lesser clergy remained in place. We should probably think of Christopher and Matthew Wren – eldest sons of key clergy figures of the old regime – as men who ordinarily would have taken orders and been preferred within the Church hierarchy. Under the extraordinary circumstances prevailing in 1660, however, they took higher qualifications in law and medicine instead, and were preferred in the secular domain, where suitable career opportunities could be made available more rapidly.[162]

We may, however, be looking unnecessarily high up the clerical hierarchy for the instigator of Wren's appointment at St Paul's. The surveying job may once again have come to Christopher Wren indirectly by way of his cousin Matthew. In 1659, after Matthew had dealt so successfully in print with James Harrington's attack on the Oxford club, Edward Hyde (in Brussels) wrote to Dr John Barwick (who was clearly close to the Wren family), asking if Matthew would undertake another print polemic, this time against Thomas Hobbes's *Leviathan*.[163] By the end of 1661, John Barwick was Dean of St Paul's, and could easily have proposed a Wren name as one of the surveyors of the Cathedral.[164]

In April 1663 letters patent were issued for a Royal Commission to oversee the repair and restoration of Old St Paul's. The tone of this document describes the undertaking in suitably reverential terms. The King instructs his Commission to rebuild St Paul's as the cornerstone of his Restoration – a return to Magnificence, after so much suffering 'by the iniquity of the late Times':

> Whereas Wee taking into our serious consideration the present state, and great decayes of the Cathedral church of St Paul in London, being the goodliest Monument, and most eminent Church of our Whole Dominions, and a principal Ornament of that our Royal City, the Imperial Seat, and Chamber of this our Kingdom . . . We having an earnest purpose and desire to provide, by all possible means, for the repairing and upholding of that magnificent Structure, and restoring the same (as time and means shall, by God's Blessing, give assistance) unto the ancient Beauty and Glory of it, which hath so much suffered by the iniquity of the late Times, that the Repair thereof is now become a Work of necessity to be undertaken.[165]

The royal warrant authorises a committee of any six of the long list of Commissioners included in the document to 'search, discover, try, and find out the true state of the said Church', and decide what to demolish and what to rebuild. That committee must include either 'the Lord Bishop of London' (Sheldon) or the Dean of St Paul's (Barwick) – the two men most likely to have favoured Wren as part of the survey team.

Sir John Denham, John Webb and Edward Marshall produced a first, dismally pessimistic report on the state of the Cathedral. The steeple and the adjacent roofs were 'wholy ruined & decayed' and needed to be demolished as a matter of urgency. The vaults in the main body of the Cathedral 'are of ye most of ym fallen in, & ye rest so ruinous, yt they cannot stand long'. The pillars of Inigo Jones's refaced portico had settled, causing strain to the supporting fabric of the main building. The roof over the south aisle had collapsed entirely, possibly causing damage to the foundations underneath.[166]

This was followed by a feasibility study for renovation works by Roger Pratt. At the time, Pratt was engaged in building a magnificent London home on Piccadilly for Edward Hyde, Earl of Clarendon. The gossip, as captured in verses entitled 'Upon Clarendon House', was that while conducting his detailed survey of the fabric of St Paul's Pratt had helped himself to quantities of Portland stone, which he reused in Clarendon's mansion:

> Here lye the consecrated bones
> Of Paules, late gelded of his stones,
> Here lyes the golden Briberies,
> The price of ruin'd Families.
> The Caviliers debenter wall
>   Built in th'excentrick Basis,
> Heer's Dunkirk Towne and Tangier hall,
> The marriage of the Queene and all,
>   The Dutchman's *Templum pacis.*[167]

Pratt's verdict on St Paul's was cautious and conservative. His advice was that 'no Alteration be permitted as to ye generall form of ye structure . . . being yt it may not only weaken it, & prove in no case correspondent to its ancient Symetrie, but necessarily produce at last other no less Expensive Charges'. He advocated recladding the body of the Cathedral, patching the steeple and renovating Inigo Jones's portico, 'wch will much illustrate ye Memory of ye Royal Founder, & being ye most spacious & exposed part of ye Building will most strongly excite ye Charity of ye people as it causes yr Admiration'.[168]

Coming as it did from a group of old-guard royal advisers, such a verdict on the St Paul's renovation project was perhaps only to be expected. But patching up the existing building was not what either Bishop Sheldon or the King had had in mind. As a result, like so many of the ambitiously idealistic projects which followed Charles's return, the St Paul's Commission ground to a halt. Then, in May 1666, a further report was produced, this time by one of the new generation, who until this point had been a mere assistant, but who had in the meantime

The Earl of Clarendon at the height of his power and influence, around the time of construction of his magnificent London palace, Clarendon House, and shortly before his disgrace and exile.

established a reputation as the architect of Pembroke Chapel and the rising Sheldonian Theatre – Christopher Wren.

Wren's 'Proposals for ye Reparation of St Paul's Cathedral' take an entirely different tone from that used by the older architects in Charles II's employ. He rejects, disparagingly, the views of those who 'fall so low, as to think of piecing up ye old fabrick, here with Stone, there with Brick & covering all faults with a coat of plaster'. That approach simply postpones the problem, 'leaving it still to ye next Posterity as a further object of Charity'. His bold contention is that there is no need to be sentimental about the old Cathedral, since it was 'both ill designed & ill built from the beginning':

> Ill designed because ye Artist[169] gave not Butment enough to counterpoise & resist ye weight of ye Roof from spreading ye Walls. For the eye alone will discover to any man yt those pillars, as Vast as they are, are bent outward at least 6 inches from

their Ist position wch being done on both sides it necessarily follows yt ye roof must Ist open in large wide Cracks along by ye walls & windows & lastly drop down between ye yeilding pillars.

This bending of ye pillars was facilitated by ye ill building: for they are only cased without & yet with small stones not one greater than a man's burden but within is nothing but a coar of small Rubbish stone & much mortar wch easily crushes & yeilds to ye weight. . . .

From hence I infer yt as ye outside of ye Church was new flagged with stone of larger size than before so ought ye inside also. And in doing this it will be easy to perform it after a good Roman Manner as to follow ye Gothick Rudness of ye old Design. & yt without placing ye face of ye new work in any part many inches further out or in than ye Superficies of ye old work or adding to ye Expense yt would arise were it performed ye worse way.

Thus also may safely be affirmed not only by an Architect taking his measures from the precept & example of the Ancients, but by a Geometrician (this part being liable to a Demonstration yt ye Roof is & ever was too heavy for its Butment). And so any part of ye old Roof new peeced will still but occasion further Ruine and ye 2nd Ruine will much sooner follow than ye first, since it is easier to force a thing already declining. It must so be either a timber roof plaistered (which in such Buildings where a little soak of wether is not presently discovered or remedied will soon decay) or else a thin & light shell of stone very geometrically proportioned to the strength of ye Butment. The Roof may be brick if it be plaistered with Stucco which is a harder plaster yt will [not] fall off with ye Dripp of a few Winters, & wch to this Day remains firm in many ancient Roman Buildings.[170]

Wren's flamboyant condemnation both of the original Cathedral building, and, above all, of Inigo Jones's remodelling was a technical, engineering response. The tone is strikingly confident (in contrast to that of the other reports), and it is from this secure foundation that – just returned from his architectural mission to Paris – Wren moves on to the much quoted proposal of replacing the ruined steeple with a dome:

> It must be concluded yt ye Tower from top to Bottom and ye adjacent parts are such a heap of deformities yt no Judicious Architect will think it corrigible by any Expense yt can be laid out upon new dressing it, but yt will still remain unworthy ye rest of ye Work, infirm & tottering: & for these Reasons (as I conjecture) was formerly resolved to be taken down. I cannot propose a better Remedy yn by cutting of ye inner Corners of ye Cross, to reduce ye middle part into a spacious Dome or rotunda with a Cupola or Hemispherical Roof & upon ye Cupola for ye outward Ornament, a Lantern with a Spire to rise proportionably tho not to ye unnecessary height of ye former Steeple of Lead burnt by Lightning. By this means ye Difformities of ye Unequall Intercolumnations will be taken away [interior columns had been added to support the sinking Tower]. Ye Church which is much too narrow for its height rendered spacious in ye middle wch may be a very proper place for a Vast Auditory. The outward appearance of ye Church will seem to swell in ye middle by degrees to a large Basis rising ito a Rotundo bearing a Cupola, & yn ending in ye Lantern: & ys with incomparable more Grace in ye remote Aspect yn it is possible for ye Lean Shaft of a Steeple to afford.[171]

Evelyn, who was also part of the St Paul's Commission, records, in his diary entry for 27 August 1666, a visit to the Old Cathedral, in the wake of Wren's self-assured report:

> I went to St. Paules Church in Lond: where with Dr. Wren, Mr. Prat, Mr. May, Mr. Tho. Chichley, Mr. Slingsby, the Bish: of Lond., the Deane of S. Paule, & severall expert Workmen, we went about to survey the generall decays of that antient & venerable Church, & to set downe the particulars in writing, what was fit to be don, with the charge thereof: giving our opinion from article to article: We found the maine building to receede outward: It was Mr. Chichleys & Prats opinion that it had been so built *ab origine* for an effect in Perspective, in reguard of the height; but I was with Dr. Wren quite of another

judgement, as indeede ridiculous, & so we entered it: We plumbed the Uprights in severall places: When we came to the Steeple, it was deliberated whither it were not well enough to repaire it onely upon its old foundation, with reservation to the 4 Pillars: this Mr. Chichley & Prat were also for; but we totaly rejected it & persisted that it requird a new foundation, not onely in reguard of the necessitie, but for that the shape of what stood was very meane, & we had a mind to build it with a noble Cupola, a forme of church building, not as yet knowne in England, but of wonderfull grace: for this purpose we offerd to bring in a draught & estimate, which (after much contest) was at last assented to, & that we should nominate a Committè of able Workemen to examine the present foundation: This concluded we drew all up in writing, and so going with my L: Bishop to the Deanes, after a little refreshment, went home.[172]

Pratt responded swiftly with the predictable opinion that Wren's ideas were ill-founded, and his plans for refurbishment over-ambitious.

Many years later, in the dedicatory letter (to Wren) attached to a newly revised edition of his own little treatise on architecture, Evelyn publicly recalled the consolidated efforts of the 'new men' against the patching up and making do advocated by Pratt and his supporters:[173]

I have named St. Paul's, and truly, not without Admiration, as oft as I Recall to Mind (as frequently I do) the sad and deplorable Condition it was in when (after it had been made a Stable of Horses and a Den of Thieves) You (with other Gentlemen, and myself) were by the late King Charles, nam'd Commissioners to Survey the Dilapidations, and to make Report to His Majesty, in Order to a speedy Reparation: You will not I am sure, forget the Strugle we had with some, who were for patching it up any how, (so the Steeple might stand) instead of New-Building, which it altogether needed: When (to put an end to the Contest) five days after, that Dreadful Conflagration happen'd (27 Aug. 2 Sept 1666) out of whose Ashes this Phoenix is Risen, and was by Providence Design'd for You.[174]

In 1663, in the same period when Wren was working on his chapel for Matthew Wren at Cambridge, and was presenting draft plans for

Fell and Sheldon's theatre at Oxford to the Royal Society, William Sancroft, Master of Emmanuel College, Cambridge, had also commissioned him to design and build a chapel for Emmanuel – once again, as a thanks-offering for God's goodness in restoring the King to England and himself to royal favour. Having been ejected from his fellowship at Emmanuel in 1651, Sancroft had spent the latter half of the Interregnum, after 1657, in exile in the Dutch Republic. Plans for Wren's Emmanuel Chapel project – considered by architectural historians to be one of his most achieved pieces of classical design – were not in fact settled until after 1665, by which time Sancroft had left Cambridge for a London promotion. It was Sancroft, nevertheless, who at every stage conducted the negotiations with Wren over what he continued to regard as 'his' building. Thus he was still very much in charge when, on 24 September 1667, the new Master wrote to him in London confirming some minor changes to the design:

> We are much pleased with the Modell of our Chappel; I yet meet with nothing to be added to your observations concerning it; onely we wish it could be raised to a greater height, and if we have not an East window (concerning which we are of my Lord Duresme's opinion) it is thought it will be necessary that ye side windows be inlarged. I shall trouble you with any exceptions which shall be made against it as it is viewed by others hereafter.[175]

Building began in March 1668, though the Chapel was not consecrated until 1677. Some of the delay was caused by the English weather – on 26 May 1668 the Bursar wrote to Sancroft: 'We are digging for the foundations of the Chappel, and had finished that peice of worke before now, had not the springs and the great rain made us some unexpected troubles which we shall soon overcome by pumping and fayr weather.' Of a total cost of £3,972, a handsome £600 was contributed by Sancroft personally.[176]

In May 1665, Sancroft became Dean of St Paul's as successor to John Barwick. It was thus Sancroft who participated in the St Paul's Commission meetings during the period of Wren's submission of his

OVERLEAF Wenceslaus Hollar's engraving, commissioned by Charles II immediately following the Great Fire, showing the area and extent of the devastation.

THE RIVER

A GENERALL M.
of the whole City of Lo
with Westminster & all
Suburbs, by which may
computed the proportio
that which is burnt, wit
the other parts standi

a. Tuttle Fielde
b. S.Iames Fielde
c. S.Martins Fielde
d. S.Gilts Fielde
e. Lincolns Inn F.
f. Grayes Inn Fieldi
g. Hatton garden
h. Moore fielde
i. Spittle Fielde
k. East Smithfield

l. Tower
n. Artillery
n. Charterh
o. Work S.
p. Clarken
q. Southgate
r. Printho
garden
s. Charon

Westminster

S. Iames Parke

South warke

S. Georges fielde

Lambeth

W. Hollar fecit 1666

'second opinion' report on the condition of the fabric of Old St Paul's, and, who following the Fire, spearheaded the now urgently required repair work to allow worship to continue in the burned-out Cathedral shell. In September 1668, Sancroft turned down the offer of the bishopric of Chester, so that he could see through the St Paul's rebuilding: 'Sept. 11th [1668]. At last the Dean of St. Paul's has absolutely desired to be excused from taking the Bishopric of Chester, being rather desirous to serve in the great work of "re-edifying" St. Paul's Church.'[177]

The person appointed Bishop of Chester instead of Sancroft was Dr John Wilkins. Thus the calamity of the destruction by fire of St Paul's Cathedral was, seen from another point of view, a God-sent opportunity for the faithful, long-serving Palatine retainer (and Wren's original and most loyal protector and father-figure) finally to regain his place in the sun.[178] As Bishop of Chester, Wilkins at last arrived back in a position of significant public prominence, from which, for the remainder of his life, he could once again preside, in suitably grand style, over his old Oxford circle. In his diary, Hooke records being entertained lavishly at the Bishop's London residence.[179]

As Evelyn vividly recalled in his 1697 dedication to Wren, five days after the August site visit to St Paul's the scrupulous structural survey, the compromise advice to patch the old Tower and the counter-challenge of Wren's cogent proposals for renovation had all become irrelevant. During the night of 2 September 1666 and the five days that followed, the Great Fire of London gutted Old St Paul's, and damaged beyond repair about seven-eighths of the City of London. On his next visit to the site Evelyn describes, in shocked tones, how the searing heat had cracked Inigo Jones's classical façade, and 'that beautiful portico now rent in pieces, flakes of vast stone split in sunder, and nothing remaining entire but the inscription in the architrave which shewing by whom it was built, had not one letter of it defaced'. 'Thus lay in ashes that most venerable church.'[180]

In 1666, the fate of St Paul's seemed providential to others, for different, equally compelling reasons. Just two months after the Fire, on 24 November, when it appeared that it would still be feasible to rebuild St Paul's around the surviving structure, Wren wrote to Sancroft expressing the view that the Cathedral would serve as the symbolic focus for the fund-raising activities vital for the rebuilding of London:

For though I despair this age should erect any more such huge piles, yet I believe the reputation of Paules and the compassion men have for its ruines may at least produce some neate fabrick, wch shall recompence in Art and beauty what it wants in bulke.[181]

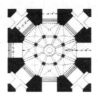

5
———

Connected in Companies

PARTICULAR FRIENDS: WREN AND EVELYN

One of those who had paid close attention to the developing career of Christopher Wren since the early Wadham days was John Evelyn. Twelve years Wren's senior, and with a lifelong interest in architecture and fine art, he had the significant advantage over his talented younger friend of having travelled widely in Europe during the 1640s, making a particular point of inspecting important buildings, going so far as to make measured drawings of several of them. It would be Evelyn who provided Wren – himself awkwardly ill-equipped to swap reminiscences with the much travelled King – with essential, first-hand knowledge of modern continental design and building methods of the kind Charles II expected of his principal professional advisers.

Echoes of Evelyn's tales of his continental travels are to be found in a letter of advice Wren wrote to his son Christopher Wren junior in the 1690s, counselling him against travelling overland to Italy. Although Wren himself had not (according to any of the evidence available) ever made the arduous alpine journey, he describes vividly to his son its dangers and difficulties:

> I hope by this time you are pretty well satisfied of the condition
> of the Climat you are in; if not, I beleive you will be ere Lent

is over, & will learne to dine upon sallad, & Morue with Egges will scarce be allowed: if you thinke you can dine better cheapre in Italy you may trie, but I thinke the passing the Alpes & other dangers of disbanded armies & abominable Lodgings will ballance that advantage.[1]

Returning from Italy in 1646 Evelyn had endured a particularly difficult crossing of the Alps. In his diary, he describes his experiences in terms which similarly stress the discomfort endured:

This night, through unacessible heights, we came in prospect of Mons Sempronius, now Mount Sampion, which has on its summit a few hutts, & a Chapell. . . . Ariv'd at our cold harbour . . . supping with Cheeze & Milke & wretched wine to bed we go in Cupbords, & so high from the floore, that we climb'd them by a Ladder, & as we lay on feathers, so are Coverd with them, that is, between two tickets stuff'd with feathers, & all little enough to keepe one warme.[2]

During the eight months he was in France in 1665 Wren confined his explorations of French culture, science and architecture to Paris and the châteaux within easy reach of the capital. Here, however, his advice to his son takes advantage of Evelyn's first-hand knowledge.[3]

Evelyn was the bridge between Wren's virtuosity and the requirements of a royal architect. He himself provides us with elegant testimony of his firm grasp on what was required, in a dedicatory letter to the King himself, printed in his translation of Fréart de Chambray's *A Parallel of the Antient Architecture with the Modern*, first published in 1664, and a manifesto statement of the close relationship between royal Restoration and a programme of building to 'restore' England to glory:

And indeed to whom could I more aptly Inscribe it? A Discourse of Building, than to so Royal a Builder, whose august attempts have already given so great a splendor to our Imperial City, and so illustrious an Example to the Nation! . . . Not with a presumption to incite, or instruct Your Majesty, which were a vanity unpardonable; but by it to take occasion of celebrating Your Majesties great Example, who use Your Empire and Authority so worthily, as Fortune seems to have consulted her reason when she poured her favours upon You; so as I never cast my

Eyes on that generous Designation in the Epigram – 'ut donem, Pastor, & aedificem'. Without immediate reflections on Your Majesty, who seem onely to value those royal advantages you have above others, but that you may Oblige, and that you may Build. And certainly, Sir, Your Majesty has consulted the noblest way of establishing Your Greatness, and of perpetuating Your Memory; since, whilest Stones can preserve Inscriptions, Your Name will be famous to Posterity, and when those Materials fail, the Benefits that are engraven in our Hearts, will outlast those of Marble.

It would be no Paradox, but a Truth to affirme, that Your Majesty has already Built and Repair'd more in three or four Years (notwithstanding the difficulties, and the necessitie of an extraordinary Oeconomy for the publick concernment) than all Your Enemies have destroy'd in Twenty; nay then all Your Majesties Predecessors have advanc'd in an Hundred, as I could easily make out, not only by what Your Majesty has so magnificently design'd and carried on at that Your antient Honour of Green-Wich, under the conduct of Your most industrious and worthy Surveyor; but in those Splendid Apartments, and other useful Reformations for security and delight, about Your Majesties Palace at White-Hall; the chargeable covering, first Paving and reformation of Westminster-Hall; care, and preparation for Saint Paul's, by the impiety and iniquity of the late confusions almost Dilapidated: With what Her Majesty the Queen Mother has added to her Palace at Sommerset House in a Structure becoming her Royal grandeur, and the due veneration of all Your Majesties Subjects for the honour She has done both this Your native City and the whole Nation.[4]

It was Wilkins who first brought the young Wren to Evelyn's notice, at probably the lowest point in Wren's career, when Wilkins was touting his talents about, looking for employment possibilities for his young, prospectless protégé. On 11 July 1654 Evelyn noted that at Wilkins's prompting he 'visited that miracle of a Youth, Mr. Christopher Wren, nephew to the Bishop of Elie'.[5] Evelyn thought of Wren, at that time, as first and foremost Bishop Matthew Wren's nephew; he also knew that side of the family. On 7 January 1657, he noted in his diary: 'Came

Mr. Mathew Wren . . . eldest sonn to the Bish: of Ely (now a Prisoner in the Tower) and a most worthy, & learned Gent: to visite me.'[6]

A few years younger than Wilkins and his circle, Evelyn falls into the category of mentor to the young Wren – one of those who at this critical point in his life showed a genuine interest in his talents. Crucially, his extensive experience of the art and architecture of mainland Europe allowed him to identify in Wren someone with the talents and temperament to lead a flowering of English cultural life to match the revival in royalist fortunes after 1660. It is worth noting, too, that in Evelyn Wren found a friend who rapidly recognised the limitations of Charles II and his court, and came to terms with a more limited set of goals for the nation.

Recollecting those dashed hopes in a letter to Pepys in 1690 (when Pepys was out of favour and Evelyn's health was failing), Evelyn conceded that the best times lay behind them:

> Whoever shall honestly compile the Historie of these prodigious and wonderfull Revolutions, (as far as concernes this miserable and unhappy Kingdome) has already the most shining and Illustrious part drest to his hand, if there be any of that profession, who dare do right to Truth in so vitious an Age, be the Event what it will; And that unless we pluck-out our owne Eyes; we must see in spite of 'em, That You, and your Collegues, have stood in the breach, when the safety of a Nation was in uttmost danger, and by whose prudence, Experience and Industrie, it can onely be yet Rescu'd from perishing now. . . .
> I have deeply, and sadly consider'd the state; and Circumstances into which we are unhappily fall'n; and that no personal Resent'ments, or reflections on the useage from ungratefull, and Wicked Men whatsoever, ought to cancel our Endeavors to support ones native Country, what ever Sacrifice we make with Honour, and a good Conscience.[7]

At the Restoration Evelyn, whose father-in-law had loyally served the future Charles II as resident ambassador in Paris throughout the Interregnum, was quickly given a modest appointment as a member of the Royal Commission to improve the condition of London's streets. Evelyn and the King's financial adviser Stephen Fox joined the new Royal Surveyor Sir John Denham in pooling their wide experience of continental cities like Paris and Rome to plan road layout and surfacing improvements for a capital city whose dirt and disorder had shocked the returning King. Wren, who as we have seen had also manoeuvred himself into a peripheral position at court, was recruited to the project, on the strength of precisely those practical talents Evelyn had admired in the early 1650s. In the preface to his translation of Fréart de Chambray's treatise on the *Art of Painting* (published in 1668) Evelyn named Wren as his example of the kind of 'universal' man of art whose virtuosity made him an 'artist' in the fullest sense:

> For a Man to arrive to its utmost perfection, He should be almost as universal as the Orator in Cicero, and the Architect in Vitruvius: But certainly some tincture in History, the Optics, and Anatomy are absolutely requisite, and more (in the Opinion of our Author) than to be a steady Designer, and skill'd in the tempering and applying of Colours, which amongst most of our Modern Workmen, go now for the onely Accomplishments of a Painter.[8]

Like Wren, Evelyn was a founder-member of the Royal Society. They sat together as 'Commissioners for reforming the buildings, ways, streets, and incumbrances', and produced plans for rebuilding London after the Fire, whose similarities, and the level of considered thought evidenced in them, suggest they had been discussing such plans together for some time previously.

In Evelyn we have a representative figure among the many who considered architecture to sit comfortably alongside their 'scientific' interests, and who thus provide the social bridge between Wren's two spheres of interest and influence well into the 1680s. It was because members of the Royal Society in London like Evelyn expected to participate in discussions, and to offer an opinion on an architectural model with equal confidence and enthusiasm to those they offered on an astronomical observation or an experiment with the air-pump, that the collaborative nature of architecture runs so deep in Wren's practice and mentality.

What makes Evelyn's interest in the young Wren particularly significant is the part he was able to play in setting Wren on the road to his ultimate career achievement – the position of Surveyor of the King's Works, and his brilliant contribution to redesigning the civic face of

London views: (*top*) perspective view of Hampton Court (before Wren's rebuilding) by the Dutch artist Hendrick Danckerts, who painted views of important buildings for a number of English patrons, including Samuel Pepys; view from Croom's Hill of Wren's Royal Observatory at Greenwich, around 1680

Dutch perspectives: (*top*) pen and ink drawing of the devastation caused by the explosion of the gunpowder arsenal in Delft in 1654; (left) Pieter Saendredam, Interior of St Bavo's Church – in Saendredam's work, precise architectural drawing is modified to provide enhanced perspectival views; Gerrit Houkgeest, perspectival architectural fantasy, with figures – Wren considered perspective a vital part of architectural design

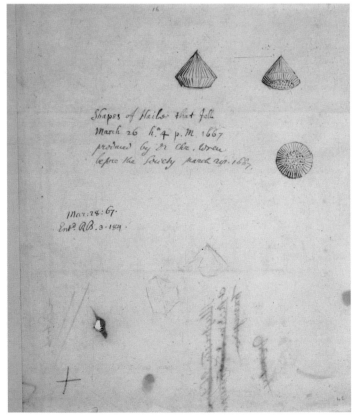

Scientific drawing: (*top*) line drawing of one version of the Wren/Hooke weather-gauge, from the record books of the Royal Society; sketch of giant hailstones, produced by Wren in March 1667, from the Royal Society records

Restoration England. For it was Evelyn who saw to the success of the mission Wren was sent on in 1665, to research the building programme currently being conducted by Jean-Baptiste Colbert for Louis XIV.

THE DEPUTY SURVEYOR'S TRIP TO PARIS

In the spring of 1665, Sir John Denham, Surveyor of the King's Works, arranged for Wren, as his deputy, to go on a trip to Paris sponsored by the court, to inspect the extensive building works currently being carried out for Louis XIV under the highly competent constructional and financial management of his chief minister Jean-Baptiste Colbert. The project Charles II was particularly interested in, in view of his ambitious plans to rebuild Whitehall, was the Louvre Palace in Paris.[9] The timing seems to have been designed to enable Wren to meet the Italian artist Bernini, who was briefly visiting Paris, primarily in order to sculpt a bust of Louis XIV. Colbert had been in correspondence with Bernini for some time over alternative designs for the completion of the Louvre, and it was known that Bernini was bringing the final set of three proposed designs with him to Paris (Bernini's was not, eventually, the scheme built).

On 4 April 1665, Evelyn, who had been told of Bernini's imminent visit to Paris by his cousin Sir Samuel Tuke, who was in Paris tutoring the children of Henry Howard, and who was himself looking for a tutor for his son John, wrote to Wren offering help with contacts there:

> You may please to remember that some time since I begg'd a favour of you in behalfe of my little boy: he is now susceptible of Instruction, a pleasant, and (though I speake it) a most ingenious and pregnant Child: My designe is to give him a good education: he is past many initial difficulties, and conquers all things with incredible industry: Do me that eternal obligation, as to enquire out and recommend to me some Young man for a Praeceptor: I will give him £20 per annum Sallary, and such other accommodations as shall be no way disagreeable to an ingenuous spirit. . . . The Boy is capable beyond his yeares; and if you encounter one thus qualified, I shall receive it amongst the greate good fortunes of my life that I obtaynd it by the

benefit of your friendship, for which I have ever had so perfect an esteeme: There is no more to be say'd, but that when you have found the Person, you direct him immediately to me, that I may receive him and value him.

Sir, I am told by Sir John Denham that you looke towards France this sommer: be assur'd I will charge you with some addresses of Friends of mine there, that shall exceedingly cherish you; and though you will stand in no neede of my recommendations, yet I am confident you will not refuse the offer of those Civilities which I shall bespeake you.

There has layne at Dr. Needhams a Copy of the Parallell [*A Parallel of the Antient Architecture with the Modern* (1664)] bound up for you, and Longsince design'd you, which I shall entreate you to accepte; not as a recompense of your many favours to mee, much lesse, a thing in the least assistant to you (who are your selfe a Master) but as a toaken of my respect, as the Booke it selfe is of the affection I beare to an art which you so hapily Cultivate.[10]

Wren looked forward eagerly to the prospect of an introduction to Bernini, as also the great French architect François Mansard. On 22 June 1665, writing to his old friend Ralph Bathurst, now President of Trinity College, Oxford, concerning designs for a new building at Trinity, he contrasted his own comparatively novice status as a designer with the expertise of the two great continental architects:

If I had skill in enchantment to represent the pile, first in one view, then in another, that the difference might be evidently seen, I should certainly make them of my opinion [that a new free-standing block would be preferable to a run of buildings completing an existing quadrangle]; or else I will appeal to Mons. Mansard, or Signor Bernini, both which I shall see at Paris within this fortnight.[11]

While he was about it, Wren remembered to ask Bathurst about a suitable young scholar to tutor Evelyn's son. That summer, Bathurst's nephew Ralph Bohun duly became John Evelyn junior's tutor.[12]

Appropriately grand travel arrangements were made for this mission. In mid-July Wren was still unclear exactly when he was to leave for France, three months after the trip had first been mooted, because he was waiting to travel with the household of the Queen Mother, Henrietta Maria (Charles I's widow), who was on the point of returning to her native France for an extended stay. She, meanwhile, was dithering:

> The queen-mother . . . was finding the cold damp English winters increasingly trying. Her catarrh was definitely getting worse and by early 1665 she was beginning to think seriously about going back to France. . . . In spite of all this, Henrietta Maria, in the words of Father Cyprien, 'wavered long irresolute', worried that she would be deserting the English Catholics. . . . By early summer, hastened by an alarming increase in reported cases of plague in the capital, Henrietta Maria was making preparations for departure and Samuel Pepys, happening to call at Somerset House on 29 June, found them all packing up, 'the Queen-mother setting out for France this day; and intends not to come [back] till winter come twelvemonths'. The king escorted his mother as far as Gravesend and the Duke of York saw her down to Dover.[13]

Wren left London with the Queen Mother's party on 29 June. In a letter written from France to 'a particular friend', he mentions that both en route and in the early stages of his visit (he was away for almost nine months in all) he had been able to take full advantage of the hospitality of those close to the Queen Mother, Henrietta Maria, herself:

> How he spent his Time, in that Place, will in Part appear from a short Account he gave by Letter to a particular Friend; wherein he returns Thanks for his Recommendation of him to [Henry Jermyn] Earl of St. *Albans*, who in the Journey, and ever since, had us'd him with all Kindness and Indulgence imaginable, and made good his Character of him, as one of the best Men in the World.[14]

With all doors open to him, Wren had been given access to all the French royal buildings and apartments he had been instructed to inspect. He had 'busied [himself] in surveying the most esteem'd Fabricks of *Paris*, and the Country round':

> The Louvre for a while was my daily Object, where no less than a thousand Hands are constantly employ'd in the Works; some

in laying mighty Foundations, some in raising the Stories, Columns, Entablements, &c. with vast Stones, by great and useful Engines; others in Carving, Inlaying of Marbles, Plaistering, Painting, Gilding, &c. Which altogether make a School of Architecture, the best probably, at this Day in *Europe*. . . . An Academy of Painters, Sculptors, Architects, and the chief Artificers of the *Louvre*, meet every first and last *Saturday* of the Month. Mons. *Colbert*, Surintendant, comes to the Works of the *Louvre*, every *Wednesday*, and, if Business hinders not, *Thursday*. The Workmen are paid every *Sunday* duly.[15]

Wren had indeed met Bernini, albeit disappointingly briefly:

Bernini's Design of the Louvre I would have given my Skin for, but the old reserv'd *Italian* gave me but a few Minutes View; it was five little Designs in Paper, for which he hath receiv'd as many thousand Pistoles; I had only Time to copy it in my Fancy and Memory; I shall be able by Discourse, and a Crayon, to give you a tolerable Account of it.[16]

Wren promised his correspondent that he would polish up all his various notes and sketches, and present them on his return as 'Observations on the present State of *Architecture*, *Arts*, and *Manufactures* in *France*'; he also notified him that he had acquired a large collection of engravings of French buildings and 'views'.[17]

The 'particular friend' to whom Wren addressed this one surviving account we have from the architect himself about his reactions to what he saw in Paris, written some time in September 1665, was undoubtedly Evelyn. Whoever that was had a high regard for Henry Jermyn and the Queen Mother. Henrietta Maria and the Earl of St Albans had paid a private visit to Evelyn's house at Deptford in 1662, staying late and eating dinner there; Evelyn's wife Mary was an old friend from the years of exile in Paris.[18] Wren's remarks about sketching what he has seen with a crayon for his friend on his return fits nicely with Evelyn's personal practice – he recounts a story of Charles II's on one occasion taking a crayon and enthusiastically sketching his own ideas for his Palace at Whitehall for Evelyn. Finally, the large collection of engravings Wren promises to return with sounds like the kind of thing to be shared

Henry Jermyn, Earl of St Albans, devoted personal secretary and confidant to Charles I's widow, Queen Henrietta Maria – it was widely rumoured that they had married secretly.

with a gentleman enthusiast like Evelyn (himself something of a collector of architectural engravings).

We have more certain evidence that Wren took up Evelyn's offers of letters of introduction to well-placed individuals in Paris, to help him gain access to royal buildings. Sir Samuel Tuke, a distant cousin of Evelyn's, was resident in Paris (in the same street in which Evelyn's wife and father-in-law had lived while Sir Richard Browne was French resident ambassador) as the tutor to Henry Howard's children.[19] In August, shortly after the arrival of the royal party, Tuke wrote to Evelyn acknowledging the letter of introduction brought to him by Wren:

> Since I writt last to you; I haue receiud 3 of yor Letters; one from My Ld Barclay who ariud heere about 10 dayes since; wch coming to my hands about 5 months after it was written, requires no answere, only to the p[ar]ticuler of the Treatise of Silkwormes & the seeds of white Mulberryes, I will enquire for them, & send them to you when I haue an oportunitye; – Another by the hands of Dr Wren to wch I can onely replye that I haue, & shall endever to serve him to the best of my capacity wch God knowes, is very little for I can neither furnish,

nor recomend; You are no stranger to my ignorance in all sorts of Litterature; – and truly since I came into this Country I neither haue nor euer will make any one Visitt, unless it be in order to these duties wch are incumbent on my present vocation; I came hither to hide my self, wch Resolution I haue faithfully pursued, my onely busines being to worke on my salvation wch according to my constitution I finde most practicable in retirement.[20]

In late October, Tuke reported Bernini's departure to Evelyn, and that 'Dr Wren, Dr Smith & Dr Grove [?] pass their time here.' Wren, he added, was intending to return shortly with Henry Jermyn:

Cavalier Bernini has left his designes for ye finishing of the Louvre & is returned wth greate rewards, & hee left greate fame for an admirable head of the King carud by him in marble. . . . Dr Wren purposes to part from here for England in the company of My Lord St Albans about 3 weekes hence. You haue all I know & part of what I guess at.[21]

In the event, Wren did not return to England till the spring. In January 1666 Tuke told Evelyn that Wren and his companions would soon return 'furnished with many of the choisest plums'.[22]

Meanwhile, the newly established Royal Society took advantage of Wren's all-expenses-paid trip to put their young protégé in touch with their counterparts in Paris, with whom they were in correspondence via Secretary Oldenburg. On 1 July Adrien Auzout told Oldenburg how delighted he was that 'your learned Mr. Wren' would soon be in Paris. 'I fear that he will not find our Company in very good shape, but if he sees nothing very splendid here, at least we shall learn much from him.'[23] In August 1665 Oldenburg reported to Boyle that Wren's trip to Paris was going well, and that he had managed to include time, as planned, with the French virtuosi of the Académie des Sciences, alongside his commitments as Deputy Surveyor of the Royal Works:

Dr Wren is well received at Paris, and conducted to some of their [the French scientists'] meetings; and made acquainted with Messieurs Auzout, Petit, and Therenot.

My correspondent tells me this: 'I took him to M. Bourdelot's house, where that day a quantity of entertaining things were discussed. He approved strongly of what was said, but he hoped that they also conducted experiments' (this is like a member of the Royal Society). 'The Queen of Poland's physician explained the nature of a disease named "plica" to which only the Poles and the Cossacks are prone. They also discussed a deaf-mute who dances in time, and several other topics, which he rather enjoyed. We also took him to meet the great architect, the chevalier Bernini. He saw the bust which he has made of the king in marble, and the designs he has made for the Louvre, which he will describe to you himself. This morning I gave him access to M. Pascal's machine, with which one can execute all kinds of rules of arithmetic.'[24]

The correspondent in question was Adrien Auzout, whose views on the path of the 1664 comet Wren had discussed with Wallis at the Royal Society in early 1665 (and whom Wren was presumably eager to meet to continue those discussions face to face). Auzout, too, was something of an expert in revived classical architecture, and it was he, apparently, who had in the end effected Wren's introduction to Bernini. Henri Justel told Oldenburg in January 1666 that he was in touch with Wren 'practically every day', and that he had introduced Wren to the best lens-manufacturers in Paris.[25]

In late September, the official portion of his visit over (and Tuke, incidentally, out of town, taking the waters with Queen Henrietta Maria and Lord Berkeley in Bourbon),[26] Wren joined up with a small group of fellow tourists to visit more buildings of architectural interest, around Paris. One of these companions was Edward Browne, son of Sir Thomas Browne, who had already spent six months in Paris the previous year and had since travelled into Italy.[27] In a letter to his father from Paris at the end of September 1665, Edward gives a delightful flavour of the sightseeing he and his friends and Wren were doing:

Three days the last week I was abroad in the country with Dr. Wren and Mr Compton. I did not thinke to see any thinge more about Paris, but was tempted out by so good company.

Dr. Wren's discourse is very pleasing and satisfactory to mee about all manner of things. I asked him which hee took to bee the greatest work about Paris, he said the Quay or Key upon the river side, which he demonstrated to me, to be built with so vast expense and such great quantity of materialls, that it exceeded all manner of ways the building of the two greatest pyramids in Egypt.

I told him that upon the banks of the river Loire for some miles, there was a wall built of square stone; but because there could not be allowed any thicknesse proportionall to the Key at Paris, hee did not know how to esteem of that, as not having ever seen it. We went the first day to Chantilly, where lives the Prince of Condy, but he was gone out, and so wee mist Abbot Bourdelot (Physician to the Prince) too: We saw the Princesse carried in a chair about the gardens, being with child. The house is old built; and belonged formerly to the Duke of Montmorancy, whose statue on horseback in bronze stands before the house; the gardens and waterworks are neat. . . .

We went from hence to Verneuil, seated upon a high hill, a very neat castel, but furnished with old fourniture. The Duke I suppose is still ambassador in England; he keeps a pack of English dogs here, and lives in a good hunting country. The house is very finely carved without side. Dr. Wren guest that the same man built this which built the Louvre, there being the same faults in one as in the other.

. . . The next day we saw Rinsy, an house belonging to the Duchesse of Longueville, sister to the Prince of Condé. The gardens and waterworks are not yet finished; the house is small but extremely neat, and the modell pleased Dr. Wren very much; the chambers are excellently well painted, and one roome with an handsome cupola in it is one of the best I have seen.

Returning to Paris, the King overtook us in chaise roulante with his Mistress La Valière with him, habited very prettily in a hat and feathers, and a *Just aucorps* [a particularly fashionable jacket].[28]

Wren was still in Paris in January 1666. Justel, arranging to send a number of scientific journals to Oldenburg, said that he would give them to Wren 'who I see almost every day, together with a number of other English gentlemen'. Justel also told Oldenburg that he was continuing to give Wren access to the most advanced work with lenses being conducted in Paris, and that he had taken him to see the famous

Bernini bust of Louis XIV.[29] By this time England and France were at war, and there must have been some danger that the French virtuosi were seen as revealing classified information to the English visitors.

Shortly thereafter, Wren prudently returned to London. He had succeeded in meeting the expectations of both his court and Royal Society patrons over the course of his trip. He had also managed to stay clear of the complex diplomatic negotiations which were going on around him, as Henrietta Maria tried to dissuade Louis XIV from declaring war on England. Henry Jermyn shuttled to and fro between Paris and London during the latter part of 1665 and the early months of 1666, brokering this attempt at royal diplomacy, and Wren may have taken advantage of any one of these trips to accompany him home.[30]

On 6 March 1666, Oldenburg reported to Boyle that 'Dr Wren is returned, and very kindly enquired after you. He is very well satisfied with the civilities he has received in France, and commends particularly Mr Auzout; and so, I think, will every ingenious and learned man.' Wren had, however, failed to bring Oldenburg all the books Justel was supposed to have given him.[31] On 23 May 1666 Oldenburg successfully proposed Adrien Auzout as a foreign member of the Royal Society.[32]

A PHOENIX RISING FROM THE FLAMES

Wren probably witnessed at first hand the Great Fire, which broke out in the early hours of Sunday, 2 September, and (after a slow start) raged uncontrollably for almost five days. On Monday, 27 August, Wren and Evelyn had been together on site at Old St Paul's Cathedral, assessing the possibilities for restoring the existing building to its ancient grandeur. The plan was to 'set downe the particulars in writing, what was fit to be don, with the charge thereof: giving our opinion from article to article' – not a job that could be completed *in situ*, so presumably there were to be further meetings and consultations during that week. On 12 September, Wren was due to present his new 'double telescope' at that week's Royal Society meeting, together with Hooke, who would present his redesigned quadrant (a presentation which never took place, on account of the Fire). Both instruments formed part of a combined proposal by Wren and Hooke together, for finding longitude at sea – a problem in which the Society was taking an intense interest – and

Hooke loyally referred to Wren's design many years later as particularly effective for the purpose.[33] Since Hooke lived at Gresham College in Bishopsgate, these discussions, too, would have taken place in London.[34] The University of Oxford was on vacation, so there was, in any case, no need for Wren to be in residence there, except to oversee construction work on the Sheldonian Theatre, which he appears largely to have left to others.

Some of Wren's closest colleagues lived in or near the area devastated by the Great Fire: in 1666 John Wilkins was vicar of St Lawrence Jewry, next door to the Guildhall (both buildings were destroyed by the fire), Sir Robert Moray and Sir Paul Neile had lodgings at Whitehall (where the fire was prevented from taking hold of Inigo Jones's Banqueting House by the Duke of York's ordering the dynamiting of a row of houses between it and the fire). John Evelyn joined the court volunteers who supervised fire-fighting efforts round the Palace.

Although Wren was not, as Samuel Pepys was, forced to evacuate his own household and possessions, his response is likely to have been that of his close friend (and fellow town-planner and lover of buildings) Evelyn:

> 2 [September 1666]: This fatal night about ten, began that deplorable fire, neere Fish-streete in Lond:
>
> 2: I had pub: prayers at home: after dinner the fire continuing, with my Wife & Sonn took Coach & went to the bank side in Southwark, where we beheld that dismal speectaccle, the whole Citty in dreadfull flames neere the Water side, & had now consumed all the houses from the bridge all Thames Streete & up-wards towards Cheape side, downe to the three Cranes, & so returned exceedingly astonishd, what would become of the rest:
>
> 3 The Fire having continud all this night (if I may call that night, which was as light as day for 10 miles round about after a dreadfull manner) when consp<ir>ing with a fierce Eastern Wind, in a very drie season, I went on foote to the same place, when I saw the whole South part of the Citty burning from Cheape side to the Thames, & all along Cornehill (for it likewise kindled back against the Wind, as well <as> forward) Tower-Streete, Fen-church-streete, Gracious Streete, & so along to

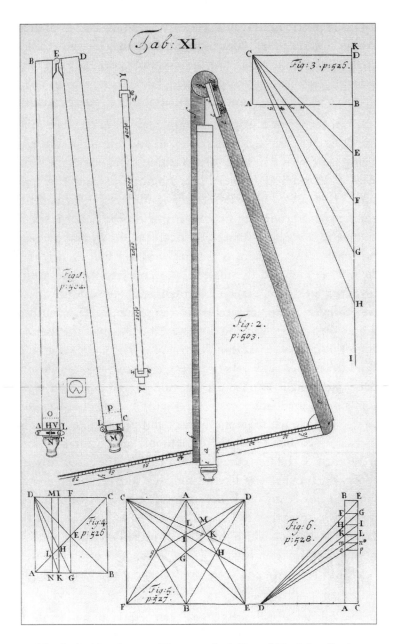

Wren's double telescope (Fig. 1, on the left), and Hooke's reflecting quadrant (Fig. 2), designed to be used together to calculate longitude at sea. The Royal Society meeting at which they should have been presented was cancelled because of the Great Fire.

Bainard Castle, and was now taking hold of St. Paules-Church, to which the Scaffalds contributed exceedingly:

The Conflagration was so universal, & the people so astonish'd, that from the beginning (I know not by what desponding or fate), they hardly stirr'd to quench it, so as there was nothing heard or seene but crying out & lamentation, & running about like distracted creatures, without at all attempting to save even their goods; such a strange consternation there was upon them, so as it burned both in breadth & length, The Churches, Publique Halls, Exchange, Hospitals, Monuments, & ornaments, leaping after a prodigious manner from house to house & streete to streete, at greate distance one from the other, for the heate (with a long set of faire & warme weather) had even ignited the aire, & prepared the materials to conceive the fire, which devoured after a<n> incredible manner, houses, furniture, & everything. . . . o the miserable & calamitous spectacle, such as happly the whole world had not seene the like since the foundation of it, nor to be out don, 'til the universal Conflagration of it, all the skie were of a fiery aspect, like the top of a burning Oven, & the light seene above 40 miles round about for many nights: God grant mine eyes may never behold the like, who now saw above ten thousand houses all in one flame, the noise & crakling & thunder of the impetuous flames, the shreeking of Women & children, the hurry of people, the fall of towers, houses & churches was like an hideous storme, & the aire all about so hot & inflam'd that at the last one was not able to approch it, so as they were force'd <to> stand still, and let the flames consume on which they did for neere two whole mile<s> in length and one in bredth: The Clowds also of Smoke were dismall, & reached upon computation neere 50 miles in length:

Thus I left it this afternoone burning, a resemblance of Sodome, or the last day: It call'd to mind that of 4 Heb: *non enim hic habemus stabilem Civitatem*: the ruines resembling the picture of Troy: London was, but is no more.[35]

Devastation by fire was a recurrent nightmare for the inhabitants of seventeenth-century towns. Two hundred and twenty-four houses were destroyed by a blaze which raged uncontrolled in Marlborough in

1653, another 238 in Southwold in 1659, and 156 at Newport, Shropshire in 1665.[36] A whole series of great houses were reduced to charred shells by fire, including Whitehall Palace itself: although saved from destruction in 1666, fire broke out at the Palace twice thereafter, in 1691 and 1693, on the latter occasion devastating the royal apartments.[37] Inigo Jones's Banqueting House was a replacement building for one which burned to the ground in 1619.[38] The 1666 Great Fire destroyed houses on the northern end of London Bridge which had only recently been rebuilt after being burned out in 1633.[39] Ten years on, in May 1676, Robert Hooke took his niece Grace to the as yet uncompleted Monument to the Great Fire, to watch the progress of yet another fire south of the river: 'With Grace at Column to see the great fire in Southrick [Southwark] which burnd 8 or 900 houses'.[40]

Abroad, the 1654 explosion of the gunpowder arsenal at Delft, in the Dutch Republic, which caused a major fire as well as substantial loss of life, became a cautionary tale for the dangers of explosives storage in built-up areas.[41] An eye-witness account of this disaster was sent to Charles II's secretary Edward Nicholas by his aunt, Elizabeth of Bohemia.[42] The major European fire most directly relevant to London's was that deliberately set by Sir Robert Holmes, as an act of war, at Vlie and Westterschelling on the Dutch coast in August 1666. Holmes fired 150 Dutch merchant vessels lying in the shelter of the islands of Vlie and Terschelling, and the adjacent towns, as the final summer manoeuvre of the second Anglo-Dutch war.[43] In the panic which followed London's Great Fire, it was widely believed that it had been deliberately set by the Dutch in retaliation.

Nevertheless, the Great Fire of London was exceptional for the sheer extent of the final devastation – more than 12,000 homes destroyed and an estimated 65,000 inhabitants made homeless, in addition to the loss of public buildings and places of worship. When finally the wind dropped and the fire was brought under control, the general response among the citizens of London to the appalling extent of the destruction and loss, as evidenced by surviving accounts, was one of stunned shock, whether or not they had sustained damage or loss themselves.

The immediate task, once the blaze was out, was to assess the damage. On 10 September, the King and his Privy Council appointed Jonas Moore and Ralph Greatorex to make an initial assessment of the losses in terms of buildings and goods.[44] In collaboration with the

Sir Jonas Moore's 1662 Survey of the Thames – his experience made him a suitable person to carry out the post-Fire survey of London.

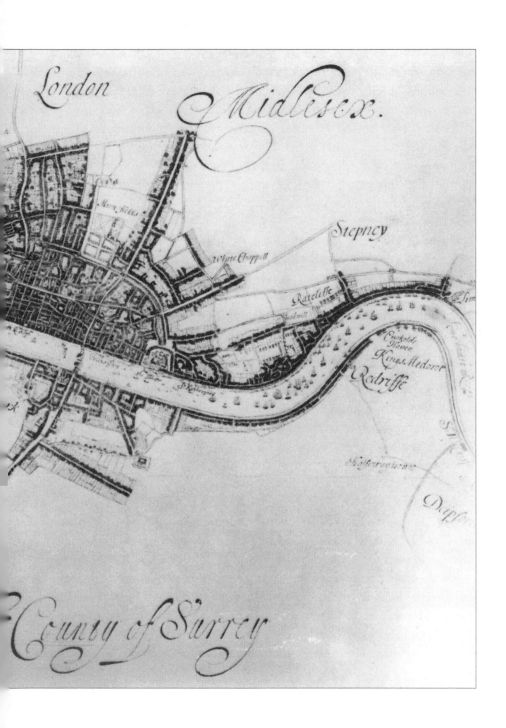

engraver Wenceslaus Hollar and his colleague Francis Sandford they were instructed to produce 'an exact plan and survey of the citiy, as it now stands after the calamity of the late fire'.[45] All were men of appropriate experience, well equipped to work under what were bound to be difficult circumstances. Moore had recent surveying experience along the Thames, as well as at Tangier. Hollar – a prolific publisher of 'views' and bird's-eye plans of major cities, including London – was able to work with his existing plates and rapidly issued graphic plans and elevations showing the full drama of the destruction.[46]

In early October the King, in consultation with the Corporation of the City of London, set up a joint Rebuilding Commission of six members – three of the Crown's own appointees and three nominated by the City – to report on a weekly basis to the Privy Council. The King chose Roger Pratt, Hugh May and Wren, while the Corporation nominated Peter Mills, Edward Jerman and Hooke. The Commission's brief included the management of the survey of ruined property, consideration of the form and scale of the new buildings, and alterations to the streets.[47]

In the meantime, institutional buildings outside the area of devastation were requisitioned to house essential activities. The City removed all its administrators and officers from the ruins of Guildhall to Gresham College in Bishopsgate, home of the Royal Society, as well as of the Gresham professors.[48] Gresham College also became the centre for the activities displaced from the gutted Royal Exchange – the vital financial heart of the City – responsibility for which rested with the Crown. Of the resident Gresham professors, only Hooke was allowed to remain, presumably because Gresham was his sole home address. When he had left Boyle's service to become Curator of Experiments at the Royal Society in 1662, Hooke's salary was set at £30 per annum plus the privilege of lodging free of charge at Gresham College. The year before the Fire he was elected Professor of Geometry at Gresham, which also included the right to reside. The Royal Society moved its activities temporarily to Arundel House, in the Strand, the home of Henry Howard.[49]

Beyond the obvious immediate practical problems, the Privy Council and the Corporation of London faced an urgent task of limiting the damage on two fronts: lessening the possibility of civil disorder caused by the displacement of so many people and loss of such quantities of assets and goods; and turning the tide of public opinion away from the idea that this was some form of divine punishment. To deal with the first of these, the authorities acted decisively, regaining control of the situation by issuing a set of directives for compensation and rebuilding with uncharacteristic speed. A series of tough legislative measures were rushed through on 13 September: these included the prohibiting of rebuilding by citizens in advance of a decision about an agreed master-plan, and a stipulation that rebuilding should be of brick or stone. A special Fire Court was established to handle boundary claims, and claims for rebuilding costs, from freeholders and tenants. In the short term, there was efficient management of the temporary housing and feeding of thousands of displaced people: special proclamations made provision for feeding the homeless, crowded into Moorfields, Lincoln's Inn and Gray's Inn Fields, the piazza at Covent Garden and the adjacent villages of Islington and Highgate.

The danger of general demoralisation was countered by a publicity campaign, orchestrated from the court, emphasising the speed with which the authorities were responding to London's crisis, the extent of the personal concern felt by the King and his brother the Duke of York for each and every Londoner involved, and above all the fantastic opportunity the natural disaster offered for effecting a real 'Restoration' in London – a new, modern world capital suitable for a new Stuart kingdom. Less than two weeks after the Fire, Evelyn – one of those assigned the task of talking up the possibilities offered by the Fire – was already developing all the key themes in a letter to an out-of-town friend:

> In the meane time, the King and Parliament are infinitely zeal-
> ous for the rebuilding of our ruines; and I believe it will univer-
> saly be the employment of the next Spring: They are now buisid
> with adjusting the claimes of each proprietor, that so they may
> dispose things for the building after the noblest Model: Every
> body brings in his Ideä, amongst the rest, I presented his Majes-
> tie my owne Conceptions with a discourse annex'd. It was the
> second that was seene, within 2 dayes after the Conflagration:
> But Dr. Wren had got the start on me: both of us did *coincidere*
> so frequently, that his Majestie was not displeased with it; and
> it caused divers alterations and truely, there was never a more

glorious Phoenix upon Earth, if it do at least emerge out of those cinders, and as the designe is layd, with the present fervour of the undertakers.[50]

Evelyn's own published proposals for a rebuilt London described the project as a golden opportunity: 'London Restored, not to its pristine, but to far greater Beauty Commodiousness and Magnificence'.[51]

Before September 1666, the versatile Wren still had several alternative careers open to him. The Fire decided him (whether as a conscious decision, or simply by force of circumstances) that his future lay as a town-planner and architect, in the direct employ of the King.

Assessment of his success in that career became, furthermore, inextricably bound up with the campaign promoting the theme of renewal and improvement associated with the disaster. Every move in the rebuilding process – above all, the rebuilding of St Paul's – was accompanied by a chorus of enthusiasm for the architects of London's Restoration, and, by implication, for the King as its main sponsor. From the outset the King's involvement was represented as a personal and passionate one. Evelyn played a particularly prominent part in constructing this image of the King as a second Augustus, who would make of London a new Rome, and Evelyn lined Wren up as the new Vitruvius who could make that royal promise a reality, itemising in his roll-call of works already carried out by the new monarch a number in which Wren had been directly involved:

It would be no Paradox, but a Truth to affirme, that Your Majesty has already Built and Repair'd more in three or four Years (notwithstanding the difficulties, and the necessitie of an extraordinary Oeconomy for the publick concernment) than all Your Enemies have destroy'd in Twenty; nay then all Your Majesties Predecessors have advanc'd in an Hundred, as I could easily make out, not only by what Your Majesty has so magnificently design'd and carried on at that Your antient Honour of Green-Wich, under the conduct of Your most industrious and worthy Surveyor [Denham]; but in those Splendid Apartments, and other useful Reformations for security and delight, about Your Majesties Palace at White-Hall; the chargeable covering, first Paving and reformation of Westminster-Hall; care, and preparation for Saint Paul's, by the impiety and iniquity of the late confusions almost Dilapidated.[52]

Wren's prominent role was in large part a consequence of his exceptional talent – a talent in which the King, and several of his Privy Counsellors, had already taken a personal interest. In part, though, it was an accident of circumstances. Of those selected under the pressure of the early days after the disaster, Wren was the man currently most closely linked to the court circle around the King; while the unique professional partnership between Wren and the indefatigable Hooke (who apparently barely ever slept) made them a force to be reckoned with within the rebuilding Commission at every stage.

All three royal appointments to the Commission were notable architects, with distinguished portfolios of great houses and public buildings to their names; their skills had been tried and tested in the six years of royal rebuilding since the King's return.[53] May and Wren had been working on refurbishing the royal palaces since 1661 (May held the post of Paymaster of the King's Works). Pratt was engaged in the final stages of building the magnificent new home he had designed for the Earl of Clarendon on Piccadilly. Of the three, Wren was, as we noted in the last chapter, the 'new', relatively young member of the team built up under Denham, directly favoured by the King. At the time of appointment the only completed building he had to his name was Pembroke College Chapel, but the Sheldonian Theatre was on site, and plans for Emmanuel College Chapel reasonably advanced.

On the City's side, Jerman and Mills were well-established architect–builders of the older generation (they were soon much in demand designing new buildings for the livery companies whose headquarters had been destroyed in the fire), and Mills was City Surveyor.

The appointment of Hooke – a comparatively unknown quantity – can be accounted for in various ways. He was already well known in City circles – the committee which had appointed him to the Gresham chair of Geometry in 1665 had been presided over by the then Lord Mayor Sir John Lawrence. He was known in London society as a gregarious individual-about-town with an infectious enthusiasm for technology. He was closely involved with Wren carrying out experiments for the Royal Society.[54] Finally, he was the man on the spot at Gresham, where the Corporation of London was in virtually permanent session dealing with the administrative consequences of the Fire (they were in late-night sittings, and Hooke was a chronic insomniac).

Roger Pratt recorded the first meetings of the Rebuilding Commission in his diary, showing that the earliest decisions were entirely concerned with improving the existing street-plan:

> His Majesty King Charles the 2nd was pleased out of his owne meere motion to appoint his Surveyour for ye present Mr. Hugh May, Doctor Renne, and myselfe to be his Commissioners to treate with such as the Citty should think fit to nominate about the more quick and orderly reedification of the citty, who sente to us Mr. Milles their Surveyour and Mr. Hooke Professor of ye Mathematics in Gresham Colledge, and Mr. Germain an experienced man in buildings.
>
> About the beginning of Octob: 1666 wee had our first meeting, wherein it beeing much controverted whether that part of the citty now burned, were commensurable or not, by reason of many difficulties then proposed, it was at last resolved that it was commensurable. Whereupon at our second meeeting about Octob: the 8, wee ordered that Surveyours should bee appointed for the measurement of each particular Ward of the citty, and that the citty should be sente too to issue out Orders commanding each Proprietor to cleere his foundations within 14 dayes at the farthest, in order to such measurement; and likewise to pitch upon some fitting sallary for each Surveyour, as 12d per howse, etc, wherewith the city most readily complyed.
>
> At our third meeeting Octob: the 11, upon the motion of some Lords of ye Council, who resolved to sitt to heare the progresse of our affaires every Tuesday in the afternoon, wee resolved the breadth of the severall future streetes.[55]

Pratt does seem to have played a prominent role in these early meetings. So much so that his cousin was convinced he would be chosen to lead the rebuilding also – especially that of St Paul's:

> I am exceeding glad the King hath commissioned you (no question in the first place) with Mr. May & Dr. Renne: they will get more secrets of your art brought from Rome, & so from Athens, then you from them. If you have a hand in repairing St. Pauls, the

most Royall peice in Christendom, it will be a Jacobs ladder to carry you to heaven beyond all profit & honour in this world.[56]

Pratt's cousin was correct in thinking that the architect of the restoration of St Paul's would earn a special place in English history (in 1666 it was still believed that a major refurbishment of the surviving building would be possible). He was quite wrong in thinking Pratt would be chosen as the man for the job. Wren had already shown greater courage, imagination and vision in relation to Old St Paul's, directly contradicting Pratt, in their surveys immediately before the Fire. Pratt's name was in any case linked with the ostentatious Palace he had just completed, with impeccable bad timing, in the very month of the Fire, for the Earl of Clarendon, whose own fortunes were about to go into rapid decline.

The inclusion of Hooke in the Commission gave Wren an advantage over the other gentleman members – something which at this early stage was probably evident only to members of the Royal Society. Writing to Boyle in Oxford, less than six weeks after the Fire, Oldenburg was already yoking their names together:

> The other grand affair about the rebuilding of the Citty, is not neglected neither; Strict injunction being now issued by the Lord Mayor, in the Kings name, wch done, the Survey and admeasurement of all such Foundations is to be forthwith taken in hand, and th[a]t by the care and management of Dr Wren and M. Hook: wch survey is to be exactly registred; for the better stating thereafter every ones right and propriety: And then the method of building will be taken into nearer consideration, and, 'tis hoped, within a short time resolved upon.[57]

It would be the 'care and management of Dr Wren and M. Hook' which eventually won the day.

MASTER-PLANS

Terrible though the damage inflicted by the Fire on the City of London was, it came as a heaven-sent opportunity to the team assembled by the Surveyor of the King's Works, whose efforts at creating a physical environment to match Charles II's early dreams of restoring the ruined

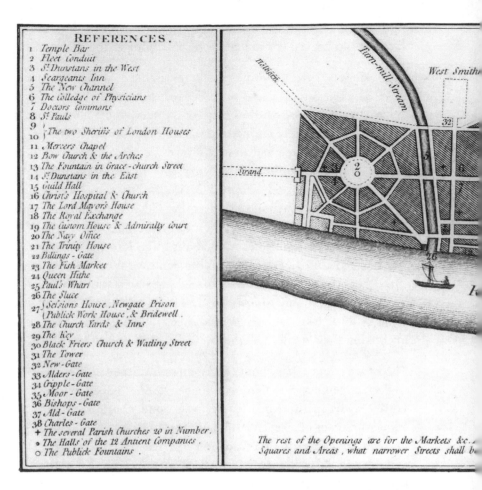

John Evelyn's plan for rebuilding London, submitted to Charles II two days after Wren had presented his, on 13 September 1666.

fabric of his realm had been largely frustrated by administrative indecision and lack of available funding. The challenge of the organised rebuilding of the City, with the potent image of a phoenix rising renewed from the flames, was a chance to reinvigorate the reign of Charles II. It was a challenge to which individuals close to the King rose with remarkable alacrity. Within days of the disaster, five individuals came forward with considered, worked-out plans for rebuilding *ab initio*, including Wren and Evelyn (As Evelyn reported, Wren's plan was with the King by 11 September; Evelyn's two days later).[58]

Fortunately when it came to proposals to exploit the utter devastation

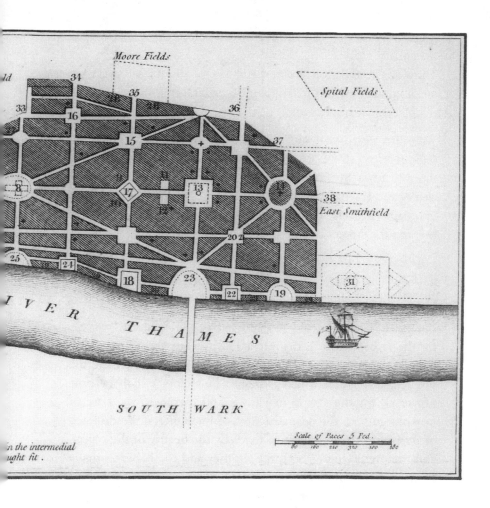

Moore Fields

Spital Fields

34

33

16

35

36

15

37

+

8

17

13

14

38

East Smithfield

10

25

24

18

23

22

19

31

20 21

R I V E R

T H A M E S

S O U T H   W A R K

Scale of Paces 5 Fed.

n the intermedial
ught fit .

in the heart of the City and redesign its layout and circulation, immediately following the Fire, this group was already well prepared. A Royal
Commission 'for reforming the buildings, ways, streets, and incumbrances, and regulating the hackney coaches in the City of London'
had been convened by the Lord Chancellor, Clarendon, and the Royal
Surveyor, Sir John Denham, in spring 1662.[59] Evelyn reports that 'there
were divers gentlemen of quality in this commission'. The Commission,
which included Sir Stephen Fox, an important figure in the King's
financial team, met regularly throughout 1663 and 1664. If Wren was
among them, it would explain why, although not named in the list of
those appointed to the Commission for Renovation of St Paul's
Cathedral two years later, both Evelyn and Wren are referred to as

'Commissioners' when called upon to participate in a feasibility study for St Paul's.

The 1662 Commission had immediately set about a rational reorganisation of circulation in the City, and a programme of repaving major thoroughfares. Evelyn reports:

> 31st [June 1662]. I sat with the Commissioners about reforming buildings and streets of London, and we ordered the paving of the way from St. James's North, which was a quagmire, and also of the Haymarket about Piqudillo [Piccadilly], and agreed upon instructions to be printed and published for the better keeping the streets clean.[60]

In a dedicatory letter to Sir John Denham, written in 1664, Evelyn acknowledged the Royal Surveyor's contribution to the Commission's work:

> But neither here must I forget what is alone due to you Sir for the reformation in the streets, as by your introducing that incomparable form of paving to an incredible advantage to the Publick, when that which is begun in Holborn shall become universal, for the saving of wheels and carriages, the cure of noysom gutters, the deobstruction of Encounters, the dispatch of Busi-ness, the cleanness of the way, the beauty of the object, and the preserving of both the mother and the babe, so many of the fair sex and their offspring having perished by mischances (as I am credibly informed) from the ruggedness of the unequal street.[61]

Thus for several years before the Fire, Evelyn and Wren had been studying the street-pattern of the capital, discussing circulation routes, the widening of streets, improvements to intersections and the paving of main thoroughfares. Denham's talent, in fact, seems to have been for town-planning – his Commission for reforming streets established the tone and temperament of the rebuilding which followed the Fire. Indeed, it was Denham who drafted the emergency regulations of 13 September.

It is not surprising, then, that Wren's and Evelyn's schemes for a London whose street-plan and layout were begun again from scratch should have resembled one another (as the King himself remarked).

Both plans showed strong continental influences, with radial streets superimposed on a grid; both treated the northern end of London Bridge as the point of entry into the City and showed three streets diverging from a large oval space containing St Paul's Cathedral, east of Ludgate. Both included an improved Fleet Ditch (see below), at right angles to a substantial 'quay' running the length of the frontage on to the Thames.[62] A fine quay was, we recall, the feature Edward Browne reported Wren as admiring most about Paris.[63]

Wren's scheme was accompanied by a document justifying and commenting upon each novel feature of his design. In it Wren represented the Fire as a golden opportunity to build a new royal city, and was typically robust about the undesirability of retaining the existing property boundaries and rebuilding to the old plan:

Consequences of Rebuilding the City upon the old Foundations

Either the Town must be built with Timber Buildings as before or with Brick on the same foundations.

The Inconveniencies of Building just as before, are too obvious to be reckon'd; the Calamities of Plague and Fire manifestly proceeding from the Closeness of the Streets and the Combustible Materials.

To Build with Brick upon the Same Foundations has These Inconveniencies.

1) The Streets will be much more Deform'd then before, unless the Fronts of Brick-Houses range by Lines.

2) Foundations that supported some houses of great rents in Timber will not serve a house of half those rents in Brick, because Timber Houses gain room by projecture of Stories, & some will be totally lost that ran over Alleys.

3) All the Inconveniencies of Stops, and ill Passage will remain.

4) It will be a Shame to the Nation, which will be thrown upon us by all our Politer Neighbours, that haveing the Opportunity in our hands of makeing This Place the most convenient City for Trade in the World, we should negligently let it slide into Its old Barbarity, for which when it is irreparable our Posterity will ~~curse~~ <blame> the ill and untractable Humours of This Age.

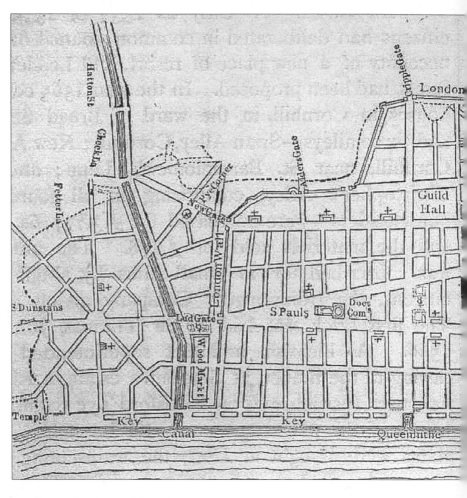

Wren's plan for the rebuilding of London, an ambitious, Paris-influenced radial design, based on an assumption of 'raze and rebuild', which smacked of the absolutism of Charles I.

5) Nothing will more Discover abroad the Weakness of our Government, both as to the discretion of our Governors, & Their Influence upon the Commonalty, then This, That haveing an Opportunity in their hands of doeing one of the greatest Benefits that can be done to the Publick, They are unable to bring it to Pass, or unwilling to be at the trouble.[64]

Parliament met in the last week of September, and debated Wren's and Evelyn's proposals as part of a wide-ranging discussion which

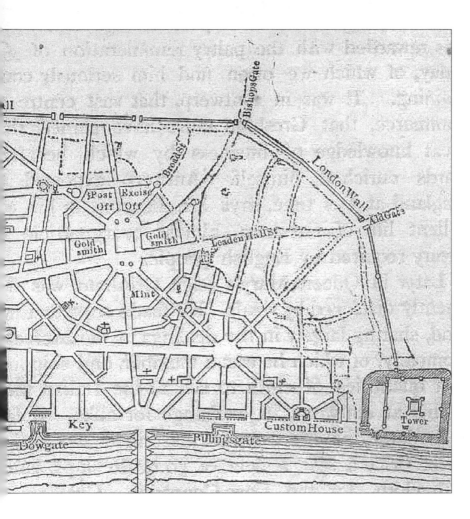

considered both limited and radical change to the City's layout. Among Wren's papers at the end of his life was what appears to be a set of memoranda based on these discussions:

Objections against the Model in 15 articles.

Those Objections answer'd, Article by Article.

The Method propos'd for Surveying the Parts of the City consumed by the Fire.

Of the Inconveniencies of the Old Town before the Fire.

To Remedy all Those Inconveniencies in the Restoration of the City.

A Middle Way propos'd to Remedy as many Inconveniencies as possible, with the least disturbance of Private Interest, and the Constitutions of the Government.

The Heads of a Power to be given a Com[m]ission by Act of Parliament, to Enable them to Transplant Proprietors, for Widening the Streets, and makeing the Key.

Heads of an Act of Parl: to Enable Commissioners to Regulate the Forms of Public & Private Buildings, & Other Things conducing to Publich Benefit.[65]

In the end Parliament reached no conclusion, although its mood seemed to favour a compromise solution. As for the Privy Council, in spite of the King's own enthusiasm for a fresh start, it was the scale of the cost of such a scheme which caused hesitation.[66] Wren's son recalled, with an edge of bitterness:

After he [Wren] had taken a Survey with all possible exactness of that Part which lay in Ashes, he Contriv'd a Model for Building the New City in a very Regular <Form,> with particular Beauty and Symmetry, suitable to so Noble a Situation, and most Commodious for Health and Trade, which was Lay'd before the King and Parliament; but he was not able to Prosecute this Design in every part, because the Generality of the Citizens and Proprietors insisted on haveing their Houses rebuilt on their old Foundations, without any deviation. This Original Plan, (Drawn by his own hand,) with References, and the Properties of it, and Answers to all Objections that have been made, are still extant, and with his other Architectonical-Works, are design'd, at a proper time, to be Engrav'd and Publish'd.[67]

The failure of nerve on the part of court and City administrations, as a result of which all the plans submitted for razing and rebuilding were rejected, may be directly related to anxiety about the appearance of absolutism. To achieve the visual aesthetic pleasure of radial avenues, vistas and grand monuments required the removal of the urban residents of the City, the compulsory purchase of their property and their enforced resettlement elsewhere. One contemporary who saw Wren's plan made precisely this point when he queried 'whether it has consulted with the populousness of a great city, and whether reason of state would have that consulted with'. This was not the kind of renovation a king who had declared himself, on returning, to be 'of the people' could be seen to endorse. It is, indeed, a measure of Wren's (and Evelyn's) continuing commitment to the old absolutist Stuart version of sovereignty that they sprang into action with models for rebuilding which for all their 'modernity' were based squarely on Laudian organisational principles.

Instead, within a month of the Fire a programme of surveying all existing sites had been undertaken, and the pegging out of new, widened streets, which took account of the existing buildings (and recompensed owners for any ground lost). Already in the 'Declaration To His City of London, Upon Occasion of the late Calamity by the lamentable Fire' issued on 13 September, the King himself set an example by proposing: 'That We may encourage men by Our Own example, We will use the expedition We can to re-build Our Custome-House in the place where it formerly stood, and enlarge it with the most conveniences for the Merchants that can be devised.'[68] Here is the tone which would be sustained throughout London's rebuilding: the new will be significantly better than the old, but it will be located exactly where 'formerly' it stood, confirming existing property ownership, and making a meticulous survey of London's past the basis for London's future.[69]

As for the river-fronting quay – vested property interests along the north side of the Thames prevented Wren's grand designs for an unloading and commercial storage area like that in Paris from being fully realised, although in 1671 he did manage to include in the specifications for a quay, 'made generally straighter', a purpose-built area for two substantial cranes to unload the Portland stone for St Paul's.[70] The City later agreed to an ambitious plan for exploiting the potential commercial value of its river banks by commissioning Wren and Hooke to design a scheme for improving the Fleet Ditch, allocating monies from the coal tax imposed for the rebuilding of the City churches. Under their direction this shallow river – running from the Thames to Holborn Bridge – was straightened and canalised. Quays forty feet wide were build alongside on both banks, backed by vaults and storehouses.[71]

In his eagerness to be the first to present his master-plan for London's rebuilding, Wren once again offended the Royal Society by taking his proposals in person directly to the King. Oldenburg (by this time the official Secretary of the Royal Society), who saw Wren's 'model' a week later and was impressed by it, made no attempt to hide his annoyance at what he regarded as a major opportunity lost for the Society. He wrote to Boyle in Oxford:

> Such a modell, contrived by him, and reviewed and approved
> by ye R Society, or a Committee thereoff, before it had come
> to the view of his Majesty, would have given the Society a name,
> and made it popular, and availed not a little to silence those,
> who aske continually, What have they done?[72]

Hooke, who had certainly been privy to Wren's deliberations during the drawing up of his own (and perhaps Evelyn's) plan, swiftly stepped in to smooth over any embarrassment Wren might have caused. Within another week Hooke had prepared and presented to the City his own plan for rebuilding.[73] Sir John Lawrence showed it to the Royal Society and reported that the Lord Mayor, Sir Thomas Bludworth, and the Court of Aldermen had approved the plan in preference to one by Peter Mills, the City Surveyor, and that they wished to present it to the King for his approval. The Royal Society responded that they would be pleased if one of their employees could be of service to his Majesty.[74]

Although in the end the decision was taken largely to retain London's old street-plan, this incident is an illuminating one for our understanding of the relationship between Hooke and Wren, and the practices they had already established in their collaborative work.

After Hooke settled at Gresham College in 1662, he and Wren had resumed the habits of close collaboration in scientific experiment and astronomical observation they had developed in the mid-1650s in Oxford. Both were in fact still toing-and-froing between London and Oxford – Wren because he still held his post of Savilian Professor of Astronomy (he finally resigned in 1673),[75] Hooke because he continued to combine his posts in London with service to Boyle, who kept a base (and a laboratory) in Oxford until 1668. At Royal Society meetings, a pattern emerged whereby Wren and Hooke proposed some chosen investigation together, and worked on it in its preliminary stages as a partnership. Hooke next put in the detailed, time-consuming practical work to move the project through development and execution, consulting Wren when necessary. He then presented the final results to the Society on his own, with fulsome acknowledgement of Wren's input.

The partnership worked because the two men had distinct, complementary skills. Wren was conceptually the more original, with a gift for identifying important theoretical issues, and the pure mathematical ability to solve difficult problems. Hooke's talents lay in the direction of design of experiments and the technical equipment necessary to conduct them. His considerable mathematical ability was firmly on the applied side (his attempts at solutions to pure mathematical problems like that of the form of the equation for the catenary curve smack of bravado). By temperament he was an inventor and engineer. Of the two, there is no doubt that Wren was the better draughtsman – Wren, indeed, drew with great natural ease and elegance from an early age, whereas Hooke's drawings tend to resemble carefully measured technical drawings.

Already by 1665–6 it was extremely difficult to decide which of the two men was the prime mover in joint undertakings. Oldenburg's correspondents, at home and abroad, regularly referred to Wren and Hooke together in one breath, as if they were a known working partnership – 'please pass these remarks to Mr. Wren and Mr. Hooke' and so on.[76] This reflected the reality of their shared participation in Royal Society experiments. When Moray proposed to the Royal Society a project for fixing the positions of the stars in the Zodiac in April 1663, Hooke and Wren volunteered to survey Taurus together.[77] A star-map of the Pleiades figures in Hooke's *Micrographia*; we also have evidence for an extended collaboration over the motion of comets a year and a half later.

In December 1664, the appearance of a comet was reported at a Royal Society meeting attended by both Wren and Hooke. Hooke was instructed to make observations and compile a 'history' (a table of results), while Wren agreed to do the same in Oxford. As in the case of the Oxford group injection and transfusion experiments, the comet observations and the subsequent generalised discussions of cometary motion were part of an organised collaboration, which in this case comprised Wren, Hooke and Wallis in London, plus two overseas observers, Adrien Auzout and Christiaan Huygens (both in Paris).

On 20 January 1665 Moray reported to Huygens that Wren was collating the English observations of the comet viewed from London. At a meeting of the Royal Society the following day Wallis presented Auzout's hypothesis, in a recently published article, that the path of the comet was a straight line, bent by a magnetic attractive force pulling it towards the sun. Wallis responded with the view that comets were emitted from the sun in a straight line, but retarded by the sun's attractive force. Given the rotation of the sun (as Wallis believed), the resulting path of the comet was an ellipse which began and ended in the sun.[78]

Wren's own contribution to this discussion, characteristically, consisted in his suggesting the geometrical problem whose solution would advance the investigation further. Suppose the comet moved in a straight line in space. The question was, how would one determine what that path looked like when viewed in the ecliptic (that is, in the plane swept by the earth around the sun)? In other words, how would one prove the comet's path on the basis of, say, four observations taken from a given location? The relevant geometrical problem, according to Wren, was to find the straight line intersected by four given straight lines, such that the ratio between the three segments thus formed was that of the time intervals between the observations.[79]

At the end of January 1665, Moray promised Huygens that Wren would shortly be producing an account based on Wren's and Hooke's combined observations, and at a meeting on 1 February, 'Dr. Wren produced some observations of the comet, with a theory.' The theory, apparently, assumed a uniform rectilinear path. Wren produced a solution to his geometrical problem, and a diagram, in which Wren used his mathematical construction to locate the comet and describe its motion in a straight line between 20 October 1664 and 20 January 1665. Hooke later published both in his *Cometa* ('Comets').

This looked like the end of Wren's active participation. By late February, Hooke was lecturing on the comet at Gresham College; by March, Wren was planning his trip to France. On 17 March, Moray told Huygens that Hooke had taken over the comet investigations from Wren. However, on 31 March Huygens reported that a new comet had appeared, and this rekindled Wren's interest. Both Hooke (in London) and Wren (in Oxford) began a fresh set of observations in the first week

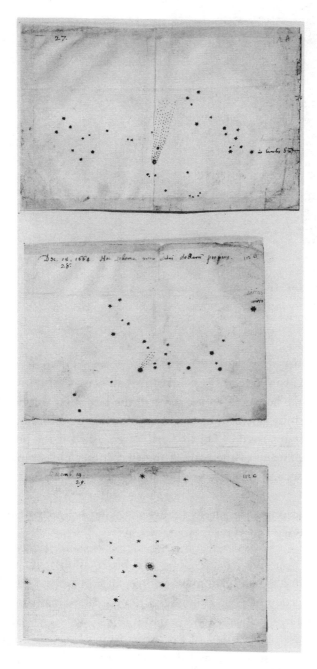

Sketches of the nightly progress of the 1664 comet, made by Hooke
as part of the co-ordinated observations he and Wren conducted for the
Royal Society.

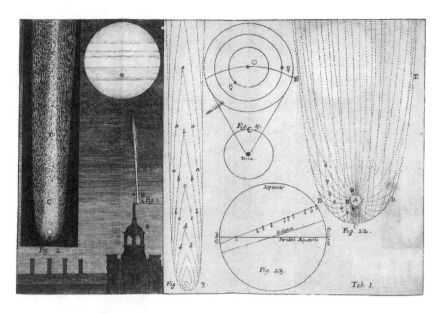

Engraved plate from Hooke's published treatise on comets (1678).

of April, and on 7 April Wren asked Moray 'if I may obtain what observations you have at Gresham of this 2d comet. Also I would desire of Mr. Hooke he would let me have all the last observations of the last Comet when he began to be stationary or slow his Motion, & when & where he disappeared.'[80] On 19 April Wren asked if the Society could return his drawing of the path of the first comet for comparison with that of the second, and Hooke duly copied the drawing for the Society's archive.

In the accompanying letter (a rare surviving example of an exchange between Hooke and Wren), Hooke wrote:

I hope you received the globe and observations which I sent you: you had had them much sooner, but, in truth, I could not get the copy of your Hypothesis, though the amanuensis was ordered by the society to have had it ready above a week before.

Those observations of my own making I have not yet had time to adjust so well as I desired; for the sun came upon me before I was aware, and so I must stay till the constellation of [Aries] appear in the morning, before I can be able to rectify the places of the telescopial stars, by which I observed the comet to pass; which I hope I may do about a fortnight hence, about which time also I expect to see both the old, or first comet, with a telescope, and second, or last comet, with my eye; for, if the motion of them be regular, as I see not the least cause to doubt, I hope to be able to design their places among the fixed stars, without erring much more than I am able to see at once with a telescope; and therefore I hope it will be no difficult matter to find either of them, unless the first may be gone so far as to disappear by reason of distance, which is, indeed, the greatest part of my fear; for, if it continue to move those ways I imagined it, whether we take the supposition of the motion of the earth, and imagine the comet to be moved in a circle, one side of which touches, or rather goes within the orb of the earth on one side, and without the orb of Saturn, or, at least, that of Jupiter on the other, whose plane is inclined to that of the ecliptic about twenty degrees, or whether we suppose the earth to stand still, and the comet to be moved in a great circle, whose convex side, is turned towards the earth (which, supposing no certain parallax has been observed, may be supposed of any bigness, keeping only the same proportion between the nearest distance of it from the earth, and the radius or diameter of that circle), it must appear again very near the same place, about a fortnight hence.

And I am apt to think the body of the comet is of a constitution that will last much longer than either a month or a year, nay, than an age; and if I can be so lucky as to meet with it again, I hope to trace it to its second appearing. But I weary you with my conjectures; and I doubt not but that before this, you have perfected the theory of comets, so as to be able to predict much more certainly what we are to expect of these comets for the future; wherefore, if at your leisure you will please to afford me a word or two, you will much oblige me.[81]

Here Hooke is clearly proposing a circular orbit for comets, in a plane angled to that containing the earth and the sun (the ecliptic). Wren responded to him:

I thank you for the freedome of your converse wch. I should be glad you would sometimes continue to me whilest I am heer though I dare not importune you to it, for I know you are full of employment for the Society wch. you allmost wholy preserve together by your own constant paines. I have not yet received the Globe & papers. . . . I shall be attent to looke for both the Comets if the Sun give us leave, though I am affrayd the 2d. runnes too fast into the South.[82]

In autumn 1665, Moray reported to Oldenburg that Hooke and Wren were working together, developing a theory of the nature and motion of comets.[83]

Hooke's diary shows that he and Wren continued to discuss cometary motion informally for a number of years. By the time he published his *Cometa* in 1678, Hooke's considered view was that cometary movement was basically rectilinear, but was modified by gravitational forces. Thus the theory, as contained in Hooke's published work, was the outcome of more than ten years of group discussion, in which Wren and he were the leading figures.

In the case of another long-running project, the weather-gauge, or weather-clock, however, the situation was reversed. Here, Wren took credit for the final instrument, in spite of the clearly documented fact that Hooke had participated throughout the design stage, and was largely responsible for turning the theoretical instrument into a practical reality.

In its final form, Wren's weather-gauge was a complex instrument for measuring various aspects of the weather over a period of time: rainfall, barometric pressure and humidity. It consisted of a clock, a barometer, a thermometer, a tipping-bucket for rainfall measurement, and a hygroscope; it also incorporated ingenious devices for recording small changes in each of the above, using pulleys, pencils and rotating drums or plates.[84] When the French aristocrat Monconys visited England in 1663 he was shown an automatic rain-gauge made by Wren ('M. Renes'). Twelve years later it was again firmly attributed to Wren in the *Philosophical Transactions* of the Royal Society, though this time with some acknowledgement of Hooke's hand in the instrument's modifications:

[Estimation of rainfall] hath been attempted here, and proposed to the *R. Society*, some years since, by *Sr. Chrs. Wren*, who by the contrivance of a Rain-bucket had taken an account of all the Water that fell for a considerable time; and by his

Weather-clock had, among other particulars, not only taken in the measuring of the quantity of Rain that falls, but also the time when it falls, and how much at each time. Which Instrument, if put into practice, would be of excellent Use, forasmuch as it may also serve, by some additions made thereunto by *Mr. Hooke*, to record the weight of the Air, the drought, moisture, heat and cold of the Weather, the Sun-shine, the quarters and strength of the Winds: And all this to be performed by one only motion, driving all the parts of the instrument; which is therefore the more considerable, that itself records its own effects.[85]

Wren seems to have been the first to devise a method of registering small changes in mercury level by using a float on the surface of the mercury, attached to a weight by a string and pulley wheel, so that the string moved an index (or a pencil) to trace a path on a sheet moved by clockwork. Hooke subsequently incorporated the device in his 'wheel baroscope' – a barometer capable of registering extremely small changes in barometric pressure, in 1678. He was encouraged to do so by difficulties he was having registering very small changes in pressure at stages down the stairway inside the recently completed 'Monument in Fish Street'.[86] In July 1663, Wren suggested that his 'circular thermometer' might amuse the King on his proposed visit to the Society, since he himself had 'pleased myself not a little with ye play of ye weather wheele (ye only true way to measure expansions of ye Aire)'.[87]

Hooke, on the other hand, was certainly responsible for the construction of the tipping water-bucket which was a crucial feature of the rain-gauge in its final form. He had been officially asked by the Royal Society to undertake further refinement of a weather-clock 'such as Dr Wren had formerly contrived' in 1670. Derham's volume of Hooke's posthumous papers (1725) includes a paper on a 'Weather-Wiser' or 'Weather-Clock', delivered to the Society in December 1678. It describes, with diagram and mathematical explanation, 'Dr. Hooke's Contrivance of a Vessel, to measure the Quantities of Rain falling'. This sets and solves the problem: 'To make a Vessel, which, when it hath received a certain Quantity of Water, shall empty itself'.[88]

Wren's weather-clock – regularly mentioned in the roll-call of extraordinary instruments devised and built by him – was thus a composite piece of scientific equipment, which in its final, working form incorporated bits of technology devised by both Wren and Hooke, and refined by either or both of them over a period of years.

The most celebrated and most striking example of the long-running and complex Wren–Hooke partnership, however, was the compilation of drawings of tiny creatures much magnified under the new microscope – that 'curiosity' which prompted the delighted King to take a personal interest in the newly formed Royal Society. The eventual end product of this particular collaboration was Hooke's single-authored best-seller, *Micrographia*, published in 1665: a lavishly illustrated folio volume combining scientific content, based on experiments conducted for the Royal Society, and eye-catching engravings of a wide range of magnified objects and organisms. Pepys was an early purchaser, and was captivated by the illustrations, noting in his diary that the following evening he 'sat up till 2 a-clock in [his] chamber, reading of Mr. Hooke's Microscopical Observations'. He commented that it was 'the most ingenious book' he had ever read.[89] Even today the *Micrographia* engravings have a particular vitality, and are much reproduced.

These 'Microscopical Observations' were a joint venture between Wren and Hooke from as early as 1655, when Hooke began working with Wilkins's group in Oxford, alongside Wilkins's protégé Wren. In that year it was Wren whom Hartlib reported to be putting together a book of his drawings:

> The 17 September Mr Wren told of a Book which hee is preparing with Pictures of observations microscopical. He counteth Reeves makes the best of any Microscopes to bee had. As likewise Tubes of which they have one at Oxford of 24. foot long. which with a thread once placed hee can manage as hee pleases. As likewise to rule the light or Sight in it according to all its diversities.[90]

In the preface to *Micrographia* in its final, published form, Hooke scrupulously acknowledged this shared ownership, as well as giving a clear account of the process of the project's development:

> If these my first Labours shall be any wayes useful to inquiring men, I must attribute the incouragement and promotion of them to a very Reverend and Learned Person, of whom this ought in justice to be said, That there is scarce any one invention, which this Nation has produc'd in our Age, but it

has some way or other been set forward by his assistance. My reader, I believe will quickly ghess, that it is Dr. Wilkins that I mean. He is indeed a man born for the good of mankind; and for the honour of his Country. In the sweetness of whose behaviour, in the calmness of his mind, in the unbounded goodness of his heart, we have an evident Instance, what the true and the primitive unpassionate Religion was, before it was sowred by particular Factions. . . . So may I thank God, that Dr. Wilkins was an Englishman, for whereever he had lived, there had been the chief Seat of generous Knowledge and true Philosophy. . . .

By the Advice of this Excellent man I first set upon this Enterprise, yet still came to it with much Reluctancy, because I was to follow the footsteps of so eminent a Person as Dr. Wren, who was the first that attempted any thing of this nature; whose original draughts do now make one of the Ornaments of that great Collection of Rarities in the Kings Closet. This Honor, which his first beginnings of this kind have receiv'd, to be admitted into the most famous place of the world, did not so much incourage, as the hazard of coming after Dr. Wren did affright me; for of him I must affirm, that, since the time of Archimedes, there scarce ever met in one man, in so great a perfection, such a Mechanical Hand; and so Philosophical a Mind.

But at last, being assured both by Dr. Wilkins, and Dr. Wren himself, that he had given over his intentions of prosecuting it, and not finding that there was any else design'd the pursuing of it, I set upon this undertaking, and was not a little incourag'd to proceed in it, by the Honour the Royal Society was pleas'd to favour me with, in approving of those draughts (which from time to time as I had an opportunity of describing) I presented to them. And particularly by the Incitements of divers of those Noble and excellent Persons of it, which were my more especial Friends, who were not less urgent with me for the publishing, then for the prosecution of them.[91]

In the same preface, Hooke described the complex manner in which his original drawings were made – line drawings from which the engravings were made under his supervision by William Faithorne:[92]

I never began to make any draught before by many examinations in several lights, and in several positions to those lights, I had discover'd the true form. For it is exceeding difficult in some Objects, to distinguish between a prominency and a depression, between a shadow and a black stain, or a reflection and a whiteness in the colour. Besides, the transparency of most Objects renders them yet much more difficult then if they were opacous.[93]

These remarks apply most evidently to plates like that of the cell structure of a section of cork, and the magnified point of a needle; they are far less apt as a description of the process which produced the drawings (and then engravings) of insects and minute life-forms. We know Hooke invented an instrument he named the 'scotoscope' to focus additional light on to scientific specimens under the microscope – enhancing light and shadow as he describes above. The complexity of living organisms, on the other hand, we learn from other sources, required repeated sketches of multiple specimens, which the draughtsman then combined into one 'ideal' specimen.[94]

Hooke's remarks are also consistent with the fact that while he was completing the *Micrographia* plates, he was also drawing experimental set-ups and pieces of equipment for a volume of Boyle's, and overseeing their production alongside his at Faithorne's shop.[95] Technical drawing, rather than virtuoso life-drawing of tiny animals, was Hooke's forte. The insect-drawings in *Micrographia* are in all likelihood Wren's. So the *Micrographia* text is (as Hooke tells us) a compilation of topics presented for discussion at the Royal Society, while the engravings are a *mélange* by Hooke and Wren. Nevertheless, the final volume bears Hooke's name alone on the title-page, and has, since its publication, always been attributed to Hooke, in spite of the internal evidence to the contrary.

Remarkably, Wren remained active in scientific research throughout the 1670s and 1680s, in spite of the increasing demands of his official work as Surveyor of the King's Works, particularly, after 1670, when he held responsibility for the design and rebuilding of all fifty-one City churches destroyed in the Fire, and for the reconstruction of St Paul's. This required considerable organisation and self-discipline on his part. Like Boyle, he fell into a pattern of letting Hooke notify him when a matter in which he had an interest was coming up, and duly attended

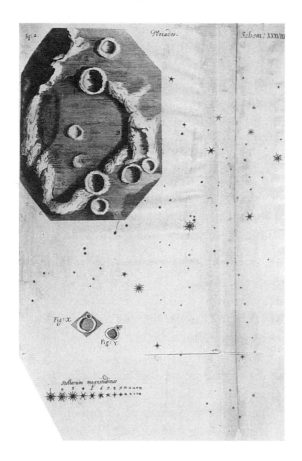

Survey of a portion of the surface of the moon, and map of the Pleiades from Hooke's *Micrographia* – some work in this popular publication was probably done collaboratively with Wren.

and contributed.[96] We misunderstand Wren's commitment to the Royal Society, therefore, if we merely note his occasional attendance at meetings from the Royal Society records. In his scientific activities, exactly as we shall shortly see was the case in his architectural practice, Wren – ever the efficient manager of his time, as of those who worked under him – economised on his presence at meetings, but kept a firm eye on the progress of the project in hand.

Meanwhile, he never lost interest in developments in areas of science to which he had once contributed himself. In 1690, for example, we find him discussing the latest in air and nitre theory with Hooke at one of their favourite coffee houses: 'With Sr. Christ. Wren at Mans: theory of Niter air flame'.[97]

In 1669 Sir John Denham died, and the job of Surveyor of the King's Works finally fell vacant. There were three old-guard contenders for the post: Webb, May and Pratt all believed they were owed the reversion by the King, for their services to architecture (and their patience in waiting for the top job). If Mills had still been alive he would presumably have expected it too. But Charles did not appoint one of the old guard. Instead, the Royal Surveyorship went to Wren. The disgruntled May told Pepys that he believed Wren's appointment had been due to the intervention of the Duke of Buckingham:

> Mr. May . . . tells me the story of his being put by by Sir John Denham's place (of Surveyor of the King's Works, who it seems is lately dead) by the unkindness of the Duke of Buckingham, who hath brough in Dr. Wren – though he tells me he hath been his servant for twenty years together, in all his wants and dangers, saving him from want of bread by his care and management, and with a promise of having his help in his advancement, and an engagement under his hand for 1000l not yet paid; and yet the Duke of Buckingham is so ungrateful as to put him by – which is an ill thing – though Dr. Wren is a worthy man.[98]

Clearly there was some ill feeling about Wren's being catapulted into the key royal architectural appointment, and promises had undoubtedly been made. Nevertheless, the most likely reason for the King's preferring Wren was because Wren's name alone of those qualified to take up the appointment was not tarnished by association with buildings designed and executed in England during the period of Charles's exile. The King needed a new man to design and build his restored capital city on a scale to match ancient Rome. Wren's profile as 'architect in waiting' in the years preceding perfectly matched the King's own as 'monarch in waiting'.[99]

Now with a residence at Whitehall, rather than bachelor rooms in an Oxford college, Wren could at last consider starting his own family. His chosen bride came from the Oxfordshire village, home of his sister Susan Holder and her husband, in which he had grown up. His marriage to Faith Coghill, daughter of Sir Thomas Coghill of Bletchingdon, in December 1669, was probably brokered by William Holder, who was on the point of launching himself into the public arena after many years as a country clergyman. The same year, 1669, in which Holder published his *Elements of Language*, with its appendix on teaching a deaf-mute to speak, and its strong contestation of John Wallis's claim that he had been the first successfully to do so (Wren, too, had had occasion to accuse Wallis of stealing ideas from him, and there was a suggestion that his continuing role as a government cryptographer gave him unreasonable advantages in matters of intellectual property and priority).[100]

From the early 1670s Holder was appointed to a succession of ecclesiastical posts at St Paul's Cathedral, under the direct patronage of the King. The records show that it was indeed on account of Wren that his brother-in-law was appointed:

> Sep. 29 1672 – Whitehall. King to Dean & Chapter of St. Pauls – recommends Wm: Holder DD for 1st canonry residential that becomes void . . . esp[ecially] because of his mathematical learning, & is also a near relative of Dr. wren, surveyor of the works & so may be of assistance to them in their building.[101]

Holder was by this time already the holder of minor posts at the Chapel Royal and St Paul's (presumably also as a result of petitioning by Wren). The next step towards his significant promotion came five years later:

> October 31 Whitehall 1678 – re. Wm Holder, sub-almoner & sub-dean of the Chapel Royal & prebendary of St. Pauls. King to Dean & Chapter of St. Pauls. Has filled a place of canon-residentiary with Tillotson (though already promised to Holder) King asks them to keep the next void place for Holder.[102]

Eight months later Holder petitioned the King to make sure the appointment as Prebend would indeed be forthcoming:

> June 18 1679 Whitehall – petition of Wm Holder DD praying to his Majesty to confirm a former promise of the next prebend of Westminster. Declaration by his majesty that he intends the petitioner shall have the benefit of the former promise.[103]

Holder subsequently sat on a number of committees associated with the rebuilding of St Paul's, right down to the 1690s.

An autograph letter concerning a damaged pocket-watch, interleaved in the Heirloom copy of *Parentalia*, has traditionally been identified, sentimentally, as a 'courtship' letter to Faith Coghill. The woman Wren addresses – evidently someone close to him – has 'drowned' a pocket-watch by somehow immersing it in water. Wren has, after some considerable lapse of time, restored the watch, with its delicate balance mechanism, to working order, and now returns it. The letter ends with an engagingly practical postscript: 'I haue put the Watch in a Box that it might Take noe harme, & wrapt it about with a little Leather, & that it might not jog, I was fain to fill up the corners either with a few shavings or wast paper.'[104]

That traditional identification of the addressee of this letter is frankly implausible. Pocket-watches were rare, expensive items, unlikely to be owned by a woman in an Oxfordshire village. This one, furthermore, is to be consulted by its female owner: 'how your time shall passe while you employ your hand in your excellent workes'. This implies that the woman in question does something of publicly acknowledged significance in the way of 'workes'. Faith Coghill, as far as we know, was at home in Bletchingdon until her marriage to Wren.

There are two further candidates as recipient of a Wren letter of this loving kind, who might have returned it to the family archive. One is his second wife Jane, about whom we know so little that it is hardly worth speculating. The other is his beloved sister Susan, who was indeed someone with recognised 'chirurgical' and medical skills, and sufficiently in the court and Royal Society circle with her husband by the 1680s (when surely this letter was written) to have owned (and dropped into water) a watch with a complicated balance mechanism. If so, it is further evidence of the depth of feeling between Wren and his one surviving close relative, who had raised him in Oxfordshire.

Wren's marriage, like so much else in his post-Restoration life, harks back to his childhood, picking up the threads of the sheltered, modest life at Bletchingdon after the Holders rescued the Wrens in 1646. He probably had known Faith as a boy, since the Holders and Coghills were neighbours. For both it was a late marriage: Wren was thirty-seven; his new wife was four years younger.[105]

Wren's first child, a son, was born on 14 October 1672, and christened

Gilbert, after Archbishop Sheldon, who may well have agreed to be his godfather. There is no doubt the birth of a son and heir was enormously important to Wren – even Hooke recorded the event in his diary.[106] In November Hooke visited, and gave the baby's nurse a generous gift of money.[107]

In 1673, Wren's position as an established figure in London court circles was confirmed when he received a knighthood from the King. Hooke, who was inevitably the first to know, recorded the event somewhat laconically in his diary: 'Friday November 14 1673. – Dr. Wren knighted and gone to Oxford.'[108] The sudden trip to Oxford was for Wren to hand in his resignation as Savilian Professor of Astronomy. The job which had been so important in marking the transformation of his prospects at the Restoration was now no more than one more pressure in his demanding public life. From now on Wren, like most of his virtuosi friends, and all of his court acquaintances, would be based in London.

Sadly, Wren's satisfaction in this period was marred by anxiety about his infant son. On 15 September 1673 Hooke noted in his diary that the nine-month-old Gilbert had been having convulsive fits while he had been visiting.[109] The baby died on 23 March 1674. Hooke again recorded the death in his diary – something he only did in the case of those he was very close to.[110] Nor was this the end of Wren's troubles. In February 1675 a second son was born and named Christopher. But just six months later, in late August, Hooke reported that Faith had been 'five days sick of small pox'; she died on 3 September. On 11 September Hooke, Wren and Faith's mother, Lady Coghill, dined together – one imagines she was caring for (and organising future care for) the infant Christopher.

On 24 February 1677, Wren (by now referred to in royal documents as 'our trusty and well-beloved Sir Christopher Wren, Knight') remarried, at the Chapel Royal, Whitehall. His second wife was Jane Fitzwilliam, daughter of William, second Baron Fitzwilliam of Lifford in Ireland. This was a more prestigious match than the first (witness the royal location for the wedding ceremony).[111] There is some evidence that Wren's new companion was interested in philosophy and religion, since on one occasion, Hooke records in his diary, he promised to produce 'Mahomet's book' (the Quran) for her.[112] She bore Wren two further children: Jane (born November 1677), Wren's favourite child, who died tragically young on 29 December 1702; and William (born 16 June 1679), to whom Evelyn stood godfather, known throughout his life to the family as 'poor Billy', on account of the chronic mental disability from which he suffered from birth.[113] On 4 October 1680, after a short illness, Wren's second wife died, leaving Wren a widower once again, with three small children.[114]

Wren thus enjoyed married life for only ten of his ninety-one years. There is no reason to think that those years were anything but typical, happy family years, during which, like other professional men of his rank, work and the company of his male friends tended to take precedence over domestic affairs. Nevertheless, Hooke's diary bears witness to the fact that married life dovetailed smoothly with the long-standing partnership Wren had developed over the years with Hooke. The extraordinarily close relationship between Wren and Hooke continued uninterrupted throughout the years of Wren's married life, as did his day-to-day habits of meeting and dining with a group of male friends with interests akin to his own. And at moments of crisis – the death of a child, the sickness of a wife – it was, apparently, to Hooke that Wren turned for emotional support.[115] He and Hooke, after all, shared a long history of devastating family losses and domestic upheavals.

Nor was the intimate relationship between Hooke and Wren confined to their shared professional business. They also socialised together, particularly when there was music to be listened to. Both were considerable music lovers. Wren had grown up in the house of William Holder, of whom Aubrey wrote: 'He is very musicall, both theorically and practically, and he had a sweet voyce. He hath writt an excellent treatise of musique, in English, which is writte both *doctis et indocti*s, and readie for the presse.' Hooke may have been a choral scholar at Christ Church, Oxford.[116]

Pepys reports their attendance at a high society musical performance together:

> To my Lord Brouncker's, and there was Sir Rob. Murray [Moray] . . . a most excellent man of reason and learning, and understands the doctrine of Music, and every thing else I could discourse of very finely. Here come Mr Hooke, Sir George Ent, Dr Wren, and many others; and by and by the music, that is to say, Seignor Vincentio, who is the master Composer, and six

more, where of two Eunuches (so tall, that Sir T. Harvy said well that he believes they did grow large, by being gelt, as our oxen do), and one woman very, well dressed and handsome enough but would not be kissed, as Mr. Killigrew, who brought the company in, did acquaint us. They sent two Harpsicons before and by and by, after tuning them, they begun; and, I confess, very good music they made; that is, the composition exceeding good, but yet not at all more pleasing to me than what I have heard in English by Mrs. Knipp, Captain Coocke, and others ... Their justness in keeping time by practice much before any that we have, unless it be a good band of practiced fiddlers.[117]

BUILDING FOR ETERNITY

Towards the end of 1666, shortly after the King had set up his Royal Commission for Rebuilding, Wren once again carried out a survey of the fabric of St Paul's. On the previous occasion, he had been alarmed by the state of the building, in spite of its apparent potential for refurbishment; now he emphasised just how little remained to sustain any fresh attempt at restoration:

> What time & weather had left intire in the old, & art in the new repaired parts of this great pile of Pauls, the late Calamity of fire hath soe weakened & defaced, that it now appeares like some antique ruin of 2000 yeares standing, & to repaire it sufficiently will be like the mending of the *Argo navis*, scarce any thing will at last be left of the old.[118]

Even before the Fire, Wren's personal view had been that no satisfactory solution could be found for restoring the Cathedral without substantial demolitions, though he conceded that Pratt's more conservative plan 'will be plausible because it will seeme to aim at great thrift'.[119] He had confided to William Sancroft that experimenting with design possibilities for a new-build cathedral had been his 'constant Recreation when Journies businesse or friends left [him] vacant', and that the satisfaction he derived from such creative efforts 'aequalls that of poetry or compositions in Musick'.[120] Now it seemed that he might indeed be called upon to provide such fresh designs, after the destruction of the Fire.

Those in charge of post-Fire emergency arrangements, however, thought otherwise. To restore public morale it was decided that a place of worship had to be created immediately, to compensate for the dozens of lost City churches. So the problem Wren was asked by Sancroft to solve at the end of 1666 was that of providing an enclosed space for worship within the burned-out ruins of the Cathedral. He likened this to a physician's attempting to prescribe a cure for a gravely ill patient – the best that will be achieved is a temporary easing of the condition:

Having shewn in part the deplorable condition of our patient wee are to consult of the Cure if possibly art may effect it, & herein wee must imitate the Physician who when he finds a totall decay of Nature bends his skill to a palliation, to give respite for a better settlement of the estate of the patient. The Question is then where bes[t] to begin this kind of practice, that is to make a Quire for present use.[121]

With characteristic pragmatism Wren identified the soundest portions of the fabric to provide such a suitable space:

I would take the lesser north & south dores [within the Body of the Church] from the entrances & leaving 2 Intercolumnations eastward & 3 or 4 westward I would there make partition walls of the fallen stone upon the place, the east part above the dores may be contrived into a Quire the west into the Auditory. I would lay a Timber roofe as lowe as the bottomes of the upper windowes with a flat fretted ceeling, the lead saved out of the burning will more then cover it: of iron & of pavement there is enough for all uses. The roofe lying low will not appeare above the walls, & since wee cannot mend this great Ruine wee will not disfigure it, but that it shall still have its full motives to work if possible upon this or the next ages: & yet within it shall have all convenience & light (by turning the 2nd story of Arches into windowes) & a beauty durable to the next 2 centuries of Yeares: & yet prove soe cheape that between 3 & 4000 £ shall effect it all in one summer.[122]

It is an indication of Wren's authority by this time, in matters of construction, that the first order for St Paul's from the Royal

Commission for Rebuilding, issued after a number of delays a year later, simply rephrased Wren's proposal as their own:

> It was this day ordered, that a Choir and Auditory for present use be forthwith set out, repaired and finished (if it may be) in the course of the next summer, in the body of the church between the West end and the second pillars above the little North and South dores (which of all the fabrick remains most entire and most easily reducible to the intended use).[123]

Wren was by now working for William Sancroft as client simultaneously on two projects: the chapel Sancroft had commissioned at Emmanuel College (for which he was still issuing the instructions on behalf of the new Master and fellows, in spite of his move to the Deanship of St Paul's), and the temporary place of worship for Londoners at St Paul's. The two men exchanged a flurry of letters in late 1667 and early 1668, as Wren shuttled to and fro between London and Oxford, about the recently completed model for Emmanuel Chapel,[124] and about a design for a pitched timber roof for the new St Paul's Choir.[125] On 25 April 1668, Sancroft wrote to Wren informing him that Wren's fears – expressed on his most recent visit to the St Paul's site – had been realised. The new structure had collapsed, and Wren was urgently summoned back to London:

> What you whispered in my Ear, at your last coming hither, is now come to pass. Our Work at the West-end of St. Paul's is fallen about our Ears. Your quick Eye discern'd the Walls and Pillars gone off from their Perpendiculars, and I believe other Defects too, which are now expos'd to every common Observer.[126]

He was, moreover, to bring with him 'those excellent Draughts and Designs you formerly favour'd us with' – the designs for a new St Paul's Cathedral which had always been Wren's preference over a refurbished building.

At this point, however, Wren, displaying the pragmatic aplomb which characterised all his dealings with patrons and potential clients, took one step back from a commission. On 24 May 1668 he wrote to Sancroft from Oxford, explaining that he could go no further with discussions of his taking full charge of rebuilding until it had been

William Sancroft, who was the client, as Master of Emmanuel College, Cambridge, for the new chapel Wren designed there, and subsequently, as Dean of St Paul's, for Wren's St Paul's Cathedral.

determined once and for all that no argument would be advanced for making further attempts to pin new build on to the unstable old fabric. There was no point, he went on, speculating further about designs on paper until it was known what sums of money were envisaged for the new Cathedral. Once Wren was given a figure, he would provide drawings to match:

> You will aske me what is then to be don, [if] noething of the old be usefull? I am very unwilling to give hasty resolutions in thinges for perpetuity, nor will the end of a Letter in wch I am already troublesome afford you satisfaction, to designe such thinges for you that will not be suitable to our age and readily practicable is to build only on paper, and I think it is silver upon wch the foundation of any worke must be first layd, least it sinke while it is yet rising. When you have found out the largenesse and security of this sort of foundation I shall presently resolve you what fabrick it will beare.[127]

In spite of Wren's firmness, it was another three years before serious demolition work was undertaken (and the old materials sold off, to clear the site and raise additional funds for rebuilding).

In 1673, a royal warrant was finally issued for the complete rebuilding of St Paul's. It clearly affirmed the symbolic importance of St Paul's as a marker for the renewed continuity of Stuart dynastic rule, and named Wren as the architect of the project:

> King Charles the Second's Commission for rebuilding the cathedral church of St. Paul, London – Dated November 12, 1673.
>
> Charles the Second, by the grace of God, King of England, Scotland, France, and Ireland, Defender of the Faith, &c.
>
> Whereas our most dear and royal grandfather and father were pleased to begin and set forward that great honourable work of upholding and repairing the cathedral church of St. Paul, in London, and granted several commissions, in order to the accomplishing of that work, with sundry good directions therein contained to that purpose; and whereas we, in pursuance of their pious and royal intentions, resolving to make a further and more effectual progress in that work, which, by the iniquity of the late times, had been so much and so long interrupted, did, by our commission, under our great seal of England, bearing date the 18th day of April, in the fifteenth year of our reign [1663], directed to the several lords, spiritual and temporal, and others the persons of eminent rank and quality therein named, authorize and empower them, or so many of them as are therein appointed and enabled to act, to proceed in that great undertaking, and to endeavour the perfecting thereof by such ways and means, and according to such rules and orders, as are therein mentioned.
>
> Since the issuing out of which commission, the late dreadful fire in London hath destroyed and consumed the said cathedral to such a degree, that no part of the ancient walls or structures can, with any safety, be relied upon, or left standing; insomuch that it is now become absolutely necessary totally to demolish and raze to the ground all the relicks of the former building, and, in the same place, but upon new foundations, to erect a

new church (which, that it may be done to the glory of God, and for the promoting of his divine worship and service therein to be celebrated, and to the end the same may equal, if not exceed, the splendour and magnificence of the former cathedral church, when it was in its best estate, and so become, much more than formerly, the principal ornament of that our royal city, to the honour of our government, and of this our realm; we have caused several designs, to that purpose, to be prepared by Dr. Christopher Wren, surveyor-general of all our works and buildings, which we have seen, and one of which we do more especially approve, and have commanded a model thereof to be made, after so large and exact a manner, that it may remain as a perpetual and unchangeable rule and direction for the conduct of the whole work).[128]

Among the dignitaries listed in the document to monitor the rebuilding were Sir Robert Hanson, Lord Mayor of London, Gilbert Sheldon, Archbishop of Canterbury, and the central political figures of Charles II's government, the Dukes of Buckingham, Albermarle, Lauderdale and Ormonde.

Only now did the gruelling work of dismantling Old St Paul's, down to its crypt and underground vaults, and the excavation of new foundations really begin. Wren's son Christopher, working to dictation at the end of his father's life, gave a vivid description of the Royal Surveyor's personal supervision of the difficult task:

The pulling down the Walls, being about 80 Feet high, and 5 Feet thick, was a great and troublesome Work; the Men stood above, and work'd them down with Pickaxes, whilst Labourers below moved away the Materials that fell, and dispersed them into Heaps: the want of Room made this Way slow, and dangerous, and some Men lost their Lives; the Heaps grew steep and large; and yet this was to be done before the Masons could begin to lay the Foundations.

The City having Streets to pave anew, bought, from the Rubbish, most of the Stone, call'd Kentish-rag, which gave some Room to dig, and to lay Foundations; which yet was not easy to perform with any Exactness, but by this Method.

The Surveyor placed Scaffolds high enough to extend his

Lines over the Heaps that lay in the Way, and then by Perpendiculars set out the Places below, from the Lines drawn with Care upon the level Plan of the Scaffold.

Thus he proceeded, gaining every Day more Room, till he came to the Middle Tower that bore the Steeple; the Remains of the Tower being near 200 Feet high, the Labourers were afraid to work above, thereupon he concluded to facilitate this Work by the Use Of Gunpowder.

He dug a Hole of about 4 Feet wide, down the Side of the North-West Pillar of the Tower, the 4 Pillars of which were each about 14 Feet diameter; when he had dug to the Foundation, he then, with Crows and Tools made on purpose, wrought a Hole 2 Feet square, level into the Center of the Pillar; there he placed a little Deal-box, containing eighteen Pounds of Powder, and no more: a Cane was fix'd to the Box with a Quick-match (as Gunners call it) within ye Cane, which reach'd from the Box to the Ground above, and along the Ground was laid a Train of Powder, with a Match: after the Mine was carefully clos'd up again with Stone and Mortar to the Top of the Ground, he then observ'd the Effect of the Blow.

This little Quantity of Powder not only lifted up the whole Angle of the Tower, with two great Arches that rested upon it, but also two adjoining Arches of the Ailes, and all above them; and this it seem'd to do somewhat leisurely, cracking the Walls to the Top, lifting visibly the whole Weight about nine Inches, which suddenly jumping down, made a great Heap of Ruin in the Place without scattering, it was half a Minute before the Heap already fallen open'd in two or three Places, and emitted some Smoke. By this description may be observ'd the incredible Force of Powder: 18 Pounds only of which lifted up above 3000 Tun, and saved the Work of 1000 Labourers.

The Fall of so great a Weight from an Height of 200 Feet, gave a Concussion to the Ground, that the Inhabitants round about took for an Earthquake.

Encourag'd by this Success, he thought to proceed this Way, but being oblig'd to go out of Town in the King's Service, he left the Management of another Mine begun, to the Care of his next Officer, who too wise in his own Conceit, put in a greater

Quantity of Powder, and neither went low enough, nor sufficiently fortified the Mouth of the Mine; and tho' it had the
Effect, yet one Stone was shot out to the opposite Side of the
Church-yard, through an open Window, into a Room of a
private House, where some Women were sitting at Work, without any Harm done; this Accident frighted the Neigbours to
that Degree, that he was importun'd to use no more Powder,
and was so directed also by his Superiors, tho' with due Caution
it might have been executed without any Hazard, and sav'd
much Time and Money.

Thwarted in his plan to bring the old fabric down with explosives,
Wren resorted to purpose-built battering rams:

He then turn'd his Thoughts to another Method; to gain Time,
prevent much Expence, and the endangering of Men's Lives;
and that was, to make an Experiment of that ancient Engine in
War, the Battering-ram.

He took a strong Mast of about 40 Feet long, arming the
bigger End with a great Spike of Iron, fortified with Bars along
the Mast, and Ferrels: this Mast in two Places was hung up
to one Ring with strong Tackle, and so suspended Level to a
Triangle-prop, such as they weigh great Guns with: thirty Men,
fifteen on a Side, vibrated this Machine to and again, and beat
in one Place against the Wall the whole Day; they believ'd it
was to little Purpose, not discerning any immediate Effect; he
bid them not despair, but proceed another Day: on the second
Day the Wall was perceiv'd to tremble at the Top, and in a few
Hours it fell. The Reason to be given for it may be this; 'tis not
by any present Violence the Ram is able to overturn a Wall
of such Bulk and Compacture, but incessantly vibrating by
equidistant Pulses, it makes a small intestine Motion through
all the insensible Parts of the Wall, and by Degrees loosens all
the Bond of the Mortar, and moves every Stone from its Bed,
and tho' not the hundredth part of an Inch at every Blow, yet
this Motion once begun hath its Effects more and more, till at
length it is quite loose and falls. He made good Use of this
Machine in beating down all the lofty Ruins; and pleas'd himself
that he had recover'd this noble Engine, of so great Service to

the Ancients in besieging of Towns; tho' great Guns have now put them out of Use, as more expeditious, and requiring fewer Men to manage.

This was not, however, the end of Wren's problems. It now transpired that at the north-east corner of the site the discovery, on excavation, of an ancient well meant that there were not adequate footings there for secure foundations. It was tantalisingly close: 'He wanted but six or seven Feet to compleat the Design, and this fell at the very Angle North-east.' Wren was not prepared to risk driving wooden piles in at this point, in case at some later date the water level should drop and expose the piles to the air: 'For, tho' Piles may last for ever, when always in Water, (otherwise tho' sometimes moist, they will rot:) His Endeavours were to build for Eternity.'

Wren's solution was a masonry pier, buried in a deep pit, with an inverted arch (the form of foundation Wren believed to be the most structurally effective in supporting heavy masonry) spanning the two ends of the remainder of the foundations:

> He therefore sunk a Pit about eighteen Feet square, wharfing up the Sand with Timber, till he came forty Feet lower into Water and Sea-shells, where there was a firm Sea-beach which confirmed what was before asserted, that the Sea had been in Ages past, where now Paul's is; he bored through this Beach till he came to the original Clay; being then satisfied, he began from the Beach a square Peer of solid good Masonry, ten Feet square, till he came within fifteen Feet of the present Ground, then he turned a short Arch under Ground to the former Foundation which was broken off by the untoward Accident of the Pit. Thus the North-east Coin of the Quire stands very firm, and, no doubt, will stand.[129]

On 14 May 1675, when funds raised by coal taxes had accumulated to a 'considerable Sum', the King approved Wren's so-called Warrant Design for a new Cathedral.[130] Even so, the royal warrant still envisaged the project as proceeding by piece-work rather than as a coherent whole – something Wren had consistently opposed:

> [The money raised] though not proportionable to the Greatness of the work, is notwithstanding sufficient to begin the same;

and . . . will put a new Quire in great Forewardness; and whereas among divers Designs which have been presented to Us, We have particularly pitched upon one, as well because We found it very artificial, proper, and useful; as because it was so ordered that it might be built and finished by Parts.[131]

There was to be no building 'by Parts' for Wren – the vagueness of the warrant simply allowed him to vary the plans attached, as the 'parts' became a coherent design whole. As far as Wren was concerned, the cathedral he had for so long wanted to build, and had consistently described as being designed 'for eternity', to stand 'in perpetuity', was at last properly under way. It would take almost forty years to complete, and, almost miraculously, the architect would live long enough to see the final touches put to London's most lasting and best loved of monuments.

And there was, in the end, something in that propaganda about a phoenix rising, in the use made of Inigo Jones's portico – so admired by Evelyn at the Restoration as a symbol of the survival of the aesthetic aspirations of Charles I, while at the same time the source of Wren's despair over the poor workmanship in its attachment to the medieval masonry which supported it. More than seventy of the huge, carved limestone blocks from the portico were incorporated into the foundations of Wren's new St Paul's. They were rediscovered during twentieth-century excavations.[132]

THE WREN–HOOKE PARTNERSHIP – THE ARCHITECTURAL FIRM

As members of the Royal Commission for Rebuilding, Wren and Hooke worked in tandem, in the months immediately following the Great Fire, contributing their expert professional advice freely wherever appropriate. Clearly, in the eyes of the court, Wren was the principal figure. Nevertheless, Hooke was essential to the success of the enterprise from the start. As the Wren family papers have it:

In order to Ease himself of some part of the great fatigue of This extraordinary Service, which at first, by his Majesties Directions, lay wholly on himself, he took to his Assistance his most ingenious friend Dr. Robert Hooke, Professor of Geometry of

Gresham College, and assigned him the Measuring and Setting of the Ground of Private Houses for the several Proprietors. Takeing on himself the Care of the Cathedral of Ste. Paul; the Parochial Churches; and all other Publick Structures.[133]

This was a national crisis, and they were part of the select group put together by the King himself to solve it. The work included inspecting existing sites and buildings, assessing the structural safety of damaged buildings, and attending regular meetings concerned with overall plans for the future rebuilding of the capital. The arrangement was an extremely fortunate one for the Corporation of London: Hooke answered directly to them, and was tireless in his work facilitating swift rebuilding by individual householders; Wren had the ear of the King, and had previous experience working with Royal Commissions on London planning issues alongside the other pivotal royal appointees in the rebuilding commission, Pratt, Denham and May.

From 1668 onwards, however, Wren's control over London's rebuilding, at the level both of individual buildings and of the operation as a whole, steadily increased. In 1668, the Earl of Clarendon fell, and Pratt, whose reputation had been irrevocably linked to his patron's since the unfortunate timing of the completion of Clarendon House in Piccadilly at the very moment when many Londoners lost all their worldly goods (and their property) in the Great Fire, took retirement.[134] The elderly Denham fell ill in that year, and Wren took over unofficially as Surveyor of St Paul's Cathedral (one of Denham's responsibilities as Royal Surveyor), before becoming Surveyor of the Royal Works in his place on his death the following year. From then on, official responsibility for all royal buildings destroyed in the Fire rested with him. Since rebuilding of public buildings had barely started at this date, this meant, effectively, that the name of Wren is associated with the entire rebuilt City, even though individual buildings like the Royal Exchange were designed and built by other royal employees (in this case, by Edward Jerman, who also died in 1668, but whose design for the Exchange was seen through to completion).[135]

The most significant change in Wren's relation to London's rebuilding, however, came with the passing of the 1670 City Churches Rebuilding Act, which detailed the procedures for the rebuilding of the City parochial churches.[136] The Act established a Commission to be responsible for this rebuilding, consisting of the Archbishop of Canterbury, the Bishop of London and the Lord Mayor of London then in office. Theirs was the final responsibility for the design and construction of the fifty-one parish churches designated for rebuilding:

> The . . . churches to be rebuilded within the said City of London . . . shall be built and erected according to such Models, and of such Dimensions, and in such Manner and Form in all Respects, as by the said Lord Archbishop of Canterbury [Gilbert Sheldon], Lord Bishop of London [Humphrey Henchman], and Lord Mayor of London for the time being [Samuel Starling] (with his Majesty's Approbation thereof) shall be directed and appointed.

One of the first decisions taken by this team – none of whom, naturally, had the expertise or inclination to concern themselves with details of the design and contracting of work for individual churches – was to appoint Wren to take responsibility on their behalf:

> We . . . doe hereby nominate constitute and appoint Dr Christopher Wren, Doctor of Lawes, Surveigher General of all his Majesty's Workes, to direct and order the dimensions, formes and Modells of the said Churches . . . to contract with . . . Artizans, builders and workmen as shall be employed . . . [to] take care for the orderly execution of the workes and accompts . . . and to receive from the Chamber of London such . . . summes of Mony as we . . . shall appoint for the constant and speedy payment.[137]

Nor did devolution of responsibility for actual building stop here. The Commissioners passed reponsibility for day-to-day direction of the surveying, site clearing, designing, hiring of skilled labour, ordering of materials and rebuilding activities, for the fifteen churches selected as those to begin the process, to a team of qualified experts:

> Dr Christopher Wren, Surveyor General of his Majesty's Works, Mr Robert Hooke and Mr Edward Woodroffe are hereby required to repair forthwith the aforesaid churches and take an account of the extent of the parishes, the sites of the churches, the state and conditions of the ruins and accordingly prepare fit models and draughts to be presented for his Majesty's approbation and also estimates proper to inform us what share and

proportion of the money out of the imposition upon coals [the coal tax] may be requisite to allow for the fabric of each church, and where any contracts have been already made by the church-wardens, the said Christopher Wren and his assistants, are hereby authorised and required to call for the said contracts, and to examine what hath been already expended upon any of the said churches that thereupon we may better judge what is further expedient to allow for the finishing of such churches.[138]

By 1670 Hooke had emerged as a scrupulous and talented surveyor, exemplary in terms of his accuracy, efficiency and acumen, fully deserving of the trust the Corporation of London had placed in him when they nominated him as one of the City's Surveyors on the original post-Fire Rebuilding Commission. Between March and May 1667, he and Peter Mills had marked out entirely the new streets of the City, starting at Fleet Street – six carpenters and seven labourers used 1220 feet of timber for stakes to do so.[139] Between late April 1667 and the end of 1671, Hooke, Mills and Oliver undertook foundation surveys, and issued rebuilding certificates, for over 8000 properties. As well as measuring and assessing individual plots, Hooke was responsible for calculating compensation for lands taken for road-widening and other adjustments, and attended a large number of sites to assemble the evidence in disputed cases (known in the period as taking 'views').[140] Judging from the careful annotations on the surviving surveys and views, Hooke's accounting was meticulous, and impeccably honest – another reason the City may have particularly valued his efforts.

Woodroffe was ten years older than Wren, also an experienced surveyor with a wealth of experience in the building industry, whose first major appointment was evidently as Surveyor to the Dean and Chapter of Westminster Abbey in 1662. In 1668 he had joined the relatively inexperienced Wren as Assistant Surveyor to St Paul's Cathedral, becoming Surveyor to the Dean and Chapter in 1669. Not surprisingly, in the church rebuilding project he took responsibility for the practical side of the rebuilding, overseeing labour and construction work, while Hooke took charge of contracts and payments, and Wren and Hooke shared the design side.[141]

Here is where we see the working relationship between Wren and Hooke crystallise into something novel and productive in the way of organisation of responsibility – something quite close to the arrangement of a modern architectural office. All three men were paid by the Commission, with Wren receiving around twice the salary of each of the other two. Starting in 1670, however, Wren began paying Hooke an additional annual salary for work undertaken directly for him, organising the day-to-day running of the work on the City churches inside the Surveyor's office at Scotland Yard (and eventually in the second office adjacent to St Paul's Cathedral).[142]

On top of all his other commitments, in 1670 Hooke took on the role of office manager in the Wren architectural practice. It was a job he was well qualified to perform, because of the long-standing, close friendship he already enjoyed with Wren, and the fact that they had worked together as scientists since the 1650s. They no doubt knew each other's ways inside out. Wren remained the senior figure, with the status and decision-making authority to match. Hooke intensified his pattern of shadowing Wren's activities, anticipating his professional needs and desires, and quietly and efficiently providing support and technical expertise whenever necessary. Wren clearly appreciated the way the arrangement worked, and that it depended on the balance of skills between himself and Hooke, together with the experienced direction of the building work itself by the third member of the team.[143]

When Woodroffe died in 1675, Hooke's proposal was that he be replaced by Sir John Hoskins – another of the Royal Society virtuosi, and a personal friend. Wren overrode him, and instead appointed John Oliver, a man much more like Woodroffe in terms of building experience.[144] When Hooke stepped down in 1693 (the same year in which he also ceased acting as City Surveyor), his job was taken by Nicholas Hawksmoor, who had joined Wren's office as a draughtsman around 1684 and, like Hooke, had learned the design aspects of architecture inside the practice.

It is because the Wren office functioned as what we would now think of as an office or firm that, where a number of the City churches are concerned, it becomes so difficult to attribute design responsibility as between Wren and Hooke. In one or two cases there is good reason to suppose that Wren took a personal interest throughout the process from drawing-board to completion, because of the prestige associated with the church in question. In such cases, Hooke acts as right-hand man to the master-architect. In other cases, and increasingly, as Wren

St Mary-le-Bow – a prestige commission among the churches rebuilt by the Wren office after the Fire of London.

got busier and Hooke became more practised as a design architect, Hooke is the lead architect, presumably taking advice from Wren where necessary, and using all the resources of the Wren office for 'his' building.

Thus St Mary-le-Bow had a special status, because it housed the Court of Arches – the Ecclesiastical Court of Appeal, chaired by Archbishop Sheldon, who, apart from being a fellow member of the Rebuilding Commission, was a personal friend, and Wren's patron for the recently completed Sheldonian Theatre. A large cohort of wealthy parishioners also ensured that funds were available on loan in advance of the public money raised from the coal tax levied for the rebuilding programme, to allow the work to get under way immediately.

Wren certainly took charge of the design and rebuilding of

St Mary-le-Bow, including, unusually, the finished tower and steeple (the steeples of most of the churches were completed later, many of them designed by the young Hawksmoor). The 'Cheapside pillar', as this tower became known, was regarded as one of the wonders of rebuilt London at the end of the seventeenth century. Nevertheless, a plan for the site between the main body of the church of St Mary-le-Bow and Cheapside survives, in Hooke's hand, part of the design decision-making as to where the Court of Arches would be located within the new building. Here we probably have a surviving trace of joint discussions between Hooke and Wren.[145]

By contrast, at St Lawrence Jewry, the church where Wren and Hooke's long-standing mentor John Wilkins had been vicar until 1668, and which served as the place of worship for the Corporation of London in the adjacent Guildhall, and where we might expect both men had attended services, architectural historians are undecided as to whom to attribute the completed church, because of signs of design work characteristic of each of them.[146] Wilkins certainly retained an interest in the rebuilding of his old church, and, as we might expect, Wren, as the senior architect, attended when the now Bishop of Chester came to visit the site. The churchwardens' accounts for the period April 1670 to March 1671 record payment of a total of £8 for 'Entertainment of Dr. Wren and Bishop of Chester'.[147]

We know, however, that both Wren and Hooke were involved with the new church at the planning stage because, owing to a dispute with the Guildhall – also under rebuilding on the adjacent site – the City Aldermen appealed to them for arbitration, in June 1671:

> The parishioners of the said parish have pressed this Court that the [north-east corner of the church land] may not be taken in [by the Corporation] but [the church] continue to be built as formerly upon the old foundations. This Court doth not think fit to grant the said petition, but doth refer it to Sir Christopher Wren and Mr Hooke to contrive the building . . . as may best answer the desires of the said parishioners, and without disappointment or hinderence, to the conveniency and ornament intended to the said Court.[148]

The Aldermen won, and the church lost a corner of its site. The resulting church is therefore asymmetrical in plan, and ingenious compromises

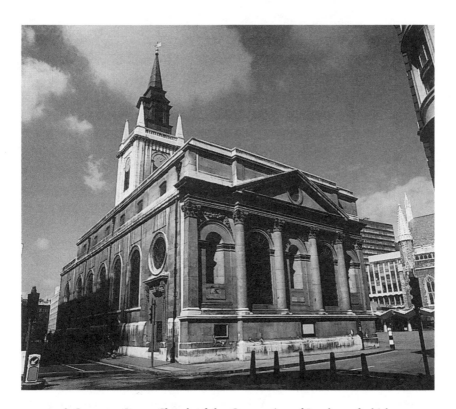

St Lawrence Jewry, Church of the Corporation of London, of which,
after the Restoration, John Wilkins was vicar until 1668.

have been made in the exterior elevations to compensate. The final
design brilliantly deceives the eye from key vantage points – notably,
when facing the imposing east front – suggesting some team-work on
the part of Wren and Hooke. Serving a particularly affluent parish and
the Corporation of London itself, the church was successful in raising
considerable funds of its own for rebuilding, as a result of which it too,
like St Mary-le-Bow, had a completed steeple by 1680.

That was, unfortunately, too late for Wilkins to take pleasure in his
rebuilt former parish church. He died in November 1672, after a brief
but painful illness, made more so by his virtuoso friends' enthusiasm
for trying a range of the latest drastic medical remedies on him.[149]
Hooke, as ever, recorded his passing precisely: 'November 19 1672. Mr.
Lee here. Lord Bishop of Chester [Wilkins] dyed about 9 in the morning
of a suppression of urine. Dr. Wren here at Dionis Backchurch. Dind
at the Bear in Birchen Lane with Dr. Wren, Controuler, Mr. Fitch.'[150]

Hooke, with characteristic loyalty to those who had helped him, had visited Wilkins assiduously during his illness; Wren seems to have been less in evidence. By 1672 Wren's professional career had taken off, he had an established public reputation, and he had resumed his place close to the royal circle, among men far more influential than his old protector. Hooke, on the other hand, stayed loyal to his old Oxford mentor to the end, just as he did to his Westminster headmaster Busby, for whom he designed and built a church at his retirement estate of Willen (near Milton Keynes) in 1678.

In a few cases of City church rebuilding there is surviving documentation to show that all three team members – Wren, Hooke and Woodroffe – were acknowledged to have had a share in the completed church. A striking example is St Stephen Walbrook, a particularly elegant rebuilt City church, with a cupola prefiguring the one at St Paul's. Here two men associated with the rebuilding were powerful City figures, and both were close colleagues of Wren. Sir Robert Hanson, patron of the living, was Lord Mayor of London in 1672, the year the foundation stone for the new church was laid. As Lord Mayor he was sitting with Wren on the Rebuilding Commission for the parochial churches at the time. Sir Thomas Chicheley, also present at the stone-laying, was another prominent City figure. With Wren and Evelyn, he had been one of the team examining the structural condition of Old St Paul's shortly before the Fire.

Significantly, the St Stephen Walbrook stone-laying also marked the low-point of Charles II's royal finances, which had been in growing crisis since 1660. In January 1672 the Crown, indeed, declared the so-called 'Stop of the Exchequer' – formally pronouncing itself insolvent. Some £1 million of capital was owed to London bankers (among them the patrons so ready to fund thanks-offering churches in their parishes), and was due for redemption that year. The 'Stop' allowed Charles to postpone capital repayment indefinitely, and to pay his creditors a fixed 6 per cent rate of interest thereafter. This was also the year in which work was abandoned on Webb's new royal palace at Greenwich. While the combination of steady tax-income and private finance sustained the City churches, the King's own building projects lurched from crisis to financial crisis. Contractors on building sites, as Wren knew so well, simply stopped work if payment was not forthcoming.[151]

The serenity and ostentatious affluence of St Stephen Walbrook

Interior of St Stephen Walbrook Church as it is today, showing the airy
central auditory and dome.

contrasts starkly with the bankruptcy of the Crown. In keeping with the prestige of the parish, and the prominence of those associated with the plans and funding for the new parochial church, St Stephen Walbrook is distinctive both for the sophistication of the design and for its structural complexity. At first entry it appears to be a nave and aisle building (particularly since in Wren's day this area was filled with box pews). Once immediately below the dome (Wren's 'auditory'), however, the church appears to the viewer to be centrally planned around the light-filled space defined by the cupola. This visual illusion is characteristic of Wren, who, like the contemporary Dutch artists Pieter Saenredam and Emmanuel de Witte, was fascinated by the eye's tendency to read spaces as symmetrical, even where, when viewed in plan, they turn out to be full of asymmetries.[152] In a surviving draft essay on architecture he particularly noted the importance for the architect of skill in perspective:

> The Architect ought, above all Things, to be well skilled in Perspective; for every thing that appears well in the Orthography, may not be good in the Model, especially where there are many Angles and Projectures; and every thing that is good in Model, may not be so when built; because a Model is seen from other Stations and Distances than the Eye sees the Building: but this will hold universally true, that whatsoever is good in Perspective, and will hold so in all the principal Views, whether direct or oblique, will be as good in great, if this only Caution be observed, that Regard be had to the Distance of the Eye in the principal Stations.[153]

The dome at St Stephen Walbrook crowns an area which is square rather than circular in plan and marked out by twelve of the sixteen central columns and the entablature. The dome is carried on arches that bridge the corners of this space, converting the square into an octagon at the higher level, before transforming to the circular base of the shallow dome. The result is a surprisingly light, airy interior, which again recalls the clarity and geometrical elegance of a Dutch painting of a contemporary church interior. Wren office teamwork is still, nevertheless, in evidence. The complicated calculations of loads and stresses required to produce this effect almost certainly required the technical brilliance of Hooke for their solution.

Records for the church do indeed confirm that at St Stephen

Walbrook the active participation of Wren, Hooke and Woodroffe as a team was visible to the client. The churchwardens' accounts show the following:

> 7 March 1673. Paid for a dinner at the Swan in Old Fish Street to entertain Dr. Wren and other surveyors with the vestry and others £9 9 0.
>
> Paid to ye Survaer Gennarall by order of Vestry 20 Ginnes [guineas] for a gratuety to his Lady to incuring and hasting ye rebuilding ye church.
>
> 1673–4. Paid Mr Hook surveyor by order of vestry, 5 Guineas.
>
> Paid for a piece of plate by order of vestry for Mr Woodriffe, £5 5s. 0d.[154]

The vestry minutes clarify further that the '20 ginneys, in a silke purse' for Lady Wren were 'in consideration of his greate care & extraordinary pains taken in ye contriving ye designe of ye church & assisting in ye rebuilding ye same', while in this case Hooke's five guineas was in gratitude for 'his paynes in surveying & measuring ye ground yt belong-eth to ye parish'. Woodroffe's five guineas was associated with the construction work itself.[155] In this case, then, the perception of the client was that Wren was the design architect, Hooke the surveyor and structural engineer, and Woodroffe the site manager.[156]

We might notice that the names of powerful figures associated with churches rebuilt early in the programme, to designs in which Wren appears to have taken a particularly keen interest, and to the detail of which he was especially attentive, reappear in the roll-call of those nominated by Charles II in the Commission for Rebuilding St Paul's Cathedral (dated 12 November, 1673). This list was headed by Sir Robert Hanson (closely associated with St Stephen Walbrook) and Archbishop Sheldon (St Mary-le-Bow). Other names on the list included Sir Robert Wiseman, Dean of the Arches (St Mary-le-Bow), and Alderman Sir John Robinson (St Stephen Walbrook).[157] As in any modern architectural office, Wren as the firm's 'name' appears to have put special effort into projects for clients who were currently discussing who was to be entrusted with a much more prestigious one in the offing.

The years of working together on the City churches rebuilding established a style of office working which Wren and Hooke sustained up until the time of Hooke's retirement in 1693. Since this became their recognised practice, it was continued when Wren worked on buildings other than those directly related to the Great Fire. Whether working for the King at Whitehall, Winchester and Newmarket, or for an educational patron at Trinity College, Cambridge, Christ Church, Oxford and Eton College, Windsor, 'Wren' buildings involve design and structural work carried out by Hooke (and, indeed, others in the office like Woodroffe, Oliver and Hawksmoor).

Equally, where, as time went on, Hooke's name is associated as design architect in the surviving documentation, he was able to take full advantage of his privileged position in the Wren office at Scotland Yard, employing carpenters and masons drawn from among those regularly employed there, and doubtless consulting Wren on design details where his special contribution would make a difference.[158]

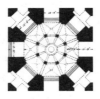

6

_____

Overlapping Interests

ARCHITECT AND ASTRONOMER:
THE ROYAL OBSERVATORY

At a moment when the Wren office was at full stretch rebuilding the City churches, and just when work was starting on site for the new St Paul's Cathedral, Wren took on an urgent commission, by royal command. The politically high-profile project brought together what by now were Wren's two main areas of professional interest – architecture and astronomy.

In December 1674 Charles II set up a Royal Commission to investigate a French claim to have solved the strategically vital problem of finding longitude at sea – that is, of determining the precise location of a vessel on the high seas (its latitude being comparatively easy to compute).[1] Determining longitude exactly was a problem of vital importance both for the safety of commercial shipping and for naval manoeuvres, particularly in times of war, and it was in fact to elude solution for another fifty years.[2] The occasion for the Commission was a claim by an entrepreneurial Frenchman that he had a method for finding longitude, based on observations of the position of the moon in relation to the fixed stars. Such a method had already been proposed in France some years earlier and had led to the setting up of the French Royal Observatory. Failing to interest the French Académie on this occasion, the Frenchman in question, Le Sieur de St Pierre, had instead approached the English King, via his current mistress, Louise de Keroualle. The Commission set up under the direction of Lord Brouncker, Sir Jonas Moore and selected members of the Royal Society with expertise in observational astronomy (including both Wren and Hooke) interviewed St Pierre and pronounced the method of little interest. The initiative, however, led to the proposal that a Royal Observatory of a calibre to match the one at Paris be established in London.

A talented young astronomer, John Flamsteed (who had already been co-opted on to the Commission to interrogate St Pierre), was appointed to the position of Astronomer Royal. The twenty-seven-year-old Flamsteed was a protégé of Sir Jonas Moore, now Surveyor-General at the Ordnance Office (the seventeenth-century equivalent of the Pentagon, responsible for national security, armaments, military training and strategic planning in time of war).[3] Many years later, Flamsteed recalled this crucial moment:

> Severall persons about the yeare 1674 pretending to the discovery of the *Longitude* and the most skillfull of them demanding the Moones distances from fixed stars in order to find it by compareing her observed place with that given by Astronomicall Tables, it was represented to his then Majestie K. C. the 2d. by the Lord Brouncker (then a principall Officer at the Navy bord). Sir Jonas Moor Surveyour Generall of the Ordnance, and severall other able Mathematicians[4] about the Court. That this method was indeed the most likely to prove usefull to our saylours because most practicable. But that the Catalogue of the fixed stars made by Tycho Brahe a Noble Dane an age agone and Now used was both erroneous and incompleat, and that the best Tables of the Moons Motions erred sometimes above 20 minutes which would Cause 15 degrees [marginal note: or 300 leagues] error in determineing the longitude, so that our saylours could expect no help from it, till both the places of the fixed stars were rectified and New Tables of the Moons motions made which might represent her places in the heavens much exacter then the old did. for which a stock of exact observations was wanting.
>
> And that therefore his Majestie would give a great and

altogeather Necessary encoragement to our Navigation and Commerce, the strength and wealth of our Nation, if he would cause an Observatory to be built, furnisht with proper Instruments, and persons skillfull in Astronomy imployd in it to take New observations in the Heavens both of the fixed stars and Planets in Order to correct the places of the stars and rectifie the Motions of the Planets the Moons especially.[5]

Such was the explicit brief Flamsteed was given in his letters of appointment: to apply 'the most exact Care and Diligence to rectifying the Tables of the Motions of the Heavens, and the Places of the fixed Stars, so as to find out the so-much desired Longitude at Sea, for perfecting the art of Navigation'.[6]

On 22 June, Wren was appointed as architect, to design and build the Royal Observatory in close consultation with Flamsteed as to its technical specifications (the building being named, accordingly, 'Flamsteed House'):

Whereas, in order to the finding out of the longitude of places for perfecting navigation and astronomy, we have resolved to build a small observatory within our park at Greenwich, upon the highest ground, at or near the place where the castle stood, with lodging-rooms for our astronomical observator and assistant. Our will and pleasure is, that according to such plot and design as shall be given you by our trusty and well-beloved Sir Christopher Wren, Knight, our surveyor-general of the place and site of the said observatory, you cause the same to be fenced in, built and finished with all convenient speed, by such artificers and workmen as you shall appoint thereto, and that you give order unto our Treasurer of the Ordnance for the paying of such materials and workmen as shall be used and employed therein, out of such monies as shall come to your hands for old and decayed powder, which hath or shall be sold by our order of the Ist of January last, provided that the whole sum, so to be expended and paid, shall not exceed five hundred pounds.[7]

Wren, in his turn, immediately appointed Hooke to act as his deputy and site manager, 'to direct [the] Observatory in Greenwich Park for

Sir J More'.[8] Apparently Hooke and Wren had already identified Greenwich as a suitable site together (rejecting the Commission's first suggestion of Chelsea College).[9] Hooke viewed the site with Flamsteed at the end of the month, 'describd' the buildings on 2 July, and 'set out' the ground-plan on July 28. The Observatory went up with inordinate speed, as required. Flamsteed records that 'the foundations [foundation stone] were laid August 10 1675; and the work carried on so well that the roof was laid, and the building occupied by Christmas'. The building was near enough to completion to be used for viewing an eclipse at the beginning of June 1676 – it had been hoped that the King might attend, but in the event he failed to appear.

The speed of completion was partly due to the site Wren had shrewdly identified. Not only was it far enough from the centre of London, and high enough to avoid the famously polluted atmosphere of the City, but it was built on the existing foundations of Duke Humphrey's Tower – a lodge erected at the highest point in the royal park in the 1430s and long since fallen into ruin. Flamsteed regretted the expedient – in 1676 he wrote to fellow astronomer Richard Towneley that 'It were much to be wished our walls might have been meridional [aligned with the zero meridian] but for saving the Charges it was thought fit to build upon the old ones which are some $13\frac{1}{2}$ degrees false and wide of the true meridian.'[10]

During the construction period, Flamsteed was lodged in Inigo Jones's Queen's House, close to the Observatory site, and he, Wren and Hooke became close collaborators, both in designs which met the technical requirements of observational astronomy, and in astronomical observation itself, since all three men were equally passionate about telescopes and star-gazing. As so often happened in Wren's life, his manner and methods of working built a trust and friendship between himself and Flamsteed that would become a matter of crucial importance (for Flamsteed specifically) a good thirty years later.[11]

The Royal Observatory at Greenwich brought together, in full public view, the two sides of Wren's professional personality. Until he resigned as Savilian Professor of Astronomy at Oxford in 1673, his professional identity had, indeed, been first and foremost as an academic astronomer (years later he referred to astronomy as his 'trade'). He continued to join his fellow astronomers to observe important astronomical events, as did Hooke. Their appointment together to the Royal Commission confirms the prominent place both were considered to occupy among practising astronomers. In the period when the Observatory was being built, Hooke was perfecting the use of his new balance-spring watch, together with a long telescope, to take precise measurements of astronomical phenomena: 'January the first, 1675, being at Sr. Jonas Mores in the Tower of London, and making use of a Telescope of eight foot, and my pocket-Watch, whose ballance was regulated with springs, I observed the Eclipse of the Moon.'[12]

The Royal Observatory was a project which the Wren office was especially well qualified to build, since its two leading architects were both virtuoso astronomical observers themselves of long standing. Both men were expert operators of the range of technical instruments used in an observatory, and therefore in a position to make sure the building matched the requirements of the astronomers who were to use it. The Royal Observatory was designed as a simple building (incorporating parts of the older building it replaced), purpose-built to facilitate the use of the astronomical instruments it was built to house. On 22 August, for example, right at the beginning of the actual construction, Hooke was at the site overseeing the space which would house a large mural quadrant which he was himself designing for the Observatory. The design of the famous Octagon Room was adjusted so that it could house two astronomical clocks, regulated by a novel escapement designed by Richard Towneley, and donated to the project by Sir Jonas Moore.

In his capacity as Curator of Experiments for the Royal Society, Hooke in 1674–75 began serious attempts to measure stellar parallax, in order to prove the movement of the earth around the sun. Wren and Neile had been interested in attempting stellar parallax measurement as early as the 1650s. In 1669 Hooke constructed a 'tubeless' telescope, by cutting a hole vertically, right through from ground floor to roof, at his lodgings at Gresham College, which had not proved stable enough for reliable measurements; we know from Hooke's diary that in the 1670s he and Wren discussed zenith telescopes together.[13]

This particular kind of observational activity depended crucially on the precision measuring of stellar distances made possible by the micrometer eyepiece perfected by Wren. For the stellar parallax experiment, observations of a selected fixed star were taken in the same night-sky position, exactly six months apart, and any minute displacement in position recorded; errors introduced by altered conditions in the observing equipment (caused by meteorological factors and so on) made detection of such hypothesised small alterations impossible.

Apparently Hooke and Wren planned another attempt at a zenith telescope site at Greenwich, in the form of a 120-foot well, adjacent to the main Observatory. An early engraved plan of the Greenwich site shows a small octagonal building, labelled 'Puteus profunditatis 120 ped. cum Tubo pro Observ. Parallaxis Terrae' ('well of depth 120 feet, for observations of stellar parallax'); another shows a section of the well, lined with masonry, and with a spiral stair leading down to a small chamber for the observer.[14] The idea of mounting a zenith telescope in a deep well was one which Hooke and other Royal Society members were actively working on in 1674–75; by using the vertical shaft of the well, it was thought, it would be possible to take accurate telescope readings on fixed stars vertically above the shaft. In March 1675, William Ball wrote to Huygens (with whom as an enthusiastic astronomical observer he had a long-standing correspondence on the rings of Saturn):[15]

> I invited o[u]r operator at Gresham Colledge [Hooke] to come to mee last November to have assisted me to sett a tube for ye like observation [of stellar parallax]; but his leisure . . . not suiting hath hitherto hindred all my endeavours towards it. . . . I hope to begin something this summer, being pretty well furnished w[i]th tools of such a worke in proportion to my small share of ye world; & a neibouring hill almost a mountaine where I might have a pitt 360 or 600 ft. deep, Mr Hooke mentions one in Surry 360; & yo[u]r selfe speake of one 28 fathom, as I remember. . . . I doe not despaire yt a few yeares diligent contrivance may doe something considerable in itt, if you can pardon this, bolder than Mr Hookes attempt, w[i]th a small encourag[emen]t.[16]

Since the budget for the Observatory was extremely tight – eventually the cost of the completed building was just over £520 – the well at Greenwich was never sunk for the zenith telescope. We shall see shortly, nevertheless, that Wren and Hooke continued to design buildings with the potential themselves to double as scientific instruments.

Wren, too, was directly involved in innovative astronomical research at the time of construction of the Greenwich Observatory. In the preface to Sir Jonas Moore's *System of Mathematics* (1681), Flamsteed explains that shortly after he was installed in the Observatory at Greenwich he discovered a graphical method of calculating eclipses, which he sent to Sir Jonas Moore, who communicated it to the Royal Society:

> It hap'ned Sir Christopher Wren was there present, who having viewed the Figure only, told him, that himself had known the same method 16 years a gone, and to assure him of it, sent him soon after a like Projection, neatly drawn on Pastboard, and fitted with several ingenious contrivances of Numbers and Scales for the Construction of Solar Eclipses in our Latitude. This Sir Jonas brought down to me, then Labouring under some Distempers, to Greenwich, whereby I was satisfied that the honour of the first Discovery of this useful invention was absolutely due to Sir Christopher Wren, whom of all Mortals I believe to have been the first that knew how to find the Times of the Beginning, Middle, Digits then darkned, Inclination of the Cusps at any Phasis, and End of a Solar Eclipse, without the Calculation of Parallaxes.

Whether or not he was the 'inventor' of the method, it is clear that Wren convincingly demonstrated a graphical method of computing eclipses to the Astronomer Royal, though, as so often where Wren was working in a team, the evidence for this is tucked away in a book by a scientific collaborator, in this case Sir Jonas Moore.[17]

On the architectural side, however, this was also a period during which Wren and Hooke were making fundamental breakthroughs in solving classic structural problems in building construction together, taking the Wren practice to the forefront of the architectural profession. They had, for example, for some time been working on the structural, load-bearing properties of stone arches, both between themselves and at meetings of the Royal Society (where both Hooke and Wren were involved in demonstrations of the properties of arches).

Only weeks before their appointment to build the Royal Observatory (and when they were already actively involved in looking for a suitable site) the two men were again discussing the ideal form for a supporting stone arch. This time the discussion was associated directly with Wren's design for St Paul's, which was on the point of going into the construction phase. On Saturday, 5 June 1675 Hooke (who was, in his turn, at work as named architect for the up-and-coming Ralph Montagu on plans for an ostentatious house in Bloomsbury) records in his diary:

> At Sir Chr[istopher] Wren. At Mr. Boyles. At Mr. Mountacues with Fitch. . . . Told Montacue of Pillers 20 foot high for £10 [altogether]. Told Sir Ch[ristopher] Wren of it. He promised Fitch at Paules. He was making up of my principle about arches and altered his module by it.[18]

In general, the scientific questions relating to the buildings were posed by Wren. They were then scrupulously and exhaustively explored, and the findings publicly explicated by Hooke. It was Hooke who undertook microscopical examinations of Kettering (or Ketton) stone, so that he and Wren could assess its strength and fracture characteristics as a building material (Wren used Ketton stone for the Wren Library at Trinity College). He also experimented with different methods for firing bricks to increase their load-bearing properties, investigated the suitability in construction of different kinds of wood, and later devised a new kind of hard-bonding plaster.[19]

Some years later, corresponding with his old friend John Fell about proposals to complete Tom Tower – the tower over the gatehouse at Fell's college, Christ Church, Oxford – Wren recalled the building of the Greenwich Observatory with evident nostalgia. He too, it seems, was aware of the neat fit, on that particular project, between his expertise as a Professor of Astronomy and that as an increasingly highly regarded architect. Fell had suggested – rather late in the day, as clients are inclined to – that the room in the Tower might be designed as an observatory. Wren responded that actually such a turret room was no longer considered the ideal location for observational activities:

> Give me leave to adde, that such a Room as this will be when built, is noe way necessary for Observations, as now they are managed. Were I to set up the Trade again I was once well acquainted with, & I thinke the world doth or may justly own some improuements of it to me, I should require nothing else but these things. First a large murall Quadrant fixt to a wall trewly built in the meridian, & this is best in an open Court or Garden, 2dly a pole to rays large Telescopes & manage them, and the like place is properest for this also. 3dly A Quadrant to

take distances fixt to a Foot soe as it may turne to all sort of plains, this having Telescope sightes & many nice Joynts & Screwes must be housed for its better preservation, but the best house will be a little house of boardes about 12 foot square & 7 foot high & noe other roofe but what may be taken quite off when the Instrument is used, as you draw off the sliding lid of a box, or upon hinges as you open the Cover of a Trunke, & this will be as well don in a Garden as the top of a Tower, for wee valewe noe observations made neer the Horizon.

This, Wren went on, was what he, Hooke and Flamsteed had done at Greenwich, where the Royal Observatory offered tailor-made observational facilities without fuss:

We built indeed an Observatory at Greenwich not unlike what your Tower will proue, it was for the Observators habitation & a litle for pompe; It is the instruments in the Court after the manner I haue described wch are used, the roome keepes the Clocks & the Instruments that are layd by.[20]

Expert in both the buildings and the instruments, Wren recalled with pride the Royal Observatory at Greenwich. He even confessed that there was an element of architectural irony in the folly-like style of the building, with its italianate scrolls and turrets – 'a litle for pompe'.[21] With complete confidence he advised Fell that an observatory in Tom Tower would be inappropriate, and besides would fatally interfere with the coherent gothic scheme Wren had devised to complete the medieval lower storeys. Fell, not surprisingly, abandoned his idea, and the Tower was completed according to Wren's original design.

ARCHITECT AND SCIENTIFIC VIRTUOSO:
THE PILLAR AT FISH STREET

For Wren and Hooke themselves, as the case of the Royal Observatory makes clear, there was no dividing line between their activities as committed and active scientists and those in the office of the Surveyor of the King's Works, where they were increasingly sought after to design important public buildings. At the Observatory their understanding of astronomical instruments dovetailed with Wren's design. At the Royal College of Physicians, another building destined for specialist scientific use (where Hooke took a leading role in the design and execution), they fed the experience gained from their thorough and continuing activities in dissection into the design discussions.[22] Buildings like these enabled them to conceive of design and function as intrinsically related, and, in the case of some of their buildings, allowed the possibility of combining the overt function with scientific functions recognised largely by themselves.

Of such buildings, the Monument to the Great Fire stands out for the fully realised nature of its double function as both architectural monument and oversized scientific instrument.

The 1670 City Churches Rebuilding Act contained money for a memorial 'the better to preserve the memory of this dreadful visitation'. From the beginning it seems to have been decided that the memorial would take the form of a pillar. It was to offer a 'vista' (a focal point at the end of an avenue) as visitors crossed over old London Bridge into the City. London Bridge is, of course, long gone from its old location, and the Monument is now hemmed in by tall buildings, erasing the intended 'prospect'. Wren submitted the first wooden model to the City for approval early in 1671. Drawings of several types of column survive in a variety of hands, including those of Woodroffe and Hooke. The one which most closely resembles the pillar as built is in Hooke's hand, and signed by Wren in his capacity as Royal Surveyor: 'With His M[ajes]ties Approbation'.

Some are of proposals for what should go on the top of the completed column – presumably those submitted to the King for scrutiny in July 1675, with an accompanying letter from Wren:

> In pursuance of an Order of the Comittee, for City Landes I doe heerwith offer the Severall designes which some monthes since I shewed His M[ajes]tie for his approbation, who was then pleased to thinke a large Ball of metall gilt would be most agreeable, in regard it would give an Ornament to the Town at a very great distance; not that His M[ajes]tie disliked a Statue; and if any proposall of this sort be more acceptable to the City I shall most readily represent th same to His M[ajes]tie.
>
> I cannot but com[m]end a Large Statue as carrying much

dignitie with it, & that wch would be more valewable in the Eyes of Forreiners & strangers. It hath been proposed to cast such a one in Brasse of 12 foot high for 1000lb I hope (if it be allowed) wee may find those who will cast a figure for that mony of 15 foot high, wch will suit the greatnesse of the pillar & is (as I take it) the largest at this day extant; and this would undoubtedly bee the noblest finishing that can be found answerrable to soe goodly a worke in all mens Judgements.

A Ball of Copper, 9 foot Diameter cast in severall peeces with the Flames & gilt, may well be don with the Iron worke & fixing for 350lb. and this would be most acceptable of any thing inferior to a Statue, by reason of the good appearance at distance, and because one may goe up into it; & upon occasion use it for fireworkes.

A phoenix was at first thought of; & is the ornament in the wooden modell of the pilar, wch. I caused to be made before it was begun, but upon second thoughtes I rejected it because it will be costly, not easily understood at that Highth and worse understood at a distance; & lastly dangerous by reason of the sayle the spread winges will carry in the winde.

The Belcony must be made of substantiall well forged worke there being noe need at that distance of filed worke, and I suppose (for I cannot exactly guesse the weight) it may be well performed & fixed according to a good designe for fourscore & ten pounds including painting. All wch is humbly submitted to your consideration.[23]

The Monument was under construction during the six years from 1673 to 1679, with Hooke taking charge of the project once it went on site, through to completion. On 19 October 1673 he recorded in his diary, 'perfected module of Piller'; on 1 June 1674, 'At the pillar at Fish Street Hill. It was above ground 210 steps'; on 7 August, 'At the Pillar in height 250 steps'; on 21 September 1675, 'At fish-street-hill on ye top of ye column'. On 11 April 1676, he was with Wren 'at the top of ye Piller'. From the precision of the elements in the column as built (the accuracy of the height of each individual stair-riser, the breadth of the circular apertures) it appears that particular care was taken with the construction of this single, vertical shaft, extending the period to completion significantly. On 14 October 1676, Hooke noted, 'scaffolds at fish-street-piller almost all struck', but a year later he went again 'to piller about scaffold' and on 26 October 1677 he 'directed corners'.[24]

Although the pillar was commissioned as part of the Royal Commission's rebuilding works, and was paid for with coal tax revenue, it was rumoured in Wren's scientific circle that the Monument had been designed with a dual purpose: as well as providing a grand memorial landmark, it would also serve as a large-scale scientific instrument. It was their third attempt at constructing a giant vertical, zenith telescope. The rebuilding money would thus, in this case, provide two structures for the price of one. In his early Life of Wren, John Ward explained:

> The monument is a pillar of the Doric order, the pedestal of which is 40 feet high and 21 square, the diameter of the column 15 feet, and the altitude of the whole 202, a fourth part higher than that of the emperour Trajan at Rome. It was begun in the year 1671, and finished in 1677. The ingenious and learned architect built it hollow, that it might serve as a tube to discover the parallax of the earth, by the different distances of the star in the head of the Dragon from the zenith, at different seasons of the year.[25]

Ward believed that the Monument had failed as a telescope whose observations would prove the movement of the earth round the sun – in fact, given the extended periods of time over which measurements are required to be taken, it would have been several years before it became clear that no vertical shaft was sufficiently stable to achieve the level of accuracy required. Since the flaming urn which crowns the Monument has a hinged 'lid', there is no reason why it could not have been used for observation of the night sky long after it had been completed.[26]

With its scientific use in mind, Wren and Hooke put considerable thought and effort into the entirely invisible portion of the building – the underground laboratory which would house the experimenter and his equipment, at foundations level, beneath the vertical shaft.

On 8 February 1673, Hooke recorded in his diary discussions he had had with Wren that day about modifying the preparatory drawings for St Paul's: 'With Mr. Haux at Pauls churchyard. at Dr. Wrens, told me the Designe of burying vaults under Paules and the Addition of Library

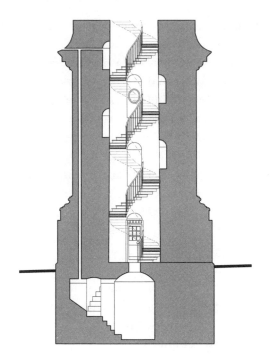

Section through the lower portion of the Monument to the Great Fire, showing the basement laboratory.

Body and portico at the west.'[27] The discussion of the 'vaults' or crypt of St Paul's envisages functional spaces below ground to support the practical needs (as well as the fabric) of the Cathedral. Two years earlier, in 1671, Hooke, designing a new building for the Royal College of Physicians, had similarly proposed that 'the Cellar under the Hall and great Stayer Case bee fitted for a laboratory with a large chimney'.[28]

A domed underground space, ample enough to offer facilities for an experimentalist working directly beneath the shaft, provides the foundation for the 'Fish Street pillar', suggesting that Wren and Hooke devised this neglected, yet structurally and functionally vital, part of the building together.[29] The underground room culminates in a round aperture at the top of its domed roof, so that the experimenter has a clear view from the basement to the top of the shaft, and, indeed, through the ornamental urn (which conveniently hinges open to the sky). Sunk twenty feet deep, covering an area exactly the dimensions of the plinth at the base of the column, and designed with openings to allow access for air (and experimental features like a vertical plumbline dropped from above), this laboratory is large enough to allow several experimenters to work at the bottom of the vertical shaft. It is also large enough for an observer to spend long periods of time comfortably and conveniently taking measurements there.[30]

Although it did not produce the desired results as a zenith telescope (neither in a deep well nor beneath the column did it prove possible to measure the tiny incremental shifts in position of the fixed stars required to provide the hoped-for proof of the earth's rotation round the sun), the Monument did prove a suitable location for more modest kinds of experiments. Hooke used it regularly for empirical work which required long vertical drops, and readily accessible, staggered experimental locations vertically above one another (for instance, for experiments with pendulums and barometers).

On 16 May 1678, Hooke recorded in his diary: 'At Fish Street pillar [Monument] tried mercury barometer experiment. It descended at the top about $\frac{1}{3}$ of an inch.'[31] On 23 May he 'directed experiment at Column. Lent Mr. Hunt a cylinder to do it.'[32] The proceedings of the Royal Society for 30 May record that Hooke measured the pressure at various stages as he came down the Monument's steps, but that he was not entirely happy with the accuracy of his equipment:

> He had observed the quicksilver to ascend by degrees, as near as he could perceive, proportional to the spaces descended in going down from the top of the column to the bottom: but because the said stations of the mercury were different from one another but very little, and so it was not easy to determine the certain proportions of the one to the other; therefore he proposed against the next meeting an experiment be tried at the same place with an instrument which would determine that distance an hundred times more exactly: which instrument also he there produced, in order to explain the manner thereof, it being made upon the same principle with the wheel barometer, but more curiously wrought.[33]

Preserved among the manuscripts of the Royal Society is an autograph paper by Hooke in which he develops his wheel barometer, explicitly in the context of these experiments conducted inside the shaft of the Monument. The paper also makes it clear that these experiments continue those begun by Wren and Boyle, thus indicating that Wren remained involved at least in spirit in the post-construction scientific uses of this Wren office architectural project.[34]

In December 1678 Hooke measured the height of the Monument – presumably the distance from the upper platform (beneath the crowning burst of gilded flames) to the floor of the basement.[35] This was the distance over which measurements could be taken for his resumed Torricellian and pendulum experiments – the series he had begun twelve years earlier at the top and bottom of Old St Paul's tower, shortly before the Great Fire destroyed his experimental location.[36]

In its final realisation the pillar on Fish Street was heralded as a fully achieved Monument to the Great Fire – arresting, elegant and an architectural *tour de force*. We might also think of it as a lasting monument to the scientific endeavours of the Wren–Hooke team – sadly, that second virtuoso part of the building, its underground domed chamber, essential to this function of the building, has, since the deaths of its architects, been almost entirely forgotten.

ARCHITECT AND INTELLECTUAL: THE WREN LIBRARY

One further architectural commission the virtuosity of whose execution can be traced to the close match between Wren's own intellectual interests and the design was the library commissioned in 1675 by the Master of Trinity College, Cambridge – Newton's mentor Isaac Barrow.[37]

Barrow had been one of those pressing Cambridge to build a University theatre, to house University graduation ceremonies, like the recently completed Sheldonian Theatre in Oxford, and to combine this with a University library and repository. When the University refused to fund this ambitious project, Barrow resolved that his college would sponsor the initiative instead. He retained Wren to redesign the building as a library for Trinity (in the spirit of the project, Wren contributed his designs without a fee).

Early in 1676, Barrow appealed for contributions to a library which would yield – according to his fund-raising brochure – 'much Ornament to the University, and some honour to the Nation'. He succeeded in raising enough money to get the building under way. Newton donated £40, slightly less than the average contribution made by the 115 past and present fellows who contributed (his friend Humfrey Babington gave a magnificent £900). Subsequent masters, however, had more difficulty in finding the finances to complete the library. Towards the end of the construction period the college was reduced to selling library duplicate volumes, raising loans from individual fellows, and, finally, selling the college plate for £1479. For some time after it was finished there were no funds properly to supplement the college's collection of books for the library; although the roof was put on in 1684–85, the building did not house the library until 1696.[38]

Dr John North, who followed Barrow as Master of Trinity, inheriting the debts accumulated by the library building, gave his brother a colourful account of the circumstances of the Wren Library commission:

> Dr. Barrow assured them that if they made a sorry building, they might fail of contributions, but if they made it very magnificent and stately, and, at least, exceeding that at Oxford, all gentlemen, of their interest, would generously contribute; it being what they desired, and little less than required of them; and money would not be wanted as the building went up, and occasion called for it. But sage caution prevailed, and the matter, at that time, was wholly laid aside. Dr. Barrow was piqued at this pusillanimity, and declared that he would go straight to his college, and lay out the foundations of a building to enlarge his back court, and close it with a stately library, which should be more magnificent and costly, than what he had proposed to them, and doubted not but, upon the interest of his college, in a short time to bring it to perfection. And he was as good as his word; for that very afternoon he, with his gardeners and servants, staked out the very foundations upon which the building now stands; and Dr. North saw the finishing of it except the classes [bookcases], which were forward, but not done, in his time; and divers benefactions came in upon that account; wherewith, and the liberal supply from the college, the whole is rendered complete; and the admirable disposition and proportion on the inside is such as touches the very soul of anyone who first sees it.[39]

The model for the library was a building which both Barrow and Wren had known intimately in London, John Webb's library for the Royal College of Physicians.[40] This elegant purpose-built library was paid for by the aged ex-royal physician William Harvey, when he retired

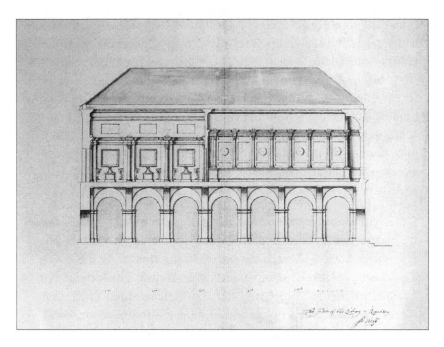

Webb's design for a library and repository at the Royal College of
Physicians, built during the Commonwealth period, and paid for by
William Harvey (1651–54).

as Lumleian Lecturer there, handing over the lucrative appointment to
Sir Charles Scarburgh. Aubrey called the building 'a noble building of
Roman architecture'.[41] The period of construction (1651–54) corresponded precisely to Wren's association with the circle of Sir Charles
Scarburgh in his formative late teens.[42] This was probably Webb's first
solo commission (he had hitherto worked as deputy to Inigo Jones),
and surely an interesting project to have watched go up. The issue of
how to distribute the significant, focused load of the bookcases and
books, particularly over an open arched loggia, was inevitably the para-
mount structural issue in this case, as also for Wren at Trinity. Webb's
building was destroyed in the Great Fire. In 1670 the Wren office undertook the rebuilding of the Royal College of Physicians, to include a
library, repository and anatomy theatre, under Hooke's direction.[43]

During the Commonwealth years, while Wren was admiring Webb's
Inigo Jones-inspired classical library in London, Barrow was travelling
abroad, visiting Smyrna, Constantinople, Florence and Venice. Like
other enforced English travellers of that period, he was fascinated by

the distinctive forms of the exotic foreign-style buildings he visited. We might regard the airy colonnaded building on which architect and client eventually settled as elegantly combining the two sets of influences – revived European classical, oriental and Venetian.[44]

In the letter Wren wrote to accompany his presentation drawings for the library, he drew Barrow's attention to innovative design features calculated to improve the functionality of the building. An entirely novel solution to the relationship between the library floor and the double-ordered façade provided a deep, windowless vertical space inside against which bookcases could be ranged without interruption:

> I have given the appearance of arches as the order required fair & lofty: but I haue layd the floor of the Library upon the impostes, wch. answar to the pillars in the cloister, & the levells of the old floores, & haue filled the Arches with relieues of stone, <where if you please you may *deleted*> of wch. I have seen the effect abroad in good building. . . . By this contrivance the windowes of the Library rise high & giue place for the deskes against the walls, & being high may be afforded to be large & being wide may haue stone mullions & the glasse pointed, which after all inventions is the only durable way in our Climate for a publique building.[45]

A second feature, though one not explicitly described in Wren's accompanying letter, was the inverted stone arches which provided the foundations, to cope with the danger of differential settlement of the ground on which the building was constructed.[46] Wren did, however, describe the technical details when conferring with John Fell, Dean of Christ Church, Oxford, over the completion there of Tom Tower. Wren was concerned about the additional load his new gothic Tower would place on the old foundations:

> I am heartily sorry the foundations are begun without that due consideration wch is requisite, so that (unlesse you take them up again) I am out of all hope this designe will succeed. I am most certain it will not without unexcusable flaws & cracks & weaknesse in the fabrick when the whole weight comes on let your workemen warrant what they will. I haue runne through a greater experience in this kind then any of them can haue, &

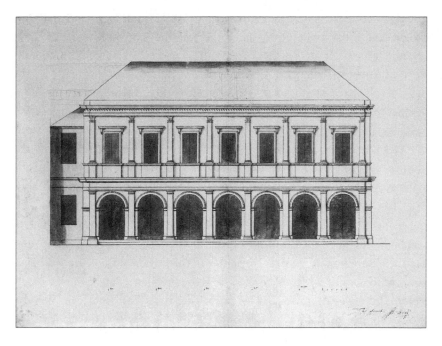

External elevation of Webb's library for the Royal College of Physicians.

tis my failings in some great fabricks where I haue not used greater caution then I beleiue they haue taken, & the constant successe where I haue used the trew waies, that makes me thus confident. . . . This is that wch I assert from Experience, that there is but two waies of making an addition of new worke to an old but that the new will part from the old if any weight depend upon the new. One way is if you haue sufficient set-offs upon the old foundations to spring substantiall arches from them under ground of large stones with deepe summering Joynts as carefully put together as you would doe aboue ground. If you haue not this opportunity . . . What is then to be don? . . . I ram[m]e the Earth though it seeme firme enough with very weighty rammers, to inure the Earth to beare, for blowes are aequipollent to weight, even to im[m]ense weightes as may be demonstrated, I lay my bed of Earth as even as possible & I lay stones at first of large beds such as old broaken Gravestones or the like, & I worke up the rest of my foundation with square stones the bedding Joynts as trew as for a good building in sight, & with thin mortars still setting them with heavy beetles, lastly I suffer a winter to passe ere I lay worke upon it.[47]

At Trinity inverted arch foundations were indeed laid, built off a bed of clunch, a hard chalk, 1394 loads of which were brought from nearby Cherry Hinton. The accounts cover payments to 'Bricklayers and other Laborers working in the Foundations'.[48]

The most difficult technical problem for the building was the floor, because it had to carry the weight of the bookcases, which projected eight and a half feet from the walls on either side. Although they were placed in line with the columns which support the floor at mid-point, there was still a span of twenty feet from wall to column, with the superincumbent weight of the bookcases bearing down on it. In November 1685 Matthew Banckes, the master carpenter of the Office of the King's Works, was sent to Cambridge by Wren to assess the problem. Payment was made to him 'by order of a meeting for surveying the Flore' and 'For ordring the workmanship of the Library Floore'. A 'moddell' whose transport from London was paid for in December may have been to demonstrate the revised method of support worked out in the Wren office. As carried out, this consisted of main girders sixteen inches square, supported at either end on cantilevers (thereby reducing the span to about twelve and a half feet), and assisted by diagonal struts which made the whole system into a kind of truss. In addition the weight of the bookcases was relieved by a series of diagonal iron bars built into the walls and bolted to a longitudinal girder running beneath the ends of the presses.[49]

The carpentry of the roof was also significantly modified during construction, to cope with the problem of the span. Wren devised a complex combination of kingposts standing on tie-beams held together by iron bolts and straps and strengthened by subsidiary queenposts and angle struts. Trusses similar to these were later used by Wren for the choir at St Paul's, where the space spanned is the same.[50]

As a lover of and collector of books himself, frequenter of the circles of those with large personal libraries, Wren understood both the requirements of the reader and the specific demands placed on a building by the need to support the localised concentrations of weight produced by many books in heavy bookcases. When we admire the Wren Library today, it is surely for this combination of the breathtaking ambition of the design with the ingenuity of its solutions to the structural problems raised.

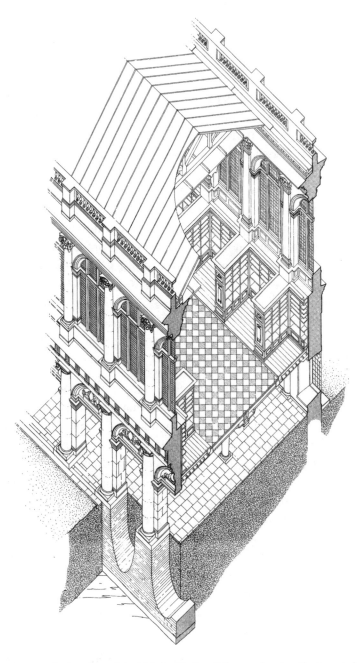

Axometric drawing of the Trinity College Library, showing the inverted arches for the foundation of the piers.

By the 1680s, Wren's distinction as the King's architect and a combination of his personal charisma in the design process, his leadership of his office and the sheer quantity of work they had produced meant that in the public sphere his professional identity as architect was formidable, and had all but overwhelmed his continuing prominence as a scientist. Those who came in contact with him, however, responded not to the holder of an important royal office, but to the possessor of an inquiring mind – talented, versatile and a fund of new ideas and possibilities. In part this can be put down to his physical appearance.

Though he was, by now, in late middle age, a widower with children, he apparently retained his disarmingly youthful appearance. Short, slight and delicate, he kept his place in the hearts of the Restoration 'returners' as the golden boy, with the future fortunes of the realm on his shoulders. Looking back on England's architectural achievements in 1697, Evelyn singled out Wren for the impact he had made, just as he had singled him out in the 1660s for his promise:

> For proof of this (without travelling far abroad) I dare report myself to any man of judgement, and that has the least taste of order or magnificence; If after he had look'd a while upon King Henry the VII's chapel at Westminster, gaz'd on its sharp angles, jetties, narrow lights, lame statues, lace and other cutwork and crinkle crankle; and shall then turn his eyes on the Banqueting-House built at White-Hall by Inego Jones after the Antient manner; as on what his majesty's present surveyor Sir Christopher Wren has lately advanced at St. Paul's; and consider what a glorious object the designed cupola, portico, colonads and other (yet unfinished) parts will then present. . . . I say, let him well consider and compare them which of the two Manners strikes the Understanding as well as the Eye with the more majesty and solemn greatness.[51]

Wren was evidently a man who made a good first impression, thanks to his personality and his manner. Throughout his career he had a reputation for candour and sincerity. After visiting Wren at Oxford in the 1660s, the French traveller Balthasar Monconys had commented, as did others who met the Savilian Professor, on Wren's small stature and slight build. Like others, too, Monconys commented on Wren's personal charm. He found him one of the most polite and frank of the scientists he had met in England; their discussions turned largely on Wren's weather-clock.[52] John Flamsteed, who was himself (like Hooke) a difficult man, wrote of him much later: 'He is a very sincere honest man: I find him so, and perhaps the only honest person I have to deal with.'[53]

By the early 1680s, however, Wren's untroubled appearance belied the reality of his life. He was once more, through no choice of his own, a bachelor, but now with three small, motherless children to care for. The childcare, of course, he left to nursemaids and female relations. For his own part, he buried himself in his work.

For two years from the beginning of 1681, Wren took on more responsibilities, and worked harder than at any other stage in his career. Given the customary pace he had set himself by this time, this is remarkable. By now he carried the responsibilities of the Surveyorship of the King's Works, with its Scotland Yard office to run, the additional demands of the Rebuilding of City Churches Commission and the Surveyorship for the rebuilding of St Paul's (which he had taken on in 1675), from a second office in the Convocation House alongside the site. He was also directing a large-scale architectural practice, whose projects by now extended countrywide, and he was continuing his involvement at a practical level with serious experimenting in medicine and mechanics at the Royal Society.

At the beginning of 1681 Wren also agreed to take on the Presidency of the Royal Society for a two-year term, chairing all but two of the twenty-nine Council meetings held during that period. On the Society's behalf, he pursued the long-running, vexed issue of what to do with Chelsea College – a collection of derelict buildings given to the Society by Charles II, but for whose renovation they could raise no funds. He was an active member of the Hudson Bay Company, attending thirty-five of its meetings in the year 1681–82 alone. Twice in 1681 he acted as Deputy Governor in the Governor's absence, taking responsibility for all Hudson Bay business. Meanwhile, he continued the demanding work as head of the Commission for rebuilding the London parochial churches, and as architect for the rebuilding of St Paul's.

The first mention of Wren's name as a potential candidate for the Royal Society Presidency came shortly after the death of Oldenburg on

5 September 1677. It was closely connected with a group of early Royal Society members who believed that the Society had lost sight of John Wilkins's original visionary plans.[54] In December 1675, a 'plot' was hatched, to re-establish the Royal Society as a club which conformed more closely to the original ambitions of the Society for the Improvement of Natural Knowledge. The first evidence is to be found, as so often, in Hooke's diary for the period. On 10 December 1675 he notes: 'Agreed upon a new clubb to meet at Joes [coffee house]. Mr. Hill, Mr. Lodowick, Mr. Aubrey and I and to joyn to us Sir Jo[nas] More, Mr. Wild, Mr. Hoskins.' By 1 January 1676 we read: 'With Wild and Hill to Wren's house. We now began our New Philosophicall Clubb and Resolvd upon Ingaging ourselves not to speak of any thing that was then reveald *sub sigillo* to any one nor to declare that we had such a meeting at all.'

Plans to oust Oldenburg and Brouncker and take control of the Society were discussed at a sequence of meetings held at Wren's official lodgings at Whitehall – details of which were recorded meticulously in Hooke's diary, since Hooke, inevitably, was prime mover in the whole affair. 'Began new Journall of Club,' he wrote on 2 January 1676; and two weeks later: 'Club at Wren's', 'Henshaw, Holder, Aubrey, Hooke at Wren's'.[55]

On 20 September 1677, less than three weeks after Oldenburg's death Hooke was 'with Mr. Evelin [Evelyn] at Sir Chr[istopher] Wrens', discussing who should be put up as Secretary to replace Oldenburg. On 10 October Hooke and Wren discussed Wren's standing for President, and the following day they successfully proposed the nomination to the other members of the 'new club'. By November, however, it was clear that there was not enough support for Wren's candidacy, and the club agreed, instead, to support the nomination of Sir Joseph Williamson.[56] Williamson was duly elected President, and nominated Wren as his Vice-President.

As Vice-President, with Hooke and Nehemiah Grew now joint Secretary (following the deaths of Wilkins and Oldenburg), Wren attended Council meetings assiduously, becoming remarkably active in the administrative business of the Society, considering the burden of his other, official duties. When he took the chair in Williamson's absence, the Council met at his house – the official residence of the Surveyor of the Royal Works in Scotland Yard, inside Whitehall Palace.

At the Royal Society's elections of November 1680, Robert Boyle was elected President in his absence. When approached, he declined, on the ground that the position required him to swear a binding oath, whereas he was conscientiously opposed to oaths of all kinds. Actually, Boyle consistently turned down all offers of high office during his lifetime, including several attempts on Charles II's part to elevate him to the House of Lords. Wren was elected in Boyle's place, and served a two-year term.[57]

In some sense the eventual success of Hooke's 'plot' to get Wren made President of the Royal Society marks, ironically, the beginning of a parting of the ways for the two friends. For Hooke the issue was to rescue the serious professional club from the control of those with special interests – court patronage, dilettante dabbling in new science. But Wren had moved, by 1680, conclusively within the court circle, and was, as we shall see, already involved in ventures like the Hudson's Bay Company with powerful financiers like Sir Stephen Fox. In 1679, during a financial dispute with the widow of one of Wren's masons, Hooke recorded in his diary that Wren was 'not kind' – a rare indication of differences having arisen between them.[58] Although the two continued to meet regularly, and to enjoy each other's company in the coffee houses they both loved frequenting, some of the passion had gone out of their relationship. By 1701, when Hooke, still only in his early sixties but in poor health, withdrew almost completely from professional life, Wren was no longer taking a close interest in his doggedly loyal lieutenant's personal affairs.

For the two years following the death of his wife Jane, Wren threw himself into every kind of work he could find for himself. This is probably all the evidence we need to tell us how keenly Wren felt Jane's loss. It also goes some way to explain his son Christopher's evident sense of distance from his father in early life – a somewhat surprising fact in view of the trust and intimacy he shared with a select band of friends outside the family.

THE ROYAL SEAT THAT NEARLY WAS

On top of his regular commitments, Wren was also, as Royal Surveyor, always on call for any project which the King chose to pursue as part of his Royal Works.

In July 1682 the corporation of Winchester placed a notice in the fashionable *London Gazette* to advertise the recreational delights of their city directly to a King addicted to horse-racing. With Winchester already well established as a racing centre (second only to Newmarket) and well known for outstanding hunting, they announced that 'the inhabitants of this city, being ambitious of the honour of his majesties presence', proposed to establish a new race, rewarded by a handsome plate, to be run on the downs at the end of August. The hope was that the King and his court would attend.[59]

The invitation was accepted, and in August the King, Queen and much of the court removed to Winchester for the race meeting and associated festivities. Large crowds of loyal citizens turned out to welcome the royal party – as they had done in 1647 when Charles I had passed through Winchester on his way to the Isle of Wight (then the Mayor and aldermen had offered the King the civic mace). Charles II was delighted with his reception, the race and the general ambience: 'The King is mightily pleased at Winchester. . . . The Duke [of York] says tis abundantly better placed for all sort of pleasure than Newmarket, and then tis neere ye forest for hunting,' a member of the royal party reported.[60]

When the city offered to sell the King the site of their medieval castle for five shillings, adding a promise to provide him with all the building timber he needed for a new palace, and to restrict leases on adjoining parcels of land until the extent of the plan was decided, he agreed without hesitation. It was an astute move on the part of Winchester Corporation. During a further short visit the following summer the King spent £1755 19s 10d locally, much of which went into the pockets of Winchester residents. On this second occasion, the Duke of York himself wrote with enthusiasm to his niece the Countess of Lichfield: 'This country is a very proper place for women to ride in, for I never saw a finer, for all field sports, the duchesse and my daughter have been several tyms a hare hunting with little beagles.'[61]

Hitherto the court had gone regularly to Newmarket for its horse-racing (Charles and James were both enthusiasts, and heavy gamblers on the outcomes) and for recreational hunting. Game in the Newmarket area had, however, become seriously depleted through over-hunting, and the accommodation there was not up to royal standards. The court blamed both, somewhat unconvincingly, on the local people:

The country people have very much spoil'd and destroy'd His Majesties Game, which, together with the moross carriage to some gent. that attend the court, and the dirtiness of the town, tis said His Majesty is not well pleas'd with it: and tis discoursed that He will not for the future spend so much time in this place as formerly.[62]

The attractiveness of Newmarket was further dimmed when, in August 1683, a serious fire gutted half of the town, and the King's residence narrowly escaped being reduced to ashes. Actually, the fire may have saved the King's life, since, following his unexpected departure, two plots against his life were uncovered. The King also complained that the finest houses in Newmarket were all occupied by prominent anti-government figures – members of the emerging Whig party. Winchester looked a far more attractive proposition. With a characteristic combination of passion and impatience, the King launched his Royal Surveyor, Wren, on the project of building a major new summer palace there for the entire court. Evelyn reported in his diary:

> 23rd September 1683. There was this day a collection for re-building Newmarket, consumed by an accidental fire, which removing his Majesty thence sooner than was intended, put by the assassins, who were disappointed of their rendezvous and expectation by a wonderful providence. This made the King more earnest to render Winchester the seat of his autumnal field-diversions for the future, designing a palace there, where the ancient castle stood; infinitely indeed preferable to Newmarket for prospects, air, pleasure, and provisions. The surveyor has already begun the foundation for a palace, estimated to cost £35,000, and his Majesty is purchasing ground about it to make a park, &c.

Responsibility for assembling a site of a suitable size for the projected Palace, its outbuildings, stables, parks and views, fell directly to Wren, who negotiated the contracts locally. By January 1683 he had paid out just short of £2000 for properties and lands which included: 'three small Tenements ... by Lease from the Citty for 80 years to come' (cost, £324); 'a hopp Ground & Cherry Orchard, held by Lease from the Citty ... for 40 years to come; with a small piece of Ground, held from the

Citty for 1000 years' (cost, £63 10s); 'A Ten Acre Close' (£160); 'A Brick house, and Orchard, without West-gate, held . . . for 1000 years' (£270).[63] Wren was present, too, at the Treasury Meeting of 16 January 1683, chaired by the King, at which the money for these transactions was advanced ahead of an agreed sum of £1000 a month for ten months, for the actual construction.[64] The cost of the Palace itself eventually exceeded substantially Evelyn's estimate. In fact, between 1683 and the beginning of 1685 Charles spent £44,000 on Winchester Palace.

In February Wren was back at Winchester, finalising the purchase arrangements, and negotiating a further substantial acquisition of land for a large park. By September 1683 expenditure had reached £7180 for land purchases alone.[65]

On 13 March 1683, Wren contracted with two of his most experienced masons, Christopher Kempster and Edward Strong, for the building of the foundations of the Palace.[66] Kempster had recently acted successfully as site manager for Wren for the completion of Tom Tower at Christ Church, Oxford – as Wren assured his client there, 'I haue used him in good workes and he is very carefull to worke trew to his designe & strong well banded worke, & I can rely upon him.'[67] A contract was also drawn up with James Grove – another Londoner, and a rising star in Wren's team – as master carpenter to the project.[68] Bricks were to be manufactured locally on a large scale (and Wren oversaw the setting up of those arrangements, changing the source of raw materials because of dissatisfaction with the quality), but further skilled labour for construction was also recruited from the London region. The management and building expertise for the royal residence was, therefore, entirely London in origin, and, for speed and reliability, direction of the project was in the hands of experienced members of the team regularly employed by the Wren office.

Winchester Palace was the first large-scale responsibility for one further trusted employee who had recently joined the Wren office. Nicholas Hawksmoor was introduced to Wren by the plaster worker Edward Gouge. He began as the Surveyor-General's personal clerk, some time around 1684, and his first recorded work for Wren was on this project.[69]

The Winchester Palace project is typical of Wren's dealings with the King as Royal Surveyor, over the royal residences. Beginning with the earliest enthusiasm for rebuilding Whitehall – which eventually resulted only in a piecemeal series of royal lodgings, rather than execution of anything like the dream of a master-plan inherited from his father – Charles settled his attention on Greenwich, Windsor, Hampton Court and finally Winchester, with ambitious and costly plans for building, in pursuit of a level of royal residential grandeur to outdo what he had seen in France, Germany and the Low Countries.[70] Webb, May and Wren were all involved in designs, and in partial executions of these plans.

Whenever Wren was involved, he would throw himself into the scheme, doing a significant amount of the preliminary work of site purchasing and contract negotiation himself. Sets of drawings poured from the Wren office to satisfy the King's excitement for whichever project currently took his attention. Work would then proceed at astonishing speed until the King lost interest, circumstances changed or the money ran out. The closest Charles came to completing any of these grand ventures was at Windsor, where Hugh May, as Comptroller of the Windsor Office of Works, had succeeded by 1680 in restoring Charles I's favourite seat to a standard suitable for the headquarters of the Order of the Garter, and where Wren was closely involved because of his historical, sentimental attachment, as his childhood home, and as the last resting place of Charles I.[71] Even there, however, as we shall see, the ambitious monument to Charles I, a project particularly dear to Wren's heart, was never executed. In each of these cases, Wren was closely involved, either as the architect or (as in the case of Windsor) as the Royal Surveyor overseeing financial and practical arrangements.

The design produced by Wren for Winchester was even more ambitious than that already undertaken some twenty years earlier, on the riverside site at Greenwich, by his rival for the Royal Surveyorship, John Webb, and left half completed at Webb's death in 1672.[72] The imposing façade, with central giant-order portico and cupola, was to be flanked by two substantial side-wings. The Palace included state apartments, privy lodgings for the King and Queen, the Duke and Duchess of York and the Duchess of Portsmouth, a Council Chamber and lodgings for the Clerks of Council, as well as over a hundred lodgings for courtiers. It was clearly intended as a major governmental centre – an alternative to Charles's other traditional non-metropolitan alternative, Oxford – rather than simply a summer hunting lodge. In autumn 1683 the King called his Royal Surveyor into a Treasury meeting at Whitehall, and asked Wren how long it would take him to complete these ambitious buildings. Wren answered that it would take two years to do the job properly but one year 'not so well, nor without great confusion, charge, and inconvenience'. Pressing him (impatiently as always), the King insisted, 'if it be possible to be done in one year, I will have it so, for a year is a great deal in my life'.[73]

Wren made every effort to comply with his royal master's wishes, and execute the Palace as quickly as possible. In making the arrangements he took special pains to ensure the job proceeded smoothly. Describing the process of producing working drawings for large teams of masons and carpenters on another project Wren explained to his client how multiple drawings taken from his master-plans would assist the skilled builders:

> If you approue the designes, let <copies be taken of them *deleted*> the mason takes his measures as much as is necessary for the present setting out of the worke & be pleased to transmit them to me again & I shall copy out partes of them at large, more proper for the use of the workemen & giue you a carefull estimate of the charge, & returne you again the originall designes, for in the handes of the workemen they will soon be soe defaced that they will not be able from them to pursue the worke to a conclusion.[74]

In the case of Winchester Palace, Wren had the good fortune to have recently taken on the talented Hawksmoor as his personal clerk – one of his responsibilities was the precise copying of drawings.[75]

There were also plans for gardens full of artificial vistas and elaborate waterworks. According to Wren's son, the purchase of extensive park lands at Winchester had been intended to provide the Palace with gardens to rival those currently fashionable in France, including an artificial river, and a stepped water-feature on a grand scale, emulating those at Rueil and Sceaux:[76]

> [The Palace] extends to the West 326 Feet, to the South 216 Feet. There was particularly intended a large Cupola, 30 Feet above the Roof, which would have been seen a great Way to the Sea; and also a regular Street of handsome Houses, leading in a direct Line down the Hill, from the Front of the Palace to the West-gate of the Cathedral; for which, and for the Parks,

the Ground was procured; and Preparations made for proper Plantations, a necessary Ornament for that open Situation. The Surveyor [Wren] had projected also to have brought from the Downs a River through the Park, which would have formed a Cascade of 30 Feet Fall.[77]

As early as 1664, Charles II had proposed a cascade (designed by Le Nôtre) at Greenwich: 'Pray lett le Nostre goe on with the modell [for the Fountaine in the Parke] . . . he may add much to the beauty of the descente by a cascade of watter.'[78] Wren had visited the Château at Rueil in 1665, where the spectacular cascade was built for Cardinal Richelieu in 1638.[79]

By August 1684, when the King and Queen arrived with a large court party (and a green damask travelling bed and Dutch mat for the Queen's lodgings in the town) to spend two months there, the shell of a substantial building was completed, and most of the main roofs on. Only the end elevation, which was to have been crowned with a substantial dome, was not quite finished. Charles was delighted with his new Palace, and anticipated spending summers there with his court on a regular basis. In January 1685 he remarked to the Earl of Ailesbury: 'I shall be most happy this week, for my building will be covered with lead.' Wren had evidently excelled himself organisationally, in successfully completing the fabric of a building on this enormous scale in under two years.

Within a week, however, the King was mortally ill, his remark to Ailesbury reinterpreted for posterity as a sinister premonition of his own death – the lead-covered building in question being identified, with hindsight, as his coffin. Work on Winchester Palace was immediately halted, and never recommenced. Two years later, James II officially decided to abandon the project.[80]

In September 1685 Evelyn visited Winchester, and described the Palace, now standing abandoned:

> I went out, to see the New Palace his late Majestie had began, and brought almost to the Covering: It was placed on the side of the Hill where formerly stood the old Castle; a stately fabrique, of 3 sides; and a Corridor, all built in brique, and Cornished, windoes, and Columns at the break and Entrance of freestone. . . . and having an incomparable prospect [view].[81]

One of the small tragedies of Wren's own long life was that he survived long enough to preside over the decommissioning of buildings on whose erection he had lavished so much loving care on behalf of his sovereign, effectively giving the lie to his determination to build 'for all eternity'. In October 1698 Wren 'and other officers of the works' were advised by Thomas Bateman 'that in his Majesty's house at Winchester there is a leak in the roof, and no local plumber available'. Wren directed Bateman to 'speak wth Mr. Roberts to Employ his men to make a report there upon wth. Estimate of the same upon view', and make good the damage.[82]

DYNASTIC DISARRAY

On the night of Sunday, 1 February 1685 King Charles II was taken suddenly and violently ill. By the morning his speech was severely impaired; as his attendant was shaving him (he rose with great regularity at 5 a.m.), he let out a piercing shriek, fell into some kind of apoplectic fit and collapsed backwards unconscious. It was obvious his condition was life-threatening. Edmund King, a physician who happened to be present, prescribed immediate bleeding, without waiting for the arrival of the royal medical team. As Evelyn records in his diary for 4 February:

> If, by God's providence, Dr. King (that excellent chirurgeon as well as physician) had not been accidentally present to let him blood (having his lancet in his pocket), his Majesty had certainly died that moment; which might have been of direful consequence, there being nobody else present with the King save this Doctor and one more, as I am assured. It was a mark of the extraordinary dexterity, resolution, and presence of mind in the Doctor, to let him blood in the very paroxysm, without staying the coming of other physicians, which regularly should have been done, and for want of which he must have a regular pardon, as they tell me. This rescued his Majesty for the instant, but it was only a short reprieve.[83]

Meanwhile, panic-stricken messages were sent to the Duke of York and the Privy Counsellors summoning them to the royal bedside. By the time they arrived Charles had had sixteen ounces of blood removed from a vein in his arm.

When Wren's old friend and mentor Sir Charles Scarburgh arrived with his team of royal physicians he took over the King's treatment. All the cathartic regimes and therapeutic practices developed during the years of medical experimentation carried out by the circle of physicians at Oxford and London were focused on trying to save the sovereign's life. The hapless man was subjected to a succession of increasingly radical treatments: he was bled again repeatedly, his head was shaved, cantharide beetles (Spanish Fly) were applied to his skin to produce blistering. The King recovered his speech briefly, but by the next day he had been prostrated by another seizure or fit, and Scarburgh's team of physicians and surgeons had embarked on a further frenzy of remedies. Charles was purged, cauterised, clystered and blistered to remove the poisons from his system. Red-hot irons were seared on to his shaven skull and his naked feet to stimulate him back into consciousness. Cupping glasses and cantharides were once again administered externally. All these attempts at curing the King were excruciatingly painful to the patient, who was once again lucid, and evidently suffering. He tolerated every attempt at cure with extraordinary fortitude and good grace. He did so in the public glare of a growing crowd of important political and court figures – by the fifth day of his illness there were no fewer than seventy-five people crowded into the royal apartments, including five bishops.

The almost unseemly efforts to revive the King with drastic remedies when in fact all hope of his recovery was gone were symptomatic of the rising panic in the inner royal circle. The entire court – the whole county indeed – was caught unawares by the King's sudden illness. He had, since his return in 1660, enjoyed a positively rude good health, with the exception of a brief, though acute, bout of fever in August 1679. But, beyond the sheer unexpectedness of his fatal illness, those around him were dismayed at having to face the problematic issue of succession many years before it had been anticipated. Charles was not yet fifty-five. His contemporaries among the 'returners', including Wren, were still struggling to understand (both emotionally and politically) what the Restoration of the monarchy had really achieved for the long-term strength and stability of the country. The wildly over-optimistic hopes of spring 1660 had given way to more realistic efforts in the 1670s to come to terms with the King's personal weaknesses – his moral laxity, his dislike of paperwork and administration, and his chronic extravagance, bringing with it persistent shortage of cash in the royal exchequer. Nevertheless, the Exclusion Crisis which dominated the political scene between 1679 and 1681 had shown just how reluctant the English were – in spite of the spectre of a future Stuart monarch (James II) who was an enthusiastic Roman Catholic – to countenance actions which might risk once again throwing the country into the turmoil of civil war.[84] By the mid-1680s the circle in which Wren moved was committed to a conscious policy of backing a monarch in the line of most direct Stuart descent, whatever his flaws, on the ground that only he could guarantee political stability.

The psychological unpreparedness for the King's death of those around him, and the subsequent turmoil into which the monarchy was inevitably thrown, is symbolised by a story frequently repeated in the weeks following Charles's death: James – summoned from his bed in haste in the early hours by news of his brother's illness – displayed an exterior calm and decorum, but was noted still to be wearing his bedroom slippers in the royal sickroom.

By the Thursday it was clear that the situation was desperate, and the King's life was ebbing away. At noon on Friday, 6 February 1685, in spite of the physicians' best efforts, he died. Conscious to the end, he received the last rites from a Catholic priest, thoughtfully provided by his brother James. According to the gentlemen with him at the end he took these freely, and apologised graciously to those attending him for taking so long to die. It should perhaps have been his doctors who begged his pardon, rather than he theirs.[85]

Since boyhood Wren had unwaveringly honoured the memory of Charles I – 'royal martyr'. At the Restoration, that commitment to the 'martyred' King had been refashioned into devoted attendance on his son, a devotion intensified by their shared early life-experiences, from charmed infancy to near destitution and dependency, covering the period from childhood to young adulthood. Extraordinary efforts had gone, as we have seen, into establishing in the public imagination a seamless continuity between the reigns of the two Charleses, father and son – efforts in which Wren had played a direct part, both as the guardian of the Garter records and as the royal architect implementing the hopes and dreams of Charles I in his designs at Whitehall and Windsor. Others in his circle – Evelyn and Ashmole, in particular – had contributed substantial printed works tracing in detail the history of sustaining Stuart rituals and institutions, which had allegedly never been interrupted during the Commonwealth or Protectorate periods, but had simply been displaced temporarily to the continent of Europe. With the death, without legitimate direct heir, either male or female, of Charles II, that illusion of dynastic continuity could no longer be sustained.

Yet sustained it had to be. Although there were those who wanted to argue that Charles II had in effect been 'married' to the commoner mother of his eldest illegitimate son, the Duke of Monmouth, legitimising him was never a real political option. It is clear that Wren had committed himself to James well before the abortive Monmouth Rebellion in June 1685.

Wren had developed a close working relationship with Charles II, as Surveyor of his Royal Works. The King and his royal architect shared a commitment to building on a grand scale, as the way to set the seal on England's restored glory. Here again, the aspiration was ably supported by John Evelyn, who published a sequence of short treatises on architecture (both original, and translated from French and Italian) the argument of whose prefatory letters was consistently that the material splendour of Charles's restored reign in Britain would match that of the glorious regime of Louis XIV in France, on the strength of Wren's magnificent plans for the royal palaces, and his grand design projects for the public buildings destroyed in the Great Fire.

With the King's unexpected death, however, what became important was a transfer of power which disrupted as little as possible an administration which had at last succeeded in bringing royal finances into good order, and in stabilising the political agenda after the hysteria of the 1678 Popish Plot.[86] In spite of the violent opposition of supporters of Charles II to his Catholic brother, which had marked the political scene for the preceding ten years, James II succeeded to the throne without incident, and old royalists like Wren (now grouped under the political designation of 'Tories', or the 'country party') committed themselves without demur to serving the man they considered, in the absence of legitimate offspring, to be the divinely sanctioned Stuart heir. They may even have hoped that the austere James's more disciplined and sober court would be more to their liking than the dissolute circle around Charles. On the day after Charles's death Evelyn reflected in his diary:

He was a prince of many virtues, and many great imperfections; debonair, easy of access, not bloody nor cruel; his countenance fierce, his voice great, proper of person, every motion became him; a lover of the sea, and skilful in shipping; not affecting other studies, yet he had a laboratory, and knew of many empirical medicines, and the easier mechanical mathematics; he loved planting and building, and brought in a politer way of living, which passed to luxury and intolerable expense. . . . He would doubtless have been an excellent prince, had he been less addicted to women, who made him uneasy, and always in want to supply their unmeasurable profusion, to the detriment of many indigent persons who had signally served both him and his father. He frequently and easily changed favourites to his great prejudice.[87]

All royal appointments, and all financial arrangements between Parliament and the monarch, fell in, and required to be renegotiated, following the death of one king and the succession of another. Technically, Wren had to be reappointed to the office of Royal Surveyor. In practice, he immediately took on the responsibility for organising the Coronation of James II, in his capacity as Royal Surveyor, just as Sir John Denham had done, spectacularly, for Charles I.[88]

FRIENDS IN HIGH FINANCIAL PLACES

Wren was apparently considered from the very start to be sympathetic to James II, because of his high Toryism – his unwavering commitment to the monarchy and his belief in obedience to the Crown, come what might. Although resolutely Anglican in his personal faith, Wren had no particular problem with a king who preferred Catholic worship in private. As we saw, his uncle Bishop Wren, and indeed his own father, had negotiated such sensitive matters with discretion and sensitivity, in relation to the personal piety of James I and the young Charles I.[89]

Accordingly, Wren was moved into place as a member of the new regime which would adopt (James hoped) a more laissez-faire set of policies with regard to Catholic office-holders. Even before Charles II's death a strategy had been adopted of issuing new charters to England's boroughs up and down the land, 'regulating' them by putting in place entirely new sets of burghers – ones who could be counted upon to support a more Catholic-leaning set of policies.[90] Winchester had been so regulated, during the very period in which the city was endeavouring to gain royal favour by making itself an attractive location for the royal summer vacation.

Another of the boroughs 'regulated' (effectively, administratively manipulated) by the new King in the run-up to the 1685 General Election was Plympton in Devon. On 11 March, just ahead of the election, Wren was nominated by the Crown as a burgess of Plympton, thereby guaranteeing him a parliamentary seat, and implying that his vote could be counted on to support the new King.[91]

One reason for Wren's firm backing for the incoming regime was his growing involvement in the 1680s with the small group of extremely wealthy men whose loans were critical for the smooth running of an administration otherwise constantly paralysed by lack of ready funds. As part of the business of ensuring a smooth cash-flow for a series of important building projects, Wren had become close to one of the most important and influential figures among those managing the King's financial affairs – Sir Stephen Fox.[92] Just as his close friendship with Robert Hooke had sustained Wren's early Restoration years, and continued to support his pressured architectural office, so now Wren turned to Fox to learn how to negotiate the unfamiliar higher reaches of commercial finance and investment.

Three years younger than Charles II, and from a humble family (possibly with a farming background), Fox had joined the royal court at Richmond in 1640, at the age of thirteen, almost by accident, as what his biographer calls 'a sort of juvenile hanger-on with no post of his own'. According to his own account, written at the end of his long life, he was frequently allowed to play with the royal children because of his closeness in age to them. After the King's declaration of war in 1642 Fox began an itinerant life as a page-boy in the service of various royalist peers, eventually winding up in Paris in 1646, where he assumed the elevated position of gentleman of the horse to Charles, Prince of Wales – probably because no one more suitable was available to the royal heir in exile. As such he was in charge of expenditure and accounts for the royal stables and travel, expenditure which during the 1650s, with Charles constantly on the move, and living much of the time hand to mouth,

Stephen Fox, brilliant financier and the man responsible for keeping Charles II's finances afloat during his years of exile – he made a personal fortune from his brokering for the King and his courtiers.

formed a significant part of the exiled court's financial outlay. Fox's astute management of the monarch's limited resources meant that he rose to become a lynchpin member of his entourage.[93] There was no question, during this period, of financial reward for the young man, but in 1658 Charles made him a grant in arms, whose preamble gave as its reason for its award:

> [That Fox] having been advanced unto ye trust and Clerke of his Majesty's Kitchen, taxeing likewise care of and ordering the expences of the Household in His Majesty's journeys and residence in these parts, hath in the execution thereof behaved himself with extraordinary diligence, fidelity, prudence and ability, to the great advantage and satisfaction of his Majesty and his service.[94]

In December 1659, just months before his unexpected recall to the English throne, Charles stood as godfather to Fox's second son, also named Charles, born in Brussels.

At the Restoration Fox was rewarded with the important post of Clerk Comptroller (Clerk of the Green Cloth) in charge of the royal household's day-to-day expenditure; he was also rewarded for his loyal, unremunerated service during the exile years with a small estate. In 1661 it was decided that for security reasons the King would continue to retain a small body of guards in royal employment, and Fox was appointed to the newly created post of Paymaster of the King's Guards.

To begin with Fox's duties as Paymaster were straightforward and unglamorous. Money was issued to him by the Exchequer, and he paid it on to the Guards, making a twopence in the pound deduction to meet the cost of the fees he had to pay to the Exchequer officials. Before long, however, lengthy delays began to occur in the issue of money to him from the Exchequer. The Guards cost nearly £123,000 a year – money over and above the £1,200,000 Parliament had undertaken to provide to meet the normal costs of the Crown's expenditure, and which, in any case, Charles's court, with its extravagant lifestyle, managed to exceed right from the beginning of his reign.[95] By May 1661 Fox was acting as unofficial banker to the Guards, borrowing the money for their pay and uniforms himself, paying it on, after deductions to cover his own interest on the loan, plus administrative costs, and a small 'risk' payment of his own. By the summer of 1662 it had been decided to regularise the arrangements by turning the business of borrowing to ensure regular payment of the Guards over to a private contractor. This proved more difficult than anticipated. It was apparently not a sufficiently lucrative proposition to be attractive to London's banking community; in the end Fox himself agreed to the 'undertaking' (as it was officially called). Fox himself describes, in a fragment of autobiography, how this came about:

At last being commanded by the King, encouraged by my Lord High Treasurer Southampton, & every day prest by the Duke of Albermarle, the Generall, I told His Grace that I would use my utmost endeavor, whereupon hee sent the chieffe officers to make a proposition to mee, which brought to my lodging seventeene officers with Coll. Russell, Chieffe Commander by being Coll. Of His Majesties first Regiment of Foot Guards, who said they were glad to be sent from the Generall with a proposall for the undertaking of a steddy constant paying of the forces commanded by them, & having considered it at a meeting of officers they resolved to give 12d. out of every 20s to ye undertaker besides the Exchequer fees of 2d. per £ that they hitherto had paid. Whereupon I told the sd Coll. & the rest of ye officers that if I could not doe it for a shilling in the pound, including the sd. Fees, I would not consent a greater deduction should be made from the establishment. To wch Coll. Russell & the rest of ye officers said they were likely to be infinitely beholding.[96]

Under the agreement drawn up in August 1662 Fox was to advance the Guards a proportion of their pay every week in order to provide them with subsistence money, and was then to pay over the remainder at the end of every 'muster' – the six- or eight-week periods into which the army year was divided for accounting purposes. In return he took a shilling in the pound (5 per cent) of all the money passing through his hands, of which two-thirds (eightpence in the pound or $3\frac{1}{3}$ per cent) was to cover interest on the money he had to borrow, and the remaining one-third (fourpence in the pound or $1\frac{2}{3}$ per cent) covered Exchequer fees and his own expenses. Although we do not know what rate of interest Fox had to pay on the money he borrowed, nor precisely where his personal profit figured in the calculations, there is no doubt at all that he became extremely rich in the process.

He increasingly extended his arrangements to other areas of the cash-impoverished administration, and to private lending to hard-pressed courtiers and politicians. In the 1670s he was lending substantial sums to key figures in Charles's Government, from the disgraced Earl of Clarendon's two sons, Lord Cornbury and Laurence Hyde, to the Dukes of Monmouth and Ormonde, and Lord Arlington. Following the marriage of William of Orange to the Duke of York's eldest daughter, Mary, in 1677, Fox also appears to have acted as William's London banker. With so many prominent court figures relying on Fox for ready money, and contracted to him for repayments, his influence at court continued to increase.[97] At the end of 1679 he became a member of the Treasury, a post to which he was appointed both on the strength of his proven financial acumen, and because of his known, unwavering loyalty to Charles II, at a time when there was high anxiety over possible undermining influences in government in the wake of the Popish Plot.[98]

From 1669, when Wren moved into the Surveyor's apartments at Whitehall, he and Fox were neighbours, occupying spacious premises on opposite sides of Scotland Yard.[99] Fox obtained permission (from the Royal Surveyor) substantially to enlarge and improve his residence, and between 1670 and 1678 he spent £1000 doing so, with Wren as his architectural adviser. By the time he had finished he had a large house on two floors, consisting of about twenty rooms on the principal floor, with five staircases, and with a river frontage of nearly a hundred feet. In 1691 Wren made a plan of this property in his capacity of Surveyor-General of the Works, responsible for all the buildings within the precinct of Whitehall, at which time Fox had incorporated the adjacent old Bakehouse building, and was hoping for Wren's permission (and design assistance) for further improving his residence.[100]

Fox also owned a fine house at Chiswick, built for him by Hugh May between 1682 and 1684. He appears to have divided his time equally between his two residences; Evelyn dined regularly with him at Chiswick on his way back from Hampton Court to his own residence at Deptford (Evelyn thought the house 'somewhat heavy & thick; and not so well understood [architecturally]').[101] Only when he retired in 1702 did Fox finally give up his Whitehall lodgings and settle permanently at Chiswick.

In 1678 Fox fell briefly from royal favour and was dismissed from his Paymaster's office. Ordered to vacate his Whitehall apartments he 'represented to His Royal Highness [the Duke of York] that they were built at my own expense'. As a consequence 'His Majesty was pleased to recall that part of his punishment'; shortly thereafter he was, in any case, restored to his old job.[102] In 1680 Fox built a row of almshouses (or 'hospital' as Fox preferred to call it) in his native village of Farley in Wiltshire, as a thanks-offering for his good fortune. The building was completed by the middle of 1682 at a cost of almost £2000; given Fox and Wren's personal closeness by this date there is good reason to suppose Wren had some hand in the design, if only in an advisory capacity. Wren's master joiner, Alexander Fort, was appointed surveyor for the hospital's construction. Edward Heldar, bricklayer, and John Hayward, carpenter, who were both also associated with the Wren office, carried out the actual work. In 1688 Fox added a new church at Farley, and once again took advantage of Wren's expertise, both with the plans and during construction.[103]

In spite of Fox's less distinguished family background, his early life, and his youthful relationship with Charles II, runs tellingly parallel to Wren's. Another fatherless boy, drawn into an adulatory relationship with the ousted Stuarts; another lifelong idoliser of the martyred

Charles I. Socially Fox's life also intersected with Wren's from the early 1680s onwards. He was a close friend of Evelyn's, a regular visitor at Sayes Court, and a prominent mourner at the funeral of Evelyn's beloved daughter Mary. The younger of Fox's two surviving daughters, Jane (born in 1669), married the nephew of Henry Compton, Bishop of London, one of the prime movers behind the invitation to William of Orange to assume the throne in 1688, and a staunch supporter of Wren's St Paul's Cathedral as a leading member of the Rebuilding Commission (Compton and Wren had known each other since the 1665 trip to Paris, when Wren had joined the young Compton and Thomas Browne's son on a châteaux-sightseeing trip).[104]

It is significant for our understanding of Wren that by all accounts Fox was an extremely pleasant man. Wren was scrupulously well behaved himself, in all his affairs, and required a high level of integrity and consideration from those with whom he did business. In his diary, Evelyn describes Fox vividly as he was at the time when Wren got to know him well:

> He is believed to be worth at least 200000 pounds honestly <gotten> & unenvied, which is next to Miracle, & that with all this he still continues, as humble, & ready to do a Courtesie, as ever he was; nay he is generous, & lives very honorably, of a sweete nature, well spoken, & well bred. . . . In a word, never was man more fortunate than Sir Stephen; & with all this he is an handsom person, Vertuous & very religious, & for whom I have an extraordinary esteeme.[105]

INTERESTS IN COMMON

It was not only Wren's known commitment to the Stuart dynasty, and his increasing involvement with those bankrolling the Government, that made him a likely candidate for supporting James II. Given the long-established task of creating memorials of lasting royal Stuart splendour, it was a matter of central importance for Wren to ensure the smooth continuation of the major building works already in progress, notably St Paul's Cathedral and the City churches. Work on Winchester Palace might have to cease, without Charles's personal enthusiasm for the project; rebuilding work for the greater glory of London must keep going at all costs.

As it happens Wren did not find this smoothing of the way towards carrying on his construction projects awkward or difficult. Indeed, because of the accidents of their personal histories, the ascent to the throne of James II left Wren quite at ease in his professional life. Wren fell quickly into as familiar a relationship with James as he had had with his elder brother. A year younger than Wren, James, Duke of York shared with him a broken childhood whose resemblance was even closer than that which had bonded Wren to Charles. Like Wren (and unlike Charles) he had been obliged to offer solace to a devastated father at an age when he was old enough to understand his pain, but too young to offer real comfort or support.[106] Perhaps as a result of their lost dream of an all-powerful father-protector, both men believed with passion in absolute and unswerving obedience to their King.

Where Charles II had been outgoing and demonstrative, having learned early in life that such a demeanour eased the way with strangers and those from whom he needed favours, James II, like Wren, tended to conceal emotion and anxiety behind a façade of relaxed yet guarded propriety. Both were described as 'charming' by those who knew them in early manhood, yet both were apparently difficult to get to know. They shared an intense religious fervour, which found comfort in the ceremonies and rituals of High Church practice (though Wren stopped short of Catholicism). Both are reported occasionally breaching their calm exterior demeanour with outbursts of intense rage, which shocked those close to them (as we saw, Hooke records at least one such angry incident involving Wren in his diary).[107]

Wren's cousin Matthew, to whom he had been close since the Commonwealth years, was secretary to James from 1667 until his death in 1672.[108] Matthew had brought Wren to Clarendon's attention as a possible candidate for the Tangier Surveyorship in 1662; he probably also acted as intermediary between Wren and James in the several circles in which they all moved, both professionally and socially.

Wren and the former Duke of York had plenty of experience of one another in the relatively informal atmosphere of London medical and scientific circles. Wren and the new King had a long-standing acquaintance as partners-in-science in the early Royal Society, where James was a regular and enthusiastic attender. Since his brother Charles was comparatively young, and in robust good health when he came to the throne, and had already produced a crop of illegitimate children (he is supposed to have spent the night of his return to England in 1660 with the Countess of Castlemaine), it could be assumed that his marriage to Catherine of Braganza in 1662 would produce an heir. James, therefore, although technically second in line of succession at the Restoration, never expected to reign. He shared his privileged position – senior royalty without the burden of future monarchy – with Prince Rupert (also a regular participant in Royal Society activities).

When Christiaan Huygens was in London in 1661 he found the Duke of York active among the Royal Society astronomers:

> 13 May [1661]. Observed the conjunction of Saturn with the moon, in the garden at Whitehall, with Mr. Neile's long telescopes. Saturn passed above very close. The Duke of York was also there.
>
> The next day he returned and with him the Duchess of York, formerly Mrs. Hyde. This time we used my lenses. I bowed deeply to the Duchess, and Mr. Neile praised me highly.[109]

Both the Duke of York and Prince Rupert were enthusiasts for the new science, and prided themselves in their close personal involvement in experimental activities in chemistry and astronomy. A note in the Wren family papers records:

> He frequently assisted his R. Highness Rupert Prince Palatine, in his Laboratory; entertaining him with various Chymical Operations, & new Experiments; <&> sometimes in the Presence of King Charles; the Prince was pleas'd to honour him with distinguishing favour and Esteem, and Placed him on the List of those Particular <Select> friends, to whom he sent annually a Present of Wine from his Appennage on the Rhine.[110]

At one of the earliest meetings of the Society, on 4 March 1661 – three days before Sir Robert Moray was formally elected its first official President – Sir Paul Neile produced 'glass bubbles' for the examination of the members. According to the minutes, 'The King sent by Sir Paul Neile five little glass bubbles, two with liquor in them, and the other three solid, in order to have the judgement of the society concerning them.' Since the communication came from the King (whom the Society

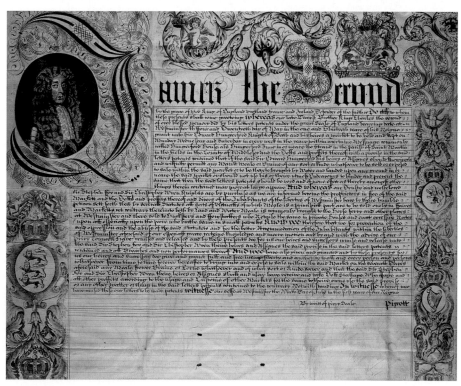

Business paperwork: (*top*) the lease for two shops and vaults on the east side of Hungerford market, issued by Sir Stephen Fox and Sir Christopher Wren to John Smalbone for seven years, sealed by Fox and Wren (Wren's seal inverted); letters patent granted by James II to Sir Stephen Fox and Sir Christopher Wren, proprietors by purchase of Hungerford market in St Martins-in-the-Fields, issued in July 1685, five months after James's accession, and a year after they had acquired the property

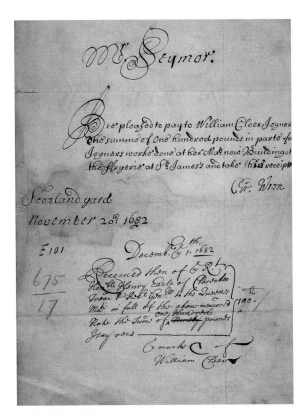

Building paperwork: (*top*) invoice issued by Wren, as Royal Surveyor, for joinery work carried out in 1682 at St James's Palace for Queen Catherine, and settled in full by the second Earl of Clarendon; plan for the redevelopment of Golden Square in London in 1673, signed off by Wren as Surveyor of the King's Works

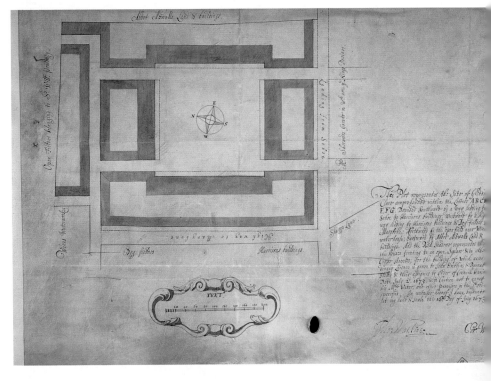

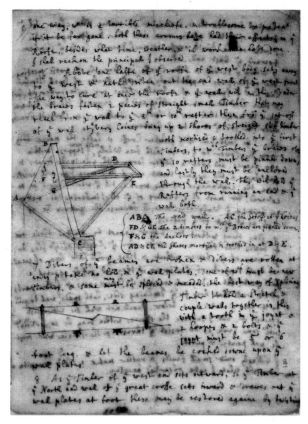

Leaving instructions: (*top*) part of a letter
from Wren to Seth Ward, Bishop of
Salisbury, advising extensive structural
repairs to Salisbury Cathedral, on the
basis of Wren's survey of the fabric;
Robert Hooke's incomplete and unsigned
will, drafted on 25 February 1703, five days
before his death

THE
INSTITUTION,
Laws & Ceremonies
Of the most NOBLE

ORDER
OF THE
GARTER.

Collected and digested into one Body
BY
ELIAS ASHMOLE of the *Middle-Temple* Esq;
WINDESOR Herald at Arms.

A Work furnished with variety of matter, relating to
HONOR and *NOBLESSE.*

LONDON,
Printed by *J. Macock*, for *Nathanael Brooke* at the *Angel*
in *Cornhill*, near the *Royal Exchange*, MDCLXXII.

B. 4.

Creating history: frontispiece from John Evelyn's copy of Elias Ashmole's monumental
compilation of archival documents and records, published at his own expense in 1672,
which established the history of the Order of the Garter – Ashmole sent out a great many
complimentary copies to those in positions of influence

was wooing in the hope of being granted a royal charter) the Society took an eager interest in the 'bubbles'. A full report of the experiments performed on them was given to the Royal Society on 14 August 1661 by Moray, which was published as an appendix to Christopher Merrett's *Art of Glass* in 1662. Hooke included a full discussion of them in *Micrographia* (1665), with illustrations.[111]

The 'bubbles' later became known as 'Prince Rupert's drops', and it appears that the examples first shown to the Society at the request of the King had indeed been brought from mainland Europe by Prince Rupert. They were glass beads in the form of a tear-drop tapering to a fine tail, made by dripping molten glass into cold water (though this was not known at the time). They exhibited a strange combination of strength and fragility: the head could withstand hammering on an anvil, or squeezing in a vice, without fracture; yet if the tail was broken with finger pressure, the whole thing exploded into powder. Hooke came close to an explanation in *Micrographia*, but the properties of these drops have continued to fascinate material scientists down to the present day.

The drops are an example of the close involvement of the court circle – a circle which included Prince Rupert and the Duke of York, and to which Neile, Moray and Wren belonged – in early Royal Society activities, and early science in general. Prince Rupert also received the credit for making the engraving technique of the mezzotint known in England. Evelyn records in his diary for 21 February 1661 that 'Prince Rupert first showed me how to grave in *mezzo tinto*.' Evelyn described the process in his *Sculptura; Or, the History and Art of Chalcography, and Engraving in Copper* (1662), including a striking example of Rupert's own work (the profile of a dark-skinned, hook-nosed man, in a folding plate),[112] but declining to explain exactly how it was achieved to prevent 'an Art so curious, and (as yet) so little vulgar' from being 'prostituted at so cheap a rate, as the more naked describing of it here, would too soon have expos'd it to'.[113] In this case, however, Rupert shares the honour with Wren himself, who apparently considered he had perfected the technique (in fact, it had begun to be developed in the 1640s in Germany, though no doubt both Rupert and Wren, possibly working together, made technical improvements to the process).[114]

Pepys recorded the King and other members of the court attending dissections in 1663: 'the other day Dr. Clarke and [Dr. Pierce] did dissect

Mezzotint of a dark-skinned man (copied from a painting), executed by Prince Rupert, who is credited with inventing the process.

two bodies, a man and a woman, before the King, with which the King was highly pleased'. In April 1665 the King attended the yearly anatomy lectures in the Harveian Building of the Royal College of Physicians, and heard George Ent lecture, knighting him at the end of the event.[115] Wren's friend Evelyn assisted at anatomical events both at the Royal Society and at the Royal College of Physicians on a regular basis.[116] In 1679, when Charles sent James to Scotland to get him out of the way in the aftermath of the Exclusion Crisis, James involved himself closely in scientific activities in Scotland, and personally established the Scottish Royal College of Physicians. The court circle took a particular interest in the development of the balance-spring watch – both Charles II and the Duke of York test-ran pocket-watches supplied by Hooke for their accuracy (a programme of testing in which Wren was also involved).[117]

Thus even though the death of Charles II, and consequent succession of the Catholic James II, caused dramatic political upheavals in England, and alarm in circles of Church and state, Wren managed astutely to avoid being caught up in the unfolding events beyond his professional interests. He was reappointed Surveyor of the King's Works, and began design work on a chapel at Whitehall for James's wife, Mary of Modena, whose Catholicism meant specific requirements in terms of church furniture. Wren had no more difficulty complying with this than he had with the corresponding commission, in the 1660s, to convert a room at Whitehall into a chapel for Charles II's Catholic Queen.

Wren's friendship with Sir Stephen Fox culminated in a joint venture which remains one of the most lastingly admired projects undertaken by the Royal Surveyor, conceptually and architecturally. The Royal Military Hospital at Chelsea, completed in 1692, demonstrates with particular elegance the way that, at their best, Wren's monumental undertakings for the Stuart monarchy brought together his exceptional mathematical and engineering talents with a deep and abiding sense of charitable obligation and good works, exercised on behalf of the Crown.

Among the surviving documents in Christopher Wren junior's hand recording details of his father's career, a synopsis of the process of design, building and organisation of the Chelsea Hospital figures no fewer than three times, in slightly different forms:

> In 1692. He finish'd the Royal Hospital at Chelsea, founded by King Charles Ye. 2d. at the latter end of his Reign for ye support of Maim'd & superannuated Soldiers. The success in the Foundation, Erection, and Settlement of this Noble Hospital <was greatly owing> to the industrious and skillfull Management of Sr. Stephen Fox & Himself, – Sr. Stephen took care of the Mony, whilst He prosecuted the Buildings; and lastly He Compil'd the Statutes, and <contriv'd ye.> Whole Oeconomy of the House.[118]

As this note suggests, it was Charles II himself who in September 1681 proposed establishing a residential hospital for discharged, invalided soldiers. The model, as so often for Charles, was probably French: Louis XIV had recently built such a charitable foundation for retired and wounded soldiers at Les Invalides in Paris, of whose designs Charles had obtained drawings, which he gave to Wren. The King originally envisaged the costs of the building being met out of royal revenue, and he raised the matter with the Treasury Committee on several occasions. There was no enthusiasm for a state-funded venture – these were, after all, employees of the Crown, whose retirement benefits should, it was agreed, fall to the royal purse. In 1681 the King asked Sir Stephen Fox to devise an alternative method of paying for his royal hospital.

The idea Fox eventually came up with was to take advantage of the twelvepence in the pound which he had been collecting as Paymaster for the Royal Guards, ever since he had been appointed to the post in the 1660s. Since the beginning of 1680, better management of royal funds had meant that Fox's old 'undertaking', for ensuring payment of the forces when Exchequer payments were late, had ceased to be necessary. Nevertheless, the shilling deduction had continued to be made from the soldiers' pay, of which two-thirds remained after expenses, and had been accumulating as assets in the royal accounts. At first Fox proposed that half that 'spare' money be earmarked for Chelsea; later he modified that to cover the entire amount, thereby doubling the revenue. Fox volunteered to pay for the acquisition of a suitable site himself.[119]

Fox clearly consulted Wren informally – as friend, as architect on several of his own private projects, and as Royal Surveyor – about a suitable site. The one they identified was twenty-seven acres in Chelsea, on part of which stood the derelict buildings of Chelsea College – founded by James I for the training of Anglican clergy, and used during the second Dutch war to house prisoners of war. In 1667 Charles II had given the College and its grounds to the Royal Society as a possible location for a permanent home (or, failing that, as a tangible asset, against which the Society could raise much-needed funds). No suitable benefactor, however, had been forthcoming, and repeated attempts to lease the buildings (one of which was in train in autumn 1681) had come to nothing. The College had sat empty, its fabric deteriorating, and local builders pilfering it for stone and other materials. Now, repurchase by the Crown would, it could be argued, benefit both sides in the sale: the Society would gain ready money; the King an inexpensive site for his hospital.

When Wren took over the Presidency of the Royal Society in January 1681, one of the long-standing pieces of business he was asked to deal with was the question of how to exploit the Chelsea College site to the Society's advantage. Having failed to raise the money to build their own permanent headquarters there, the Society had, over a period of almost fifteen years, also failed to find a tenant for it. Wren visited the site several times in the first half of that year to assess various claims on the land on the basis of customary use currently being asserted by local residents.

Thus when he and Fox began discussing a possible location for the

Royal Chelsea Hospital for the 'support of Maim'd & superannuated
Soldiers', built through the charitable efforts of Fox, Evelyn and Wren.

King's Royal Hospital it was not likely to have been long before Wren
suggested the Chelsea site, and proposed that it be repurchased. Wren and
Fox discussed the matter together at length and agreed that all parties
concerned would benefit from the arrangement. By the end of the
summer all that was at issue was the price.

Since Wren had recently been elected President of the Royal Society,
and therefore could be considered to have a conflict of interests regarding Chelsea, the formal approach on behalf of the Surveyor's office had
to be made by someone else. Evelyn was the obvious person. Evelyn,
who shared confidences with both men, had been devastated, since his
appointment as Commissioner for Sick, Wounded and Prisoners in 1664
(he personally designed a seal depicting the Good Samaritan, with the
motto 'do likewise'), at the inadequacy of the money and facilities
available for the horribly mutilated soldiers brought out of successive
military engagements. His diary entries during the second Dutch war
in 1665 – when he had responsibility for wounded prisoners as well as
home casualties – record his dismay at what he saw, 'poor creatures',
'several with legs and arms off; miserable objects, God knows'.[120] He
and Pepys confided to one another how 'vexed' they were 'to see how
little heed is had to the prisoners and sick and wounded'.[121] Together

the two men had tried repeatedly and unsuccessfully to raise the money for an 'infirmary':

> [Mr. Evelyn] intertained me with discourse of an Infirmery which he hath projected for the sick and wounded seamen against the next year, which I mightily approve of – and will endeavour to promote, it being a worthy thing – and of use and will save money.[122]

Provision for sick and wounded seamen was not in fact made until the completion of Greenwich Hospital in 1704. Evelyn would, though, certainly have been equally delighted to assist in taking forward practical arrangements for charitable support of disabled and retired soldiers.

On 14 September 1681 John Evelyn and Fox dined together, and Fox proposed that Evelyn broker his repurchase of Chelsea College from the Royal Society, of which Evelyn was an active member, for the explicit purpose of establishing an 'infirmary for soldiers' there:

> Dined with Sir Stephen Fox, who proposed to me the purchasing of Chelsea College, which his Majesty had sometime since given to our Society, and would now purchase it again to build an hospital; or infirmary for soldiers there, in which he desired my assistance as one of the Council of the Royal Society.[123]

As agreed at the dinner, Evelyn informally sounded out the Council of the Royal Society. In October the President, Wren, announced that Fox had approached him to ascertain whether the Society would agree to sell the Chelsea College buildings back to the King for a royal building project: 'The President acquainted the Council with some treaty which he had lately with Sir Stephen Fox concerning Chelsea College.'[124] It was agreed and minuted that:

> The President and Mr. Evelyn be desired to treat with Sir Stephen Fox about selling the house and the whole concerns of the College (Sir Stephen having by letter to the President declared that he would not treat for the house alone without all the concerns of the Society in Chealsea), and the President and Mr. Evelyn were empowered to get a price for the house and land, viz. £1,500 if it might be agreed, but not under £1,400.[125]

Negotiations for obtaining the site having now begun, Fox was able to inform the King that the Hospital project could proceed. On 7 December he was appointed Treasurer of the Hospital by royal warrant, and on 22 December letters patent were issued publicly announcing the royal intention to build a Hospital 'for the relief of old, lame, and infirm soldiers', and setting up the formal arrangements for Fox in his capacity as Paymaster for the Royal Guards to dispense the money to pay for it to the Hospital Trustees – effectively to himself with his 'Treasurer of the Hospital' hat on.[126]

On 11 January Wren informed the Council that the deal had been completed, and the Chelsea site bought by Sir Stephen Fox on behalf of the Crown for the sum of £1300 – paid directly out of Fox's own pocket. Nobody mentioned the fact that the sale price was £100 less than Wren had been authorised to accept, and gratitude to the President was minuted for successfully completing the sale.

Wren was apparently already busy designing the buildings even as the deal was being done. The Chelsea College site was transferred to the King's name on 8 February 1682; the foundation stone of the Hospital was laid by Charles II on 16 February.[127] By May, Evelyn, Fox and Wren were ready to escort the Archbishop of Canterbury – Wren's old friend and building associate Sancroft – to visit the site, and walk him over the proposed building to gain his support and approval:

> 25th May. I was desired by Sir Stephen Fox and Sir Christopher Wren to accompany them to Lambeth, with the plot and design of the College to be built at Chelsea, to have the Archbishop [of Canterbury]'s approbation. It was a quadrangle of 200 feet square, after the dimensions of the larger quadrangle at Christ-Church, Oxford, for the accommodation of 440 persons, with governor and officers. This was agreed on.
>
> 4th August. With Sir Stephen Fox, to survey the foundations of the Royal Hospital begun at Chelsea.

Among Fox's family papers is a document drafted by Wren, describing the amenities of the building he had designed:

> The Royall Hospitall at Chelsey is pleasantly seated on a plane of gravell overlooking the Meadowes and the River Thames, which lies to the South, and having the prospect of the City and a pleasant view of the Country on all sides. It consists of

a large Courte built on three sides, the 4th side next the Thames lying open to the Gardens and Meadowes.

... The whole Building is 382 foot long from North to South, and 348 from East to West. The Galleries are 12 foote high in the cleer; each side hath on the middle, both within the Court and without, frontispeices of the Dorick order, with Pilasters of Portland Stone answering the Columnes of the great Porticoe; the lesser Porticoes and principal doorways are Portland Stone. The rest of the Fabrick is brick, and the whole pile well and durably built with good materialls.

Adjoyning are enclosures of brickwalls for Walks, Gardens, Kitchin garden, Back Courte and Buriall place. The Garden hath a terrace overlooking the Meadowes and river. A Water Gate at the Thames leads cross the Meadowes to the Terrace.[128]

Internally, the old soldiers were to be amply provided for. There were private spaces 'divided off with partitions of wanscot' for 416 men, with communal facilities like hot water and heating. There was an infirmary and a laundry, and substantial accommodation for a governor and officers. Among the more formal – positively palatial – spaces were a chapel and a communal dining hall, both 'vaulted Underneath for Cellars and conveniences'. No provision is specified here, however, for a library – one of Evelyn's pet projects during the preliminary discussions concerning the setting up of the Hospital, on the ground that now the old soldiers would have leisure time for reading and self-improvement.

The layout and facilities proposed by Wren for Chelsea Hospital reflect the wholeheartedly philanthropic spirit in which Fox, Wren and Evelyn committed themselves to Chelsea as a charitable work, and their shared emotional investment in the scheme. Beyond the fact that the King had expressed a desire to see such a project realised, for them it represented an act of benevolence and thanks to those who had borne the brunt of social upheaval in successive civil and foreign wars. Once again, this abiding sense of responsibility for those less fortunate than themselves is typical of devout men who had known hard times before the Restoration, and who also had their problems with the decadence of Charles II's court. After the accession of James, in changed times, they continued to pursue the project with determination. When Fox was replaced by Richard Jones, Earl of Ranelagh (and Robert Boyle's nephew) as Paymaster of the Forces, and Treasurer of Chelsea, this necessitated their staying close to his manipulative and Catholic-leaning administration, in spite of the dangers of their thereby becoming suspected of being active sympathisers. Significantly, Fox became so closely associated with James's regime that he found himself left out of the reorganisation of the Treasury after the arrival of William of Orange, even though he had probably acted as William's personal banker in England in the 1670s.

Fox's personal financial commitment to Chelsea Hospital over the years was substantial. Because most of the money was to be obtained by regular deductions from military personnel's pay, guarantees had to be provided up front, before Wren could negotiate contracts with the various masons, carpenters and suppliers involved. Fox promised to lend, free of interest, as much money as was required by the progress of the work. Because the building made such good progress, Fox at one point was forced to lend £6000 to meet the payments that fell due – the cost in terms of waived interest over several years may have been as much as £2000. His private memoirs put the figure of the largest advance he made for this purpose at £10,000 – his funeral oration put the figure at £13,000.[129]

From the earliest discussions with Evelyn and Wren, Fox made it clear that he would continue to fund the activities of the Hospital beyond the expenditure on the building. In late January 1682 Fox and Evelyn were already planning the way the finished Hospital would be organised and run:

> This evening, Sir Stephen Fox acquainted me again with his Majesty's resolution of proceeding in the erection of a Royal Hospital for emerited soldiers on that spot of ground which the Royal Society had sold to his Majesty for 1300*l.*, and that he would settle 5000*l.* per annum on it, and build to the value of 20,000*l.* for the relief and reception of four companies, namely, 400 men, to be as in a college, or monastery. I was therefore desired by Sir Stephen (who had not only the whole managing of this, but was, as I perceived, himself to be a grand benefactor, as well it became him who had gotten so vast an estate by the soldiers) to assist him, and consult what method to cast it in, as to the government.

Evelyn thoroughly approved of Fox's charitable commitment – after all, it was the eight clear pence in the pound deducted from serving soldiers' pay which had made Fox a rich man. Before adjourning to enjoy a pleasing musical performance by a fashionable counter-tenor, the two men made notes on the eventual structure of the hospital's administration:

> So, in [Fox's] study we arranged the governor, chaplain, steward, house-keeper, chirurgeon, cook, butler, gardener, porter, and other officers, with their several salaries and entertainments. I would needs have a library, and mentioned several books, since some soldiers might possibly be studious, when they were at leisure to recollect. Thus we made the first calculations, and set down our thoughts to be considered and digested better, to show his Majesty and the Archbishop [of Canterbury]. He also engaged me to consider of what laws and orders were fit for the government, which was to be in every respect as strict as in any religious convent.[130]

Shortly after plans were complete for its establishment in 1682, Evelyn was, in fact, offered the future Governorship of Chelsea Hospital by Sydney Godolphin (a Treasury Lord alongside Fox, and a close personal friend of Evelyn's). Evelyn had been lobbying Godolphin for an immediate government post, to alleviate his serious financial difficulties. Evelyn reluctantly turned down the Chelsea offer, because the job's prospects lay some way off – it was barely half built, and it would be years before anyone was needed to supervise its occupants. Charmingly, however, he did indicate that should he ever take up the post he envisaged sharing the duties with his beloved wife, just as he had once before proposed to Robert Boyle in connection with a monastic foundation for the Royal Society:[131]

> Since you have had me in your thoughts, you have me in your dispose. . . . There's nothing shall be wanting in my Endeavors to render me Competent: it suits with my Yeares, my Genius, my Formalitie, and the greate disposition I have to be usefull to brave men [at Chelsea]; & I have (you know) some other habitudes that may not disqualifie me. As to my private Circumstances I can decently resigne my present dwelling to my son

Interior of the Governor's House at Chelsea – Evelyn was offered
the job by Godolphin, but refused it because it would be several
years before the buildings were complete and the appointment
could be taken up.

& his pregnant family: My wife could realy on this occasion be
a meete Assistant Matron as now she is, not unexperienc'd in
Oeconomical functions, & of extraordinary Charity and
pious. . . . If it be my Lot, Ile boukle to it cordialy, & intend it
wholy, and think in so doing I may do Gods & his Ma[jes]tys
Service. . . .

Yet the successe of that, as tis Contingent, & but in Idea;
so it cannot take place these two or three yeares at the soonest,
& that's a very long day in my Kalendar. There is therefore in
the mean time an Opportunity in which you may Effectually
assist me, with a Considerable kindness . . . viz – were it to be
a farmer I assure you I would flie from it, but since what I
mention is (I heare) to be manag'd by Commissioners . . . Make
one harty attempt for your old friend & defer it not.[132]

He was right in anticipating a long wait before any governor took
up his post. In August 1691 a commission was established by royal
warrant 'to place such contracts and make such other arrangements as

might be necessary to open the Royal Hospital'. The three Commissioners appointed were the Archbishop of Canterbury, Fox and Wren. Between them they drew up the 'Statutes and whole Oeconomy of the House'. Wren was closely involved in the terms of these administrative rules, and they in turn set an important precedent for the naval hospital at Greenwich. The two institutions adopted the same type of constitution, similar rules governing diet and clothing, fund-raising, staff conditions and charitable exemptions from taxation.[133] Wren remained active on the Board which administered Chelsea Hospital until 1712, when the Board was reorganised and he ceased to be a member.[134] Nevertheless, in November 1713, it was the compassionate Wren, as ever, who was summoned, urgently, to deal with a crisis at the Hospital:

> Several of the Lords Commiss[ion]ers of the Hosp[ita]ll being out of Towne His Grace [the Duke of Ormonde] desires you not fail to meet Him at the time abovemen[tione]d in Order to give directions for the Cloathing of the Invalide Companys who are in a Perishing Condition for want thereof, they not having been Cloathed for near three Years Past.[135]

In June 1693 Wren was paid £1000, 'for his great Care and Paines in Directing and Overseeing the Building of [Chelsea] Hospitall and in Stating and Settling the Workemen's Bills relating thereto for ten years past'.[136] The settlement came, predictably, many years in arrears. While Ranelagh had, from his assumption of the Treasurership at Chelsea in 1686, taken commission on suppliers' payments, accumulating a tidy profit on his own behalf, and had also had a house built for himself in the grounds, at Hospital expense, Wren had, as usual, derived no personal financial advantage of any kind.[137]

BUSINESS PARTNERS

One of those courtiers to whom Sir Stephen Fox had been lending extensively during the 1680s was Sir Edward Hungerford, who sat with Wren as one of the foundation charter members of the Hudson's Bay Company, a prominent if disreputable figure in court circles. Aside from a generally extravagant lifestyle, Hungerford was apparently a compulsive gambler, who borrowed increasingly large sums from Fox to cover his debts. By July 1683 Hungerford owed Fox £40,000. As he fell increasingly far behind on his interest payments it became clear that he would have to sell lands in order to settle.

Among Hungerford's assets, the one Fox had his eye on, and which may, indeed, have encouraged him to extend his loans to Hungerford well beyond the bounds of prudence, was Hungerford House, located on a substantial site between the Strand and the river (roughly where Charing Cross Station now stands), conveniently close to Fox's Whitehall residence. The house itself had been destroyed by fire in 1669, and in 1670 Hungerford had obtained letters patent from Charles II to convert it to commercial use, demolishing the house and replacing it by a colonnaded market space, containing stalls and storage for retailers, who paid rents to the owner. By 1684, when Hungerford was obliged to transfer ownership of the site to Fox in settlement of the major part of his debts, Hungerford Market was a thriving commercial venture of stalls, shops and houses, attracting custom from the army of court officials and hangers-on at Whitehall, down the road.[138]

Two months after he had acquired Hungerford Market, in July 1684, Fox transferred a quarter share in it to Wren. On paper Wren paid £6250 for his share in the operation, but it seems more likely that the quarter share transferred to Wren was in settlement for monies advanced towards their previous joint project, Chelsea Hospital.[139] The two men had become something of a team through the ups and downs of that project, as Evelyn's diary entries show – at all stages in the decision-making process they acted in tandem.

Nor was this a mere paper transaction in settlement of some kind of financial obligation. From the surviving records it is clear that Fox and Wren managed Hungerford Market together, as a partnership, with Sir Stephen, as the senior financial member and majority shareholder, taking the lead, but with both men putting their names and seals to documents. Five months after the accession of James, the new King regularised Fox and Wren's position by issuing them with new letters patent for trading (suggesting that until this point they had been conducting their business under Edward Hungerford's old ones):

James the Second by the grace of God King of England Scotland France and Ireland Defender of the faith *To All* to whom these presents shall come greeting *whereas* our late Dearest Brother

King Charles the second of ever blessed memory did by his letters patents under the great seale of England beareing date at Westminster the Four and Twentyeth day of May in the one and Thirtyeth yeare of his Reigne [1680] grant unto Sir Edward Hungerford Knight of Bath and his heires a market to be held and kept on Munday Wednesday and Saterday in every week in the yeare within a certaine Messuage commonly called Hungerford House als Hungerford June in or neare the Strand in the parish of Saint Martin in the fields in the County of Middlesex and the Tolls and proffits thereof with a proviso in the said letters patents conteined that if the said Sir Edward Hungerford his heires or Assignes should knowingly and wilfully permitt any Mault Meale or Graine of any sort of kinde whatsoever to be sold or exposed to sale within the said market or to be thereto brought by Water and landed upon any ground in or neare the said market or should not use his or theire utmost Endeavours to hinder and prevent the same that then the said letters patents should be voyd and of none effect as thereby amongst other things therein conteined may more at large appeare *And whereas* our trusty and welbeloved Sir Stephen Fox and Sir Christopher Wren Knights are by purchase as we are informed become the proprietors in Fee of the said Markett and the Tolls and proffits thereof and divers of the Inhabitants of the libertys of Westminster have by theire humble petic[i]on sett forth that by serverall Statutes all sorts of Victualls of which Meale is a principall part are to be sold onely in Faires and Marketts yet contrary thereunto both by Land and Water Meale is commonly brought to the Horse ferry and other places at Westminster and there sold to Hucksters and Forestallers who Retaile the same in private houses and exact excessive Rates upon all especially upon the poore who buy the same in small parcells *know yee* therefore that we for prevention of the said oppression and the abuse of the said statutes and for the better Accommodation of the Inhabitants within the liberties of Westminster aforesaid of our especiall grace certeine knowledge and meere mocion and by and with the advice of our Privy Councell Have revised and released and by these presents doe for us our heires and successors revise and release unto the said Sir Stephen

Fox and Sir Christopher Wren theire heires and Assignes the said proviso in the said letters patents conteined and all Breaches and non performances thereof *And wee* have also given and granted and by these presents for us our heires and successors doe give and grant full and free licence liberty and authority to all and every person and persons whatsoever from time to time forever hereafter to bring into and expose to sale within the said Market on the several Dayes aforesaid any Meale flower Graine or Corne whatsoever and of what sort or kinde soever and that the said Sir Stephen Fox and Sir Christopher Wren their heires or Assignes shall and may have receive and take Toll Stallaye Wharfaye and all other proffits according to the usage and Custome of other Markets for the same to theire owne use the said proviso or any other matter or thing in the said letters patents conteined to the contrary Notwithstanding *In witnesse* whereof wee have caused these our letters to be made patents *witnesse* our selfe at Westminster the Ninth Day of July in the first yeare of our Reigne.[140]

Fox and Wren continued to administer Hungerford Market together for many years, though it did not prove as lucrative an investment as either had probably hoped.[141] In 1686 it was providing an annual return on their investment of around 6 per cent. By 1716 the capital value had fallen by 4 per cent, but income had remained fairly steady. This performance was markedly worse than that of most of Fox's other investments, which mattered less to him than to Wren, who held a much smaller portfolio. The failure of Hungerford Market to take off commercially in the later 1690s in the way Fox had expected may have been due to the tremendous success of Covent Garden Market near by. It may also have been a consequence of the fire which destroyed White-hall Palace in 1698, after which the large number of potential customers for the market and shops moved into the fashionable areas around St James's.[142]

The Hungerford Market venture was not Wren's only attempted at property venture. In 1688, after fire destroyed the home of the Earl of Bridgewater in the Barbican, Wren and Robert Jackson together raised £4400 to purchase the shell, and built Bridgewater Square speculatively on the site. Among those to whom plots were sold were Wren's clerk and rising architectural collaborator, Nicholas Hawksmoor and the masons Edward Strong and Samuel Fulkes. Again, there is no record of whether any substantial profit was made by Wren on this venture.[143]

WONDERS OF THE WORLD

We are coming increasingly to understand how influential in the seventeenth century, in all kinds of areas of life and thought, were the detailed accounts – and images – of new cultures brought home by enthusiastic travellers.[144] Architects of the period, in particular, were receptive to the possibilities of architectural inspiration and models drawn from unfamiliar cultures. Wren himself consulted merchant friends about building construction methods at Smyrna and Constantinople, as well as reading extensively in the rapidly expanding specialist travel literature. Hooke records in his diary on 14 November 1677: 'To Sir Chr Wr. At Mans with him and Mr. Smith, a description of S[an]ta Sophia' – Thomas Smith, a fellow of the Royal Society, had lived in Constantinople for two years from 1699. (Studies of Hagia Sophia in plan and section, possibly in Hawksmoor's hand, have recently come to light).[145] In his second Tract on architecture (probably written in the 1680s, at a time when Wren was beginning to instruct his clerk Hawksmoor in design), Wren draws on oriental examples in his discussion of the construction of arches and domes:

> Another Way, (which I cannot find used by the Ancients, but in the later eastern Empire, as appears at St. Sophia, and by that Example, in all the Mosques and Cloysters of the Dervises, and every where at present in the East) and of all others the most geometrical, is composed of Hemispheres, and their Sections only: and whereas a Sphere may be cut all manner of Ways, and that still into Circles, it may be accommodated to lie upon all Positions of the Pillars [Wren is here describing a dome on pendentives].[146]

It is not surprising, therefore, that Wren shared with others in favour in the circle of James II a considerable optimism about the business opportunities afforded by the opening up of markets in new commercial worlds, both to the east and west of Europe. From the

Restoration, Charles II's brother James (Duke of York) was a very considerable shareholder in the new joint-stock companies which proliferated in the City of London, adding to his portfolio at every opportunity right up to his accession to the throne (and, in fact, beyond). His investments spanned the globe: from the East Indies to Africa, and from the Americas to Hudson's Bay. He sat as the Governor on the boards of three major trading companies – the Royal Fishery Company, the Royal African Company and (after the death of Prince Rupert in 1682) the Hudson's Bay Company – directing their business from his offices in Whitehall.[147]

It was Prince Rupert who first interested James in speculative overseas trade; driven on to the west coast of Africa during a sea-chase in 1652 (pursued by Commonwealth gunships) he had found tribesmen trading gold from inland mines with the Dutch merchants at the head of the Gambia River. In 1660 he launched a scheme to mine Gambian gold commercially, under the Royal African Company. Early backers were James's sister Henrietta of Orléans, Mary of Orange, and Lord Craven (the Winter Queen's long-standing, and extremely wealthy protector). The Duke's name was used liberally to advertise the financial gains to be made by investing in African stock, and by the autumn of 1662 he had consolidated his position as the Company's largest single shareholder. He pledged an investment of some £3600, as against £800 each from Prince Rupert, Charles II and the Duke of Buckingham. His appointment as Governor in July 1664 increased the perceived significance of the Company, offering City merchants direct access to the court.

The gold-mining scheme turned out to be impractical, and the company quickly moved into the 'black gold' trade – slaves. Throughout the 1670s, James headed an organisation capturing men and women and trafficking them from Africa to the New World plantations with absolute unscrupulousness. James was apparently unconcerned about the nature of the trade in which he was so deeply involved, and was delighted when, by the 1680s, he began to see a substantial annual return on his investment, as also on his investments in the East India Company and the Royal Fishery Company. On the death of Charles II, James sought to retain his full and perpetual title as Governor of his African holdings, in spite of a general view that such involvement in business was inappropriate for the monarch, and he embarked on a fresh round of speculative investments in the City, paving the way financially for his apparently bright future as king.

James originally held only a nominal £300 share in the stock of the Hudson's Bay Company, which was fundamentally Prince Rupert's venture, but was elected Governor after Rupert's death.

Wren was discussing the possibility of investing in the Hudson's Bay Company over coffee with Hooke in July 1679, around which time he made his first purchase of stock. For four years, from November 1679 to November 1683, he was one of the Committee of seven who, with the Governor and the Deputy Governor, directed the affairs of the Company. One of his responsibilities – as so often in his dealings with building works on behalf of the Crown – was to negotiate large loans from individuals on behalf of the Company. At the end of December 1679, and again in February 1680, he approached leading financier (and Lord Mayor of London) Sir Robert Clayton to arrange fresh loans and organise repayments on monies still outstanding. Wren remained active in the Company until March 1684.[148]

Wren was Deputy Governor at the time of Prince Rupert's death in November 1682. After James's election as Governor in the following January, it was Wren who was directed, with two other members of the Committee, to 'attende his Royall Highness with the notice of this Election, and the Right honourable the Earle of Craven a Member of this Company is Desired to Introduce yem to his Royall Highness humbley to Desire his gratious Acceptance of the Government and that he wold be pleased to take the Company under his Patronage & protection'. Although James was not especially active in the Company, all his dealings with it during the following twelve months were carried out via Wren. James resigned the post on his accession to the throne, in response to a suggestion from the Company that this was appropriate, 'seeing our Governour is now our Sovereigne Lord the King'.

Wren was a regular attender at the frequent Committee meetings that were held, and often chaired meetings as a Committee member, in the absence of the Governor, even before he became Deputy Governor himself. Wren's holding in the Company's stock commenced with £200 in 1679, and was increased by subsequent purchases to a total of £1200 in 1683, at which date the total stock was £10,500 and the number of shareholders about thirty. Wren lent substantial sums to the Company to fit out ships setting out for Hudson's Bay. As ever, he does not appear to have benefited greatly from these speculative investments. Unlike the Royal African Company, however, the Hudson's Bay Company produced modest returns on investment for its shareholders – once again, Wren's involvement helped make his circumstances more comfortable, but did not bring him the wealth that others of his generation had accumulated since the Restoration.

As always, Wren threw himself into the rituals of membership of an exclusive organisation. When the Company decided it needed an oath, to be sworn by members on joining, it was Wren who was asked to draft a suitable document, just as his father, all those years earlier, had devised and drafted equivalent rituals in his capacity as Register of the Order of the Garter:

> Sir Christopher Wren having been desyred to overlooke & correct ye forme of an Oath to be given to those who shall enter into ye service of ye Company, hath produced it to this Committee who have allowed of ye same, and Mr. Hayward is desyred to get severall coppys of ye Same printed yt they may be bound up together and every particular person may signe his particular paper.

At some level, then, Wren was temperamentally more of James's party even than he had ever been of Charles II's. James recognised this in his immediate conferring of yet more honours and commissions on Wren at his accession. Once again Wren drew a veil over this preferment (and his compliant undertaking of plans for elaborate work on a Catholic chapel for Mary of Modena) after James's short reign was abruptly terminated.

Wren's involvement in a whole raft of overseas ventures aimed at making large profits on investments was part of his lifelong ambition to turn individual talent, and above all 'industry', into capital assets (an ambition which he significantly never realised). We may recall his draft charter for the Royal Society in the early 1660s:

> The Way to so happy a Government, we are sensible is in no Manner more facilitated than by the promoting of useful Arts and Sciences, which, upon mature Inspection, are found to be the Basis of civil Communities, and free Governments, and which gather Multitudes, by an *Orphean* Charm, into Cities,

and connect them in *Companies*; that so, by laying in a Stock, as it were, of several Arts, and Methods of Industry, the whole Body may be supplied by a mutual Commerce of each others peculiar Faculties; and consequently that the various Miseries and Toils of this frail Life, may, by the Wealth and Plenty diffused in just Proportion to every one's Industry, that is, to every one's Deserts.[149]

Wren never became rich on the basis of his business ventures, any more than he did from his dedicated and high-profile service to the Crown. There was, it turned out, no justice in the world of money, no guarantee that 'the various Miseries and Toils of this frail Life' could be alleviated 'by the Wealth and Plenty diffused in just Proportion to every one's Industry, that is, to every one's Deserts'. Individuals like his friend Sir Stephen Fox, who could amass a personal fortune without forfeiting their integrity, were the exceptions rather than the rule (and even in his case there were those who did not share Evelyn's admiration for the great financier). In Restoration England, scoundrels like Richard Jones made personal fortunes, while industrious individuals like Petty – exemplary in their application of their skills to the good of the nation – felt increasingly sidelined by a nation which continued to reward birth and family connection before talent.

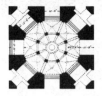

7

Standing the Test of Time

A TALENT FOR ORGANISATION

On 21 April 1685, Wren was once again confirmed as Surveyor of the King's Works, and as Controller of Works at Windsor Castle. The smoothness of the transition from serving Charles II to serving James II, in spite of the drastic differences others detected between their manners of ruling, depends to a large extent on Wren's extraordinary gift for managing people and situations discreetly and with tact. In these latter years of his career, his avoidance of faction and 'party' (explicit alliance with Whig or Tory political interests) was vital for his survival in public office. Nowhere is this more evident than in his handling of the rebuilding programme for the City churches during this period.

In the years 1686 to 1688, Henry Compton, Bishop of London was in dispute with the new King, both on doctrinal matters and because they candidly disliked one another. Compton had been the tutor in charge of the education of James's daughters Mary and Anne during their girlhoods, entrusted with the task of raising them (as required by Charles II) in the Protestant faith. Apart from the Bishop's public stance against James's preferment of practising Catholics to positions of power, his continuing influence over Mary and Anne greatly annoyed the King.[1]

Eventually James removed Compton from office, ostensibly as a result of his refusal to dismiss the rector of St Giles-in-the-Fields, who

Henry Compton, Bishop of London – Compton's suspension by James II precipitated the political crisis which led to James's abdication.

had preached a sermon of which James disapproved. This should have had immediate repercussions for Wren's rebuilding activities, since Compton was one of the Commissioners required to sign all orders associated with the church rebuilding under the 1670 Act. In fact, Wren, in his capacity as convener of the Commission quietly sidestepped the issue. Direct orders of the Commissioners simply ceased at this point, and Wren assumed direction of operations himself, taking decisions personally as necessary. Possibly he consulted each of the Commissioners individually and informally, including Compton, or he may have fashioned decisions based on his assessment of the kind of support he could elicit from the Commissioners, and presented them with a *fait accompli*. Either way, he preferred not to commit decisions to paper, so we are left with surmise only as to his successful method.[2] The seamlessly continuous process of rebuilding the City churches was not in fact halted until the civil disruption of the Glorious Revolution of 1688, when all construction works on the site temporarily ceased.

At the same time, Wren, who was an old and close friend of

Compton's, managed to avoid being implicated in the Bishop's disgrace. The Royal Surveyor's likeable nature, his discretion and his easy access to a large network of senior figures in and around the court enabled him to smooth the way to decision-making vital to the successful completion of rebuilt London, at a moment when that might otherwise have stalled. We might recall here Wren's early association with William Petty, who has been called the 'prototype of the English bureaucrat' – a man with innovative ideas about organising large numbers of people to collect and process data, first in Ireland and later in early work on mortality rates and actuarial statistics. At the Restoration Petty turned his attention to devising tax-strategies based on data on life-patterns and income-variation, and is claimed as the founder of modern economic theory.[3]

Remarkably, Petty succeeded in persuading successive governments, from the politically volatile 1650s down to the rapidly changing regimes of the late 1680s, of the importance of what he called his 'Political Arithmetick' for planning and policy.[4] He achieved public prominence under Cromwell (first as a physician, and then as a surveyor and statistician), and retained his administrative positions under Charles II, although towards the end of the reign he complained he was not sufficiently honoured for his work. Wren's remarkable ability to see projects through, commenced under one administration and completed under an entirely different one, owes something at least to Petty's example of bureaucratic competence combined with level-headed avoidance of sensitive political issues.[5]

Petty's and Wren's paths had continued to cross, and, characteristically, Wren remained devoted to the man who had placed his confidence in him, and supported him materially, during his youth when he had few influential figures to turn to. Wren and Petty were both founder members of the Royal Society, where in the early days they had collaborated on experiments for improving shipping – the design of vessels and of sails, as well as navigational instruments.[6] They shared interests in the Society's activities in the spheres of anatomy, practical inventing and mathematical problem-solving. The two stayed close right up to the time of Petty's death in 1687.

Some of the projects in which they both became involved were engagingly optimistic, and it was probably only their reputation for careful inquiry and conscientious assessment of data and evidence which ever allowed them to be undertaken. In 1680, Petty and Hooke proposed

Sir William Petty in later life – in spite of the wealth he accumulated he felt that he had not received the recognition he deserved.

military uses of English wool, as an economic solution to a chronic wool surplus and falling prices. After somewhat comical, dead-pan discussions of experiments to see if densely packed wool could act as portable bullet-proofing for buildings and personnel (all the experiments failed), it was proposed that a committee headed by Wren examine the feasibility of further experiments and development.[7] In 1683, Petty arbitrated a complaint by Hooke against Sir John Cutler, supposedly sponsor of his Cutlerian lectureship at Gresham College, that he had not been paid, and Cutler's counter-claim that Hooke had failed to fulfil the conditions of the appointment. Petty ruled that Hooke should be paid in full, provided he agreed to co-operate over the lectures.[8]

Petty's commitment to the statistics and organisation of people depended not just on mobilising large numbers of co-workers on any single project, but on collecting and analysing data uninterruptedly over extended periods of time. There are obvious analogies between this and the activities Wren was required to master to mount large-scale construction projects, with numerous craftsmen and workmen to organise, management decisions to be taken rapidly and consistently over long periods, and commitment to arithmetical and accounting accuracy to ensure steady progress, whatever the current political conditions. Passing remarks by several of Wren's contemporaries testify to the extraordinary level of his participation in building projects like St Paul's to whose successful execution he had a particularly intense commitment. Roger North recorded weekly visits with his brother Dudley to watch the progress of the Cathedral:

> He [Dudley North] was so great a lover of building, that St. Paul's, then well advanced, was his ordinary walk: there was scarce a course of stones laid, while we lived together, over which we did not walk. And he would always climb to the uttermost heights.... We usually went there on Saturdays, which were Sir Christopher Wren's days, who was the Surveyor; and we commonly got a snatch of discourse with him, who, like a true philosopher, was always obliging and communicative, and, in every matter we inquired about, gave short, but satisfactory answers.[9]

At the beginning of the eighteenth century, when the Duchess of Marlborough was contesting a bill from her surveyor at Blenheim (where her husband had retained Sir John Vanbrugh as architect, rather than Wren, whom she had used for her house in London), she told him 'that Sir Christopher Wren, while employed upon Saint Paul's, was content to be dragged up to the top of the building three times a-week in a basket, at the great hazard of his life, for only 200l. a-year'.[10]

WEATHERING THE GLORIOUS REVOLUTION

The 1680s were not auspicious years for an architect with a number of important building projects under way, whose ordered execution depended on political and administrative stability to guarantee patronage and consistent levels of funding. Having successfully negotiated his way back into a position from which smoothly to conduct his architectural business on behalf of the Crown, while retaining a discreet distance from James II's policies, the equilibrium of Wren's professional, day-to-day activities was disturbed once again in the autumn of 1688, with the news of the imminent arrival of invading forces of the Prince of Orange, rumours concerning which began in late August.

Dissatisfaction with James II's regime, with its flagrant disregard for parliamentary strictures against the promotion to high office of practising Catholics, reached a peak in the summer of 1688. Until this point, the failure of James and his second wife to produce a male heir had meant that the crown would eventually pass to his daughters by his first marriage, Mary and Anne, both (thanks to Bishop Compton) staunchly Protestant. On 10 June 1688, however, Mary of Modena gave birth, prematurely, to a healthy boy, James Edward, who took dynastic precedence over Mary and Anne. Such was the political convenience for James that it was widely held that the baby was a substitute for a still-born child (Mary had had a number of unsuccessful pregnancies), brought into the Queen's lying-in chamber by a midwife, in a warming pan.

Throughout the summer, prominent figures in the English administration either left for The Hague, where James II's eldest daughter Mary's husband, William of Orange, was rumoured to be mustering an army to invade, or distanced themselves from the regime. Compton left London for Yorkshire with the excuse that he was going to visit his sisters. From there he kept closely in touch with Mary's sister Anne in London, eventually arranging safe accommodation for her with his nephew, the Earl of Dorset, when she fled the court to join her sister's supporters.[11]

By August London was full of rumours of a sizeable army assembling at The Hague, preparing to invade England under the command of William of Orange. On 23 August Evelyn recorded in his diary that 'the Dutch make extraordinary preparations both at sea and land'. On 18 September he went to London and 'found the Court in the utmost consternation upon report of the Prince of Orange's landing; which put Whitehall into so panic a fear, that I could hardly believe it possible to find such a change'.[12]

In fact, William finally landed at Torbay on 5 November 1688. The ship on which he had sailed flew a flag embroidered with the words 'I will maintain the Protestant religion and the liberties of England'. In the days that followed, according to Hooke's diary, Wren and Hooke anxiously trawled the London coffee houses, seeking reliable news and opinions on the political situation.

James II's infant son, Prince James Francis Edward Stuart – so convenient was his birth for James's ambitions to establish a Catholic succession that it was rumoured that the baby had been brought into the delivery room and substituted for one that had been still-born.

On 5 November itself, Hooke recorded:

Dutch seen off the Isle of Wight. DH [dined home]. At Jon[a-than's] coffee house. Henshaw, Hally [Edmond Halley, FRS], Gof [Sir Godfrey Copley, FRS], Lod [Francis Lodwik, FRS], Pif [Alexander Pitfield, FRS], Wall [Richard Waller, FRS]. In vault did little. At Jon[athan's]. Dutch sayd to be landed at Pool. Tison and HH [Henry Hunt] here tea, choco[late]. A mystick letter Aubrey. Horn at Jon[athan's]. D m D [God defend us]. Candles.[13]

Hooke had been at his local coffee house no fewer than three times that day, gathering gossip and news about the Dutch invasion. He proceeded, over the following weeks, to spend as much time as he could between professional duties, in one or other of the fashionable meeting spots. More often than not, he notes that Wren was with him.

On 12 November Wren and Hooke met at William Holder's house. Wren's brother-in-law was now a widower – Wren's beloved sister Susan had died that June. The three men repaired to Jonathan's where there was 'news of yesterdays and this days riots of Rabble'.[14] On Saturday, 17 November, Wren and Hooke were at Man's coffee house at Charing Cross, when they learned that King James had gone to Windsor, having sent his wife and baby son to Portsmouth. On the following Wednesday, 21 November, Wren chaired the weekly meeting of the Royal Society. Hooke recorded in his diary that news of more landings of Dutch invading forces and of the Prince of Orange's Declaration of his intention to accept an invitation to take the English throne was a topic of conversation. On 29 November, according this time to Evelyn, the Royal Society postponed the election of its next President, 'by reason of the public commotions, yet dined together as of custom this day'.[15]

On 4 December Hooke was 'at Wallers' when he heard 'News of seasing Gloster, Bristol, of the sinking 3, taking 2, stranding 1 French ships; and escape by 8 dutch vnder Herbert'. He dined with his old teacher Busby (as he did regularly during this period), then repaired as usual to a coffee house where he 'Mist Sr. C. Wren' – in other words, they had both been there in search of confirmation of the day's events.[16] Wren's friends Evelyn and Fox were, during this same period, in a rather higher state of anxiety about the possibility of the imminent abdication of James, and (because closer to the King's inner circle) somewhat better informed about William of Orange's movements:

> 1st November. Dined with my Lord Preston againe, with other company, at Sir Stephen Foxes. Continual al'arms of the Prince of Oranges landing, but no certainty: reports of his greate losses of horse in the storme; but without any assurance . . .

> 2nd. It was now certainly reported by some who saw the Prince imbarke and the fleete, that they sailed from Brill on Wednesday Morning, and that the Princesse of Orange was there to take leave of her Husband . . .

> 8th. I went to London: heard the newes of the Prince being landed at Torbay with a fleet of 700 sail, so dreadful a sight, passing through the Channell with so favorable a Wind, that

our Navy could by no meanes intercept or molest them: This put the King and Court into greate Consternation. . . . These are the beginnings of Sorrows, unlesse God in His Mercy prevent it, by some happy reconciliation of all dissentions amongst us.[17]

On 11 November, with William already at Exeter, Fox, foreseeing his imminent dismissal from office, hastily approached Wren for confirmation of the works he had carried out on his Whitehall lodgings ten years earlier, under Wren's supervision, at a cost of £1000. Wren obliged with the certification of expenditure, and on 17 November Wren issued a royal warrant guaranteeing Fox the right to remain in his Whitehall house until he had been repaid the £1000.[18]

Once again, the transition from James II to William and Mary was, for Wren, on the face of it a smooth one. On 25 April 1689, Wren was confirmed in his old post of Surveyor of the King's Works, and Surveyor for St Paul's.[19]

In fact, the drama of dynastic interruption, however tactfully handled in publicity terms, had serious repercussions for the financing of public works, specifically major building programmes. James II had caused a certain amount of ill will by assuming that he could rely on income allocated to his brother, even before Parliament met to reconfirm the sums concerned. There was, however, never any constitutional doubt about the fact that such an agreement would be reached. With the arrival of a monarch from overseas, who had effectively invaded England and laid claim to the throne, deposing the legitimate incumbent, no such assurances could be given, and all administrative arrangements went into abeyance.

The difference between the two administrative transitions can be clearly seen in the case of the continuing construction of St Paul's and the last of the rebuilt City churches. After the accession of James II in 1685, an approach was made to the House of Commons and leave given to bring in a Bill to extend the tax on coal to the year 1700, primarily to continue the work on the Cathedral. The Commons referred the Bill to a committee (which included the new Member for Plympton, Sir Christopher Wren), who were empowered 'to bring in a clause to

OVERLEAF Plan of Whitehall Palace after the Restoration – the properties occupied by Fox and Wren were almost adjacent to one another in Scotland Yard.

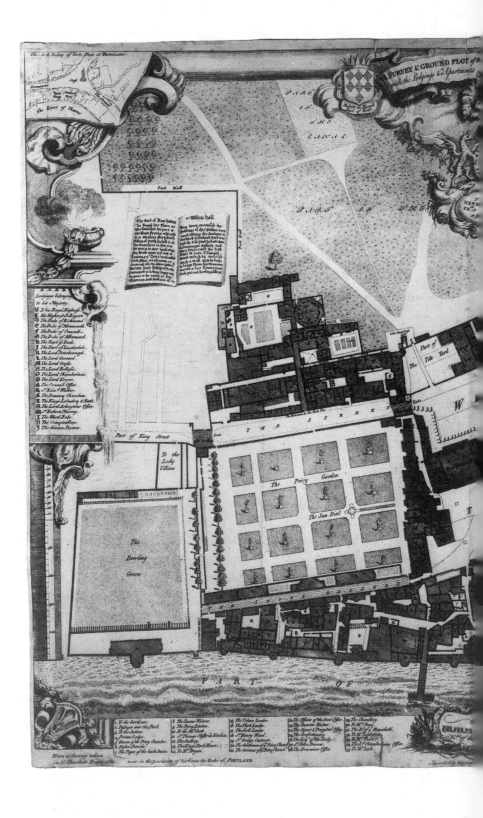

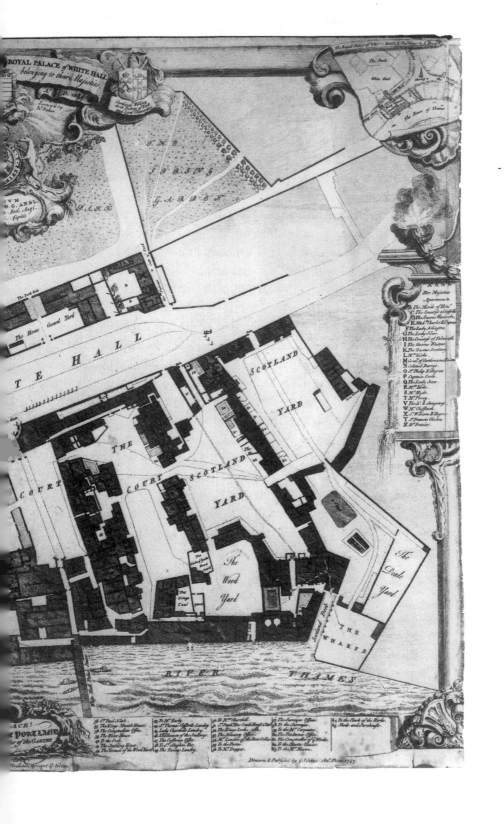

be added to the said Bill, for Provision for Finishing of Four Churches within the Walls of London'. Royal assent to the Bill was given on 2 July 1685, leaving the Commissioners and Wren, for the first time, with adequate funding for London's rebuilding: having completed the rebuilding of most of the parish churches they now had an assured and regular income down to the year 1700. With this income Wren was able to complete the churches to which the Commons referred, to attend to the towers which had been boarded over, and to consider what else remained to be done.

In 1688, by contrast, the dynastic hiatus caused a major funding crisis. Work on the remaining churches came to an abrupt halt at the end of that year with the last four churches still not finished. It was not until the end of 1689, with the financial and administrative crisis over, that life began to return to normal. The four remaining churches were completed by 1694.[20]

The fortunes of St Paul's mirrored those of the City churches. In 1685, less than a week after the first sitting of the new Parliament on 19 May, leave was given to present a Bill for rebuilding and finishing St Paul's. The accession of James, in spite of his Catholicism, caused barely an interruption in the programme. A full meeting of the Commission for Rebuilding on 29 April 1686 had agreed 'that the summe of £4000 should be Borrowed upon the credit of the Act of Parliament for the imposition upon Coals betweene this & Midsummer next, in order to ye more speedy & vigorous prosecution of the Work'.[21] In September 1686, the Bishop of London, Henry Compton, disappeared from the Commission and its working Committee (on which Wren and William Holder also sat), having been suspended by James for failing to enforce his pro-Catholic policies, but the work of the Committee went on. The 16 September meeting resolved:

> [Tha]t the summe of £5000 should be forthwith borrowed for 6 months upon the Credit of the Act of Parliament, for the more speedy Carrying on of this Worke & Sir Peter Rich & Sir Chr Wren were desired to undertake the management thereof and to advise with Sir John Holt, Recorder of ye City of London, and whom else he shall desire to be joined with him about drawing up of Security for the same.[22]

At the Committee meeting held on 13 January 1687, Wren and two of his colleagues were instructed to 'waite upon the Judges tomorrow at the Sessions House & desire their opinions upon ye Clause in the Act of Parliament concerning the borrowing of money thereupon, whether the said Clause doth Warrant the payment of reasonable interest for Money so to be borrowed'.[23] Arrangements for loans totalling £5000 were eventually finalised on 5 May 1687. At the next meeting on 4 July, it was ordered 'That £4000 more be immediately borrowed upon Credit of the Act of Parliament'.[24]

Given the complexity of the financial borrowings in hand – all of which depended upon Acts of Parliament which were now null and void – it is hardly surprising that the first meeting of the Committee following the flight from England of James II, and his replacement by William and Mary, on 11 February 1689 (with the Bishop of London back in place), found itself financially embarrassed:

> Ordered: The State of the Account for Rebuilding St Paul's was this day examined & it appears yt there is still due to severall persons of whom money was borrowed on ye credit of ye Act of Parliament £5,150, and that there is also due to ye Workmen for materialls & workmanship till Xmas last, which is already Stated and Measured, £5,575. and also for Mason's Work, not yet Stated and Measured, by Estomate £3,500. In all £14,225. And ye Ld Bp of London was desired by Sir Chr Wren to give his Opinion, what method should be taken for ye ensuing year, which was, That ye money borrowed should still be continued at Interest, and more taken up at Interest to pay off ye Workmen's Debt, and that ye Work should still vigorously go on.[25]

By the end of 1689, though, the affairs of the Commission for Rebuilding seem to have regained their equilibrium – the arrangements for the substantial outstanding loans had been regularised by the new Parliament, and payment of contractors could recommence.

ANOTHER CORONATION

Even before his official reappointment as Royal Surveyor by William and Mary, Wren was responsible in his official capacity for the physical arrangements for their Coronation – a unique occasion in English history, since it involved the solemn rites of succession being administered

Engraving of the Coronation of William and Mary, showing the joint
monarchs on adjacent thrones, with matching regalia.

to two monarchs at once. Although, as Hooke and Evelyn learned from
government gossip and recorded in their diaries, it had been suggested
that either William become regent, or that Mary, as direct Stuart heir,
be made queen in her own right, William declined the former suggestion,
and the proposal that he might be prince consort, on the ground that
it would make him 'his wife's gentleman usher', while Mary wrote
sharply to Lord Danby that she was the Prince of Orange's wife, and
would never be 'other than what she would be in conjunction with him
and under him'.[26] Accordingly, at the Coronation, Mary was raised into
an identical throne alongside William, the Sword of State was girded
on her also, and she too was handed the orb and sceptre and Bible.

Wren was in charge of all the physical arrangements at Westminster,
to accommodate the vast number of peers and officials who assisted at
the ceremony – the raked seating, platforms and 'scaffolds' which created
the grand ceremonial space at Westminster, recorded in contemporary
engravings of each post-Restoration Coronation in turn:[27]

> At the Councell Chamber in Whitehall the-5th-of March. 1689
>
> By the Rt Hono'ble the Comittee appointed to consider of the
> time & man[n]er of the Coronac[i]on of their Maj[es]ties.
>
> It is this day ordered by their Lo[rdshi]pps that Sr Christopher

Wren Knt. Surv[ey]er gen[era]ll of their M[ajes]tes workes Doe prepare an acct. of the Expences in erecting the Scaffolds at the last Coronac[i]on in Westminster Hall and in the Aby and for raising and Gravilling the Streets and other Disbursm[en]tes out of the office of the workes on that Occasion, And that the same may be sent to the Clarke of the Councill attending their Lord[shi]ps into the Councill Chamber on Wednsday morning next, that it may be presented to the Committee who are to meete in the afternoone.

Ever punctilous where money was concerned, Wren provided meticulous financial estimates for the expenditure incurred:

Estimate of the charge in the Office of Workes of preparing for their Ma[jes]ties Coronac[i]on In Westminster Hall & Roomes adjoyning: Takeing downe the Courts of Indicature; makeing of the floores over the Courtes of the Kings Bench & Chancery for the King and Queene to dine upon w[i]th steps and table; makeing 2 Galaryes on each side of the Hall of the whole length w[i]th 3 degrees in each Galary; makeing a Galary cross the lower end of the Hall for the Drums & trumpets; Boarding on the pavement the whole length – 15 ft. wide for the Ld Steward Ld Marshall the Champion &ca to ride upon. Makeing Tables on each side the whole length of the Hall for the Nobillity to Dine at; makeing . 16. sideboards & Cupboards & fitting up the Confecc[i]onery In the Excheq[u]er side; Fitting up the Celler under the Excheq[u]er for the use of the Cookes.

In St Stephens Courte makeing kitchens & Larders. In Mr Squibbs garden: makeing sheds and fitting up his house at the End of the garden for the Poultrey. In Mr Powells garden: Fitting up some sheds for a scalding house. In the new Palace yard: makeing the Champions Stable. Raising the way from Westminster Hall to the Abby doore and gravelling the Same. Setting up againe all the Courts of Indicature.

In Westminster Abby: makeing a Scaffold over the whole Choire upon which the Throne is to be set for the King and Queene and seates for the whole Peerage of England Lords & Judges. Fitting up the Alter proper for the Solemnity. makeing Degrees on each side the Choire for the Privie Councell and for the Ld Maj[o]r and Ald[erm]en.

Makeing Degrees over them on both sides for the Peeres of Scotland and Ireland & for the Ladyes.

Makeing a standing over the Choire Doores for the Drumms and Trumpetts [inserted] makeing scaffolding for the Prince & Princes & over that for the Forragne Ministers.

Makeing of Scaffolding on the other side w[i]thout, A Scaffold for the Muisick, and against that a Scaffold for the Orgainist and Organist.

Setting up a Pulpitt. Inclossing all King Edwards Chappell and makeing tables & Partic[i]ons, & Traversses there. Makeing Scaffolding in the North & South Ailes

The total for this work was £1670 0s 7d. Wren had, of course, overseen precisely the same arrangements, in the same capacity only four years earlier, for James II. In 1689, at the end of his typically fastidious accounting for the materials and labour required, Wren pointed out that there had been significant inflation since James's Coronation, increasing the current costs correspondingly:

This is the exact Charge of the last Coronac[i]on taken out of the Bookes of the Office of the workes. But in regard Timber and boards are at this time dearer one fifth parte, It properly may raise the charge to £1800. Signed Chr: Wren. 60. Mar. 1689. A Coppie of this was likewise delivered to the Trea[su]ry Mar. 15°. 1689.

These records are a vivid reminder of the alacrity with which someone in Wren's position – an office-holder and public servant, with time-consuming practical duties to be performed – was required to respond to instructions from new masters, and sucked back into the machinery of each successive royal regime. There was little time for Wren to reflect on the political nuances of change, particularly since duties like the Coronation arrangements came on top of the onerous responsibilities he was still carrying for major building contracts which it was important should not come to a halt due to altered political circumstances.

We might compare Wren's discreet 'trimming' to accord with the times, and adjust to the new sovereigns with his old friend Bishop Sancroft's fortunes and conduct over the same period. Sancroft was one of the seven bishops who had stood out against James II's preferment of Catholics to important clerical positions, and had thereby been instrumental in forcing the King's abdication. Subsequently, however, he felt unable to swear the oath of allegiance to William and Mary, as required by legislation rapidly passed by Parliament in the early months of their reign. He was deposed as Archbishop of Canterbury in 1690, and died in retirement on 24 November 1693.

LASTING LOYALTY TO 'THIS UNFORTUNATE FAMILY'

In terms of the complex and intense relationship Wren and men like him had sustained with the Stuart brothers Charles and James since the Restoration, the arrival of James's daughter Mary and her Dutch husband William of Orange marked another potentially disruptive turn in events. Here was another change of rule, in this case the outcome of an invasion by a foreign power. Yet the new regime was still one closely identified with and shaped by the events of the (for Wren and his circle) traumatic period during the 1640s and 1650s. Since the moment of his birth, William III's fortunes – not simply dynastic, but also private and personal – had been inextricably bound up with those, first of Charles I and then of his sons Charles and James.

While Charles I fought a war against his own people in England, his daughter Mary lived a protected, luxurious life in Holland, as the wife of William II of Orange. William had become Stadholder and Captain-General of the States-General on his father's death in March 1647, when he was not quite twenty-one and his wife was fifteen and a half. The new Stadholder and his wife were barely grown up – spoiled children, self-willed and extravagant. They spent much of their time amusing themselves, and poured out money on jewels, clothes, furnishings, entertainments and works of art. Foreign envoys complained that the only hope of doing business with the Stadholder was to waylay him in the hunting field, on the tennis court or at the theatre.[28]

This was the household where Princes Charles and James Stuart found temporary refuge after their father's execution, and where the

Elector Palatine stopped off with his English entourage on his way home to Heidelberg in the spring of 1649. William received all his visitors with lavish generosity, and lent the royal princes large sums of money.

In October 1650, however, William went down with smallpox; Mary was heavily pregnant, and could not be allowed into the sickroom, remaining instead shut up in her own apartments. On 6 November William died, and a week later Mary gave birth to a son, William, in a household so deep in mourning that even the cradle was hung with black. Nor did the family misfortunes end at this point. William was third in line to the English throne, a direct dynastic threat to the new republican administration in England. Under pressure from Cromwell, the States-General not only refused to recognise any hereditary right on William's part to the title of Stadholder, but passed an Act of Seclusion, in a hurried secret session, barring the House of Orange from all its former offices. John Evelyn's cousin Samuel Tuke in a letter from The Hague in early 1651 describing this new set of adversities facing Stuart progeny, referred to the children of Charles I as 'this unfortunate family'.

William was raised and educated by Sir Constantijn Huygens (father of Wren's competitor in scientific virtuosity, Christiaan) and Frederik van Nassau-Zuijlenstein, both of whom were considerable anglophiles (as we have seen, William Frederick's wife was Mary Killigrew, one of Mary's English ladies in waiting). In keeping with this English orientation to his upbringing, one of the first international pieces of business conducted by Charles II, even before he left The Hague to take possession of his throne, was to persuade the States-General to rescind the Act of Seclusion, thus paving the way to his nephew William's eventual installation as Stadholder. On 29 September, Mary joined her brother in London for a triumphant celebration of the family's restored fortunes, leaving William in Holland. On Christmas Eve she died of the same smallpox that had carried off her husband, leaving her ten-year-old, orphaned son in the care of her Dutch relatives. He grew up with a robustly Dutch sensibility, but an ease and fluency with English and English ways. When James II's daughter Mary (William's first cousin) married the Prince of Orange in November 1677, apparently reluctantly, his early self-conscious upbringing as a Stuart prince (and his good spoken English) may have helped effect the rapid rapprochement between the newlyweds.

By the time William and Mary arrived in England, and jointly took possession of the throne in 1689, theirs was an unusually close and harmonious royal marital relationship (in spite of notorious sexual infidelity on his part).

Theirs was also the first royal household since the Restoration with a private, domestic life, in a sense we can understand today. Whereas Wren's clients heretofore had been the successive male monarchs, now the Queen dealt with matters like royal accommodation, on behalf of the two of them, as a couple. Mary 'mothered' her husband, as he had never been able to be mothered as a child. It was she who decided as soon as they arrived in London that the thick smog (generated by coal-burning, which ensured that the coal tax provided amply for rebuilding St Paul's) made it impossible for the asthmatic William – and therefore the royal household – to reside at Whitehall Palace. (The smog was also responsible for discolouring the Portland stone of St Paul's to a dull grey, even as it was being built.)[29]

In her dealings with her Royal Surveyor, we see Mary taking a close interest in the actual living arrangements, as opposed to visible pomp and ceremony, quite unlike that of previous regimes. The personal tastes of the future residents became an issue, as well as the formal and ceremonial requirements for the built spaces. Mary, for instance, was an enthusiastic collector of china and porcelain. Among the many interior-décor drawings produced for her, exquisitely executed by Hawksmoor, is a delightful sketch of a proposed mantelpiece arrangement for some of her porcelain pieces.[30]

Shortly after accepting the Crown, in February 1689, the new King and Queen abandoned Whitehall for the cleaner air and more private setting of Hampton Court Palace. Two days later, Wren attended them there, and was instructed to draw up plans for suitable new accommodation to supplement the largely Tudor apartments, which had last been renovated for the honeymoon of Charles II. The couple had decided that this would be their official out-of-town residence. Early in March it was reported that 'the bed of state is removed from Windsor to Hampton Court, and Sir Christopher Wren hath received orders to beautify and add some new building to that fabric'.[31]

Wren presented the King and Queen with predictably elegant drawings, showing his vision of a completely new-build palace. He proposed replacing all the existing buildings, retaining only the Tudor great hall, and creating four grandiose ranges of buildings round a large rectangular privy court, aligned on the long canal constructed for Charles II in 1668. As usual, financial stringencies curtailed the plans. In this case there was the additional problem of William's asthma, which dictated that he should not be obliged to climb long flights of steps to reach his accommodation. His state apartments were set as low as possible, above a ground storey only twelve foot six inches high, instead of the sixteen feet Wren had wanted. Nevertheless, demolitions began immediately to make way for the new royal apartments – Mary in particular was impatient to take up residence as soon as possible. A temporary apartment was created for the Queen in the east range of the Tudor Fountain Court, and she moved in to supervise operations.[32]

Still, royal business required that William and Mary should also have a residence within easy reach of Whitehall. In early June 1689, the Treasury purchased the Earl of Nottingham's house at Kensington, on the western edge of Hyde Park, for the royal couple – a moderate-sized 'villa', standing in modest gardens, whose beauty Evelyn admired.[33] The Queen was delighted because it afforded her complete privacy, while being within walking distance of Whitehall.[34] Wren was instructed to enlarge this simple, rectangular, two-storeyed building into a discreet family home. Kensington Palace was to be a modest, functional building, to offset Hampton Court's ostentation – a suburban retreat from the intense public scrutiny to which the King and Queen were exposed at Whitehall (where traditionally the monarch even took his meals in public). Here too, work began immediately, and was progressed with extraordinary speed, in order to fulfil the Queen's wishes that she should have an extensive set of private apartments there as soon as possible.[35]

It was Mary who took charge of all the building arrangements, both exterior and interior. She spent time regularly on site at Hampton Court and Kensington Palaces with her Royal Surveyor, walking the grounds and discussing plans and details. She also pressed Wren to speed up construction at both locations. On 11 December 1689, the roof over the almost completed first range of buildings at Hampton Court collapsed, killing two carpenters and injuring eleven others. Hooke noted Wren's dismay in his diary: '[Sir Christopher Wren] troubled about fall at Hampton Court'.[36] Another contemporary diarist recorded that there had been a similar accident at Kensington Palace a month earlier: 'The additional buildings to the King's house at Kensington, being newly covered with lead, fell down on a sudden, and hurt several people and killed some, the Queen was herself there but little before.'[37] The Hampton Court collapse, he reported, had been caused by inadequate masonry: 'Part of the new buildings at Hampton Court are fallen down, occasioned by the slightnesse of the wall.'[38]

The Queen was genuinely shaken by what had happened, and openly admitted that it was she who had been urging Wren and his construction team to work too fast. She wrote to her husband that God was clearly humbling her for presumption:

> I was so unsettled at Holland House [her temporary accommo-
> dation] I could not do as I would. This made me go often to
> Kensington to hasten the Worckmen and I was too impatient
> to be at that place, imagining to find more ease there. This I
> often reproved my self for and at last it pleased God to shew
> me the uncertainty of all things below: for part of the house
> which was new built fell down. The same accident happened at
> Hampton Court. All this, as much as it was the fault of the
> Worckmen, humanly speacking, yet shewed me plainly the hand
> of God was in it, and I was truly humbled.[39]

Thereafter, building continued at a more reasonable pace, though we might ask ourselves how much close supervision Wren was in a position to give to either project, in view of the critical point that had been reached at St Paul's in the same period. Hooke was no longer available to bear the burden of site supervision and make the important on-the-spot decisions, though Hawskmoor had by now taken his place in the same capacity.

The following June, William set off on his Irish campaign, leaving Mary in sole charge of the realm, and of the royal building works. Two hindrances to rapid completion in the case of the latter particularly preoccupied her, 'want of money and Portland Stone' – the difficulty in getting adequate supplies of Portland stone because of hostile French ships in the English Channel. On 24 June 1690 Mary wrote to William:

> As for the building [at Hampton Court and Kensington Palaces]
> I fear there will be many obstacles; for I spoke to Sir J. Lowther
> this very day, and hear so much use for money, and find soo
> little, that I cannot tell whether that of Hampton Court will
> not be a little the worse for it, especially since the French are

in the Channel, and at present are between Portland and us, from whence the stone must come; but in a day or two I hope to give you a more certain account; this being only my only conjecture.[40]

In fact, in his customary accommodating, pragmatic fashion, Wren had quietly resolved the problem of possible delays caused by lack of access to the stone quarries at Portland, by electing to construct the first range of buildings at Hampton Court out of English mainland stone – most of it from Headington (outside Oxford), supplemented by stone from Reigate and Beer, reserving Portland stone for plinths and cornices. In the short term this solved the pressing problem of pleasing the Queen; in the longer run it caused its own problems, since the stone used deteriorated badly over time, unlike the later parts of the Palace in which Portland stone predominated.[41]

There is something particularly touching about the idea that Wren, aged sixty and lacking a full family life of his own, found himself, with the accession of William and Mary, shifting his attention as Royal Surveyor from designing grandiose monuments of Stuart dynastic rule to presiding over the creation of a home environment to suit the comfortable lifestyle of the Dutch royal family. Mary's letters to William are full of homely details about the progress of the works – 'your closet [at Kensington] as yet smells of paint, for which I will ask pardon when I see you':

> The outside of ye house is ye fideling work wch takes up more time than one can imagin and while ye schafolds are up the windows must be boarded up but as sone as yt is done your own apartment may be furnisht and tho mine can not possible be ready yet awhile, I have found out a way if you please, wch is yt I may make use Lord Portland's & hee ly in some of ye other roomes, we may ly in your chamber & I go throw ye councel roome down or els dresse there.[42]

William associated this home-making (which he had never had the good fortune to experience as a child) closely with his wife. When she died, he shut up Hampton Court Palace completely; in spring 1695 he decided to expand his own accommodation at Kensington, and to remodel the apartments Mary had created with such enthusiasm – her withdrawing room, supping room, chocolate room, privy apartments and 'little garden' – to suit his own, now bachelor, needs. As usual Wren was put in charge, and as usual it was a rush job. In mid-August Lord Godolphin reported that 'the joyners are now in every roome of the house, and Sir Chr. Wren who lies there, told mee last night they should be out in one months time'.[43]

CHARITABLE DESIGNS:
A HOME FOR DERELICT SEAMEN

Although James II (who had served as Admiral of the Fleet since the early days of the Restoration) had reportedly resolved in 1687 to give his half-completed Palace at Greenwich to the nation, 'to be fitted for the service of impotent sea commanders and others', it was his daughter, Queen Mary II, who actually put the plan into effect. Beyond the care and attention she gave to domestic building plans for herself and her husband, Mary – much criticised in the early days after her arrival for lack of seriousness, and smiling too much – was probably the most serious and conscientious of Wren's royal architectural patrons. Certainly of Wren's royal clients she was the most committed to charitable good works, something that weighed increasingly with him.[44] Her death from smallpox in December 1694, at the age of thirty-two, was another in a long line of small but significant disappointments in the career of the Royal Surveyor.

In 1691 the Queen 'signified her pleasure to the Treasury Lords that the house at Greenwich shall be converted and employed as a hospital for seamen'. Her commitment – and that of dedicated advocates of substantial long-term support for wounded and retired seamen like Evelyn – intensified after the English victory over the French at the Battle of La Hogue in 1692, when large numbers of wounded from both sides flooded into the country. As during the wars against the French and Dutch of the 1660s and 1670s, when Evelyn had vainly tried to deal with thousands of desperately sick men in his capacity as Commissioner for the Sick and Wounded and Prisoners of War, available facilities for housing and tending the casualties were woefully inadequate.[45]

In January 1693 Wren visited the King's House – John Webb's building, left incomplete when funds for a new royal palace dried up in 1672, and which had subsequently been allocated to the Ordnance and was currently being used as a gunpowder store – to assess its suitability to house the new charitable foundation.

Webb had begun to build the first range of what was intended to be a two-, and possibly three-range palace for Charles II at Greenwich to complement the Inigo Jones Queen's House in 1664.[46] The single, two-storey Portland stone building alone cost Charles £36,000 by the time the shell was completed in late 1669. Webb wrote hopefully that he was now 'at leasure, until his Majesty shall be gratiously pleased to proceed towards the perfecting of his new Royall Palace at Greenwich', but in fact the King had both run out of money and lost interest in the project, which promised to be at once too ostentatious (in the wake of the Great Fire and the economic difficulties it had brought to his sub-jects) and too slow in execution. From then on the interior decoration went at a snail's pace, largely because of lack of money to pay the craftsmen and to buy materials like the fine marble for paving stones and fireplaces. The account was officially closed on 31 October 1672, the day after Webb died, although payments continued to be made for another year for completion of essential interior works: completing the balustrade, painting door-cases, windows, rails and balusters, and plastering ceilings.[47]

It was Mary who decided, when the project was taken up again in the early 1690s, that it would be profligate to demolish Webb's King Charles building – a perfectly sound structure, readily adaptable to its new purpose – in order to make way for Wren's first proposal for a new, integrated set of buildings, thereby necessitating a complete redesign.

It was Mary, too, who insisted that Inigo Jones's Queen's House must retain its river access and view, and not be obscured or over-whelmed by the new buildings. Having accompanied Wren to Greenwich on a number of occasions to discuss the design of the Hospital, she insisted that 'the ground, 115 feet long, now staked out for a way or passage through the premises to and from the Thames and to and from their Majesties' house called the Queen's House' be reserved in perpetuity for the Crown. Nor should we overlook the fact that in treating the proposed buildings sympathetically in the round – as a collection of palatial buildings in a riverside garden landscape – Mary was carrying over her recent experience in questions of design at her

Greenwich Royal Hospital for retired and disabled seamen, seen from
the Thames – as Queen Mary insisted, Inigo Jones's Queen's House
retains its unimpeded view of the river.

Dutch summer palace at Apeldoorn, Het Loo (completed in 1686). She
continued to be closely involved with planning the gardens there, after
her arrival in England, although she was never able to return herself to
enjoy the results.[48]

Hawksmoor was site architect for the Wren office throughout the
long building period, first under Wren as Surveyor, and then under his
successor Sir John Vanbrugh. Writing on the completion of the Hospital
in 1728, five years after Wren's death, he both recalled the impact on
the final design of Queen Mary's two astute pieces of foresight and
captured the 'pleasure and cheerfulness' with which she and Wren
debated plans for Greenwich together:

> Sir Christopher Wren, being then the King's Architect General,
> was nominated Surveyor of this great Undertaking; and with
> great Pleasure and cheerfulness engaged in it, Gratis.
>
> Her Majesty, ever sollicitous for the Prosecution of the Design,
> had several times honour'd Greenwich with her personal Views
> of the Building erected by King Charles II, as Part of his Palace,
> and that built by Mr. Inigo Jones, called the Queen's House,
> &c. On which Views, she was unwilling to demolish either, as
> was propos'd by some. This occasioned the keeping of an
> Approach from the Thames quite up to the Queen's House, of
> 115 Feet broad, out of the Grant that was made to the Hospital,
> that her Majesty might have an Access to that House by Water
> as well as by Land; and she retained a Desire to add the Four

Pavilions to that Palace, according to Inigo Jones's Design, that she might make that little Palace compleat, as a Royal Villa for her own Retirement, or from whence Embassadors, or publick Ministers, might make their Entry into London. . . .

Her Majesty's absolute Determination to preserve the Wing built by her Uncle King Charles II; to keep the Queen's House, and the Approach to it, on the Considerations above mention'd, naturally drew on the Disposition of the Buildings, as they are now placed and situated.[49]

Mary's determination (and persuasiveness) did indeed have a dramatic impact on the final form of the Royal Hospital. The constraints she imposed meant that Wren (like Webb before him) was forced to abandon the idea of a three-range design, dominated by a lantern and cupola at the centre of the river-facing range, in favour of mirrored runs of buildings, framing the Queen's House and making it the focal point of the view from the river. Wren's inspired solution, completed by Hawksmoor to Wren's designs in 1724, creates symmetrical ranges without any hierarchical centrepiece apart from the distant Queen's House. The King Charles Building faces the mirroring Queen Anne Building. In place of a third range at right angles, two further buildings (the King William and Queen Mary Buildings) face each other beyond these two. Each has an imposing lantern and cupola at the corner closest to the earlier buildings, giving from the river a formal view down a long avenue of the Queen's House framed by the twin domes. The result lies somewhere between landscape, perspective painting and formal baroque assemblage of buildings. As a solution to a difficult design problem necessitated by the site, it is a Wren triumph. As a functioning residential institution for old seamen it was an unqualified success, setting the standard for all such institutions for at least a century thereafter.

In 1694 a royal warrant was issued, granting the land for a large-scale charitable project:

For the reliefe and support of Seamen serving on board the Shipps or Vessells belonging to the Navy Royall who by reason of Age, Wounds or other disabilities shall be uncapable of further Service at Sea and be unable to maintain themselves. And for the sustentation of the Widows and the Maintenance and

Education of the Children of Seamen happening to be slain or disabled in such service and also for the further reliefe and Encouragement of Seamen and Improvement of Navigation.[50]

Plans for the Hospital were almost immediately interrupted, however, when the Queen was taken gravely ill. With her death in December the most passionate advocate at court for the Hospital was lost. Those around the distraught King were, however, able to represent the Greenwich project as an undertaking especially dear to her heart, which must be brought to completion in her memory. The transformation of Greenwich Hospital from abandoned royal palace into a sumptuous refuge for retired and invalided seamen would, it was suggested to him, be a fitting memorial to the charitably minded Queen. William was persuaded, and a Royal Commission was established early in 1685 to oversee construction. The plans for Greenwich were ratified at the beginning of the new year, the order backdated to 25 October, the last quarter-day of the legal year, to expedite the financing arrangements, and to allow the charter to be issued in the joint names of both monarchs. George, Prince of Denmark (husband of Mary's sister Anne, now heir to the throne) and the new Archbishop of Canterbury, Thomas Tenison, were nominally in charge of the Hospital project. Evelyn was Treasurer; Wren gave his services as Surveyor free of charge.

Meanwhile Wren had broken off his work at Greenwich to deal with designs more urgently connected with the Queen's death. In keeping with the general dismay at her premature end – in particular on the part of her devoted husband – her royal funeral was the most lavish and ostentatious of the century; Evelyn judged it 'infinitely expensive, never so universal a Mourning'.[51] Wren designed a magnificent funeral car, or chariot, to convey Mary's body to Westminster Abbey, and an elaborate wooden catafalque, made by the carpenter John Churchill, with carvings by Grinling Gibbons, beneath which she lay in state. Hawksmoor was paid £5 'for his extraordinary paines in copying designes by the direction of Sir Christopher Wren for the Mausoleum in the Abbey and for the Chariot of state' for the craftsmen's use.[52]

The team which set out to build Greenwich Hospital consisted of Wren, Evelyn, Fox and Pepys – old friends, all of them by now well beyond middle age, and committed to a grand benevolent gesture to crown their achievements in public office. Pepys, a year younger than

Wren, was the youngest at sixty-two; Evelyn was seventy-five. The model was inevitably Chelsea, with some acknowledgement of the influence exerted on the whole project by Louis XIV's similar grand project at Les Invalides in Paris. The anonymous translator of a short French treatise on the institutions and regulations at Les Invalides, published in 1695, just as the project was beginning, dedicated it to King William in terms reminiscent of Evelyn's *Parallel*:

> That which has made me presume to lay the following Discourse at Your Majesty's Feet, is the Noble Resolution You have formed of providing an Habitation and Relief for Your Disabled and Distressed Seamen, by converting one of Your Royal Mansions into an Hospital, and of endowing it with Revenues sufficient for their Maintenance and Entertainment, which will be one of the most Illustrious and most Useful Monuments of Your Majesty's Wisdom and Piety, as well as of Your Power and Greatness.
>
> After-Ages will no less admire the Provident Care Your Majesty takes for the Comfortable Subsistence of the *Poor Seamen*, than the Present does what You have done already for the Disabled and Superannuated Land-Soldiers, by perfecting and establishing the Royal Hospital near *Chelsea*, begun and carried on in the Two last Reigns; but with this advantage, that to Your Majesty the Glory was reserved of beginning and finishing a Work, so much wanted and wished for by Your *Royal Ancestors*.[53]

Pepys, in particular, had been lobbying for years for some kind of provision to be made for retired seamen who had given honourable service in the Dutch and French wars, just as Evelyn had done for retired soldiers. They had run over the arguments on many occasions; now, seeing support coming from the court, they rapidly marshalled them again. Pepys wrote to Evelyn in November 1694 that he was 'recollecting his old thoughts on the matter' so that he could comment on the plans, and that Fox had done the same. He did not feel competent to comment on the architectural detail of any of Wren's alternative, ambitious plans, which ranged from a fairly basic conversion of the King Charles Building into an infirmary to a grandiose new-build scheme with wings, 'an Invalides for the sea', including a complex range of accommodation for widows and orphans as well as facilities for the aged and incapacitated. Nevertheless, he wrote, he would give it his full support: 'the work is too near akin to me, and to the Commands I have heretofore had concerning it, to let it want any degree of furtherance I can give it'. He was adamant that the money must be voted from a Parliament 'as little disposed to deny as any I sat in'.[54]

The Commissioners met for the first time on 9 May; on 24 May Evelyn 'made report of the state of Gr[eenwich] House, & how the standing part might for 6000 pounds be made servicable at present & what Ground would be requisit for the whole design'.[55] Just over a year later, Evelyn recorded a meeting at Wren's Scotland Yard office to agree payment arrangements for starting work on site:

> A Comitty meeting at W[hite]hall, about the Hospital at Greenewich at Sir Chr: Wrenn, his Majesties Surveyor Gen: We made the first agreement with divers Workemen & for Materials, & gave the first Order for the proceding on the foundations, ordering payments to be Weekly to the Workmen & a general Accompt to be monethly: I then received Orders from the Lords of the Tressury for the Kings 2000 pounds to be employed on that work.[56]

The foundation stone was laid three weeks later, on 30 June, by Evelyn and Wren together, at precisely five o'clock in the afternoon 'after we had dined together'. The precision as to the time was achieved by Royal Astronomer John Flamsteed, an old and good friend of Wren's, 'observing the punctual time by Instruments', which he had brought from the neighbouring Observatory for the purpose.[57]

Wren's friend Evelyn drove the Greenwich project forward – a somewhat remarkable fact given his age.[58] Indeed, the continuing collaboration between Evelyn and Wren is a striking feature of both Chelsea and Greenwich Hospitals, since the two projects are generally regarded as combining beauty and function especially successfully, admired for their execution and for the appropriate way they served the needs of their early residents. Here, as at Chelsea, we have a partnership in which a knowledgeable enthusiasm for architecture and a deep, compassionate commitment to charitable good works were brought into play together at all stages.

The partnership celebrated in these collaborations went back to the early years of Wren's involvement with architecture – Evelyn was the *éminence grise* behind Wren's trip to France in 1665, and his extensive collection of continental architectural engravings (additional contributions to which Wren brought back on that occasion) gave Wren further knowledge of recent buildings abroad. Evelyn was himself an invaluable guide: in his own lengthy travels in France and Italy in the 1640s he had become something of an expert in architectural aesthetics and construction methods. Evelyn was the one with the time to study the published engravings of Les Invalides, as well as the account of the rules for its day-to-day organisation, in the 'Pattern of a Well-Constituted and Well-Governed Hospital'.[59] The design for the King William Building refers specifically to 'necessary places (as it is at the Invalides at Paris) on each floor at the west end of the south dormitory'.[60]

As ever, Greenwich was tediously slow in reaching completion (Les Invalides, by comparison, was built in four years). Fortunately, as planned, the King Charles Block was already complete, requiring only internal modifications before it could be put into use. The plan of the King Charles Building as agreed in 1696 provided for the accommodation of up to 350 seamen in large wards, with residents arranged as at Chelsea. In the main block, the east side of the ground floor of Webb's range was opened out to form two large dining rooms between the entrance vestibule and the pavilions. A new floor was inserted above Webb's long gallery, to provide a single, long, heated ward with cabins placed to each side. In the base wing, the cabins were arranged as at Chelsea, on either side of the spine wall, giving on to well-lit open galleries. A system of wards and cabins, with each cabin containing a bed and a chest for possessions, was adopted from the start.[61]

The humane attention to detail testifies to the careful thought that had gone into designing these interiors, which Wren and Evelyn understood to be every bit as important as the exterior grandeur. Nevertheless, the importance of the physical surroundings for the morale of the residents was recognised by Wren's contemporaries. Commenting on the shared concerns of Les Invalides and Greenwich in 1730, a visitor to the former wrote:

> I have often heard it observed that in acts of Charity of this publick nature for the encouragement of souldiers or sea men, the money which is thus thrown away as it were on building

and outward ornament had better have been spared towards
making a more ample supply of Provisions and necessaries, and
that more beef and worse beds would give greater contentment
to these wretches[.] however true this may be as to the English,
tis not wholely so as to the french, who are generally more
taken with outward show and appearance; I believe tis with
chearfulness these men abate a pound of meat in a week, for
the sake of being so magnificently lodged.[62]

The charitable plans for the Hospital became increasingly ambitious
as the programme went along. Originally it was envisaged simply as an
almshouse, without even purpose-built medical facilities. Eventually,
however, the King William Building included an infirmary and accommodation for a surgeon, physicians, a matron and a dispenser of medi-
cincs. By 1701, a plan by Hawksmoor allocates space in the Princess
Anne (afterwards Queen Anne) Block for 'the Mathematics, Navigation,
and Writting schools', a library of 'books, mappes and charts', and a
gallery of 'Modells of Ships, Gallys, Brigantines', indicating that the
stipulation in the original charter that provision should be made for
the 'sustenation of the Widows and . . . Education of the Children of
Seamen' was by now being taken seriously. The same plan calculates
that the completed Hospital would accommodate a total of 2044 retired
seamen, plus officers and staff.[63] By 1728, however, Hawksmoor had
reduced the estimate to 1352, with an additional 200 in the infirmary.

The success of Greenwich depended on the commitment of its
non-royal champions. If it had been left to the Crown, the Army or the
Navy Office, neither Chelsea nor Greenwich Hospitals would have
reached successful completion. Fox and Evelyn made substantial financial contributions to Chelsea and Greenwich respectively, as well as
using all the political influence they could (it was they who secured the
levy against active soldiers' and seamen's pay – effectively an early
compulsory insurance payment – which made the financing possible).
Wren seems to have brought out the best in both men, his warm nature
and commitment helping transform Evelyn's and Fox's dislike of the
selfish, extravagant court and its decadent ways into creative energy for
major philanthropic works. Wren turned their dreams into bricks and
mortar. In the end, Chelsea and Greenwich Hospitals are lasting memorials to a trio of benevolent friends – Wren, Fox and Evelyn – each of

The Painted Hall at Greenwich – the palatial accommodation occasioned
much comment about the high standard of living provided for mere
retired sailors.

whom believed himself to have been blessed by God with long life and prosperity in times of danger, uncertainty and political upheaval.

PERSPECTIVE AND ARCHITECTURE

The close collaboration between highly cultivated gentlemen at Chelsea and Greenwich reveals a shared aesthetic which deserves a brief comment here, as it sheds light on Wren's architectural practice. In his few, fragmentary writings on architectural theory and above all practically, in his buildings, Wren attached particular importance to 'perspective' – how the building looks, from particular positions, as opposed to the reality of plan and elevation.

In Tract IV of his unpublished architectural tracts, Wren remarks that 'the *Romans* guided themselves by Perspective in all their Fabricks'. 'Why', he continues, 'should not Perspective lead us back again to what was Roman?'[64] In Tract I, he expands on this theme, in ways which irresistibly call to mind advice on perspective from contemporary treatises on painting:

> The Architect ought, above all Things, to be well skilled in Perspective; for, everything that appears well in the Orthography, may not be good in the Model, especially where there are many Angles and Projectures; and every thing that is good in Model, may not be so when built; because a Model is seen from other Stations and Distances than the Eye sees the Building. . . .[65]

Wren goes on to propose a rule for the visual success of buildings:

> this will hold universally true, that whatsoever is good in Perspective, and will hold so in all the principal Views, whether direct or oblique, will be as good in great, if this only Caution be observed, that Regard be had to the Distance of the Eye in the principal Stations.[66]

The advice Wren gives the reader, concerning detailed design features, takes the eye of the beholder resolutely as its starting point, and as the measure of success:

> In Things to be seen at once, much Variety makes Confusion, another Vice of Beauty. In Things that are not seen at once, and

have no Respect one to another, great Variety is commendable, provided this Variety transgress not the Rules of *Opticks* and *Geometry. . . .*

Things near at hand may have small and many Members, be well furnished with Ornaments, and may lie flatter; on the contrary, all this Care is ridiculous at great Distances; there bulky Members, and full Projectures casting quick Shadows, are commendable: small Ornaments at too great Distance, serve only to confound the Symmetry, and to take away the Lustre of the Object, by darkening it with many little Shadows.[67]

These remarks might almost be read as instructions for viewing St Paul's.[68] They match closely the kinds of things his friends Evelyn and Pepys recorded in their diaries, concerning the fashion for 'perspectives' in polite London circles. On 1 July 1664, Evelyn visited the house of Thomas Povey, a wealthy gentleman with a passion for *trompe l'oeil*:

Went to see Mr. Povey's elegant house in Lincoln's-Inn-Fields, where the perspective in his court, painted by Streeter, is indeed excellent, with the vases in imitation of porphyry, and fountains; the inlaying of his closet; above all, his pretty cellar and ranging of his wine-bottles.[69]

Pepys, too, dined with Povey on many occasions. On 19 May 1664 (a couple of months before Evelyn's visit) he writes:

With Mr. Povy home to dinner, where extraordinary cheer. And after dinner up and down to see his house. And in a word, methinks for his perspective upon his wall in his garden and the springs rising up – with the perspective in the little closet – his room floored above with woods of several colours, like, but above the best Cabinet-work I ever saw – his grotto and vault, with his bottles of wine and a well therein to keep them cool – his furniture of all sorts – his bath at the top of his house – good pictures and his manner of eating and drinking, doth surpass all that ever I did see of one man in all my life.[70]

Povey owned several perspective paintings by Dutch artist Samuel van Hoogstraten. Illusionistic art which depended on a scientific understanding of light, vision, perspective and reflection, like van Hoogstraten's own, was all the rage with the scientific community in London.

Van Hoogstraten lived and worked in London from 1662 to 1667, and recounted with pride how he dined as an equal with several gentlemen members of the Royal Society at the house of Thomas Povey. Povey owned van Hoogstraten's *Perspective from a Threshold* (1662). The painting is a household interior, in which a long black-and-white-tiled corridor, complete with glimpses of furnishings and household pets, stretches, in exaggerated perspective, away from the viewer. Pepys records in his diary that Povey had *Perspective from a Threshold* hung in such a way that he could reveal it to guests by opening the door of his ground-floor closet. He describes how delighted and amazed he was to discover that no real corridor lay before him, and that 'there is nothing but only a plain picture hung upon the wall'.[71]

It was Povey who advised Pepys when the diarist decided to embark on his own collection of perspective landscape paintings:

20 January 1669: This afternoon before the play, I called with my wife at Dancre's [Hendrick Danckerts] the great lanskip-painter, by Mr. Povy's advice, and have bespoke him to come to take measure of my dining-room panels.[72]

22 January 1669: And here at the Change I met with Mr. Dancre. The famous lanskip painter – with whom I was on Wednesdy; he took measure of my panels in my dining-room, where in the four I intend to have the four houses of the King – White-hall, Hampton-court, Greenwich – and Windsor.[73]

1 February 1669: Up and by water from the Tower to White-hall. . . . I went to a Committee of Tanger, but it did not meet; and so I meeting Mr. Povy, he and I away to Dancres to speak something touching the pictures I am getting him to make for me. And thence he carried me to Mr. Streeters the famous history-painter over the way, whom I have often heard of but did never see him before; and there I found him and Dr. Wren and several virtuosos looking upon the paintings which he is making for the new Theatre at Oxford; and endeed, they look as they would be very fine, and the rest things better then those of Rubens in the Banqueting-house at White-hall, but I do not so fully think so – but they will certainly be very noble, and I am mightily pleased to have the fortune to see this man and his work, which is very famous – and he a very civil little man

Perspective painting owned by Thomas Povey and hung behind a door
at the end of a corridor to create a *trompe-l'oeil* illusion – it is described
by Pepys in his diary.

and lame, but lives handsomely. So thence to my Lord Bellasses and met him within; my business only to see a chimney-piece of Dancre's doing in distemper with egg to keep off the glaring of the light, which I must have done for my room; and endeed it is pretty, but I must confess I do think it is not altogether so beautiful as the oyle pictures; but I will have some of one and some of another.[74]

When Pepys visited Greenwich shortly afterwards, he sought out the 'view' Danckerts was proposing – the location from which Danckerts had advised 'viewing' the Greenwich buildings, in order to see them at their best. This is precisely the aesthetic attitude to which Wren appeals in his remarks on perspective and design. For Wren and his circle, perspective and the aesthetics of built form are part of one and the same sensibility.

ST PAUL'S: TRIUMPH OF MIND OVER MATTER

By the time Wren was again confirmed in post as Surveyor of the Royal Works at the beginning of William and Mary's reign in 1689, and embarked on the demanding programme of conversion, modification and rebuilding required by the royal couple, he had risen to become a prominent and highly respected figure in polite London circles. He was a devoutly observant High Anglican, a man of substance, holding significant public office, with investments in a range of commercial ventures. He was prosperous, though not wealthy, and ran a busy and successful architectural office. He was active in London scientific and medical circles, and sat on a number of formal and *ad hoc* scientific committees. He had also been in effective sole charge of plans for rebuilding St Paul's for over twenty years, and the new Cathedral was still nowhere near completion.

Wren's preparedness to take on administrative burdens to oblige his friends and colleagues was by now having serious consequences for the efficiency with which major projects directed by him were executed. He had commitments and burdensome responsibilities across an unmanageably wide range of different types of public project – from anatomical dissection to managing the affairs of the Hudson's Bay

Company. Combined with the fresh round of Royal Works which followed the arrival of William and Mary, all this was starting to interfere with his ability to keep up momentum at St Paul's.

Matters were made worse in 1696, when a catastrophic cliff collapse caused by heavy rains destroyed the loading platforms (together with all the cranes and equipment) on the Island of Portland, Wren's main supplier of quality stone, making it impossible to load and ship the huge stone blocks for the Cathedral.[75] Here, too, however, we find evidence of Wren's tendency to see to all matters himself, however tangential to his project. A year on from the original landslide, on 18 May 1697, supplies were still at a standstill, and the St Paul's Commission (on which Wren sat) decided that the only way to resolve the problem was to send a team to Portland to advise the owners of the stone quarry there on how best to repair the wharves and loading bays. Wren volunteered to go himself, taking with him Hawksmoor and Edward Strong.[76] The workable solution they proposed in a report presented to the Commission on 30 May over Wren's signature was not, however, in the end the one adopted, making clear the way in which by this time Wren's investment in terms of time, energy and effort was no longer proportionate to the task in hand.[77] In 1697 the Commission decided to withhold half of Wren's annual £200 salary until the work was completed.

By the turn of the century, the slow pace of construction at St Paul's had become something of a London joke – or at least an extreme example other people could gesture towards to justify their own poor performance record. The first Astronomer Royal John Flamsteed invoked it, at the height of his long-running quarrel with Newton, over his refusal to publish the results for the positions of the fixed stars and observations of lunar orbit he was producing at the new Greenwich Observatory.

The exchange, on an occasion which already involved Wren in his capacity as moderator of quarrels among his scientific colleagues, at a time when Sir Isaac Newton had become a prominent London figure and Master of the Mint, is recorded in a letter from Flamsteed to his friend John Lowthorp, written in 1700.[78] Newton badly needed access to the astronomical data collected by Flamsteed at the Greenwich Observatory, as part of his own theoretical investigations of lunar motion. For years he had been pressuring Flamsteed to get his tables of corrected observations into the public domain, as required (according to Newton) under the terms of his contract as Royal Astronomer. Flamsteed describes the bad-tempered exchange between them on this occasion particularly vividly:

> I would not hear him [Newton] but onely desir'd that he would oblige me so far as to come down hither with Sir C. Wren some morning alone and take a Dinner with me, and he should then see in what forwardness my Work was and we could consider how to forward it to the Press[.]
>
> [W]hen I urg'd this againe that he would come down he ask't me a little *Quick, what for?* my reply was as before, but I added that by his seeing what was done I hoped to stop the Mouths and Clamours of some People that ask't why *I did not Print*, that it was soon said, but requir'd some consideration before it could be done, that it was a Popular Reflection, and apt to take and therefore to be timely obviated, but that my Work was like the building of St. Paul's, I had hew'd the Materials out of the Rock, brought them together and formed them but that hands and Time were to be allowed to perfect the building and Cover it.[79]

There are other reports of Flamsteed reaching, under pressure, for St Paul's as an excuse when called upon to justify the time it was taking to bring his work to fruition: 'They may as well ask why St. Paul's is not finished,' he is supposed to have retorted.[80]

The slow progress of England's first Anglican cathedral nevertheless brought with it certain advantages. It offered a whole series of opportunities for Wren and Hooke to put into practice solutions to problems concerning the stability of built form, based on the deepening understanding of materials and structures they could draw upon, from their scientific explorations at the Royal Society. Wren had been determined from the outset that, in spite of anxiety over raising sufficient funds, St Paul's should not be built 'in parts' – that what went on site should be a properly conceived whole, whose integrated elements might see completion, for convenience, at somewhat different rates. Like any practising architect, however, he anticipated occasions during construction when the design would need to be modified as structural and design problems arose. Paper plans and elevations, however meticulous, are often aspirational studies as the architect struggles to resolve the three-dimensional reality of the built form. Also, as a constructionally minded architect, Wren erred on the side of structural caution from the outset, and prudently gave himself opportunity in his design for later revision. It was pointed out many years ago that the size of the main piers, set with the laying of the Cathedral's foundations, was greater than required for the scale of building suggested by the warrant design approved by Charles I.[81]

From the very first designs for the new Cathedral (and, indeed, from the time of the proposed renovation of Old St Paul's before the Great Fire) Wren was determined that the Cathedral would be completed with a major dome. Hence the fact that the eight central pillars whose foundations were laid right at the beginning of construction were given a diameter significantly greater than that required to support the more modest crowning structure specified in the plans approved by Charles II. At various points during the building process, however, Wren adjusted his ideas as to precisely how the load would be distributed, in response to the obvious difficulties in raising a hemispherical dome to the height needed if it was to be as striking a landmark on London's horizon as the spire of Old St Paul's – long gone, but for which the London clergy consistently expressed communal nostalgia.[82]

In the 1690s, the future best-selling author Daniel Defoe (then simply Mr Foe) ran a tile and brick factory at Tilbury, supplying the bricks for a number of Wren projects (including Greenwich Hospital), until the business failed in 1703. In his popular gazetteer, *A Tour through England and Wales*, he staunchly defends the design of St Paul's, and records as a matter of fact – evidently on the basis of conversations he had had with Wren – that the central columns at St Paul's had always been intended to support the enormous load of a dome and lantern. There are those, he writes in 1724 (a year after Wren's death), who complain that the columns supporting the dome, 'that mighty arch', are 'too gross, that the work looks heavy'. The architect, he reports, had explained at the time the Cathedral was being built that the columns were designed in anticipation of the exceptional load they would ulti-mately carry in the form of a dome and lantern that would dominate the sky-line:

> Those gentlemen who in Parliament opposed Sir Christopher
> Wren's request, of having the dome covered with copper, and

who moved to have had the lanthorn on the top made shorter, and built of wood; I say, those gentlemen pretending skill in the art, and offering to reproach the judgment of the architect, alledged, That the copper and the stone lanthorn would be too heavy, and that the pillars below would not support it.

To which Sir Christopher answered, That he had sustained the building with such sufficient columns, and the buttment was every where so good, that he would answer for it with his head, that it should bear the copper covering and the stone lanthorn, and seven thousand ton weight laid upon it more than was proposed, and that nothing below should give way, no not one half quarter of an inch; but that, on the contrary, it should be all the firmer and stronger for the weight that should be laid on it; adding, That it was with this view that the work was brought up from its foundation, in such manner, as made common observers rather think the first range of the buildings too gross for its upper part; and that, if they pleased, he would undertake to raise a spire of stone upon the whole, a hundred food higher than the cross now stands.[83]

Evelyn, too, was consistent in his support for Wren's unashamedly continental (and High Church) design. On 2 October 1694 he visited the completed choir and pronounced: 'Certainly a piece of Architecture without reproch'.[84] On 5 December 1697, the first Sunday following the Peace of Ryswick, Evelyn attended a thanksgiving service in the new Cathedral, the first, he records, 'since it was Consumed at the Conflagration of the Citty; 1666: which I my selfe saw'. The choir was completely finished; the organ, he added, 'esteemed the best in Europe'.[85]

The rebuilding of St Paul's under the direction of a single master architect over a period of almost forty years (from conception to completion) was a constructional triumph of epic proportions. But we should not forget that alongside the modifications constituting structural improvements, made while the work was in progress, other changes of heart represented moments when Wren's grand conception faltered, and the fabric failed. Those much criticised piers, for example, still turned out to have been under-specified, when the Cathedral had barely risen above ground level. The rubble core proved to be insufficiently dense to support the vertical loads, causing early fracturing of the surface.[86]

St Paul's Cathedral, as imposing today as when it was first built.

Sir Dudley North, whose brother's account of Wren's practice at St Paul's was cited earlier, describes how Wren modified details in the design in response to structural failure during the building process:

> He [Dudley North] was so great a lover of building, that St. Paul's, then well advanced, was his ordinary walk: there was scarce a course of stones laid, while we lived together, over which we did not walk. And he would always climb to the uttermost heights. . . .
>
> We . . . commonly got a snatch of discourse with [Sir Christopher Wren], who, like a true philosopher, was always obliging and communicative, and, in every matter we inquired about,

gave short, but satisfactory answers. . . . He used to observe the ordinary decays of building, and where strength was most needed. He took notice that compass arches did not press uniformly; for, at the key or crown, the joints at the upper sweep, or outside, pinched hard, and gaped underneath; and contrarily, at the shoulders, those underneath pinched, and those above gaped; and for that the material, as rubbed brick, usually crushed there; and that the pinching below tends to rising. Wherefore, to secure a compass arch, it was necessary by weight, or some other means, to keep down the shoulders, which rising, let the crown, or key, fall in. . . .

He observed that the great arches at the floor of St. Paul's, after the centres were struck, fell in twice; and he was much puzzled to find out the reason of it; which he did, and then fancied the builders themselves did not know it, till after the second fall had showed it them. It seems such things were not to be talked of there, and no subject of discourse with the workmen. The middle vault was cast in three, as a middle and side aisles; and the moulds were parabolic; so as the narrow aisles, on each side, keyed as high as the middle. Then it was apparent that the thrust of the middle arch bore upon the voids on the two sides; and those yielding but little, let the middle break from its truth; and then down they must come.[87]

This kind of analysis produced the solution which eventually meant that stable supporting arches were successfully constructed. And whatever the intentions in the original plans, the roof of the choir as built adapts a solution arrived at in the process of erecting the roof of the Wren Library in Cambridge – one which had required special attention from the structural engineers in Wren's office, sent to Cambridge for the purpose.[88]

DOUBLE DOMES FROM THE EAST

Structurally, Wren's decision to use a 'cupola' to crown St Paul's was the most challenging possible choice, for which there were no precedents in English architecture, particularly given the height to which it needed to be raised if it was to provide the kind of landmark the Church authorities demanded (as a replacement for the steeple and tower of Old St Paul's):

Among all the Composures of the Ancients, we find no Cupolas raised above the necessary Loading of the Hemisphere, as is seen particularly in the Pantheon. In after Ages the Dome of Florence, and of the great Church of Venice, was raised higher, The Saracens mightily affected it, in Imitation of the first most eminent Pattern, given by Justinian, in his Temple of Sancta Sophia, at Constantinople. Bramante would not fall short of those Examples; nor could the Surveyor [Wren] do otherwise than gratify the general Taste of the Age, which had been so used to Steeples, that these round Designs were hardly digested, unless raised to a remarkable Height.

Thus St. Paul's is lofty enough to be discerned at Sea Eastward, and at Windsor Westward; but our Air being frequently hazy, prevents those distant Views, except when the Sun shines out, after a Shower of Rain has washed down the Clouds of Sea-coal Smoke that hang over the City from so many thousands of Fires kindled every Morning, besides Glass-houses, Brewhouses, and Founderies, every one of which emits a blacker Smoke than twenty Houses.[89]

In his search for architectural precedents, Wren, like others of his contemporaries, turned not only to great classical and Italian domes described in works of architectural theory like Vitruvius and Serlio, but also to examples from Byzantine and Islamic architecture. To build a basilica worthy of the true, restored Anglican Church, Wren believed, he needed precedents from the cradle of Christianity. For the vaulting of St Paul's Cathedral, he explains in his second tract on architecture, he followed the dome-building technique used at Hagia Sophia, and which is 'yet found in the present Seraglio [the Topkapi Saray]'.[90]

Wren's interest in the dome construction of Hagia Sophia extended beyond the mere mentions to be found in works we know he consulted, like Evelyn's English version of Fréart's *Parallel*. There was, indeed, a surprising amount of hard information available for consultation. In 1680, Guillaume-Joseph Grelot published a book of his close architectural studies of buildings in Constantinople, entitled *Relation nouvelle d'une voyage de Constantinople enrichie de plans levés par l'auteur*.[91] An English edition appeared in 1683 under the title *A Late Voyage to Constantinople*. Grelot's fourteen engraved plates, based on drawings done *in situ*, were widely influential, recording both interior and exterior detail of Hagia Sophia. Grelot had managed to secure permission to take measurements inside the ancient basilica, now a mosque.

Grelot's patron was John Chardin, who was in England, direct from his travels in the East, in 1680, and gave a presentation on his oriental experiences at a meeting of the Royal Society which both Wren and Evelyn attended.[92] Evelyn's account of Chardin's visit conveys graphically the excitement he brought to the Royal Society, and Wren's part in the proceedings:

August 30 [1680]: Lond: I went to visite a French Stranger, one Monsieur Jardine [Chardin] [since Knighted by his Majesty & made Denison of England] who having been thrice at the East Indias, Persia & other remote Countries, came hither in our returne ships from those parts; and it being reported he was a very curious man, & knowing, I was desir'd by the Ro: Society in their name, to salute him, & to let him know how glad they should be to receive him, if he pleased to do them the honour: &c: There were appointed to accompanie me Sir Jo: Hoskins & Sir Chr: Wren &c.

We found him at his lodging, in his Eastern habite, a very handsom person, extreamely affable, not inclin'd to talke Wonders, but exceedingly modest, & a well bred man. . . . We told him, we much desired an account of the extraordinary things he must have seene; having (as we understood) trav<e>ld over land, those places, where fiew, if any northern Europeans used to go, as about the Black & Caspian Sea, Mingrelia, Bagdat, Ninive, <persepolis> &c: He told us the things most worthy of our sight, would be, the draughts he had caused to be made of some noble ruines &c: for that (besides his little talent that way) he had carried two very good Painters along with him to draw Landskips, Measure, and designe the remainders of the Palace which Alexander burnt in his frolique at Persepolis, with divers Temples, Columns, Relievos, & statues, yet extant.[93]

Shortly after this visit, Chardin settled permanently in London.[94] On 23 February 1684 Evelyn visited him at home, to give him his professional assistance 'for the ingraving of the plates, the translation & Printing of his historie of that wonderfull Persian monument neere Persepolis, & other rare Antiquities, which he had Caus'd to be drawne from the originals'. Wren accompanied Evelyn on this occasion, and afterwards they visited Dr Thomas Tenison (later Archbishop of Canterbury) to discuss his plans to fund and build a public library in London; Evelyn thought that Tenison's library should be housed 'at St. Paules, the West end of that Church, (if ever finish'd)'.[95] Shortly thereafter Evelyn dined at the Lord Keeper's and then 'brought him to Sir John Chardin, who showed him his accurate drafts of his travels in Persia'.

Chardin is likely to be the source for three remarkable drawings

Drawing of the double dome of Hagia Sophia in Istanbul, possibly by Hawksmoor, based on drawings brought to London by John Chardin, who settled there in the 1680s.

associated with Wren (and possibly in Hawksmoor's hand) of Hagia Sophia in plan (two corner details) and cross-section, which resurfaced in the late 1980s. They first came to light at St Paul's, discovered 'among some Drawings of Sr. Cr. Wren which were evidently *Studios* for St. Pauls, London' by Robert Milne, Surveyor at St Paul's from 1766. These papers in their turn had belonged to Henry Flitcroft, Milne's predecessor. Thus they were originally discovered by Flitcroft somewhere at St Paul's Cathedral itself.[96]

The cross-section shows the double-dome construction which is a feature of early oriental basilicas and mosques. It is a freehand pencil drawing, and is not directly based on any of those in Grelot's printed version. Rather, it appears to derive from conversations, and to be based on drawings, shared with Wren by Chardin, including the measured drawings in Chardin's possession, which Evelyn refers to. However the drawing came to be made, its discovery among drawings for St Paul's reveals that during the 1680s Wren was aware of the oriental precedent for double-dome construction, and that they are likely to have played some part in the discussions which produced Wren and Hooke's success- ive modifications of their ideas for a cupola, which eventually produced the sensational soaring outer dome and inner hemisphere at St Paul's.[97]

The double vaulting of domes was not the only aspect of exotic construction techniques communicated by oriental enthusiasts to attract Wren's interest. When he came to the problem of how best to hang the lead cladding for the outer wooden dome for durability, while adding as little additional weight as possible, Wren again found himself with convenient access to non-Western alternatives. This time it was Sir Dudley North, who was himself something of an amateur in architecture and who had spent twenty years in government service at Smyrna, who supplied Wren with the relevant information:

> Our merchant [North] was a builder himself; and no foreigner ever looked more strictly into the manner of the Turkish buildings than he had done. But he could not give Sir Christopher Wren satisfaction about their covering their vaults with lead. For, when he had the covering of the great dome of St. Paul's in deliberation, he was pleased to inquire of that matter. The merchant informed him so far, as to assure him, the Turks never laid lead upon wood, but upon loam, or mere clay only: but how they fastened it he could not tell. . . .
>
> Our merchant told us, that the ordinary covering of porticoes were half-sweep vaults, which stood like mole-hills in a row; and that all public buildings whatever were covered with vaults, and leaded upon loam. And that lead lasted 2000 years; when upon wood it would be corrupted into white lead in half the time. It is hard to say, why our plumbers should not, for so great an advantage, make the experiment of house-lead upon loam. The merchant told us, that the very metal of lead, that had hung anciently upon loam, was worth much more money than new lead. So much was it purified by the weather, and no white lead ever found under it, as upon oak, which eats the sheets of lead to paper in a few years: and what remains of the metal is not so much improved.

In this case, however, Wren was not convinced. The matter was critical – the load of the outer wooden structure had to be as light as possible, given the huge weight of the inner masonry dome, cone and lantern – and he decided in favour of a shell of narrow horizontal wooden lathes, to which the lead sheets were nailed:

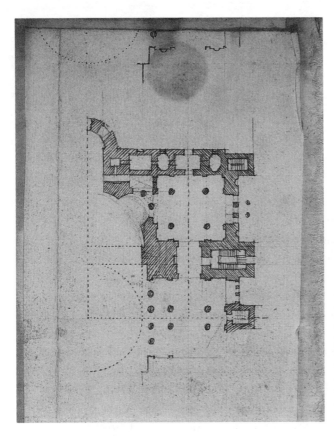

Details of the plan of Hagia Sophia, possibly by Hawksmoor– Chardin showed drawings and plans from his oriental travels at the Royal Society.

Sir Christopher was not satisfied, that the lead would hang upon loam, and not slip, without some fastening; wherein lay the whole difficulty: for if it was done with iron nails, or spikes, the iron would rust and lose its hold. It is not impossible but lead, dressed home upon loam, may hang by a sort of union, as the weight and friction together might make. But, as I said, the architect would scarce venture what was not absolutely secure, in a place so exposed; and caused the shell to be boarded, and plates of lead let in and nailed to the board, and the sheets to be a little opened, and then soldered to those plates; and so it hangs.[98]

A near-contemporary carpentry manual by Francis Price contains a plate showing the form of the wooden structure for the outer dome, and, in the accompanying text, draws particular attention to the originality of Wren's solution for hanging the lead:

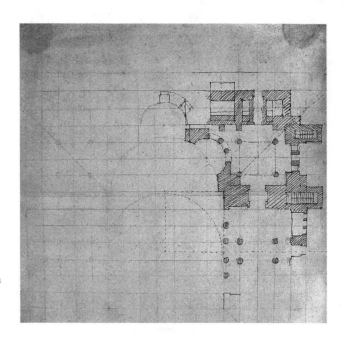

Details of the plan
of Hagia Sophia,
possibly by
Hawksmoor.

> This Dome has not Purlins in it, but is prepared with small
> Ribs that lie horizontally; so that the Boards that are nailed
> thereon, stand as it were upright. In so large a Work, these said
> Ribs ... are placed so as that their Sides tend to the Center of
> the Dome, and which gives the Center for their proper Sweep,
> or Curve.[99]

The narrow horizontal 'ribs' which ultimately support the lead of the
outer dome can still be seen today in unrestored areas not accessible to
the public. In Wren's final decision for the structure of the outer dome,
the juxtaposition of a proposed Eastern alternative with methods drawn
from traditional English carpentry produces, in the end, a typically
unusual solution which combines lightness with supporting strength.

THE STRUCTURAL ENGINEER ON
THE ST PAUL'S DOME

As in the case of the outer dome, Wren characteristically combined his
close study of Eastern and Western dome prototypes with structural
(or, as he would have it, 'geometrical') solutions based on the most

up-to-date knowledge drawn from science and mathematics. As always, it was with Hooke that he discussed each successive version of the proposed construction, modifying it in the light of Hooke's particular flair for structural engineering. Although the final design was probably not fixed until 1704, the year after Hooke's death, it undoubtedly incorporates crucial design features which draw on Hooke's advice.

As Wren rose to public prominence, Hooke figured less often and less prominently in the public side of matters associated with Wren's architectural projects, including St Paul's. He continued, nevertheless, to play an important advisory role in the engineering involved in the construction process, particularly as designs were modified in response to what was happening on the site. We know from Hooke's diary that he was regularly at St Paul's, and that he frequently met with Wren there (and afterwards in one of their favourite coffee houses) to discuss design modifications, or solve problems which had emerged as the building rose. The inevitable adjustments to details, involving decisions taken in consultation with the master masons and master carpenters who took direct responsibility for the building's construction, were often, presumably, made by Hooke, or by Hooke and Wren in collaboration. In particular, the final resolution of the problem of the dome as a whole was largely a result of the mathematical advances in understanding stresses in arches which Wren and Hooke arrived at together in the late 1670s.

Shortly after Wren's appointment to the post of Chief Surveyor, Hooke made a model for him of an inverted dome out of chain links held in shape by the force of gravity. Hooke added weights and additional links until he had achieved an aesthetically pleasing bell-like shape.[100] He then imagined the dish-shape inverted, so it stood with its aperture facing downwards. The tension forces would now, he contended, reverse into pure compressions, whose distribution would perfectly simulate those of a completed masonry-constructed dome, with buttresses to support trusses at critical points (inverting the added weights into pressures). In fact, we know today that the stable equilibrium of the dish becomes unstable when inverted, so that minute errors of construction are likely to cause distortion and cracking. Nevertheless, the engineer's imaginative move here is an importantly innovative one, translating pure geometry into statics – in practical terms, transforming the idea on the page into built form.[101]

Hooke first raised the subject of optimised load-bearing arches in his weekly experimental presentations to the Royal Society in early December 1670. On 12 January Oldenburg (as ever preoccupied with matters of priority, and oblivious to the possibility of collaborative investigation) mentioned that Wren also had a demonstration of the distribution of load; Hooke and Wren together made an oral presentation at a Royal Society meeting on 19 January 1671. Presumably Hooke then went off to do the long-term experimental work necessary to take the topic further. A year after his original announcement, on 7 December 1671, Hooke 'produced the representation of the figure of the arch of a cupola for the sustaining such and such determinate weights, and found it to be a cubico-paraboloid conoid'.[102] He added that 'by this figure might be determined all the difficulties in architecture about arches and butments'.[103] On the same day, Evelyn recorded in his diary that he had spent the afternoon at the Royal Society, where 'were examined some draughts of arches to sustaine a Cupola'.[104] The Royal Society's own records tell us that:

> Mr. Hooke produced the representation of the figure of the arch of a cupola for the sustaining such and such determinate weights, and found it to be a cubico-paraboloid conoid; adding that by this figure might be determined all the difficulties in architecture about arches and butments.[105]

On Saturday, 5 June 1675 Hooke records in his diary: 'At Sir Chr[istopher] Wren. . . . He was making up of my principle about arches and altered his module by it.'[106]

Hooke recorded his rationale for such a masonry dome-shape based on the imagined inversion of a hanging catenary, in an anagram inserted at the end of the 1676 printed version of his 1674 Cutlerian lectures ('To fill the vacancy of the ensuing page I have here added a decimate of the centesme of the Inventions I intend to publish, though possibly not in the same order, but as I can get opportunity and leasure . . .'). Decoded the formula ran: 'As it hangs in a continuous flexible form, so it will stand contiguously rigid when inverted.'[107]

Hooke's solution to the technical problem posed by Wren's ambitious design for the dome of St Paul's displays engineering virtuosity on a grand scale. The inner 'cone' supports the seventy-foot lantern, which weighs a formidable 850 tons. The columns which support this are angled inwards, taking the thrust of the masonry directly. The further buttresses at the foot of this 'cone' are concealed by the peristyle; it also bears the weight of the wooden trusses which support the external dome. Even so, Wren made further provision for the huge outward thrust at the base of his dome:

> Altho' the Dome wants no Butment, yet, for greater Caution, it is hooped with Iron in this Manner; a Chanel is cut in the Bandage of Portland-stone, in which is laid a double Chain of Iron strongly linked together at every ten Feet, and the whole Chanel filled up with Lead.[108]

Taken together, all these – to some, almost brutal – engineered solutions to the phenomenal load of the dome structure respond to Hooke's original understanding that, for stability, the masonry of an arch must accommodate within it the curve of a pure catenary.

The unique dome construction makes a further connection between Wren and Hooke's more conventionally Royal Society-style scientific activities and their collaborative work in structural engineering. The cone supporting the St Paul's outer dome has a small 'oculus' or light-admitting aperture at its top; below this is the perfect hemisphere of the inner dome, with a considerably larger oculus.[109] Light enters the upper oculus indirectly, via gaps in the outer dome. The larger aperture gives the illusion, however, that light is flooding into St Paul's – the arrangement resembled the two apertures of a microscope with one lens stopped down to reduce the coloured fringes of chromatic aberration, and indirect side-illumination of a kind Hooke invented, and of which he prints a picture in *Micrographia*. To the observer with his microscope, the reduced aperture does not alter the illusion that light is filling the eyepiece lens, as long as there is further ambient light available; similarly, the person standing beneath the dome of St Paul's believes the lower aperture to be 'filled' with light.[110]

If the structure of the dome of St Paul's is lasting testimony to the scientific and mathematical knowledge of its architect, the Cathedral as a whole is also a memorial to the union in Wren's mind of architectural beauty and multi-purpose functionality. Successive designs for St Paul's evidence a sustained pragmatic commitment to a belief that the most important buildings constructed since the Fire should serve a dual purpose – as national monuments and as over-sized scientific instruments.[111]

We know that Wren hoped to use the south-west tower at St Paul's as a telescope during the lengthy period when the Cathedral was under construction. Since the south-west tower was designed to house a clock with a long pendulum, its vertical shaft was suitable to serve as a telescope right up to the point at which it was finally roofed (and the clock fitted). The Royal Society Council Minutes for February 1704 record that Wren proposed using lenses with a 123-foot focal length, supplied by Constantijn Huygens junior (Christiaan's brother, and secretary to William III) in 1692, but that it had proved difficult to use them effectively: 'Sir Christopher Wren proposed that the Telescope given by Mr Huygens to ye Society should be set up in [St.] Pauls and astronomicall observations made. The Councell thanked him & desired him to take care of it.'[112] The attempt is confirmed in another contemporary account:

> As to St. Paul's church, the first stone was laid on the 21 of June 1675, and the body of it finished, and the cross set up, in the year 1711; tho many other works, necessary to perfect and adorn that magnificent structure, were done afterwards. And here Sir Christopher designed to make use of the hollow in the great staircase on the fourth side, being in height 96 feet 10 inches, for the like purpose as the Monument, by the assistance of the great telescope presented to the royal society by Mr. Huygens; and his kinsman, the ingenious mathematician, Mr. James Hodgson was to have made the observations. But finding that instrument, which is 123 feet long, too large for his use, and not being able to procure any other of a proper sise, he was prevented likewise from the execution of that design.[113]

James Hodgson was a talented young astronomer whom Wren had recommended to Flamsteed to help take observations at the Royal Observatory, and who later became something of a celebrity giving public lectures on astronomy in London coffee houses.[114] A man of resolutely practical bent, Wren could rely on him to carry out his observations amid the chaos and inconvenience of a construction site, unlike the astronomers at the Royal Observatory, who demanded undisturbed tranquillity for theirs.

Front elevation of St Paul's, showing the south-west tower (on the right), which Wren hoped to use during construction as a zenith telescope.

BUILT TO LAST

In spite of Wren's insistence that he built for eternity, and his meticulous attention to structure as the key to monumental permanency, repeated, calamitous outbreaks of fire in major buildings with whose construction he had been involved saw to it that significant examples of his work perished in his lifetime. There was a fire at Whitehall Palace, where Wren had first exercised his architectural talents in royal employment, in both 1691 and 1698. The 1691 fire was limited in its extent and consequences, but the conflagration of 4 January 1698 devastated the King's and Queen's lodgings at Whitehall, and left few buildings intact. The fire started on the waterside, and moved west. As in 1691, gunpowder was used to try and prevent the flames from spreading and workmen were 'forced to blow up the treasury office, and on the other side the water-gate, and the buildings adjoining the chapel'. The precious Banqueting Hall was thereby saved, but practically nothing else. James Vernon wrote that 'Except the banqueting house and the great gate all is burnt down or blown up on the privy garden side.'

On being told of the fire William III vowed that 'if god would give him leave he would rebuild them much finer than before'. Yet again, plans were revived for a major royal and administrative building complex at Whitehall. A contemporary diarist noted in March 1698 that 'His Majesty has given directions to Sir Christopher Wren to erect a range of buildings at the end of the banqueting house next the privy gardens; but the rest will be omitted until the parliament provide for the same.' Once again the undertaking foundered; although Wren produced two alternative schemes for the rebuilding of Whitehall, other building commitments, foreign wars and the accompanying inevitable shortage of ready funds prevented them from getting beyond the drawing-board. Queen Anne also entertained the idea of rebuilding the palace she had occupied as princess of Denmark: 'Tis said that her majesty has given Kensington to prince george for his life; and she designs to rebuild whithal [Whitehall], and for that purpose will set aside £100,000 per annum out of her revenue, which will finish the same in 6 years.' But nothing came of this either.[115]

In spite of the rhetoric of Restoration and continuity, the experience of Wren and those to whom he was close at court and in the City, in the years following the return of Charles II, was of a precarious, fickle world of public affairs. Shifting times and changing monarchies left them with a compulsion to establish lasting monuments. This is evident from shortly after the Restoration, and becomes a defining feature of the reigns of James, William and Mary, and Anne. The more precarious the situation, the more robustly the claim is made that the outcome of an undertaking will be a 'lasting monument' to whatever is being proposed. In some curious way, Wren's specific talents in the domains of both architecture and science meant that he was looked to to provide both material monuments to the age and its intellectual 'monuments' – lasting evidence of the advances in knowledge produced in England after 1660.

It has to be said that many such attempts were resounding failures. One need only instance the magnificent Clarendon House, built by Sir Roger Pratt to serve as a lasting monument to Henry Hyde, first Earl of Clarendon, Chancellor to Charles I, and father of James, Duke of York's first wife Anne. Completed in 1666, and hugely admired by connoisseurs of continental architecture like Evelyn, it was pulled down in 1683, following Clarendon's fall from political favour and exile.

Nevertheless, in July 1668 Pratt was knighted for his services to architecture (the first man thus to be elevated), largely on the strength of the Clarendon commission.

John Evelyn has recorded for us both the splendour of the original building and general sentiments among gentlemen-about-town regarding its demolition. Shortly after the house was finished (though not yet fitted), in January 1666, he wrote:

> Here is state and use, solidity and beauty most symetrically combin'd together. Seriously there is nothing abroad pleases me better, nothing at home approaches it. . . . When I had seriously contemplated every roome (for I went into all of them, from the cellar to the plat-forme on the roofe) seene how well and judiciously the walls were erected, the arches cut and turned, the timber braced, their scantlings and contignations disposed, I was incredibly satisfied, and do acknowledge myselfe to have much improved by what I observed. What shall I add more? Rumpatur invidia, I pronounce it the first Palace of England, deserving all I have said of it, and a better Encomiast.[116]

Seventeen years later, on 18 August 1683, Evelyn reflected with emotion on the disappearance of what had, comparatively recently, seemed like a permanent landmark to Clarendon's magnificence:

> After dinner I walked to survey the sad demolition of Clarendon House, that costly and only sumptuous palace of the late Lord Chancellor Hyde, where I have often been so cheerful with him, and sometimes so sad. . . . The Earl his successor sold that which cost £50,000 building, to the young Duke of Albermarle for £25,000 to pay debts which how contracted remains yet a mystery. . . . He sold it to the highest bidder, and it fell to certain rich bankers and mechanics, who gave for it and the ground about it £35,000. . . . 'Tis said they have already materials towards it [St James's Square] with what they sold of the house alone, more worth than what they paid for it. See the vicissitudes of earthly things!

Pratt did not belong to the circle of London virtuosi – indeed, Evelyn was careful, even as he praised Clarendon House elaborately, to register certain reservations about his design ability. Wren, by contrast, had established a reputation, as early as the late 1660s, as creator of lasting memorials, both intellectual and material.

Nevertheless, as far as ordinary Londoners were concerned, St Paul's as completed in 1711 was, and always would be, that fabulous phoenix risen from the ashes of the Great Fire, promised them by Charles II in 1666. Its symbolic promise of revival, figured in the phoenix, and the inscription 'resurgam' – I shall rise again – beneath, has become, indeed, the motto and aspiration of the City of London itself.[117] For them, the dome is not so much a triumph of engineering or a tribute to the birth of modern science as a reminder, glimpsed unexpectedly from so many points in the crowded city streetscape, of regeneration born out of determination never to submit to tyranny.

As told in *Parentalia*, the story of the origin of the motto 'Resurgam' does indeed link the heroic process whereby London's Cathedral rose again specifically with the dome:

> In the Beginning of the new Works of St. Paul's, an Incident was taken notice of by some People as a memorable Omen, when the Surveyor in Person had set out, upon the Place, the Dimensions of the great Dome, and fixed upon the Centre; a common Labourer was ordered to bring a flat Stone from the Heaps of Rubbish, (such as should first come to Hand) to be laid for a Mark and Direction to the Masons; the Stone which was immediately brought down for that Purpose, happened to be a Piece of a Grave-stone, with nothing remaining of the Inscription but this single word in large Capitals, RESURGAM.[118]

Symbolically, it is indeed the soaring cupola, whose centre Wren apocryphally marked out with the original foundations, which elicits the phoenix-like 'I will rise again' promise of the inscription. And it was the putting in place of the 'highest or last Stone' of the dome's lantern which marked the Cathedral's completion (though, as in all buildings, much remained to be done, in terms of external elaboration and interior finish). That final act was carried out, with due ceremony, by Wren's son Christopher:

428 · ON A GRANDER SCALE

The highest or last Stone on the Top of the Lantern was laid by the Hands of the Surveyor's Son, Christopher Wren, deputed by his Father, in the Presence of that excellent artificer Mr. Strong, his Son, and other Free and Accepted Masons, chiefly employed in the Execution of the work.[119]

Hooke had by this time been dead for more than seven years, and at seventy-nine Sir Christopher himself was past climbing all those stairs, though his mind remained as sharp as ever. Christopher Wren junior's deputising on this solemn occasion was particularly appropriate, because it marked the close of a project which had in reality spanned two generations. For the same reason, Edward Strong, master mason on so many of Wren's most important projects, was accompanied at the ceremony by his son, Edward Strong junior, who had followed his father as a mason in Wren's regular employ, and had, indeed, been responsible for the building of the St Paul's lantern.[120]

Since the death in close succession of both Hooke and Wren's favourite child, Jane, Christopher junior had finally managed to build a close relationship with his previously distant and remote father, agreeing to an appointment as Chief Clerk in the Office of Works, though earlier he had resisted following his father into architectural practice. After 1703, Christopher substituted for his father in all kinds of public activities, not only those involving his architectural expertise, but also those involving the wide range of public committees on which he sat. With increasing regularity, Christopher Wren junior was appointed to Royal Society committees alongside his father, to assist his father in carrying out whatever tasks were required of him. Beginning in 1710, for instance, Wren junior effectively ran the project to build a 'repository' for the Royal Society at its new premises in Crane's Court, to Wren senior's design. He – but not his father – sat on the committee which drew up the brief, and on 28 March he wrote to the Secretary:

By my father's direction a Modell is made of the room for ye Repository of ye. Royal-Society in Crane Court, wch. may give ye Gentlemen a better idea, then the designe on paper: It will be very light, very commodious, and the cheapest building that can be contrived: I have sent the Joyner with it to you, that you may take yr. Opportunity to show it to ye. Councill; it will be necessary not to loose the season of ye. year in ye. execution. I shall indeavour to attend at ye. next meeting.[121]

On such occasions, Wren's son's lack of personal charisma or (apparently) ambition made him the ideal amanuensis and facilitator. He invariably implemented his father's wishes to the letter, assiduously and without causing any kind of friction – something Hooke, in spite of his devotion to Wren, could never have achieved. Hooke may have been the most loyal of friends, but unquestioning obedience was simply not in his nature.

To grasp the change to the tenor of Wren's life once his diffident son took Hooke's place as his second-in-command, we might reflect on a single incident, referred to earlier, right at the beginning of the process which led to the rebuilding of St Paul's. In 1673, when Wren began supervising the demolitions at the St Paul's site, he expedited the arduous and difficult work of taking down the existing fabric by using carefully controlled charges of explosives. Having established the procedure, he was called away on Royal Surveyor's business. In *Parentalia*, his son Christopher records what happened next:

> [Wren] left the Management of another Mine begun, to the Care of his next Officer, who too wise in his own Conceit, put in a greater Quantity of Powder, and neither went low enough, nor sufficiently fortified the Mouth of the Mine; and tho' it had the Effect, yet one Stone was shot out to the opposite Side of the Church-yard, through an open Window, into a Room of a private House, where some Women were sitting at Work, without any Harm done; this Accident frighted the Neigbours to that Degree, that he was importun'd to use no more Powder, and was so directed also by his Superiors, tho' with due Caution it might have been executed without any Hazard, and sav'd much Time and Money.[122]

The person who accidentally blew up the houses adjacent to St Paul's during demolitions while Wren was away – 'his next Officer', who was 'too wise in his own Conceit' – was, of course, Hooke. Quite incapable of implementing Wren's careful orders without some input of his own (in this case, increasing the charge), his intervention meant that thereafter Wren was obliged to use more conventional methods to take down

Old St Paul's, at considerable cost in terms of time and effort.[123] Yet, in spite of such occasional disasters, out of the inventive dialogue between Wren and Hooke came solutions to practical problems of great collaborative originality, throughout the two men's careers. There are no such moments of creative ingenuity in Wren's relationship with his dutiful and invariably obedient son Christopher.

8

Ambitious to Leave Great Monuments

FRIEND AND CHAMPION:
THE WREN–HOOKE ROYAL SOCIETY LEGACY

By the time St Paul's finally reached completion, Wren's son Christopher had stepped discreetly and competently into the shoes of his father's trusted professional colleague Hooke. Hooke, nevertheless, was irreplaceable; his death deprived Wren of his closest and truest companion. Wren had turned seventy the autumn before Hooke's death in spring 1703. The loss of the friend with whom he had shared almost every aspect of his career since adolescence was the second emotional blow within the space of a year – Wren's beloved daughter, the talented Jane, had died the previous year aged only twenty-six. Two other members of the close circle with whom he socialised regularly, Fox and Evelyn, had recently retired from public life to the country.[1] Since adolescence Jane Wren had been her father's companion and amanuensis with whom he shared whatever intimacy was to be had at home. Hooke was Wren's unstintingly loyal and supportive colleague at work, the person to whom he had always turned with both his professional and his private problems.

Hooke died on 3 March 1703. His later years had been dogged by illness; for the last year of his life he had been confined to home and virtually bedridden.[2] Although he had stepped down from his

432

professional responsibilities in the Wren architectural office and at the Royal Society in the mid-1690s, after several bouts of ill health, he had carried on with his social life and his intellectual activities – including his passionate discussions of scientific problems with friends like Wren – at least until 1699.[3] His funeral was an appropriately grand occasion, and a fitting finale for one of the founding figures of London Restoration science. As his biographer and friend Richard Waller wrote: 'His Corps was decently and handsomely interr'd in the Church of St. Hellen in London, all the Members of the Royal Society then in Town attending his Body to the Grave, paying the Respect due to his extraordinary Merit.'[4]

Why, then, given Wren's lifelong commitment to the memory of those he loved and admired, did he leave no enduring memorial to Robert Hooke? Tributes to those who had nurtured and supported Wren are liberally scattered throughout his written remains, yet nowhere do we find the heartfelt acknowledgement of the crucial role Hooke had played. The answer may have been that, as far as Wren himself was concerned, he had indeed created a lasting monument to Hooke, in the form of the purpose-built premises for the Royal Society which had been Wilkins's and Hooke's dream since the 1660s, and into which the Society moved its collection of rarities, and its experimental activities, in summer 1712.

In the last year of Hooke's life, during the summer of 1702, shortly after the accession of Queen Anne, Wren had once again become involved in plans by the Royal Society to expand their home at Gresham College.[5] The Gresham College authorities applied for permission to completely rebuild the College's premises. This created the opportunity to make the facilities there used by the Royal Society match their needs more closely, including creating a repository (or exhibition space) to house their collection of rarities and instruments, and laboratory space for their experimental activities. Wren submitted a 'Proposal for Building a House for the R. Society' to the President, John, Lord Somers (formerly Lord Chancellor, under William III, and a figure of some political influence):

It is proposed as absolutely necessary for the continuing the Royal Society at Gresham College, that they should have a place so Seated in the said Ground, that the Coaches of the Members (some of which are of very great Quality) may have easy access, and that the Building consist of these necessary parts.

1. A Cellar under Ground so high above it, as to have good lights for the Use of an Elaboratory and House-keeper.
2. The Story above may have a fair Room and a large Closet.
3. A Place for a Repository over them.
4. A Place for the Library over the Repository.
5. A Place Covered with Lead, for observing the Heavens.
6. A good Stair Case from bottom to Top.
7. A reasonable Area behind it, to give light to the Back Rooms.

All which may be comprized in a Space of Ground Forty Foot in Front and Sixty Foot Deep.[6]

Almost immediately, however, the prospects for expansion as part of the rebuilding of Gresham College were abruptly halted with the death of Hooke, since the Society's continued occupancy of the Gresham premises was contingent on his residency there. Hooke's position as a Gresham professor entitled him to residential accommodation in the buildings. As a sitting tenant, he had in fact taken court action the previous year to prevent the Gresham trustees from evicting him to begin demolitions and the rebuilding programme for which they were seeking parliamentary permission.

Three week's after Hooke's death, on 24 March, the trustees of Gresham College notified the Royal Society that they were to remove themselves and their belongings from the College forthwith, and return the keys to Hooke's lodgings. It would undoubtedly have amused Hooke, could he have known, that his death immediately presented the new President, Newton (who had refused to have anything to do with the Society as long as Hooke was active within it), with the serious problem of where to house the Society.

A hastily assembled committee, to which Wren was appointed, succeeded in negotiating a stay of execution of the Society's eviction from Gresham until new premises could be found. A year later, in February 1704, at a meeting at which Wren was present, the Council voted to place the matter of finding them new accommodation explicitly in Wren's hands:

> They also desired Sir Christopher Wren that he would please to take the trouble of viewing the design and project and

consider what accommodation the Society wanted and to resolve by Changing or purchasing Ground fit for their affairs to add to what the Committees offer for their accommodation.

It was not until 1710 that a property that met with the committee's approval became available.[7] On 8 September Newton informed the Council that there was an opportunity to purchase 'the late Dr. Browns House in Crane Court in Fleet Street being now to be sold being in the middle of the Town out of Noise'. The Dr Browne in question was none other than the Edward Browne (son of Sir Thomas Browne) who had accompanied Wren on his sightseeing trip to the region outside Paris in 1665. Evidently it was Wren and his son, Christopher Wren junior, who decided it was suitable. On 13 September 1710 Newton wrote to Sir Hans Sloane, the Society's Secretary:

> [I] am glad Sr Christopher & Mr Wren like the house [&] hope they like the price also. I have inclosed a Note [to] Mr Hunt to call a Council on Saturday next at [twe]lve a clock, & beg the favour that you would send [it] to him by the Porter who brings you this.[8]

On 2 November Wren, his son, and Richard Waller (the Society's Curator) were authorised to negotiate with a Mr Brigstock, the house's tenant, to purchase any fittings which might suit the Society: 'Sir Christopher Wren, Mr. Wren and Mr. Waller were Appointed a Committee to see what Mr. Brigstock leaves in the House that may be usefull to the Society and of what Value they may be.' The committee reported back on 30 November: 'Mr. Brigstock was Ordered to have thirty Guineas for the Wainscot and other things he leaves in the House at Crane Court according to the Report of Sir Christopher Wren, Mr. Wren and Mr. Waller.' Wren senior appears to have been closely involved in the renovations needed to make the new accommodation habitable, in spite of the fact that he was by now seventy-eight years old (as with a number of other projects in these years, his son Christopher, appointed alongside him for the purpose, often deputised for him).[9]

In March 1711 it was agreed that in addition to refurbishment of the existing house, the Society would build a 'New Repository' at Crane Court. Wren senior was asked to design it. On 28 March Wren junior wrote to the Secretary:

By my father's direction a Modell is made of the room for ye Repository of ye. Royal-Society in crane Court, wch. may give ye Gentlemen a better idea, then the designe on paper: It will be very light, very commodious, and the cheapest building that can be contrived: I have sent the Joyner with it to you, that you may take yr. opportunity to show it to ye. Councill. . . .[10]

Now, however, the project stalled. As on every previous occasion when accommodation specially built for its purposes had been considered, the Royal Society was unable to come up with the money needed to get the building started. Contracts had to be negotiated with masons and carpenters, and these could only be commenced once cash, and regular settlement of bills, could be guaranteed. There had already been problems covering the purchase of Crane Court and seeing to its repairs. When Wren's design was costed, the figure was almost exactly twice the £200 the Society had budgeted for their new Repository. This time, however, two active members of the Society stepped in and saved the day. Richard Waller gave £300 to get the project moving, and £100 in the course of construction.[11] Hunt, the Society's Operator, in charge of the existing, run-down Repository, contributed the astonishing sum of £900 (as two separate donations).[12]

The Repository was finished in a year, and on 8 April 1712 a committee was appointed 'to take care of the due placing of the Curiosities in the New Repository built by Mr. Waller'. The very last building actively designed by Wren became the first real, properly appointed home for the Royal Society, in whose foundation and rise the architect had played such a prominent part.

In Wren's own mind (and among those in his immediate circle), it is likely that the Royal Society Repository building stood as a final and fitting memorial to his lifelong friend Robert Hooke. The evidence for this is to be found in the surprise production of that £1300 which turned the new Crane Street building from pipe-dream to reality.

The committee convened to handle the Crane Court accommodation problems following Hooke's death consisted of his oldest and dearest friend Sir Christopher Wren, Wren's son (Clerk of the Royal Works, and by now substituting for his father's regular attendance at meetings of all kinds), and Richard Waller, Hooke's closest friend and confidant at the time of his death. Waller was the person who, in the absence of near relatives, took charge of Hooke's post-mortem affairs, and who edited the 1705 edition of his *Posthumous Works*, which includes a Life of Hooke.[13] The other crucial player in the successful completion of the building was Henry Hunt, Hooke's protégé, and employee of the Royal Society (their clerk and demonstrator), who had spent his entire adult life in Hooke's service, and who (as the diary entries for the period after 1688 show) attended Hooke every day in the later years of his life, as companion and amanuensis.[14] On the basis of their involvement in the events that followed, it can be claimed with some confidence that the Crane Street Repository was in fact the final scientific and architectural collaboration between Wren and Hooke.

At Hooke's death, we are told, he left just under £10,000 in cash, in an iron chest (perhaps the one in which he had brought his father's books to London from the Isle of Wight in 1648).[15] Although he died intestate, there was an unsigned will, drafted five days before his death, which is now lodged alongside the probate inventory in the Public Record Office.[16] It indicates that Hooke intended to divide his considerable wealth (in cash) between four friends (unspecified: referred to in the draft simply as A, B, C, D), and that they had instructions on how to dispense certain sums. Waller recorded that Hooke had told him he wanted his money to go, at his death, to the Royal Society, so that new quarters, meeting rooms, laboratories and a library might be constructed:

> I indeed, as well as others, have heard him declare sometimes that he had a great Project in his Head as to the disposal of the most part of his Estate for the advancement of Natural Knowledge, and to promote the Ends and Designs for which the Royal Society was instituted: To build an handsome Fabrick for the Societies use, with a Library, Repositary, Laboratory, and other Conveniences for making Experiments, and to found and endow a perpetual 'Physico-Mechanick Lecture' of the Nature of what himself read.[17]

Waller and Wren together were responsible for the arrangements immediately following Hooke's death which led to the provision of a purpose-built repository and library at Crane Street, which contemporary guide books describe as 'in a little paved Court' behind the main house at 'Two Crane Court in Fleetstreet'. It continues: 'The Repository of Curiosities is a Theatrical Building, resembling that of Leyden in Holland.' Hooke would have been delighted with the Dutch influence, and with the allusion to the theatre he had himself designed for the Royal College of Physicians.

A cousin of Hooke's (who signed her name with a cross in the probate documents) inherited the major part of his fortune. Some of the money, however, inevitably found its way to his close friend Waller, for the sorting out of his affairs, disposing of his substantial library, and editing and publishing his *Posthumous Works*. It seems reasonable to assume that Hunt too received some kind of financial gift, as the person who had cared for Hooke throughout his final illness, providing him with a measure of company and affection; Hunt may even have received some kind of recompense directly from Hooke, during his last days.

The Royal Society Repository project was Hooke's known last wish, vehemently expressed as such to those around him. The substantial sums in cash which Waller and Hunt produced to save Wren's Repository project from being shelved, as all previous Society building projects had been (Waller not a wealthy man, and Hunt a mere employee), were surely from Hooke's funds. But since Sir Isaac Newton, the President of the Royal Society, could – notoriously – not bear the mention of Hooke's name, the benefaction necessarily remained anonymous. Newton had recently dealt savagely with another long-term adversary, John Flamsteed, expelling him from the Royal Society. It is unlikely that an appeal for posthumous clemency for Hooke would have fared any better.

It was in the course of the move of the Society's rarities from Gresham College to the new Repository at Crane Court that the Royal Society portrait of Hooke, seen by a foreign visitor to the Society a year earlier, and his instruments were lost. Was the portrait perhaps appropriated by someone who believed that under Newton's Presidency Hooke's legacy of scientific instruments would be so neglected as to endanger their survival? Henry Hunt was in charge of the removals from Gresham to Crane Court: in late June 1711 the Council ordered Hunt to remove the Society's 'curiosities' from Gresham College and transfer them to Crane Court 'with what convenient speed he could'.[18]

If Hunt did quietly remove the portrait as a reminder of his old mentor and friend (and because Newton's animus towards Hooke meant it would never be looked after), it is still possible that it will one day

Sir Isaac Newton in maturity, after he had left his reclusive life at Trinity College Cambridge, and become a powerful figure in London, Master of the Mint and President of the Royal Society.

reappear. Then, at last, we will have a visual image of the exceptional man who was such an important part of the life and career of Sir Christopher Wren – a man who, though described by Waller as emaciated and unkempt at the end of his life, was something of a dandy in his heyday, to judge by the numbers of visits to his tailor and wig-maker he recorded in his diary, not to mention his fondness for social gatherings, concerts, plays and coffee shops

FRIEND AND CHAMPION:
MODERATING QUARRELS IN ASTRONOMY

Wren may have become less physically mobile in the last two decades of his life, but his energy and enthusiasm for all kinds of intellectual projects continued unabated. He was still active in London scientific circles well into his eighties, and still contributing regularly to current scientific and mathematical debates until at least 1714. Furthermore, this involvement was far more than nominal – his continued participation in events relating to the field of his early scientific virtuosity, observational astronomy, in particular, had serious repercussions for developments in the field after Sir Isaac Newton became President of the Royal Society in 1704. Without the presence of Wren, Newton's ability to antagonise and alienate other scientists might well have arrested important progress, particularly in the continuing quest for resolution of the problem of determining longitude at sea.

All this was at a time when Wren was still fully responsible as Royal Surveyor, with Greenwich Hospital under construction and St Paul's in the final stages of completion. His responsibilities included a fresh set of concerns at Westminster Abbey, where he had been appointed Surveyor in 1698. That Wren still controlled day-to-day running of all these projects is clear from the strategic way in which his trusted deputies were deployed as each new commission came in to the Wren office. In 1698, when Wren was called on to present Bishop Thomas Pratt with a detailed survey of Westminster Abbey, Hawksmoor was appointed Clerk of Works at Greenwich. In 1713, Wren 'prepared perfect Draughts and Models' for a programme of works at Westminster Abbey which included adding a tower and steeple at the crossing and completing the unfinished West Front.[19] It was agreed that Hawksmoor and John James would from now on take responsibility for drawing up contracts with the masons and preparing the account books at Greenwich, since he was 'too busy elsewhere on the queen's business'.[20]

The considerable part Wren played in settling a series of long-running scientific feuds among members of the Royal Society is a tribute to the esteem and trust in which he was by this time held by those from different walks of life, and across the political spectrum. Wren had always shown an extraordinary capacity for friendship. His natural dignity, personal warmth and mild demeanour inspired confidence in others, and eased the progress of his own career, even in the dark years of the civil war and their aftermath. In youth and maturity these were traits which had helped him build strong working relationships both with his intellectual and social equals and with those he employed as skilled workmen.

After 1702, when Queen Anne – sister of Queen Mary, niece of

Charles II and a Stuart monarch in the old style before William and Mary – followed her sister's husband to the throne, and when political antagonisms sharpened and those harbouring differences became more intransigent with one another, the septuagenarian Wren was called upon to use these personal gifts as bridge-builder and peace-maker. Now Wren's expertise in a diversity of specialist spheres made him an ideal arbitrator to call in to resolve conflict. The most notorious and protracted of these disputes was that between John Flamsteed, the Astronomer Royal, and Sir Isaac Newton, Warden of the Mint and (after 1704) President of the Royal Society. It included, as minor players, two more of Wren's close colleagues, Edmond Halley and (until his death) Robert Hooke.

In championing Flamsteed, Wren took on the task, once again, of protecting an outstandingly scientifically gifted individual, with a particular talent for observational astronomy and an unwavering commitment to the pursuit of knowledge. Like his own, Flamsteed's rise to the position of Astronomer Royal had depended on the patronage of a well-placed man of means (in this case Sir Jonas Moore) with influence at court, who had promoted his talents astutely so as to gain him secure employment. As with Hooke, Flamsteed's rise was hampered by his difficult personality, as well as by his lack of family connections to back up the opportunities of patronage. Like Hooke, too, Flamsteed, however high he rose, continued throughout his career to think of himself as marginal – an outsider – constantly thwarted by others more fortunate than himself (perhaps that is why Hooke and Flamsteed found it so hard to get on with one another).

The Astronomer Royal had never been an easy man to deal with. Secretive by temperament, his obsession with accuracy in his astronomical observations and subsequent calculations made him permanently reluctant to release the tables for the positions of the fixed stars, of lunar and planetary movements, and any other data he generated at the Royal Observatory. The difficulties this caused, in view of the fact that he had been appointed precisely in order to produce such tables and measurements rapidly, began very shortly after his appointment in 1675. Sir Jonas Moore, who had proposed him as Astronomer Royal, was impatient for improved star charts for navigation, to assist the military, and unsympathetic with Flamsteed's reluctance to publish anything short of the complete set of the most precise observations possible.

John Flamsteed, first Astronomer Royal at the Royal Greenwich Observatory, a man temperamentally unsuited to the pressure put on him, first by Sir Jonas Moore and then by Newton, to publish his observations.

Already on 11 December 1675 Flamsteed wrote to fellow astronomer Richard Towneley: 'I would gladly have had the observations [I have made] laien by till wee had a greater number and better but Sir Jonas thinkes it requisite to publish these to satisfie some persons that enquire oft what wee are doeing, that wee are not Idle.' Relations between the two men were soon strained, and Flamsteed's natural reticence developed into a truculence verging, when provoked, on the belligerent.

The defensive attitude Flamsteed quickly developed was further exacerbated by misunderstandings from the outset between himself and the Royal Society.[21] Flamsteed had made overtures to the Royal Society from 1669 onwards, and even assured its Secretary, Oldenburg, that he was prepared to communicate astronomical observations for the private use of the Society.[22] When news broke in 1674 that Sir Jonas Moore proposed financing a Royal Observatory, it was hoped that this would take advantage of the site the Society owned at Chelsea, and it was assumed that it would be established as an integral part of the Society's activities:

Mr. Hooke acquainted the council, that Sir Jonas Moore had been with him at Chelsea College, and made an overture of engaging a gardiner, a sufficient man, to take a lease of the house and land about it, for a considerable number of years, on condition of repairing the house and wall in the land, and paying a yearly rent for it; allowing withal to the Society a power to make hortulan experiments there; as also to build an astronomical observatory; which latter Sir Jonas Moore himself would undertake to do at his own charge, to the value of an hundred and fifty or two hundred pounds. The proposition was well accepted by the council, and Mr. Hooke was desired to prosecute the business, by urging Sir Jonas Moore to proceed farther in this affair.[23]

Fellows anticipated formal and sustained relations between the two scientific institutions, along the lines of those recently established between the French Académie des Sciences and the Paris Observatory. A week after Hooke's presentation the members elected Sir Jonas Moore to the Royal Society.[24]

Even when the Royal Observatory designed and built by Wren and Hooke was completed in summer 1676, and the Astronomer Royal was settled at Greenwich, the members of the Society acted on the understanding that there would be some formal relationship between the two institutions. In January 1677 they lent a number of astronomical instruments to Flamsteed, and on 8 February they elected the Astronomer Royal to their number.[25] On the first anniversary of the loan, however, Sir Joseph Williamson, the President, 'inquired, why the Society did not receive some account from Mr. Flamsteed: to which Sir Jonas Moore answered, that he would within a fortnight be ready to produce a book of his observations'. Shortly afterwards the inquiry was repeated, the Society asking 'what was become of the instruments of the Society, that had been carried to Greenwich; and it was desired, that they might be returned to the repository, in order that they might be ready for the use of the Society'.

Moore's sudden death on 26 August 1679 added urgency to the request, as it was feared that Sir Jonas's family would claim the instruments, along with those that had been specifically bought for Flamsteed by Moore. On 22 September, the Council ordered 'that Mr. Hunt take care to have all the instruments of the Society now in the custody of Mr. Flamsteed at Greenwich immediately removed to Gresham College; and that Sir Christopher Wren and Mr. Hooke be desired to go thither, and take what care they can in it; and that in the mean time Mr. Hooke write to Mr. Moore [junior] about the same, and desire to have them carefully sent home; and that the committee meet about this affair on the Friday following'. Hooke did as instructed, recording in his diary of 26 September 1679: 'To Flamsteads, I brought back by Hunt and Crawly, Iron Screw quadrant, little brasse screw quadrant, wooden quadrant and ring, 3 reflecting rules. Flamstead mad.' From this point onwards, Flamsteed's relations with Hooke in particular were decidedly tense. Since Hooke was the main point of contact between the Observatory and the Society this further distanced them from one another. Nevertheless, not all the Society's instruments were returned. The affair was still rumbling on in March 1680, when 'Dr. Gale moved, that the Society's instruments at the observatory at Greenwich might be brought back to their repository.'[26]

Flamsteed's friendship with Wren, however, was unaffected by the tension between him and other members of the Royal Society. Warm references to Wren are to be found scattered through Flamsteed's prolific correspondence with other astronomers. When Towneley complained of a smoking chimney, Flamsteed remembered that Wren had a solution for the problem, and consulted Sir Jonas Moore:

> I informed Sir Jonas Moore of Your smokeing Chimny and that you desired to understand from him what was that remidie of Sir C. Wren made use of. Which hee described to me thus. To your Chimny you fasten a tin tube so contrived as you may understand by this figure [Flamsteed drew a diagram]. The lowest part of the tube is so inserted into the next above it as not to touch it but to leave a space of about an inch [marked 'a' on the diagram] betwixt both. This is inserted into the next above it in the same manner, so if the wind shall catch and stop the smoke in the top of the uppermost, it descends not back into the chimny but voyds it selfe in the hollows 'a' 'a' left betwixt the two tubes.[27]

Relations between the Royal Society and the Astronomer Royal improved significantly when Wren became President in late 1680. Wren, who had remained close to Flamsteed ever since their collaborations over the building of the Royal Observatory at Greenwich, was one of the few who, over the years, had managed to retain the Astronomer Royal's trust and affection.[28] Flamsteed – never particularly gregarious – began to play a more active part in the Royal Society's meetings.[29] In February 1681 he delivered to Wren as President the observations Edmond Halley had made of the exceptionally bright comet that had appeared at the end of the previous December (Halley, who acted as Flamsteed's assistant, was at this point in Paris).[30] In January 1682 he wrote to William Molyneux that 'The Society at Gresham Colledge encreases, and I hope in a short time will make good improvements.'[31] The following April Flamsteed described the Society's activities to Molyneux with quite uncharacteristic enthusiasm:

> The Royal Society now grows wealthy [Wren had just success-fully negotiated the sale of Gresham back to the Crown] and I hope from their Stock wee may in some time expect much better thinges then formerly[.] Sir Christopher Wren our President is a person both admirable knowing and discreet[.] hee pushes on all opportunityes for improveing knowledge vigorously.[32]

In the same letter, however, he responded to Molyneux's inquiry as to whether Hooke has succeeded with his many proposed scientific initiatives with the assertion that 'for Mr Hookes vast promises of Inventions I looke upon them onely as boasts or a peece of Contrivance to Magnifie him selfe'.[33] For Flamsteed Wren was a uniquely 'honest' person; towards most others in the Royal Society circle he continued to feel only mistrust and hostility.

The early 1680s was the period during which Flamsteed's friendship with Wren was cemented, and the only period during which Flamsteed interacted with comparative ease with other members of the Royal Society. In June 1682 Flamsteed was actually persuaded to dine out with Wren and the inner circle of his close Society colleagues. Afterwards Wren set him a (for once) recreational astronomical problem. Keen to impress Wren, Flamsteed appealed to Towneley to help him solve it:

> Yesterday I dined with our President Sir Christopher Wren at our Club who as wee were parteing proposed this Problem to me. A person is left on an unknowne Island without any

Mathematicall Instrument. Onely hee has a Catalogue of fixed stars and line and Plumet. With a Clock that will goe true for an hour hee observes two stars in the same Azimuth, and after 40' minutes of time two other stars in another Azimuth. What is his latitude and the true Azimuths of each payre. . . . I could wish you would thinke of this problem at your leasure.[34]

As suggested in Flamsteed's comments to Molyneux, however, the abrasiveness of his relationship with Wren's close friend Hooke continued unabated. When Hooke presented 'a mechanical way of finding the focus of all parallel rays falling upon the spherical superficies of a more dense refracting medium ... by the motion of a certain circle upon a point in its diameter excentrically taken, according to a proportion assigned', following this by showing 'the geometrical ground and demonstration of the same', at a Royal Society meeting in early November 1681, Flamsteed immediately rose to deny the demonstration as 'false and impossible'. Hooke persisted and boasted in the following two weeks that Flamsteed had conceded he was wrong. Three months later, Hooke appealed to Wren for support, declaring at the meeting of 15 February 1682 that Flamsteed's 'cavills' against his method of describing a parabola were unfounded, and that 'it was true and certain, and the best way yet known of describing that curve, and never published before'.

The quarrel between Hooke and Flamsteed rumbled on into 1684, when, during a Council meeting, Flamsteed demanded 'that the journal-book in 1682 might be altered as to some expressions reflecting upon him entered by Mr. Hooke. This was referred to another time.' A few months later, after Flamsteed again complained 'that he had been reflected upon by Mr. Hooke in the minutes of the Society, it was ordered, that a line should be drawn through the places complained of, and that there should be written on the side, cancelled by order of council: and that the journal-book should be brought to the next meeting of the council, who should see it done'.[35]

Throughout this period, Flamsteed and Edmond Halley managed to remain on reasonably good terms. At the outset of his career, the nineteen-year-old Halley had talked his way into a job working with Flamsteed on his observations at Greenwich, by writing to him to point out glaring errors in the current star charts.[36] Though very different in temperament – Halley was as brash, extroverted and entrepreneurial

Paper monuments:
(*top*) manuscript, in
Christopher Wren junior's
hand, of the account for the
Parentalia volume of Sir
Christopher Wren's
proposed Mausoleum to
Charles I at Windsor;
presentation drawing of a
design for a statue of the
'martyred' Charles I in
triumph for the proposed
Mausoleum at Windsor –
'but (alas! because of the
condition of the times)
never built'

Presentation drawings for royalty: (*top*) Wren's presentation drawing of a partial proposed elevation for Whitehall Palace, 1664; drawings by Hawksmoor of designs for fireplaces at Hampton Court Palace – one shows an arrangement for part of Queen Mary's collection of porcelain, while the other two incorporate Garter insignia, and a bust of Charles I

OPPOSITE
Presentation drawings for dons: plans and elevations for the final design of Trinity College Library, presented by Wren to the Master and Fellows of Trinity

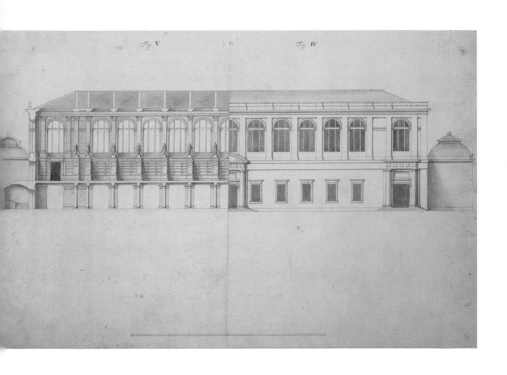

Fig. V.   Fig. IV

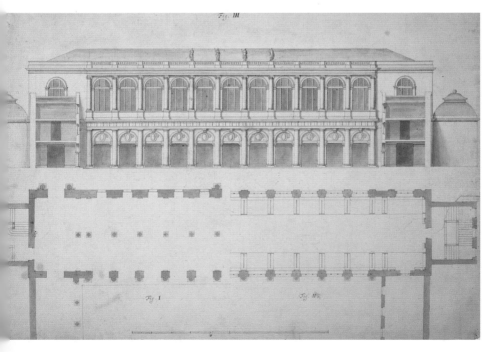

Fig. III

Fig. I   Fig. II

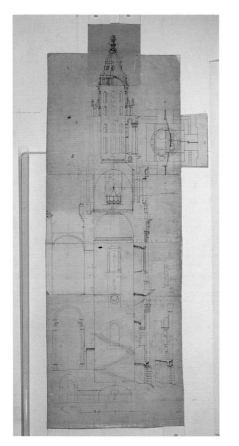

12

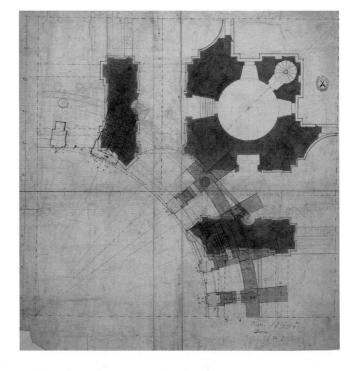

Designs for St Paul's:
(*top left*) drawing of the
south-west tower of St
Paul's, showing the
cantilevered stone staircase
and the position of the
clock; (*top right*) drawing to
study the relationship of the
stone lantern to the masonry
cone for the dome of St
Paul's; drawing with colour
wash, showing one of the
four massive piers for the
dome at ground floor level,
with the levels above
superimposed

as Flamsteed was withdrawn – they had arrived at some kind of an understanding during their periods working in close proximity at the Royal Observatory. After Halley stopped observing regularly at Greenwich, Flamsteed continued to correspond with him, and to refer to him with affection in his letters to others. In February 1682, for example, Flamsteed wrote to Molyneux to report a successful observation of an eclipse of the moon, with Halley's assistance:

> I have receaved your . . . account of the lunar Eclipse: by which
> I perceive that the heavens were as cleare with you then as with
> us. wee had not a cloud in the skyes all that time nor any wind
> to hinder us. My Freind Mr Halley a very Ingenuous person
> whom I beleive you have heard of was with mee.[37]

In 1683 Halley and Flamsteed were both elected to the Council of the Royal Society.[38]

In 1684, however, a chance remark of Wren's prompted Halley to seek out Newton for a meeting which had important consequences for mathematics, but proved fatal for Halley's relationship with the Astronomer Royal. On the evening of 14 January 1684, Wren, Hooke and Halley were discussing planetary motion, when Hooke with characteristic bravura announced that he could prove that the movement of planets was governed by an inverse square law of attraction towards the sun. As Halley later related it: 'Falling in discourse about it, Mr Hook affirmed that upon that principle [the inverse square law] all the Laws of the celestiall motions were to be demonstrated, and that he himself had done it.' Halley confessed that he had never managed to arrive at a satisfactory proof, while Wren offered 'a present of a book of 40s.' to the person who could bring him a mathematical demonstration.

In August, Halley, still preoccupied with the problem, though the deadline for Wren's bet had expired, was passing through Cambridge and called on the reclusive Newton (whom he had met once before in 1682). Newton's own recollection of what happened, recounted to Abraham De Moivre much later, is well known:

> In 1684 Dr Halley came to visit him in Cambridge, after they
> had been some time together, the Dr asked him what he thought
> the Curve would be that would be described by the Planets sup-
> posing the force of attraction towards the Sun to be reciprocal to

Edmond Halley, talented astronomer, mathematician and adventurer, through whose efforts Newton was persuaded to complete and publish his *Principia* – Flamsteed disliked his coarse ways and bad language.

the square of their distance from it. Sr Isaac replied immediately that it would be an Ellipsis, the Doctor struck with joy & amazement asked him how he knew it, why saith he I have calculated it, whereupon Dr Halley asked him for his calculation without any farther delay. Sr Isaac looked among his papers but could not find it, but he promised him to renew it, & then to send it him.[39]

In the event, it took a further three years for Newton to prove the proposition to his own satisfaction, and the result was his *Philosophiae naturalis principia mathematica* – Newton's *Principia* – an epoch-making work, published under the auspices of the Royal Society in 1687, which changed the face of mathematics and mechanics. Newton's contemporary, Alexander Pope, expressed the permanent alteration the *Principia* had made in his epitaph for the great scientist and mathematician:

> Nature and Nature's laws lay hid in night;
> God said, 'Let Newton be!' and all was light.

As far as the highly competitive and litigious Hooke was concerned, however, Newton was simply one more colleague to challenge for scientific supremacy. While Newton worked obsessively on an entire new world system, Hooke made the claim that it was he who had first given Newton the idea of the inverse square law, and that Newton's forthcoming publication would constitute plagiarism.

On 27 May 1686, Halley wrote to Newton to give him the good news that the Royal Society had voted a week earlier to publish Newton's great work themselves 'in quarto in a fair letter' (in fact, since the Royal Society had no funds to speak of, Halley already knew he would have to finance the publication himself). Unfortunately, he continued, anticipating a reaction from the sensitive and (at this stage in his life) generally uncommunicative Newton, there was further news, which Halley was anxious should not reach him from any other source. Halley was obliged to inform Newton, with as much tact as he could, 'that Mr Hook has some pretensions upon the invention of ye rule of the decrease of Gravity, being reciprocally as the squares of the distances from the Center. He sais you had the notion from him.' 'Mr Hook seems to expect you should make some mention of him, in the preface, which, if it is possible, you may see reason to praefix.'[40]

Newton, who had already tangled with Hooke in 1674, when, in his capacity as Curator of the Royal Society, Hooke had seen fit to criticise an early paper of his on optics, was outraged. Rather than be forced to acknowledge what he regarded as an utterly false claim, he threatened to withdraw the third book of his *Principia* (which dealt with his laws of motion) even before the work had been published. He wrote back to Halley rejecting Hooke's claim in no uncertain terms. After rehearsing in minute detail what had taken place at the meeting between Hooke and himself, at which Hooke had allegedly given him the clue to planetary motion, he himself announced that in any case Wren had discussed the same idea with him several years before the occasion Hooke was citing. If anyone deserved the priority claim, he maintained, it was Sir Christopher Wren:

> This is the summe of w[ha]t I remember. If there was any thing more materiall or any thing otherwise, I desire Mr Hooke would help my memory. Further that I remember about 9 years since, Sir Christopher Wren upon a visit Dr Done and I gave him at his Lodgings, discoursd of this Problem of determining the Hevenly motions upon philosophicall principles. This was about

a year or two before I received Mr Hooks letters. You are acquainted wth Sr Christopher. Pray know when & whence he first Learnt the decrease of the force in a Duplicate Ratio of the Distance from the Center.[41]

Halley, who had taken on a significant supporting role with Newton, in order to ensure that the *Principia* did indeed eventually see the light of day, replied in as conciliatory a fashion as he could. He had indeed consulted Wren, who had confirmed that Hooke had been nowhere close to a solution to the problem at the time he claimed to have alerted Newton to the inverse square law:

> According to your desire in your former, I waited upon Sr Christopher Wren, to inquire of him, if he had the first notion of the reciprocall duplicate proportion from Mr Hook, his answer was, that he himself very many years since had had his thoughts upon making out the Planets motions by a composition of a Descent towards the sun, & an imprest motion; but that at length he gave over, not finding the means of doing it. Since which time Mr Hook had frequently told him that he had done it, and attempted to make it out to him, but that he never satisfied him, that his demonstrations were cogent.

Halley then recounted to Newton the story of how he, Wren and Hooke had come to be discussing planetary motion and the inverse square law in 1684, and this had led to his original visit to Newton in Cambridge. He went on to offer his own confirmation of Newton's priority:

> The August following when I did my self the honour to visit you, I then learnt the good news that you had brought this demonstration to perfection, and you were pleased, to promise me a copy therof, which the November following I received with a great deal of satisfaction from Mr Paget; and therupon took another Journey down to Cambridge on purpose to conferr with you about it, since which time it has been enterd upon the Register books of the Society as all this past Mr Hook was acquainted with it; and according to the philosophically ambitious temper he is of, he would, had he been master of a like demonstration, no longer have conceald it, the reason he

told Sr Christopher & I now ceasing. But now he sais that this is but one small part of an excellent System of Nature, which he has conceived, but has not yet compleatly made out, so that he thinks not fit to publish one part without the other. But I have plainly told him, that unless he produce another differing demonstration, and let the world judge of it, neither I nor any one else can belive it.[42]

Halley had now become something between a mathematical assistant and a minder for Newton, nursing him through to producing his great work. One of his tasks was to collect and compute astronomical observations needed by Newton to confirm his hypotheses concerning the motion of the moon, in particular. One of his sources was his old colleague the Astronomer Royal at Greenwich. He became increasingly exasperated at Flamsteed's inability to understand how vital rapid release of his observational data had now become. It was during this period that intense hostility developed between Halley and Flamsteed, and between Flamsteed and Newton.[43] Flamsteed accused Halley of stealing his observations and passing them to Newton; Newton accused Flamsteed of withholding vital observations unreasonably; Flamsteed in his turn felt that Newton was pressuring him to produce data prematurely, and that Newton failed to treat him with due seriousness as a fellow mathematician (Newton did indeed think Flamsteed was no more talented a mathematician than Hooke). Thereafter, Flamsteed went to elaborate lengths to prevent Halley gaining access to any of his data, preferring to deal directly with Newton.

However, in the early 1690s, as Newton became more insistent, following the publication of the *Principia*, on having more and better data on the movement of the moon, Flamsteed's relations with Newton also deteriorated. In the face of Newton's increasingly insistent requests, Flamsteed became yet more unco-operative. Wren, meanwhile, continued on friendly terms with all three men individually. There are indications that he made some effort to reconcile the feuding parties. Writing in 1702, Flamsteed rejected an attempt on Wren's part to coax him out of his resolute hostility towards Halley:

But I am sorry, I must tell you, this will not make me and Mr Halley freinds[.] I have some papers in my hands that prove him guilty of disingenious practises and know more of him

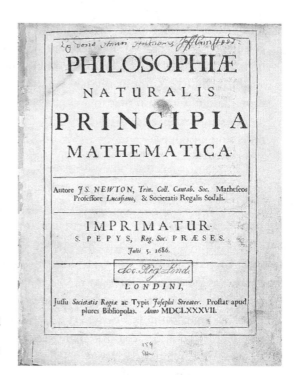

PHILOSOPHIÆ

NATURALIS

PRINCIPIA

MATHEMATICA·

Autore *JS. NEWTON,* Trin. Coll. Cantab. Soc. Mathefeos
Profeffore Lucafiano, & Societatis Regalis Sodali.

IMPRIMATUR·
S. PEPYS, *Reg. Soc.* PRÆSES.
Julii 5. 1686.

Soc. Reg. Lond.

LONDINI,

Juffu *Societatis Regiæ* ac Typis *Jofephi Streater.* Proftat apud
plures Bibliopolas. *Anno* MDCLXXXVII.

Flamsteed's inscribed
copy of Newton's
Principia, a gift from
the author.

then the generality of the World does. he knows I cannot cover
dishonesty or bear with any thinge by what is sincerely just
honest and true.[44]

Wren does not appear to have held Flamsteed's continuing hostile
remarks regarding Halley against him (his years of closeness to Hooke
must have taught him to ignore the dyspeptic rantings of gifted eccen-
trics).[45] Flamsteed, recognising Wren's goodwill towards him, began to
couch his resistance to Newton's demands in such a way as to bring
Wren in as advocate on his side. In a letter of 10 May 1700 Flamsteed
described to a friend how he had resisted Newton's accusations of
deliberate delay on his part:

> I would not hear him [Newton] but only desir'd that he would
> oblige me so far as to come down hither with Sir C. Wren some
> morning alone and take a Dinner with me, and he should then
> see in what forwardness my Work was and we could consider
> how to forward it to the Press ... and I obtein'd a promise
> that he would accompany Sir Christopher. with whom he would

agree a Time that might be convenient for both them and me. thus we parted, you see I have promis'd him nothing nor he me; since he is so reserv'd I think it concerns me to be no less so; but when he comes hither I shall not be averse to impart more Lunar Observations to him provided that he withdraw what he has imparted to [Halley and Gregory], or stop their reflecting discourses and own before Sir Chris: what he has already receiv'd and What I then imparted to him, but if otherways, I know what I have to doe, and still am resolv'd I will give him no cause to Quarrell with me. We will Part as good Friends as we Meet and I will Leave time (the Mother of Truth) to vindicate me to the World.[46]

It was natural, therefore, that when matters between Newton and Flamsteed came seriously to a head, Wren should have been drafted on to a series of official bodies brought into being to help resolve the Astronomer Royal's continuing inability to bring himself to publish his results.

In February 1692, in response to several requests from Newton for additional data on lunar movement, Flamsteed wrote a long letter of self-justification, which he redrafted a further three times before sending the final version to Newton. Each version includes a paragraph singling out Wren as the person Flamsteed can rely on: 'I shall give Sir Christopher Wren a Copy of it another I shall convey to Oxford and one to our Society after which I shall no longer heed our Men of Tricks but proceed with what I have under my hands';[47] 'I make you judge. With Sir Christopher Wren and Mr Casewell. Whether I ought to publish some part of my observations before the rest.'[48] In the version finally sent this becomes:

I despise their Calumnies and if you and Sir Christopher Wren and my freind Mr. Caswell to whome I shall send copies of this letter and one or two more ingenuous men of my Acquaintance Approve of my proceedings. I value not the little tricks or suggestions of any Malitious or envious pretender to what he understands not.[49]

From this point on, Wren figures repeatedly as an 'unprejudiced Judge' in Flamsteed's increasingly defensive correspondence. As far as Flamsteed was concerned, such trustworthy, honourable individuals were hard to find. In April 1695, Wren came up to expectations, when he finally found Flamsteed a properly qualified and reliable assistant at the observatory, James Hodgson.[50]

In 1696 Newton moved permanently to London, where he became a powerful figure in London society, and a formidable opponent for Flamsteed. When Newton became President of the Royal Society in 1704, he was at last in a position to remedy Flamsteed's persistent withholding of his observations. He persuaded Queen Anne's consort, Prince George, to sponsor publication of Flamsteed's star catalogues (the complete set of observations to date), in the interests of improving navigational safety by their means, and arranged the appointment of a scrutiny committee, or committee of referees, to coerce Flamsteed into complying. On 18 December 1704, Newton wrote to Flamsteed, summoning him to appear before the newly formed committee:

> I received last night a letter from the Prince wherein his Highness expresses that he is unwilling that your Observations designed for the benefit of Navigation and encouraged so well in the beginning should want any necessary assistance to bring them to perfection and therefore desires me, Mr [Francis] Roberts, Sir Chr. Wrenn and some others of your friends to inspect your papers and consider what is fit for the Press and when his Highness knows our Opinions he is ready to do any thing that may conduce to the making your Observations of Use to the publick. ... And to morrow Mr Robers Sir Chr. Wrenn and the rest of the Gentlemen to whom his royal Highness has referred the inspection of your papers, are to dine with me in order to consider this matter and speak with you about it. And therefore I desire the favour of your company at dinner with them, and if you please to come in the morning and bring your papers with you or such parts or specimens of them as may be sufficient you will oblige me and the rest of your friends to whom the inspection of them is referred.[51]

In spite of the civilities, this was an order. When Flamsteed procrastinated, Newton wrote again: 'I am sorry your servant is ill, but if you do not bring your papers there will be nothing done.' By mid-1705, Flamsteed had been forced into getting at least some of his material into what the committee considered to be publishable form. Although

Prince George of
Denmark, husband
of Queen Anne,
who was persuaded
by Newton to
sponsor Flamsteed's
star charts, because
of their importance
for navigation.

Wren clearly went along with the others – who included court physician
(and author) John Arbuthnott and astronomer David Gregory – Flamsteed continued to believe in his integrity. In August 1705 he wrote to
Sharp:

> Sir Christopher Wren is gone down to Winchester to view the
> buildings there which the Queen [Anne] has a mind to finish.
> he will not be in towne again this 10 days after his return we
> shall conclude about printing [the star catalogues]. he is a very
> sincere honest man I find him so and perhaps the onely honest
> person I have to deale with.[52]

Newton's committee finally forced Flamsteed to sign 'Articles of
Agreement between the referees and Flamsteed', on 17 November 1705.
The document bears the signatures of all the members. A note by
Flamsteed, written on the letter from Newton of 14 November, summon-
ing him to 'meet at my house to finish the agreement and sign the

Articles . . . and that you will be pleased to dine with me', records that 'Dr Arbuthnot was there with Mr Roberts & Mr Churchill but neither Sr Ch: Wren nor Dr Gregory.'[53] Perhaps Wren and Gregory were unwilling to participate in such an unpleasant occasion. They signed the document, in front of witnesses, as required, some days later. Undaunted, Flamsteed wrote a personal letter to Wren 'to prevent the designed effect of this malitious order or agreement'. He, at least, believed that Wren was not wholehearted in his support of Newton.[54]

Perhaps Wren did intervene. Nothing more happened until October, when Prince George died, and the project necessarily came to a halt. Newton vented his frustration by expelling Flamsteed from the Royal Society in 1709: 'Mr Flamsted his Name was ordered to be left out of the List of the Society for next year, for not having complied with the Order of Councell made the 12th of Jan. 1708.' The ostensible reason was non-payment of dues – though there were plenty of others no less in arrears. Flamsteed had, in any case, long since stopped attending meetings.[55]

In December 1710 Newton made a further attempt to take control of Flamsteed's work. By order of Queen Anne, the Royal Society was directed to appoint Visitors to supervise the organisation and activities of the Royal Observatory. The Observatory had at last been brought directly within the control of the Society. The Society appointed Newton, Sir Hans Sloane, Robartes, Arbuthnott, Halley and Wren as 'Constant Visitors'.[56] Five months later the Society 'directed' (that is, ordered) Flamsteed to 'observe the Eclipses of the Sun and Mon this Year, and particularly that of the Sun of July the 4th ensuing; and We desire You to send such Your Observations to us at Our Meeting at the House of the Royal Society'.[57] Thirty-five years after the establishment of the Royal Observatory, there was no longer any ambiguity concerning its relationship to the Royal Society. On this occasion also, however, Wren did not sign the coercive letter. Once again, too, Flamsteed emerged victorious – a year later the Royal Society was still demanding to be sent the observations it had requested.[58]

Although Wren appears to have behaved entirely correctly throughout this long-running saga, under sometimes difficult circumstances, it is hard to avoid concluding that in his anxiety not to offend any of the parties he ultimately let Flamsteed down. Wren certainly would not have felt comfortable at being closely associated with the signing of the 'Articles of Agreement between the referees and Flamsteed', on 17 November 1705. Nevertheless, Flamsteed would surely have valued his presence. As it was, by Wren's discreetly absenting himself, Flamsteed was left entirely isolated, surrounded by those wholeheartedly of Newton's party. Flamsteed's correspondent Sharp clearly thought Flamsteed, for all his difficult nature, deserved better, when he wrote in 1706:

> I am not a little troubled at the account you give me of your own proceedings. . . . I hope Providence will in a little time extricate yow and direct to such Methods as may be advantageous and successfull; I had hop'd Sir Cr: Wren would have appeard more for yow of whose integrity you have better assureance.[59]

Sharp's disappointment at Wren's behaviour is surely fair, and ought to prompt us to reflect on just what caused Wren to fail to take a stand on Flamsteed's behalf. By 1706 Wren was a figure of consequence in polite London circles, generally revered for his rebuilding of London, and treated with respect both for his intellectual achievements and for his considerable successes managing organisations like the Royal Society and the Hudson's Bay Company. In spite of his age, he continued to hold senior positions in royal employment, and attempts by Whig and Tory faction-mongers alike apparently made little dent on his public prestige.

But, even at this pinnacle of personal success, Wren continued to avoid challenging those in positions of power, just as he had done at every point in his rise to secure position and professional fame. Both in the case of the Royal Society Repository and in arbitrating the Astronomer Royal's grievance, he stepped back from confronting Sir Isaac Newton, despite the fact that the Royal Surveyor undoubtedly commanded as much respect, and could call upon just as powerful supporters, as the President of the Royal Society and Master of the Mint. One can only conclude that that personal 'charm' to which contemporaries liked to refer masked in Wren an inability to take a strong personal stand, with conviction, where any real risk was involved.

Some small intimation of such a criticism is to be found, tucked in among the largely eulogistic tributes to Wren's achievement, compiled by Wren's son. In 1709, London's opinion-forming magazine *Tatler* compared Wren to Nestor of Athens, another 'skilful Architect' renowned for his modesty and self-effacement. In both cases, the *Tatler* writer proposed, reluctance to put themselves forward, to make a public stand on behalf of themselves and their reputation, ultimately detracted from their achievement:

> Yet Nestor's Modesty was such, that his Art and Skill were soon disregarded for want of that Manner with which Men of the World support and assert the Merits of their own Performances. . . . This bashful Quality still put a Damp upon his great Knowledge, which has as fatal an Effect upon Men's Reputations, as Poverty.[60]

IN PURSUIT OF THE LONGITUDE PRIZE

The fatal effect of 'bashfulness' on an altogether successful career, referred to in *Tatler*, was, in any case, combined in Wren's case with a real anxiety about money, which further inhibited his outspokenness in public matters. Perhaps, in the end, his aversion to risk-taking – to destabilising, however slightly, the position to which he had risen – can be put down to the fact that Wren never succeeded in amassing the kind of personal wealth which would have cushioned even a minor blow to his public esteem. He had known poverty in boyhood; he avoided any career move which might set him once again on the path to hardship in adult life.

As we have had occasion to note, his personal integrity prevented his taking financial advantage of his posts and positions, beyond his salary or other legitimate rewards. Nor was he a successful speculator in the property ventures which enhanced the wealth of others in his immediate circle. Right to the end of his life he pursued the dream of making money by his own 'industry' – that is, as a result of some discovery or invention into which he had put his own labour and intellectual effort, on his own behalf and in his own time. The longest-running of these dreams, which he shared with a number of other practising mathematicians and astronomers, was that of solving the problem of how to calculate longitude at any point on the globe.

At the heart of the long-running quarrel between Flamsteed and Newton lay the question of determining longitude at sea. Like Wren,

Newton believed that the solution was most likely to lie with an astronomical method, combining observations of the moon (or the moons of Jupiter) with accurate tables of their predicted positions. There were, Newton submitted in a report to Parliament, three plausible methods of determining longitude: a watch that kept time perfectly, eclipses of the satellites of Jupiter, and the positions of the moon. The first was rendered difficult by the motion of the ship and variations of temperature and weather (all of which would interfere with the accuracy of any clock).[61] The second required a long telescope, which was hard to use on the deck of a tossing ship. The theory of the moon was currently accurate enough only to fix longitude within two or three degrees. Other methods proposed were idiosyncratic or of only local value.[62]

For much of his life, Newton worked on perfecting a theory of the moon which would increase the accuracy of its predictions for establishing longitude. His pursuit lay at the heart of his bitter feud with Flamsteed, who in Newton's view wilfully prevented him from making advances, both by refusing him access to measurements already made and by diverting resources at the Observatory to his own charting of the positions of the fixed stars, at the expense of observations of the moon and its eclipses. Flamsteed's observations of the movement of the moon over long periods, corrected for parallax and aberration, represented easily available, state-of-the-art data, an essential part of the complex calculations of the orbit of the moon under the gravitational influence of both the sun and the earth. By withholding his observational values, and by procrastinating over the corrections, Flamsteed ultimately prevented Newton from ever completing his lunar orbit theory.

On 20 July 1714, in response to increasing concern at the general failure to devise workable methods, the English Parliament passed an Act, 'Providing a Publick Reward for such Person or Persons as shall Discover the Longitude at Sea'. The expert committee advising Parliament included both Newton and Halley. They recommended 'that a Reward be settled by Parliament upon such Person or Persons as shall discover a more certain and practicable Method of ascertaining Longitude than any yet in Practice; and the said Reward to be proportional to the Degree of Exactitude to which the said Method shall reach'. The 1714 Act offered the full prize of £20,000 only if the longitude could be determined to an accuracy of half a degree.[63]

Wren, aged eighty-two, saw, in the prize offered under the 1714 Longitude Act, one final chance at the fortune gained with integrity, which had eluded him in his professional career and in his business ventures. He had always been interested in the problem.

On 20 November 1714 he wrote to Newton, submitting his own proposed solution, enclosed with a letter:

> I Present to the Royal-Society, a Description of three distinct Instruments, proper (as I conceive) for Discovering the Longitude at Sea: They are describ'd in Cypher, and I desire you would, for Ascertaining the Inventions to the Rightfull Author, Preserve them among the Memorials of the Society, which in due time shall be fully explain'd by yr Obe[dien]t. Humble Serv[an]t. Chr: Wren.[64]

In the earliest version of *Parentalia*, Christopher Wren junior has added the heading 'He [Sir Christopher Wren] Presented to the Royal-Society a Packet seal'd up; together with this Letter to the President.'[65] Halley confirms that, though it was the younger Christopher who delivered the parcel and letter to the Society, it was his father who was author of the inventions.[66]

The solution to the longitude problem submitted by Wren in 1714, in cypher, was later found among Newton's papers.[67] It was in three parts. Decoded, the first ran, 'Pipe screwe moving wheels from beake'. It proposes a device to be fixed to the prow ('beak') of the ship, with the flow of water turning a helical pipe to measure actual speed through the water. The second cypher, 'Wach magnetic balance wound in vacuo', related to the direct method of carrying standard time by a marine chronometer, the difference between the time at a standard meridian and the local time being a direct measure of difference in longitude. In February 1662, at the Royal Society, 'Dr Wren proposed to try a watch in Mr. Boyle's [vacuum pump] engine.'

Wren's third solution involved a technique for improving the stability of a telescope, used in the lunar (or moons of Jupiter) method of determining longitude, and was the one Wren had thought about a number of times in his scientific career: 'Fix head hippes hands poise tube on eye'. Three things were needed for this method: an instrument for taking angular measurements at sea, an accurate lunar theory, and an accurate chart of the fixed stars. Ever since the setting up of the

Greenwich Observatory, its pursuit had been the goal of London's astronomers. Wren himself had undertaken investigation of some such method in 1662, for Pepys's patron the Earl of Sandwich.[68] The cypher relates directly to the instrument to be used, and Wren had thought about its design before. In December 1704 David Gregory recorded: 'Sir Christopher Wren says he doubts not but a 5 foot Telescope made (by two reflecting plain mirrors) twenty inches long and braced to the head & orbits of the Eye, might at sea discover Jupiter's Satellites.'[69] At that time Wren had been testing his arrangement in a moving coach, applying a method for shortening telescopes (thereby making them easier to use in motion) which Hooke had suggested. The telescope was combined with a finder, or second eyepiece, viewed with the other eye. Hooke and Wren had been intending to demonstrate such a longitude-finding method at the Royal Society, but the Great Fire interrupted normal Society activities; Waller provided an illustration of the double telescope in his *Posthumous Works* of Hooke.[70]

Christopher Wren junior tells us that during the very last years of his life, when Wren was spending much of his time meditating on higher things (or perhaps just taking life a little easier), he continued to search for a solution to the longitude problem:

> Part of his Thoughts for Discovery of the Longitude at Sea ...
> had a Share in the Employment of those Hours he could spare
> from Meditations and Researches in holy Writ, during his last
> Retreat; when it appeared, that though Time had enfeebled his
> Limbs, (which was his chief Ailment) yet had it little Influence
> upon the Vigour of his Mind, which continued, with a Vivacity
> rarely found at that Age, till within a few Days of his Dis-
> solution.[71]

The longitude prize, however, eluded Wren, as had all lucrative rewards he had pursued throughout his life. His son later asked James Hodgson about his father's proposed solution: 'Pray what do you make of the Longitud. I should be curious to know.' Perhaps Wren had told him that the large legacy he had hoped for, but failed to accumulate to pass on to his only surviving child, might finally, after all, materialise.[72]

Here again, we may attribute Wren's financial difficulties (as he certainly saw them) to his temperament and upbringing. Industrious to the end, Wren was permanently reluctant to claim adequate recompense for his labours. We might recall his expressed diffidence, in his inaugural lecture for his very first public appointment at Gresham College, at the idea of 'earning a living', rather than making a genteel (unremunerated) contribution to the common weal. Much of the work he did in these years was, in any case, of its nature, without financial reward. His salaried work as Royal Surveyor was poorly paid, and even then the Crown was notoriously slow in paying what it owed. In *Parentalia*, Wren junior was at pains to remind his readers that his father had asked only the most modest of financial rewards for his work rebuilding St Paul's Cathedral:

> The Surveyor's Salary for building St. Paul's, from the Founda-tion to the Finishing thereof, (as appears from the publick Accounts) was not more than 200 l. per Annum. This, in Truth, was his own Choice, but what the rest of the Commissioners, on the Commencement of the Works, judged unreasonably small, considering the extensive Charge; the Pains and Skill in the Contrivance; in preparing Draughts, Models, and Instruc-tions for the Artificers, in their several Stations and Allotments; in almost daily overseeing and directing in Person; in making Estimates and Contracts; in examining and adjusting all Bills and Accounts, &c. Nevertheless, he was content with this small Allowance, nor coveted any additional Profit, always preferring the publick Service to any private Ends.[73]

Even this modest remuneration was reduced by half, in 1697, in the course of a series of disagreements between Wren and the Cathedral Commission (on which of course he sat) concerning building progress.[74] In spite of his public success, there are regular signs during Wren's life of his being financially embarrassed. A year after the salary cut, Wren wrote to Christopher Wren junior, travelling abroad: 'The little I have to leave you is unfortunately involved in trouble, & your presence would be a comfort to me, to assist me not only for my sake but for your own.'[75]

In June 1708, Wren acted to ensure that he would at least leave his son a substantial family residence, even though he himself had lived comfortably in tied accommodation for most of his life, and had failed to acquire the kind of lands or properties Wren junior might have expected to inherit at his father's death.[76] Wren petitioned to acquire a long lease on the house at Hampton Court which he occupied in his capacity as Royal Surveyor, in lieu of an outstanding sum in salary owing to him (he maintained) by the previous monarch. The Queen granted Wren's request, although the house, on Hampton Court Green, was well within the grounds of the Palace, and a special clause therefore had to be added stipulating, 'The Lessee is by a Special Clause to have free Ingress and Regress from Hampton Court Green through the Store House-Yard to his Coach-house and Stable at all times during the term to be granted':

> Mem[orandum] Indorsement on Sr. Chr. Wrens Petition to Her Most Excellent Majesty Queen Anne, Praying the Grant of a House and Garden Parcel of the Honour of Hampton-Court.
>
> Read before the Queen, 19th. June 1708.
>
> Her Majesty Observes that when Sr. Chr. Wren Dies, the House will goe to his Executor's, and consequently the Surveyor of the Works will have no House at Hampton Court; Nevertheless, in Regard of his Long and Eminent Services – the Queen will Gratify him in his Request.
>
> Let a Lease be prepar'd to Pass the Exchequor Seal of all and Singular the Premisses, with Their and Every of Their Appertinances &c[ete]ra.[77]

Wren himself then signed a document acknowledging that he accepted the fifty-year lease on the Hampton Court house as full settlement for what he was owed by William III, and renouncing all further claims:

> Wren, Sir Christopher: A messuage [property] and Store Yard, etc. at Hampton Court. With plan. 7 Anne [1708]
>
> To all to whom these presents shall come Sr. Christopher Wrenn Kn:t Sends Greeting

Whereas there is due and owing to me from his late Ma[jes]ty King William the third of Glorious Memory the sum of Three hundred Forty one Pounds Three Shillings and four pence upon the Books in the Office of his said late Ma[jes]tes: Service as Surveyor Generall of the Workes According to a Certificate in that behalfe from the said Office of the said Workes

Now Know Yee That I the said Sr: Christopher Wrenn for good and valuable Causes and Considerac[i]ons Me hereunto moveing have Remised Released and for ever quitt Claimed And do by these presents for me my Heires Executors Administrators and Assignes and every of them Clearly and Absolutely Remise Release and for ever Quitt Claime unto the Queens most Excellent Ma[jes]ty that now is her heires and Successors the said sume of Three hundred Forty One Pounds Three Shillings and four pence and every part and parcell thereof So due and in Arreare to me from his said late Ma[jes]ty upon the Books in the said Office of the Workes for My Wages on attendance on his said late Ma[jes]tes Service as Surveyor Generall of the Workes as aforesaid.[78]

'The continued Aim of his whole Life', his son recorded, was '(in his own Words) *beneficus humani generi* [the benefit of mankind]; for his great Humanity appeared to the last, in Benevolence and Complacency.'[79] Considering the vast personal fortunes accumulated by many around Wren by the beginning of the eighteenth century, there was clearly a penalty to be paid, in London society, for the kind of propriety and integrity Wren had resolutely shown in the course of his long career.

ARTISAN EXPERTISE

It may have been Wren's understanding throughout his career of the importance of 'earning a decent living', caused by his own persistent shortage of money, which shaped his relationship with the paid labour on which his buildings depended. Ever since his own early days as a laboratory assistant to Scarburgh, and his formative encounters with that master-planner of projects that employed unskilled labour, Sir William Petty, Wren had had a particular knack in directing the activities of his masons and carpenters. The era after the Great Fire gave long-term shape to London building practices, and Wren was at the heart of that process. The proliferation of manuals and instruction books for those in the building trade, published in the decades after Wren's death, are testimony to the change in working attitudes brought about during the period when Wren was overseeing most of the major public building works in London.

Evelyn, too, attached particular importance to graded instruction in the craft skills needed for construction, and handbooks on architecture for artisans. He wrote in his 1664 dedicatory letter to the then Royal Surveyor, John Denham, attached to his translation of Fréart's *Parallel*:

> Sir, I am not to instruct you in the merits and use of this excellent Piece; but it is from your approbation and particular influence, that our Workmen ought to esteem it, and believe me too when I affirme it: That the Ten Authors in this Assembly, which compose both so many, and (for not being vulgar) unintelligible Volumes, will neither afford them so full instructions in the Art, nor so well inable them to judge, and pronounce concerning the true Rules and Maximes of it as this one little, but incomparable, Collection.[80]

In the second edition of the *Parallel* (1706), in a new preface addressed to Wren himself, Evelyn made it even more clear that the purpose of handbooks such as his was first and foremost to assist skilled craftsmen in their work:

> The *Parallel* (to which this was Annex'd) being out of Print, I was Importun'd by the Book-Seller, to add something to a New Impression; but to which I was no way Inclin'd, till not long since, going to St. Paul's, to Contemplate that August Pile, and the Progress You have made, some of Your Chief Work-men, gratefully Acknowledging the Assistance it had afforded them; I took this Opportunity of doing my self this Honour.[81]

On rare occasions, Wren's assumptions about mature, reasonable, mutually respectful working practices are revealed precisely when he found it impossible to act on the basis of such practices. When he became Royal Surveyor in 1669, one of his first official acts was to regulate arrangements at the quarries at Portland on which London depended for its supplies of quality stone. In 1677 extra privileges with regard to control of the labour force and activities at Portland were granted to him (including control of the loading pier and crane).[82] These special powers gave Wren direct authority over the Portland workforce. When the quarry workmen at Portland failed, on one occasion, to comply with his instructions to the letter, he wrote:

> Though you will not be sensible of the advantage you receive by the present working of the quarries yet, if they were taken from you, I believe you might find the want of them in very little time; and you may be sure that care will be taken both to maintain the Queen's right and that such only will be employed in the quarries as will work regularly and quietly, and submit to proper and reasonable directions, which I leave you to consider of.[83]

In exchange for regular and quiet working, and submission to proper and reasonable directions, Wren was prepared to allow his workforce a certain amount of leeway in their internal organisation and working practices.

The accusations of abuse of position and protectionism in working practices at St Paul's, levelled indirectly against Wren in a pamphlet entitled *Frauds and Abuses at St. Paul's*, in 1712, arose as a direct consequence of his respect for the skilled construction labour he employed.[84] At the centre of the dispute was Wren's master carpenter, Richard Jennings, accused of protective practices in hiring, and of claiming more for work done than he paid out. Jennings had been responsible for the centring of the brick cone supporting the outer dome of St Paul's. The precision of his setting out of the wooden scaffolding frame against which the cone was built was critical for the successful execution of the entire, structurally sensitive, triple-layered cupola. It was also Jennings who supervised the construction of the timber outer dome, whose structure is sufficiently original for it to have merited its own handsome plate in Francis Price's 1635 manual for master carpenters, *The British Carpenter*.[85]

There was, for Wren, no question of dismissing a master carpenter of Jennings's calibre, on whose skills the success of vital elements in the project had depended. Charges of inefficiency and corruption in the management of the works were mere politics, and of no consequence,

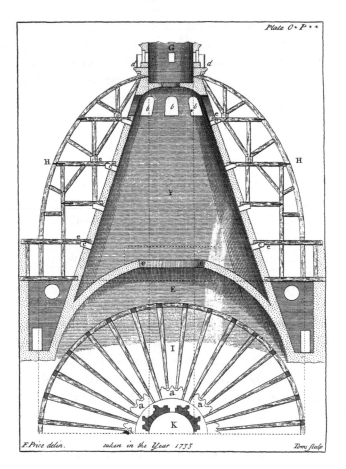

Plate from Francis Price's *The English Carpenter* (1735, second edition 1753), showing the innovative use of structural carpentry to support the outer dome of St Paul's.

compared to the complex, established patterns of administration and construction which had brought the great Cathedral to the point of completion.[86]

The scurrilous pamphlet followed a period of difficulty between Wren and the members of the St Paul's Commission, which ended in the disbanding and reforming of the Commission in 1711, the year in which the Cathedral was finished, and Wren was finally able to claim the half of his annual salary withheld since 1697. The author of *Frauds and Abuses* appears to be one of the committee which was dissolved for undue influence and hindrance of the architect's proceedings, or someone writing on their behalf. The pamphlet hints at charges of corruption against Sir Christopher Wren, insinuating that it was 'well enough known' that corrupt practices were in operation at St Paul's, where allegedly marking up of prices, claiming for work not done and taking back-handers in exchange for hiring had produced 'sweet gains and assumed power of some persons employed in the work'.[87] Richard Jennings was named as the perpetrator of the illegal employment practices. Wren was accused of turning a blind eye.

Such accusations were run of the mill in England in the faction-ridden years just before the arrival of George I to succeed Queen Anne in 1714. Wren was closely associated with the Tory cause, and therefore, in political terms, anathema to political Whigs, in spite of his general talent for not provoking displeasure. When the Duke of Marlborough was deciding on an architect for Blenheim Palace, he 'cast his eye upon the Board of Works', Vanbrugh tells us, 'and there (for reasons best known to himself) not inclining to engage Sir Christopher Wren, he fix'd upon the next officer to him'. The choice of Sir John Vanbrugh rather than Wren caused some raised eyebrows, but was assumed to have been made on political rather than artistic grounds. 'I suppose, my Lord,' Lord Ailesbury observed to the Duke sardonically, 'you made choice of him because he is a profound Whig,' almost adding the words which were, so he confessed, at his 'tongue's end', 'You ought as well to have made Sir Christopher Wren Poet Laureate.'[88]

The exchanges that followed the *Frauds and Abuses* pamphlet tell us less about the propriety of Wren's conduct than about the kind of understandings that inevitably existed between a demanding architect and the talented masons and carpenters who were responsible for construction. Wren refused to dismiss Jennings, and, when pressed, simply had him rehired under a sub-contract for which he was notionally not himself responsible. John James, who already held a position of responsibility for the Wren office on the Greenwich Hospital project, was eventually appointed as a senior site manager at St Paul's, at a salary of £200 (matching the salary Wren himself had received throughout the rebuilding).[89]

It may also have been Wren's profound understanding of carpenters, masons and the clubs to which they belonged to protect themselves and their skills which led to his agreeing to become a freemason. Wren joined the fraternity of London speculative freemasons in 1691, in a ceremony associated with St. Paul's Cathedral itself:

Memorandum. This day (May the 18th. being Munday 1691 after Rogation Sunday) is a great Convention at St Paul's Church of the Fraternity of the Adopted Masons where Sr. Christopher Wren is to be adopted as a Brother: and Sr. Henry Goodric ... of the Tower & divers others. There have been kings, that have been of this Sodality.[90]

This may have been the ceremony by which the 'Lodge of Antiquity', to which Wren is known to have belonged, was established.[91]

In this period before proper records, it is difficult to judge the importance for Wren's career of this move. There is some suggestion that in this period 'speculative' masons were nonetheless associated with 'operative' masonry, and the skilled practices of stone and stone-working. Sir Robert Moray – Wren's earliest court patron after the Restoration – was a free (or speculative) mason. Moray had spent the Commonwealth period at Maastricht, where (Edward Browne tells us in his 'Travels') there was a particularly important stone quarry, and associated skilled stone-cutting and carving. Moray helped Constantijn Huygens design his house at The Hague; he was asked repeatedly to supply a History of Masonry for the Royal Society's projected 'History of Trades', though as far as we know he never complied.

The earliest English masonic document dates from 1659 and is in the library of the Royal Society in London. It contains a list of masonic signs and the text of the mason's oath. It makes the claim that the masons' ancient status derives from their knowledge of geometry, the chief of all liberal sciences.[92] By the 1720s members of the Royal Society figured prominently in the London masonic lodges.

John Wallis – a problematic figure in the story of the Royal Society, and of Wren, on account of his shifting political associations, and his activities as a cryptographer, apparently, for all parties – was a fellow free-mason, as we discover from a letter from Wren to his friend David Gregory at Oxford. At the end of a letter to Gregory advising on repairs to the Divinity Schools and the Bodleian Library, in July 1700, Wren added the postscript: 'My humble service to M.r Vicechancel[er] and my Brother Wallis, to whom & such ingenious persons as your selfe this is submit-ted.'[93] 'Brother' identifies Wallis as a fellow mason, and furthermore suggests that Gregory too is a 'brother' (since it would not have been appropriate to make such a reference in the presence of a non-mason).

There are also credible near-contemporary reports that Wren was Master of his London lodge for the second time in 1710, and that he held that post until 1716. He was by now eighty-four years old. His great age adds authenticity to a further story told about the early history of the London masonic lodges. On 24 June 1717, four London lodges came together at the Goose and Gridiron Ale House in St Paul's Churchyard, where they formed themselves into a Grand Lodge under a Grand Master and Grand Wardens. The reason given for this occasion, which marks the beginning of 'organised' freemasonry, was that the Master of one of the lodges, referred to as the 'oldest Mason', was of extreme age, and beginning to be infirm. Rather than hurt this Master Mason's feelings by removing him from his post, it was decided that the four London lodges would amalgamate, under a Grand Master, who would be drawn from each lodge in rotation. Anthony Sayer was duly appointed, thereby relieving Wren (presumably the ancient Master Mason) of his office.[94]

EASED OF THE BURDEN OF BUSINESS

Meanwhile, in spite of his quite remarkable longevity, Wren's own career was finally drawing to a close. In 1718, William Benson replaced Wren as Surveyor of the Royal Works. Wren's reappointment to the Surveyorship by George I, upon arrival in England in 1714, had been something of a courtesy. He had remained, nevertheless, in post.[95] As Wren put it:

> It was his Majesty's pleasure, on his happy accession to the Throne to continue me in the office of Surveyor of the works: but soon after, in regard of my great age, He was pleas'd of his Royal Clemency to ease me of the burden of the business which was under such regulations and restrictions, as that alltho' I had the honour to be first nam'd with the old title of Surveyor, yet in acting I had no power to over-rule, or give a casting-vote.[96]

He owed his reappointment to the tact of Vanbrugh, newly knighted by the King, and in a position to press for the post of Royal Surveyor, should he have wished. As he reminded a colleague four years later (when he was eventually passed over for the Surveyorship in favour of Benson), 'I might have had [the post of Surveyor] formerly, but refus'd

Sir John Vanbrugh, playwright and gentleman, who designed Blenheim Palace for the Duke of Marlborough (1705–22) – at the end of Wren's life, Vanbrugh, as Comptroller of the Works, effectively acted for the Royal Surveyor.

it, out of Tenderness for Sr. Chr: Wren.'[97] Instead Sir John Vanbrugh, newly appointed Comptroller of the Works, sat alongside Wren on the Board, acting as his deputy, and undoubtedly doing most of the work. For the first time in the Board's history, regular minutes were to be kept, and Vanbrugh arranged for Hawksmoor to get the job, at a salary of £100 a year. Hawksmoor was also promoted to Clerk of the Works at Whitehall, Westminster and St James's (he was already in charge at Greenwich). Thus as Wren gradually eased out of his responsibilities, the work was taken over by gifted architects (one, Hawksmoor, wholly trained by Wren) respected by the Royal Surveyor, and in turn respectful of him. Wren nevertheless continued to attend meetings of the Board regularly, missing only 43 of the 200 meetings in the three years 1715 to 1718.[98]

Both Vanbrugh and Wren must have assumed that in due course Wren would bow out, and Vanbrugh would become Royal Surveyor in his place. Instead, in April 1718 it was announced that Wren was to be dismissed in order that his place might be given to the architectural amateur and patron William Benson.

Wren withdrew to his house at Hampton Court Green, but immediately found himself drawn back into the politics of the Surveyor's Office. Benson laid charges of mismanagement in which Wren, Vanbrugh and Hawksmoor were all implicated. At the beginning of 1719 Wren expressed his hurt and concern, 'that after haveing served the Crown and the Publick above Fifty years, and at this great Age, I should be under a necessity of takeing a Part in answering a Memorial Presented by Mr. Benson to your Lordships, charging some Mismanagements on the late Commissioners of the Board of Works'. He went on:[99]

> I am perswaded, upon an impartial view of Matters, & fairly distinguishing all particulars, with due consideration had to long protracted payments of artificers, there will be no just grounds for the censuring former Managements; and as I am Dismiss'd, haveing worn out (by God's mercy) a long Life in the Royal service, and haveing made some Figure in the world, I hope it will be allow'd me to Die in Peace.[100]

No further action was taken against Wren or his former colleagues on the Board. Wren withdrew again to the calm of Hampton Court, where he was by now ready for a little real repose, 'as well pleased to die in the shade as in the light'. In April 1719 it was judged that 'the Office of His Majesty's Works is in very great Disorder'; Benson was dismissed from his post in July.

Still by temperament as gregarious as ever, even at over ninety Wren continued to travel to London on business, staying at the house he leased in St James's Street, at the heart of fashionable residential London. He remained Surveyor for Westminster Abbey, and was advising Hawksmoor on proposals for renovation and rebuilding there. His intellectual acumen was as sharp as ever, and it is clear that his views continued to be sought in all the areas in which he had been active so successfully throughout his career.

It was at St James's Street, on 25 February 1723, sitting peacefully in his armchair, that he failed to wake from an early-evening nap. 'Haveing made some Figure in the world', he had finally been allowed 'to Die in Peace'.

Wren's funeral was magnificent, the eulogies uttered proclaiming the central role he had played, both actually and symbolically, in the regeneration of London after the Great Fire. He was buried with all pomp and ceremony in London's first Anglican Cathedral, over whose construction he had presided for most of his architectural career. 'Look up and wonder', wrote a 'St. Paul's scholar', in a Latin poem composed for the occasion, at this 'vast edifice', whose architect is made 'twice immortal' by his work.[101]

Wren's official epitaph is the one carved over his tomb in St Paul's, inviting the visitor to look around for his lasting monument. The most telling lines commemorating him, however, were written twenty-five years earlier, by one of those who understood him best. It was John Evelyn who, more than anyone else, created Wren's lasting reputation as the architect of England's grandeur. He was also among Wren's oldest friends, sharing with him his enthusiasm for science and architecture, from the Restoration until Evelyn's own death in 1706. His memorial lines on Wren, which appeared in the form of a dedicatory letter prefaced to the second edition of his *Parallel*, published in the year of his death, are characteristically clear-headed and well informed about Wren's achievements.

Evelyn identified Wren's genius with new London, after 1666. That renewed City, he maintained, 'Rebuilt and Beautified' by Wren, served to 'Eternize' not only Wren's architectural talents, but also his 'Vertues and Accomplishments . . . thro' all the learned Cycle of the most Usefull Knowledge and Abstruser Sciences'. London, in other words, was a City of Beauty, but also a City of Science, Enterprise and Modernity, and Wren was the architect of both:

> I have . . . an Ambition of Publicly Declaring the great Esteem I have ever had of Your Vertues and Accomplishments, not only in the Art of Building, but thro' all the learned Cycle of the most Usefull Knowledge and Abstruser Sciences, as well as of the most Polite and Shining: All which is so justly to be allow'd You, that You need no Panegyric, or other History to Eternize them, than the greatest City of the Universe, which You have Rebuilt and Beautified.[102]

The rebuilt St Paul's Cathedral belonged, for Evelyn, to a subtly different moment – that of the restoration of the Anglican Church as the established Church of England. For him, as for Wren, the dismantling of that Church following the English civil wars was a mark of the spiritual iniquity of the Commonwealth. The defacing of Old St Paul's, and the desecrating of its consecrated space, by using it as a parliamentary barracks, symbolised, for High Anglicans of Evelyn's generation, the Commonwealth's abandonment of true religion and its descent from civilised values into barbarity.[103]

This is also the way St Paul's figures in William Dugdale's *History of St. Paul's Cathedral* – a work closely comparable with Ashmole's *Institution of the Order of the Garter* (especially in its second, post-Restoration edition) in its cataloguing of materials relating to the period before Cromwell's sacrilegious desecration, so as to celebrate the endurance and continuity of important pre-Commonwealth institutions.[104] When Wren's contemporaries and near-contemporaries praise him specifically for St Paul's, of all the great buildings for which he was responsible, they are alluding directly to his known piety, and commitment to the High Anglican Church in which he was raised, and in which he continued to worship throughout his life.[105]

LIFELONG NOSTALGIA
FOR THE RESTORATION MOMENT

By the standards of any age, Wren's lifetime achievement was awesome in its scale and extent. Yet this was not just any age. Wren's life began in what was probably the most acute political crisis in England's history. He grew up through times of extraordinary political and social turmoil – civil war, regicide, international isolation, economic turbulence – the after-effects of which shaped the world in which he lived, worked and made his reputation. In mature middle age, dynastic accident and doctrinal difference threatened on at least three further occasions (the accession of James II, the arrival of William and Mary, the Hanoverian succession) once again to destabilise the fragile political and social equilibrium on which the continuity of Wren's architectural project depended. Nevertheless, Wren succeeded in sustaining exceptional careers in science and architecture, leaving lasting legacies in mathematics, medicine, astronomy and built form.

That success was achieved at considerable personal and emotional cost. Such was the intensity of the memories of the Commonwealth and Protectorate for those from Wren's kind of background that the men who shared them formed lifelong bonds of friendship. They also rarely talked explictly about their childhood or adolescence, preferring to draw a veil over their activities then, whether that meant forgetting long periods of deprivation and dearth, or being vague about whether they had spent the 1650s in England or 'travelling' abroad.

The defining moment, for Wren, remained the return of the King in May 1660. That was the moment of hope and promise for the future. At the end of his life, even when he had been hailed by men like Evelyn for his 'extraordinary Genius', who had 'Rebuilt and Beautified' 'the greatest City of the Universe', Wren seems to have felt that somehow that promise had failed to materialise.

A shared ethos of regret for the faded promise of the Restoration tinges remarks made by men who had shared Wren's history and fortunes. It can be found in Wren's brother-in-law William Holder's *A Discourse Concerning Time* (London, 1694), where Holder explains the way the measurement of time is used to identify key moments in history. The moment he chooses is Charles II's Coronation Day:

> We measure the Beginning, and Progress, and End of the Year, by these Months, and the Days of which they consist; we Date all Affairs, Actions, and Accidents of Humane life, and Reflect back upon them, by the help of this certain character of Time, when joyned with other Measures: as, Such a Day of such a Month, of such a Year in some certain Period of *Epocha. Ex. Gr.* King CHARLES the Second was Crowned on the 23^d Day of the Month of *April*, in the Year of our Vulgar Christian *Aera* 1661; and the time elapsed to this, is so many Years, Months, and Days; as may be found by Computing. Likewise for time to come; There will be an Eclipse of the Moon, the 27th Day of *June*, 1694.[106]

That moment of return by the Stuart King is singled out by Holder – the only historical event cited in the entire book – as a date to be remembered by all right-thinking Englishmen, for ever.

For Wren many of the dashed hopes and disappointments following the Restoration had taken the form of grand royal architectural schemes designed but never built, or begun and abandoned, or completed and left to decay. At the beginning of one of his unpublished architectural treatises Wren described vividly the role he believed architecture should play in 'establishing a Nation' and 'holding together a People . . . through infinite Changes':

> Architecture has its political Use; publick Building being the Ornament of a Country; it establishes a Nation, draws People and Commerce; makes the People love their native Country, which Passion is the Original of all great Actions in a Commonwealth. The Emulation of the Cities of *Greece* was the true Cause of their Greatness. The obstinate Valour of the Jews, occasioned by the Love of their Temple, was a Cement that held together that People, for many Ages, through infinite Changes. . . . Architecture aims at Eternity.[107]

He also wrote, 'Great Monarchs are ambit[i]ous to leave great Monuments behind them, and this occasions great Inventions & Mechanicks Arts.'[108]

The failure of each of his royal patrons in turn (but particularly of Charles II) to see through to completion the great buildings Wren designed for them as their 'great Monuments' was symptomatic of their failure to give moral leadership and provide the foundation of a united, God-fearing nation under them. It led Wren increasingly to look back, like Holder, to that golden moment when everything seemed possible, when Charles II was presented with the extravagant plans for rebuilding Whitehall Palace on the grandest of scales – designed by Webb and shown to his father on the Isle of Wight – and announced that he would build that Palace himself.

In those final years at Hampton Court, after Wren's official retirement in 1719, he and his son Christopher began to assemble a paper monument with which to memorialise him. Their model was clearly those Garter records which Wren's father and uncle had so lovingly assembled, documenting for posterity the glory of the ancient Order of the Garter.[109] After Wren's death, Christopher continued to add materials, to transcribe originals into a text for publication, and to edit what had already been transcribed. His manuscript, further edited by his own son Stephen, was published in London in 1750, under the title *Parentalia* ('Family matters'), 'completing the work of his late father,

Christopher Wren Jnr., and realizing an ambition that had been cherished for at least thirty years'.[110]

Parentalia is the richest compilation of Wren-related materials we have. It also carries the clear marks of Sir Christopher Wren's retrospective view of his own life, at its very close. *Parentalia*, in other words, may be treated both as a compilation of edited documentary evidence and as a skeletal autobiography. I have drawn on *Parentalia* repeatedly in this book, observing the usual kind of caveats about emended documents, inaccuracies, unreliable word-of-mouth and omissions. Here what concerns me is that autobiographical strand.

Three manuscripts related to the printed text of *Parentalia* survive – in the British Library, the Royal Society Library and the Codrington Library at All Souls College, Oxford. Only one of these, the British Library manuscript, dates from Wren's lifetime; it is largely in Christopher Wren junior's handwriting. The title-page is marked 'Collected, and Collated; An°: 1719', and at two places in the text Christopher junior refers to the fact that Wren is still working on the problem of longitude.[111] Marginal dates in the work as printed indicate that Wren's son was working on the material in the late 1720s, after his father's death.[112] The Royal Society's is a fair copy, with later corrections and emendations, and appears to have been assembled around 1741. It contains a large amount of material not in the British Library's fragmentary manuscript, but it also omits some material included there.[113]

Both the British Library collection of fragments and the Royal Society copy of the *Parentalia* text contain material omitted from the printed edition. In both cases the omissions appear, not surprisingly, to be intended to show Wren senior in the best possible light. To that extent the final document is a 'constructed' version of Sir Christopher Wren's life and career, as scholars have often warned before.

Almost all references to Wren's close friendship with Hooke, and their extensive collaborations in both science and architecture, are omitted from the printed *Parentalia*. For example, at the end of the lengthy description of Wren's work on redesigning London, following the Great Fire, the British Library manuscript version has the following:

> After he had taken a Survey with all possible exactness of that Part which lay in Ashes, he Contriv'd a Model for Building the New City in a very Regular <Form,> with particular Beauty

and Symmetry, suitable to so Noble a Situation, and most Commodious for Health and Trade, which was Lay'd before the King and Parliament; but he was not able to Prosecute this Design in every part, because the Generality of the Citizens and Proprietors insisted on haveing their Houses rebuilt on their old Foundations, without any deviation. . . .

In order to Ease himself of some part of the great fatigue of This extraordinary Service, which at first, by his Majesties Directions, lay wholy on himself, he took to his Assistance his most ingenious friend Dr. Robert Hooke, Professor of Geometry of Gresham College, and assigned him the Measuring and Setting of the Ground of Private Houses for the several Proprietors. Takeing on himself the Care of the Cathedral of Ste. Paul; the Parochial Churches; and all other Publick Structures.[114]

This entire passage is omitted from the printed text. We might care to remember that Christopher Wren junior, who put together the *Parentalia* papers with his octogenarian father, and then worked on them further following his death, had been left motherless at the age of six months in 1675. From Hooke's diary we know how little of his time Wren spent at home, following his wife's death, and much of his time – both professional and social – was spent in the company of Hooke. In his later years (when he was past seventy) Wren had established a strong professional bond with his son, and a close personal relationship – a relationship largely discovered after the death of Christopher's half-sister Jane in 1702 and Hooke's death in March 1703. It is hardly surprising that Christopher Wren junior should (consciously or unconsciously) have edited out of his father's biography the dear friend who had deprived him of his father's attention and companionship for the first thirty years of his life.

In doing so, however, Wren junior made it much more difficult for us to understand the very special achievement, in a very special age, which was that of Sir Christopher Wren. By restoring Hooke alongside Wren, as also by restoring to both of them an abiding commitment to a 'martyred' King of England, whom they devotedly served, and his legacy, I have tried to give back meaning to an otherwise truncated story. In the same way, by recovering Wren's filial commitment to the Order of the Garter, and the ceremonial practices which confirmed

Stuart continuity in spite of the interruption of the Commonwealth and Protectorate, I have also tried to provide Wren and his circle together with a historically specific motivation for their single-minded pursuit of 'fame' on behalf of the English Crown. However we care to define the magnificence of Wren's achievement today, these were the parameters within which it was originally shaped, and in terms of which it took its final form.

FINALE: CHARLES I'S PAPER MAUSOLEUM

To the extent that *Parentalia* is a self-conscious construction – a carefully crafted version of the great man in which he himself participated – it tells us a great deal about how Wren and the Wren family wished posterity to remember him. It also gives us a sense of what was on Wren's mind during his final years. Most unexpected is the steady refrain of continuing commitment – to the point of apotheosis – to the memory of the 'martyred' Charles I. The inclusion of a large amount of material relating to Dean Christopher Wren and his brother Matthew's terms as Register of the Garter also makes clear that the family regarded the continuation of the Wren family tradition of service to the Order – a prime source for a hagiography of Charles I – as no less important than Sir Christopher Wren's reputation as scientist, virtuoso and architect of rebuilt London.[115]

There are a number of passages, distributed right through the pages of *Parentalia*, which form part of a conscious hagiography of Charles I. We are alerted to this theme early on, by a curious item about premonitions and omens, tucked away in the 'Appendix of Records' to the Bishop Matthew Wren section. It contains premonitions of the death of Charles I:

> King Charles the First, by a Prescience, like that of Bishop Andrews, and divine Instinct, after he was condemned, did tell Colonel Tomlinson, 'That he believed the English Monarchy was now at an End.' About half an Hour after, he told the Colonel, 'That now he had an Assurance, by a strong Impulse on his Spirit, that his Son should reign after him.' His Majesty meekly resign'd to God, his own private, and the publick Cause;

and by a divine Spirit, foretold the happy Recovery of both. *'Nemo vir magnus, sine aliquo afflatu divino unquam fuit'*, was the Observation of Tully.[116]

A note tells us that this story is taken from 'Doctor Sprat's Sermon before the House of Commons, Jan. 30, 1677/8' – the Sermon, passionately regretting the fact that Charles I was still without an official grave or monument, delivered on the anniversary of Charles I's execution in 1678, on the day after Parliament had voted a huge sum for the building of a Windsor Mausoleum to the King's memory.

On 29 January 1678 the House of Commons optimistically voted £70,000 'for a solemn Funeral of his late Majesty King Charles the First, and to erect a Monument for the said Prince of glorious Memory; the said Sum to be raised by a Two Months Tax'. The money was never forthcoming, but a design for a monument was. Although it was decided to erect the monument at Windsor on the site of the Tomb-house at the east end of St George's Chapel, its design was entrusted not to May (Surveyor at Windsor, and in charge of Royal Works there) but to the Surveyor-General, Wren. Three days after the resolution in the House of Commons, Hooke noted in his diary, 'with Sir Chr. Wren about Kings tomb chappell at Windsor'.[117]

Parentalia includes an account of Wren's involvement in designing what he in all likelihood considered the most important monument of his career, in the course of which Christopher Wren junior as narrator quotes again from Sprat's 1678 sermon:

> I intended to have complained, that the present Age had not made that Use of him [King Charles] which it ought. . . . But, blessed be God, I am happily prevented in one Part of the Complaint . . . by that much desired, long expected, Yesterday's Vote; in which you have given a Resurrection to his Memory, by designing magnificent Rites to his sacred Ashes.
>
> So that now, for the future, an Englishman abroad will be able to mention the Name of King Charles the First, without blushing; and his heroick Worth will be delivered down to Posterity, as it always deserved to be, not only freed from Calumny, or Obscurity, but, in all Things, most illustrious; in all Things to be commended; in most Things to be imitated; in some Things scarce imitable, and only to be admired.[118]

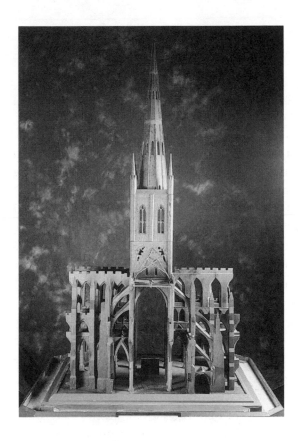

Wooden model of Westminster Abbey, showing the unbuilt new spire, which Wren maintained would provide vital structural stability.

Wren's magnificent baroque Mausoleum for Charles I was never built, because the money voted by Parliament was never in fact forthcoming. Nothing could be more symbolic, in the reign of the martyred King's son, Charles II – in whom so many like Wren had placed so much hope – of the yawning gap between the highest of good intentions and their fulfilment. Perhaps, too, in the difficult years around the time of the Popish Plot, a monument which, by its iconography, represents the executed King as part of a Church Militant, trampling the enemies of the true faith, and declaring his own triumphant, was thought too provocative.[119]

What is made abundantly clear in Wren junior's account is that, as far as Wren was concerned, the *Parentalia* volume itself had become a paper monument where, in spite of Wren's best efforts, no physical one had been created. The *Parentalia* account closes with a passage taken from Lucan and adapted slightly to fit the contemporary circumstances.

Wren drawing of the interior of his planned Mausoleum to Charles I.

It insists that a paper memorial will, in the end, last longer than anything built in marble or bronze:

> Meanwhile, let us mark on paper the place of your empty tomb, in order to note your grave. He who wishes may make atonement to your spirit and give you [your] due of funeral honours. One day it will prove a gain that no lofty pile of massive marble was raised here to last for ever. For a short space of time will scatter the little heap of dust; the grave will fall in; and all proof of your death will be lost. A happier age will come, when those who point out that stone will be disbelieved, and perhaps our descendants will consider Windsor as false in her tale of Charles's tomb as Crete when she claims the tomb of Jupiter.[120]

'Meanwhile let us mark on paper the place of your empty tomb.' It was the paper monuments of the Order of the Garter, assembled and preserved secretly by Dean Wren during the Commonwealth years, which bore lasting testimony to Stuart continuity – from martyred father to restored son. On those paper memorials, the elaborate edifice of justification and reconstituted tradition of Charles II's Restoration rule, had been largely based. By means of them, too, Christopher Wren had started to rebuild a life shattered by the civil war, when he presented the Garter records to the returning King, on behalf of his dead father, in summer 1660.

In St Paul's Cathedral, Wren had built an enduring monument to his own lifetime achievement: 'Reader, if you require a monument, look around you.' In *Parentalia*, he and his son had done their utmost to provide as lasting a paper monument to the memory of their spiritual inspiration on earth, upholder of their quintessentially English values and beliefs, Defender of the Anglican faith, King Charles I.

NOTES

Preface

1 'Lector, si Monumentum requiris, Circumspice'. *Parentalia*, p. 347.
2 'Viator, si Tumulum requiris, Despice, / Si Monumentum, Circumspice'. *Parentalia*, p. 347.
3 The alternative version has 'for his country'. *Parentalia*, p. 347.
4 The producer of the TV programme was James Runcie. The attendant at the Monument that morning was Martin Witziers. My thanks to them both for their wisdom and encouragement.
5 H. Robinson and W. Adams (eds), *The Diary of Robert Hooke* MA MD FRS *1672–1680* (London: Taylor & Francis, 1935), p. 307.

CHAPTER 1: *Loyal Sons of Delinquent Fathers*

1 Three younger children, James, Duke of York, Elizabeth and Henry remained at St James's Palace. C. Carlton, *Charles I: The Personal Monarch* (second edition; London: Routledge, 1995), p. 234.
2 *A Deep Sigh Breathed through the Lodgings at Whitehall* (164?), cit. Carlton, *Charles I*, p. 236.
3 This account is based on Carlton, *Charles I*; R. Hutton, *Charles the Second King of England, Scotland, and Ireland* (Oxford: Clarendon Press, 1989); S. Coote, *Royal Survivor: A Life of Charles II* (London: Hodder & Stoughton, 1999).
4 Carlton, *Charles I*, p. 249. One of Charles I's 'party tricks' at court as a young man had been to stage martial

feats of bravery before delighted audiences of foreign dignitaries. See e.g. Carlton, *Charles I*, p. 27. Active combat must have come as a shock to father as to son.
5 Typically for a regime returning after long-term exile, anyone who had done a favour in the 'old days' merited consideration. Sir Jonas Moore, who had briefly tutored the thirteen-year-old James, Duke of York, while he and two of his younger siblings were in the custody of parliamentary forces in St James's Palace in 1647, for example, rose rapidly at the Restoration. It is Moore of whom Aubrey records that, encountering James again at Charles II's court, 'The Duke of York said that "Mathematicians and physicians had no religion": which being told to Sir Jonas More, he presented his duty to the Duke of York and wished "with all his heart that his highness were a mathematician too"': this was since he was supposed to be a Roman Catholic.' See F. Willmoth, *Sir Jonas Moore: Practical Mathematics and Restoration Science* (Woodbridge: Boydell Press, 1993), pp. 37–41. On royal reappointments connected with the King's Works (the area in which Wren found preferment) immediately following the Restoration, see H. M. Colvin, *The History of the King's Works*, 7 vols (London: Her Majesty's Stationery Office, 1963–82) 5, chapter 1.
6 Charles I stood five foot four inches tall; Charles II was a massive (for the times) six foot two fully grown.

7 The swarthy complexion raises the vexed question of James I's parentage. James's daughter Elizabeth of Bohemia's first son was also unusually dark-skinned (she too referred to him as a 'black boy'). Given what we now know about genetics, this points to the possibility that the dark-skinned Rizzio, Mary Queen of Scots's secretary, fathered James, not her then husband Darnley. General court gossip right down to the arrival of William and Mary (as recorded in John Evelyn's diary) had it he was 'Rizzio's boy'. (E.g. 30 October 1688, 'The Duke told us many particulars of Mary Queen of Scots, and her amours with the Italian favourite, &c.')

8 Coote, *Royal Survivor*, p. 6.

9 Hutton, *Charles the Second*, p. 2.

10 Coote, *Royal Survivor*, p. 6.

11 Hutton, *Charles the Second*, p. 2. There is an evocative picture of the boy Charles in all his finery, with his brothers and sisters, reproduced in Coote, *Royal Survivor*, facing p. 130 ('artist unknown').

12 Over all this he wore a beautifully crafted, ornate breastplate and marvellously contrived helmet in burnished black metal. His mount was 'a very goodly white horse', with which he had been presented at York, its richly studded velvet trappings reaching nearly to the ground and embroidered all over 'with burning waves of gold'. Coote, *Royal Survivor*, pp. 29–30.

13 Cit. K. Sharpe, *The Personal Rule of Charles I* (New Haven: Yale University Press, 1992), p. 220: 'The king ordered all knights of the order always to wear their George; the badge is prominent in nearly all the paintings of Charles himself. Charles rebuked the Prince of Orange for not wearing his Garter and reminded him of his obligation to wear it daily (*CSP Venice 1632–6*, p. 557). He exempted the Garter alone in the 1640s from the ban on ornaments to clothing. He minted the first money on which the emblem

appeared.' On the reverse of Charles's George was a miniature of Henrietta Maria (see Ashmole, *Institution of the Order of the Garter*, p. 182). There is a sketch by Van Dyck of a Garter feast-day procession, intended to become a painting or a cartoon for tapestries for Banqueting House walls. The project was abandoned after the procession was dropped.

14 Charles I continued his father James I's tactic of bestowing the Order of the Garter on those foreign sovereigns who fought successfully on the side of the Palatinate during the thirty years war – a war precipitated by the expulsion from the throne of Bohemia (Czechoslovakia) and the Palatinate of James's son-in-law Frederick and his daughter Elizabeth, but into which England consistently refused to be drawn.

15 *Parentalia*, p. 142.

16 We can date this complaint to some time shortly after 1636 by the fact that that was the year in which 'the crown established a saltpetre monopoly, and to ensure adequate supplies of a key raw material of gunpowder, authorized its agents to raid pigeon lofts for hoarded supplies of this obnoxious, but efficacious, compound' (Carlton, *Charles I*, pp. 190–1). The problem of irresponsible digging for saltpetre persisted throughout the civil war period, when there was inevitably an acute shortage for munitions purposes. In 1647 Boyle wrote to Worsley (a colleague who had been granted a new patent for saltpetre manufacture) complaining that 'those undermining two-legged moles, we call saltpetermen', had dug up his pigeon-house. R. G. Frank, Jr, *Harvey and the Oxford Physiologists: A Study of Scientific Ideas* (Berkeley: University of California Press, 1980), p. 121.

17 Ashmole, *Institution of the Order of the Garter*, p. 231.

18 Wren's three sisters' married names were Fishborne, Brounsell and Holder. Christopher Wren junior, in

his remarks concerning Wren's unbuilt tomb for Charles I at Windsor, notes that some questioned whether Charles's body was in fact in the vault at Windsor, but 'Mr. Fishborne, Gent. of Windsor, a Relation of Sir Christopher Wren's, was among those who were present at the Interment of the King, went into the Vault and brought away a Fragment of King Henry's Pall; he observed the Vault was so narrow, that it was some Difficulty to get in the King's Coffin by the side of the others' (*Parentalia*, p. 330).

19 The source of this information is a collection of damaged copies of originals, in the hand of Christopher Wren junior, now in the British Library (BL Add. MS 25071). The list of births there is apparently transcribed from an original by Dean Christopher Wren. BL MS *Parentalia*, fol. 25 recto [and fol. 26 verso – two recensions of the same document].

20 The details concerning Matthew Wren's children are compiled out of his jottings in his almanac, reproduced in *Parentalia*, pp. 133–4. The most poignant piece of evidence concerning Bishop Wren's political downfall and imprisonment in the Tower of London comes in the form of the lives and deaths of his children, as recorded in this almanac. Up until his imprisonment, with his family living in comfort and affluence, Bishop Wren had eleven children (and one still-birth), the last, Alicia, having been born just ten days before his arrest and imprisonment. One of the twins, Francis, who we may assume had always been sickly, died at the beginning of his troubles in July 1642. Alicia died in July 1643. The two children born to Matthew in captivity (we therefore assume his wife was with him) both survived for less than a month. Meanwhile his twelve-year-old daughter Eliza died in Ely in February 1643. Having lost three children in the space of eighteen months, Wren recalled his

emotional state in his almanac for 10 January 1645 (the date of the death or burial of his infant daughter 'Eliza 2') with the words 'Parce, o Deus, requisitor sanguinis' ('O God, please diminish your demand for blood!'). His wife Eliza died in 1646.

21 See house identified on Hollar bird's-eye view in Ashmole, *Institution of the Order of the Garter*, p. 131.

22 Ashmole, *Institution of the Order of the Garter*, p. 342.

23 *Parentalia*, p. 140.

24 *Parentalia*, p. 183.

25 *Parentalia*, p. 183. Matthew Wren junior, in his *Monarchy Asserted, or the State of Monarchicall & Popular Government in Vindication of the Considerations upon Mr. Harrington's Oceana* (Oxford, 1659) (dedicated to Wilkins), specifically refers to the study of lice under a microscope as having been carried out in Wilkins's circle at Wadham (fols A7v–A8r).

26 Charles II cherished the fact that he was the youngest ever to be installed as a Garter Knight. He recalled this when, following his father's execution, he, as the new Sovereign of the Order of the Garter, bestowed the honour of Garter Knighthood upon his two-year-old nephew William of Orange. On Wren's early education see *Parentalia*, p. 181.

27 Apparently the Bishop of Ely and Oliver Cromwell had crossed swords directly and personally while Cromwell was based in Ely.

28 According to Matthew Wren's almanac, he had already been imprisoned in the Tower for a short time the previous year, along with other bishops. For the details of his impeachment and imprisonment (including his own lengthy defence) see *Parentalia*. By the time Matthew Wren junior moved on to study for his MA at Oxford, his father could no longer afford the fees for full residence, and he lodged 'nor in a College or Hall, but a private House' (*Parentalia*, p. 53).

29 The term was conveniently borrowed

from its usage to designate those identified as Roman Catholics by English Protestant administrations under Elizabeth I.

30 See *Parentalia* and Ashmole, *Institution of the Order of the Garter*.

31 *Parentalia*, p. 139. Among the Ashmole manuscripts in the Bodleian Library are three that relate to the looting of Dean Wren's home at Windsor. W. H. Black, *A Descriptive, Analytical, and Critical Catalogue of the Manuscripts Bequeathed unto the University of Oxford by Elias Ashmole, Esq., M.D., F.R.S., Windsor Herald . . .* (Oxford: At the University Press, 1845): MS 1111, column 768, item 43: 'Memoriall of the goodes and monumentes belonging to the Kings chappell and treasury at Windsor, till Octob' 23, 1642', when the plate was taken away by Capt. Fog. 'Ex autogr. penes Dr: Chr: Wren.' Item 44: 'Memorial of ye goods and monumts belonginge to ye Ks chappel, and ye college of Windsor 1643' and a note of Col. Venn's taking the keys from the Dean, in May, 1643. 'The original by Dr. C. Wren's hand: the first half is half cut off: the second is indorsed "Doctr Wrenns papr concerning ye Kts. of ye garter." ' Item 45: 'An inventory taken by William Shephard, of goodes left in Dr. Wrens house, when he left Windsor castle, for the preservation and restituc[i]on whereof Colonell Ven promised to be accountable.'

32 See the letter preserved among the Ashmole manuscripts: Black, *A Descriptive, Analytical, and Critical Catalogue*: MS 1132, column 939, item 81: 'Warrant of Charles I. commanding the Dean of Windsor to "sweare James Maxewell and Alexander Thayne esqrs Gentlemen Ushers of ye Black Rodd in ordinary," and dispensing with any custom or order to the contrary. (Court at Derby, 14 Sept. 1642)', 'Apparently written by Sir. Fra. Crane; signed "Charles R." and indorsed by Dr. Wren, "Ks mandate

to mee, to admit Mr. Thane Usher of ye Parliament".' This shows Dean Wren was in Derby in September 1642.

33 William Holder was husband of Susan Holder, Wren's second surviving daughter. Dean Wren may have retained access to the parsonage at Knoyle Magna for some years after the looting of the Deanery at Windsor.

34 Though Aubrey has a story about Christopher Wren junior dreaming the defeat of Charles II at Worcester in 1651, at 'Knoyle'.

35 His last 'official' duty seems to have been a final appeal to the Garter Knights of both Houses of Parliament, just before the King's arrest in January 1647. See below, chapter 2.

36 Cit. J. Adair, *By the Sword Divided: Eyewitness Accounts of the English Civil War* (Bridgend: Sutton Publishing, 1998), pp. 219–20.

37 Carlton, *Charles I*, pp. 318–19.

38 Such hints are all that survives of Oglander's commitment to seeing the King returned to power. One of the difficulties with Oglander's diary and account books – as with other documents from this period – is that they have been discreetly censored, pages taken out with a sharp knife at the binding, presumably to avoid further grief during the Commonwealth and Protectorate periods.

39 'Afterwards, I took Mr. Hooke, curate of Brading, into my house to teach him his accidence, in which my own care and pains were not wanting. Then not long after growing to more expenses, I procured Mr. Elgor, schoolmaster of Chichester School, to come to Newport and there I placed him, where he continued 4 years. Thence I sent him to Oxford and for love of his tutor, one Mr Reynolds, Fellow of Merton College, I placed him as a fellow commoner, where he profited very well under Mr Reynolds . . .' *A Royalist's Notebook*.

The Commonplace Book of Sir John Oglander Kt. Of Nunwell. Born 1585 died 1655, Transcribed and edited by Francis Bamford (London: Constable, 1936), p. 177. See also the Oglander account book (1622–3OG 90/1): 'Given to him that teacheth my boys astronomy – 2 – 0 – 0', May 20th 1623 [p. 192] 'To Mr Hooke for my privie [??] tithe – 3 – 0 – 0'.

40 At the time of John Hooke's death, the vicar of Freshwater was Cardell Goodman. '1623 March 24th The patronage of [Freshwater] Church conveyed to The Master, Fellows and Scholars of St. John's College Cambridge by the Bishop of Lincoln to whom it had been granted by James I.'

41 For the details of Hooke's family see H. Nakajima, 'Robert Hooke's family and his youth: some new evidence from the will of the Rev. John Hooke', *Notes and Records of the Royal Society* 48 (1994), 11–16. Confirmed by Rachel Jardine following her trip to the Isle of Wight and the Hampshire record office.

42 *A Royalist manifesto drawn up by Island gentlemen in 1642, is signed by (among others) Sr Wm. Hopkins & Sr John Oglander.* Newport Corporation Manuscripts *Convocation Book* vol. 1 [1609–59], p. 426. See also J. D. Jones, *The Royal Prisoner: Charles I at Carisbrooke* (Northumberland Press, 1965).

43 Carlton, *Charles I*, p. 331.

44 Cit. Carlton, *Charles I*, p. 327.

45 *A Royalist's Notebook*, pp. 120–1.

46 On the damaging level of fines for delinquents during this period see P. H. Hardacre, *The Royalists during the Puritan Revolution* (The Hague: Martinus Nijhoff, 1956), chapter 2, 'The delinquents, 1643–1649', pp. 17–38. For the penalties paid by Anglican clergy see chapter 3, 'The religious victims of the Long Parliament, 1642–1649', pp. 39–63.

47 *A Royalist's Notebook*, p. 120.

48 Robert Hooke records such boasts in his diary: Sunday, 2 September 1677,

'Sir Jonas More and Lingar here, he told me of an absconding freind in the Isle of Wight, of his voyage with the King to Plinmouth.' Loyal royalists on the Isle of Wight were responsible for saving important artworks associated with the monarchy. See S. E. Lehmberg, *Cathedrals under Siege: Cathedrals in English Society, 1600–1700* (Exeter: University of Exeter Press, 1996), p. 65: 'The cathedral at Winchester had not been severely damaged in the [civil] war, so most of the work there involved either adornments or normal maintenance. Shortly after the Restoration the bishop, Brian Duppa, paid £100 to retrieve Le Sueur's statues of James I and Charles I, which had been buried in a garden on the Isle of Wight.'

49 Carlton, *Charles I*, pp. 331–2.

50 Parish Register entry obtained by Rachel Jardine, August 2000. Although as far as we know Robert Hooke never returned to the Isle of Wight, his mother continued to live there until her death. Newport Parish Register has: 'Buried June 12th 1665 Mrs Cissely Hooke Widow'.

51 Nakajima, 'Robert Hooke's family', pp. 12–13.

52 Since a) a suicide could not receive burial on consecrated ground (John Hooke is buried at Freshwater Church), there would be no record of 'suspicious circumstances'. Still, John Hooke might have hastened his own end by some (chemical) means. John Hooke junior (who hanged himself) received a private burial, and his family was given a special dispensation to be allowed to inherit his goods (which were technically impounded in the case of suicide). On John Hooke's suicide see now the full (if a tad sensational) website: 'The Tragedy of John Hooke, Being the Strange and Shocking Story of Robert Hooke's Brother', research and text by Dr Stephen Johnson, P. van Elven and Rob Martin, for The Isle of Wight History Centre, to be

found at http://freespace.virgin.net/
ric.martin/vectis/hookeweb/start.htm.
See also now, Rachel Jardine's
transcription from the PRO of the
John Hooke–Oglander lawsuit, in
early 1678.
53 Nakajima, 'Robert Hooke's family',
p. 14.
54 When Robert Hooke went to Christ
Church, Oxford, sponsored by
Westminster School (then as now
schools had special arrangements with
particular colleges), he was entered in
the record as 'servant to Mr
Goodman'.
55 Sir Peter Lely was born in Germany
to Dutch parents. His real name was
Pieter van der Faes; Lely was a family
nickname deriving from his
grandfather's house, which had a lily
on its gable and which was in the de
Lelye area of The Hague, in the
Netherlands. After serving his
apprenticeship in Holland, Lely came
to England some time in the early
1640s. Within a very few years, he
had become England's leading
portrait painter. He was patronised by
Charles I and later by Oliver
Cromwell. In 1661, he was appointed
Principal Painter to King Charles II.
He became an English subject in 1662
and in 1680 received the honour of a
knighthood. He died in the same year
and was buried in St Paul's Church in
Covent Garden.
56 In the inventory of sale for Hooke's
extensive library, auctioned after his
death in 1704, are a number of the
kind of general books (including
arithmetic and the classics) which
might have come from his father's
library, as his legacy to Hooke in
1648. The most striking entry on this
list, however, is a folio Italian Bible
which fetched the top price in the
auction for a single volume, at
£2 0s 0d. The inventory entry reads:
'La Sacra Biblia da Giov[anni]
Diodati fol[io] deaur[ata] cart[arium]
Maj[estatis] Reg[is] con medes[imi]
Comment[arii] – 1640' ('The Bible of
Giovanni Diodati in folio, gilded,

from the collection of his Majesty the
King and with annotations by the
same'). See A. N. L. Munby (ed.),
*Sale Catalogues of Libraries of Eminent
Persons*, vol. 11 (London: Mansell
Publishing, 1975), pp. 37–56; 50. I find
it irresistible to think that this
precious 'relic' of King Charles I was
acquired by John Hooke in 1647–48
and passed, as part of his legacy, to
Robert.
57 'John Hoskins (1590–1664/5)
originally trained as a portrait painter
with William Larkin. His earliest
miniatures bear the influence of
Nicholas Hilliard and Isaac Oliver,
but later he was very much
influenced by the arrival of Van Dyck
in England in 1632. Hoskins was
Limner to King Charles I making
many miniatures of the royal family
and also miniature copies of pictures
in the royal collection.'
58 Rachel Jardine thinks Oglander may
have had a portrait done during this
period.
59 See Hooke's diary.
60 Eyewitness account of John
Rushworth, cit. Adair, *By the Sword
Divided*, p. 236.
61 In fact the account of Charles I and
his Great George – richly symbolic
though I am arguing it is – already
fudges the record, as one might
expect from its place in royal
martyrology. Carlton has the
following story from the eve of the
King's execution: 'That evening,
Colonel Matthew Tomlinson,
commander of the king's guard, let
Edward Seymour deliver a letter from
Prince Charles written but four days
before. The messenger was so
overcome with grief that he swooned
wailing to the floor, grasping his
sovereign's knees, and had to be
prised off. Following this distressing
exhibition, Charles took an emerald
and diamond ring from his hand and
gave it to Herbert, telling him to slip
past the guard and deliver it to Mary
Wheeler, his laundress, who now
lived in Channel Row. In return she

gave him a small cabinet, which Herbert brought back to the king. He opened the box. When all he found was several diamonds and precious stones, mainly bits from broken-up badges of the Garter and St George, Charles sadly told his servant, "You see all the wealth now in my power"' (Carlton, *Charles I*, p. 350). See A. MacGregor (ed.), *The Late King's Goods: Collections, Possessions and Patronage of Charles I in the Light of the Commonwealth Sale Inventories* (London and Oxford: Oxford University Press, 1989): 'Charles I's own Garter, "which is said late Majesty wore upon his Leg at the time of his Martyrdom", also had the motto picked out in diamonds, "to the number of 412". It came into the hands of Captain Preston, one of Cromwell's Captains of Horse, who delivered it to the Trustees. They in turn sold it to John Ireton, a Lord Mayor of London, for £205. . . . Fortunately Ashmole caused Hollar to engrave in 1665 for his book on the Garter the most interesting of all these Georges, that worn by Charles "at the time of his Martyrdom". He describes it as ". . . curiously cut in an *Onix*, set about with 21 large Table Diamonds, in the fasion of a *Garter*: on the back side of the *George* was the picture of his *Queen*, rarely well limn'd, set in a Case of Gold, the lid neatly enamel'd with Goldsmiths work, and surrounded with a like number of equal sized Diamonds, as was the foreside"' (p. 272).

62 Secret societies, secret ceremonies and bonds between men of different faiths, classes or political persuasion proliferate in the first half of the seventeenth century. The Royal Society was only one among several 'sodalities' which, it was claimed after the Restoration, straddled the periods of 'misrule' from the reign of Charles I to that of his son. Freemasons, Rosicrucians and the Order of the Garter all pretended continuities and sustained, rule-bound organisation

which rose above the disorder of the times.

63 An account of the returning in full ceremony to the Chapel at Windsor in 1638 of the Great George and Mantle which Charles I had presented to the King of Sweden, as recorded by Christopher Wren senior, is to be found in *Parentalia*.

64 *Parentalia*, pp. 63, 157.

65 G. P. V. Akrigg (ed.), *Letters of King James VI & I* (Berkeley: University of California Press, 1984), letter 195, p. 397.

66 Akrigg, *Letters of King James*, p. 397. For the Wren family comments see BL MS *Parentalia*, fol. 3 recto: 'Dr. Matthew Wren, Ld. Bishop of Ely, and Count Palatine [margin: sic in Sched:], was Born Ano: 1585 & being an eminent s[c]holar in his Youth, became first a student in Pembroke Hall Cambridge; then Greek Scholar, and Fellow of the House; and in 1615, Chaplain to Lancelot Andrewes – Bp. of Winchester; then Rector of Teversham, Cambridgeshire; in 1621 sworn Chaplain to his Royal Highness Charles Prince of Wales, – Whom, <(by K. James special Directions> in 1623, he attended in His Journy to Spain; in 1624, <he was presented to the> Rectory of Bingham in Nottinghamse.; in 1625 <Elected> Master of Peter-House, Camb: and Vice Chancellor of that University; Prebendary of Winchester; Dean of Windsor, in which honourable Dignity he was Installed 240. July 1628.' [sideways down the front edge] 'As first Chaplain entrusted by the special appointment of K. James with the care of his Conscience.'

67 *Parentalia*, pp. 45–7, 'A Transcript of a certain Narrative, written by the late Bishop of Ely [Dr Matthew Wren] with his own Hand, of that remarkable Conference, which, after his Return from Spain with Prince Charles (Anno 1623,) he had with Dr. Neale, then Bishop of Durham; Dr. Andrews, Bishop of Winchester, and

Dr. Laud, Bishop of St. David's, touching the said prince; whereat, something prophetical was then said by that reverend Bishop of Winchester [Ex MS. Dugd. (in Musaeo Ashmoliano) E 2. sub finem, published by Mr. Thomas Hearne, Oxford, at the Theatre, 1725. in the Publisher's Appendix to his Preface to Peter Langtoff's Chronicle, Page ccviii]'.

68 *Parentalia*, p. 10.

69 'About August 20 [1635], the King without any Warning given, remov'd to Oatlands, and seeing the Bishop [Matthew Wren] go thither the next Day, he smiled, and said, I'll reward your Diligence, I hear the Bishop of Norwich is dead, and I'll remove you thither, (giving him his Hand to kiss.)' (*Parentalia*, p. 50).

70 *Parentalia*, p. 133: 'May 2. Mariam principem junxi cum Wmo. Aurasionis Princ. 1641.'

71 *Parentalia*, p. 135. Matthew Wren had tried earlier, with less success, to pass on his good fortune to his brother. When he resigned as Master of Peterhouse he attempted to get his brother elected in his place. In the event the fellows preferred the other candidate. See *Parentalia*, p. 44.

72 Colvin, *The History of the King's Works* 3, 331–2: 'In 1638, the king's clock-maker, David Ramsey, provided a clock and dial to be placed on the gatehouse [at Windsor] between the Middle and Upper Wards. It was to be cased in a "pyramid or lanthorne" for which Ramsey furnished a "moddell" which the surveyor was directed to follow. In the previous year the recently appointed dean, Dr. Christopher Wren (the father of the future architect), obtained permission to make a window in a part of the castle wall on which the Deanery abutted and to rebuild a chimney stack at his own expense, simultaneously making some necessary repairs to the wall.'

73 Bishop Matthew Wren's 1631 autograph draft statutes for the Order

are inserted into the St Paul's Cathedral copy of *Parentalia* (the provenance of this volume is unknown). The header on this document is identical with that transcribed in *Parentalia*, p. 63. I am grateful to Jo Wisdom, Librarian of St Paul's Cathedral Library, for bringing this copy of *Parentalia* and its manuscript inserts to my attention.

74 *Parentalia*, p. 152. The full account is given (in Latin), pp. 150–7.

75 The Queen watched the entire proceedings 'e fenestris camerae quae ad euro-australem angulum apellae propendet'. Dean Wren (the father of a small boy himself) comments in his account on how proud she must have been, and how amazed by his stamina (*Parentalia*, 154).

76 The installation of Prince Charles had been intended to be yet more lavish. Originally Charles I had planned to make the Prince a Knight of the Order of the Bath at Westminster Abbey, and then proceed in procession all the way from Westminster to Windsor. Ashmole, *Institution of the Order of the Garter*, p. 341.

77 For further details on the investiture of Prince Charles, the proposed procession and a reproduction of Van Dyck's drawing, see Sharpe, *Personal Rule*.

78 Even before the events which followed 1642, Prince Charles's installation as Garter Knight was commemorated with full public (as well as private, royal) pomp. At least two commemorative medals were struck to celebrate the occasion (see engravings, Ashmole, *Institution of the Order of the Garter*, p. 366).

79 I believe this was Thomas Rowe.

80 *Parentalia*, p. 153. The loss of the Great George and Garter of King Gustav Adolph, seized by parliamentary forces during the civil war, returns as a kind of plangent refrain throughout *Parentalia*, as also in Ashmole, *Institution of the Order of the Garter*: 'But the Dean failed of

the like Success in his best Endeavours to preserve the George and Garter, of the great Gustavus Adolphus, King of Sweden; these Jewels containing four Hundred ninety-eight Diamonds, great and small, were returned after his Decease, by a solemn Embassy, (pursuant to the Statutes of the Order,) and by the Sovereign's Command, (24 May, Ann. 14 Car. I.) committed to the Custody of the Dean and Chapter of Windsor, to be layed up in the Treasury, "for a perpetual Memorial of that renowned King, who died in the Field of Battle, wearing some of those Jewels, to the great Honour of the Order, and as a true martial Prince, and Companion thereof." The Dean to prevent the irretrievable Loss of such valuable Ensigns, by the Plunder of the Rebels, in the Year 1642, took the extraordinary Care, with Hazard of Life, to bury them under the Floor of the Treasury; and deposited a Note in the Hands of a worthy Person, intimating where they might be found, in case of Death. In this Place they remained securely, till about the Beginning of March, 1645, when being discovered by Cornelius Holland, a Regicide, and taken thence by Colonel Ven, a Regicide, the then Governor of the Castle, and afterwards delivered to Colonel Whitchcott, (who succeeded him in that Government) were at length fetched away by John Hunt, Treasurer to the Trustees appointed by the long Parliament for the Sale of his Majesty's Goods, and sold by them to Thomas Beauchamp their then Clerk' (Ashmole, *Institution of the Order of the Garter*, pp. 203–4 and 641; cit. *Parentalia*, p. 136).

81 *Parentalia*, p. 137.

82 Contemporary lampoons took advantage of the grand aspirations of the Garter Knights, and the contrasting poor performance of individual Knights in military confrontations, to poke merciless fun

at James I and Frederick, Elector Palatine. Frederick appealed to James (his father-in-law) for military assistance when the Habsburgs drove the Winter King and Queen out of Bohemia. Instead, James made Frederick a Garter Knight (*in absentia*), and sent him a lavish, bejewelled Great George and Garter. When Frederick and Elizabeth fled from Prague, these were left behind (perhaps because Frederick was infuriated at the inappropriateness of the gesture at that critical political moment). This became common knowledge, and pamphlet cartoons of Frederick thereafter depicted him with one stocking falling down – because of the absence of his 'garter'.

83 *Parentalia*, pp. 139–40.

84 *Parentalia*, p. 136.

85 *Parentalia*, p. 136.

86 It was he who conveyed the Garter appointments to the two-year-old William of Orange, and other close relatives of the Stuarts on whom Charles, for want of more substantial gifts, bestowed the Order during his years of exile. See below, chapter 3.

87 *Parentalia*, pp. 135–6.

88 Ashmole also records consulting Garter records with Bishop Matthew Wren, in 1666.

89 *Parentalia*, p. 138.

90 *Parentalia*, p. 138. A copy of the order is preserved among Ashmole's manuscripts. See Black, *A Descriptive, Analytical, and Critical Catalogue*.

91 'Ex ipso Autogr. Penes praef. Jac. Palmer', Ashmole, *Institution of the Order of the Garter* [Appendix, s.p.].

92 Through an accident of bad timing which was probably coincidental, Charles received the news of the surrender of Bristol shortly after he had been informed that Parliament had agreed a pension of £8000 per annum for the Elector Palatine and his mother. It seemed possible that the Elector Palatine and his family held out some hope of being installed as the royal line of England in place

of the Stuarts, because of their greater commitment to the Protestant cause.

93 Carlton, *Charles I*, p. 289.

94 Carlton, *Charles I*, p. 289.

95 Carlton, *Charles I*, p. 291. It is not quite clear when or whether Rupert leaves – he is still offering 'abject apologies' in Oxford in December 1645.

96 *Parentalia*, p. 139.

97 Matthew Wren's almanac contains the following heartbreaking series of entries for this period: 'July 22. Denascitur Alicia F, 1643 [born August 22, 1642]. / Dec. 23. Francis. 2 dus F. 20 die natus, 1643. / Jan. 25. Franc. 2dus denat, 1643/4. / Feb. 27. Eliza F. denascitur Eliae. 9. vesper. 1643/4.' The State Papers Domestic contain a reference to Matthew Wren's family having to move their lodgings in the Tower because their old ones were needed for storing Spanish bullion. 1644. Dec. 15. Eliza 2. F. nata, 1644, & denata die 17.

98 C. Petrie (ed.), *King Charles, Prince Rupert, and the Civil War from Original Letters* (London: Routledge & Kegan Paul, 1974), p. 152.

99 For Rupert's movements during this period see the appendix to L. Brodsley, C. Frank and J. Steeds, 'Prince Rupert's drops', *Notes and Records of the Royal Society* 41 (1986), 1–26. From Rupert's point of view, the fact that the younger brothers of the Elector Palatine had been given neither role nor territories by the settlement of the Treaty of Westphalia in 1648 (which restored the lower Palatine to Karl Ludwig) no doubt influenced his decision permanently to throw in his lot with Charles in England. He had also quarrelled badly with Karl Ludwig, and permanently exiled himself from Heidelberg.

100 Coote, *Royal Survivor*, p. 174.

101 When Lodewijck Huygens (Christiaan Huygens's brother) visited London in 1651 as part of an embassy from the Dutch States-General, he saw some of Charles I's works of art up for sale at Somerset House. They had apparently been given to those who had outstanding royal debts, in lieu of cash, and the new owners were trying to sell them on as quickly as possible. See A. G. H. Bachrach and R. G. Collmer (eds), *Lodewijk Huygens: The English Journal 1651–1652* (Leiden: Brill, 1982), p. 61: 'We went to Somerset House again and saw a number of beautiful things, among them the most costly tapestries I ever saw. One room was valued at £300. In that same room were many antique and modern statues, though nearly all damaged. There was also a unicorn cane as thick as an arm, with a large crystal knob. In a gallery above, we saw a very large number of beautiful paintings, but all so badly cared for and so dusty that it was a pitiable sight. There was an admirable portrait by Van Dyck of King Charles sitting on a white horse, which could be obtained for £150. Five or six Titians, however, surpassed everything else there, and yet these also could be purchased at a very reasonable price. All these goods, brought together from several of the King's houses, had been given in payment to some creditors of the late Sovereign, who did their best now to get rid of them.'

102 *Parentalia*, p. 136. Ashmole records identical procedures for the successive investitures of Dean Matthew Wren, Dean Christopher Wren and Bruno Ryves, thus symbolically continuing the Garter seamlessly across the 1650s. Ashmole, *Institution of the Order of the Garter*, p. 249.

CHAPTER 2: *Precocious Students at Invisible Colleges*

1 See Adair, *By the Sword Divided*, chapter 5, 'Cavaliers in Oxford'.

2 R. G. Frank, Jr, 'John Aubrey FRS, John Lydall, and science at Commonwealth Oxford', *Notes and Records of the Royal Society* 27 (1972–3), 193–217; 196.

3 Carlton, *Charles I*, p. 294.

4 Moray became a leading courtier at Charles II's court after the Restoration. See below.

5 Carlton, *Charles I*, pp. 299–300, and 401 n.: 'Photo in *Archaeologia*, LII (1892) plate VIII. Sheldon immediately buried the promise, and dug it up at the Restoration.'

6 Dean Wren's composition as a delinquent is preserved in BL Add. MS 22,085. 'Register of the Committee of Sequestrations for co. Wilts; containing the compositions of delinquents etc.; from 1645 to 1648, with their signatures. Amongst them are C[ecil Calvert] 2nd Lord Baltimore, ff. 15b, 75; Dr. Christopher Wren [Dean of Windsor and father of the architect], f. 24; and Lady Blanch Arundell [widow of Thomas, 2nd Lord Arundell], f. 29. Paper. Small Folio.'

7 Both letters are in the Heirloom copy of *Parentalia* [item 11 following p. 158].

8 Facing p. 194 in the Heirloom *Parentalia*.

9 For a vivid account of the lives of royalists in this period see Hardacre, *The Royalists during the Puritan Revolution*.

10 L. M. Soo, *Wren's 'Tracts' on Architecture and Other Writings* (Cambridge: Cambridge University Press, 1998), pp. 103–4.

11 See Dean Wren's list of the birth-dates of his children transcribed by Christopher Wren junior in *Parentalia* (manuscript copy), BL MS Add. 25,071, fol. 25 recto [and fol. 26 verso – two recensions of the same document].

12 Figures for Matthew Wren's children and their demise based on his almanac jottings, transcribed in *Parentalia*, pp. 133–4.

13 For an illustration showing one of these early seed drills see J. Morrill, *Stuart Britain: A Very Short Introduction* (Oxford: Oxford University Press, 2000), p. 8.

14 Hardacre, *The Royalists during the Puritan Revolution*, p. 78. See also

p. 79: 'Confinement to a small area in the country proved irksome; and there must have been many who complained, with one of Dugdale's correspondents, of their "five mile tether" [*Life of Dugdale*, ed. Hamper, p. 243].'

15 On Harvey's work on the circulation of the blood, conducted around Charles I's hunting trips, see L. Jardine, *Ingenious Pursuits: Building the Scientific Revolution* (London: Little, Brown, 1999).

16 Orders were issued for the safekeeping of the King's property in the outer and privy lodgings at Whitehall in 1643, 1644, 1645 and 1648. See S. Thurley, *Whitehall Palace: An Architectural History of the Royal Apartments, 1240–1690* (New Haven and London: Yale University Press, 1999), p. 97. 'Following Charles's execution in January 1649, his "kingly office" was abolished and Parliament ordered the valuation of royal "honours, manors, castles, houses, messuages, parks and lands". Preparatory to their sale, Whitehall was exempted from this process on account of its importance, but on 4 July 1649 Parliament passed an Act for the sale of the "goods and personal estate of the late king" which did include the contents of Whitehall. However, there was a proviso for items to be reserved for the use of the state not exceeding the value of £10,000. A second Act in 1651 doubled the amount that could be reserved, and eventually over £50,000-worth of goods were not sold. These items were used by Parliament and later the Lord Protector' (Thurley, *Whitehall Palace*, p. 98). On the inventorying and sale of the King's possessions see also MacGregor, *The Late King's Goods*, and O. Millar (ed.), 'The inventories and valuations of the King's goods, 1649–1651', *Walpole Society* 43 (1970–2).

17 As in the case of Dean Wren, it is not clear when Harvey abandoned his service of the doomed King. It looks

as if he joined the King in Newcastle but was forced to leave the King's service when he was handed over to the parliamentary army and was not allowed to go to him when he was imprisoned in the Isle of Wight. After the execution of the King, Harvey compounded, rather than lose his assets entirely, and the committee at Goldsmiths' Hall which determined levels of composition allocated Harvey a fine of £2000 and forbade him access to London for a period of two years; £2000 is a huge fine, giving us some idea of Harvey's assessed wealth. Such fines were, however, often reduced later, since the depletions in income of the civil war period simply made it impossible for those fined to pay. See Hardacre, *The Royalists during the Puritan Revolution*.

18 On compounding see Hardacre, *The Royalists during the Puritan Revolution*, especially chapter 4, 'The Royalists under the Commonwealth 1649–1653'.

19 'Ent published a defence of Harvey, *Apologia pro circulatione sanguinis*, 1641, in which he showed the influence also of hermetic authors and concepts of innate heat, which seem to look forward to Mayow' (Westfall, Rice University Galileo project website).

20 For the crucial general importance of Commonwealth scientific activity in laying the foundations for the 'scientific revolution' at the Restoration, see C. Webster, *The Great Instauration: Science, Medicine and Reform 1626–1660* (London: Duckworth, 1975). I am extremely grateful to Charles Webster for allowing me to read the introduction to his new edition of *The Great Instauration* (in press), in typescript.

21 Richard Westfall, Rice University Galileo project website.

22 See Jardine, *Ingenious Pursuits*.

23 It is a feature of these kinds of circumstances that physicians are reluctant, later, to admit that the misfortunes of others caught up in war afforded wonderful opportunities to the doctors for medical advance.

24 This point is made allusively, as it were, by way of the story, which circulated widely and excited great popular interest, that Petty and others in the Oxford circle had revived a hanged woman, who was perceived to be breathing as they commenced a dissection.

25 Ent persuaded Harvey to publish and saw the volume through the press. The *History of Generation* carries a dedication to Robert Boyle (of whom more in chapter 3), dated 15 May 1651: 'You have, Sir, so inricht your tender years with such choice principles of the best sorts, and even to admiration managed them to the greatest advantage; that you stand both a pattern and a wonder to our Nobility and Gentry . . . you have not thought your blood and descent debased, because married to the Arts. You stick not to trace Nature in her most intricate paths, to torture her to a confession; though with your own sweat and treasure obtained.' Cit. R. E. W. Maddison, 'Studies in the life of Robert Boyle FRS. Part VI', *Notes and Records of the Royal Society*, 18 (1963), 104–24; 114–15. Maddison goes on: 'Highmore was a neighbour of Boyle, and practised at Sherborne, near Stalbridge; a fact which is sufficient to explain how the dedication came to be made to Boyle.'

26 Nathaniel Highmore, *Corporis humani disquisitio anatomica* (The Hague, 1651), sig. A1r. See Frank, 'John Aubrey FRS, John Lydall, and science at Commonwealth Oxford', p. 195. Frank cites Highmore's notebooks, British Museum MSS Sloane 577 and 579 for evidence that the material for his anatomy was compiled during his time as a fellow of Trinity.

27 On the research activities of the Oxford medical men during this period see Frank, *Harvey and the Oxford Physiologists*.

28 The Queen actually lived in Merton College, where Harvey was briefly appointed Warden in 1645.

29 For Dean Wren marginalia see J. A. Bennett, *The Mathematical Science of Christopher Wren* (Cambridge: Cambridge University Press, 1982), pp. 14–15.

30 George Bathurst was killed at the Battle of Farringdon in 1644. Frank says that Ralph Bathurst changed from divinity to medicine because of the parliamentary victory.

31 Aubrey, cit. Frank, 'John Aubrey FRS, John Lydall, and science at Commonwealth Oxford', p. 195. On Harvey's lost research see Westfall: 'Harvey planned a vast program of publication on respiration, the functions of the brain and spleen, animal locomotion, and comparative and pathological anatomy. All he actually published were *De motu* and *De generatione*, plus his essay defending *De motu* against Riolan. Many of his manuscripts were destroyed when his chambers in Whitehall were sacked in 1642, and then later in the great fire which consumed the library of the Royal College of Physicians. The manuscripts of his lecture notes (on anatomy, in the Royal College) and of "De musculis" and "De motu locali animalium" survive. He completed his second great work, *De generatione*, in about 1638, and ultimately published it in 1651. It was a fundamentally new view of generation in which oviparous generation, rather than viviparous, became the general model. His lecture notes show that he had dissected more than eighty different species of animals. His planned book on morbid anatomy was to have been based on post-mortem examinations. He also planned one on the effect that the concept of the circulation of the blood would have on the practice of medicine. The final section of *De generatione* is virtually a textbook on midwifery. He also composed a work on the generation of insects, which

was among the manuscripts destroyed in 1642' (Richard Westfall, Rice University Galileo project website). See also Frank, *Harvey and the Oxford Physiologists*.

32 See below, chapter 4.

33 Cit. Willmoth, *Sir Jonas Moore*, p. 53. On the details of compounding during the civil war and from 1649 under the Commonwealth see Hardacre, *The Royalists during the Puritan Revolution*.

34 See C. Webster, 'The College of Physicians: "Solomon's House" in Commonwealth England', *Bulletin of the History of Medicine* 41 (1967), 393–412.

35 For a full account of the activities of the Society of Physicians during this period see Webster, *The Great Instauration*; R. G. Frank, Jr, 'The physician as virtuoso in seventeenth-century England', in B. Shapiro and R. G. Frank, Jr (eds), *English Scientific Virtuosi in the 16th and 17th Centuries* (Los Angeles: William Andrews Clark Memorial Library, 1979), pp. 59–103.

36 *Parentalia*, p. 185.

37 When Christiaan Huygens's father Constantijn managed to get his son attached to the household of Maurice of Nassau, during the period immediately following the unexpected death of his own employer, William II of Orange, he stressed the fact that he would be unable to pay for his son's accommodation. See below, chapter 3.

38 *Parentalia*, pp. 184, 185.

39 'After deciphering a coded letter for the parliamentary authorities, Wallis was rewarded with the sequestered living of St Gabriel, London. He exchanged this living for St Martin in Ironmonger Lane in 1647' (Westfall, Galileo project website). There is a link between Wallis as cryptographer for Parliament around 1643 and Wilkins doing the same job for the Palatinate. This link explains how after the Treaty of Westphalia (and the reopening of Heidelberg University in 1652), and the

establishing of the English Protectorate, both England and the Palatinate continued with mathematical developments grounded in cryptography and associated mathematical advances. Wilkins and Haak continued to communicate regularly with the court of Karl Ludwig in Heidelberg; Wallis and Wilkins worked together in Oxford throughout the 1650s.

40 See the account given by Aubrey to Hobbes, Letter 199, 24 June 1675: 'When Mr Oughtreds Clavis Math was printed at Oxford, Dr Wallis had the Care of ye Impression: In ye place [preface?], Mr Oughtred makes honourable mentions of severall ingeniose persons, and amongst others Dr Wallis, of whom he sayd "a sharp-witted, pious, and hard-working man, very well versed in all literature of the more recondite sort, and perceptive in mathematical letters", this the good old Gent: [Oughtred] thought very faire, if not too much; but the Dr thought it not enough, but adds "and with an astonishing ability to unravel and explain writings which have been hidden and concealed in the most elaborate of cyphers – a sign of an extremely fine intelligence". This impudence of his extremely disobliged Mr Oughtred of wch he has often complayned to the Bp of Sarum [Seth Ward], and others that I know.' N. Malcolm (ed.), *Correspondence of Thomas Hobbes* (Oxford: Clarendon Press, 1994) 2, pp. 753–4. See also Aubrey, *Brief Lives*, pp. 328–9.

41 See Willmoth, *Sir Jonas Moore*, p. 52. 'In the epistle to the reader of the 1647 English Key [*Clavis*] Oughtred said that Ward had personally sought him out and "by a gentle violence induced me to publish again my former Tractate in a manner new moulded and perfected"; in the 1652 Latin edition the acknowledgements begin with a tribute to him expressed in similar terms' (ibid.). Willmoth

points out that this epistle refers to 'unspeakable wrongs' done to Oughtred shortly before publication of the 1647 edition of his arithmetic, and that this refers to moves to confiscate Oughtred's benefice because of his delinquent status. According to Willmoth the arithmetic helped ensure that Oughtred was not thus deprived (Willmoth, *Sir Jonas Moore*, pp. 56–7).

42 Willmoth, *Sir Jonas Moore*, p. 53. On Robert Wood see below.

43 Cit. Bennett, *The Mathematical Science*, p. 18. According to Bennett, Oughtred presented Wren with an inscribed copy of the 1652 *Clavis* (ibid.).

44 In the Royal Society manuscript draft of *Parentalia*, Christopher Wren junior writes: 'There was found among [Scarburgh's] Papers, a Latin Anonymous Treatise *de Motu Musculorum*. Printed in 1664. Lond: which the Collector cannot assent to have been His.' Wren junior attributed this work to his father, but it is now clear it was William Croone's *De ratione motus musculorum*, the first edition of which was published anonymously. Although the attribution of such a treatise to Wren does not figure in the printed version of *Parentalia*, the suggestion that such a work existed continues to circulate in the secondary literature on Wren. For the versions of *Parentalia*, and the limitations on Wren junior's reliability, see J. A. Bennett, 'A study of *Parentalia*, with two unpublished letters of Sir Christopher Wren', *Annals of Science* 30 (1973), 129–47.

45 On the Oughtred 'school' of mathematics see Willmoth, *Sir Jonas Moore*, pp. 43–61. On the 1652 *Clavis* edition's role in bringing together a group of like-minded aspirants to academic office under the Commonwealth administration see especially p. 54: 'It seems that interest in the *Clavis* was shared by many members of this Oxford-based circle,

and that (as J. A. Bennett has argued) the sponsoring of the 1652 edition was in some sense an expression of their joint aspirations. They were certainly using it as an advanced teaching text, and the likelihood is that young men like Wren and Rooke became acquainted with it through their contact with Ward and other members of the Wadham circle.'

46 See Willmoth, *Sir Jonas Moore*, pp. 50–1.

47 A similar exercise had been conducted at Cambridge – which had declared for Parliament – in 1644. Seth Ward was one of those who lost his fellowship at Cambridge. In 1649 he was, however, appointed by the Parliamentary Commissioners to the post of Savilian Professor of Astronomy at Oxford.

48 Carlton, *Charles I*, pp. 313, 350. *Calendar of State Papers Venetian etc. Vol. 28 1647–1652*, p. 90: March 19th 1649. 'Senato, Secreta. Dispacci, Munster. Venetian Archives. no. 245. Alvise Contarini, Venetian Ambassador to the Congress of Munster to the Doge and Senate. Encloses summary of the report made in Holland by the Ambassador Pau on his return from England. Enclosure 246: . . . "the Prince Palatine wished to visit him [the King] but the Bishop of London made his excuses on account of the distress he was in from the sight of his children."' p. 110 July 27 1649 no. 311 source as above to Michael Morosini, colleague in France [in Italian] 'In the negotiations with Brun [Antonio Brun, Spanish Plenipotentiary] about the Palatine there was some suggestion of a separate agreement between Spain and the Palatine, with a hint of including the English also. If this were true it would join with the alliance between Denmark and the Dutch. It is said that on the mention of England the one negotiating for the Palatine immediately drew back, because of the close connection

between the prince and the King of England [. . .]'.

49 Although the Elector Palatine was restored to his title lands, the Treaty of Westphalia explicitly denied any titles to the other male members of his line. Thus Rupert and Maurice were permanently excluded from lands or revenues in Germany, and hence continued to depend on subsidy from England – in the continuing expectation that one of them might eventually accede to the throne of England (as staunchly and reliably Protestant), should the monarchy be restored. Maurice was lost at sea during one of the brothers' merchant adventurer voyages to the West Indies. After the Restoration, as we shall see, Rupert became a member of Charles II's Privy Council, and a prominent member of the Royal Society. It was the son of Rupert's younger sister Sophie who, as George I, eventually became King of England.

50 See B. J. Shapiro, *John Wilkins, 1614–1672: An Intellectual Biography* (Berkeley and Los Angeles: University of California Press, 1969); H. Aarsleff, 'John Wilkins', *Dictionary of Scientific Biography* 14 (1976). Westfall says Wilkins was 'chaplain to William Fiennes, Lord Saye and Sele, 1637–c.1640; by 1641 until 1644 chaplain to Lord George Berkeley; chaplain to the Elector Palatine Charles Louis, the King's nephew, 1644–8'. Lord Saye and Sele was a notorious critic of Charles's excise tax (the tax Elias Ashmole was appointed to collect in 1644). Wilkins became Warden of Wadham College, Oxford in April 1648, following the inspection of the University by the Parliamentary Visitors, who ejected all notable royalists from their offices. Nevertheless, it is certainly worth taking seriously Aubrey's assertion that 'he was chaplain to his Highnesse [Charles Louis] Prince Elector Palatinate of the Rhine, with whom he went (after the peace

concluded in Germany was made) and was well preferred there by his Highnesse. He stayed there not above a yeare' (Aubrey, *Brief Lives*, p. 341).

51 On the scientific interests of the Palatinate court in exile see F. Yates, *The Rosicrucian Enlightenment* (London: Routledge & Kegan Paul, 1972), passim. Wilkins's early publications were as follows: *The discovery of a world in the moone, or, a discourse tending to prove, that 'tis possible there may be another habitable world on that planet*, with *A discourse concerning the possibility of a passage thither* (1638); *A discourse concerning a new planet, tending to prove that 'tis probable our Earth is one of the planets* (1640); *Mercury, or the secret and swift messenger, showing how a man may with privacy and speed communicate his thoughts to a friend at any distance* (1641); *Mathematical magick, or the wonders that may be performed by mechanical geometry* (1648). He is best known for his *An essay towards a real character and a philosophical language* (1667), a book much admired by the early Royal Society, the first print-run of which was entirely lost in the Great Fire of London in 1666, on which see *Ingenious Pursuits*. On these publications of Wilkins's see E. J. Bowen and H. Hartley, 'The Right Reverend John Wilkins, FRS (1614–1672)', *Notes and Records of the Royal Society* (1960), 47–56.

52 On Haak see P. R. Barnett, *Theodore Haak, FRS (1605–1690)* ('sGravenshage: Mouton & Co., 1962). Haak was a scientific 'intelligencer', an active correspondent who functioned as a link, first between Hartlib's circle and the so-called 'invisible college' and the continent (primarily Mersenne), later between the Royal Society and the continent. John Wallis stated that Haak was the person who originally proposed weekly meetings of the invisible college. Wilkins proposed Haak for membership of the Royal Society in 1677.

53 For Haak's activities on behalf of the Elector Palatine and his subsequent work for the English Parliament (rewarded with the proceeds of fines on sequestered Royalists) see Barnett, *Theodore Haak*, pp. 89–113.

54 Charles Louis's mother Elizabeth repudiated the parliamentary government as soon as Charles I was executed – and had her pension from London stopped forthwith (causing one more financial crisis in her crisis-ridden life in exile). Charles Louis prevaricated, and kept his pension for a further period.

55 It was on this basis that Cromwell appointed Wilkins as one of the three senior Oxford appointments entrusted with recruitment and appointment after the Commissioners had left Oxford.

56 *Parentalia*, p. 140.

57 Aubrey thought that Wilkins was chaplain to Viscount Say and Seale in 1640–41. Aubrey also has an illuminating comment on Wilkins's early career in the court circle: 'He sayd oftentimes, that the first rise, or hint of his Rising, was from accidentally a courseing of a Hare: where an ingeniose Gentleman of good quality falling into discourse with him, and finding him to have very good partes, told him, that he would never gett any considerable preferment by continuing in the University: and that his best way to betake him selfe to some Lord's, or great person's House, that had good Benefices to conferre. Sayd Mr John Wilkins, "I am not knowne in the world; I know not to whom to addresse myselfe upon such a designe." The Gentleman replied, "I will recommend you myselfe", and did so, to (as I thinke) the Lord Viscount Say and Seale, where he stayed with very good likeing till the late Civill warres, and then he was chaplain to his Highnesse [Charles Louis] Prince Elector Palatinate of the Rhine' (Aubrey, *Brief Lives*, pp. 340–1).

58 Bennett, like me, is tempted to make Wilkins, as Charles Louis's personal chaplain, one of those who stayed at the Dean's house in Windsor and ate at the Dean's table, as well as participating in the entertaining intellectual discussions there. Westfall says that Wilkins only became chaplain to the Elector Palatine in 1644.

59 Petty's publications in economics largely date from after the Restoration (he was too busy working directly for Cromwell during the Commonwealth and Protectorate years to publish). They include: *A Treatise of Taxes and Contributions*, written and printed 1662; *Verbum Sapienti [a word to the wise], or an Account of the Wealth and Expences of England, and the Method of raising Taxes in the most Equal Manner*, written 1665, printed 1691; *The Political Anatomy of Ireland*, written 1671–2, printed 1691; *Political Arithmetick, or a Discourse concerning the Extent and Value of Lands, People, Buildings . . . etc. As the same relates . . . to the Territories of . . . Great Britain . . . Holland, Zealand, and France*, written 1672–6, printed 1690 (and surreptitiously by a 'pirate' of those days in 1683); *Quantulumcunque concerning Money*, written 1682, printed 1695 (and perhaps 1682. Writings, ii. 438, 639); *Another Essay in Political Arithmetick concerning the Growth of the City of London*, written 1682, printed 1683 (the first essay is lost); *Observations (and further Observation) upon the Dublin Bills of Mortality*, written and printed 1683 and 1686; *Two Essays in Political Arithmetick concerning London and Paris*, 1687; *Observations upon the Cities of London and Rome*, 1687; *Five Essays in Political Arithmetick*, 1687; *Treatise of Ireland*, written 1687, printed 1899.

60 Willmoth, *Sir Jonas Moore*, says 1652; other sources give 1654 for the patent, which seems to me too late.

61 I. Masson and A. J. Youngson, 'Sir William Petty FRS (1623–1687)', *Notes and Records of the Royal Society* (1960), 79–90; 83–4.

62 Robert Wood became 'Accountant General of Ireland'. M. Hunter, *The Royal Society and its Fellows 1660–1700: The Morphology of an Early Scientific Institution*, revised edition (Oxford: Oxford University Press, 1994). So the fact that Wren takes advantage of his travelling to Ireland to send his letter of thanks to Petty might help date the letter. Bennett dates the letter to 1656, which is too late, as Petty returned to England in that year. In any case, Wren implies in the letter that he has already been supported by Petty in residence at Wadham for some time.

63 B. Little, *Sir Christopher Wren: A Historical Biography* (London: Robert Hale, 1975), p. 26.

64 Frank, *Harvey and the Oxford Physiologists*, p. 61.

65 Bennett, 'A study of *Parentalia*', pp. 146–7. Hartlib records in his 'Ephemerides' that Wood has visited him on 3 July 1656, before his departure to Ireland (Frank, *Harvey and the Oxford Physiologists*, p. 333, n. 41). After a successful career as a civil servant in Ireland, Wood later became headmaster of Christ's Hospital School, but stood down on grounds of ill health when inspection revealed the training of the boys to be distinctly mediocre.

66 *Parentalia*, p. 53. For Matthew Wren's place of residence in Oxford see Frank, *Harvey and the Oxford Physiologists*, pp. 88–9.

67 *Parentalia*, p. 55.

68 See below, chapter 4.

69 'The Marquis of Winchester and Bishop Wren are to remain in everlasting prisons, who, with those banished (already signified to you), and such as have assisted in the Irish affairs, have not leave to compound. The rest have thus: All within eighty miles of London, filing their petitions at Goldsmiths' Hall by the 1st of April; all more distant, within six

weeks, and if beyond the seas, by the 1st of June; after which time, to forfeit their estates.' John Evelyn, letter from London to Paris dated 22 March 1649. W. Bray (ed.), *Diary and Correspondence of John Evelyn FRS* (London: George Routledge & Sons, n.d.), p. 551.

70 The Wren family was not the only one to make contingency plans in March 1649. A draft letter survives from Robert Boyle to an unidentified lady soliciting her aid to secure a passport from the French ambassador for his brother Roger, Lord Broghill, to travel abroad to join Charles II in exile (in the event the passport was not needed as Broghill changed sides and became an important Cromwellian supporter). See Maddison, 'Studies in the life of Robert Boyle', p. 113.

71 Letter dated 6 April, 1649. *Parentalia*, p. 195. 'Extract [sic] of a Letter written, as it seems, in the Year 1649, and 17th of his Age'.

72 There is no copy or original of this letter in the earliest collection of *Parentalia* documents in the BL. In the RS manuscript, the opening sentence of the letter has two words heavily crossed out, with substitutions: 'Humanissimo ~~Tantorum~~ [?] <Sum[m]orum> Amicorum hospitio ~~illegible~~ / <receptus>, Ferias hasce Pascatis transegi'. The strikings out may be in order further to conceal the identity of the persons with whom Wren spent this visit. 'Tantus amicus', 'so highly esteemed friends', suggests protectors of high status.

73 By which Aylesbury means Bletchingdon. See Aubrey: 'The parsonage-house at Bletchingdon, was Mr Christopher Wren's home, and retiring-place. Here he contemplated, and studied, and found-out a great many curious things in Mathematiques. About this house he made severall curious Dialls with his owne handes which are still there to be seen. Which see, as well worthy to

be seen' (Aubrey, *Brief Lives*, pp. 158–9). Nevertheless, there seems to be some suggestion that Dean Wren retained access to his Knoyle Magna residence even after he had been deprived of his living there. See Evelyn's recollection of Wren's dream of the outcome of the Battle of Worcester there (1651). One possibility is that (as happened in other cases) the living was allocated to someone sympathetic to Dean Wren, who allowed him limited access.

74 'Of his Tract abovementioned, intitled, *Sciotericon*, and other Inventions, and Experiments, at the Age of Sixteen, relating to *Gnomicks*, is a memorable complimental Account from an eminent Mathematician of that Time, as follows' (*Parentalia*, p. 184). Thomas Aylesbury was a royalist minister, and an active Clubman (member of the group resisting both sides in the civil war conflict, on grounds of the damage they were causing non-combatants). 'When in July 1646 the Committee for Plundered Ministers took evidence regarding delinquent ministers one witness said that: "the said Mr Aylesbury was very forward in the Club business". Whether Thomas Aylesbury was amongst those taken at Shaftesbury, or later on August 4th at Hambleton Hill, near Shrawton, I cannot tell but the former seems more likely. He was certainly held in London for at least a year before being freed. The Committee for Plundered Ministers' report to the House of Commons on 28th March 1646 refers to Mr Alesbury's claim of a Prebendary at Heytesbury whence revenue of £10 per annum was reserved to be paid to the Minister of Heytesbury, Mr Gracious Frankelyn. During Aylesbury's imprisonment in London, his wife, Joan, was granted funds to support herself and eight children. Thus on 12th June 1646 she was granted £16 per annum (one fifth of

the rent of Kingston Deverill) and on 27th July of that year this income was supplemented by the granting of the residue of "all the tithes unto glebe lands and Easter booke" of Kingston Deverill. By contrast with the family's former income the deprivation was severe. It seems likely that Thomas Aylesbury, junior, who was to become Rector of Great Corsley was born in 1647/8 at Cloford following his father's return from imprisonment in London.' After Dean Wren's death in 1658, Aylesbury obtained his East Knoyle living, which he retained at the Restoration (additionally regaining his own confiscated livings), though he died shortly thereafter.

75 The Aylesbury letter may have been written as an open 'academic reference' for Wren, to assist him in gaining a university place. It resembles the letters written by influential friends of the Locke family, cited in Maurice Cranston's biography of John Locke, which facilitated his gaining a King's scholarship to Christ Church, Oxford. See M. Cranston, *John Locke: A Biography*, revised edition (Oxford: Oxford University Press, 1985).

76 Indeed, it has proved a handicap for all historians of science, that activities in the years 1642–51 are vague or invisible for most of the early scientists in England. This is strikingly the case in Westfall's register of early scientists on the Rice University Galileo project website.

77 Evelyn eventually secured Browne's house, Sayes Court in Deptford, for himself and his wife, in 1653.

78 Bray, *Evelyn Diary*, p. 167.

79 Bray, *Evelyn Diary*, p. 168. His letters for this turbulent period include vivid eye-witness accounts of events. On 18 December 1648, for instance, he writes that 'soldiers have marched into the city, and seized on the public treasures; they have been pretty quiet as to much action, only they extremely insinuate themselves into the town, where they pretend to be at free-quarters until their arrears be fully paid. In the mean time they have garrisoned Blackfriars (which likewise they have fortified with artillery); Paul's Church [i.e. Old St Paul's Cathedral], which, with London House, they have made stables for their horses, making plentiful fires with the seats; also Barnard's Castle, with divers other considerable places in the body and rivage of the city.' Bray, *Evelyn Diary*, p. 549.

80 Two references in the State Papers allow us to glimpse the departure arrangements. *Calendar of State Papers: Domestic 1649–50*, p. 31 [SP Vol. I no. 18] 1649 March 9 Council of State Day's Proceedings: 'The lodgings formerly let to the Prince Elector in Somerset House to be reserved for the service of the public. This order to be sent to the committee for ordering the houses belonging to the commonwealth.' *Calendar of State Papers: Domestic 1649–50*, p. 37 [SP Vol. I no. 24] 1649 March 13 Council of State Day's Proceedings: 'Sir Henry Mildmay to report to the House that the Prince Elector intends travelling to his own country on Thursday, and to inquire whether persons should not be sent to offer the civilities usual on the departure of princes and their ambassadors' [I. 62 pp. 82–7].

81 Reported in a letter smuggled to his father-in-law Sir Richard Browne in Paris on 22 March 1649: 'The Prince Elector (with some ceremony) is gone for Holland, from whence Mr. Strickland writes word that Monsieur Pau, the Ambassador (returned, not long since, out of England) hath made a very favourable relation of his noble usage here: and that the States will not interpose in the difference between the Prince and Parliament, with matter to the same effect' (Bray, *Evelyn Diary*, pp. 551–2).

82 Rhenen had been built for the Winter King and Queen between 1629 and 1639

to house their court in exile. It was a palace of some splendour, but by the late 1640s it had fallen into disrepair, externally and internally, due to the precarious finances of the widowed Queen. For a drawing of the Palace, with its magnificent tower, in 1644, by Pieter Saenredam, see G. Schwartz and M. J. Bok, *Pieter Saenredam: The Painter and his Time* (The Hague: SDU Publishers, 1990), p. 194.

83 'When Charles Louis made a decidedly ignominious reappearance at the Hague in the April after the tragedy [April 1649], his mother enclosed him with her, in her bedchamber, for an interview so unpleasant that he recalled it with resentment five years later. . . . She proceeded to dictate his conduct. He must pay his court to the new King of England, and refrain from visiting the Parliamentary agent to the States General. Charles Louis, who had left London requesting his friends there to continue his pension, suggested that his cousin might not wish to see him. But the very ugly French-looking youth of nineteen who was now Charles II had particularly easy manners, and a family party at Rhenen, engineered by Elizabeth, passed off without a hitch. Charles Louis then departed. . . . At Cleves [Kleve, further down the Rhine], a letter from his mother, upbraiding him for neglecting to condole with the widow of King Charles the Martyr, enlivened the journey of the Elector Palatine towards his devastated principality.' C. Oman, *The Winter Queen: Elizabeth of Bohemia* (London: Phoenix Press, 1938), pp. 374–5. For the correspondence between Charles Louis and his mother see G. Bromley, *Collection of Original Royal Letters* (London, 1835). Charles Louis's sister Sophie put a somewhat different interpretation on the meeting between her brother and Charles II in two letters to her absent brothers Rupert and Maurice (fighting in

Ireland) which were intercepted by parliamentary intelligence. She implied that Charles Louis had had a complete change of heart and repudiated the parliamentary regime. *Calendar of State Papers: Domestic 1649–50*, p. 85 [SP Vol. I no. 53] April 13 1649: 'Princess Sophia to her brother Prince Rupert. We have no news about "Rupert the devil" except what comes out in print. My brother the Prince Elector is here, and cares no more for those cursed people in England, for he has done his duty to the king, which he might have avoided, as his affairs require him in Cleves. The Scotch Commissioners are here also, and bring every day some new proposal to the King, full of impertinency. They would not that he should keep any honest man about him; they are in great favour with the Princess of Orange, who declares much for the Presbyterians, and says Percy is the honestest man the King has about him.' [Holograph, French, 2 pages. Endorsed: Sophia to Rupert, intercepted.] *Calendar of State Papers: Domestic 1649–50*, [SP Vol. I no. 54] April 13 1649: 'Princess Sophia to Prince Maurice. The Prince Elector is here, and is now altogether, as we are, against the knaves; he will soon go to his country. Peace in France is made. My brother Edward has taken no employment. Prince Ratzevil is deadly sick in Poland; it is said Marquis Gonzaga has poisoned him. The States have forbidden all the ministers to pray for Kings in the churches, but the French will not desist. With note of compliment from Charles Louis, Elector Palatine.' [Holograph, German, 2 pages. Similarly endorsed.]

84 See Ashmole, *The Institution, Laws & Ceremonies*.

85 The fact that Charles Louis became Karl Ludwig once more when he returned to his German Palatine territories further complicates any attempt to reconstruct his curiously shadowy history.

86 I believe this is Rutger van Haersolte, Governor of the Overijsel region. He was a strong supporter of of William of Orange, backing up Princess Mary in her declaration of her infant son William III as Stadholder, in opposition to the Dutch States-General's opposition of the post following the untimely death of her husband William II in 1650.

87 26. Mart. [1649]. Transcribed from University of Leiden website.

88 30. Mart. [1649]. Transcribed from University of Leiden website.

89 See C. D. Andriesse, *Titan kan niet slapen: een biographie van Christiaan Huygens* (Amsterdam: Contact, 1993), French trans. D. Losman, *Christiaan Huygens* (Paris: Albin Michel, 1998), p. 93.

90 This evidence is circumstantial. But (a) the tone and vocabulary of Constantijn Huygens the Elder's poems match closely the language of Wren's letter to his father; (b) Klarenbeeck is convincingly on the route the Palatine party would have taken to Kleve, and (c) the fact that Huygens writes three intense poems about Charles I's execution immediately following his stay there adds substance to the suggestion he had met the party coming from England there.

91 In fact, Wilkins's book on cryptography, *Mercury or the Secret and Swift Messenger* (1641), is dedicated to 'The Right Honourable George Berkeley, Baron of Berkeley', and signed 'Your Lordship's Servant and Chaplain'.

92 Aubrey, *Brief Lives*, pp. 340–1.

93 Montague Burrows (ed.), *The Register of the Visitors of the University of Oxford from AD 1647 to AD 1658* (London, 1881), p. 22, cit. Aarsleff, 'John Wilkins', p. 364.

94 For the complexity of the Palatine relations with the English during the civil wars see above, chapter 1.

95 *Parentalia*, p. 183.

96 *Parentalia* marginal note: 'Suppos'd Dr. Wilkins'.

97 *Parentalia*, p. 183.

98 Although the Palatinate Palace at Heidelberg remained intact (it was eventually burned to the ground by the French in 1698), the University did not reopen until 1652, which may have contributed to the decision to bring Wren back to England. When it did it once more became one of the great centres for mathematics in Europe.

99 *Parentalia*, p. 7. The marginal gloss to this reads: 'Anno 1622. ex schedis C. W. et Helvici Chron. p.158'. Elsewhere in *Parentalia* this Helvicus volume crops up again, with Dean Wren's marginal annotations, as particularly associated with his son Christopher. It is in this volume that Dean Wren notes Christopher Wren's birth, with the information that there was a transit of Mercury in that year (*Parentalia*, pp. 147–8). He further notes on the title page (according to *Parentalia*) that the anonymous tract on calculating years according to the Julian calendar printed in this 1651 edition and later Oxford editions was in fact by Christopher Wren junior (aged nineteen): 'Tractatulus ad periodum Julianam spectans, Chronologiae summe utilis. This short Tract, which contains a Method to find any particular Year requir'd, upon giving the Cycles, is inserted in the Prolegomena of Helvicus's *Theatrum historicum & chronologium*, Ed. Oxon. 1651. And continu'd in the later Editions. The Author's Name is not mention'd; but that it was written by Mr. Wren, is manifest from a Note indorsed on the Title-page of the Book, in the Hand of his Father, the Dean, now in the Possession of Christopher Wren, Esq; The Words are these: "Denique filio meo modestius renitenti incentivum adhibui, ut tractatulum illum algebraicum; Julianae periodo (e cyclis in historia datis) expiscandae accommodatissimum, sudante jam hoc praelo Oxoniensi, praefigi sineret." By the Time, in which this

Tract was first publish'd it appears, that Mr. Wren could not be more than nineteen Years of Age, when he wrote it.' *Parentalia*, p. 244; see also p. 195.

100 The only strong argument against Wren's having left England is the absence of documentary evidence. In the case of Hooke, of whom it is also claimed that he never visited the continent, there is much circumstantial evidence to support the view that he travelled at least as far as The Hague. There is in fact evidence that he may have been to Paris, too. Hooke's *Diary* records: '8 July [1676] Met Sir J. Hoskins at Childs. Resolved upon new Society, and to go into France with Mr. Montacue.'

101 See Wood, *Athenae Oxonienses*, ed. Philip Bliss, 3 (London, 1817), col. 971, cit. Aarsleff, 'John Wilkins', p. 375. Aarsleff adds, 'Wood's information is also in Walter Pope, *Life of Seth Ward* (London 1697), p. 29.'

102 See M. Keblusek and J. Zijlmans, *Princely Display: The Court of Frederik Hendrik of Orange and Amalia van Solms* (Zwolle: Historical Museum, The Hague, 1997).

103 For the influence of Dutch architecture on Wren's collaborator, Hooke, see A. Stoesser-Johnston, 'Robert Hooke and Holland: Dutch influence on his architecture', *Bulletin KNOB* 99 (2000), 121–37.

104 Bennett, *Mathematical Science*, p. 16; Little, *Sir Christopher Wren*, p. 25.

105 On Samuel Hartlib see M. Greengrass, M. Leslie and T. Raylor (eds), *Samuel Hartlib and Universal Reformation* (Cambridge: Cambridge University Press, 1994); J. Bennett and S. Mandelbrote (eds), *The Garden, the Ark, the Tower, the Temple: Biblical Metaphors of Knowledge in Early Modern Europe* (Oxford: Museum of the History of Science, 1998), pp. 33–41; Webster, *Great Instauration*, passim.

106 Bennett, *The Mathematical Science*, p. 17. In another letter Wallis tells Hartlib that Wren 'besides divers other fine inventions and contrivances, hath found out a way to measure the moistnesse and dryness of the air exactly' (ibid.).

107 Bennett, *The Mathematical Science*, p. 18.

108 See M. Greengrass, 'Archive refractions: Hartlib's papers and the workings of an intelligencer', in M. Hunter (ed.), *Archives of the Scientific Revolution: The Formation and Exchange of Ideas in Seventeenth-Century Europe* (Woodbridge: Boydell Press, 1998), pp. 35–47, especially figure 2, p. 41, which shows a significant dip in the volume of surviving letters in the correspondence for the years 1649–56.

109 L. Hunter, 'Sisters of the Royal Society: the circle of Katherine Jones, Lady Ranelagh', in L. Hunter and S. Hutton (eds), *Women, Science and Medicine 1500–1700* (Stroud: Sutton Publishing, 1997), pp. 178–97; 186.

110 J. Buchanan-Brown (ed.), *John Aubrey, Brief Lives* (London: Penguin Books, 2000), p. 253.

111 Frank, 'John Aubrey, FRS, John Lydall, and science at Commonwealth Oxford', p. 202.

112 Frank, 'John Aubrey, FRS, John Lydall, and science at Commonwealth Oxford', p. 202.

113 Frank, 'John Aubrey, FRS, John Lydall, and science at Commonwealth Oxford', p. 215.

114 *Parentalia* has Petty's patent of the double-writing machine as 1647 'for seventeen years' (p. 216).

115 On Boyle and Broghill, and the importance of the Anglo-Irish gentry in the Commonwealth and Protectorate periods see below, chapter 3.

116 Cit. Maddison, 'Studies in the life of Robert Boyle', p. 112.

117 BM MS 25,071 ff. 42–3. J. A. Bennett, 'Studies in the life and work of Sir Christopher Wren' (University of Cambridge: PhD dissertation, 1974) [PhD 8750], 21–7. (Two new Wren letters from the British Library copy of *Parentalia*.) Jim Bennett suggests

this letter is written to Matthew Wren junior in the period 1651–54 (which is unlikely, since he too was in Oxford with Christopher at that time).

118 *Parentalia*, pp. 214–15.

119 *Parentalia*, p. 215.

120 *Parentalia*, pp. 215–16. It seems reasonably clear here that it is Petty who has laid claim to the perfected instrument: 'I am beholding to the Person who, by vindicating it to be his own, has put me again in Mind of it [i.e. claiming credit for the final developed instrument].'

121 On the organisation of Wren's office and the pattern of production of sets of drawings see below, chapter 5.

122 *Parentalia*.

123 'Ad Regem, feliciter Reducem / Diffluit en Gemino Quam prodiga Sepia Ductu, / Ut cadat in Titulos, Carole Magne Tuos / Marte, ac Consilio nam Te Bis Scribere Magnum, / Unica si nequeat Dextera, Dupla valet.' RS MS *Parentalia*, fol. 235v. Similarly arch verses were attached by Wren to his lunar globe, also presented to the King.

124 Cit. *Parentalia*, p. 212.

125 See Bennett, *The Mathematical Science*, p. 73. Monconys visited Wren himself, and captured his physical appearance in 1663 for us as follows: 'i'y allay encore plus voir M. Renes grand Mathematicien quoy que petit de corps, mais des plus ciuils & des plus ouuerts que j'aye trouuez en Angleterre' (Bennett, *The Mathematical Science*, p. 25).

126 See Jardine, *Ingenious Pursuits*.

127 Bennett, *The Mathematical Science*, p. 133, n. 8.

128 Bennett, *The Mathematical Science*, p. 73.

129 Matthew Wren junior, *Monarchy Asserted*, fol. A7v–A8r.

130 For Wren's micrometer and the lunar globe which he constructed with its help see below, chapter 3.

131 Matthew Wren junior, *Monarchy Asserted*, fol. A2r.

CHAPTER 3: *Making the Most of One's Talents*

1 Cit. Coote, *Royal Survivor*, p. 137.

2 Cit. Coote, *Royal Survivor*, p. 128.

3 Cit. A. Bryant, *King Charles II* (London: Collins, 1955), p. 31. Hyde's own circumstances were not much better: 'I am sure the King himself owes for all he hath eaten since April, and I am not acquainted with one servant of his who hath a pistole in his pocket. Five or six of us eat together one meal a day for a pistole a week, but all of us owe for God knows how many weeks to the poor woman that feeds us' (*Cl. S. P.*, III. 174, cit. Bryant, *Charles II*, p. 33).

4 Compare, for example, the magnificent Arundel collection of paintings and marbles (sold off to support the family during the Commonwealth years), and indeed Charles I's own art collection, with the coveted Tradescant Ark collection of exotic rarities, collected by a mere gardener, and which Elias Ashmole was so anxious to acquire in 1659. See O. Impey and A. MacGregor (eds), *The Origin of Museums: The Cabinet of Curiosities in Sixteenth- and Seventeenth-Century Europe* (Oxford: Clarendon Press, 1985).

5 Meanwhile his father retreated into copiously annotating the pages of books in his personal library, interrogating the texts he read, and turning his intellectual energies to such topics as schemes for a universal language and curiosities of natural history. See Wren senior's annotations in Sir Thomas Browne, *Pseudoxia epidemica: or, Enquiries into Very Many Received Tenets, and Commonly Preserved Truths* (London, 1646) and Francis Bacon, *Sylva Sylvarum* (London, 1631 edition). The former are discussed in Bennett and Mandelbrote, *The Garden, the Ark, the Tower, the Temple*, pp. 126–7; the latter in P. Gouk, *Music Science and Natural Magic in Seventeenth-Century England* (New Haven and London:

Yale University Press, 1999), p. 161. See also R. L. Colie, 'Dean Wren's marginalia and early science at Oxford', *Bodleian Library Record* 6 (1960), 541–51.

6 BL MS *Parentalia*, fol. 21 verso.

7 A. Powell (ed.), *Brief Lives and Other Selected Writings by John Aubrey* (London: The Cresset Press, 1949), pp. 180–2.

8 Little, *Sir Christopher Wren*, p. 35. See John Ward, *The Lives of the Professors of Gresham College* (London, 1740), pp. 109–10: 'Sir Christopher had a sister, named Susan, married to Dr. William Holder, subdean of the chapel to his majesty king William, subalmoner of St. Paul's, and canon of Ely, who was a man of great learning and fine parts. Nor was she less eminent for her great virtues, and rare accomplishments; for besides her exemplary prudence, piety, and other charities, expressed on her sepulchral monument, "in compassion to the poor she applied herself to the knowledge of medicinal remedies, wherein God gave so great a blessing, that thousands were happily healed by her, and no one ever miscarried; King Charles the second, queen Catharine, and very many of the court, had also experience of her successful hand." She died on 30 of June 1688, aged 61 years, forty five of which she had happily passed in a conjugal state, and lies buried with her husband in the vault under St. Paul's church, near Sir Christopher, her brother.'

9 Cit. Bowen and Hartley, 'John Wilkins', p. 53.

10 The statue of Colly Cibber in Soho Square is to this day fitted with such a device.

11 Cit. Bowen and Hartley, 'John Wilkins', pp. 50–1. The stained marble presages Wren's later interest in such features as part of the interiors of his public buildings.

12 Bray, *Evelyn Diary*, pp. 570–1.

13 See Bennett and Mandelbrote, *The Garden, the Ark, the Tower, the Temple*, pp. 162–3: 'This work included a contribution from Arnold Boate, on the generation of bees, as well as pieces by other members of the Hartlib circle. In particular, it printed several letters detailing new designs of beehive, of which the most striking was the transparent beehive developed by William Mewe, a Gloucestershire clergyman, following a model mentioned in Pliny. Mewe's invention had been further modified by John Wilkins and his young protégé, Christopher Wren. Hartlib illustrated Wren's design, executed in May 1654, for a three-storey, transparent beehive. The bees were able to move between the various layers of the hive, and glass panels set into the structure allowed an observer to see the honey cascading down inside it. Although Wren's construction had not been an immediate success (due to a failure to realise that bees worked downwards), it offered the prospect of an ever-increasing stock of bees and honey within the same hive. Sir Cheney Culpeper was enthusiastic about the possibilities of transparent hives, "wherein the whole way of woorkinge of that little creature might be seene; by which wee might (I am confidente) haue vnsophisticated wines of our owne, cheaper & better then from other nations".'

14 If beehives are a special emblem in relation to the Freemasons, that may be another reason for Wren (by 1710 Grand Master of the London Lodge) accepting credit for the apiary design.

15 Charles W. Colby (ed.), *Selections from the Sources of English History*, (London: Longmans, Green & Co., 1920), pp. 196–9.

16 'We learn of these illustrious guests from a letter of Haak's, which was carried to France by a German friend of his at the beginning of July' (Barnett, *Theodore Haak*, p. 87).

17 It was Robert Boyle who apparently coined the phrase 'invisible college'.

See below, chapter 3. The coinage relates to 'club' here because Boyle was heavily into alchemy and early chemistry, where secret, and invisible societies were the order of the day. Webster links the 'invisible college' both with Boyle and with scientific activities specifically linked to a Boyle–Ranelagh scientific circle in Ireland (*Great Instauration*, pp. 57–67).

18 See OED: A club as 'A clique: a secret society' given up to 1730 as an introduced word. For the verb: 'To gather into a club-like mass. 1625; hence to gather together 1641'. 'To combine togther', 'introduced' in 1649 (from French). 'To combine or contribute to a common end 1632'; (1612) 'club-law' or law of the physically stronger. For 'Club-man' (1597) a man armed with a club and 'A member of a club' (1851?). 'Club-riser' (1645) = club-man 'Eng. Hist.'.

19 On playing cards see Rachel Jardine, MA thesis. Thanks to Rachel Jardine for picking up the reference to the term 'club-men', and its relationship to 'The bloody game of cards' pamphlet (and derivation from card suits).

20 On the historical club-men see J. Morrill, *Revolt in the Provinces: The People of England and the Tragedies of War 1630–1648*, second edition (London and New York: Longman, 1999), pp. 132–51.

21 See above, chapter 2.

22 Cit. Frank, 'John Aubrey FRS, John Lydall, and science at Commonwealth Oxford', p. 203.

23 H. W. Robinson, 'An unpublished letter of Dr. Seth Ward relating to the early meetings of the Oxford Philosophical Society', *Notes and Records of the Royal Society* 7 (1949), pp. 69–70; G. H. Turnbull, 'Samuel Hartlib's influence on the early history of the Royal Society', *Notes and Records of the Royal Society* 10 (1953), 101–30; 113. Cit. M. Feingold, 'Of records and grandeur: the archive of the Royal Society', in M. Hunter

(ed.), *Archives of the Scientific Revolution: The Formation and Exchange of Ideas in Seventeenth-Century Europe* (Woodbridge: Boydell Press, 1998), pp. 171–84; pp. 172–3.

24 For Dean Wren's marginalia see Bennett, *The Mathematical Science*, pp. 14–16.

25 Dr Samuel Johnson's biographer James Boswell was a direct descendant of Alexander Bruce and his aristocratic Dutch wife. Cornelis van Aerssen van Sommelsdyck, Bruce's wife's brother, became Governor of Surinam in the 1680s.

26 See Brodsley, Frank and Steeds, 'Prince Rupert's drops', p. 22. F. Kitson, *Prince Rupert: Admiral and General-at-Sea* (London: Constable, 1998), pp. 124–5: 'Rupert's inventive labours during the period [1656–59] include the making of a quadrant for measuring altitude at sea and the design of a machine for raising water. He was also working on the production of high-quality gunpowder with vastly improved explosive power, which he demonstrated in England soon after the Restoration. But the work for which Rupert is most famous today was his development of the engraving process known as mezzotint.'

27 See J. Sargeaunt, *Annals of Westminster School* (London: Methuen & Co., 1898). Since Hooke was not a King's scholar at Westminster School (he lacked the means), he cannot have been one of the three Westminster scholars sent annually to Christ Church. Westminster also sent choral scholars, and Hooke had musical talents, so may officially have held a choral scholarship.

28 See Hooke's *Diary*.

29 In 1672 Busby retired from Westminster School, and purchased the manor at Willen, where he commissioned a new church, designed by Hooke.

30 This was a standard arrangement for a category of student called a Town

boy. See Sargeaunt, *Annals of Westminster School*, p. 122.

31 Thus, according to Aarsleff, Wilkins is also the intermediary between Hooke and Wren. 'While still at the Westminster School, Robert Hooke received a copy of Mathematical Magick as a gift from the author; and when a few years later he became a student at Oxford, he attended the scientific meetings and sought Wilkins' advice on his experiments on the art of flying and the making of artificial muscles.' Aarsleff, 'John Wilkins', p. 369. The source cited in the footnote is R. T. Gunther, *Early Science at Oxford*, 6 (Oxford, 1930), *The Life and Work of Robert Hooke*, pp. 5–9.

32 Thanks to Rachel Jardine for spotting this connection.

33 Cit. Frank, *Harvey and the Oxford Physiologists*, p. 165.

34 See below, chapter 4.

35 Petty, 'The Raising of Anne Greene', 14 December 1650, in Marquis of Lansdowne (ed.), *The Petty Papers: Some Unpublished Writings*, 2 vols (London: Constable and Co., 1927) 2, 157–67.

36 Frank, *Harvey and the Oxford Physiologists*, pp. 50, 53.

37 Frank, *Harvey and the Oxford Physiologists*, p. 50.

38 His father Samuel Fell had retired to the country after his ejection from the Deanship of Christ Church, and died in 1648.

39 The couple resemble other high–low male partnerships after the civil war like Finch and Baines, and Ray and Willoughby (all of whom are members of the Royal Society).

40 Aubrey, *Brief Lives* (Penguin edition), p. 13.

41 Letter from Evelyn to Boyle, Sayes-Court, September 3, 1659. Bray, *Evelyn Diary*, pp. 590–2. Evelyn is coyly explicit about the celibacy: 'If I and my wife take up two apartments (for we are to be decently asunder; however I stipulate, and her inclination will greatly suit with it,

that shall be no impediment to the Society, but a considerable advantage to the economic part)' (ibid. p. 591). Evidently this part of the plan did not meet with Boyle's approval – we may assume from the tone of Evelyn's next letter that the rest of his response to the plan, detailed down to the costs of the building and rules of the society, was positive. Evelyn's long letter of 29 September is a long, elaborate defence of love and matrimony, and how intelligent wives can be a positive support to their husbands' intellectual endeavours (ibid., pp. 592–5).

42 Evelyn's proposal for a monastic college apparently included a plan and elevation for the proposed building. As we shall see, Wilkins had already provided a rudimentary kind of 'college' building in the form of modified space in the Schools Quadrangle at Oxford. Evelyn's more grandiose scheme belongs to discussions of a range of possibiities for purpose-built accommodation for a 'society' or 'college', in which Wren undoubtedly took part. See below.

43 Bray, *Evelyn Diary*, p. 596. The 'observations' Evelyn was sending concerned the encouraging of a regular ring system in trees whose wood would later be used for joinery ('I doubt not but by some art [English trees] might be made to have their circles as orderly as those we find in Brasile, Ebene [Ebony], &c.').

44 Cit. A. Plowden, *Henrietta Maria: Charles I's Indomitable Queen* (Stroud: Sutton Publishing, 2001), p. 237.

45 Frank, *Harvey and the Oxford Physiologists*, p. 165. According to the DNB an edition of the *Diatribae duae* was also published in The Hague. If this was the case, might Hooke, as Willis's 'cousin' and scientific assistant, have taken it there for printing?

46 'Willis's doctrine of fermentation was founded upon a compromise

between chemistry and atomism. He saw matter as divisible into ultimate particles, but he ascribed to these particles separate identities based on their *chemical composition*, and not upon their shape and size, as did the purely mechanical atomists' (Frank, *Harvey and the Oxford Physiologists*, p. 165).

47 See above, chapter 2.

48 *Some considerations touching the usefulnesse of experimental naturall philosophy* (Oxford, 1663), Part II, pp. 57–60, cit. Frank, *Harvey and the Oxford Physiologists*, pp. 170–1.

49 Wallis to Oldenburg, November 1675, cit. Frank, *Harvey and the Oxford Physiologists*, p. 170.

50 This account of the development of experimental techniques and accompanying theory concerning intravenous injection and blood transfusion is indebted to Frank's brilliant reconstruction of the team researches of the Oxford physicians in *Harvey and the Oxford Physiologists*, particularly chapter 7.

51 BL Add. MS 25,071 ff. 92–3, also f. 45. See Bennett, 'A study of *Parentalia*', pp. 146–7.

52 Frank, *Harvey and the Oxford Physiologists*, pp. 171–2. Neile to Oldenburg, 15 December 1667: *Correspondence* IV, 54–7.

53 Frank, *Harvey and the Oxford Physiologists*, p. 172.

54 R. Latham and W. Matthews (eds), *The Diary of Samuel Pepys*, 11 vols (London: Bell & Hyman, 1972, reissued HarperCollins, 1995) 5, 151.

55 Frank, *Harvey and the Oxford Physiologists*, pp. 172–3.

56 Cit. Frank, *Harvey and the Oxford Physiologists*, p. 177.

57 See Jardine, *Ingenious Pursuits*, chapter 3.

58 This account, from Willis's *Cerebri anatome*, is taken directly from Frank, *Harvey and the Oxford Physiologists*, p. 174. See also pp. 182–3.

59 Lower to Boyle, 4 June 1663; *Works* VI, 467. Cit. Frank, *Harvey and the Oxford Physiologists*, p. 174.

60 Cit. Frank, *Harvey and the Oxford Physiologists*, p. 174. There is no doubt in my mind that this association is deliberate. Throughout the pages and pages of descriptions of experiments in injecting opium into dogs, no mention is made of the possibility of injecting it into a man, let alone oneself. However, since Wren and Hooke did every other possible kind of self-experiment, it is hard to see why they would have resisted this one. In 1689 Hooke wrote a small treatise on the therapeutic efficacy of cannabis, in which he highlighted the efficacy of cannabis to induce sleep. As a chronic insomniac himself, he had presumably tried the remedy he advocated with such enthusiasm.

61 Taken from the 1681 English edition of *The Anatomy of the Brain* (1681) (reprint, USV Pharmaceutical Corporation, Tuckahoe, New York, 1971), p. 4.

62 J. A. Bennett, 'A note on theories of respiration and muscular action in England c. 1660', *Medical History* 20 (1976), 59–69; Frank, *Harvey and the Oxford Physiologists*, p. 181. See *Parentalia*, following p. 350, 'Actorum D[ivi]ni Ch. Wren': '1667: Epistola ad Doc[tore]m Carol[u]m Scarborough, De Ossibus Brachii &c. MS.'

63 Frank, *Harvey and the Oxford Physiologists*, pp. 179–80. See also Richard Westfall's entry for Willis on the Rice Galileo project website.

64 BL MS *Parentalia*, fol. 38 verso: 'At the desire of Sr. C. Scarborough he Discours'd larg'ly on the Motions of the Muscles, Explaining the Anatomy by Models form'd in Pastboards. Hence it was, that in the latter part of his life, he has been often heard to complain; That King Charles the 2d. had done him a disservice in takeing him from the pursuit of Those Studies, and obliging him to spend all his time in Rubbish; (the expression he had for Building:) for, had he been permitted to have follow'd the Profession of Physick, in

all probability he might have Provided much better for his Family.' At the end of his life William Petty, too, expressed regret that he had not continued to pursue his original profession as a physician. See F. Harris, 'Ireland as a laboratory: the archive of Sir William Petty', in M. Hunter (ed.), *Archives of the Scientific Revolution: The Formation and Exchange of Ideas in Seventeenth-Century Europe* (Woodbridge: Boydell Press, 1996), pp. 73–90.

65 Daniel Whistler was actually a physician, friend and colleague at the College of Physicians of Scarburgh and others. In 1645 he discovered the nutritional cause of rickets.

66 Robina French had previously been married to Peter French of Christ Church, 'also a man of some importance in the university' (Aarsleff, 'John Wilkins', p. 378). Most sources maintain that personal intervention by Cromwell was necessary to allow the head of house of an Oxford college to marry. However, Aarsleff, 'John Wilkins', rebuts this: 'It is an often repeated error that Wilkins on this occasion gained permission to marry from Cromwell, then chancellor of the university; the Wadham statutes had already been altered in 1651 so as to permit the warden to marry – one wonders whether Wilkins contemplated marriage at that time or whether he was acting on principle [in changing the statutes].' The story in the academic community was that Wilkins had married out of pure altruism, to protect middle-of-the-road scholars from Cromwell and the parliamentarians. This seems unlikely.

67 For the history of Gresham College see R. Chartres and D. Vermont, *A Brief History of Gresham College 1597–1997* (London: Gresham College, 1997); F. Ames-Lewis, F. Baden-Powell et al., *Sir Thomas Gresham and Gresham College* (London: Ashgate Publishing, 1999).

68 W. S. C. Copeman, 'Dr. Jonathan Goddard, FRS (1617–1675)', *Notes and Records of the Royal Society* 15 (1960), 69–77.

69 Bray, *Evelyn Diary*, p. 215.

70 Bennett, *The Mathematical Science*, p. 21.

71 The previous day, 10 February 1656, Evelyn had 'heard Dr. Wilkins preach before the Lord Mayor in St. Paul's'. On 11 February Evelyn 'went with Dr. Wilkins to see Barlow, the famous painter of fowls, beasts, and birds.' Bray, *Evelyn Diary*, p. 214.

72 It would have been out of the question for Wilkins's new wife to set up house within the all-male precincts of Wadham College.

73 8 May 1656 entry in Evelyn's diary: 'went to visite Dr. Wilkins at Whitehall, where I first met with Sir P: Neile famous for his optic-glasses'. E. S. de Beer, *The Diary of John Evelyn*, 6 vols (Oxford: Clarendon Press, 1955) 3, 172.

74 T. Carlyle (1904), vol. 2, p. 493.

75 In the light of Ward's career after the Restoration, when he moved rapidly into the close circle round the King – including successfully claiming the coveted position of Chancellor of the Order of the Garter for himself, in his capacity as Bishop of Salisbury (see below, chapter 4), Cromwell's instincts here were probably correct.

76 This interpretation is supported by the following, from a history of the Gresham Professors written a generation later: 'But upon the 7 of August 1657 Dr. Whistler, the geometry professor in Gresham college, resigning that place, Mr. Rooke was permited [sic] to exchange the astronomy professorship for that of geometry, and upon surrendering the one was immediately chosen into the other. As astronomy continued always his favorite study, it may be difficult to conceive, what could induce him to desire that exchange; unless it was the conveniency of the lodgings (for the observatory was not then built) which opened behind the reading hall, and by that means were

proper for the reception of those gentlemen after the lectures, who in the year 1660 formed the royal society there' (Ward, *The Lives of the Professors of Gresham College*, Life of Laurence Rooke, p. 91).

77 Bennett has Cromwell intervening affirmatively in this affair, but admits that this is slightly odd, in view of Wren's family history: 'The appointments of Rooke and Goddard to chairs at Gresham, illustrate again the links between London and Oxford, and Wren was to follow them in 1657. Circumstantial evidence points to a very interesting and, in view of his Royalist background, perhaps surprising conclusion about Wren's appointment' (Bennett, *The Mathematical Science*, pp. 20–1).

78 English version of Wren's Gresham inaugural lecture, *Parentalia*, p. 200.

79 Letter from Wren to Sir Paul Neile, from Oxford, October 1, 1661. RS Letter Book I, 16. Cit. J. Elmes, *Memoirs of the Life and Works of Sir Christopher Wren* (London: Priestly & Weale, 1823), pp. 88–91. See also C. A. Ronan and Sir H. Hartley, FRS, 'Sir Paul Neile, FRS (1613–1686)', *Notes and Records of the Royal Society* 15 (1960), 159–65.

80 *Parentalia*, p. 254.

81 *Parentalia*, p. 255.

82 These were, presumably, the very apartments recently vacated by Neile's old friend, Cromwell's brother-in-law John Wilkins. Both Moray's and Neile's apartments are marked on Ralph Greatorex's 1670 survey of Whitehall Palace – Moray's on the river and Neile's in Scotland Yard. The Scotland Yard Lodgings of the King's Surveyor are also shown on this plan – by 1670 these were occupied by Christopher Wren. See Thurley, *Whitehall Palace*, plate 128, pp. 122–3.

83 See A. Van Helden, 'Christopher Wren's *De corpore Saturni*', *Notes and Records of the Royal Society* 23 (1968), 213–29; 215: 'Neile's early association with the Oxford astronomers is attested to by the reference to him in the preface of Ward's *In Ismaelis Bullialdi Astronomiae Philolaica Inquisitio Brevis* of 1653. It appears that Jonathan Goddard, who was also mentioned in the same preface, was replaced by Neile as provider of telescopes.'

84 Webster, *Great Instauration*, p. 170. 'The records also show that during the 1650s a declinatory instrument was constructed, and a sextant repaired, for this observatory. At this time the observatory also benefited from instruments donated by the Greaves family in memory of the first two Savilian astronomy professors, John Bainbridge and John Greaves. Thus a modest collection of instruments was recorded with a catalogue prepared at the end of the century. Conspicuous in this list were three telescopes, the largest being a fifteen-foot instrument with three lenses.'

85 Bennett, *The Mathematical Science*, p. 18.

86 Cit. Webster, *Great Instauration*, p. 171.

87 William Neile too was a keen astronomer, making astronomical observations using instruments on the roof of his father's house at White Waltham in Berkshire. He died there, prematurely and much mourned, at the age of thirty-two.

88 On Ball's contributions to the Saturn discussions see A. Armitage, 'William Ball FRS (1627–1690)', *Notes and Records of the Royal Society* 15 (1960), 167–72.

89 On Huygens see Andriesse, *Christiaan Huygens*.

90 Elmes, *Memoirs of Wren*, pp. 88–91.

91 Van Helden, 'Wren's *De corpore Saturni*', pp. 220–1.

92 Bennett, *Mathematical Science*, pp. 28–9.

93 Bennett, 'A study of *Parentalia*', pp. 146–7.

94 Société Hollandaise des Sciences, *Oeuvres complètes de Christiaan Huygens*, 22 vols (The Hague:

Martinus Nijhoff, 1888) 1, 392, 396 [eps 272, 277].

95 *Oeuvres complètes de Christiaan Huygens* 1, 401–3 [ep. 280].

96 *Oeuvres complètes de Christiaan Huygens* 1, 424: 'NB. Deceperat me [pseudoanagramma] confingens Wallisius; nam literis quas confuso ordine miserat, tunc demum cum mei anagrammatis explicationem accepisset, similem utcunque sensum effinxit, ut postea confessus est.'

97 *Oeuvres complètes de Christiaan Huygens* 2, 329–31 [ep. 574].

98 This was probably a poor judgement on Wren's part. Huygens was interested in the mathematics of the arc of a cycloid because he was in the process of designing cycloidal cheeks for his pendulum clock, to increase its precision. If the two had collaborated a joint project might have emerged for a precision chronometer.

99 Bennett, *Mathematical Science*, p. 30; Van Helden, 'Wren's *De corpore Saturni*', p. 216.

100 Elmes, *Memoirs of Wren*, pp. 88–91.

101 'Frederick Henry and Amalia van Solms did not delegate the acquisition of art to an extensive network of agents, diplomats and acquainted collectors – as other rulers did – instead they employed a single intermediary: Constantijn Huygens. Huygens was a remarkably sophisticated figure, both a poet and an art collector. He was also a leading authority on music and a composer. And he was the personal secretary of the Stadholder with responsibility for the latter's correspondence. All contacts with artists went through Huygens, which enabled Huygens to influence the allocation and execution of commissions. Indeed, the royal collection reflects in part the tastes of Constantijn Huygens' (Keblusek and Zijlmans, *Princely Display*).

102 See S. Alpers, *The Art of Describing: Dutch Art in the Seventeenth Century* (Chicago: University of Chicago Press, 1983), pp. 1–2: 'Constantijn Huygens

(1596–1687) was the son of the secretary to the first stadholder of the new Dutch Republic and succeeded his father in that position. He combined service to the state and religious orthodoxy with a variety of intellectual and artistic skills. The lute, globes, compass, and architectural plan on the table beside him in the portrait by Thomas de Keyser refer to only a few of Huygens's interests and accomplishments. He was trained in the classics, was a writer, a poet, a translator of Donne, and had a library almost half the size of that of the king of France. He was well traveled and when still young was invited to perform on the lute before the English king [James I]. He was vitally interested in both art and contemporary science.' See also Andriesse, *Christiaan Huygens*, pp. 18–37.

103 Wren's mother gave birth to his youngest sister in 1643, and was still alive a couple of years later, when Dean Wren helped hide fleeing royalist soldiers at East Knoyle; Wren seems to have been motherless by the time the family moved to the Holder household. Huygens's mother died in 1637, when Christiaan was eight (his father complained that the little boy would not give up wearing mourning for her).

104 Both Bishop Wren and his son, Wren's cousin Matthew, did land significant early commissions for Christopher Wren.

105 To give some idea of the privileged position of the Huygens family, their family home stood next door to the great Mauritshuis built by John Maurice of Nassau at The Hague, and the two gardens shared a common fence. In 1646 Christiaan wrote to his brother Constantijn: 'Le plus grand passetemps que j'aij me donne le craijonner, que j'exerce a toute force et de toute façon; J'aij peint en nostre jardin des grandes figures comme le vif, avecq du charbon mis dans de

l'huijle et du craijon blancq, contre les aijs qui separent nostre jardin d'avecq celuij du Conte Maurice' (*Oeuvres complètes de Christiaan Huygens* 1, 17).

106 John Maurice of Nassau (1604–79) was a distinguished Dutch general and colonial administrator, a prince of the house of Nassau-Siegen. He was grandnephew of William the Silent. In 1636 the Dutch West India Company appointed him governor-general of its newly acquired possessions in Brazil. He conquered north-east Brazil from the Portuguese and, in order to ensure the supply of slave labour, seized several Portuguese strongholds on the Guinea coast of Africa. An able administrator, John Maurice consolidated Dutch rule in Brazil. He built up the state of Pernambuco and rebuilt the city of Recife. He supported science and arts in the colony: pioneering studies on the botany, zoology and diseases of Brazil were published by his court physician and a German naturalist, while artists including Frans Post painted Brazilian scenes. Rising Portuguese hostility and Dutch criticism of his expenses led him to request he be recalled in 1643. He subsequently held commands in Europe in the thirty years war, governed, after 1647, Cleves, Mark, and Ravensburg for the elector of Brandenburg, and in 1652 was made a prince of the Holy Roman Empire. Despite his advanced age, he won new distinction in the Dutch wars. After his retirement in 1675 he lived at Cleves. He was known for his patronage of the arts, and his residence at The Hague is the celebrated Mauritshuis.

107 Friedrich Wilhelm Elector of Brandenburg, 1640–88. Born 6 February 1620 Berlin. Died 29 April 1688 Potsdam. Married (1) 7 December 1646 The Hague, Countess Louise Henriette von Nassau, daughter of Frederik Hendrik, Prince of Orange, Count of Nassau and Countess Amalia zu Solms-Braunfels. Born 27 November 1627 The Hague. Died 6 June 1667 Berlin.

108 *Oeuvres complètes de Christiaan Huygens* 3, 254–5. There is a wonderful example of the tight bond between diplomatic service and pursuit of science in the lives of the Huygens brothers in a letter from Constantijn to Christiaan of 10 February 1661, when Christiaan was in Paris and Constantijn in The Hague: 'Mon Pere est revenu de Cleue bien satisfait de l'accueil qu'il y a receu, mais n'ira pas en Angleterre ou Monsieur l'electeur envoye le Prince Maurice [John Maurice of Nassau] et le Sieur Wyman [Daniel Weimann] comme sans doubte mon Pere vous mande, et de mesme comment il a dessein de vous faire passer dans le dit païs pour y aller trouver ce Prince, chose dont je m'asseure que serez trescontent, deuant auoir l'occasion par là tant pour vous perfectionner dans la langue comme pour aller voir touts ces faiseurs d'Almanacs et de lunettes d'approche, qui sont de votre connoissance. . . . Je ne doubte pas que n'ayez veu le nouveau Comete qui paroist icy depuis quelques jours du coste de l'Orient. Je me levay hier a 3 heures et montay par un grand froid au hault de nostre maison sans le pouvoir trouver, estant encore trop proche de l'horizon, mais depuis y estant retourné a 5. je le vis d'abord qui estoit desja esleué de quelque 30. degrés, et reconnoissable mesme sans lunettes d'approche, auec lesquelles je le puis voir de ma chambre à l'aise. Je l'ay veu avec les grandes que nous avons, mais par ce que sa lumiere est assez foible, je trouve qu'avec celles de cinq pieds on en decouvre tout autant de perfection qu'avec les autres' (*Oeuvres complètes de Christiaan Huygens* 1, 237).

109 *Oeuvres complètes de Christiaan Huygens* 3, 267, 28 April n.s., Constantijn informs Christiaan he has sent lenses as requested.

110 *Oeuvres complètes de Christiaan Huygens* 22, 572–6.

111 Cit. Andriesse, *Christian Huygens*, p. 225 [my translation].

112 Bray, *Evelyn Diary*, 15 December 1670: 'To Lond[on] It was the thickest, & darkest fogg on the Thames, that was ever know<n> in the memory of man, & I happned to be in the midst of it: I supped with Monsieur Zulestein late Governor of the Young Pr: of Orange, with severall other greate persons, & had a greate entertainement: next day, at the Ro: Society.'

113 See Huygens website, poems for 1671. He also apparently spent some time in Paris.

114 *Horologium oscillatorium* (1673) [Huygens, O. C. XVIII], pp. 202–5.

115 P. de la R. Du Prey, *Hawksmoor's London Churches: Architecture and Theology* (Chicago: Chicago University Press, 2000), p. 149, n. 39.

116 *Parentalia*, p. 215.

117 'June 14 [1652]. 11 a.m. Dr Wilkins and Mr Wren came to visit me at Blackfriars, this was the first time I saw the doctor.' R. T. Gunter, *The Diary and Will of Elias Ashmole, edited and extended from the original Manuscripts* (Frome and London: Butler & Tanner, 1927), p. 48.

118 Ashmole, *Institution of the Order of the Garter*, preface (fo. A2r). Ashmole is a shady character, about whom we will learn more later. He typifies the less deserving who flourished with the return of Charles II. Ashmole had insinuated himself into royalist favour at Oxford in the 1640s, when he accepted the post of collector of the deeply unpopular excise tax for the King in 1644. He rocketed to prominence after the Restoration precisely with his re-establishing of the old Ceremonies and Orders, and specifically with his publication of the Wren records of the Order. Notoriously, we remember him because of his appropriation of the Tradescant rarities, and their presentation to the University of Oxford under his own name (see Jardine, *Ingenious Pursuits*).

119 25 May 1659: 'I went to Windsor, and took Mr Hollar with me to take views of the Castle &c.' (Ashmole, *Diary*, p. 63). These are the views which were eventually to illustrate Ashmole's *Institution of the Order of the Garter*.

120 Apart from the juvenilia reproduced in *Parentalia*. All the other engravings are inscribed 'W. Hollar delineavit et fecit', mostly without dates, though 1667 seems a reasonable date for these engravings too (when the publishing project was properly under way). One Hollar engraving of the interior of St George's Chapel is dated 1663. The engraving of the Garter regalia on p. 202 (which include a representation of the George with painting of Henrietta Maria inside it which is said by Ashmole to be the one Charles I wore on the scaffold) is dated 1666. Wren's view is reproduced without comment in Colvin, *The History of the King's Works*.

121 Wren–Hollar engraving of the *Prospect of Windsor Castle from the North*, Ashmole, *Institution of the Order of the Garter*, p. 134.

122 Wilkins had attended Richard Cromwell at his installation, briefly, as Protector in succession to his father. The Trinity post may have been a reward for this public support.

123 This either means 'with all his goods [in baskets]' or 'with his chum(s)'. Either way it suggests a domestic shift of residence. Robina Wilkins lived until 1689; they had no children.

124 Bennett, *The Mathematical Science*, p. 126, n. 16. If the 'library' in question was the Bodleian Library, adjacent to the Schools, here is further confirmation that Wilkins had been responsible for some kind of conversion of existing buildings to house an embryo scientific 'College'. See below, chapter 4.

125 On the fortunes of Whitehall Palace after 1658 see Thurley, *Whitehall Palace*, p. 98.

126 Since, as we know, Wilkins managed to be politically acceptable to both parties, he was quietly given a London

living, and eventually raised to Bishop
of Chester.

127 Hutton, *Charles the Second*, p. 135.

128 One link here is Bishop Matthew
Wren, who had been responsible for
the planning and building of the
Chapel at Peterhouse, Cambridge,
while he was Master in the 1630s
(completed and dedicated 1633). On
Peterhouse Chapel see T. Mowl and
B. Earnshaw, *Architecture without
Kings: The Rise of Puritan Classicism
under Cromwell* (Manchester:
Manchester University Press, 1995),
pp. 193–4.

129 Cit. Webster, *Great Instauration*, p. 171.

130 To whom Boyle entrusted the first
attempt at building an air-pump in
England.

131 Mowl and Earnshaw, *Architecture
without Kings*, p. 194.

132 Cit. Webster, *The Great Instauration*,
p. 171.

133 Bray, *Evelyn Diary*, pp. 578–9.

134 Webster, *The Great Instauration*,
pp. 171–2. 'At the Restoration' is
consistent with Wilkins leaving Oxford
for Cambridge 'cum pannie' in 1659. In
that year Evelyn wrote to Boyle with a
much enlarged proposal for a new-
build semi-monastic college for virtuosi
scientists (Evelyn to Boyle, 3 September
1659, Bray, *Evelyn Diary*, pp. 590–2).

135 Frank, *Harvey and the Oxford
Physiologists*, p. 46.

136 *Parentalia*, p. 338. A pen-and-ink
drawing of Wallis's innovative roof
structure (copied from Wallis's *De
motu*, and in turn copied from Serlio,
On Architecture, Book 1) survives in
the RS MS *Parentalia* volume. The
juxtaposition of Wallis's mathematical
solution to spanning large spaces
and Serlio's unrelated design is first
made, apparently in Plot's *History of
Oxfordshire*, from where Wren junior
mistakenly took it. See below,
chapter 4.

137 Cit. M. Hunter, 'The work-diaries of
Robert Boyle: a newly discovered
source and its internet publication',
Notes and Records of the Royal Society
55 (2001), 373–90; 377.

138 Bray, *Evelyn Diary*, p. 267. The Old
Schools stand directly next door to
the Sheldonian.

139 Mowl and Earnshaw, *Architecture
without Kings*, pp. 196–7.

140 M. Hunter, 'A "College" for the
Royal Society: the abortive plan of
1667–1668', *Notes and Records of the
Royal Society* 38 (1984), 159–86; 161.

141 Hunter, 'A "College" for the Royal
Society', p. 179.

142 Hunter, 'A "College" for the Royal
Society', pp. 172–3.

143 The account which follows is indebted
to Thurley, *Whitehall Palace*.

144 Webb had been Inigo Jones's deputy
for twenty years (as he states in his
petition to the King), trained in the
expectation he would take over on
Jones's retirement. In the event, Jones
was deprived of his post by
Parliament in 1643, and Webb, who
remained with the court at Oxford,
was appointed by the King to take
over the post.

145 For the plan see Thurley, *Whitehall
Palace*, p. 102, fig. 109. 'The ambition
of the scheme can be seen by noting
that the existing banqueting house [by
Inigo Jones] is shown at the bottom
of the plan, centrally placed in the
range to the left of the central,
pillared hall' (Thurley, caption to
109). Webb had had something of an
obsession with rebuilding designs for
Whitehall throughout much of the
period during which he worked as
Inigo Jones's deputy. See Mowl and
Earnshaw, *Architecture without Kings*,
pp. 81–95. Mowl and Earnshaw are
incorrect in believing that Webb's
account of taking Whitehall plans to
the Isle of Wight was 'most
improbable and likely to be a bold lie'
(p. 85).

146 *Wren Society*, 18, 155–6. Simon
Thurley gives the dates of these two
documents as May 1661.

147 Cit. in Appendix II to J. Bold, *John
Webb: Architectural Theory and
Practice in the Seventeenth Century*
(Oxford: Clarendon Press, 1989),
pp. 181–2.

148 Bold, *John Webb*, pp. 181–2.

149 Webb's case was not helped by his having worked for a sequence of prominent parliamentary clients during the Commonwealth and Protectorate periods. Charles noticeably preferred the loyal subjects he 'restored' not to have collaborated. See Mowl and Earnshaw, *Architecture without Kings*, pp. 81–95.

150 Cit. E. McKellar, *The Birth of Modern London: The Development and Design of the City 1660–1720* (Manchester: Manchester University Press, 1999), p. 18. For Denham's transformation of London see John Kip's engraving, *A Prospect of City of London, Westminster and St James's Park* (1710), reproduced in McKellar, *The Birth of Modern London*, p. 16.

151 Cit. McKellar, *The Birth of Modern London*, p. 25. Denham was an early member of the Royal Society, elected at the same meeting as Henry Oldenburg. See Hunter, *The Royal Society and its Fellows*, pp. 142–3.

152 Thurley, *Whitehall Palace*, p. 99. Thurley assumes that 'modells' means a three-dimensional model, rather than a set of plans.

153 'In 1661 he was paid £2 by the Paymaster of the King's Works "for drawing the draughts with the uprights for the intended Building at Greenwich" [PRO, WORK 5/2, under Whitehall, July 1661]. . . . Willem was still living in London in 1674, and in 1678 was admitted to the Masons' Company as a "foreign member" [D. Knoop and G. P. Jones, *The London Mason in the Seventeenth Century*, 1935, 71], but the place and date of his death are not known'. H. Colvin, *A Biographical Dictionary of British Architects 1600–1840*, third edition (New Haven and London: Yale University Press, 1995), p. 299. Willem de Keyser designed a number of buildings in the Netherlands which survive, including the Academie van Bouwkunst building in Amsterdam. Willem's brother Thomas painted the portrait of Constantijn Huygens senior

and his clerk, now in the National Gallery, London. All the de Keysers (father and sons) were painters and sculptors as well as architects.

154 On the Greenwich rebuilding plans see S. Thurley, 'A country seat fit for a King: Charles II, Greenwich and Winchester', in E. Cruickshanks, *The Stuart Courts* (Stroud: Sutton Publishing, 2000), pp. 214–39.

155 Thurley, *Whitehall Palace*, p. 106.

156 Thurley, *Whitehall Palace*, pp. 114–15.

157 'The events which followed strongly suggest that by the autumn of 1664 another architect was already involved. We learn from the accounts of the Office of the Works that between January and June 1665 another elaborate model for the rebuilding of Whitehall was being made. One of the drawings for this model survives and, interestingly, it is in the hand of Christopher Wren. Evidently Wren, even before his appointment as Surveyor, and in collaboration with his precursor, Sir John Denham, the paymaster Hugh May and Webb, was helping Charles II visualize a new Whitehall'. S. Thurley, *The Whitehall Palace Plan of 1670* (London Topographical Society Publication no. 153, 1998), p. 6. See also K. Downes, 'Wren and Whitehall in 1664', *Burlington Magazine* 113 (1971), 89–92.

158 Thurley, *Whitehall Palace*, p. 99. Wren drawing p. 105.

159 Cit. in Appendix II to Bold, *John Webb*, pp. 182–3.

CHAPTER 4: *Preferred Routes to Success*

1 This process was helped by the fact that in the latter years of his court-in-exile Charles II had effectively re-created his father's administration. In 1660 there was therefore a general tendency to put back in place figures like Moray and Neile, even though they had not formed part of the intervening court circle. See Hutton, *Charles the Second*, pp. 118–19.

2 See 1670 plan of Whitehall Palace,

reproduced in Thurley, *Whitehall Palace*, pp. 122–3.

3 'brought in by Sr. R[obert] Nov. 9. 1664'. Royal Society archives, C1.P.VI.17. I have chosen to leave 'wee', although Moray has replaced these in the manuscript by 'they' throughout, to turn the personal account into a paper appropriate for Royal Society presentation.

4 Cit. Bennett, *The Mathematical Science*, p. 24.

5 Bennett, *The Mathematical Science*, p. 24.

6 See above, chapter 3. Rooke, Wren, and Goddard were all Gresham professors; Wallis was both a court and university figure: Savilian Professor of Geometry at Oxford and chaplain to the King.

7 Pepys, *Diary* 1, 156–7: 'Up and made myself as fine as I could with the Linning stockings and wide Canons that I bought the other day at Hague. Extraordinary press of Noble company and great mirth all the day. There dined with me in my Cabbin ... Dr. Earle and Mr. Hollis, the King's Chaplins. Dr. Scarborough, Dr. Quarterman, and Dr. Clerke, Physicians; Mr. Darcy and Mr. Fox (both very fine gentlemen), the King's servants. Where we had brave discourse.'

8 Though the royal charter was not awarded until 1662, and reissued in 1663.

9 See Hutton, *Charles the Second*: 'As the summer of 1658 opened, Charles and his brother Henry had to pawn their jewelled badges symbolizing the Order of the Garter. ... [Following the death of Cromwell] they expected that the Protectorate ... would now collapse on itself. ... The results of all these hopes and efforts was a disappointment as crushing as any before. ... England, far from being in chaos, proved to be, in the opinion of one royalist agent, more peaceful than ever before' (p. 113).

10 Anne Hyde's pregnancy and James's insistence on making an honest woman of her had somewhat tarnished celebrations of the Restoration towards the end of 1660.

11 Cit. A. Plowden, *The Stuart Princesses* (Stroud: Sutton Publishing, 1996), p. 91. As late as 1658 Charles was regarded as so poor a marriage prospect that the Dowager Princess of Orange refused him the hand of the third daughter (Hutton, *Charles the Second*, p. 113).

12 Rumour had it that he had married his mistress Lucy Walter, mother of the Duke of Monmouth, in 1648, largely because she (unlike Elizabeth Killigrew) gave birth to a royal boy.

13 See Hutton, *Charles the Second*: '[In autumn 1660] Charles yielded to pressure of London mercantile opinion, and took his first step away from a policy of greater friendship with the United Netherlands: he ordered the East India Company to seize Pulo Run [in the East Indies]. In the case of Spain, the deterioration in relations was much more spectacular. ... Next to the Catholic religion, Felipe [of Spain]'s driving passion was for the recovery of all the lands which he had inherited in 1621, and his pride would not permit him to write off Dunkirk and Jamaica. For his own part, Charles dared not hand back these prizes for fear of a massive loss of popularity in his newly recovered realm. ... Felipe's sentiments regarding his inheritance applied with particular force to his rebel kingdom of Portugal, and in 1660, with his French and English wars over, he could at last concentrate his strength against it. In their desperation the Portuguese were prepared to bid for help at a fabulous price, and from Charles, who had as yet made no diplomatic commitments, above all. ... In late July [1660, the Portuguese envoy] seems to have offered him the hand of Catherine, daughter of the man whom the Portuguese had crowned. With her, apparently, was dangled the

bait of the richest dowry brought by any Queen of England' (pp. 157–8).

14 Hutton, *Charles the Second*, p. 160.

15 Willmoth, *Sir Jonas Moore*, pp. 130–1; see also E. M. G. Routh, *Tangier: England's Lost Atlantic Outpost* (London, 1912).

16 *Parentalia*, p. 260.

17 BL MS *Parentalia*, fol. 43v: 'Of the Apparatus; in pursuance of the Com[m]and of the Rt. Honle. the Earle of Sandwich, which were these. That in the Azimuth 270 40' SW. The Moon's Altitude should be observ'd. together with her apparent Place for certain days together, from the first Quarter till the Full Moon, in the Months of Jan: & Feb: 1662. the Fix'd Starrs from when the Distance was to be taken being prescrib'd. To know by memory the true Place of the [sun] in the Zodiack ye. 10/20th of June or 02 days after the Aequinoctial of V (for ever.) Upon supposition the Calendar to be rectified by leaving out for the future the Intercalar days. &c.'

18 *Parentalia*, p. 260 (where the letter is wrongly dated 1663). Bryan Little gives the date of the letter as late 1661, on the ground that Dr Baylie (mentioned in the letter) retired from his post as Vice-Chancellor in summer 1662. Since Baylie's complaint is Wren's absence 'so long after the Beginning of the Term', this suggests a date in late October or November, and that Wren has failed to take up his duties as the newly appointed Professor (he was appointed at the end of the previous academic year). See Little, *Sir Christopher Wren*, p. 39.

19 He may even have sought Petty's advice before doing so. Petty returned to London in 1660, and was quickly knighted by the King for his services in Ireland. Perhaps the offer was never more than mooted in the lost letter from Matthew Wren. Jonas Moore was already known to, and working for, Sandwich by early 1662.

20 For details of the fen drainage project, see Willmoth, *Sir Jonas Moore*, pp. 88–120.

21 Willmoth, *Sir Jonas Moore*, p. 127. See also Jardine, *Ingenious Pursuits*.

22 PRO WORK 38/331, cit. Willmoth, *Sir Jonas Moore*, p. 128. The royal warrant itself was dated 7 February 1662.

23 Willmoth, *Sir Jonas Moore*, p. 134.

24 Willmoth, *Sir Jonas Moore*, p. 135.

25 Willmoth, *Sir Jonas Moore*, p. 133. Moore, Hooke and Wren were also all involved in surveys immediately following the Great Fire, and in building the Fleet Ditch in 1672. See Willmoth, *Sir Jonas Moore*, and below, chapter 5.

26 See below, chapter 6.

27 Bombay, by contrast, was more lastingly important for England's imperial ambitions. In 1668 the Crown leased it to the East India Company, which thenceforth successfully exploited it as England's centre of operations for colonial ventures in the region. See J. H. Parry, *The Age of Reconnaissance: Discovery, Exploration and Settlement 1450–1650* (London: Weidenfeld & Nicolson, 1963 [Phoenix Press edition, 2000]): 'In 1664 the Marathas raided Surat. They sacked the town, but were beaten off by the company's men from the walls of the English factory. For the first time the Mughal had failed to protect his clients, and the company began to look round for means to defend itself. The first requirement was a defensible base, if possible outside the imperial jurisdiction. Such a base lay ready to hand. Bombay had come into Charles II's hands as part of Catharine of Braganza's dowry. His ships had taken possession in 1665, after a protracted dispute with the resident Portuguese, and in 1668, finding the town an expensive liability, he leased it to the company' (p. 256).

28 Jardine, *Ingenious Pursuits*. Willmoth, *Sir Jonas Moore*, p. 133. See also E. Chappell (ed.), *The Tangier Papers*

of Samuel Pepys, Navy Records Society 73 (1935).

29 Wren's other close colleague, Seth Ward, also worked his way gradually back via ecclesiastical preferment, in spite of having been ejected from his academic post at the Restoration.

30 Aarsleff, 'John Wilkins', p. 371.

31 Wilkins's political resilience is truly remarkable, if we bear in mind the fact that beyond serving Oliver Cromwell, and marrying his favourite sister, it was he who escorted Richard Cromwell at his installation in office in September 1658, and advised the new appointee until May 1659.

32 Cit. Barnett, *Theodore Haak*, p. 121. On 17 February 1660, Evelyn wrote to Wilkins, 'President of our Society at Gresham College': 'Sir – Though I suppose it might be a mistake that there was a meeting appointed to-morrow (being a day of public solemnity and devotion), yet because I am uncertain, and would not disobey your commands, I here send you my trifling observations concerning the anatomy of trees, and their vegetative motion' (Bray, *Evelyn Diary*, p. 596). See above, chapter 3.

33 Royal Society, Journal Book, vol. I, pp. 1–2, cit. M. Purver, *The Royal Society: Concept and Creation* (London: Routledge & Kegan Paul, 1967), p. 131. Although Purver's quest to make precise the origins of the Royal Society now seems quaintly anachronistic, her compilation of all the surviving documentary evidence concerning the Society and its foundation is invaluable.

34 Aarsleff, 'John Wilkins', p. 371.

35 Purver, *The Royal Society*, p. 131.

36 Lord Brouncker became the active President at the time of issue of the first royal charter to the Society in 1662.

37 *Parentalia*, pp. 210–11. In addition to the approach from Neile and Moray, Wren received a personal note from Henry Powle (Master of the Rolls): 'I am commanded by the Royal Society to acquaint you, that his Majesty expects you should prosecute your Design of making the Representation of the Lunar Globe in *Solido*; and that you should proceed in drawing the Shapes of little Animals as they appear in the Microscope; and that he doth expect an Account of this from you shortly' (*Parentalia*, p. 210).

38 Bennett, *The Mathematical Science*, p. 39.

39 Wren apparently added adjustable knife-edges or wires to a magnifying eyepiece incorporating a graduated ruler. Sprat says Wren 'added many sorts of Retes, Screws and other devices to Telescopes, for taking small distances and apparent diamets to Seconds' (cit. Bennett, *The Mathematical Science*, p. 39).

40 The Oxford 'Act' or Graduation Ceremony took place in July. See Evelyn's *Diary*.

41 *Parentalia*, pp. 224–5. In *Parentalia* this letter is dated 1661, but described as addressed to Lord Brouncker (who did not become President of the RS until 1662). The partial copy in BL MS *Parentalia*, fol. 47 recto, however, contains a final sentence, omitted in the printed version, as follows: 'I must needs acknowledge I am only indebted to the Society, but most particularly to Yr. Ld.ship, to whom I ow a double duty both as our President & as my very good Ld. & Patron.' This makes it clear that the letter is to Robert Moray, who was indeed President of the Society (not yet Royal) in 1661.

42 Transcribed from RS MS 249, fols 233v–235v. See also *Parentalia*, p. 211. The identity of Vander Driver is not known (his name never appears again). In his *Sculptura* (1662), Evelyn mentions with approval Vander Douse, one of an important family of Dutch engravers (p. 111), who may be intended here.

43 *Parentalia*, p. 211. '*Unus non sufficit orbis*' was the motto of the sixteenth-century Spanish Habsburg King Ferdinand.

44 Oldenburg to Huygens, 7 September

1661. This is uncharacteristically clear for Oldenburg, and suggests that he is drawing on a written (or oral) description which Wren did present at a Royal Society meeting. R. Hall and M. B. Hall (eds), *The Correspondence of Henry Oldenburg*, 13 vols (Madison: University of Wisconsin Press, 1965–86) 1, 422.

45 'fort plaisante a veoir avec toutes ses taches et petites vallees rondes' (cit. Bennett, *The Mathematical Science*, p. 40).

46 See J. Bennett, 'Sphere No. 11: Christopher Wren's Lunar Globe', http://wee/mhs.ox.ac.uk/sphaera/issue11/artic19.htm.

47 Hall and Hall, *Oldenburg Correspondence* 1, 422.

48 Aarsleff, 'John Wilkins', p. 364.

49 Cit. *Parentalia*, p. 212.

50 Aarsleff, 'John Wilkins', p. 371. Aarslef suggests that the slump in the Royal Society's activities in the early 1670s was directly related to Wilkins's death in November 1672. Wilkins left the Royal Society £400 in his will. Sprat was a close personal friend of Wren (he refers to him as 'Kit' in surviving letters, unlike anybody else). It is not surprising that he puffs Wren so resoundingly in the *History*.

51 Purver, *The Royal Society*, p. 136.

52 See Hunter, *The Royal Society and its Fellows*, pp. 134–53.

53 Wren's draft document may also have been discarded because of the intensity of its expressed feelings in support of Charles I (a politically sensitive issue in 1662): 'Not that herein, we [i.e. Charles II] would withdraw the least Ray of our Influence from the present established Nurseries of good Literature, and Education, founded, by the Piety of our Royal Ancestors, and others, to be the perpetual Fountains of Religion, and Laws; that Religion, and those Laws, which, as we are obliged to defend, so the holy Blood of our martyr'd Father hath inseparably endear'd to us' (*Parentalia*, p. 197).

54 *Parentalia*, pp. 196–7.

55 Cit. M. Hunter, *Science and Society in Restoration England* (Cambridge: Cambridge University Press, 1981), p. 131.

56 See Hunter, *Science and Society*, passim, for a negative account of the impact of the Royal Society in its early years.

57 Sir Charles Scarburgh, too, was evidently part of the group of keen royalist enthusiasts for astronomical observation.

58 Purver, *The Royal Society*, p. 135.

59 Royal Society, Journal Book, vol. I, p. 4, cit. Purver, *The Royal Society*, p. 132.

60 Purver, *The Royal Society*, p. 132.

61 W. Charlton, *The Immortality of the Human Soul, Demonstrated by the Light of Nature* (London, 1657), pp. 34–5; cit. Frank, *Harvey and the Oxford Physiologists*, p. 24.

62 Frank, *Harvey and the Oxford Physiologists*, pp. 24–5.

63 Although Scarburgh was elected a member of the Royal Society in January 1661 (together with William Holder, both presumably at Wren's suggestion), he took no part in its meetings, and failed to pay his dues after 1663, resulting in his expulsion in 1666. Hunter, *The Royal Society and its Fellows*, pp. 142–3. In 1672–75, however, it was Scarburgh who acted as client for the new Royal College of Physicians building and anatomy theatre built by the Wren office. See for instance, Hooke, *Diary*, 7 August 1674: 'Propounded open theater. Agreed to. Sir Ch. Scarborough pleasd.'

64 Royal Society, Journal Book, vol. I, p. 6, cit. Purver, *The Royal Society*, p. 133.

65 Purver, *The Royal Society*, p. 133.

66 Purver, *The Royal Society*, p. 133.

67 Hunter, 'A "College" for the Royal Society', p. 163.

68 See below, chapter 6, for further details of Wren's proposals.

69 On the whole affair see M. Hunter, 'A "College" for the Royal Society', pp. 159–86.

70 T. Birch, *A History of the Royal Society of London for Improving Natural Knowledge, from its first Rise*, 4 vols (London, 1756–7) 2, 289.

71 Hall and Hall, *Oldenburg Correspondence* 4, 454–5.

72 Bray, *Evelyn Diary*, 19 June 1662: 'I went to Albury in surrey, to visite Mr. Henry Howard [since Duke of Norfolk], soone after he had procured the Dukedome to be restored &c. [after Charles II's Restoration]: this Gent: had now compounded a debt of neere 200000 pounds, contracted by his Grandfath<e>r: I was much obliged to that great virtuoso and to this young Gent: so as I staied a fortnight with him.' G. de la Bédoyère, *Particular Friends: The Correspondence of Samuel Pepys and John Evelyn* (Woodbridge: Boydell & Brewer, 1997), p. 142.

73 Bédoyère, *Particular Friends*, p. 294.

74 Hall and Hall, *Oldenburg Correspondence* 5, 117–18.

75 Hall and Hall, *Oldenburg Correspondence* 5, 125.

76 See the original papers in the RS letter books, detailing exchanges on a theory of motion, 1668, with both Wren and Huygens telling Oldenburg that they do not have time to pursue it though they do each have papers on the topic (which they could polish) – and could they see each other's work. LBO.LBC.2.346.

77 See below, chapter 8.

78 It was, however, the Wren office (with Hooke as leading design and site architect) which was responsible for the new Royal College of Physicians building.

79 *Diary*, 7 September 1660.

80 See above, chapter 1.

81 On Boyle see Michael Hunter (passim).

82 On the first Earl of Cork see N. P. Canny, *The Upstart Earl: A Study of the Social and Mental World of Richard Boyle first Earl of Cork 1566–1643* (Cambridge: Cambridge University Press, 1982).

83 At which point Francis enlisted to fight in Ireland, as captain of one of the foot companies, on the basis of a personal recommendation to the Lord Lieutenant there, leaving Robert stranded alone in France. See *Commons Journals*, 14 October 1642, vol. II, p. 809.

84 *The Life of the Honourable Robert Boyle* by Thomas Birch, MA and FRS, London: Printed for A Millar, over-against Catharine-Street in the Strand MDCCXLIV [this later appears as the first part of vol. I of the *Works*]. For Francis's marriage, see p. 34: 'Towards the end of this summer [1638], the kingdom having now obtained a seeming settlement by the King's pacification with the Scots, there arrived at *Stalbridge* Sir *Thomas Stafford*, gentleman usher to the Queen, with his lady, to visit their old friend, the earl of *Cork*, with whom, ere they departed, they concluded a match betwixt his fourth son, Mr. *F:B:* and *E:K:* (*Killigrew*) daughter to my lady *S:* by Sir – *K.* and then a maid of honour, both young and handsom. To make his addresses to this lady, Mr: *F:* was sent (and *Philaretus* in his company) before up to *London*.' And see p. 35: 'Not long after his arrival, *Philaretus*'s brother having been successful in his addresses to his mistress, was, in the presence of the King and Queen, publickly married at court, with all the solemnity, that usually attends matches with maids of honour. But to render their joy as short as it was great, *Philaretus* and his brother were within four days after commanded away for *France*, and after having kissed their Majesty's hands, they took a differing farewel of all their friends; the bridegroom extremely afflicted to be so soon deprived of a joy, which he had tasted but just enough to to encrease his regrets, by the knowledge of what he was forced from; but *Philaretus* as much satisfied to see himself in a condition to content a curiosity, to which his

inclignations did passionately addict him. With these differing resentments of their father's commands, accompanied by their governor, two French servants, and a lacquey of the same country, upon the end of *October* 1638, they took post from *Rye* in *Sussex*, where the next day hiring a ship, though the sea was not very smooth, a prosperous puff of wind did safely by the next morning blow them into *France*.' [From Boyle's manuscript memoirs, drawn up shortly after his return from his travels, but which end very abruptly at the point at which they were stranded in Marseille, in 1642.]

85 *Lords Journal*: 'Boyle et al – pass to go to Holland, 22. Car. 1 viii 468 a. "Ordered, That Mr. Boyle and his Wife shall have a pass to go in to Holland; carrying with them Servants, and such Necessaries as are fit for his Journey."' This was exactly the moment when Charles II left Jersey to join his mother at the French court, and when Henrietta Maria was in negotiations with Ireland to raise forces to support the King. There was a steady to and fro between the courts at Paris and The Hague thereafter.

86 'In February 1647–8, made a voyage to *Holland*, partly to visit the country, and partly to accompany his brother *Francis* in conducting his wife from the *Hague*. But he did not stay long there, for on the 15th of April, 1648, he was at *London*; and on the 13th of May at *Stalbridge*, whence he wrote to his sister *Ranelagh*, giving her an account, that he should possibly soon send her his thoughts upon the subject of *Toleration*, in an essay of his, intitled, *Of* Divinity' (Birch, *Life of Boyle*). Birch adds the footnote: 'Mr. *Boyle*'s letter to Mr. *Marcombes*, dated from *London*, Febr. 22, 1647–8, in which he mentions his intentions of setting out for *Holland* the next day.'

87 Letter from Boyle to Marcombes, 22 February 1648 (This letter is now

lost – or was destroyed.) See Maddison, 'Studies in the life of Robert Boyle', n. 27.

88 See Maddison, 'Studies in the life of Robert Boyle'.

89 The court of William II and Mary (he twenty-one, she fifteen and a half in March 1647 when William became Stadholder) was lavish and self-indulgent. 'Both were still in many ways spoiled children, self-willed and extravagant. They spent much time amusing themselves, and poured out money recklessly on jewels, clothes, funishings, entertainments and works of art. . . . [William] had a passion for French plays and . . . French actresses. . . . He received his exiled brothers-in-law, Charles and James, with lavish generosity.' N. A. Robb, *William of Orange: A Personal Portrait* (London: Heinemann, 1962), pp. 49–50.

90 Charlotte's birth-date is generally given as 'around 1650', since the actual birth took place discreetly, and her status as a royal bastard was not made public till many years later.

91 William III had been born a month after his father's death from smallpox. When Mary, also, died in 1660, the Nassau-Zuijlensteins became yet more influential.

92 'This evening come Mr Boyle on board, for whom I writ an order for a ship to transport him to Flushing. He supped with my Lord, my Lord using him as a person of honour.'

93 See T. C. Barnard, 'The political, material and mental culture of the Cork settlers, 1650–1700', in P. O'Flanagan and C. G. Buttimer (eds), Cork: *History and Society* (Dublin, 1993).

94 In its first version the function of this work as consoling a man whose lady has let him down is clear. My thanks to Professor Michael Hunter for lending me his copy of the early manuscript version.

95 See above, chapter 3.

96 *Seraphic Love* was substantially expanded for publication in 1659, and

in its reworked form some more direct 'clues' to the original occasion are added, including reference to a sudden storm at sea, during the crossing to The Hague.

97 Presumably the Ranelaghs separated, since Viscount Ranelagh was too distinguished to take a back seat (grandson of Thomas Jones, Archbishop of Dublin and Lord Chancellor of Ireland d. 1619 – and son of Roger Viscount Ranelagh). On the other hand, I suppose he may have chosen to reside primarily in Ireland. Henry Oldenburg became their son Richard Jones's tutor in 1655, which was his entry into the elite Oxford science circle.

98 Cit. Maddison, 'Studies in the life of Robert Boyle', p. 112. On the double-writing instrument dispute see above, chapter 2.

99 On the relationship between expatriate Anglo-Irish and the 'Invisible College', see C. Webster, 'New light on the Invisible College', *Transactions of the Royal Historical Society* 5th Series, 24 (1974), 19–42. On significant scientific developments in Ireland, see T. C. Barnard, 'The Hartlib circle and the cult and culture of improvement in Ireland', in M. Greengrass, M. Leslie and T. Raylor (eds), *Samuel Hartlib and Universal Reformation: Studies in Intellectual Communication* (Cambridge: Cambridge University Press, 1994), pp. 281–97.

100 Maddison, 'Studies in the life of Robert Boyle', p. 116. There is, however, contact with the group earlier. Nathaniel Highmore, *History of Generation* (1651) carries a dedication to Boyle, dated 15 May 1651: 'You have, Sir, so inricht your tender years with such choice principles of the best sorts, and even to admiration managed them to the greatest advantage; that you stand both a pattern and a wonder to our Nobility and Gentry . . . you have not thought your blood and descend debased, because married to the Arts. You stick not to trace Nature in her

most intricate paths, to torture her to a confession; though with your own sweat and treasure obtained.' Cit. Maddison, 'Studies in the life of Robert Boyle', pp. 114–15. Maddison goes on: 'Highmore was a neighbour of Boyle, and practised at Sherborne, near Stalbridge; a fact which is sufficient to explain how the dedication came to be made to Boyle.'

101 Boyle to Hartlib, 14 September 1655, cit. Aarsleff, 'John Wilkins', p. 363.

102 Cit. Aarsleff, 'John Wilkins', p. 369.

103 Mr Crosse, whose house it was, was 'an apothecary and great friends of Dr. John Fell', according to Birch.

104 An interesting letter from Boyle to Clodius (written some time in 1653, from Ireland) picks up on precisely the list of activities which Wren described to the Elector Palatine, suggesting that Petty is 'managing' scientific activities in Ireland to dovetail with those of Wilkins in Oxford. Boyle thanks Clodius for sending the processes of *mercurius vitae*, and continues by explaining that in the absence of the right equipment to conduct his chemical researches he is taking his scientific interests in other directions: 'I live here in a barbarous country, where chemical spirits are so misunderstood, and chemical instruments so unprocurable, that it is hard to have any hermetick thoughts in it, and impossible to bring them to experiment. . . . For my part, that I may not live wholly useless, or altogether a stranger in the study of nature, since I want glasses and furnaces to make a chemical analysis of inanimate bodies, I am exercising myself in making anatomical dissections of living animals: wherein (being assisted by your father-in-law's friend Dr Petty, our general's physician) I have satisfied myself of the circulation of the blood, and the (freshly discovered and hardly discoverable) *receptaculum chyli*, made by the confluence of the *venae lactae*; and have seen (especially in the

dissections of fishes) more of the variety and contrivances of nature, and the majesty and wisdom of her author, than all the books I ever read in my life could give me convincing notions of' (cit. Maddison, 'Studies in the life of Robert Boyle', pp. 118–19).

105 For the Willis circle's work see above, chapter 3. It should be noted that Wren was closely involved in Willis's work at exactly the same time that he was also in demand for building works in Oxford, Cambridge and London.

106 See Frank, *Harvey and the Oxford Physiologists*, pp. 121–8.

107 Cit. Frank, *Harvey and the Oxford Physiologists*, p. 128.

108 S. Shapin and S. Schaffer, *Leviathan and the Air-Pump: Hobbes, Boyle, and the Experimental Life* (Princeton: Princeton University Press, 1985), p. 231; Frank, *Harvey and the Oxford Physiologists*, p. 130.

109 R. Waller, *Robert Hooke: Posthumous Works* (London, 1705), p. iii; cit. Purver, *The Royal Society*, p. 114.

110 Son of Robert's eldest brother, Sir Richard 'the Rich' Boyle, second Earl of Cork, first Earl of Burlington, Viscount Dungarvan, Baron Clifford of Londesborough. Sir Richard's London residence was Burlington House on Piccadilly, next door to which Pratt soon began building Clarendon House.

111 Frank, *Harvey and the Oxford Physiologists*, pp. 131–2. All the quotations are from Boyle's *New experiments physico-mechanicall touching the spring of the air* (Oxford, 1660).

112 Bray, *Evelyn Diary*, p. 132.

113 Shapin and Schaffer, *Leviathan and the Air-Pump*, pp. 30–1.

114 Cit. E. T. Drake, *Restless Genius: Robert Hooke and his Earthly Thoughts* (Oxford: Oxford University Press, 1996), p. 21.

115 As ever, Huygens emulated the London scientists in his use of the air-pump to attract royal sponsorship. Huygens, who had been invited from The Hague to become a founder member of the French Académie des Sciences in Paris in 1666, brought his own air-pump with him when he moved into Louis XIV's royal library (the early home of the Académie). He introduced the machine to his French colleagues with some simple botanical experiments – evacuating the receiver and watching the effect on plant germination and growth over a period of days. Botany was a particular focus of interest among the members of the Paris Académie. The air-pump produced far less spectacular effects on plants (which simply failed to prosper) than the amusing experiments tried in London with animals (which collapsed and died). Accordingly, Huygens's air-pump never achieved the symbolic centrality in Paris of its counterpart in London. See A. Stroup, *A Company of Scientists: Botany, Patronage, and Community at the Seventeenth-Century Parisian Royal Academy of Sciences* (Berkeley: University of California Press, 1990), pp. 160–5.

116 Westfall, Rice University Galileo project website.

117 Bray, *Evelyn Diary*, pp. 252–3.

118 M. M. 'Espinasse, *Robert Hooke* (London: Heinemann, 1956), pp. 51–2.

119 See Robb, *William of Orange*.

120 See Pepys, *Diary*, I, pp. 160–1; pp. 196–7. Hutton, *Charles the Second*, p. 135.

121 On Petty's post-Restoration disappointment, see Harris, 'Ireland as a laboratory'.

122 Ashmole and Evelyn were both gold-diggers and treasure-seekers, Evelyn hanging on Sir Richard Browne's and Arundel's coat-tails (ultimately to the advantage of the Royal Society, since it got them his house and library), Ashmole literally cashing in on the Garter treasures . . . was he looking for Great Georges and Garters when he started researching with Dean Wren in the 1650s? Ashmole was a freemason by the 1640s; Sir Christopher Wren became a freemason in 1691, and later Grand Master of the London Lodge.

123 He had been King of Arms since 1644,

and had retained his post throughout the Commonwealth period alongside Charles II in exile, and presided over the formal bestowing of Garters throughout that period.

124 It was on 11 August that Bruno Ryves signed for receipt of the precious Garter Record books, delivered to him in person on behalf of his deceased father, by Christopher Wren (see above, chapter 1). Thus receipt of the restored Garter Records was the first official business performed by the newly sworn-in officers of the Garter.

125 Ashmole, *Diary*, pp. 64–8.

126 See Jardine, *Ingenious Pursuits*.

127 All accounts of the Garter ceremonies, for example, go back no further than Ashmole's *Institution of the Order of the Garter* – a carefully concocted reworking of the surviving fragments into a baroque whole whose pedigree supposedly ran continuously back to Edward III.

128 C. H. Josten (ed.), *Elias Ashmole (1617–1692)*, 5 vols (Oxford: Clarendon Press, 1966) 3, 846–7.

129 London, 1672. For an inventory of the manuscripts, now in the Bodleian Library, see Black, *A Descriptive, Analytical, and Critical Catalogue*.

130 Wren expresses admiration for the Cathedral in his introduction, particularly for the lack of interior fussiness: 'The Pillars and ye Spaces between them are well suited to ye highth of the Arches, the Mouldings are decently mixed with large planes without an affectation of filling every corner with ornaments, which, (unlesse they are admirably good), glut ye eye, as much as in Musick, too much Division Cloyes ye eare, the Windows are not made too great, nor yet ye Light obstructed with many mullions and transomes of Tracery-worke which was ye ill fashion of he next (following) age: our Artist knew better that nothing could adde beauty to light, he trusted in a stately and rich Plainenesse that which his Marble Shafts gave his Worke' (*Wren Society* 11, 21).

131 *Wren Society* 11, 24.

132 Including clear technical drawings of the bits of equipment needed for the bracing, and how to splice beams – reproduced in Soo, *Wren's 'Tracts' on Architecture*.

133 Facsimile letter between pp. 236 and 237, in E. P. Warren, 'Sir Christopher Wren's repair of the Divinity School and Duke Humphrey's Library, Oxford', in *Sir Christopher Wren AD 1632–1723. Bicentenary Memorial Volume published under the auspices of the Royal Institute of British Architects* (London: Hodder & Stoughton, 1923), pp. 233–8. On the proposed Bodleian repairs see also *Parentalia*, p. 342. On the mathematician David Gregory see below, chapter 8.

134 Ashmole, *Institution of Order of the Garter*, pp. 241 3.

135 Ashmole, *Institution of Order of the Garter*, p. 242.

136 I first noticed the inscription on a slide shown by Michael Cooper during his Royal Society Lecture on Hooke, delivered at Gresham College on Wednesday, 4 April 2001.

137 See James Campbell, 'Architect as engineer: Sir Christopher Wren, the Royal Society and structural carpentry in the late seventeenth century', Gresham College Lecture, 23 October 2000 (draft).

138 Here it should be recalled that Wren was in The Hague and elsewhere in the Dutch Netherlands in 1649. I shall also argue that Hooke, who was a leading figure in the Wren architectural office, was importantly influenced by Dutch classical building. See below, chapter 6.

139 On Peterhouse Chapel in relation to Wren, see Mowl and Earnshaw, *Architecture without Kings*, pp. 193–4.

140 Rather than at Ely Cathedral.

141 James Campbell, personal communication (March 2002). There is a similar Wren-designed burial vault under St Lawrence Jewry church.

142 Soo, *Wren's 'Tracts' on Architecture*, pp. 112–13.

143 For a fascinating account of

Vanbrugh's experience of edge-of-town burial grounds in Surat in India, and the mausolea in them, see R. Williams, 'Vanbrugh's India and his Mausolea for England', in C. Ridgway and R. Williams (eds), *Sir John Vanbrugh and Landscape Architecture in Baroque England 1690–1730* (Stroud: Sutton Publishing, 2000), pp. 114–30.

144 Although the costs of the Sheldonian were almost halved – from £25,000 to £14,000 in the course of the scheme's execution. See *Wren Society* 19, 91–9.

145 Fell had an ulterior motive for backing the building, which from the outset was designed also to house the University printer: 'Immediately after the opening, Fell, with his usual energy, set about fitting up the printing presses in the cellars, a work which, Anthony Wood tells us, was completed by September 6th. Fell had already established a type foundry and assisted in fitting up a paper mill at Wolvercote. The first book printed and published at the Theatre came out in the October, being a folio of verses on the death of the Queen Mother, who had died at the end of August. The press was put in charge of a committee of delegates, with Dr. Fell as "supervisor and corrector of books". According to Wood, Fell was a forerunner of the late Poet Laureate in that he – "made it his design to correct the English and Latin tongues, as in English sic for sick, site for scite, contemt for contempt, throu for thorough. But printing many books without frugality and without overseeing or examining accompts (they) run themselves into debt and were forced to sell the Theatre to London booksellers in 1678."' (C. Hussey, 'The Universities of Oxford and Cambridge: The Sheldonian Theatre Oxford – II', *Country Life*, 24 May 1930, 750–5; 754–5).

146 Birch, *History of the Royal Society* 1, 230. Letter from Abraham Hill to John Brookes, 19 May 1663, cit. C. Saumarez-Smith, 'Wren and Sheldon',

Oxford Art Journal 6 (1983), 45–50; 46.

147 See J. Summerson, *The Sheldonian in its Time* (Oxford: Clarendon Press, 1964), p. 5. In practice the space above Wren's unique roof was used as a store for the printer's stock.

148 *Wren Society* 19, 91.

149 *Parentalia*, p. 338.

150 See above, chapter 3.

151 RS MS 249 *Parentalia* facing fol. 457r.

152 When Wren was corresponding with John Fell in 1681 about the possibility of incorporating an observatory into his designs for Tom Tower, Christ Church, he once again mentioned the importance of flat open space for telescope use: 'A Change it will be of the whole designe; for the Loft for the Bell aboue the ringing loft must be higher considerably & with large Windowes & still I doubt the Bell will be somwhat lowe to be well heard; then the octogonall Tower must be flat on the Top with a levell Ballaster (for pinnacles will do injury) the windowes also must be only wooden shutters without Mullions or barres, these things considered it will necessarily fall short of the beauty of the other way, for having begun in the Gothick manner wee must conclude aboue with flats & such proportions as will not be well reconcilable to the Gothick manner.' W. D. Caröe, *'Tom Tower' Christ Church Oxford: Some Letters of Sir Christopher Wren to John Fell, Bishop of London* (Oxford: Clarendon Press, 1923), p. 31.

153 *Parentalia*, pp. 339–42. Hooke boasted of the same thing in the house he designed for Charles Montagu, and there is a suggestion that the 'auditory' at St Paul's has exceptional acoustic qualities.

154 Cit. A. T. Friedman, 'John Evelyn and English Architecture', in T. O'Malley and J. Wolschke-Bulmahn, *John Evelyn's 'Elysium Britannicum' and European Gardening* (Dumbarton Oaks Publications, 1998), pp. 159–60.

155 Just as all subsequent accounts of the

Order of the Garter go back to Ashmole, so all accounts of the history of St Paul's depend on William Dugdale's *History of [Old] St. Paul's cathedral in London, from its foundation untill these times*, first published in 1658, and reissued after the Restoration. Its magnificent engravings of the intact Cathedral became a symbol for the revival of the grandeur of monarchy, and shaped Wren's aspiration to rebuild a monument of equivalent significance. As it happens, Ashmole's third wife was Dugdale's daughter, and the two men parcelled up a variety of projects for recording the seamless history of England (passing as swiftly as possible over the Interregnum) during the latter part of the seventeenth century.

156 Jonas Moore took part in a structural survey of the fabric in the mid-1650s. In 1657 a Convocation House was build behind the Cathedral. See *Wren Society* 13, 12.

157 *Parentalia*, p. 260.

158 In addition to loyally supporting Charles II in exile, Sheldon had contributed significant sums of money to the King's cause. Wren and Hooke's old school headmaster Busby also officiated at the Coronation.

159 Willis dedicated his *Cerebri anatome* (1664) to Sheldon.

160 DNB. See Chapter 2.

161 DNB.

162 The title of Doctor of Civil Law was conferred on Christopher Wren by Oxford in 1661; his LLD was awarded by Cambridge in 1673. Thomas Wren, second son of Matthew Wren, was created 'Doctor of Physick' in August 1660, 'by virtue of the Chancellor's Letters', on the ground that he had been prevented by his father's circumstances from pursuing normal studies at Oxford during the 1650s (*Parentalia*, p. 55). See above, chapter 2.

163 *Parentalia*, p. 54. Matthew Wren apparently declined, although at the end of July 1659 Hyde still hoped he would undertake the rebuttal.

164 Hyde's letter mentions a problem with an ordination – possibly Barwick's. For Barwick's appointment as Dean of St Paul's see Willmoth, *Sir Jonas Moore*, pp. 127–8.

165 *Wren Society* 13, 13.

166 *Wren Society* 13, 13–14.

167 MS Ashmole 36, fo. 117. Cit. R. T. Gunther (ed.), *The Architecture of Sir Roger Pratt, Charles II's Commissioner for the Rebuilding of London after the Great Fire: Now Printed for the first time from his Note-Books* (Oxford: Oxford University Press, 1928), p. 135. Roger Pratt's notes on Clarendon House include: 'May 2 1664 Payd to St Paules of ye first stone 60 Tunns', indicating that some of the stonework of Clarendon House had come from the old Cathedral. Other stone, however, came from Mr Switzer from Portland, also presumably in 1664, in five consignments (p. 140).

168 *Wren Society* 13, 14–15.

169 'Artist' is the term used by all concerned with St Paul's (and all other projects) for the design architect. 'Architect' is used (correctly according to its etymology) for a person with technical, construction expertise.

170 *Wren Society* 13, 15–16.

171 *Wren Society* 13, 16–17. Wren goes on explicitly to describe how the ruined tower and its supporting scaffolding can be left in place during the building of the dome, both to save expense in scaffolding, and 'because ye expectation of persons is to be kept up (for many unbelievers would bewail the loss of the old Paul's Steeple & despond if they did not see a hopefull successor rise in its stead)' (*Wren Society* 13, p. 17).

172 G. de la Bédoyère (ed.), *The Diary of John Evelyn* (Bangor: Headstart History, 1994), p. 171.

173 *An Account of Architects and Architecture*, appended to Evelyn's translation of Fréart de Chambray's *A Parallel of the Antient Architecture with the Modern* (second edition, 1707), letter dated 1697.

174 *Wren Society* 13, 37.
175 *Wren Society* 5, 29. The College Chapel accounts note: 'For the module of the designe in wainscot, 13.5.0. Carriage from London. 0.7.8'.
176 *Wren Society* 5, 30–1.
177 *Wren Society* 13, xviii.
178 Inevitably, Wilkins's biographers have tended to look for more reasonable grounds for his appointment (rather than a mere accident of fate): 'At the beginning of 1668, Wilkins once more became involved in church affairs. After the fall of Clarendon, during the closing months of the previous year, the way was open for an attempt to bring at least some groups of nonconformists into communion with the church, a policy Wilkins had long supported in accordance with the promise made by the king in the Declaration of Breda shortly before his return to England. It was also advocated by the duke of Buckingham, now the king's first minister. Richard Baxter was approached, but he found himself unable to accept the initial terms of negotiation and requested instead that "two learned peaceable divines" be nominated "to treat with us, till we agreed on the fittest terms". One of them was Wilkins, who drew up a proposal that was revised during further deliberations. Baxter's detailed account shows that Wilkins was a skillful negotiator who tried his best to find a compromise that would satisfy all parties. This proved impossible, and when it became known that a bill for comprehension was ready, Parliament refused to accept it. But Wilkins had Buckingham's patronage, and when the see of Chester fell vacant in August, he was soon appointed and duly consecrated on 14 November 1668' (Aarsleff, 'John Wilkins', p. 371).
179 There were strings attached to any prominent public office under Charles II – returned favours for benefits bestowed, replacing his father's old-style absolutism. As new Bishop of Chester, Wilkins led the arguments in the House of Lords in the Roos divorce case (on Charles II's behalf) in 1668 – Sheldon opposed the divorce. See Callow, *Charles II*, p. 170.
180 Bédoyère, *Evelyn Diary*, pp. 173–4.
181 *Wren Society* 13, 45. Wren was equally devoted to Sancroft. On hearing of his being made Archbishop of Canterbury at the death of Sheldon, Wren wrote a fervent letter of congratulation (on 30 December 1677): 'Most Reverend, I am soe many ways Concerned, and soe much in Duty bound to rejoyce in the Good News (which, though I wished long since, I heard but to day) that I cant defir to congratulate our Church in generall and particularly St Paules: that his Majestie hath made so wise and exact a choyce for the service both of them and himselfe. I want expression for my Zeale as I doe Herauldry for my superscription and time to kiss Your Grace's handes (being sent abroad upon former appointment) but I presume upon Yr Grace's Clemency, and that you will accept a sincere profession of Duty from Your Grace's Most humble and most obliged servant Chr Wren' (*Wren Society* 13, 51).

CHAPTER 5: *Connected in Companies*

1 *Parentalia*, after p. 194. Wren goes on to his son in terms more familiarly sceptical of the advantages of seeing buildings 'in the flesh': 'but the seeing of fine buildings I perceive temptes you, & your companion Mr Strong whose inclination and interest leades him, by neither of which I can find you are moved; but how doth it concerne you? you would haue it to say hereafter that you haue seen Rome Naples & other fine places, a hundred others can say as much & more; calculate whither this be worth the Expence & hazard as to any advantage at your returne.'
2 Evelyn, *Diary*, April 1646.
3 It is still possible that Wren did cross the Alps to Italy during his nine

months abroad in 1649. It is a curious irony that, because of the comparative wealth of documentation concerning Wren's life that survives, in the Wren Society and elsewhere, absence of documentary evidence is taken as conclusive evidence that an event did *not* take place.

4 Fréart, *A Parallel of the Antient Architecture with the Modern*, trans. John Evelyn (London, 1664), 'The Epistle Dedicatory', fols A2r–A3r.

5 'Supped at a magnificent Entertainement in Waddum Hall, invited by my excellent & deare Friend Dr. Wilkins, then Warden [now Bishop of Chester]: on the Eleventh was the Latine Sermon which I could not be at, invited, being taken up at All-Soules, where we had Music, voices & Theorbes perform'd by some ingenious Scholars, where after dinner I visited that miracle of a Youth, Mr. Christopher Wren, nephew to the Bishop of Elie: then Mr. Barlow [since Bishop of Lincoln] Bibliothe<c>arius of the Bodlean Library, my most learned friend, who shewd me, together with my Wife, The rarities of that famous place, Manuscrip<t>s, Medails & other Curiosities.' De Beer, *Diary of John Evelyn*, 3, pp. 105–6.

6 De Beer, *Diary of John Evelyn*, 3, p. 186.

7 Bédoyère, *Particular Friends*.

8 *An idea of the perfection of painting: demonstrated from the principles of art, and by examples conformable to the observations, which Pliny and Quintilian have made upon the most celebrated pieces of the antient painters, parallel'd with some works of the most famous modern painters, Leonardo da Vinci, Raphael, Julio Romano, and N. Poussin* (1668), sig. b7v.

9 See Thurley, Whitehall Palace, p. 101: 'That Bernini was to arrive in Paris in June 1665 was probably known to Charles II and to Wren, and the coincidence of the completion of Wren's first Whitehall model and his trip to meet Bernini and Mansart in July 1665 are no accident of history. . . . These events suggest that Wren's trip was . . . specifically aimed at gleaning ideas for Whitehall.'

10 Ep. 236, 4 April 1665. Transcription from the Letter Copybooks courtesy of Douglas Chambers, from the complete John Evelyn edition in progress. I would like to express my gratitude to Douglas Chambers for making these letters available to me in definitive form.

11 *Wren Society* 5, 14.

12 John Evelyn junior's tutor had until this point been Milton's nephew, Edward Phillips. He was replaced in the summer of 1665 by Ralph Bohun. On Bohun see Frank, *Harvey and the Oxford Physiologists*, pp. 239 and 68–9. For further evidence of the Wren connection in Bohun's appointment see a 1668 letter from Bohun to Evelyn's wife Mary, with whom Bohun corresponded regularly after his appointment: 'Dr Bathurst has importun'd me in the company of Dr Wren to shew some of your admirable letters to confirm his character of you.' Cit. F. Harris, 'The letterbooks of Mary Evelyn', *English Manuscript Studies* (1998), 202–15; 211. Wilkins also apparently recommended Bohun to Evelyn.

13 Plowden, *Henrietta Maria*, p. 251.

14 *Parentalia*, p. 261. Henry Jermyn, Earl of St Albans, was Henrietta Maria's closest personal attendant and adviser – gossip had it that the two were secretly married. Detailing the many marvels and rarities he has seen in the French capital, Wren tells his correspondent that the best of these 'now furnish the Glorious Appartment of the *Queen Mother* at the *Louvre*, which I saw many Times'. Some confusion is caused by the fact that there was also a French 'Queen Mother' in residence (mother of Louis XIV), but she was mortally ill (she died in Februrary 1666), so the reference is clearly not to her. The fact that Wren's son reports here that

the 'particular friend', Wren's correspondent, thought especially highly of Earl St Albans narrows down the possibilities to someone in the 'French party'.

15 *Parentalia*, p. 261.

16 *Parentalia*, p. 262.

17 At the time of writing Wren planned to return in December: 'My Lord *Berkley* returns to *England* at *Christmas*, when I propose to take the Opportunity of his Company.' This was George Berkeley, who had, while himself in Paris with Henrietta Maria, lent his house at Durdans, Epsom to Wilkins, Hooke and others, as a refuge during the summer 1665 plague outbreak. On 30 November, Edward Browne reported in a letter that 'Dr. Wren is at Lord Barclays' (*Wren Society* 18, 178). However, Wren stayed in France until the end of February.

18 '14th. [August 1662]. This afternoon, the Queen-Mother, with the Earl of St. Alban's and any great ladies and persons, was pleased to honour my poor villa with her presence, and to accept of a collation. She was exceedingly pleased, and staid till very late in the evening' (Bray, *Evelyn Diary*, p. 255).

19 'Samuel Tuke, Mary Evelyn's cousin, was a warm supporter of his work and from Paris sent him welcome news of architectural developments, reporting on Louis XIV's summons to Bernini. Evelyn had sent Wren to visit Tuke bearing a letter of introduction and October he reports that Bernini has gone home, leaving his designs for the finishing of the Louvre (and a marble head of the king). Wren and his companions would return, he considered, "furnished with many of the choisest plums". (The previous year he had tried to coax reports of Bernini's work at St Peters from his nephew George, on his Grand Tour, with no great success.)' Gillian Darley, 'Evelyn, Greenwich and the Sick and Wounded', paper delivered to the John Evelyn conference, British Library, London, September 2001.

20 BL MSS JE A8 (2). 'Letters from Sir Samuel Tuke, 1st Bart., 1649–1672', Letter from Tuke to Evelyn, Paris, 12 August 1665. I am extremely grateful to Gillian Darley for bringing Tuke's letters to my attention, and to Frances Harris of the British Library for her help with the Evelyn archive.

21 BL MSS JE A8 (2) 'Letters from Sir Samuel Tuke, 1st Bart., 1649–1672', Letter from Tuke to Evelyn, 23 October 1665.

22 Tuke to Wren, 13 January 1666, f. 1302.

23 Hall and Hall, *Oldenburg Correspondence* 2, 480.

24 Part of this letter is in French: 'Le medicin de la reyne de Pologne y explique la nature d'une maladie, nommé plica à lequelle les Polonois & les Cosques seul son sujets on y parla d'un sourd & muet qui danse en cadence & des plusiers autres choses, qui lui plurent assez nous l'avons aussi mené chez le grand architecte le chevalier Bernini. Il a vu le buste, qu'il fait du roi en marble, & le dessein qu'il a fait du Louvre, dont il vous entretiendra, Je luy ay fait voir ce matin la machine de monsieur Pascal, avec laquelle on peur faire toutes sortes de règles d'arithmetique' (*Wren Society* 13, 44).

25 Hall and Hall, *Oldenburg Correspondence* 3, 12.

26 See Plowden, *Henrietta Maria*, p. 251.

27 See R. Iliffe, 'Foreign bodies: travel, empire and the early Royal Society of London. Part 1. Englishmen on tour', *Canadian Journal of History* (1998).

28 *Wren Society* 18, 180.

29 'Je donnerai tous que ie ne vous ai pas envoye a M. Vren que je vois presque tous les iours et quantite dautres Messieurs Anglois. Je luy ai faict voir depuis peu ce qua faict Mignard au Vol de grant, qui est un ouvrage digne de l'estime des curiouex. Nous avons aussi le buste du Roy faict par Bernin qui est une belle piece' (Hall and Hall, *Oldenburg Correspondence* 3, 11).

30 The Venetian ambassador reported in

September 1666: 'Accordingly the queen, as if on her own motion, has despatched to England my lord Germen, her major domo, who has been employed on similar affairs on other occasions' (Plowden, *Henrietta Maria*, p. 253).

31 *Wren Society* 13, 44.

32 Hunter, *The Royal Society and its Fellows*, pp. 174–5.

33 The problem of longitude is mentioned in the Royal Society's founding charter of 1662. The Royal Society meeting in question did not take place in its usual form, because of the Fire. It had, in any case, lost its accommodation at Gresham College, and was meeting temporarily in the lodgings of Dr Walter Pope, Gresham Professor of Astronomy. Instead of the prearranged meeting there was a general discussion of the form the Society's response should take to the Fire, to prove its usefulness. When Hevelius claimed that telescopic sights had never been tried on large instruments in 1679, Hooke repled that he had used several: 'and particularly one of Sr. Christopher Wren's invention, furnished with two Perspective Sights of 6 foot long each, which I made use of for examining the motions of the Comet in the year 1665' (Bennett, *Mathematical Science*, p. 42).

34 The previous summer, during a major plague outbreak in London, Hooke and Wilkins (who as incumbent at St Lawrence Jewry, next door to the Guildhall, was also at risk) took refuge together on the estate of Lord Berkeley in Epsom. Wren was abroad in France at the time.

35 De Beer, *Diary of John Evelyn*, 3, pp. 450–4.

36 S. Porter, *The Great Fire of London* (Stroud: Sutton Publishing, 1996), p. 3. On the Great Fire and rebuilding in general see J. P. Malcolm, *Londinium Redivivium*, 4 vols (London, 1802–7); T. F. Reddaway, *The Rebuilding of London after the Great Fire* (London: Jonathan Cape, 1940).

37 Thurley, *Whitehall Palace*, pp. 142–3.

38 Thurley, *Whitehall Palace*, p. 82.

39 Porter, *The Great Fire of London*, p. 37.

40 Hooke, *Diary*. Actually the toll was 624 houses – a classic example of the exaggerations associated with natural disasters (see Porter, *The Great Fire of London*, p. 155).

41 Among those killed in the blast was the Dutch landscape and still-life painter Carel Fabritius (1622–54), who had trained in Rembrandt's studio, and his colleague Mathys Spoors.

42 Plowden, *The Stuart Princesses*, p. 102.

43 See Porter, *The Great Fire of London*, p. 33.

44 See Willmoth, *Sir Jonas Moore*, pp. 136–7.

45 Cit. Porter, *The Great Fire of London*, p. 68.

46 Hollar images reproduced in Porter, *The Great Fire of London*, pp. 68–9, 72–3.

47 Porter, *The Great Fire of London*, p. 105.

48 'On 7 September 1666 the City had ordered the lodgings of Dr Jonathan Goddard, FRS, Gresham Professor of Physic to be taken and used by the City Chamberlain, and the rooms formerly occupied by Dr Horton to be taken by the Deputy Town Clerk and the City Swordbearer for lodgings and offices. There seems to have been some resistance to this order, for on the next day, Saturday 8 September, the City reordered Horton's former lodgings and some other rooms to be cleared by Monday morning: "And in case of any contempt or neglect of this Order the Citty Artificers are to breake open the Doors and see it executed accordingly."' M. Cooper, 'Robert Hooke's work as surveyor for the City of London in the aftermath of the Great Fire. Part one: Robert Hooke's first surveys for the City of London', *Notes and Records of the Royal Society* 51 (1997), 161–74; 162–3.

49 All Royal Society arrangements with Arundel were brokered by Evelyn, who had been in the service of the Earl's grandfather.

50 Ep. 277. Transcription from the Letter Copybooks courtesy of Douglas Chambers, from the complete John Evelyn edition in progress.

51 *Londinium Redivivum*, 1666.

52 Fréart, *A Parallel of the Antient Architecture with the Modern*, trans. John Evelyn (London, 1664), prefatory letter fol. A2r–A2v.

53 For May's and Pratt's earlier buildings see Mowl and Earnshaw, *Architecture without Kings*; McKellar, *The Birth of Modern London*.

54 In the mid-1660s Hooke, like Oldenburg, was still in Boyle's service (and in all likelihood still paid by him).

55 Gunther, *The Architecture of Sir Roger Pratt*.

56 Gunther, *The Architecture of Sir Roger Pratt*.

57 Oldenburg to Boyle, 16 October 1666. Hall and Hall, *Oldenburg Correspondence* 3, 245.

58 For Wren's and Evelyn's rebuilding schemes see Porter, *The Great Fire of London*, pp. 98–101.

59 '14th May [1662]. To London, being chosen one of the Commissioners for reforming the buildings, ways, streets, and incumbrances, and regulating the hackney coaches in the City of London, taking my oath before my Lord Chancellor [Clarendon], and then went to his Majesty's Surveyor's Office [Denham], in Scotland-Yard, about naming and establishing officers, and adjourning till the 16th, when I went to view how St. Martin's Lane might be made more passable into the Strand. There were divers gentlemen of quality in this commission' (Bray, *Evelyn Diary*, p. 253).

60 Bray, *Evelyn Diary*, p. 254.

61 'Epistle to Sir John Denham', *A Parallel of the Antient Architecture with the Modern, written in French by Roland Fréart, sieur de Chambray,*

made English . . . by John Evelyn, (London, 1664; 1701 edition), n.p. Cit. Friedman, 'John Evelyn and English Architecture'.

62 Both men had spent significant periods in Paris (Wren the previous year, Evelyn regularly since the 1640s), a city replanned and rebuilt on a grand scale under the absolutist regime of Louis XIV. For the comparison of the two plans see Porter, *The Great Fire of London*, pp. 98–9.

63 'I asked him which hee took to bee the greatest work about Paris, he said the Quay or Key upon the river side, which he demonstrated to me, to be built with so vast expense and such great quantity of materialls, that it exceeded all manner of ways the building of the two greatest pyramids in Egypt.' See above, chapter 4.

64 BL MS *Parentalia*, fol. 53 verso. See also, fol. 50 verso down the side and partly trapped in the binding [along the description of Wren's plan for rebuilding London]: 'The only obstruction at last that prevented the execution of it being the obstinacy of the generality of proprietors & citizens by persisting to have their [rest lost].' This whole document has been tactfully omitted from the printed text of *Parentalia*, where we find only the following, p. 269: 'The Practicability of this whole Scheme, without Loss to any Man, or Infringement of any Property, was at that Time demonstrated, and all material Objections fully weigh'd and answered: the only, and as it happened, insurmountable Difficulty remaining, was the obstinate Averseness of great Part of the Citizens to alter their old Properties, and to recede from building their Houses again on the old Ground and Foundations. . . . By these Means, the Opportunity, in a great degree was lost, of making the new City the most magnificent, as well as commodious for Health and Trade of any upon Earth.' This is clearly

retrospectively based on the document quoted here.

65 BL MS *Parentalia*, fol. 53 verso.

66 Porter, *The Great Fire of London*, pp. 104–5.

67 BL MS *Parentalia*, fol. 54 recto (compare *Parentalia*, p. 269).

68 Cit. C. Wall, *The Literary and Cultural Spaces of Restoration London* (Cambridge: Cambridge University Press, 1998), p. 43.

69 For a fully articulated argument of this democratic case for retaining London's old property ownership patterns see Wall, *The Literary and Cultural Spaces of Restoration London*, passim.

70 *Wren Society* 13, 50. Wren to Sancroft, 16 September 1671: 'The City are falling upon making the wharf from the Temple to ye bridge . . . at Paules Wharfe it will be about 30 foot [into the Thames]. . . . This is the designe but it cannot be effected without a Grant under the broad seale to the City of soe much of the soyle of the River as shall be taken in by this new line. . . . I interposed that there might be an exception of soe much ground upon this Key as might serve for 2 good cranes for the building of St Paules, that is about 100 foot between Barnard's Castle and the Staires which is all before yr own Tenants.'

71 Porter, *The Great Fire of London*, pp. 156–7. 'The scheme was designed under Wren's direction and in consultation with Robert Hooke and John Oliver, acting for the City, and was completed by the end of 1674 at a cost of £51,307.' The improvements were a success in technical and construction terms, but in the end failed as a commercial venture since the rents and dues raised by traffic on the Fleet failed to raise the sums needed for the canal's upkeep. [There is a docket for works on the Fleet Ditch, signed by Wren, Hooke and Oliver, in the Pierpont Morgan Library.

72 18 September 1666. Hall and Hall, *Oldenburg Correspondence* 3, 230–1.

73 Waller, *Robert Hooke*, p. xiii.

74 Cooper, 'Robert Hooke's work as surveyor for the City of London in the aftermath of the Great Fire. Part one', p. 162.

75 For some years before his actual resignation Edward Bernard, appointed by Wren as his deputy, lectured in his place (Bennett, *The Mathematical Science*, p. 89).

76 Hall and Hall, *Oldenburg Correspondence*.

77 Bennett, *The Mathematical Science*, p. 51. Hooke included a map of the Pleiades in his *Micrographia* (pp. 241–2).

78 Bennett, *The Mathematical Science*, p. 65.

79 'Problema: Datis quatuor lineis utcunque ductis (quarum nec tres sunt parallelae neque ab eodem puncto ductae) quintam ducere quae a quatuor primo datis in tres partes secetur ratione et positione datas' (cit. Elmes, *Memoirs of Wren*, Appendix, p. 60).

80 RS MS EL W.3 no. 5, cit. Bennett, *The Mathematical Science*, p. 67.

81 London, May 4, 1665. cit. Elmes, *Memoirs of Wren*, pp. 164–5.

82 RS MS EL W.3 no. 6, cit. Bennett, *The Mathematical Science*, p. 67. I have reversed the order of these letters, in spite of the dates given, since Wren's appears to answer Hooke's.

83 Moray to Oldenburg, 28 September 1665. Hall and Hall, *Oldenburg Correspondence* 2, 529. Bennett, *The Mathematical Science*, p. 64.

84 See Bennett, *The Mathematical Science*, pp. 84–6; A. K. Biswas, 'The automatic rain-gauge of Sir Christopher Wren, FRS', *Notes and Records of the Royal Society* 22 (1967), 94–104.

85 Cit. Biswas, 'The automatic rain-gauge of Sir Christopher Wren', p. 96.

86 'In the prosecution of which conjecture, I did first contriue a way to make those alterations more sensible by means of a flote mouing upon the subjacent surface of the [mercury] and that flote hauing a

counterpoising weight suspended by a small thread layd over a pully caused the motion of an index or hand which served to magnify, as it were, this effect, the point of this index being thereby made to moue as many feet as the [mercury] did inches, which I have particularly described in in [sic] ye preface to my micrography. p. 10. and some additions to it in the transactions ['A new Contrivance of Wheel-Barometer, much more easy to be prepared, than that, which is described in the *Micrography*; imparted by the Author of that Book.' Phil. Trans. 1, 218–219 (1666)].' Cit. W. E. K. Middleton, 'A footnote to the history of the barometer: an unpublished note by Robert Hooke, FRS', *Notes and Records of the Royal Society* 20 (1965), 145–51. There is another description by Hooke of his 'Contrivance to augment the Divisions of the Barometer' in W. Derham (ed.), *Philosophical Experiments and Observations of the late Eminent Dr. Robert Hooke* (London, 1726), pp. 302–3.

87 Cit. Bennett, *The Mathematical Science*, p. 85.

88 Derham, *Philosophical Experiments and Observations*, pp. 41–7.

89 Pepys, *Diary*, 6, p. 18.

90 Hartlib Papers 1655 part 4. I am extremely grateful to Jessica Ratcliff for supplying this reference at the critical moment. See also Bennett, *The Mathematical Science*, p. 73 (although there is a misprint, 1655 being rendered, confusingly, 1665).

91 *Micrographia* page reference.

92 For Faithorne as the engraver of the plates for *Micrographia* see Jardine, *Ingenious Pursuits*, chapter 2.

93 *Micrographia* page reference. Hooke does go on to discuss the fly's eye, but largely on the basis of Power's interpretation of what is actually being seen.

94 The exquisite drawings produced in this way by the Dutch microscopist Antoni van Leeuwenhoek were made by professional artists in his native Delft, since he himself had no artistic talent. See Jardine, *Ingenious Pursuits*, chapter 3.

95 Jardine, *Ingenious Pursuits*, chapter 2.

96 For Boyle's pattern of intermittent attendance, and his practice of sending Hooke to represent him when necessary, see Frank, *Harvey and the Oxford Physiologists*.

97 Hooke, *Diary*, cit. Frank, *Harvey and the Oxford Physiologists*, p. 282.

98 Pepys, *Diary* 9, 491.

99 Wren also had the administrative toughness needed – note on Portland stone legislation the same autumn.

100 See Aubrey to Hobbes, Letter 199, 24 June 1675: 'He [Wallis] makes it his Trade to be a common-spye. Steales from every ingeniose persons discourse, and prints it: viz from Sr Chr: Wren God knows how often, from Mr Hooke [one and a half lines deleted] etc. he is a most ill-natured man, an egregious lyer and back-biter, a flatterer, and fawner on my Ld Brouncker & his Miss: that my Ld may keepe up his reputation' (Malcolm, *Correspondence of Thomas Hobbes* 2, 753–4).

101 SP Dom Ch II p. 667, Entry Book 35b f. 24.

102 SP Dom Ch II p. 496, Entry Book 47 f. 79.

103 SP Dom Ch II Jan 1679–Aug 1630 p. 183, Entry book 55 p. 24. In May 3 1692, 'Wm Holder DD' appears in a long list of people appointed commissioners for carrying on and completing the furnishing and adorning of St Paul's (SP Dom Wm & Mary 1691–2 p. 287).

104 'Madam, The Artificer having never before mett with a drowned Watch; like an ignorant physician has been soe long about the care, that he hath made me very unquiet that your comands should be soe long deferred. however I have sent the Watch at last, & envie the felicity of it, that it should be soe neer your side, & soe often enjoy your Eye, & be consulted by you how your time

shall passe while you employ your hand in your excellent workes. But haue a care of it. for I haue put such a Spell into it that every Beating of the Ballance will tell you. 'tis the pulse of my Heart which labours as much to serue you and more trewly then the Watch. for the Watch I beleeve will sometimes lie, & sometimes perhaps be idle & unwilling to goe, having receiued so much injury by being drenched in that briny bath, that I dispair it should ever be a trew servant to you more: But as for me (unlesse you drown me too in my teares) you may be confident I shall never cease to be Your most affectionate humble Servant Chr: Wren' (*Parentalia*, following p. 194).

105 In 1694 Wren brought a lawsuit laying claim to the Coghills' old home, the Great House at Bletchingdon, on the ground that the late Earl of Anglesey, who had bought the estate in 1666, had mortgaged it to him. Faith's parents had been forced by Commonwealth sequestration to sell up their home at Bletchingdon and move to a smaller farm property, Old House, next door to William Holder's church. Wren's attempt to acquire a country home in the village of his boyhood, however, failed.

106 'October 14 1672. . . . Dr. Wrens son born about 8 at night.'

107 'November 2 1672. . . . Dr. Wrens, dind, gave nurse 5s.'

108 Hooke, *Diary*, p. 69.

109 'September 15 1673. . . . at Garways with Oldenburg. at Dr. Wrens his child in convulsion fits.'

110 'Monday March 23 1674. . . . Sir Chr. Wrens child died suddenly.'

111 Like several other important figures in Wren's story, Jane's father was Irish nobility.

112 Little, *Sir Christopher Wren*, pp. 100–1.

113 Little, *Sir Christopher Wren*, p. 107.

114 Little, *Sir Christopher Wren*, p. 114. Christopher, the eldest, was five and a half, and from this point onwards would be raised by nurses and

relatives. Small wonder that he and his father were not close.

115 On more than one occasion Hooke's diary records Wren dining with him shortly after the event.

116 They also went to the theatre: 'Saturday June 20, 1674. . . . To Sir Ch. Wren. Dind with him. Woodroof there. To Hoskins with Sir Ch. Wren. By water with him to the Playhouse. Saw Tempest [Dryden's fashionable revival].'

117 Pepys, *Diary*, 8, p. 64.

118 Transcribed from the original manuscript in L. M. Soo, *Wren's 'Tracts' on Architecture*, p. 56.

119 Wren to Sancroft, 7 May 1666, *Wren Society* 13, 44.

120 Wren to Sancroft, 5 August 1666, *Wren Society* 13, 45.

121 Soo, *Wren's 'Tracts' on Architecture*, p. 56.

122 Soo, *Wren's 'Tracts' on Architecture*, p. 59.

123 *Wren Society* 13, 23. Dated 15 January 1668.

124 See above, chapter 4.

125 *Wren Society* 13, 45–6 (dating the two letters more plausibly to 1667, not 1666 as postulated by the editors).

126 *Wren Society* 13, 46.

127 *Wren Society* 13, 47–8.

128 Elmes, *Memoirs of Wren*, Appendix, pp. 77–90.

129 *Parentalia*, pp. 283–7.

130 *Wren Society* 13, 31.

131 *Wren Society* 13, 31.

132 'More than 70 carved stones from the western portico of London's Old St. Paul's Cathedral have been found beneath the present cathedral, according to John Schofield, head of archaeology for the Museum of London. The portico was built during the 1630s by Inigo Jones (1573–1652), the father of English classical architecture, as part of a remodeling of the medieval cathedral. The entire structure was badly damaged during the English civil war (1642–1648) and again in the Great Fire of London (1666). Between 1675 and 1710 it was replaced by the current St. Paul's,

designed by Sir Christopher Wren (1632–1723), who reused blocks from the portico in his foundations. Jones's makeover of the medieval building included covering the outside with a layer of limestone masonry in the classical style and adding a portico with ten columns capped by a frieze and architrave with statues along the top. This design combined details of the second-century AD Temple of Antoninus and Faustina in Rome with a reconstruction of the Temple of Venus and Rome (built ca. AD 121– 135), also in Rome, by the Italian Renaissance architect Andrea Palladio (1508–1580). Parts of the portico's fluted Corinthian columns have now been found; their dimensions suggest that the columns originally stood 56 feet tall.' (*Archaeology*, Vol. 50 No. 2 March/April 1997).

133 BL MS *Parentalia*, fol. 54 recto.

134 On Pratt's career, see Gunther, *The Architecture of Sir Roger Pratt*. 'In 1664, while still heavily engaged upon work at Kingston Lacy and at Horseheath, Pratt undertook a third and yet larger mansion for Edward Hyde, Earl of Clarendon. The site chosen lay on the north side of the "rode to Reading", now Piccadilly, between Burlington House and Devonshire House. Pratt devoted himself most assiduously to the planning of this house and has left very full notes as to his building practice. The building took three years and was valued at £35,000, but it was not fated to stand long, for it was demolished in 1683, having been in existence less than twenty years. In the interval the place had acquired a site value and had become mature for development. A speculative builder purchased the materials of the house at house-breakers' prices, and many of Pratt's bricks are doubtless below the foundation of Bond Street' (see Gunther, pp. 9–14).

135 It is striking that, from immediately after the Fire, Jerman was extensively occupied with commissions for

rebuilding from livery companies and guilds, which presumably further lessened his involvement with the overall rebuilding plans. In addition to the Royal Exchange, Jerman designed new buildings for the goldsmiths, fishmongers, weavers, drapers and mercers (Porter, *The Great Fire of London*, p. 131). May, meanwhile, was Paymaster for the Royal Works, thus fully occupied with the financial side of rebuilding operations.

136 The account that follows is largely based on P. Jeffery, *The City Churches of Sir Christopher Wren* (London: Hambledon Press, 1996).

137 Cit. Jeffery, *The City Churches*, p. 27.

138 Cit. Jeffery, *The City Churches*, p. 31.

139 For a comprehensive account of Hooke's activities staking out the new, wider streets of London, see M. Cooper, 'Robert Hooke's work as surveyor for the City of London in the aftermath of the Great Fire. Part one', Robert Hooke's first surveys for the City of London, *Notes and Records of the Royal Society*, 51 (1997), pp. 161– 74.

140 For a comprehensive account of Hooke's surveying and 'viewing' activities, see Cooper, 'Robert Hooke's work as surveyor. Part two: certification of areas of ground taken away for streets and other new works', *Notes and Records of the Royal Society* 52 (1998), 25–38, and 'Robert Hooke's work as surveyor. Part three: settlement of disputes and complaints arising from rebuilding', *Notes and Records of the Royal Society* 52 (1998), 205–20.

141 Jeffery, *The City Churche*s, pp. 37–8.

142 It looks as if the figure was £50 per annum plus occasional payments pro rata. Hooke records these payments – or rather Wren's accumulating debt, due to his slowness in paying – at regular intervals in his diary. Since Woodroffe also did work in the Wren office directly for Wren, he too may have received additional remuneration. However, he died in 1675, and was replaced by John Oliver. See below. By

1670, Hooke was receiving £150 a year from the Corporation of London for his work as City Surveyor (see Cooper, 'Robert Hooke's work as surveyor. Part one', p. 170).

143 For the evidence from Hooke's diary of his close involvement with the City churches see M. I. Batten, 'The architecture of Dr Robert Hooke FRS', *Walpole Society* 25 (1936–7), 83–113: 'Nearly all of [the City churches] are mentioned in the Diary, those he visited most frequently being St. Benets Finck, St. Laurence [Jewry], St. Magnus, St. Stephen's Walbrook, Bassingshaw Church, St. Anne's and St Agnes, and St. Martin's Ludgate. The entries are continuous and show him visiting them with Wren and without him, passing accounts and attending meetings of the parish councils. A typical church visiting day is the following: "April 13th, 1675; Sir Chr. Wren and Mr Woodroof here. To Dionis Backchurch, Buttolphs, Walbrook, Coleman Street, St. Bartholomews. Dind at Levets. With Sir Ch. Wren to Paules." A few days later we get "I was several times about accounts at Sir Ch. Wren with Woodroof. I transacted the business of St. Laurence Church with Mr. Firman." In April 1676 Hooke "agreed with Marshall about St. Bride's Church Tower". In July 1674 is the entry, "with St. Martins Parish at the Greyhound. . . . Saw all things concluded what to doe." He gives a list of those present and Wren's name is not among them. Besides the very many references to the churches themselves there are many others relating to payments from Wren to Hooke "on ye City Churches account". These appear in the Diary separately from the payments that Hooke was receiving from the City of London for his work as City Surveyor. From November 1674 to October 1681 Hooke received something over eight hundred pounds, though as some of the entries are "due from Sir Chr. Wren" and others are "received",

sometimes after an interval of several months, it is difficult to be sure of the precise amount.'

144 See Jeffery, *The City Churches*, pp. 38–9. Hoskins was a member of the 'new club' Hooke and Wren were plotting at this time. See above, chapter 4.

145 Jeffery, *The City Churches*, pp. 93–4.

146 In this case, unusually, I disagree with Jeffery, who attributes the church to Hooke, largely on the ground that it is assymetrical. St Lawrence Jewry achieves the remarkable feat of creating an illusion of symmetry, in spite of pronounced asymmetries in both the main body of the church and the tower. This makes it more likely to be Wren's design.

147 *Wren Society* 19, 26.

148 Jeffery, *The City Churches*, pp. 107–8.

149 '16 November 1672: Lord Chester desperately ill of the stone, stoppage of urine 6 dayes. oyster shells 4 red hot quenched in cyder a quart and drank, advisd by Glanvill. Another prescribed *flegma acidum succini rectificatum cum sale tartari*. Dr Godderd advisd Blisters of cantharides applyd to the neck and feet or to the vains' (Hooke, *Diary*, p. 13).

150 Hooke, *Diary*, p. 13.

151 On Charles II's successive financial crises see G. Holmes, *The Making of a Great Power: Late Stuart and Early Georgian Britain 1660–1722* (London: Longman, 1993), chapter 5.

152 On Saenredam's deliberate creation of illusions of symmetry from asymmetrical spaces see Schwartz and Bok, *Pieter Saenredam*. De Witte's paintings of church interiors even more closely resemble Wren spaces like that at St Stephen Walbrook. At the time when Wren visited The Hague in 1649, William II of Orange owned at least one large Saenredam painting, his 1648 painting of the Great Church at Bavokerk in Haarlem. On 21 May 1648, Saenredam wrote to Constantijn Huygens senior, William's secretary and cultural adviser from Haarlem: 'It pleases me

very much to hear that His Highness has begun to take pleasure in paintings, that he indeed desired to see my recently completed great church, and that he wanted to have it shipped now, in which I foresee, on the basis of continuous experience, difficulties of such magnitude, too long to relate, that I do not dare ship it or take that risk. Nonetheless I cordially wished that His Highness saw the same with his own eyes, as has happened with you, My Lord. I have had this piece along with five more of the largest brought to Monsr Vroons. The family tree of the house of Brandenburg will now also progress again. As for the price of the church, I trust that Your Excellency still recalls our oral discussion' (Schwartz and Bok, *Pieter Saenredam*, p. 206).

153 Soo, *Wren's 'Tracts' on Architecture*, p. 155.

154 *Wren Society* 10, 114–15.

155 Jeffery, *The City Churches*, pp. 56–7.

156 For the detailed information of St Stephen Walbrook on which this discussion is based see Jeffery, *The City Churches*, pp. 337–42.

157 For the complete text of the Commission see Elmes, *Memoirs of Wren*, Appendix, pp. 77–90.

158 On Hooke's architecture see Stoesser-Johnston, 'Robert Hooke and Holland'. See also Batten, 'The architecture of Dr. Robert Hooke FRS'. However, although Batten usefully collates the architectural material from Hooke's diary, to establish the importance of Hooke's contribution to the Wren office, she tends to suppress references to Wren (as having been overemphasised in the past), thereby somewhat skewing the picture of Hooke's actual prominence and autonomy.

CHAPTER 6: *Overlapping Interests*

1 For a full account of the planning and building of the Royal Observatory at Greenwich see D. Howse, *Greenwich Time and Longitude*, second edition (London: Philip Wilson, 1997).

2 On the history of solutions of the problem of longitude see W. J. H. Andrewes, *The Quest for Longitude* (Cambridge, Mass.: Harvard University Press, 1996); Howse, *Greenwich Time and Longitude*; D. Sobel, *Longitude: The True Story of a Lone Genius Who Solved the Greatest Scientific Problem of his Time* (London: Fourth Estate, 1995).

3 The Ordnance Office remained responsible for paying the Astronomer Royal's salary down to the nineteenth century (Willmoth, 'Mathematical sciences and military technology', pp. 129–30).

4 Sir Samuel Morland, Sir Christopher Wren, the courtier Colonel Silius Titus, John Pell and Robert Hooke are named in the royal patent of appointment preserved in the British Library (Add. MS. 4393, fol. 89r).

5 Flamsteed's 'Account of the Observatory' [late 1699]. E. G. Forbes, L. Murdin and F. Willmoth (eds), *The Correspondence of John Flamsteed, The First Astronomer Royal*, vol. 2 (1682–1703) (Bristol and Philadelphia: The Institute of Physics Publishing, 1997), letter [unsent – no addressee, but probably a self-justification addressed to the Archbishop of Canterbury] 803, pp. 797–800; 797.

6 See Willmoth, *Sir Jonas Moore*, pp. 176–92.

7 *Wren Society* 19, 113.

8 Hooke, *Diary*, cit. *Wren Society* 19, 114.

9 The altered choice caused long-term difficulties between Flamsteed and the Royal Society. Had Chelsea been the site, there would have been a formal connection between the Observatory and the Society. See below, chapter 8.

10 J. Bold, *Greenwich: An Architectural History of the Royal Hospital for Seamen and the Queen's House* (London: Yale University Press, 2000), p. 21.

11 See below, chapter 8.

12 Hooke, *A Description of Helioscopes, and some other Instruments* (London: John Martyn, Printer to the Royal Society, 1676), reprinted in Gunther 8, 142.

13 See Bennett, *The Mathematical Science*, pp. 41–2.

14 A. R. Hinks, 'Christopher Wren the astronomer', in *Sir Christopher Wren AD 1632–1723. Bicentenary Memorial Volume published under the auspices of the Royal Institute of British Architects* (London: Hodder & Stoughton, 1923), pp. 239–54; 252–4. In the case of the section, the label reads, '*Puteus 100 pedum ad Parallaxes Terrae observandas. pr paratus*'. The engraved cross-section is reproduced in Willmoth, *Sir Jonas Moore*, p. 191.

15 See above, chapter 3.

16 Armitage, 'William Ball FRS (1627–1690)', pp. 170–1. In fact, insufficient light would have entered at the top of the well for these projected telescopes to have worked.

17 Hinks, 'Christopher Wren the astronomer', pp. 250–1.

18 For the classic structural problems in architecture see J. Heyman, *The Science of Structural Engineering* (London: Imperial College Press, 1999).

19 See D. Hull, 'Robert Hooke: A fractographic study of Ketteringstone', *Notes and Records of the Royal Society* 51 (1997), 45–55.

20 Caröe, '*Tom Tower*' *Christ Church, Oxford*, pp. 31–2.

21 'There is in Wren's design an element of knowing fantasy that predates the "castle air" to which Sir John Vanbrugh was later to aspire' (Bold, *Greenwich*, p. 21).

22 Batten puts together quotes from Hooke's diary to argue that Hooke was the architect of the College. However, she leaves out the many entries where both men are involved. E.g.: 'Friday August 15 1673. D[ined] H[ome]. went with Dr. Wren to Scotland Yard and to Mr. Boyles and Mr Oldenburgs at Physitians colledge about the dreine, turret. at the

controulers with Dr. Wren.' (p. 55) 'Friday May 15, 1674. . . . To Sir G. Ents. To Sir Ch: Wrens and Sir J. Cutlers. Dind there. With Sir Christopher to Colledge by water.' 'Wednesday May 20, 1674. . . . At Sir Ch: Scarborough [who was acting as representative of the College for the building] with Sir Chr. Wren and Dr. Holder.'

23 Chr: Wren July 28th 1675 [verso:] Report of Dr. Wren / concerning the Monument / 28 July 75. BL Add. MSS 18,898.

24 Hooke also had trouble with the inscription: on 17 June 1678, he 'saw Monument inscription now finished', but as late as 10 April 1679, he writes, 'At Fish Street Piller. Knight cut wrong R. for P.'

25 Ward, 'Life of Christopher Wren', p. 105.

26 'Finding it was liable to be shaken by the motion of coaches and carts almost constantly passing by, he laid aside that thought; and would have set the statue of king Charles the second on the top of it, which was over ruled, and a flaming urn placed there' (Ward, 'Life of Christopher Wren', p. 105).

27 Hooke, *Diary*, p. 27.

28 A. Stoesser, 'Robert Hooke and Holland: Dutch Influence on Hooke's Architecture' (Utrecht University: doctoral dissertation, 1997), p. 45.

29 Although he did not know about the domed basement, Professor Heyman indicated to me that he did not find it surprising that it should exist, since the pillar as built requires substantial, spanning foundations for stability. Personal communication, July 2001.

30 See Preface.

31 Hooke, *Diary*, p. 358.

32 Hooke, *Diary*, p. 359.

33 Birch, *History of the Royal Society* 3, 409–10.

34 See W. E. K. Middleton, 'A footnote to the history of the barometer: an unpublished note by Robert Hooke, FRS', *Notes and Records of the Royal Society* 20 (1965), 145–51.

NOTES · 541

35 Hooke, *Diary*, p. 388. Since the circular opening at the very top of the flaming urn also hinges open, allowing an operator to stand in the open air above the shaft, it would theoretically be possible to conduct experiments from that height also.

36 See L. Jardine, 'Monuments and microscopes: scientific thinking on a grand scale in the early Royal Society', *Notes and Records of the Royal Society* 55 (2001), 289–308. The inscription on the Monument's base explains that its height was calculated to have symbolic significance – 202 feet, the distance from it to the baker's shop where the Great Fire had started. It is worth pointing out, however, that Wren and Hooke chose the location of the Monument in order to satisfy their scientific requirements for as tall a tower as was consistent structurally with his classic column design. Once one adds in the distance from ground level to the operator in the basement room beneath, the height of the Monument matches that to the cross-beams of Old St Paul's, where Hooke had previously been conducting his barometer and pendulum experiments.

37 This account is closely based on H. Colvin, 'The building', in D. McKitterick (ed.), *The Making of the Wren Library, Trinity College, Cambridge* (Cambridge: Cambridge University Press, 1995), pp. 28–49, with additional help from James Campbell.

38 R. Westfall, *Never at Rest: A Biography of Isaac Newton* (Cambridge: Cambridge University Press, 1980), pp. 335–7.

39 Roger North, *The Lives of Francis North, Baron Guildford and Sir Dudley North*, 1826 edition, vol. iii, p. 365.

40 On Webb and the Royal College of Physicians see Bold, *John Webb*.

41 R. G. Frank, 'Viewing the body', in W. G. Marshall (ed.), *The Restoration Mind* (London: Associated University Presses, 1997), pp. 65–110; 89.

42 See chapter 2.

43 Once again, Scarburgh was closely involved with the project. Stoesser, 'Robert Hooke and Holland', pp. 44–9. The rejected, circular design for the Wren Library, at the centre of the open end of Nevile's Court, may have been intended, like Hooke's equivalent circular building for the Royal College of Physicians, to have been flanked by two curve wings connecting back to the existing wings of the Court.

44 See Colvin, 'The building', pp. 33–4.

45 'Appendix: Letter by Sir Christopher Wren', in McKitterick, *The Wren Library*, pp. 142–5.

46 The use of inverted arches for foundations is recommended by Alberti in his *De re aedificatoria* (1486). On the inverted arches foundations at Trinity see Colvin, 'The building', p. 41.

47 11 June 1681, letter from Wren to Bishop Fell, in Carӧe, *'Tom Tower' Christ Church, Oxford*, pp. 25–6.

48 Colvin, 'The building', p. 41. The arches as built did not precisely correspond to the piers they were supposed to support, somewhat limiting their effectiveness.

49 Taken from Colvin, 'The building', p. 43.

50 James Campbell, personal communication.

51 Fréart, *Parallel*, 1707 edition, pp. 10–11 (letter dated February 1697).

52 Little, *Sir Christopher Wren*, p. 38.

53 Flamsteed to Abraham Sharp (formerly his Observatory assistant), letter 1022, 26 or 27 August 1705. Flamsteed, *Correspondence* 3, 204–5.

54 I am grateful to Professor Moti Feingold for bringing the 'new club' discussions to my attention, and for identifying for me the relevant portions of Hooke's *Diary*. It may be significant that these machinations took place around the time of the Popish Plot, in a general atmosphere of political mistrust.

55 Sir John Hoskins joined later meetings. On 24 June, Boyle 'desird

to be of clubb. Wren promised to come. Met at Childs [coffee house].' By 2 July the club had become a 'new Decimall Society' – comprising 'Boyle, More, Wren, Hoskins, Croon, King, D[aniel]. Cox, Grew, Smethwick, Wild, Haak', and presumably Hooke, 'for chemistry, anatomy, Astronomy and opticks, mathematics and mechanicks'. On 4 July Hooke was at Ranelagh House: 'To Mr. Boyles much discourse with him about new clubb, Sir W. Petty there.' On 13 July, Hooke 'Dined with Sir Chr. Wren. At Mr. Boyles . . . Sir J. Hoskins. Hill. Grew. Contrived new club at Garaways [coffee house].'

56 'To Williamson there Wren, Holder, Henshaw, Whistler, Pett, King, Evelyn. Whistler, Evelyn and Hooke spoke to him, as well as Aubrey and Smith, Sir Joseph himself. We were nobly treated and bid about accepting the presidentship, very kindly welcome, all unanimous for chusing him president.' Hooke, *Diary*, pp. 208–328. 'Historians have tended to assume that Hooke simply referred to yet another club or two that he belonged to, but an awareness of the Society's affairs – as well as the rapidly deteriorating relations between Hooke and Brouncker/ Oldenburg, places the plethora of references during 1676–7 in new light. Starting on 10 Dec. 1675 you find: "Agreed upon a new clubb to meet at Joes. Mr. Hill, Mr. Lodowick, Mr. Aubrey and I and to joyn to us Sir Jo: More, Mr. Wild, Mr. Hoskins." By 1 Jan. 1675/6 we read: "With Wild and Hill to Wren's house." "We now began our New Philosophicall Clubb and Resolvd upon Ingaging ourselves not to speak of any thing that was then reveald *sub sigillo* to any one nor to declare that we had such a meeting at all." For the next year and a half it's clear that Wren's house became the center of the alternative society and that quite a few fellows were associated. What exactly transpired at the Society itself is not quite clear but

it's telling that Brouncker is conspicuously absent throughout 1677' (Moti Feingold, personal communication, 2000).

57 There is no modern biography of Boyle. For the clearest picture available of the man see M. Hunter, A. Clericuzio and L. M. Principe (eds), *The Correspondence of Robert Boyle*, 6 vols (London: Pickering and Chatto, 2001).

58 Hooke, *Diary*, 7, 11, 16 January 1679. There had been earlier unease in 1675, when Wren was reluctant to see Hooke in lodgings inside Whitehall, where he, as Royal Surveyor, now resided.

59 S. Thurley, 'A country seat fit for a king', in E. Cruickshanks (ed.), *The Stuart Courts* (Stroud: Sutton Publishing, 2000), pp. 214–39; 226. At the Restoration Brian Duppa, a Laudian and High Anglican, was created Bishop of Winchester. 'Shortly after the Restoration the bishop, Brian Duppa, paid £100 to retrieve Le Sueur's statues of James I and Charles I, which had been buried in a garden on the Isle of Wight. Some plate was also returned. When Archbishop Juxon visited Winchester in 1663, he was able to record that "the Cathedral Church is well repayred". More than £1,100 had been spent by the end of 1667' (Lehmberg, *Cathedrals under Siege*, p. 65).

60 Thurley, 'A country seat fit for a king', p. 227.

61 Thurley, 'A country seat fit for a king', p. 238.

62 Thurley, 'A country seat fit for a king', p. 227.

63 *Wren Society* 7, 19–20.

64 *Wren Society* 7, 45–6.

65 *Wren Society* 7, 51.

66 *Wren Society* 7, 28–30. See also pp. 32–43. The building was to be of local-made brick (for which contracts had already been drawn up in January 1683), and Portland stone. The contracts for the stone were drawn up directly with the Portland suppliers in July 1683.

67 Caröe, *'Tom Tower' Christ Church Oxford*, p. 24.

68 Grove was later a central figure in the completion of Greenwich Hospital, under Hawksmoor. See Bold, *Greenwich*, pp. 119–25.

69 V. Hart, *Nicholas Hawksmoor: Architecture and Ornament* (London: Yale University Press, in press) (read in manuscript), MS pp. 45–6. Although it was claimed in Hawksmoor's obituary that 'under [Wren] he was assisting, from the Beginning to the Finishing of that grand and noble Edifice the Cathedral of St. Paul's', his involvement at St Paul's post-dated both the warrant design and the Great Model.

70 The 1698 Whitehall fires destroyed the new buildings designed by Wren since 1660. See Thurley, *Whitehall Palace*, pp. 142–5.

71 Colvin, *The History of the King's Works* 3, 316–17: 'The reconstruction [at Windsor] was carried through in two clearly defined phases. Between September 1675 and the late summer of 1678 new apartments for the king and queen were constructed and decorated in the north range of the Upper Ward, and the duke's and duchess's [of York] apartments in the south range of the same ward were remodelled. A single account was declared for these three years, showing receipts of £69,782 18s. 3¾d. (including only £10,689 19s. 1¾d. from the Exchequer, as against moneys "voluntarily charged", which included £13,000 from the Navy Office and £44,000 through William Chiffinch, of which £18,000 came from the king's subsidy from the King of France), and expenditure which amounted to £74,209 4s. 3¼d. At the end of these three years the Court was able to spend August and September of 1678 at Windsor, and thereafter throughout the rest of Charles II's reign the Court spent several months of each year in residence there. In the second phase the chapel and St. George's Hall were rebuilt, the rest of the east and south ranges remodelled and the terrace walk extended round on the outer side of these ranges. Structural work was largely completed by 1680: Evelyn on 24 July of that year saw the Upper Ward and assumed it to be "now neere finished". The accounts however show that the decoration of St. George's Hall was not completed until the period 1682–4. During the first two years of this second phase the work was largely financed by payments of £1000 per month out of the Irish revenue of £27,000 per annum reserved for the king's use, on the authority of a royal warrant of 8 October 1678. May, as Comptroller of the Windsor Works, constantly pressed the Vice-Treasurer of Ireland, the Earl of Ranelagh, for regular payment, with such success that by 30 September 1680 Ranelagh had transmitted £28,846 for the Windsor works. The sum total of expenditure declared for this second phase, the six years ending 30 September 1684, when work was virtually complete and the king had but a few months to live, was £53,520 9s. 5¼d., together with a further £3500 odd spent on making an avenue from the castle to the Great Park.'

72 On Webb see Bold, *John Webb*. Work had begun on a three-range royal palace at Greenwich to Webb's designs in the early 1660s, but by 1672 work had stopped, with only one side wing (known as the King's House) completed. See Bold, *Greenwich*, pp. 79–81.

73 Thurley, 'A country seat fit for a king', p. 228. See North, *The Lives of Francis North, Baron Guildford and Sir Dudley North* vol. iii, p. 156: 'It was not long before that dismal loss (death of Charles II) that the King came into the Treasury Chamber, to settle the maintenances of his children, whom, as he told his Commissioners, my Lord Shaftesbury had declared he expected to see running about the streets like link-boys. And he having in mind to

finish the new house at Winchester in a short time, thinking that air to be better for his health than Windsor was, caused Sir Christopher Wren, the Surveyor-General of this buildings, to attend, and pressed him to say how soon it might be done. He answered, "In two years". The King urged him to say if it might not possibly be done in one year. "Yes", said the Surveyor-General, "but not so well, nor without great confusion, charge, and inconvenience," and however diligent they were, he feared disappointments would happen. "Well," said the King, "if it be possible to be done in one year, I will have it so; for a year is a great deal in my life." By such passages as these, one would think men had presages of their later end: at least by this, that his Majesty had; for he lived not many weeks after. And what else should make him so solicitous for time and posterity?'

74 Wren to Barrow, McKitterick, *The Wren Library*, pp. 144–5.

75 Hart, *Nicholas Hawksmoor*, MS p. 45.

76 See J. Roberts, 'Stephen Switzer and water gardens', in C. Ridgway and R. Williams (eds), *Sir John Vanbrugh and Landscape Adventure in Baroque England 1690–1730* (Stroud: Sutton Publishing, 2000), pp. 154–71. See also K. Woodbridge, *Princely Gardens: The Origins and Development of the French Formal Style* (New York: Rizzoli, 1986). For images see R. Strong, *The Artist and the Garden* (London and New Haven: Yale University Press, 2000), pp. 192–3.

77 *Parentalia*, p. 325.

78 Cit. Bold, *John Webb*, p. 129.

79 Wren, 'Letter from Paris', *Parentalia*, p. 261.

80 In 1688 building materials from Winchester to the value of £1200 were transported for use at Hampton Court. *Wren Society* 7, 12.

81 De Beer, *Diary of John Evelyn*, 4, pp. 471–2.

82 PRO Office of Works: Miscellaneous Letter Books 1685–1923, fol. 9v.

83 King was not prosecuted for his unauthorised treatment of Charles, but the £1000 he was later promised for trying to save his Majesty was apparently never paid.

84 For a clear account of the politics of this period see Holmes, *The Making of a Great Power*.

85 For a luridly full account of Charles's death see A. Fraser, *King Charles II* (London: Weidenfeld & Nicolson, 1979 and 1993).

86 Briefly disturbed again by the 1683 Rye House conspiracy against the lives of both Charles and the Duke of York.

87 Evelyn, *Diary*, pp. 420–1.

88 PRO, Treasury Books 1660–7, p. 232 1661 Apr 3: 'Warrant for £1000 to John Denham, surveyor General of the Works, for an intended building of a throne & other necessary works against the Coronation'.

89 See above, chapter 1.

90 Wren's cousin Matthew had benefited from this tactic immediately after the Restoration. He served as an MP in the 1661 Parliament, as a result of his appointment as a burgess of St Michael's in Cornwall, a post he gained after its restructuring, through his patron the Earl of Clarendon (*Parentalia*, p. 53).

91 *Calendar of State Papers: Domestic James II Feb–Dec 1685*, Entry Book 336, p. 28: 'Wren: Sr Chr: named Burgess of Plympton' (363). March 11 Warrant for renewing the Charter of Plympton, Devon. Minute. Annexed: 'Paper of heads. That the borough now be incorporated by the name of the Mayor and Burgesses of the Stannery town and borough of Plympton'. On manipulation of newly regulated boroughs by Charles II and James II see Holmes, *The Making of a Great Power*, p. 168.

92 For a definitive account of Stephen Fox's life and career, see C. Clay, *Public Finance and Private Wealth: The Career of Sir Stephen Fox, 1627–1716* (Oxford: Clarendon Press, 1978).

93 Clay, *Public Finance*, chapter 1.

94 Clay, *Public Finance*, pp. 15–16.
95 On the failure of Charles II's court to balance its budget see A. Barclay, 'Charles II's failed Restoration: administrative reform below stairs, 1660–4', in Cruickshanks, *The Stuart Courts*, pp. 158–70.
96 Clay, *Public Finance*, p. 33.
97 Clay, *Public Finance*, p. 168.
98 Clay, *Public Finance*, chapter 9.
99 See map in *Wren Society* 7, plate VI.
100 Fox also had offices one courtyard away from his main residence at Whitehall, in the Tilt Yard, for his financial dealings.
101 Cit. Clay, *Public Finance*, p. 263.
102 *Wren Society* 19, xi.
103 Clay, *Public Finance*, pp. 308–10.
104 Even during the period when Compton was suspended from his bishopric, it looks as if Wren quietly went on using his signature on important documents connected with the Cathedral and the City churches (particularly loan documents), though Compton did not attend committee meetings. See Jeffery, *The City Churches*.
105 Evelyn, *Diary*, 6 September 1680.
106 '[James's] sense of burning injustice was . . . fuelled by a series of interviews with his father, which were conducted between June and November 1647, at Hampton Court Palace. . . . The impact of these long interviews upon the Duke of York cannot be overstated. Twice, or even three times a week, he was ushered into the presence of the King and was offered a degree of intimacy, and an insight into the private thoughts of the fallen monarch, which previously would have been unimaginable. The cult of the royal family was firmly re-established as Percy employed Sir Peter Lely to produce a series of paintings to commemorate their meetings, and as Charles I seized the opportunity to stress the need for his family to remain united in the face of adversity.' J. Callow, *The Making of King James II: The Formative Years of a Fallen King* (Stroud: Sutton Publishing, 2000), pp. 46–7.

107 See above.
108 See above, chapter 4. *Parentalia*, p. 53.
109 *Oeuvres complètes de Christiaan Huygens* 22, 576.
110 BL MS *Parentalia*, fol. 47 verso.
111 See Brodsley, Frank and Steeds, 'Prince Rupert's drops'.
112 See illustration on following page.
113 Cit. M. Hunter, *Science and the Shape of Orthodoxy: Intellectual Change in Late Seventeenth-Century Britain* (Woodbridge: Boydell Press, 1995), p. 81.
114 Mezzotint is a reverse engraving process used on a copper or steel plate to produce illustrations in relief with effects of light and shadow. The surface of a master-plate is roughened with a tool called a rocker so that, if inked, it will print solid black. The areas to be white or grey in the print are rubbed down so as not to take ink.
115 Cit. Frank, 'Viewing the body', p. 97.
116 Frank, 'Viewing the body', pp. 94–5.
117 See Jardine, *Ingenious Pursuits*, chapter 4.
118 BL MS *Parentalia*, fol. 113 verso [compare *Parentalia* p. 327]. See also fol. 57 recto: 'In the Year 1692. He Finished the Royal-Hospital at Chelsea, Founded by King Charles the Second, for the Support of Maim'd & Superannuated Soldiers: the success of the Foundation, Erection, and Settlement of this Noble Hospital, was greatly owing to Himself and Sr. Stephen Fox; Sr. Stephen, being then a Lord of the Treasury, took care for the payment of the work, whilst He vigorously prosecuted his part in the Building; and lastly, He Compil'd the Statutes, and settled the whole Oeconomy of the House.' Also fol. 61 verso: 'This Royal Hospital Founded by King Charles the Second for the support of maim'd and superannuated soldiers, was Finished <in> the year 1692. The Success in the Founding, Erection, and Settlement of this Hospital was greatly owing to the Surveyor and Sr. Stephen Fox; Sr. Stephen <who> being then a Lord of

ye. Treasury, took care for the payments of the Work, whilst the Surveyor vigorously prosecuted his Part in the Building; & lastly – compiled the Statutes, and Settled the whole oeconomy of the House; which for Cleanliness, Health, and Convenience is deservedly reckon'd one of the best dispos'd in Europe.' Finally, down side of fol. 54 recto: 'In 168- He was appointed surveyor Generall and Commisioner joyntly with ye. Earle of Ranelagh & Sr. Stephen Fox, for Building and Establishing ye. R. Hospital of Chelsea. In 1698 he was appointed surveyor and Controller of the Greenwich Hospital.'

119 The King instructed Fox to add the sum of £6787 to the total, which he was holding against one-off disbursements on the King's behalf (a job he had done since the Restoration). On the financial arrangements for Chelsea see Clay, *Public Finance*, pp. 132–5.

120 See Darley, 'Evelyn, Greenwich and the sick and wounded'. I am extremely grateful to Gillian Darley for letting me read a typescript of her paper.

121 Pepys, *Diary* 6, 275.

122 Pepys, *Diary* 7, 29.

123 De Beer, *Diary of John Evelyn*, 4, p. 257.

124 *Wren Society* 19, 63.

125 *Wren Society* 19, 63.

126 *Wren Society* 19, 63.

127 *Wren Society* 19, 64. See also C. Stevenson, *Medicine and Magnificence: British Hospital and Asylum Architecture, 1660–1815* (London: Yale University Press, 2000), p. 56.

128 Earl of Ilchester's MSS, cit. *Wren Society* 19, 64–5.

129 Clay, *Public Finance*, p. 137.

130 Evelyn, *Diary*, 27 January 1682.

131 See above, chapter 3.

132 Evelyn Papers BL MSS JE A1 (letterbook 2), Evelyn to Sidney Godolphin, 19 Nov. 1682 (copy). My thanks to Dr Frances Harris, Curator of Manuscripts at the British Library,

for drawing this letter to my attention, and providing me with the transcription.

133 See Bold, *Greenwich*, p. 101.

134 *Wren Society* 19, 86.

135 *Parentalia*, preceding p. 195.

136 *Wren Society* 19, 69–70.

137 *Wren Society* 19, 68–9. In 1712 Richard Jones, Earl of Ranelagh (b. 1638, d. 5 January 1712), Lady Ranelagh's son and Boyle's nephew, was indicted for embezzelling £150,000 as Paymaster-General. Nevertheless, Jones was critical to Wren and Evelyn in providing funding for both Chelsea Hospital and Greenwich Hospital.

138 Clay, *Public Finance*, pp. 180–2.

139 Clay suggests that some of the money loaned to Hungerford had been Wren's, but this seems unlikely. Wren had no history of lending money to individuals, only of advancing it against building works (he did so regularly over the years to allow workmen to be paid at St Paul's). See Clay, *Public Finance*, p. 182.

140 PRO RAIL 1073/60. *Letters patent granted by James II to Sir Stephen Fox and Sir Christopher Wren, proprietors by purchase of the market in St. Martins-in-the-Fields 1685 July 9.*

141 See, for example, PRO C 112/4 John Ramsay deceased c. 1668 – collection of papers concerning him and his estate. Item 100, lease by Sir Stephen Fox and Sir Christopher Wren to John Smalbone of 2 shops and vaults in Hungerford Market, 1690 – also no. 101. Lease, 5 June 1690, by Sr Stephen Fox and Sir Chr. Wren to John Smalbone of 2 shops and vaults on east side of market in the parish of St. Martin in the Fields, London, for 7 years.

142 Figures from Clay, *Public Finance*. On the reasons for the market's failure to prosper see also Clay, *Public Finance*, p. 192, n. 1. Ironically, Hungerford Market became a booming commercial centre in the nineteenth century.

143 See Little, *Sir Christopher Wren*, p. 157; Guildhall Library MS 2461.

144 See, for example, among architects, John Webb's excitement about China, largely based on Nieuhoff's *An Embassy from the East India Company of the United Provinces to the Grand Tartar Cham emperour of China* (English edition, 1669) (see Bold, *John Webb*, pp. 36–47), and Vanbrugh's time spent in Surat on the coast of India, as an employee of the East India Company (see Williams, 'Vanbrugh's India and his Mausolea for England').

145 See below, chapter 7. The Wren studies of Hagia Sophia are in the collection of Queen's University at Kingston, Ontario. See Du Prey, *Hawksmoor's London Churches* (where the hand is identified as Wren's).

146 Soo, *Wren's 'Tracts' on Architecture*, p. 163.

147 See Callow, *The Making of King James II*, pp. 238–63.

148 Sir William Schooling, 'Sir Christopher Wren Merchant Adventurer', in *Sir Christopher Wren AD 1632–1723. Bicentenary Memorial Volume published under the auspices of the Royal Institute of British Architects* (London: Hodder & Stoughton, 1923), pp. 255–64.

149 *Parentalia*, pp. 196–7.

CHAPTER 7: *Standing the Test of Time*

1 See, e.g., C. Hibbert, *The Marlboroughs: John and Sarah Churchill 1650–1744* (London: Viking, 2001), pp. 37–8.

2 See Jeffery, *The City Churches*, pp. 28–9.

3 The quote is from S. Schama, *A History of Britain: The British Wars 1603–1776* (London: BBC Worldwide, 2001), p. 234.

4 Among Petty's ground-breaking works in economics and statistics were his *Treatise of Taxes and Contributions* (1662), his *Verbum sapienti* [*A Word to the Wise*] (c. 1665, published posthumously, 1691) which contains the first estimate of national income, his *Political Anatomy of Ireland* (c. 1672, published 1691) which advocates an economic policy supported by economic geography. And his actuarial work, *Political Arithmetick* (c. 1671–6, published 1690). He was closely associated with John Graunt and his *Natural and Political Observations* (1662), which started the sciences of demography and statistics.

5 There may be a closer link. Petty chose the Augustinian triad 'number, weight, measure' as his basis for truth: 'Now the Observations or Positions expressed by Number, Weight, and Measure, upon which I bottom the ensuing Discourses, are either true, or not apparently false, and which if they are not already true, certain, and evident, yet may be made so by the Sovereign Power, *Nam id certum est quodcertum reddi potest*, and if they are false, not so false as to destroy the Argument they are brought for; but at worst are sufficient as Suppositions to shew the way to that Know-ledge I aim at.' *Political Arithmetick* (London, 1690). Wren also chose this phrase as his personal motto, as did his brother-in-law William Holder.

6 19 December 1660: 'That Dr. Petty and Mr. Wren be desired to consider the philosophy of shipping, and to bring in their thoughts about it to the society' (cit. Bennett, *Mathematical Science of Christopher Wren*, p. 45). Wren was also involved in Petty's long-running attempt to design a stable sea-going vessel with a double keel or hull.

7 BL Add. MSS 72897. *Petty Papers*, vol. 48, ff. 47–54.

8 BL Add. MSS 72898. *Petty Papers*, vol. 49, ff. 34–43. The case was not in fact settled satisfactorily until 1696. See Waller, *Robert Hooke*, p. xxv: 'On the 18th of July 1696. being his Birth Day, his Chancery-Suit for Sir John Cutler's Salary, was determin'd for him, to his great satisfaction, which had made him very uneasy for several Years.' Hooke was not the only one

to suffer because of unfulfilled financial promises made by Cutler – at Cutler's death his executors demanded repayment in full, with interest, of monies given for the post-Fire Royal College of Physicians building. For a full account of the Hooke/Cutler dispute see M. Hunter, *Establishing The New Science*, chapter 9.

9 North, *The Lives of Francis North, Baron Guildford and Sir Dudley North* vol. iii, p. 42 (reprinted in *Wren Society* 19, 116–18).

10 On Wren and the Marlboroughs see Hibbert, *The Marlboroughs*.

11 For an assessment of the Anglo-Dutch implications of the Glorious Revolution, see D. Hoak and M. Feingold (eds), *The World of William and Mary* (Stanford: Stanford University Press, 1996).

12 De Beer, *Diary of John Evelyn*, 4, p. 597.

13 Gunther, *Early Science in Oxford* 10, 70.

14 Gunther, *Early Science in Oxford* 10, 72.

15 De Beer, *Diary of John Evelyn*, 4, p. 608.

16 Gunther, *Early Science in Oxford* 10, 79. William Stukeley wrote in his commonplace book: 'Sir Christ Wren & Mr. Hook great drinkers of Coffee. Dr. Gale drank 2 dishes twice a day . . . Dr. W. Cole was as great a coffee drinker as smoaker'. Cit. Gunther, *Early Science in Oxford* 10, xxv–xxvi.

17 De Beer, *Diary of John Evelyn*, 4, pp. 604–6.

18 *Calendar of Treasury Books* 8, pp. 2126, 2129. From Hooke's *Diary*, above, we know the King himself fled to Windsor on that Saturday.

19 Both in 1685 and in 1689, Wren was reconfirmed in post within days of the Feast of St George's, 23 April – the Feast Day of the Order of the Garter.

20 Jeffery, *The City Churches*, p. 50.

21 *Wren Society* 16, 54.

22 *Wren Society* 16, 55.

23 *Wren Society* 16, 56.

24 *Wren Society* 16, 57.

25 *Wren Society* 16, 62.

26 Plowden, *The Stuart Princesses*, p. 202.

27 See conveniently the images in The Guildhall Library online image gallery, collage.nhil.com.

28 Robb, *William of Orange*, p. 49.

29 Thanks to historian of London Geoffrey Palmer for drawing this to my attention.

30 Soane Museum Hawksmoor drawing.

31 Colvin, *The History of the King's Works* 5, 155.

32 Colvin, *The History of the King's Works* 5, 155–8.

33 Evelyn, *Diary*, 25 February 1690.

34 *Wren Society* 7, 137.

35 Colvin, *The History of the King's Works* 5, 183–7.

36 Gunther, *Early Science at Oxford* 10, 171.

37 *Wren Society* 7, 135.

38 *Wren Society* 4, 72. The new palace was built with a spine wall between two banks of staterooms, whose floors it supported on both sides. Because of the many passages and fireplaces which weakened this spine wall it collapsed (James Campbell, personal communication).

39 *Wren Society* 7, 135.

40 *Wren Society* 7, 136.

41 Colvin, *The History of the King's Works* 5, 158.

42 *Wren Society* 7, 136.

43 Colvin, *The History of the King's Works* 5, 190.

44 See Evelyn: 'Supped with the B[ishop] of Lichfield . . . who related me the pious behaviour of the Queen in all her sickness, which was admirable & the noble designe she had in hand, her expensive Charity, never enquiring of the opinion of the partys if objects of charity' (*Diary*, 5 March 1695).

45 See Darley, 'Evelyn, Greenwich and the sick and wounded'.

46 Webb made minor modifications to the Queen's House in 1662–63, but the integrity of the Jones building

remained intact. See Bold, *Greenwich*, chapters 2 and 3.

47 Bold, *John Webb*, pp. 141–6.

48 On Anglo-Dutch garden design in this period, see J. D. Hunt and E. de Jong (eds), *The Anglo-Dutch Garden in the Age of William and Mary* (London: Taylor & Francis, 1988) (special double issue of the *Journal of Garden History*); W. Kuyper, *Dutch Classicist Architecture: A Survey of Dutch Architecture, Gardens, and Anglo-Dutch Architectural Relations from 1625 to 1700* (Delft: Delft University Press, 1980).

49 Hawksmoor, 'Remarks on the founding and carrying on the buildings of the Royal Hospital at Greenwich', reprinted in *Wren Society* 6, 19–21. See also *Parentalia*, p. 328. Christopher Wren junior modifies the opening sentence to read: 'Her Majesty Queen Mary, the Foundress of the marine Hospital, enjoin'd Sir Christopher Wren to build the Fabrick with great Magnificence and Order; and being ever sollicitous . . .'.

50 Bold, *Greenwich*, p. 95.

51 Evelyn, *Diary*, 5 March 1695.

52 Colvin, *The History of the King's Works* 5, 455. See also Soo, *Wren's 'Tracts' on Architecture*, p. 309.

53 Anon. [J. Fraser], *A Pattern of a Well-Constituted and Well-Governed Hospital: Or A Brief Description of the Building, and Full Relation of the Establishment, Constitution, Discipline, Oeconomy and Administration of the Government of the Royal Hospital of the Invalids Near Paris* (London, 1695).

54 See Darley, 'Evelyn, Greenwich and the sick and wounded'.

55 Evelyn, *Diary*, 9 May 1695.

56 Evelyn, *Diary*, 4 June 1696.

57 Evelyn, *Diary*, 30 June 1696.

58 Part way through the project, in 1703, Evelyn handed over the important job of Treasurer to the project to his son-in-law, William Draper (Bold, *Greenwich*, p. 121).

59 Bold, *Greenwich*, p. 100.

60 Bold, *Greenwich*, p. 100.

61 Bold, *Greenwich*, p. 105.

62 Cit. Bold, *Greenwich*, p. 105.

63 Bold, *Greenwich*, p. 107.

64 Soo, *Wren's 'Tracts' on Architecture*, p. 182.

65 Soo, *Wren's 'Tracts' on Architecture*, p. 155.

66 Soo, *Wren's 'Tracts' on Architecture*, p. 155.

67 Soo, *Wren's 'Tracts' on Architecture*, pp. 154–5.

68 See Soo, *Wren's 'Tracts' on Architecture*, and Hart, *Nicholas Hawksmoor*.

69 Evelyn, *Diary*, 1 July 1664.

70 Pepys, *Diary* 5, 161–2.

71 See Jardine, *Ingenious Pursuits*, chapter 3; C. Brusati, *Artifice and Illusion: The Art and Writing of Samuel Van Hoogstraten* (Chicago: University of Chicago Press, 1995), 92–3.

72 Pepys, *Diary* 9, 421.

73 Pepys, *Diary* 9, 423.

74 Pepys, *Diary* 9, 434–5.

75 See the account in Royal Society Journal Book 8, p. 332.

76 *Wren Society* 16, 86.

77 *Wren Society* 16, 88–9.

78 For Wren's role as moderator see below, chapter 8.

79 10 May 1700. Forbes, Murdin and Willmoth, *The Correspondence of John Flamsteed, The First Astronomer Royal*, vol. 2 (1682–1703), letter 813, pp. 816–19; 818.

80 Cit. W. J. Ashworth, ' "Labour harder than thrashing": John Flamsteed, property and intellectual labour in nineteenth-century England', in F. Willmoth, *Flamsteed's Stars: New Perspectives on the Life and Work of the First Astronomer Royal (1646–1719)* (Woodbridge: Boydell Press, 1997), p. 216. On the quarrel between the Astronomer Royal, John Flamsteed and Sir Isaac Newton over publication of definitive star-charts under the auspices of the Greenwich Observatory see Westfall, *Never at Rest*; Jardine, *Ingenious Pursuits*, chapter 4.

81 M. D. Whinney, *St. Paul's Cathedral* (London: Lund, Humphries, 1947).

82 To explain the fact the Wren never had any intention of building the Cathedral to the plans approved by the Royal Commission, it is unnecessary to claim actual collusion between Wren and the King. Both were sufficiently High Church in their beliefs, and continental in their experience and aspirations, to have been in tacit agreement that something less parochial and more comparable to St Peter's at Rome was required.

83 Daniel Defoe, *A Tour through England and Wales, Divided into Circuits or Journies*, 2 vols, Everyman edition (London: J. M. Dent and Sons, 1927) 1, 332–3. The original edition of the *Tour* also contains a description of Wren's proposed building for Whitehall, and Wren's views on it, which is not found elsewhere, and supports the view that Defoe is drawing on first-hand conversations with Wren.

84 Evelyn, *Diary*, 2 October 1694.

85 Evelyn, *Diary*, 5 December 1697.

86 Whinney, *St. Paul's Cathedral*.

87 North, *The Lives of Francis North, Baron Guildford and Sir Dudley North*, p. 210.

88 Inigo Jones's Banqueting House roof is the model for the Wren Library. D. Yeomans, 'Inigo Jones's roof structures', *Architectural History* 29 (1986), pp. 85–101.

89 *Parentalia*, p. 292.

90 Soo, *Wren's 'Tracts' on Architecture*, p. 163.

91 The account that follows is based on Du Prey, *Hawksmoor's London Churches*, pp. 41–6.

92 Du Prey, *Hawksmoor's London Churches*, p. 43.

93 Evelyn, *Diary*, 30 August 1680. The Society did not see the drawings on this occasion 'his things, not yet out of the ship'.

94 On his first visit Chardin told Evelyn he had the intention 'to be suddenly back againe ... the persecution in France not suffering Protestants, & such he was, to be quiet'.

95 Evelyn, *Diary*, 23 February 1684. Evelyn was godfather to Chardin's son, also named John, in October 1687.

96 The drawings were authenticated as Wren's by Kerry Downes in 1988 but have been reattributed by Geraghty.

97 The other drawings of Hagia Sophia, showing studies of a corner of the basilica, with its internal staircases, are strikingly reminiscent of equivalent corner constructions at St Paul's.

98 North, *The Lives of Francis North, Baron Guildford and Sir Dudley North* vol. iii, p. 42 (reprinted in *Wren Society* 19, 116–18).

99 F. Price, *The British Carpenter: Or, a Treatise on Carpentry. Containing the most concise and authentick Rules of that Art*, second edition (London, 1735), p. 30, and plate O*, P**. See also plate O.

100 This is precisely the form taken by Christiaan Huygens's proof of the form of a hanging chain in his juvenile work '*De catena pendente*' (1646). On Huygens's catenary, and the subsequent discussions with Jakob Bernouilli, see J. G. Yoder, *Unrolling Time: Christiaan Huygens and the Mathematization of Nature* (Cambridge: Cambridge University Press, 1988), pp. 108–11. Hooke's library contains (unbound) the issue of the *Acta eruditorum* in which Jakob Bernouilli challenged mathematicians to find the true shape of the catenary (June 1690). See A. N. L. Munby (ed.), *Sale Catalogues of Libraries of Eminent Persons*, vol. 11 (London: Mansell Publishing, 1975). Several scholars have proposed a 'thought experiment' whereby the chain shape would be dipped in plaster and inverted so that 'all the tension forces reverse to become purse compressions with a distribution ideal for masonry' (E. C. Hambly, 'Robert Hooke, the City's Leonardo', *City University* 2 (1987), 5–10; 9). However, whereas the inverted form is in stable

equilibrium, the inverted shape is fundamentally unstable. I am extremely grateful to Professor Jacques Heyman, both for providing me with a copy of Hambly's article and for explaining to me the instability of the plaster-dipped, catenary-shaped dome.

101 I am grateful to Professor Jacques Heyman for discussing arches, domes and catenaries with me in the context of the Hooke–Wren conversations. See Heyman, *The Science of Structural Engineering*, chapter 3. Also to Professor John Knott of the University of Birmingham, for sharing with me his thoughts on Hooke, catenaries, domes and chains.

102 As late as 1665, Newton also believed that a cubic equation gave a parabola-like shape, because of confusion about negative solutions. See Westfall, *Never at Rest*. Wren may have discussed catenaries and load-bearing arches with Newton. See the jotting by David Gregory, May 1694, detailing topics discussed with Newton or Fatio: [Latin original] 'on sails for big and little ships, on the figure of a ship and a book on these topics. Whence the differential calculus of Leibniz. The transparency of Water. Wren's problem about a loaded arch. On the length of [? a curved] line. A new Thermometer. The Catenary. A property of the Circle.' (Cit. H. W. Turnbull, J. F. Scott, A. R. Hall and L. Tilling (eds): *The Correspondence of Isaac Newton*, 7 vols (Cambridge: Cambridge University Press, 1959–77) Newton 3, 387.

103 Further entries on load-bearing arches: 8 December, 15 December, 12 January. 'Mr Oldenburg mentioned that Dr. Wren had also a demonstration of it. It was desired that these demonstrations might be both delivered and opened together by the president': 19 January 1671 (both men presented their versions). Hooke may well have seen the Huygens catenary proof. Huygens shows by the thought-experiment of

hanging weights on a catenary that it becomes paraboloid *only* when such weights are added. Hooke inverts the diagram for that proof, and uses it to solve the structural problem of supporting weights on an arch. By the time Wren and Hooke came to the final design for the dome and its supporting catenary cone, after 1702, Bernouilli and others had publicly produced the equation for the pure catenary. Even if the masons could only approximate a catenary incorporating the inward-leaning inner peristyle and arch-supported dome above, the intention to follow an inverted hanging chain is still an engineering innovation.

104 Evelyn, *Diary*, 7 December, 1671.

105 Birch, *History of the Royal Society* 2, 984. See Jardine, *Ingenious Pursuits*, chapter 4.

106 On Hooke's claim that the hanging chain is a 'cubico-parabolical conoid' see J. Heyman, 'Hooke's cubico-parabolical conoid', *Notes and Records of the Royal Society* 52 (1998), 39–50.

107 ibid. 131. The announcement runs: 'The true Mathematical and Mechanichal form of all manner of Arches for Building, with the true butment necessary to each of them. A Problem which no Architectonick Writer hath ever yet attempted, much less performed. [cypher <translated>: ut pendet continuum flexile, sic stabit contiguum rigidum inversum]' (Gunther 8, 151). In his diary for Sunday, 26 September 1675 Hooke himself gives this as follows: 'Riddle of arch, of *pendet continuum flexile, sic stabit grund Rigidum.*' On the general problem see Heyman, *The Science of Structural Engineering*, chapter 3, 'Arch bridges, domes and vaults', pp. 25–48.

108 *Parentalia*, p. 292.

109 The cone is pierced with windows at regular intervals; the outer dome admits light where it meets the lantern at points, rather than continuously. Thus additional light enters the lower oculus indirectly,

apparently emanating from the upper oculus.

110 See Jardine, *Ingenious Pursuits*, chapter 2: 'In order to make the exquisitely detailed drawings upon which *Micrographia*'s illustrations were based, it turned out that he needed a brighter light-source than sunlight or candlelight to illuminate his specimens, to sharpen the quality of the image seen through his microscope eye-piece. Undaunted, and with characteristic improvisatory flair, Hooke had invented a purpose-built piece of image-enhancing apparatus. He placed a light-condensing brine-filled globe between his lamp light-source and his specimen, then narrowly focused the lamp's intensified beams by means of a convex lens. By adjusting the relative positions of lamp, globe and lens he found he could improve the magnified image of his subject considerably. He called it his "scotoscope".' See also R. H. Nuttall, 'That curious curiosity: the scotoscope', *Notes and Records of the Royal Society* 42 (1988), 133–8.

111 Wren's proposed recladding of Old St Paul's before the Fire and his 'warrant' (approved by King Charles) design for St Paul's Cathedral both incorporate vertical shafts within a spire, accessible via a circular staircase, and allowing for access, ascent and experimental result-taking at various levels. In the case of the Old St Paul's design, the open-work 'pineapple' on the top of the spire might have allowed for use as a zenith telescope.

112 Cit. M. Feingold, 'Astronomy and strife: John Flamsteed and the Royal Society', in Willmoth, *Flamsteed's Stars*, pp. 31–48; 48. Bennett gives the date as February 1703 (Bennett, *The Mathematical Science*, p. 42).

113 Ward, 'Life of Christopher Wren', p. 104.

114 See L. Stewart, 'Other centres of calculation, or, where the Royal Society didn't count: commerce, coffee-houses and natural philosophy

in early modern London', *British Journal of the History of Science* 32 (1999), 133–53.

115 Thurley, *Whitehall Palace*, pp. 142–4.

116 On Clarendon House see Gunther, *The Architecture of Sir Roger Pratt*, pp. 9–14. The building was valued at £35,000.

117 See, for example, P. Ackroyd, *London: The Biography* (London: Chatto, 2000), pp. 777–9.

118 *Parentalia*, p. 292.

119 *Parentalia*, pp. 292–3.

120 All those involved may also have been Speculative Freemasons, and the topping out ceremony may have included masonic rituals. See below, chapter 8. Wren junior and Strong junior had travelled together through France and Italy in 1698 (*Wren Society* 19, 119).

121 Cit. J. A. Bennett, 'Wren's last building?', *Notes and Records of the Royal Society* 27 (1972–3), 107–18; 111. Also, concerning the acquisition of the Crane's Court building: 'Sir Christopher Wren, Mr. Wren and Mr. Waller were Appointed a Committee to see what Mr. Brigstock [the tenant] leaves in the House that may be usefull to the Society and of what Value they may be' (p. 109). See also below, chapter 8.

122 See above, chapter 5.

123 We can make this inference from the fact that Sir John Vanbrugh designates himself in the Office of Works as Wren's 'next Officer' when occupying the same post in the early decades of the eighteenth century. See Hibbert, *The Marlboroughs*, pp. 167–8.

CHAPTER 8: *Ambitious to Leave Great Monuments*

1 Evelyn was twelve years older than Wren, and also suffering from ill health by 1700; both Evelyn's son John and his brother George died in 1699, and thereafter he devoted himself to the managing of the Evelyn estate on behalf of his grandson. Evelyn died in 1706. Fox, who also

latterly devoted himself to family affairs, died in 1716.

2 'Thus he lived a dying Life for a considerable time, being more than a Year very infirm, and such as might be call'd Bed-rid for the greatest part' (Waller, *Robert Hooke*, p. xxvi).

3 See the volume of Hooke papers in the archives of the Royal Society, RS Cl. P. XX, which contain 'in progress' works, including work for the Society, down to May 1699 – latterly reading and producing synopses of new scientific books, in increasingly tiny, obsessive writing.

4 Waller, *Robert Hooke*, p. xxvi.

5 The account which follows takes as its starting point Bennett, 'Wren's last building?'

6 RS Register Book RBC.9.143. The letter is undated, but is copied between letters dated May 1702 and September 1702. The whole volume is strictly chronological.

7 It may have been that political quarrels within the Society forced a move on the Society in that year. See Westfall, *Never at Rest*, pp. 671–9.

8 Newton, *Correspondence* 5, 61, letter 802 Newton to Sloane, 13 September 1710.

9 See e.g. the letter from Wren junior to Sloane (Secretary of the Royal Society): 'I have given directions to [par]ticular Workmen, Persons I know well & trust, to take an Exact Survey of all the necessary repairs of ye House; when [they] have made their Report; and my Father [has] examin'd their several Rates, I will [place] the whole before you, and ye Workmen [m]ay begin when you shall think proper' (Bennett, 'Wren's last building?', p. 110). All the workmen employed came from Wren's office.

10 Cit. Bennett, 'Wren's last building?', p. 111.

11 Hunt advanced £464 for the project in its early stages; four months later he lent a further £450, making a total of £900 – an enormous sum for any individual to provide. It matches the largest single donation made by a Fellow towards the Trinity College library. At Hunt's death in June 1713 he was still owed £650. See Westfall, *Never at Rest*, pp. 676–7. In Waller's case, various arrangements were made for the Royal Society to repay some of the costs of the Repository, but Waller received nothing during his lifetime. His widow, however, received from Newton 'two hundred and fifty pounds and fifty three pounds in full Interest' (Bennett, 'Wren's last building?', p. 113).

12 'Henry Hunt (d. 1713) served Robert Hooke as a boy assistant and was trained by him. Soon after the death of Richard Shortgrave, the Society's first operator, Hunt was appointed to succeed him (2 November 1676); he also carried on the making of meteorological instruments for Fellows and others that Shortgrave had commenced. On 14 January 1679/80 his salary was raised from £10 to £40 p.a. (the same as Hooke's) in return for his devoting all his time to the Society's affairs. In 1696 he was appointed Keeper of the Library and Repository. By the time of his death the Society owed him £650 advanced by him for the purchase and fitting out of Crane Court' (note in Newton, *Correspondence* 5, 62).

13 At the end of the manuscript of Hooke's *Diary*, now in the Guildhall Library, there is a note in Waller's hand saying that Waller could prove, were it a proper time, that Hooke was the first to invent or hint of those things about which great heroes of renown had contested the priority. Waller also left us the most affectionate portrait of Hooke, which includes the observation: 'He was in the beginning of his being made known to the Learned, very communicative of his Philosophical Discoveries and Inventions, till some Accidents made him to a Crime close and reserv'd. He laid the cause upon some Persons, challenging his Discoveries for their own, taking

occasion from his Hints to perfect what he had not; which made him say he would suggest nothing until he had time to perfect it himself, which has been the Reason that many things are lost, which he affirm'd he knew'.

14 Gunther, *Early Science in Oxford* 10, passim.

15 He also left properties on the Isle of Wight.

16 'This is the Last Will & Testament of me Robert Hooke M.D. Professor of Geometry & Experimental Pholosophy [sic] in Gresham College London & Survayor of the City of London &c. Made the [blot] twenty fifth day of – February 1702/3 for the notification of the Persons to whome I do bequeath all the several parts of such goods real & Personal as it shall please God to bless me withall at the time of my decease, with the Quallifications & quantities of them. First I doe bequeath & give to my – good friends A, B, C, & D. my whole Estate Real & Personal together with all debts owing to me yet unpaid, upon trust – and Confidence that they shall & will dispose & pay unto the said persons nominated in a sedule [sic] anexed to this present will signed & sealed by me the several sums therein particularised And also discharge the Charges or Expences of my funeral which I would not have to exceed the vallue of forty pounds, And the Remainder to be equally distributed between the foresaid A. B. C & D. In testimony whereof I have here unto Subscribed my name & affixed my Seale, & declared the same to be my Act & deed to the Persons following [rest of sheet blank] [Title on back of sheet says:] Testam[en]tum Rob[er]ti Hook M D defuncti.' PRO Prob 20/1315. My gratitude to Rachel Jardine, who first spotted the unsigned will at the PRO.

17 Richard Waller, 'The Life of Dr. Robert Hooke', reprinted in Gunther, *Early Science in Oxford* 6, 1–68; 59–66.

18 Bennett, 'Wren's last building?', p. 113.

19 *Parentalia*, p. 302. For Wren's report see *Parentalia*, pp. 295–303. For a model of the proposed spire (c. 1720), see T. Cocke, *900 Years: The Restorations of Westminster Abbey* (London: Harvey Miller Publishers, 1995), p. 131.

20 Bold, *Greenwich*, p. 142.

21 The following is based on M. Feingold, 'Astronomy and Strife'. I am grateful to Moti Feingold for sharing with me some of his research in progress on the history of the early Royal Society.

22 Flamsteed, *Correspondence* 1, letter 5, pp. 12–26; letter 27, p. 63: 'If it seems appropriate that this informative if not highly accurate observation, together with other papers I gave you, should become both public property and privately that of the Royal Society, I shall make a formal present of them.'

23 Birch, *History of the Royal Society* 3, 139; cit. Feingold, 'Astronomy and Strife', p. 37.

24 Feingold, 'Astronomy and Strife', pp. 37–8.

25 'Despite his early association, he was not elected until 8 February 1676/7, and then under rather peculiar circumstances. As the minutes read: "Mr. John Flamsteed was elected, Sir Jonas Moore and Mr. Daniel Colwall affirming, that he had been formerly proposed, though it appeared not upon the Journal, that he had been so." More curious still was the fact that Flamsteed was not actually admitted until 13 February 1678/9, two full years later. It is likely that some, or all, of the above factors caused discord and forced a controversy over the legality of his candidacy and election' (Feingold, 'Astronomy and Strife', pp. 39–40).

26 Feingold, 'Astronomy and Strife', pp. 40–3.

27 Flamsteed, *Correspondence* 1, letter 332, p. 617. Halley remembered Wren's smoking-chimney remedy

when the Royal Society discussed the general problem in 1691. According to Halley, Wren had used it in a building in Whitehall.

28 On the beginning of their relationship see above, chapter 6.

29 In November 1679 he wrote to Towneley: 'I goe once a weeke usually to London to the meeting of the R. Society' (Flamsteed, *Correspondence* 1, letter 369, p. 714), but he rarely contributed to the discussions.

30 Flamsteed, *Correspondence* 1, letter 398, p. 762. Newton was also communicating his observations of this comet, and the one which had appeared some months earlier (in fact one and the same) to Flamsteed. See Flamsteed, *Correspondence* 1, letters 399–403, and Jardine, *Ingenious Pursuits*, chapter 1.

31 Flamsteed, *Correspondence* 1, letter 434, p. 851.

32 Flamsteed, *Correspondence* 1, letter 445, p. 887.

33 Flamsteed, *Correspondence* 1, letter 445, p. 886.

34 Flamsteed, *Correspondence* 2, letter 451, p. 1: 'I have had little time to Consider this probleme but it seemes to require a new sort of Trigonometrie to solve it in which lesser circles and theire arches must be considered,' Flamsteed confided.

35 Feingold, 'Astronomy and Strife', pp. 44–5.

36 Flamsteed *Correspondence* 1, letter 216, Flamsteed to Towneley, 29 April 1675, p. 348: 'Mr Edmond Halley an ingenuous Young man from Oxford sent mee the tender of a friendly correspondence and wee have changed some letters.' A. Cook, *Edmond Halley: Charting the Heavens and the Seas* (Oxford: Clarendon Press, 1998).

37 Flamsteed, *Correspondence* 1, letter 439, Flamsteed to Molyneux, 27 February 1681/2, p. 861.

38 The following account of Halley's relations with Flamsteed and Newton after 1684 is based on Cook, *Edmond Halley*, and Westfall, *Never at Rest*.

39 Westfall, *Never at Rest*, p. 403; Cook, *Edmond Halley*, p. 149.

40 Westfall, *Never at Rest*, p. 446.

41 Newton, *Correspondence* 3, 433–4, letter 286, Newton to Halley, 27 May 1686.

42 Newton, *Correspondence* 3, 441–2, letter 289, Halley to Newton, 29 June 1686.

43 See Cook, *Edmond Halley*, pp. 382–3.

44 Flamsteed, *Correspondence* 2, letter 881, p. 982. This letter appears twice (once with the passage quoted here omitted) in *Parentalia*. The original manuscript, together with those of two other letters (880 and 719) are bound into the Royal Society MS version of *Parentalia*. From these it is clear that Christopher Wren junior omitted portions of letters to or from his father which he was transcribing, if they contained gossip or innuendo.

45 Halley signs a letter of 1711 to Flamsteed, 'Your quondam friend and not yet your profligate Enemy (as you call me)', suggesting he did not himself take Flamsteed's hostility entirely to heart. Flamsteed, *Correspondence* 3, letter 1302, p. 618.

46 Flamsteed, *Correspondence* 1, Letter 813, Flamsteed to Lowthrop, pp. 816–19; 818. See also letter 809, Flamsteed to Wren, 28 March 1700, p. 814: 'You are both [Wren and Newton] my Friends both Zealous for the honour of the king and Nation.'

47 Flamsteed, *Correspondence* 2, letter 636, pp. 448–53.

48 Flamsteed, *Correspondence* 2, letter 638, p. 463.

49 Flamsteed, *Correspondence* 2, letter 639, p. 467.

50 'I have got but halfe a score observations of the Moone this 3 moneths. Sir Ch: Wren has helpt me to a servant [James Hodgson] of whom I have very good hopes' (Flamsteed, *Correspondence* 2, letter 688, p. 582).

51 Flamsteed, *Correspondence* 3, letter 965, pp. 116–17.

52 Flamsteed, *Correspondence* 3, letter 1022, p. 205.

53 Flamsteed, *Correspondence 3*, 14 November 1705, letter 1043, p. 242.

54 Newton did eventually succeed in forcing a partial printing of Flamsteed's work, by breaking an undertaking to Flamsteed that 175 pages of observations submitted to him and sealed in the presence of Wren (at Flamsteed's request) should remain undisclosed. Flamsteed later succeeded in having all the copies recalled, however, and the final version of the *Historia coelestis* was published after Flamsteed's death, by his widow.

55 Westfall, *Never at Rest*, p. 667; see also Feingold, 'Astronomy and Strife'.

56 See Flamsteed, *Correspondence 3*, pp. 573–7.

57 Flamsteed, *Correspondence 3*, letter 1301, p. 617.

58 Flamsteed, *Correspondence 3*, letter 1318, p. 640.

59 Flamsteed, *Correspondence 3*, letter 1077, 9 March 1705/6, p. 300.

60 *Parentalia*, p. 349.

61 Newton, and the rest of the 1714 Longitude Committee, all of whom were astronomers, were particularly sceptical about the likelihood of anyone constructing a suitable timepiece, hence Harrison's difficulty in interesting subsequent committees in his solution. See Andrewes, *The Quest for Longitude*.

62 Westfall, *Never at Rest*, pp. 834–5.

63 See Howse, *Greenwich Time and Longitude*; A. J. Turner, 'In the wake of the Act, but mainly before', in Andrewes, *The Quest for Longitude*, pp. 116–27.

64 Newton, *Correspondence 6*, 193.

65 BL MS *Parentalia*.

66 Newton, *Correspondence 6*, 193.

67 The cypher submitted ran: 'O Z V C V A Y I N I X D N C V O C W E D C N M A L N A B E C I R T E W N G R A M H H C C A W. Z E I Y E I N O I E B I V T X E S C I O C P S D E D M N A N H S E E P R P I W H D R A E H H X C I F. E Z K A V E B I M O X R F C S L C E E D H W M G N N I V E O M R E W W E R R C S H E P C I P'. If we reverse the letters in each sentence and omit every third letter, the sentences now read: 'W A C H

MAGNETIC BALANCE WOVND IN VACVO. / FIX HEAD HIPPES HANDS POISE TUBE ON EYE. / PIPE SCREWE MOVING WHEELS FROM BEAKE'. The omitted letters spell: CHR WREN MDCCXIVZ.

68 See the fragment in BL MS *Parentalia*, fol. 43 v: 'Of the Apparatus; in pursuance of the Com[m]and of the Rt. Honle. the Earle of Sandwich, which were these. / That in the Azimuth 270 40' SW. The Moon's Altitude should be observ'd. together with her apparent Place for certain days together, from the first Quarter till the Full Moon, in the Months of Jan: & Feb: 1662. the Fix'd Starrs from when the Distance was to be taken being prescrib'd. / To know by memory the true Place of the [sun] in the Zodiack ye. 10/20th of June or 02 days after the Aequinoctial of V (for ever.) Upon supposition the Calendar to be rectified by leaving out for the future the Intercalar days. &c.'

69 Bennett, *The Mathematical Science*, pp. 52–3.

70 See above, chapter 5.

71 *Parentalia*, p. 346.

72 Bennett, *The Mathematical Science*, p. 54.

73 *Parentalia*, p. 344.

74 The halving of Wren's salary was recognised as unnecessarily punitive at the time. A few months later his old and close friend Thomas Sprat, Dean of Westminster, organised a new position of Surveyor of Westminster at £100 per annum, to which Wren was appointed, thereby restoring his salary to its old level.

75 *Parentalia*, following p. 194.

76 Wren owned a house in St James's.

77 BL MS *Parentalia*.

78 PRO E 367/3866.

79 *Parentalia*, p. 346.

80 Fréart, *A Parallel of the Antient Architecture with the Modern*, trans. John Evelyn (London, 1664), fols A5r–A6v.

81 Preface to J. Evelyn, *An Account of Architects & Architecture, together with*

An Historical, and Etymological
Explanation of certain Tearms
particularly affected by Architects
(London, 1706 [thus on separate t-p]),
in Fréart, A Parallel of the Antient
Architecture with the Modern, trans.
John Evelyn (London, 1707).

82 Colvin, The History of the King's
Works 5, 61.

83 Cit. J. Lang, Rebuilding St. Paul's
(Oxford: Oxford University Press,
1956), p. 204.

84 For the sequence of pamphlets see
Wren Society 16, 146. See also Elmes,
Memoirs of Wren.

85 Wren Society 16, 141; Price, The British
Carpenter, plates O* P**.

86 See Lang, Rebuilding St. Paul's,
pp. 250–2.

87 Elmes, Memoirs of Wren, pp. xxx–
xxxi.

88 Hibbert, The Marlboroughs,
pp. 167–8.

89 Wren Society 16, 141–71. The
documents collected here give a clear
picture of the sophistication and
complexity of work practices at the
level of craftsmanship required at
St Paul's.

90 Naturall Historie of Wiltshire. John
Aubrey [1626–97] manuscript: 1685
[Bodleian Library, Oxford], transcript
by Clerk to the Royal Society, Mr.
B. G. Cramer, additional notes in
Aubrey's hand: 1691. [Archives of the
Royal Society, Misc. MS. 92, f. 277.
373 pages.]

91 'On the Engraved List of Lodges of
1729, the Goose and Gridiron Lodge
No. 1, known after as the Lodge of
Antiquity, is said to have dated from
1691' (Masonic Short Talk Bulletin, 7
(January 1929, consulted online). I
am grateful to Professor Andrew
Prescott, University of Sheffield, for
his assistance with information
regarding Wren and early
freemasonry.

92 M. C. Jacob, Living the Enlightenment:
Freemasonry and Politics in
Eighteenth-Century Europe (Oxford:
Oxford University Press, 1991),
pp. 87–8.

93 Warren, 'Sir Christopher Wren's
repair of the Divinity School and
Duke Humphrey's Library, Oxford',
pp. 233–8; facsimile letter between
pp. 236 and 237.

94 'Having put into the Chair the oldest
Master Mason (now the Master of a
Lodge), they constituted themselves a
Grand Lodge pro Tempore in Due
Form, and forthwith revived the
Quarterly Communication of the
Officers of Lodges (Call'd the Grand
Lodge) resolv'd to hold the Annual
Assembly and Feast, and then to
chuse a Grand Master from among
themselves, till they should have the
Honour of a Noble Brother at their
head' (Jacob, Living the
Enlightenment, p. 92). There is a
masonic engraving among those
inserted into the Heirloom copy of
Parentalia. It has been argued that
this is due to Wren junior, an
enthusiastic freemason, but Wren
junior followed his father
scrupulously in everything.

95 For a full account of the political
machinations surrounding the final
years of Wren's tenure of the Royal
Surveyorship see Colvin, History of
the King's Works 5, chapter 4, 'The
end of Wren's regime'.

96 Colvin, History of the King's Works
5, 52.

97 Colvin, History of the King's Works
5, 52.

98 Colvin, History of the King's Works
5, 55.

99 Colvin, History of the King's Works
5, 60.

100 Colvin, History of the King's Works
5, 61.

101 Parentalia, pp. 347–8.

102 Dated 'Wotton. 21. / Feb. 1696/7'.
Preface to J. Evelyn, An Account of
Architects & Architecture, together with
An Historical, and Etymological
Explanation of certain Tearms
particularly affected by Architects
(London, 1706 [thus on separate t-p]),
in Fréart, A Parallel of the Antient
Architecture with the Modern, trans.
by John Evelyn (London, 1707). This

work is referred to by Wren/Wren junior in *Parentalia*, p. 307: 'The ingenious Mr. Evelyn, makes a general and judicious Comparison, in his Account of Architecture, of the ancient and modern Styles, with Reference to some of the particular Works of Inigo Jones, and the Surveyor; which in a few Words, gives a right Idea of the majestick Symmetry of the one, and the absurd System of the other.'

103 This is the running theme of Ashmole's *Institution of the Order of the Garter*. Evelyn's copy of Ashmole is in the British Library. It is inscribed on the title-page: 'Catalogo Evelyni inscriptus. to kalon katechete [*το καλον κατεχετε*] Ex dono Authoris'. There is a single marginal note in Evelyn's hand.

104 W. Dugdale, *The history of St. Paul's Cathedral in London, from its foundation : Extracted out of original charters, records, leiger-books, and other manuscripts. Beautified with sundry prospects of the old fabrick, which was destroyed by the fire of that city, 1666. As also with the figures of the tombs and monuments therein, which were all defac'd in the late rebellion. Whereunto is added, a continuation thereof, setting forth what was done in the structure of the new church, to the year 1685. Likewise, An historical account of the northern cathedrals, and chief collegiate churches in the province of York* (London, 1658, second edition, 1716). Just like Ashmole's *Institution of the Order of the Garter* the second edition of Dugdale's book is worked backwards from the rebuilt Wren Cathedral, so that the story on paper of the Cathedral itself is the tale of the fortunes of the monarchy from the reign of James I to that of Charles II (including some rather fanciful reconstructions of Old St Paul's in all its original glory, long-gone by the seventeenth century).

105 The annual Boyle Lectures, on a religious topic associated with science and the Royal Society, founded by benefaction of Robert Boyle in 1694, were delivered at St Paul's.

106 W. Holder, *A Discourse Concerning Time* (London, 1694), pp. 103–4.

107 Soo, *Wren's 'Tracts' on Architecture*, p. 153.

108 'Discourse on Architecture. By Sr. C: W:', p. 7, inserted in *Parentalia* following p. 366.

109 A copy of the Statutes for the Order drawn up by Matthew Wren, dated 1631 and in his hand, is bound into the St Paul's Cathedral Library copy of *Parentalia*. Ashmole has had access to this, since he cites it in his *Institutions of the Garter*. On its front page are jottings by Matthew Wren for an etymology of 'Windes-Oure'. Throughout this manuscript corrections have been made to remove all references to Catholic observance – for example, references to 'masses for the dead' have been replaced by 'Matins', and the 'blessed Virgin Mary' deleted. 'An ancient copy' of the 'Incorporation of the Chapel of Windsor by K. Ed. III' is also bound in to this copy of *Parentalia*. Christopher Wren junior's hand is to be found in the descriptions of the manuscripts on their front pages. I am grateful to Jo Wisdom, Librarian at St Paul's, for his kindness and help with material at St Paul's.

110 Bennett, 'A study of *Parentalia*'. Bennett's is the only full treatment of the three versions of *Parentalia*. Since he is interested only in the scientific content Bennett does not, however, on the whole record the discrepancies between the BL fragments and the printed text. Lydia Soo also has a treatment of the three manuscripts, but does not appear to have examined either the BL or RS manuscripts very closely. See Soo, *Wren's 'Tracts' on Architecture*, pp. 8–17.

111 BL Add. MS 25,071, fols 89, 115.

112 See, e.g., the date 1628 in the margin on p. 269 of the printed *Parentalia*.

113 Because the Codrington Library is

under renovation, I have not been able to inspect the All Souls copy, and have relied here on Bennett and Soo.

114 BL MS Add. 25,071, fol. 54 r.
115 Wren and the Royal Society fellows' involvement with the building of the Church of King Charles the Martyr for the fashionable spa town of Tunbridge Wells demonstrates how this undercurrent of continued attention to the memory of the executed King figured. The church was built at first as a chapel in 1678 and was further enlarged and beautified in 1682 and 1696. A long list of Royal Society fellows donated money for the construction. Since Wren's name does not figure, he was probably involved in the design, waiving his fee as usual. I am grateful to Sir Alan Cook for making his list of Royal Society subscribers available to me.
116 *Parentalia*, p. 55.
117 Colvin, *History of the King's Works* 5, 324.
118 *Parentalia*, p. 331. For a full account of Wren's designs for the Charles I Mausoleum, see J. D. Stewart, 'A militant Stoic monument: the Wren–Cibber–Gibbons Charles I Mausoleum project: its authors, sources, meaning, and influence', in W. G. Marshall (ed.), *The Restoration Mind* (Newark: University of Delaware Press, 1997), pp. 21–64; R. A. Beddard, 'Wren's Mausoleum for Charles I and the cult of the Royal Martyr', *Architectural History* 27 (1984), 36–47.
119 Stewart, 'A militant Stoic monument', p. 36.
120 For translation see Stewart, 'A militant Stoic monument', p. 54. In the Royal Society copy of the *Parentalia* MS (copied c. 1741) this Lucan passage is on a separate, additional sheet, in a different hand from that of the copyist.

ILLUSTRATIONS ACKNOWLEDGEMENTS

ILLUSTRATIONS IN THE TEXT: (page x) St Paul's during the Blitz: Hulton Archive; (xiii) Monument to the Great Fire: John Hare; (5) Infant Charles II by an unknown artist, 1630: by courtesy of the National Portrait Gallery, London; (6) Charles II and his brother James by William Dobson, 1642: National Gallery of Scotland; (8) Ceremonial portrait of Charles I by Sir Anthony Van Dyck: Staatliche Kunstsammlungen, Dresden; (11) Engraved view of Windsor Castle (detail) drawn by Wren and engraved by Wenceslaus Hollar, Elias Ashmole, 1672, eve. c.10 (p. 134): The British Library; (25) Garter Regalia, Elias Ashmole, 1672, eve. c.10 (p. 202): The British Library; (34) Aerial engraved view of Windsor Castle, Elias Ashmole, 1672, cvc. c.10 (p. 131): The British Library; (38) Prince Rupert by Sir Anthony Van Dyck, c.1637: by courtesy of the National Gallery, London; (51) Dr Richard Busby by an unknown artist, after 1695: by courtesy of the National Portrait Gallery, London; (55) William Harvey after an etching attributed to Richard Gaywood: by courtesy of the National Portrait Gallery, London; (61) John Wallis after Sir Godfrey Kneller, 1701: by courtesy of the National Portrait Gallery, London; (62) Seth Ward by David Loggan, 1678: by courtesy of the National Portrait Gallery, London; (65) John Wilkins by Mary Beale: © The Royal Society; (68) William Petty by Isaac Fuller, c.1649–50: by courtesy of the National Portrait Gallery, London; (78) Charles Louis, Elector Palatine by Sir Anthony Van Dyck, c.1637: by courtesy of the National Gallery, London; (81) Sir Constantijn Huygens by Thomas de Keyser: by courtesy of the National Gallery, London; (91) Experimental seed drill from *Systema Agriculturae* by J.W. Gent, 1675, 1505.110 (p. 47): The British Library; (98) Engraving of flea: from Robert Hooke's *Micrographia*, 1665; (104) Edward Hyde, after Adriaen Hanneman, c.1648–55: by courtesy of the National Portrait Gallery, London; (108) Beehive from *The Commonwealth of Bees* by Samuel Hartlib, 1655, 972.i.27 (p. 8): The British Library; (121) Seventeenth-century engraved plan of Oxford; Christiaan Huygens: Library of Congress; (144) Grinling Gibbons, after Sir Godfrey Kneller, c.1690: by courtesy of the National Portrait Gallery, London; (148) Engraved view of Windsor Castle drawn by Wren and engraved by Wenceslaus Hollar Elias Ashmole, 1672, eve. c.10 (p. 134): The British Library; (156) Plan for the rebuilding of Whitehall Palace by John Webb, c.1648: Devonshire Collection, Chatsworth, reproduced by permission of the Duke of Devonshire and the Chatsworth Settlement Trustees; (160) Sir John Denham, Engraving by Le Goux, after an unknown artist: Mary Evans Picture Library; (160) Lady Denham by Charles Turner, after an unknown artist, published 1811: by courtesy of the National Portrait Gallery, London; (169) Edward Montagu, after Sir Peter Lely, c.1660: by courtesy of the National Portrait Gallery, London; Map of Tangier, (173) Jonas Moore, 1664: MAPS K117.79.11 TAB., The British Library; (181) Portrait of Wren by Sir Godfrey Kneller, c.1708: Sheldonian Library, Oxford; (183) William Brouncker, 2nd Viscount Brouncker by an unknown artist: by courtesy of the National Portrait Gallery, London; (191) John Evelyn, diarist and (200) Boyle's air pump, 1659: © The Royal Society; (208) Elias Ashmole, after John Riley, c.1687–89: by courtesy of the National Portrait Gallery; (211) Sketch of ironwork by Wren: by kind permission of the Dean and Chapter of Salisbury, photograph by Simon Eagar; (214) Wooden model of roof structure: by courtesy of Pembroke College, Cambridge; (218) Drawing of Wallis's diagram in *Parentalia*: © The Royal Society; (220) Engraving of Old St Paul's by Wenceslaus Hollar, 1657: by courtesy of the Guildhall Library, London; (222) Archbishop Gilbert Sheldon, Studio of Sir Peter Lely, *c.*1665: by courtesy of the National Portrait Gallery, London; (225) The Earl of Clarendon by David Loggan, 1666: by courtesy of the National Portrait Gallery, London; (230) Engraving of plan of London by Wenceslaus Hollar, 1666: by courtesy of the Guildhall Library, London; (243) Henry Jermyn, after Sir Peter Lely: by courtesy of the National Portrait Gallery, London; (249) Wren's Double Telescope and Hooke's Reflecting Quadrant, 1705: L35/56, TAB VIII. The British Library; (252) Survey of the Thames by Jonas Moore, 1662: © Public Record Office/Museum of London; (260) Plan of London by John Evelyn, *c.*1790: by courtesy of the Guildhall Library, London; (264) Wren's plan for the rebuilding of London; (271) Sketches of the 1664 comet by Robert Hooke: © The Royal Society; (272) Engraved plate on comets by Robert Hooke, 1674: 233.h.5, TAB 1. The British Library; (279) Survey of a portion of the surface of the moon by Robert Hooke, 1665: *Micrographia*; (288) William Sancroft by Edward Lutterel, *c.*1688: by courtesy of the National Portrait Gallery, London; (299) St Mary le Bow: © Valerie Bennett/Architectural Association Photo Library; (301) St Lawrence Jewry: © Valerie Bennett/Architectural Association Photo Library; (303) Interior of St Stephen Walbrook: © Richard Turpin/Arcaid; (319) Section through the Monument to the Great Fire: John Hare; (323) Design for a library and repository at the Royal College of Physicians by John Webb, *c.*1651: by courtesy of Worcester College Oxford and The Conway Library, Courtauld Institute of Art; (325) External elevation of the library at the Royal College of Physicians by John Webb, *c.*1651: by courtesy of Worcester College Oxford and The Conway Library, Courtauld Institute of Art; (327) Axonometric drawing of the Trinity College Library by Edward Impey after Donald Insall and Partners; (344) Stephen Fox by Sir Peter Lely; (352) Dark-skinned man, Mezzotint (after a painting) by Prince Rupert, Count Palatine: by courtesy of the National Portrait Gallery, London; (355) Royal Chelsea Hospital: © E.R. Jarrett/Architectural Association Photo Library; (361) Interior of the Governor's House at Chelsea: © Canon Parsons/ Architectural Association Photo Library; (372) Henry Compton by Sir Godfrey Kneller, *c.*1712: by courtesy of the National Portrait Gallery, London; (374) Sir William Petty by Edwin Sandys, 1683: by courtesy of the National Portrait Gallery, London; (377) Prince James Francis Edward Stuart by John Smith, after Sir Godfrey Kneller, *c.*1688: by courtesy of the National Portrait Gallery, London; (380) Plan of Whitehall Palace, 1680: Museum of London; (384) Engraving of William and Mary by Jakob Van der Schley, after Hubert François Gravelot (or Bourguignon): by courtesy of the National Portrait Gallery, London; (395) Greenwich Royal Hospital: © Alex Bartel/Arcaid; (402) The Painted Hall at Greenwich: © Canon Parsons/Architectural Association Photo Library; (406) Perspective painting by Samuel Van Hoogstraeten, *c.*1662: © Derrick E. Witty/National Trust Photographic Library; (412) St Paul's Cathedral: © Roy Rainford/Robert Harding Picture Library; (417) Drawing of the double dome of Hagia Sophia: from an illustrated volume by Julien-David Le Roy, Paris 1764: by courtesy of W.D. Jordan Special Collections & Music Library, Queen's University at Kingston, Canada; (419) Details of the plan of Hagia Sophia, from an illustrated volume by Julien-David Le Roy, Paris 1764: by courtesy of W.D. Jordan Special Collections & Music Library, Queen's University at Kingston, Canada; (420) Details of the plan of Hagia Sophia, from an illustrated volume by Julien-David Le Roy, Paris 1764: by courtesy of W.D. Jordan Special Collections & Music Library, Queen's University at Kingston, Canada; (425) Front elevation of St Paul's: © C. Bowman/Robert Harding Picture Library; (439) Sir Isaac Newton: © The Royal Society; (442) John Flamsteed by Thomas Gibson, 1712: © The Royal Society; (448) Edmond Halley, by Thomas Murray: © The Royal Society; (452) Flamsteed's inscribed copy of Newton's *Principia*, 1686: © The Royal Society; (455) Prince George of Denmark, after John Riley, *c.*1687: by courtesy of the National Portrait Gallery, London; (467) Plate from *The English Carpenter* by Francis Price, 1735, second edition 1753; (471) Sir John Vanbrugh by Sir Godfrey Kneller, *c.*1704–10: by courtesy of the National Portrait Gallery, London; (481) Wooden model of Westminster Abbey: © Dean and Chapter of Westminster, photograph by Andrew Dunsmore; (482) Drawing of Wren's planned Mausoleum to Charles I: by courtesy of the Warden and Fellows of All Souls College, Oxford.

PLATE SECTION: The five eldest children of Charles I by Sir Anthony Van Dyck: The Royal Collection © 2002, Her Majesty Queen Elizabeth II; Charles I by Sir Anthony Van Dyck: The Royal Collection © 2002, Her Majesty Queen Elizabeth II; Wedding portrait of Princess Mary and William of Orange by Sir Anthony Van Dyck, c.1642: © Rijksmuseum, Amsterdam; Charles I and the Duke of York by Sir Peter Lely: by courtesy of The Northumberland Estates; James, Duke of York by Henri Gascard: © National Maritime Museum Picture Library; William III by an unknown artist, after Cornelius Johnson, 1657: by courtesy of the National Portrait Gallery, London; James, Duke of York and Anne Hyde, Duchess of York by Sir Peter Lely, c.1660–69: by courtesy of the National Portrait Gallery, London; Charles II in later life, attributed to Thomas Hawker, c.1680: by courtesy of the National Portrait Gallery, London; Charles Louis and Prince Rupert by Sir Anthony Van Dyck, 1637: Louvre/Bridgeman Art Library; Charles II's sister Mary by Adriaen Hanneman: Royal Cabinet of Paintings, Mauritshuis The Hague; Wren in maturity by Johann B. Closterman © The Royal Society; Robert Boyle, by Johann Kerseboom, 1692: © The Royal Society; Sir John Chardin by an unknown artist, c.1700–05: by courtesy of the National Portrait Gallery, London; Sir Robert Viner and family by John Michael Wright, 1673: by courtesy of the National Portrait Gallery, London; Hampton Court Palace by Hendrick Danckerts: © The Royal Collection © 2002, Her Majesty Queen Elizabeth II; The Royal Observatory, Seventeenth-century English School: © National Maritime Museum; View of Delft by Saftleven: The Metropolitan Museum of Art, Purchase, Bequest of Helen Hay Whitney, by exchange, and The Munchin Foundation, Mr and Mrs David M. Tobey, and Werner H. Kramarsky Gifts, 1995. (1996.197), photograph: © 2000 The Metropolitan Museum of Art; Interior of St Bavo's by Pieter Saenredam: National Gallery of Scotland; Architectural fantasy with figures by Gerrit Houkgeest: National Gallery of Scotland; Wren/Hooke weather gauge: © The Royal Society; Drawings of hailstones observed by Wren in 1667: © The Royal Society; Lease issued by Sir Stephen Fox and Wren: © Public Record Office; Letters patent to Sir Stephen Fox © Public Record Office; Invoice issued by Wren: © Public Record Office; Plan for Golden Square: © Public Record Office; Letter from Wren to Seth Ward: by kind permission of the Dean and Chapter of Salisbury, photograph by Simon Eagar; Robert Hooke's Will: © Public Record Office; Order of The Garter frontispiece, Elias Ashmole, 1672, eve. c.10 (p. 202): The British Library; Parentalia: The Warden and Fellows of All Souls College, Oxford; Design for triumphalist statue of Charles I: The Warden and Fellows of All Souls College, Oxford; Presentation drawing for Whitehall Palace by Wren, 1664: The Warden and Fellows of All Souls College, Oxford; Drawings by Hawksmoor of Wren's proposed fireplace at Hampton Court Palace: by courtesy of the Trustees of Sir John Soane's Museum; Presentation drawing of Trinity College Library by Wren: The Warden and Fellows of All Souls College, Oxford; Presentation drawing and plan of Trinity College Library by Wren: The Warden and Fellows of All Souls College, Oxford; Wren drawing of the south-west Tower of St Paul's Cathedral: Guildhall Library/St Paul's Cathedral, photograph by Geremy Butler; Wren drawing of lantern detail: Guildhall Library/St Paul's Cathedral, photograph by Geremy Butler; Wren drawing of the base of the dome of St Paul's Cathedral: Guildhall Library/St Paul's Cathedral, photograph by Geremy Butler.

We have tried to trace and contact all copyright holders before publication. If notified the publisher will be pleased to make any necessary arrangements at the earliest opportunity.

BIBLIOGRAPHY

WREN MATERIALS

Wren Society, 20 vols (Oxford: printed for the Wren Society at the University Press, 1924–43)

Wren, Stephen *Parentalia: or, Memoirs of the Family of the Wrens; viz. Of Mathew Bishop of Ely, Christopher Dean of Windsor, &c. but chiefly of Sir Christopher Wren, Late Surveyor-General of the Royal Buildings, President of the Royal Society, &c. &c.* (London: T. Osborn and R. Dodsley, 1750; reprinted Gregg Press, 1965 [the 'heirloom' copy])

BL MS *Parentalia*, BL Add. MS 25,071

RS MS *Parentalia*, RS MS 249

Royal Society Registers, Journals and Letter Books, passim

Downes, K. *Sir Christopher Wren: Catalogue of an Exhibition at Whitechapel Art Gallery* (London: Trefoil, 1982)

Downes, K. *Sir Christopher Wren: The Design of St Paul's Cathedral* (London: Trefoil, 1988)

Downes, K. *Sir Christopher Wren and the Making of St. Paul's* (London: Royal Academy of Arts, 1991)

Elmes, J. *Memoirs of the Life and Works of Sir Christopher Wren* (London: Priestly & Weale, 1823)

Poley, A. F. E. *St Paul's Cathedral / measured, drawn, and described* (London, printed for the author, 1927)

SOURCE MATERIALS BEFORE 1800

Ashmole, Elias *The Institution, Laws & Ceremonies of the most Noble Order of the Garter. Collected and digested into one Body by Elias Ashmole of the Middle-Temple Esquire Windesor Herald at Arms. A Work furnished with variety of matter, relating to honor and noblesse* (London, 1672)

Bamford, F. *A Royalist's Notebook. The Commonplace Book of Sir John Oglander Kt. Of Nunwell. Born 1585 died 1655, Transcribed and edited by Francis Bamford* (London: Constable & Co., 1936)

Beer, E. S. de *The Diary of John Evelyn*, 6 vols (Oxford: Clarendon Press, 1955)

Birch, T. *A History of the Royal Society of London for Improving Natural Knowledge, from its first Rise*, 4 vols (London, 1756–7)

Black, W. H. *A Descriptive, Analytical, and Critical Catalogue of the Manuscripts Bequeathed unto the University of Oxford by Elias Ashmole, Esq., M.D., F. R. S., Windsor Herald . . .* (Oxford: At the University Press, 1845)

Bray, W. *Diary and Correspondence of John Evelyn: to which is subjoined the private correspondence between King Charles I and Sir Edward Nicholas . . .* (London: George Routledge, [1906])

Defoe, D. *A Tour through England and Wales, Divided into Circuits or Journies*, 2 vols, Everyman edition (London: J. M. Dent and Sons, 1927)

Derham, W. (ed.) *Philosophical Experiments and Observations of the late Eminent Dr. Robert Hooke* (London, 1726)

Dugdale, W. *The history of St. Paul's Cathedral in London, from its foundation : Extracted out of original charters, records, leiger-books, and other manuscripts. Beautified with sundry prospects of the old fabrick, which was destroyed by the fire of that city, 1666. As also with the figures of the tombs and monuments therein, which were all defac'd in the late rebellion. Whereunto is added, a continuation thereof, setting forth what was done in the structure of the new church, to the year 1685. Likewise, An historical account of the northern cathedrals, and chief collegiate churches in the province of York* (second edition, London, 1716)

Evelyn, J. *A Character of England, As it was lately presented in a Letter, to a Noble Man of France* (London, 1659)

Forbes, E. G., L. Murdin and F. Willmoth (eds) *The Correspondence of John Flamsteed, The First Astronomer Royal*, 3 vols (Bristol and Philadelphia: The Institute of Physics Publishing, 1995–2001)

Fréart, R. *A Parallel of the Antient Architecture with the Modern*, trans. John Evelyn (London, 1664) (facsimile reprint, London: Gregg International Publishers, 1970)

Gunther, R. T. *The Diary and Will of Elias Ashmole, edited and extended from the original Manuscripts* (Frome and London: Butler & Tanner, 1927)

Gunther, R. T. *Early Science in Oxford*, 15 vols (Oxford: printed for the author, OUP, 1920–67)

Gunther, R. T. (ed.) *The Architecture of Sir Roger Pratt, Charles II's Commissioner for the Rebuilding of London after the Great Fire: Now Printed for the first time from his Note-Books* (Oxford: Oxford University Press, 1928)

Hall, A. R. 'Wren's problem', *Notes and Records of the Royal Society* 20 (1965), 140–4

Hall, A. R. and M. B. Hall (eds and trans.) *The Correspondence of Henry Oldenburg*, 13 vols: vols 1–9 (Madison: University of Wisconsin Press, 1965–73); vols 10–11 (London: Mansell, 1975–6); vols 12–13 (London: Taylor & Francis, 1986)

Hart, V. and P. Hicks (trans. and eds) *Sebastiano Serlio on Architecture*, 2 vols (New Haven and London: Yale University Press, 1996–2001)

Holder, W. *A Discourse Concerning Time* (London, 1694)

Hooke, R. *Micrographia, or some Physiological Descriptions of Minute Bodies* (London, 1665)

Hunter, M. and E. B. Davis (eds) *The Complete Works of Robert Boyle*, 14 vols (London: Pickering & Chatto, 1999–2001)

Hunter, M. A. Clericuzio and L. M. Principe (eds) *The Correspondence of Robert Boyle*, 6 vols (London: Pickering & Chatto, 2001)

Huygens, C. *Oeuvres complètes de Christiaan Huygens*, 22 vols (The Hague: Martinus Nijhoff, 1888–1950)

Josten, C. H. (ed.) *Elias Ashmole. His Autobiographical and Historical Notes, his Correspondence, and other Contemporary Sources relating to his Life and Work*, 5 vols (Oxford: Clarendon Press, 1966)

Lansdowne, Marquis of (ed.) *The Petty Papers: Some Unpublished Writings*, 2 vols (London: Constable and Co., 1927)

Latham, R. and W. Matthews (eds) *The Diary of Samuel Pepys*, 11 vols (London: Bell & Hyman, 1972, reissued HarperCollins 1995)

Malcolm, N. (ed.) *The Correspondence of Thomas Hobbes*, 2 vols (Oxford: Clarendon Press, 1994)

Moore, J. *A New System of Mathematics* (London, 1681)

Moore, J. *A Mathematical Compendium, or, Useful Practices in Arithmetic, Geometry, etc.* (London, 1681)

Munby, A. N. L. (ed.) *Sale Catalogues of Libraries of Eminent Persons*, vol. 4: *Architects* (London: Mansell Publishing, 1972) [Wren]

Munby, A. N. L. (ed.) *Sale Catalogues of Libraries of Eminent Persons*, vol. 11: *Scientists* (London: Mansell Publishing, 1975) [Hooke]

Newton, I. *Philosophiae naturalis principia mathematica* (London, 1687)

Oughtred, W. *Clavis mathematicae* (Oxford, 1652)

Price, F. *The British Carpenter: Or, a Treatise on Carpentry. Containing the most concise and authentick Rules of that Art*, second edition (London, 1735)

Robinson, H. and W. Adams (eds) *The Diary of Robert Hooke MA MD FRS 1672–1680* (London: Taylor & Francis, 1935)

Sprat, T. *The History of the Royal Society of London* (London, 1667)

Turnbull, H. W., J. F. Scott, A. R. Hall and L. Tilling (eds) *The Correspondence of Isaac Newton*, 7 vols (Cambridge: Cambridge University Press, 1959–77)

Waller, R. *The Posthumous Works of Robert Hooke* (London, 1705)

Wallis, J. *Mechanica: sive, De motu, tractatus geometricus, etc.* (London, 1670–1)

Ward, J. *Lives of the Gresham Professors* (London, 1740)

Wilkins, J. *The discovery of a world in the moone, or, a discourse tending to prove, that 'tis possible there may be another habitable world on that planet, with A discourse concerning the possibility of a passage thither* (London, 1638)

Wilkins, J. *A discourse concerning a new planet, tending to prove that 'tis probable our Earth is one of the planets* (London, 1640)

Wilkins, J. *Mercury, or the secret and swift messenger, showing how a man may with privacy and speed communicate his thoughts to a friend at any distance* (London, 1641)

Wilkins, J. *Mathematical magick, or the wonders that may be performed by mechanical geometry* (London, 1648)

Wilkins, J. *An essay towards a real character and a philosophical language* (London, 1667)

Wren, Jr, Matthew *Monarchy Asserted, or the State of Monarchicall & Popular Government in Vindication of the Considerations upon Mr. Harrington's Oceana* (Oxford, 1659)

SOURCES AFTER 1800

Aarsleff, H. 'John Wilkins', *Dictionary of Scientific Biography* 14 (1976), 364

Ackroyd, P. *London: The Biography* (London: Chatto, 2000)

Adair, J. *By the Sword Divided: Eyewitness Accounts of the English Civil War* (London: Sutton Publishing, 1998)

Akrigg, G. P. V. (ed.) *Letters of King James VI & I* (Berkeley: University of California Press, 1984)

Alpers, S. *The Art of Describing: Dutch Art in the Seventeenth Century* (Chicago: University of Chicago Press, 1983)

Ames-Lewis, F., F. Baden-Powell et al., *Sir Thomas Gresham and Gresham College* (London: Ashgate Publishing, 1999)

Andrewes, W. J. H. *The Quest for Longitude* (Cambridge, Mass.: Harvard University Press, 1996)

Andriesse, C. D. *Titan kan niet slapen: een biografie van Christiaan Huygens* (Amsterdam: Contact, 1993), French trans. D. Losman, *Christiaan Huygens* (Paris: Albin Michel, 1998)

Archer, I. W. 'Social networks in Restoration London: the evidence from Samuel Pepys's diary', in A. Shepard and P. Withrington (eds), *Communities in Early Modern England* (Manchester: Manchester University Press, 2000) pp. 67–94

Armitage, A. 'William Ball FRS (1627–1690)', *Notes and Records of the Royal Society* 15 (1960), 167–72

Ashworth, W. J. ' "Labour harder than *thrashing*": John Flamsteed, property and intellectual labour in nineteenth-century England', in F. Willmoth (ed.), *Flamsteed's Stars: New Perspectives on the Life and Work of the First Astronomer Royal (1646–1719)* (Woodbridge: Boydell Press, 1997), pp. 199–216

Aylmer, G. 'Patronage at the court of Charles II', in E. Cruickshanks (ed.), *The Stuart Courts* (Stroud: Sutton Publishing, 2000), pp. 191–202

Bachrach, A. G. H. and R. G. Collmer (eds) *Lodewijk Huygens: The English Journal 1651–1652* (Leiden: Brill, 1982)

Barclay, A. 'Charles II's failed Restoration: administrative reform below stairs, 1660–4', in E. Cruickshanks (ed.), *The Stuart Courts* (Stroud: Sutton Publishing, 2000), pp. 158–70

Barnard, T. C. 'The Hartlib Circle and the cult and culture of improvement in Ireland', in M. Greengrass, M. Leslie and T. Raylor (eds), *Samuel Hartlib and Universal Reformation: Studies in Intellectual Communication* (Cambridge: Cambridge University Press, 1994), pp. 281–97

Barnett, P. R. *Theodore Haak, FRS (1605–1690)* ('sGravenshage: Mouton & Co., 1962)

Batten, M. I. 'The architecture of Dr Robert Hooke FRS', *Walpole Society* 25 (1936–7), 83–113

Beddard, R. A. 'Wren's Mausoleum for Charles I and the cult of the Royal Martyr', *Architectural History* 27 (1984), 36–47

Bédoyère, G. de la *Particular Friends: The Correspondence of Samuel Pepys and John Evelyn* (Woodbridge: Boydell & Brewer, 1997)

Bennett, J. A. 'Wren's last building?', *Notes and Records of the Royal Society* 27 (1972–3), 107–18

Bennett, J. A. 'A study of *Parentalia*, with two unpublished letters of Sir Christopher Wren', *Annals of Science* 30 (1973), 129–47

Bennett, J. A. 'Studies in the life and work of Sir Christopher Wren' (University of Cambridge: PhD dissertation, 1974)

Bennett, J. A. 'Hooke and Wren and the system of the world', *British Journal for the History of Science* 8 (1975), 32–61

Bennet, J. A. 'A note on the theories of respiration and muscular action in England c. 1660', *Medical History* 20 (1976), 59–69

Bennett, J. A. 'Robert Hooke as mechanic and natural philosopher', *Notes and Records of the Royal Society* 35 (1980), 33–48

Bennett, J. A. *The Mathematical Science of Christopher Wren* (Cambridge: Cambridge University Press, 1982)

Bennett, J. A. and S. Mandelbrote (eds) *The Garden, the Ark, the Tower, the Temple: Biblical Metaphors of Knowledge in Early Modern Europe* (Oxford: Museum of the History of Science, 1998)

Birch, T. (ed.) *The History of the Royal Society of London*, 4 vols (London, 1756–7)

Biswas, A. K. 'The automatic rain-gauge of Sir Christopher Wren, FRS', *Notes and Records of the Royal Society* 22 (1967), 94–104

Bold, J. *John Webb: Architectural Theory and Practice in the Seventeenth Century* (Oxford: Clarendon Press, 1989)

Bold, J. *Greenwich: An Architectural History of the Royal Hospital for Seamen and the Queen's House* (London: Yale University Press, 2000)

Bold J. and E. Chaney (eds), *English Architecture Public and Private* (London: Hambledon Press, 1993)

Bowen, E. J. and H. Hartley, 'The Right Reverend John Wilkins, FRS (1614–1672)', *Notes and Records of the Royal Society* (1960), 47–56

Brodsley, L., C. Frank and J. Steeds, 'Prince Rupert's drops', *Notes and Records of the Royal Society* 41 (1986), 1–26

Bromley, G., *Collection of Original Royal Letters* (London, 1835)

Brusati, C. *Artifice and Illusion: The Art and Writing of Samuel Van Hoogstraten* (Chicago: University of Chicago Press, 1995)

Buchanan-Brown, J. (ed.) *John Aubrey: Brief Lives* (London: Penguin Books, 2000)

Bryant, A. *King Charles II* (London: Collins, 1955)

Callow, J. *The Making of King James II: The Formative Years of a Fallen King* (Stroud: Sutton Publishing, 2000)

Campbell, J. W. P. 'Sir Christopher Wren, the Royal Society and the development of structural carpentry, 1660–1710 (University of Cambridge: PhD dissertation, 2000)

Campbell, J. W. P. 'Architect as engineer: Sir Christopher Wren, the Royal Society and structural carpentry in the late seventeenth century', Gresham College Lecture, 23 October 2000 (draft)

Canny, N. P. *The Upstart Earl: A Study of the Social and Mental World of*

Richard Boyle first Earl of Cork 1566–1643 (Cambridge: Cambridge University Press, 1982)

Carlton, C. *Charles I: The Personal Monarch*, second edition (London: Routledge, 1995)

Caröe, W. D. *'Tom Tower' Christ Church Oxford: Some Letters of Sir Christopher Wren to John Fell, Bishop of London* (Oxford: Clarendon Press, 1923)

Chambers, D. 'John Evelyn and the construction of the scientific self', in W. G. Marshall (ed.), *The Restoration Mind* (London: Associated University Presses, 1997), pp. 132–46

Chappell, E. (ed.) *The Tangier Papers of Samuel Pepys*, Navy Records Society 73 (1935)

Chartres, R. and D. Vermont, *A Brief History of Gresham College 1597–1997* (London: Gresham College, 1997)

Clay, C. *Public Finance and Private Wealth: The Career of Sir Stephen Fox, 1627–1716* (Oxford: Clarendon Press, 1978)

Cocke, T. *900 Years: The Restorations of Westminster Abbey* (London: Harvey Miller Publishers, 1995)

Colby, C. W. (ed.) *Selections from the Sources of English History* (London: Longmans, Green & Co., 1920)

Colie, R. L. 'Dean Wren's marginalia and early science at Oxford', *Bodleian Library Record* 6 (1960), 541–51

Colvin, H. M. 'Roger North and Sir Christopher Wren', *Architectural Review* 111 (1951), 257–60

Colvin, H. M. *The History of the King's Works*, 7 vols (London: Her Majesty's Stationery Office, 1963–82)

Colvin, H. *A Biographical Dictionary of British Architects 1600–1840*, third edition (New Haven and London: Yale University Press, 1995)

Colvin, H. 'The building', in D. McKitterick (ed.), *The Making of the Wren Library, Trinity College, Cambridge* (Cambridge: Cambridge University Press, 1995)

Cook, A. *Edmond Halley: Charting the Heavens and the Seas* (Oxford: Clarendon Press, 1998)

Cooper, M. 'Robert Hooke's work as surveyor for the City of London in the aftermath of the Great Fire. Part one: Robert Hooke's first surveys for the City of London', *Notes and Records of the Royal Society* 51 (1997), 161–74

Cooper, M. 'Robert Hooke's work as surveyor. Part two: certification of areas of ground taken away for streets and other new works', *Notes and Records of the Royal Society* 52 (1998), 25–38

Cooper, M. 'Robert Hooke's work as surveyor. Part three: settlement of disputes and complaints arising form rebuilding', *Notes and Records of the Royal Society* 52 (1998), 205–20

Coote, S. *Royal Survivor: A Life of Charles II* (London: Hodder & Stoughton, 1999)

Copeman, W. S. C. 'Dr. Jonathan Gooddard, FRS (1617–1675)', *Notes and Records of the Royal Society* 15 (1960), pp. 69–77

Cranston, M. *John Locke: A Biography*, revised edition (Oxford: Oxford University Press, 1985)

Cruickshanks, E. (ed.) *The Stuart Courts* (Stroud: Sutton Publishing, 2000)

Darley, G. 'Evelyn, Greenwich and the sick and wounded', paper delivered at the British Museum Evelyn Conference, October 2001 (in preparation)

Dickinson, H. W. *Sir Samuel Morland, Diplomat and Inventor, 1625–1695* (Cambridge: Cambridge University Press, 1970)

Downes, K. *Hawksmoor* (London: Thames & Hudson, 1969)

Downes, K. 'Wren and Whitehall in 1664', *Burlington Magazine* 113 (1971), 89–92

Downes, K. *Christopher Wren* (London: Allen Lane, 1971)

Downes, K. *Vanbrugh* (London: Zwemmer, 1977)

Downes, K. 'Sir Christopher Wren, Edward Woodroffe, J. H. Mansart and Architectural History', *Architectural History* 37 (1994), 37–67

Drake, E. T. *Restless Genius: Robert Hooke and his Earthly Thoughts* (Oxford: Oxford University Press, 1996)

Du Prey, P. de la R. *Hawksmoor's London Churches: Architecture and Theology* (Chicago: Chicago University Press, 2000)

'Espinasse, M. M. *Robert Hooke* (London: Heinemann, 1956)

Feingold, M. 'Astronomy and strife: John Flamsteed and the Royal Society', in F. Willmoth (ed.), *Flamsteed's Stars: New Perspectives on the Life and Work of the First Astronomer Royal (1646–1719)* (Woodbridge: Boydell Press, 1997), pp. 31–48

Feingold, M. 'Of records and grandeur: the archive of the Royal Society', in M. Hunter (ed.), *Archives of the Scientific Revolution: The Formation and Exchange of Ideas in Seventeenth-Century Europe* (Woodbridge: Boydell Press, 1998), pp. 171–84

Field, J. V. and F. A. J. L. James, *Renaissance and Revolution: Humanists, Scholars, Craftsmen and Natural Philosophers in Early Modern Europe* (Cambridge: Cambridge University Press, 1993)

Fleming, J., H. Honour and N. Pevsner (eds), *The Penguin Dictionary of*

Architecture and Landscape Architecture, fifth edition (London: Penguin Press, 1999)

Frank, Jr, R. G. 'John Aubrey FRS, John Lydall, and science at Commonwealth Oxford', *Notes and Records of the Royal Society* 27 (1972–3), 193–217

Frank, Jr, R. G. 'The physician as virtuoso in seventeenth-century England', in B. Shapiro and R. G. Frank, Jr (eds), *English Scientific Virtuosi in the 16th and 17th Centuries* (Los Angeles: William Andrews Clark Memorial Library, 1979)

Frank, Jr, R. G. *Harvey and the Oxford Physiologists: A Study of Scientific Ideas* (Berkeley: University of California Press, 1980)

Frank, Jr, R. G. 'Thomas Willis and his circle: brain and mind in seventeenth-century medicine', in G. S. Rousseau (ed.), *The Languages of Psyche: Mind and Body in Enlightenment Thought* (Berkeley: University of California Press, 1990), pp. 107–46

Frank, Jr, R. G. 'Viewing the body: reframing man and disease in Commonwealth and Restoration England', in W. G. Marshall (ed.), *The Restoration Mind* (London: Associated University Presses, 1997), pp. 65–110

Fraser, A. *King Charles II: His Life and Times* (London: Weidenfeld & Nicolson, 1979 and 1993)

Friedman, A. T. 'John Evelyn and English Architecture', in T. O'Malley and J. Wolschke-Bulmahn, *John Evelyn's 'Elysium Britannicum' and European Gardening* (Dumbarton Oaks Publications, 1998), pp. 159–60

Friedman, T. ' "Behold the proud stupendous pile": 18th century reflections on St. Paul's Cathedral', in J. Bold and E. Chaney (eds), *English Architecture Public and Private* (London: Hambledon Press, 1993), pp. 134–46

Geraghty, A. 'New light on the Wren city churches: the evidence of the All Souls and Bute drawings' (University of Cambridge: PhD dissertation, 1999)

Geraghty, A. 'Introducing Thomas Laine, draughtsman to Sir Christopher Wren', *Architectural History* 42 (1999), 240–5

Geraghty, A. 'Nicholas Hawksmoor and the Wren City church steeples', *Georgian Group Journal* 10 (2000), 1–14

Gingerich, O. *The Great Copernicus Chase and Other Adventures in Astronomical History* (Cambridge: Cambridge University Press, 1992)

Gouk, P. *Music Science and Natural Magic in Seventeenth-Century England* (New Haven and London: Yale University Press, 1999)

Greengrass, M. 'Archive refractions: Hartlib's papers and the workings of an intelligence', in M. Hunter (ed.), *Archives of the Scientific Revolution: The Formation and Exchange of Ideas in Seventeenth-Century Europe* (Woodbridge: Boydell Press, 1998), pp. 35–47

Greengrass, M., M. Leslie and T. Raylor (eds) *Samuel Hartlib and Universal*

Reformation: Studies in Intellectual Communication (Cambridge: Cambridge University Press, 1994)

Hambly, E. C. 'Robert Hooke, the City's Leonardo', *City University* 2 (1987), 5–10

Hardacre, P. H. *The Royalists during the Puritan Revolution* (The Hague: Martinus Nijhoff, 1956)

Harris, E. *British Architectural Books and Writers, 1556–1785* (Cambridge: Cambridge University Press, 1990)

Harris, F. 'Ireland as a laboratory: the archive of Sir William Petty', in M. Hunter (ed.), *Archives of the Scientific Revolution: The Formation and Exchange of Ideas in Seventeenth-Century Europe* (Woodbridge: Boydell Press, 1996)

Harris, F. 'The letterbooks of Mary Evelyn', *English Manuscript Studies* (1998), 202–15

Harris, F. 'Living in the neighbourhood of science: Mary Evelyn, Margaret Cavendish and the Greshamites', in L. Hunter and S. Hutton (eds), *Women, Science and Medicine 1500–1700* (Stroud: Sutton Publishing, 1997), pp. 198–217

Hart, V. *St Paul's Cathedral: Sir Christopher Wren* (London: Phaidon, 1995)

Hart, V. *Nicholas Hawksmoor: Architecture and Ornament* (London: Yale University Press, in press)

Hart, V. with P. Hicks (eds), *Paper Palaces: The Rise of the Renaissance Architectural Treatise* (London: Yale University Press, 1998)

Hazelhurst, F. H. *Gardens of Illusion: The Genius of André Le Nostre* (Nashville: University of Tennessee Press, 1980)

Heilbron, J. L. *The Sun in the Church: Cathedrals as Solar Observatories* (Cambridge, Mass.: Harvard University Press, 1999)

Heyman, J. 'Hooke's cubico-parabolical conoid', *Notes and Records of the Royal Society* 52 (1998), 39–50

Heyman, J. *The Science of Structural Engineering* (London: Imperial College Press, 1999)

Hibbert, C. *The Marlboroughs: John and Sarah Churchill 1650–1744* (London: Viking, 2001)

Hinks, A. R. 'Christopher Wren the Astronomer', in *Sir Christopher Wren AD 1632–1723. Bicentenary Memorial Volume published under the auspices of the Royal Institute of British Architects* (London: Hodder & Stoughton, 1923), pp. 239–54

Hoak, D. and M. Feingold (eds), *The World of William and Mary* (Stanford: Stanford University Press, 1996)

Holmes, G. *The Making of a Great Power: Late Stuart and Early Georgian Britain 1660–1722* (London: Longman, 1993)

Howse, D. *Greenwich Time and Longitude*, second edition (London: Philip Wilson, 1997)

Hull, D. 'Robert Hooke: A fractographic study of Kettering-stone', *Notes and Records of the Royal Society* 51 (1997), 45–55

Hunt, J. D. *Greater Perfections* (London: Thames & Hudson, 2000)

Hunt, J. D. and E. de Jong (eds), *The Anglo-Dutch Garden in the Age of William and Mary* (London: Taylor & Francis, 1988) (special double issue of the *Journal of Garden History*)

Hunt, J. D. and P. Willis (eds) *The Genius of the Place: English Landscape Garden, 1620–1820* (New York: Harper & Row, 1975)

Hunter, L. 'Sisters of the Royal Society: the circle of Katherine Jones, Lady Ranelagh', in L. Hunter and S. Hutton (eds), *Women, Science and Medicine 1500–1700* (Stroud: Sutton Publishing, 1997), pp. 178–97

Hunter, L. and S. Hutton (eds), *Women, Science and Medicine 1500–1700* (Stroud: Sutton Publishing, 1997)

Hunter, M. *John Aubrey and the Realm of Learning* (London: Duckworth, 1975)

Hunter, M. *Science and Society in Restoration England* (Cambridge: Cambridge University Press, 1981)

Hunter, M. 'Early problems in professionalizing scientific research: Nehemiah Grew (1641–1712) and the Royal Society. With an unpublished letter to Henry Oldenburg', *Notes and Records of the Royal Society* 36 (1982), 189–209

Hunter, M. 'A "College" for the Royal Society: the abortive plan of 1667–1668', *Notes and Records of the Royal Society* 38 (1984), 159–86

Hunter, M. *Establishing the New Science: the Experience of the Early Royal Society* (Woodbridge: Boydell Press, 1989)

Hunter, M. *The Royal Society and its Fellows 1660–1700: The Morphology of an Early Scientific Institution*, revised edition (Oxford: Oxford University Press, 1994)

Hunter, M. *Science and the Shape of Orthodoxy: Intellectual Change in Late Seventeenth-Century Britain* (Woodbridge: Boydell Press, 1995)

Hunter, M. (ed.) *Archives of the Scientific Revolution: The Formation and Exchange of Ideas in Seventeenth-Century Europe* (Woodbridge: Boydell Press, 1998)

Hunter, M. 'The work-diaries of Robert Boyle: a newly discovered source and its internet publication', *Notes and Records of the Royal Society* 55 (2001), 373–90

Hunter, M. and S. Schaffer (eds) *Robert Hooke: New Studies* (Woodbridge: Boydell Press, 1989)

Hussey, C. 'The Universities of Oxford and Cambridge: The Sheldonian Theatre Oxford – II', *Country Life* 24 May 1930, 750–5

Hutchison, H. F. *Sir Christopher Wren: A Biography* (London: Gollancz, 1976)

Hutton, R. *Charles the Second King of England, Scotland, and Ireland* (Oxford: Clarendon Press, 1989)

Iliffe, R. ' "In the warehouse": privacy, property and priority in the early Royal Society', *History of Science* 30 (1992), 29–68

Iliffe, R. ' "Material doubts": Robert Hooke, artisanal culture and the exchange of information in 1670s London', *British Journal for the History of Science* 28 (1995), 285–318.

Iliffe, R. 'Mathematical characters: Flamsteed and Christ's Hospital Royal Mathematical School', in F. Willmoth (ed.), *Flamsteed's Stars: New Perspectives on the Life and Work of the First Astronomer Royal (1646–1719)* (Woodbridge: Boydell Press, 1997), pp. 115–44

Iliffe, R. 'Foreign bodies: travel, empire and the early Royal Society of London. Part 1. Englishmen on tour', *Canadian Journal of History* (1998)

Iliffe, R. 'Foreign bodies: travel, empire and the early Royal Society of London. Part II. The land of experimental knowledge', *Canadian Journal of History* (1999)

Impey O. and A. MacGregor (eds) *The Origin of Museums: The Cabinet of Curiosities in Sixteenth- and Seventeenth-Century Europe* (Oxford: Clarendon Press, 1985)

Jacob, M. C. *Living the Enlightenment: Freemasonry and Politics in Eighteenth-Century Europe* (Oxford: Oxford University Press, 1991)

Jardine, L. *Ingenious Pursuits: Building the Scientific Revolution* (London: Little, Brown, 1999)

Jardine, L. 'Monuments and microscopes: scientific thinking on a grand scale in the early Royal Society', *Notes and Records of the Royal Society* 55 (2001), 289–308

Jeffery, P. 'Where are they now? Wren drawings from the Bute Collection', *Society of Architectural Historians of Great Britain Newsletter* 50 (1993), 4–5

Jeffery, P. *The City Churches of Sir Christopher Wren* (London: Hambledon Press, 1996)

Jones, J. D. *The Royal Prisoner: Charles I at Carisbrooke* (Northumberland Press, 1965)

Keblusek, M. and J. Zijlmans, *Princely Display: The Court of Frederik Hendrik of Orange and Amalia van Solms* (Zwolle: Historical Museum, The Hague, 1997)

Kitson, F. *Prince Rupert: Admiral and General-at-Sea* (London: Constable, 1998)

Kuyper, W. *Dutch Classicist Architecture: A Survey of Dutch Architecture, Gardens, and Anglo-Dutch Architectural Relations from 1625 to 1700* (Delft: Delft University Press, 1980)

Lang, J. *Rebuilding St. Paul's* (Oxford: Oxford University Press, 1956)

Lawrence, C. and S. Shapin (eds) *Science Incarnate: Historical Embodiments of Natural Knowledge* (Chicago and London: University of Chicago Press, 1998)

Lehmberg, S. E. *Cathedrals under Siege: Cathedrals in English Society, 1600–1700* (Exeter: University of Exeter Press, 1996)

Liedtke, W. with M. C. Plomp and A. Rüger, *Vermeer and the Delft School* (New Haven and London: Yale University Press, 2001)

Little, B. *Sir Christopher Wren: A Historical Biography* (London: Robert Hale, 1975)

MacDougall, E. B. and F. H. Hazelhurst (eds) *The French Formal Garden* (Washington, DC: Dumbarton Oaks Trustees for Harvard University, 1974)

MacGregor, A. (ed.) *The Late King's Goods: Collections, Possessions and Patronage of Charles I in the Light of the Commonwealth Sale Inventories* (London and Oxford: Oxford University Press, 1989)

MacGregor, A. (ed.) *Sir Hans Sloane: Collector, Scientist, Antiquary, Founding Father of the British Museum* (London: British Museum Press, 1994)

McKellar, E. *The Birth of Modern London: The Development and Design of the City 1660–1720* (Manchester: Manchester University Press, 1999)

McKitterick, D. (ed.) *The Making of the Wren Library, Trinity College, Cambridge* (Cambridge: Cambridge University Press, 1995)

Maddison, R. E. W. 'Studies in the life of Robert Boyle FRS. Part VI', *Notes and Records of the Royal Society* 18 (1963), 104–24

Malcolm, J. P. *Londinium Redivivium*, 4 vols (London, 1802–7)

Maré, E. de *Wren's London* (London: Folio Society, 1975)

Marshall W. G. (ed.) *The Restoration Mind* (London: Associated University Presses, 1997)

Masson I. and A. J. Youngson, 'Sir William Petty FRS (1623–1687)', *Notes and Records of the Royal Society* (1960), 79–90

Middleton, W. E. K. 'A footnote to the history of the barometer: an unpublished note by Robert Hooke, FRS', *Notes and Records of the Royal Society* 20 (1965), 145–51

Millar, O. (ed.) 'The inventories and valuations of the King's goods, 1649–1651', *Walpole Society* 43 (1970–2)

Morrill, J. *Revolt in the Provinces: The People of England and the Tragedies of War 1630–1648*, second edition (London and New York: Longman, 1999)

Morrill, J. *Stuart Britain: A Very Short Introduction* (Oxford: Oxford University Press, 2000)

Mowl, T. and B. Earnshaw, *Architecture without Kings: The Rise of Puritan Classicism under Cromwell* (Manchester: Manchester University Press, 1995)

Nakajima, H. 'Robert Hooke's family and his youth: some new evidence from the will of the Rev. John Hooke', *Notes and Records of the Royal Society* 48 (1994), 11–16

Nichols, R. *Robert Hooke and the Royal Society* (Sussex: The Book Guild, 1999)

Nuttall, R. H. 'That curious curiosity: the scotoscope', *Notes and Records of the Royal Society* 42 (1988), 133–8

Ollard, R. *Man of War: Sir Robert Holmes and the Restoration Navy* (London: Phoenix Press, 2001) (first published Hodder & Stoughton, 1969)

O'Malley, T. and J. Wolschke-Bulmahn, *John Evelyn's 'Elysium Britannicum' and European Gardening* (Dumbarton Oaks Publications, 1998)

Oman, C. *The Winter Queen: Elizabeth of Bohemia* (London: Phoenix Press, 1938)

Parry, J. H. *The Age of Reconnaissance: Discovery, Exploration and Settlement 1450–1650* (London: Weidenfeld & Nicolson, 1963 [Phoenix Press edition, 2000])

Petrie, C. (ed.) *King Charles, Prince Rupert, and the Civil War from Original Letters* (London: Routledge & Kegan Paul, 1974)

Plowden, A. *The Stuart Princesses* (Stroud: Sutton Publishing, 1996)

Plowden, A. *Henrietta Maria: Charles I's Indomitable Queen* (Stroud: Sutton Publishing, 2001)

Porter, S. *The Great Fire of London* (Stroud: Sutton Publishing, 1996)

Powell, A. (ed.) *Brief Lives and Other Selected Writings by John Autrey* (London: The Cresset Press, 1949)

Principe, L. M. *The Aspiring Adept: Robert Boyle and his Alchemical Quest* (Princeton: Princeton University Press, 1998)

Purver, M. *The Royal Society: Concept and Creation* (London: Routledge & Kegan Paul, 1967)

Reddaway, T. F. *The Rebuilding of London after the Great Fire* (London: Jonathan Cape, 1940)

Ridgway, C. and R. Williams (eds) *Sir John Vanbrugh and Landscape Architecture in Baroque England 1690–1730* (Stroud: Sutton Publishing, 2000)

Robb, N. A. *William of Orange: A Personal Portrait* (London: Heinemann, 1962)

Roberts, J. 'Stephen Switzer and water gardens', in C. Ridgway and R. Williams (eds), *Sir John Vanbrugh and Landscape Architecture in Barogue England 1690–1730* (Stroud: Sutton Publishing, 2000)

Robinson, H. W. 'An unpublished letter of Dr. Seth Ward relating to the early meetings of the Oxford Philosophical Society', *Notes and Records of the Royal Society* 7 (1949), 69–70

Robinson, H. W. and W. Adams (eds) *The Diary of Robert Hooke MA MD FRS 1672–1680* (London: Taylor & Francis, 1968)

Ronan, C. A. and Sir H. Hartley, FRS, 'Sir Paul Neile, FRS (1613–1686)', *Notes and Records of the Royal Society* 15 (1960), 159–65

Rousseau, G. S. (ed.) *The Languages of Psyche: Mind and Body in Enlightenment Thought* (Berkeley: University of California Press, 1990)

Routh, E. M. G. *Tangier: England's Lost Atlantic Outpost* (London, 1912)

Rowen, H. H. *The Princes of Orange: The Stadholders in the Dutch Republic* (Cambridge: Cambridge University Press, 1988)

Sargeaunt, J. *Annals of Westminster School* (London: Methuen & Co., 1898)

Saumarez-Smith, C. 'Wren and Sheldon', *Oxford Art Journal* 6 (1983), 45–50

Schaffer, S. 'Regeneration: the body of natural philosophers in Restoration England', in C. Lawrence and S. Shapin (eds), *Science Incarnate: Historical Embodiments of Natural Knowledge* (Chicago and London: University of Chicago, 1998), pp. 83–120

Schama, S. *A History of Britain: The British Wars 1603–1776* (London: BBC Worldwide, 2001)

Schooling, Sir William 'Sir Christopher Wren Merchant Adventurer', in *Sir Christopher Wren AD 1632–1723. Bicentenary Memorial Volume published under the auspices of the Royal Institute of British Architects* (London: Hodder & Stoughton, 1923), pp. 255–64

Schwartz, G. and M. J. Bok, *Pieter Saenredam: The Painter and his Time* (The Hague: SDU Publishers, 1990)

Shapin, S. *A Social History of Truth: Civility and Science in Seventeenth-Century England* (Chicago: University of Chicago Press, 1994)

Shapin, S. and S. Schaffer, *Leviathan and the Air-Pump: Hobbes, Boyle, and the Experimental Life* (Princeton: Princeton University Press, 1985)

Shapiro, B. J. *John Wilkins, 1614–1672: An Intellectual Biography* (Berkeley and Los Angeles: University of California Press, 1969)

Sharpe, K. *The Personal Rule of Charles I* (New Haven: Yale University Press, 1992)

Shepard, A. and P. Withrington (eds) *Communities in Early Modern England* (Manchester: Manchester University Press, 2000)

Sobel, D. *Longitude: The True Story of a Lone Genius Who Solved the Greatest Scientific Problem of his Time* (London: Fourth Estate, 1995)

Soo, L. M. *Wren's 'Tracts' on Architecture and Other Writings* (Cambridge: Cambridge University Press, 1998)

Stevenson, C. *Medicine and Magnificence: British Hospital and Asylum Architecture, 1660–1815* (London: Yale University Press, 2000)

Stewart, J. D. 'A militant Stoic monument: the Wren–Cibber–Gibbons Charles I Mausoleum project: its authors, sources, meaning and influence', in W. G. Marshall (ed.), *The Restoration Mind* (London: Associated University Presses, 1997), pp. 21–64

Stewart, L. 'Other centres of calculation, or, where the Royal Society didn't count: commerce, coffee-houses and natural philosophy in early modern London', *British Journal of the History of Science* 32 (1999), 133–53

Stoesser, A. 'Robert Hooke and Holland: Dutch influence on Hooke's architecture' (Utrecht University: doctoral disseration, 1997)

Stoesser-Johnston, A. 'Robert Hooke and Holland: Dutch influence on his architecture', *Bulletin Ku\u0304ncklijk Nederlands Oudheidkundig Bond* 99 (2000), 121–37

Strauss, E. *Sir William Petty. Portrait of a Genius* (London: Bodley Head, 1954)

Strong, R. *The Artist and the Garden* (New Haven and London: Yale University Press, 2000)

Stroup, A. *A Company of Scientists: Botany, Patronage, and Community at the Seventeenth-Century Parisian Royal Academy of Sciences* (Berkeley: University of California Press, 1990)

Summerson, J. *The Sheldonian in its Time* (Oxford: Clarendon Press, 1964)

Summerson, J. (ed.) *Concerning Architecture: Essays on Architectural Writers and Writing Presented to Nikolaus Pevsner* (London: Allen Lane, 1968)

Thrower, N. J. W. (ed.) *The Three Voyages of Edmond Halley in the Paramore 1698–1701* (London: The Hakluyt Society, 1981)

Thrower, N. J. W. (ed.) *Standing on the Shoulders of Giants: A Longer View of Newton and Halley* (Berkeley: University of California Press, 1990)

Thurley, S. *Whitehall Palace: An Architectural History of the Royal Apartments, 1240–1690* (New Haven and London: Yale University Press, 1999)

Thurley, S. *The Whitehall Palace Plan of 1670* (London Topographical Society Publication no. 153, 1998)

Thurley, S. 'A country seat fit for a king: Charles II, Greenwich and Winchester', in E. Cruickshanks (ed.), *The Stuart Courts* (Stroud: Sutton Publishing, 2000), pp. 214–39

Tinniswood, A. *His Invention So Fertile: A Life of Christopher Wren* (London: Jonathan Cape, 2001)

Turnbull, G. H. 'Samuel Hartlib's influence on the early history of the Royal Society', *Notes and Records of the Royal Society* 10 (1953), 101–30

Turner, A. J. 'In the wake of the Act, but mainly before', in W. J. H.Andrewes, *The Quest for Longitude* (Cambridge, Mass.: Harvard University Press, 1996), pp. 116–27

Van Helden, A. 'Christopher Wren's De corpore Saturni', *Notes and Records of the Royal Society* 23 (1968), 213–29

Wall, C. *The Literary and Cultural Spaces of Restoration London* (Cambridge: Cambridge University Press, 1998)

Waller, R. *Robert Hooke: Posthumous Works* (London, 1705)

Ward, J. *The Lives of the Professors of Gresham College* (London, 1740)

Warren, E. P. 'Sir Christopher Wren's repair of the Divinity School and Duke Humphrey's Library, Oxford', *Sir Christopher Wren AD 1632–1723. Bicentenary Memorial Volume published under the auspices of the Royal Institute of British Architects* (London: Hodder & Stoughton, 1923), pp. 133–8

Waterhouse, P. et al. *Sir Christopher Wren AD 1632–1723. Bicentenary Memorial Volume published under the auspices of the Royal Institute of British Architects* (London: Hodder & Stoughton, 1923)

Wear, A. 'William Harvey and the "way of the anatomists"', *History of Science* 21 (1983), 223–49

Webster, C. 'The College of Physicians: "Solomon's House" in Commonwealth England', *Bulletin of the History of Medicine* 41 (1967), 393–412

Webster, C. 'New light on the Invisible College', *Transactions of the Royal Historical Society* 5th Series, 24 (1974), 19–42

Webster, C. *The Great Instauration: Science, Medicine and Reform 1626–1660* (London: Duckworth, 1975)

Weiser, B. 'Access and petitioning during the reign of Charles II', in E. Cruickshanks (ed.), *The Stuart Courts* (Stroud: Sutton Publishing, 2000), pp. 203–13

Westfall, R. *Never at Rest: A Biography of Isaac Newton* (Cambridge: Cambridge University Press, 1980)

Whinney, M. D. *St. Paul's Cathedral* (London: Lund, Humphries, 1947)

Whinney, M. D. 'Sir Christopher Wren's visit to Paris', *Gazette des Beaux-Arts* 51 (1958), 229–42

Whinney, M. D. *Wren* (London: Thames & Hudson, 1971)

Whiteside, D. T. 'Wren the mathematician', *Notes and Records of the Royal Society* 15 (1960), 107–11

Williams, R. 'Vanbrugh's India and his Mausolea for England', in C. Ridgway and R. Williams (eds), *Sir John Vanbrugh and Landscape Architecture in Baroque England 1690–1730* (Stroud: Sutton Publishing, 2000), pp. 114–30

Williamson, T. *Polite Landscapes: Gardens and Society in Eighteenth-Century England* (Baltimore: Johns Hopkins University Press, 1995)

Willmoth, F. *Sir Jonas Moore: Practical Mathematics and Restoration Science* (Woodbridge: Boydell Press, 1993)

Willmoth, F. (ed.) *Flamsteed's Stars: New Perspectives on the Life and Work of the First Astronomer Royal (1646–1719)* (Woodbridge: Boydell Press, 1997)

Woodbridge, K., *Princely Gardens: The Origins and Development of the French Formal Style* (New York: Rizzoli, 1986)

Yates, F. *The Rosicrucian Enlightenment* (London: Routledge & Kegan Paul, 1972)

Yeomans, D. 'Inigo Jones's roof structures', *Architectural History* 29 (1986), pp. 85–101

Yoder, J. G. *Unrolling Time: Christiaan Huygens and the Mathematization of Nature* (Cambridge: Cambridge University Press, 1984)

INDEX

Page numbers in *italic* indicate illustrations and captions

country, 432; on supervision of workmen, 465; memorial lines on CW, 473, 475; *Parallel*, 398, 465, 473; *Sculptura*, 351

Evelyn, John, Jnr, 240

Evelyn, Mary (John's daughter), 348

Fairfax, General Thomas, 3rd Baron, 40, 45, 64

Faithorne, William, 277

Farley, Wiltshire, 347

Fell, John: conducts High Anglican services, 118; made Dean of Christ Church, 127; and building of Sheldonian Theatre, 154, 215, 229; and completion of Tom Tower, Oxford, 314–15, 324

Fell, Revd Samuel, 116

Fen Drainage Company, 171

Fitch, John, 314

Fitzcharles, Charlotte Jemima Henrietta, 195

Fitzwilliam, William, 2nd Baron, 283

Flamsteed, John: and building of Greenwich Naval Hospital, 299; appointed Astronomer Royal, 308, 310; and determination of longitude, 308–10; and building of Royal Observatory, 310, 313, 315; calculates eclipses, 313; personality, 329, 441, *442*, 452, 457; praises CW's personal qualities, 329; disputes with Newton, 408–9, 439, 441, *448*, 451–4, 457–9; invokes slow progress on St Paul's, 408–9; withholds astronomical data, 408, 451, 453–4, 456, 459; CW recommends Hodgson to, 424; elected to Royal Society, 443, 445; antagonism towards Hooke, 444–6; friendship with CW, 444–6; and Halley, 446–51; on Council of Royal Society, 447; receives gift copy of Newton's *Principia*, 452; Newton forces publication of star catalogues, 454–6; expelled from Royal Society, 456; Royal Society supervises, 456–7

Fleet Ditch, London: improvement plan, 267

Flitcroft, Henry, 417

Fogg, Captain, 13

Fort, Alexander, 347

Foster, Samuel, 109

Fox, Charles (Sir Stephen's son), 344

Fox, Sir Stephen: on Commission for improving London streets, 237, 261; and

Hudson's Bay Company, 331; background and career, 343–8, *344*; CW's relations with, 343, 346–8, 353, 363; wealth, 346, 348, 370; backs building of Chelsea Royal Hospital, 353–60, *355*, 401; dropped from William of Orange's administration, 359; Hungerford borrows from, 362–3; acquires and manages Hungerford Market, 363–5; and Glorious Revolution, 378–9; Whitehall property, 379, *379*; and building of Greenwich Naval Hospital, 397–8; retirement, 432

France: Charles II's exile in, 6–7, 42; Clarendon's exile in, 103, 168, 295, 426; *see also* Paris

Frauds and Abuses at St. Paul's, 466–8

Fréart de Chambray, Roland: *Art of Painting*, 238; *A Parallel of the Ancient Architecture with the Modern*, 235, 240, 415

Frederick, Elector Palatine (and King of Bohemia), 10, 24, 56, 65, 388

Frederick Henry, Prince of Orange, 139

Frederick William, Elector of Brandenburg, 140

freemasonry, xvi, 468–70

Fulkes, Samuel, 366

Gale, Thomas, 444

Garter, Order of: CW's association with and devotion to, xvi, 209, 478–9; Charles I and, 7, 23–4, 37–40; Ashmole's history of, 10, 25, 31, 33, 36, 207–9, *208*; ceremonial and statutes, 12, 24–6, 31, 33, 38–40, 140–1; Charles II installed as Knight Companion, 12, 30–2, 40–2; treasures and records ransacked and destroyed by Parliamentarians, 13, 33, 36, 44; regalia, 25; CW's father's duties as Register, 31, 33, 36, 41–2, 48–50, 484; records, 31; Knights support Charles I in Civil War, 37–8; CW returns records to Charles II, 44–5, 165, 483; Seth Ward's Chancellorship, 211–12; and improvements to Windsor Castle, 335

George I, King of England, 168, 468, 470

George, Prince of Denmark (husband of Queen Anne), 397, 426, 454, *455*, 456

Gibbons, Grinling, 144–5, *144*, 397

Glisson, Dr Francis, 109

Glorious Revolution (1688), 372, 375–6

Hooke, Robert – *cont.*
331; on CW's outburst of anger, 349; on
glass bubbles, 351; watch-making, 352;
on Smith's description of Hagia Sophia,
366; and CW's financial investments,
368; works with Petty, 373–4; on
Glorious Revolution, 376–8; on
accession of William and Mary, 384;
and CW's dismay at roof collapse at
Hampton Court, 390; and building of
St Paul's, 409, 421–3; and St Paul's
dome, 417; death and funeral, 429,
432–4; and demolition of old St Paul's,
430; memorialised in New Repository
for Royal Society, 433, 436–7; Newton's
hostility to, 434, 438, 448–9; estate and
will, 437–8; Waller writes life of, 437;
portrait lost, 438; Flamsteed's hostility
to, 444–6; retrieves instruments from
Flamsteed, 444; on calculation of
planetary motion, 447, 449–50; and
telescope improvement, 461;
collaborative work with CW omitted
from *Parentalia*, 477–8; achievements
and reputation, 478; *Cometa*, 270, 274;
Micrographia, 97, *98*, 182, 276–8, *279*,
351, 423; *Posthumous Works*, 437–8, 461
Hopkins, William, 18–19
Hopkins, Mrs William, 19
Hoskins, Sir John, 22, 298, 330, 416
Howard, Henry (*later* 6th Duke of
Norfolk), 189–90, *190*, 239, 254
Hudson's Bay Company, 331, 362, 367–9,
407
Hungerford, Sir Edward, 362–4
Hungerford Market, 363–5
Hunt, Henry, 377, 436, 438, 443
Huygens, Christiaan: in father's poem, 80;
shown CW's microscopic drawings, 97;
astronomical observations, 133, 136–8,
141–2, 186; CW meets, 138–9, 141, 143,
166; portrait, *138*; background and
career, 139–40; in England, 140–3, 145,
166; attends Garter ceremony, 142–3;
and CW's lunar globe, 180–1; and laws
of motion, 192; operates Boyle's air-
pump, 202; studies cometary motion,
270; Ball corresponds with, 312; on
James, Duke of York, 350; *De Saturni
luna* (*On a moon of Saturn*), 135–6;
Horologium oscillatorium, 145
Huygens, Sir Constantijn, 79–80, *81*,
138–9, 142, 144–5, 388, 469

Huygens, Constantijn, Jnr, 80, 139, 424
Huygens, Lodewijck, 80, 143
Hyde, Anne *see* Anne, Queen of James II
Hyde, Laurence, 346

Invalides, Les (Paris), 353, 398, 400
Ireland: forfeited land in, 69–70; Petty in,
71–2, 171, 196, 373; William III
campaigns in, 391; *see also* Down survey
Isham, Sir Justinian, 113

Jackson, John, 154
Jackson, Robert, 365
James I, King, 24, 26, 342
James II, King (*earlier* Duke of York): and
beginning of Civil War, 2; portrait, *6*;
upbringing, 6; Matthew Wren Jnr serves
as secretary, 30, 72, 99, 167–8;
appointed Garter Knight, 38–9, 41; in
Paris during Commonwealth, 85;
marriage to and children by Anne
(Hyde), 103, *104*, 167; scientific interests,
114, 142, 174; attends Royal Society
meetings, 125, 349; deposed and exiled,
139, 376, 379, 383, 387; affair with
Denham's wife, 159; as Sir Jonas
Moore's patron, 172; return from exile,
204; saves Whitehall Banqueting House
in Great Fire, 248; concern for
Londoners after Great Fire, 255; on
attractions of Winchester, 332; and
death and succession to Charles II, 338,
340–1, 349–50, 352, 474; Catholicism,
342–3, 371; Coronation, 342, 386; CW
supports, 348–9, 369; background and
character, 349; grants letters patent to
Fox and CW on Hungerford Market,
363–4; investments in joint-stock
companies, 367–8; involvement in slave
trade, 367; CW works under, 371–2, 375;
dispute with Compton, 371–2, *372*, 382;
stays with aunt Mary in Holland, 387
James Edward Stuart, Prince ('the Old
Pretender'), 376, *377*
James, John, 440, 468
Jennings, Richard, 466, 468
Jerman, Edward, 254, 257, 295
John Maurice, Prince of Nassau, 140–1
Jones, Inigo: death, 155; Whitehall
Banqueting House, *156*, 251, 328; and
John Webb's plans for Whitehall Palace,
157–8; serves Thomas Howard (2nd Earl
of Arundel), 190; refurbishes old

St Paul's, 219, 224, 226; St Paul's portico, *220*, 294; designs Queen's House, Greenwich, 394–6, *395*

Jones, Richard, 370

Justel, Henri, 245–7

Juxon, William, Archbishop of Canterbury (*earlier* Bishop of London): at Charles I's execution, 23–4, 64; power and authority, 30, 222; at Charles II's installation ceremony as Garter Knight, 32; Archbishopric, 222

Karl Ludwig (*earlier* Charles Louis), Elector Palatine: lodges at Dean's House, Windsor, 10–11, 29, 50; letter from CW on seed-sowing machine, 52; Wilkins serves as chaplain to, 64–7, *65*, 82; as possible successor to English throne, 66, 83; travels to continent, 77, 79, 82, 85; portrait, *78*; CW addresses letter to, 83–4, 89; and beginnings of Royal Society, 111; witnesses Charles I's execution, 139

Kempster, Christopher, 334

Kensington Palace, 390, 392

Keroualle, Louise de (Duchess of Portsmouth and Aubigny), 308

Keyser, Hendrick de, 161

Keyser, Willem de, 161

Kincardine, Alexander Bruce, 2nd Earl of, 115

King, Edmund, 338

Knoyle Magna, Wiltshire, 7, 9, 14

La Hoge, Battle of (1692), 393

Langbaine, Gerard, 113

Laud, William, Archbishop of Canterbury: power and authority, 30, 213; Canterbury Quad at St John's, 154; on Oxford graduation ceremonies, 215

Lauderdale, John Maitland, 1st Duke of, 290

Lawrence, Sir John, 257, 268

Lawson, Sir John, 169

Legge, George (*later* 1st Baron Dartmouth), 174

Legge, William, 17

Lely, Sir Peter, 22, 190, 204

Le Nôtre, André, 337

Lichfield, Charlotte, Countess of, 332

Lodowick, Francis, 330

London: Royal Commission to improve streets (1662), 237–8, 261–2; Rebuilding Commission following Great Fire, 254–61, 281, 285, 373; Evelyn's plan for, *260*; Wren's rebuilding plans for, 262–8, *264–5*; City churches rebuilt, 278, 295–302, 348, 372, 382; smog from coal-burning, 389, 415; *see also* Great Fire of London

London churches: St Lawrence Jewry, 175, 300–1, *301*; St Mary-le-Bow, 299–301, *299*; St Stephen Walbrook, 302, *303*, 304–5

longitude: CW attempts determination of, 248–9, 458–61; Royal Commission on (1674), 307–9

Louis XIV, King of France: and Charles II's exile, 3; building projects, 86, 239, 341, 353, 398; CW sees in Paris, 246; Bernini bust of, 247

Louvre, Paris, 239, 241–2, 244

Lower, Dr Richard, 89, 122, 125–7

Lowther, Sir John (1st Viscount Lonsdale), 391

lunar globe: CW designs for Charles II, 180–3, *181*, 186

Lydall, John, 91

Mansard, François, 240

Marlborough, John Churchill, 1st Duke of, 468

Marlborough, Sarah, Duchess of, 375

Marshall, Edward, 223

Marvell, Andrew, 3

Mary II, Queen (*earlier* Princess): exile in Netherlands, 1–2; upbringing, 5; marriage, 30, 346, 388; in The Hague, 86; parentage, 103; accession, 139, 379, 383, 387–9, 474; in line of succession, 276; overseas investments, 367; Compton teaches, 371; Coronation, 383–7, *384*; domestic life and homes, 389–93; relations with CW, 389–90, 392; death and funeral, 392–3, 397; approves continuation of building at Greenwich, 393–7, *395*; charitable works, 393, 397

Mary of Modena, Queen of James II, 352, 369, 376

Mary (Stuart), Princess Royal (Charles I's daughter), 53, 139, 195, 205, 207, 387

Maurice, Prince, 43, 64

May, Hugh: works on Whitehall Palace, 162; on Rebuilding Commission following Great Fire, 254, 257–8, 295; as candidate for Surveyor of King's Works,

May, Hugh – *cont.*
280; palace designs for Charles II, 335; builds Chiswick house for Stephen Fox, 347; and monument to Charles I, 480
Merrett, Dr Christopher, 109; *Art of Glass*, 351
Mersenne, Marin, 111
mezzotint, 351–2, *352*
microscopy, 97–100
Mildmay, Sir Henry, 77
Millington, Dr Thomas, 122, 126–7
Mills, Peter: on post-Great Fire Rebuilding Commission, 254, 257; plans for London rebuilding, 268, 297; death, 280
Moivre, Abraham de, 447
Molyneux, William, 446–7
Monck, General George *see* Albemarle, 1st Duke of
Monconys, Balthasar de, 97, 181, 274, 328–9
Monmouth, James Scott, Duke of, 341, 346
Montagu, Edward *see* Sandwich, 1st Earl of
Montagu House, Bloomsbury, 314
Montagu, Ralph, 313
Monument (to Great Fire): CW co-designs with Hooke, xi–xii, xiv, 316–21; as scientific instrument, xii, *xiii*, 275, 318–21, *319*; Hooke visits with niece, 251
Moore, Sir Jonas: designs Tangier defences, 171–3, *173*; assesses losses after Great Fire, 251; Survey of Thames, 252–3, 254; on Commission to determine longitude, 308; and founding of Greenwich Royal Observatory, 310–11; and Flamsteed's calculation of eclipses, 313; and reform of Royal Society, 330; as patron of Flamsteed, 441, *442*; and Chelsea College premises, 443; elected to Royal Society, 443; and Towneley's smoking chimney, 444; *System of Mathematics*, 313
Moray, Sir Robert: negotiates peace at end of Civil War, 47–8; status, 67; scientific experimentation in Holland, 115; at Whitehall Palace, 132; meets Huygens, 141, 166; and Great Fire, 148; contributes to Royal Society building, 154; in Charles II's court, 164, 167; informs Charles II of founding of Royal Society, 175; elected President of Royal Society, 176, 350; requests lunar globe from CW for Charles II, 176, 179, 182; promotes

Royal Society, 183; and accommodation for Royal Society, 187; and astronomical projects for Royal Society, 269–70, 272, 274; and glass bubbles, 350–1; freemasonry, 469
Mylne, Robert, 417

Naseby, Battle of (1645), 40
Nassau-Zuijlenstein, Frederik van, 195, 388
Nassau-Zuijlenstein, Mary van (*née* Killigrew), 195, 388
Needham, Walter, 122
Neile, Sir Paul: scientific interests and activities, 129–33, 136–7, 351; as CW's patron, 133–5, 137, 145, 167; meets Huygens, 141–2, 166, 350; and CW's design for Royal Society building, 154; in Charles II's court, 164, 166; and early meetings of Royal Society, 175; requests globe from CW for Charles II, 176; promotes Royal Society, 183; long telescopes, 186; and accommodation for Royal Society, 187; and Great Fire, 248; astronomical interests and researches, 311
Neile, William, 61, 67, 115, 124, 132
Netherlands: royal exiles in, 1–3, 42; Elector Charles Louis visits, 77, 79; CW visits with Wilkins, 86; scientific experimentation in, 115
New Philosophical Club, 330
Newcastle, Margaret Cavendish, Duchess of, 202
Newmarket, 332–3
Newport, Treaty of (1648), 18
Newton, Sir Isaac: and laws of motion, 192, 447–50; contributes to Wren library, Cambridge, 321; disputes with Flamsteed, 408–9, 438, 441, *442*, *448*, 451–4, 457–8; hostility with Hooke, 434, 438, 448–50; and housing of Royal Society, 434; Presidency of Royal Society, 434, 439–40, 454; portrait, *439*; Halley assists, 451; forces Flamsteed to publish star catalogues, 454–5; expels Flamsteed from Royal Society, 456; and supervision of Royal Observatory, 456; CW avoids confrontation with, 457; and determination of longitude, 458–60; *Principia*, 448–51, *452*
Nicholas, Sir Edward, 41, 171, 251
Nicholas, Matthew, Dean of St Paul's, 171
Norfolk, 6th Duke of *see* Howard, Henry

North, Sir Dudley, 375, 412, 418
North, Sir John, 322
North, Roger, 375
Nottingham, Daniel Finch, 2nd Earl of, 390

Oglander, George, 18
Oglander, Sir John, 15, 17–20
Oldenburg, Henry: on injection for therapeutic purposes, 125; on Wilkins's appointment as president of Royal Society, 175; on CW's lunar globe, 180, 182; and accommodation for Royal Society, 187–9; and Huygens work on laws of motion, 192; on Boyle, 201; recommends Hooke as Royal Society's Curator of Experiments, 202; on CW's plans for Sheldonian Theatre, 215; corresponds with scientists in Paris, 244–5; on CW's return from Paris, 247; as official Secretary of Royal Society, 268; on CW-Hooke partnership, 269; and CW's work with Hooke on comets, 274; death, 329; on CW's structural demonstrations, 422; Flamsteed and, 442
Oliver, John, 297–8, 306
Ormonde, James Butler, 1st Duke of, 290, 346
Oughtred, William, 59; *Key to Arithmetic*, 60–3
Owen, Colonel, 43
Oxford: in Civil War, 14, 40–1, 46–7, 154; physicians in, 55–6; scientific and medical studies at, 56–62, 72, 88–9, 121, 147, 196–7; under Commonwealth supervision, 63–4; 'club' and beginnings of Royal Society, 109–14; town plan, *121*; CW appointed Savilian Professor of Astronomy, 166–7; CW resigns Savilian Professorship, 283, 310; as Charles II's alternative government centre, 335; *see also* All Souls College; Brasenose College; Christ Church; Sheldonian Theatre; Wadham College
Oxford Philosophical Society, 100

Palmer, Sir James, 37
Parentalia (Wren family papers): on Garter rituals, 25; on Matthew Wren in Oxford, 71; and CW's travel abroad, 73, 76; on double-writing machine, 96; on Susan Holder, 104; and CW's declining

design to defences at Tangier, 170; and Wallis's calculations for CW's Sheldonian Theatre, 216–18, *218*; CW's supposed courtship letter to Faith in, 282; on motto 'Resurgam' for St Paul's, 428; on demolition of old St Paul's using explosives, 430; and CW's attempt to determine longitude, 460; on CW's finances, 462; assembled and published, 476–8; as source, 477–9, 483; on CW's design for Charles I monument, 480–2
Paris: CW visits, 52, 86, 213, 226, 235, 239–47, 263, 348, 400; influence on London rebuilding, 263, *264*, 267; *see also* Invalides, Les; Louvre
Pascal, Blaise, 245
Pell, John, 175
Pembroke College, Cambridge: CW designs chapel for, 212–14, *214*, 228, 257
Pepys, Samuel: at Charles II's restoration, 43; attends Royal Society meetings, 125, 202; attends Charles II's Coronation, 142; on Gibbons's carvings, 145; appointed to naval office by Montagu, 159, 205; on Scarburgh's travelling to Charles II in Netherlands, 166; frames engraving of Tangier Mole, 172, *173*; at destruction of Tangier Mole, 174; and negotiations for Charles II's return to England, 195; letter from Evelyn on declining circumstances, 237; and Henrietta Maria's return to France, 241; evacuates home in Great Fire, 248; praises Hooke's *Micrographia*, 276; at musical evening, 284; and treatment of wounded servicemen, 355; and building of Greenwich Naval Hospital, 397–8; on perspective, 404–5, *406*, 407
perspective (artistic), 404–5, *406*, 407
Peterhouse College, Cambridge, 29, 213
Petit, Pierre, 244
Petty, Sir William: as CW's mentor, 67, 70–2, 85, 131; academic and official career, 68–70, 72, 171, 373–4; portrait, *68*; in Ireland, 71–2, 171, 196, 373; scientific and technological projects, 89–96, 113, 196; helps Matthew Wren at Oxford, 101; and beginnings of Royal Society, 109–11; CW assists, 115, 464; appointed Tomlins Reader in anatomy at Oxford, 117; revives apparent corpse, 117; and CW's experiments on live dogs, 123–5; experiments in blood transfusion,

434, 439–40, 454; relations with Flamsteed and Royal Observatory, 442–4, 456; Flamsteed expelled from, 456; and attempts to determine longitude at sea, 460–1; and freemasonry, 469; holds manuscript fair copy of *Parentalia*, 477; *Philosophical Transactions*, 274

Rueil (France), 336–7

Rupert, Prince, Count Palatine of the Rhine: Civil War actions, 13, 40, 64; appointed Knight of Garter, 38–9, 41; portrait, *38*; banished, 40–1; and Charles's Restoration, 42–3; scientific interests, 114–15, 174, 350; attends Royal Society meetings, 203, 350–1; returns to England, 204; Ashmole on, 207; status, 350; and glass bubbles, 351; and mezzotint technique, 351, *352*; overseas investments, 367; death, 368

Ryswick, Peace of (1697), 411

Ryves (Reeves), Bruno, 44, 165

Saenredam, Pieter, 304

St Albans, Henry Jermyn, 1st Earl of, 159–60, 241, *243*, 247

St Paul's Cathedral (old): proposed renovations, 219–21, *220*, 223–9, 232, 247, 258–9, 261, 286; damaged in Great Fire, 232, 250; CW surveys and reports on, 285–7; dismantled, 290–3, 430–1; spire, 410, 413

St Paul's Cathedral (new): as CW's monument, ix, 473–4, 483; illustrated, *x*, *412–13*, *425*; CW reconstructs, 278, 329; CW's plans for, 287, 289–90, 313; costs and financing, 288–9, 293, 383; royal warrant for complete rebuilding, 289, 410; CW's Warrant Design for, 293; Commission for Rebuilding, 304, 467; structural features, 313–14, 411–13, 418–20, 422; crypt (vaults), 318–19; building progress and delays, 348, 375, 391, 407–10, 412; new legislation for rebuilding (1685–7), 382; building stone supplies, 408; Hooke's involvement in building of, 409, 421–3; dome, 410–11, 413–14, 417–24, 438, 466, *467*; as scientific instrument, 424, *425*; completed, 428; as permanent monument, 428; CW's payments for, 462, 467; charges of corruption and protectionism at, 466–8; John James

appointed site manager at, 468; CW buried in, 473

St Pierre, Le Sieur de, 308

Salisbury Cathedral: CW reports on fabric for Ward, 209–11, *211*

Sancroft, William, Archbishop of Canterbury: commissions CW to design chapel for Emmanuel College, Cambridge, 229, 287; supervises rebuilding of St Paul's, 232; and rebuilding of St Paul's, 285–8, *288*; portrait, *288*; visits site of Chelsea Royal Hospital, 357, 360; deposition as Archbishop and death, 387

Sandwich, Edward Montagu, 1st Earl of: appoints Pepys to naval office, 159, 205; and fortifications at Tangier, 169–70, *169*; as patron of Sir Jonas Moore, 172; and determination of longitude, 461

Saturn (planet), 133–7, 186

Sayer, Anthony, 470

Scarburgh, Dr (Sir) Charles: medical practices and research, 54, 57, 127, 128; CW studies with, 57–60, 63, 122, 464; status, 67; as CW's mentor and patron, 85, 115, 133; Susan Holder converses with, 104–5; appointed royal physician to Charles II, 166–7; and early meetings of Royal Society, 175; astronomical observations, 186; position at Royal College of Physicians, 188; succeeds Harvey as Lumleian Lecturer at Royal College of Physicians, 323; attends dying Charles II, 339

seed-sowing machine, 52, 89–91, *91*

Serlio, Sebastiano, 217, *218*, 415

Shannon, Elizabeth, Viscountess (*née* Killigrew; Francis's wife), 194–5

Shannon, Francis Boyle, 1st Viscount (Robert Boyle's brother), 194–5

Sharp, Abraham, 457

Sharrock, Thomas, 199

Sheldon, Gilbert, Archbishop of Canterbury (*earlier* Bishop of London): and proposed peace settlement for Charles I, 48; on Commission of Parliamentary Visitors at Oxford, 63; supports Willis's appointment to professorship, 127; officiates at Charles II's Coronation, 141–2, 221; Huygens visits, 145; CW designs Oxford building for, 154, 191, 215–16, 219, 222, 299; background and career, 215, 221–2, *222*;

Willis, Dr Thomas – *cont.*
127; on circulation of blood, 126–7;
appointed Professor of Natural
Philosophy at Oxford, 127; medical
reputation, 127; helps Hooke, 194;
anatomical research, 199; *Cerebri
anatome* (*Anatomy of the Brain*), 126–7,
146; *De fermentatione*, 121
Willoughby, Francis, 125
Winchester: invites Chales II and court to
race meeting, 332; Palace planned and
designed, 333–7; Palace building
abandoned, 337–8, 348; regulated by
new charters, 343; Queen Anne
considers finishing, 455
Windsor: Wren family at, 7–11, 29; Karl
Ludwig stays at, 10–11, 29, 50; view of,
11; Castle requisitioned and desecrated
by Parliamentarians, 13, 36; Castle,
34–5; CW draws Castle for Hollar,
146, *148*; Charles II improves Castle,
335
Wiseman, Sir Robert, 305
Witte, Emmanuel de, 304
Wood, Anthony à, 86, 201
Wood, Robert, 62, 121
Woodroffe, Edward: and rebuilding of
City churches, 296–7, 302, 305; death,
298; collaborates with CW, 306; plan for
Monument to Great Fire, 316
Wren, Anna (CW's sister), 9, 52
Wren, Catharine (CW's sister), 9, 52
WREN, SIR CHRISTOPHER: co-designs
Monument to Great Fire, xi–xii, xiv,
315–21; superstitions, xv–xvi; devotion
to Garter order, xvi, 209, 478; birth, 9;
childhood at Windsor, 9–10, 12; attends
Wadham College, 11, 87, 109, 145;
juvenile scientific inventions and
drawings, 11–12, 52, 59, 89; friendship
and collaboration with Hooke, 21–2,
117–18, 203, 257, 268–70, *271*, 273–4,
276–9, 284, 297–8, 305–6, 343, 423, 431,
478; returns Garter records to Charles
II, 44–5, 165, 483; schooling, 50, 53;
suffers poverty in youth, 50–3;
practicality, 52; visit to Paris, 52, 213,
226, 235, 239–47, 400; medical interests
and experimentation, 57, 63, 122–8; frail
health, 58; mathematical gifts, 58–9,
62–3; studies with Scarburgh, 58–60;
constructs sundials, 60, 70; mastery of
Latin, 60; All Souls fellowship, 63, 70–1;

supposed travel abroad with Wilkins
under Commonwealth, 72–4, 76, 79,
81–2, 85–7, 145; applies to Elector
Palatine for post, 83–4; assists Petty
with technological projects and
inventions, 89–96, 464; microscopic
drawings, 97–8, *98*, 100, 182, 185–6, 276,
278; inventions and practical designs,
104, 106–9; and London-Oxford groups
in origins of Royal Society, 111–12; and
Oxford philosophical club, 115;
anatomical drawings, 126–7; Charles II
employs for building projects, 128,
150–1; unsuccessful candidature for
Gresham chair of geometry, 128–30;
appointed Professor of Astronomy at
Gresham, 130–1; financial position and
earnings, 131, 173, 458, 462–4;
astronomical observations and interests,
132–7, 310–13; Sir Paul Neile supports,
133; relations with Christiaan Huygens,
137–9, 141, 143–5, 166; draws Windsor
Castle for Hollar, 146, *148*; and building
projects at Wadham, 151–4; works on
Whitehall Palace designs, 162–3; as
Surveyor of the King's Works, 163, 238,
280, 295, 315, 329, 331; excursion with
Neile and Moray, 164–5; favoured by
Charles II after Restoration, 164–7;
succeeds Ward as Savilian Professor of
Astronomy at Oxford, 166–7; declines
commission for fortification of Tangier,
170, 172–3, 220; and founding of Royal
Society, 174; designs scientific device for
Charles II, 176–80, 193; makes lunar
globe for Charles II, 180–3; portrait, *181*;
writes draft of Royal Society charter,
184; and accommodation for Royal
Society, 187–9, 191; prominence in Royal
Society, 193, 351; assists Boyle, 201;
connection with Garter Order, 209;
report on Salisbury Cathedral for Ward,
209–10; designs chapel for Pembroke
College, Cambridge, 212–14, *214*, 228;
designs Sheldonian Theatre, Oxford,
215–16, 218, 248; concern for acoustic
qualities of buildings, 218–19; proposed
restoration of old St Paul's, 219–20, 223,
225–8, 232; attempts determination of
longitude, 248, *249*, 458–61; on
Rebuilding Commission following Great
Fire, 254, 256–9, 285, 294; on Royal
Commission for improving London

streets, 262; master-plan for London rebuilding, 263–8, *264–5*; draughtsmanship, 269; on cometary motion, 270, *271*, 272–4; weather-gauge design, 274–6, 329; first marriage (to Faith) and children, 280–3; knighthood, 283; resigns Savilian Professorship, 283, 310; second marriage (to Jane), children and widowerhood, 283–4, 331, 478; love of music, 284; plans for and supervision of new St Paul's Cathedral, 287, 289–90, 314, 407–12, 418–23; supervises demolition of old St Paul's, 290–3; and rebuilding of City churches, 296–7, 299–301, 304–5, 372, 382; organisation and office management, 298, 304, 328; collaborators on buildings, 306; designs Royal Observatory, 309, 314, 443; designs Wren Library, Trinity College, Cambridge, 321–6, *326*; on laying foundations, 324–6, *327*; appearance and manner, 328–9, 349; as Vice-President of Royal Society, 330; designs and plans for Charles II, 331–5; Presidency of Royal Society, 331, 354–5, 444; relations with son Christopher, 331, 429–32, 478; weakening relations with Hooke, 331; designs (uncompleted) Winchester Palace, 333–8; royalist/Tory sentiments, 340, 342, 348, 369, 468, 479; organises James II's Coronation, 342, 386; as MP for Plympton, 343, 379; relations with Stephen Fox, 343, 346–8, 353, 363; religious practices, 349; develops mezzotint technique, 351; re-appointed Surveyor of King's Works under James II, 352, 371; negotiates and designs Royal Military Hospital, Chelsea, 353–4, 356–60, 362; part-ownership of Hungerford Market, 363–5; property investments, 365; foreign influences on, 366; financial investments and business ventures, 368–70, 458; avoids political factionalism, 371; relations with Petty, 373–4; and Glorious Revolution, 377–8; confirmed as Surveyor of King's Works under William and Mary, 379, 383, 407; guarantees Fox's occupation of Whitehall house, 379; Whitehall property, *379*; plans Coronation of William and Mary, 383–7; relations with William and Mary, 389–90, 392; improvements to Hampton Court

Palace, 390–1; works on Greenwich Palace and Naval Hospital, 395–9; on architectural theory and aesthetics, 403–4, 407, 415, 476; in social and official circles, 407; supposed drawings of Hagia Sophia, *417*, *419*, *420*; and scientific use of St Paul's, 424; plans long-lasting buildings, 425–8, 476; and completion of St Paul's, 429; and death of daughter Jane, 429, 432; and Hooke's death, 432–3, 437; designs Crane Court premises for Royal Society, 434–7; activities and appointments in later life, 439–40, 472; as peacemaker and arbitrator, 441, 451–2, 455–7; relations with Flamsteed, 444–6; Newton discusses heavenly motions with, 449; as Visitor to supervise Royal Observatory, 456; avoids confrontations, 457–8; compared with Nestor, 457–8; granted long lease on house at Hampton Court, 463–4; and supervision of workmen and artisans, 464–6, 468; accused of corrupt practices at St Paul's, 468; freemasonry, 468–70; succeeded as Surveyor of King's Works by Benson, 470–2; Benson accuses of mismanagement, 472; death and funeral, 472; retires to Hampton Court, 472, 476; achievements and reputation, 473–9; designs mausoleum for Charles I, 480–1, *482*; *De corpore Saturni*, 133, 138

Wren, Christopher, Dean of Windsor (CW's father): as Dean of Windsor and Register of Order of the Garter, 7–10, 12, 25, 30, 209, 479, 483; ambitions for children, 12, 147; in Civil War, 13–14, 41; at Bletchingdon, 14; duties for Garter Order, 31, 33, 36, 41–2, 44, 48–50; at Charles II's installation as Garter Knight, 32; death, 44, 53, 150; land and livings forfeited by Parliamentarians, 48, 50, 53; and CW's education, 53, 58–9; and medical research, 57; and Wilkins's appointment to Wadham, 66–7; sends CW abroad, 72, 74, 85, 87; on library at Heidelberg, 85; scientific marginalia, 114, 147; interest in action of poisons, 122; supplies material to Ashmole for history of Garter Order, 146; on rejection of CW's London rebuilding plan, 266; in *Parentalia*, 479

Wren, Christopher, Jnr (CW's son):
proposes tombstone inscription for
father, ix; on father's being introduced
to Elector Palatine, 83; on defences at
Tangier, 170; CW advises against
travelling overland to Italy, 234; birth,
283; on CW's supervision of
dismantling old St Paul's, 290; relations
with father, 331, 429–31, 478; and
building of Winchester Palace, 336; and
completion of St Paul's, 428–9;
architectural career, 429–30; and
building of Royal Society premises,
435–6; and father's attempts to
determine longitude, 460–1; on father's
financial position, 462; assembles family
papers for *Parentalia*, 476–8, 480, 483;
on memorial for Charles I, 480
Wren, Faith (*née* Coghill; CW's first wife):
background, 281; courtship and
marriage, 281–2; death, 283
Wren, Francesca (CW's sister): birth and
death, 14
Wren, Gilbert (CW's son): birth and
death, 282–3
Wren, Jane (CW's daughter by Jane):
birth, 283; death, 284, 429, 432
Wren, Jane, Lady (*née* Fitzwilliam; CW's
second wife): anonymity, 282; marriage
and children, 283; death, 284, 331, 478;
receives gift from St Stephen Walbrook
church, 305
Wren, Mary (*née* Cox; CW's mother): at
Windsor, 14; children, 52
Wren, Matthew, Bishop of Ely (CW's

uncle): as Dean of Windsor and
Register of Garter Order, 7–8, 25, 29,
479; family, 9, 12, 52; imprisoned in
Tower, 12–13, 42, 72–3, 237;
accompanies Prince Charles to Spain,
26–8; career and appointments, 29–30,
222; at Charles II's installation as Garter
Knight, 32; released from Tower and
reinstated at Ely, 44, 139, 167; in old
age, 150, 167; requests CW to design
Oxford building, 154; and building of
chapel at Pembroke College,
Cambridge, 212–14, *214*, 219, 228; death,
214; and Charles I's religious piety, 342;
in *Parentalia*, 479
Wren, Matthew, Jnr (CW's cousin):
friendship with CW, 9, 72; at Pembroke
College, Cambridge, 12, 168; career and
appointments under Charles II, 30, 72,
99, 167–8, 349; lodges in Oxford, 71–2;
in Wadham circle, 98–101; answers
Harrington, 99, 167, 223; scientific
interests, 147; contributes to Royal
Society building, 154; and Tangier
defences, 170; promotes Royal Society,
183; and accommodation for Royal
Society, 187; and CW's commission for
chapel at Pembroke College,
Cambridge, 213; death and burial, 214;
secular career, 222
Wren, Stephen (Christopher junior's son),
476
Wren, Thomas (CW's cousin), 71, 168

York, James, Duke of *see* James II, King